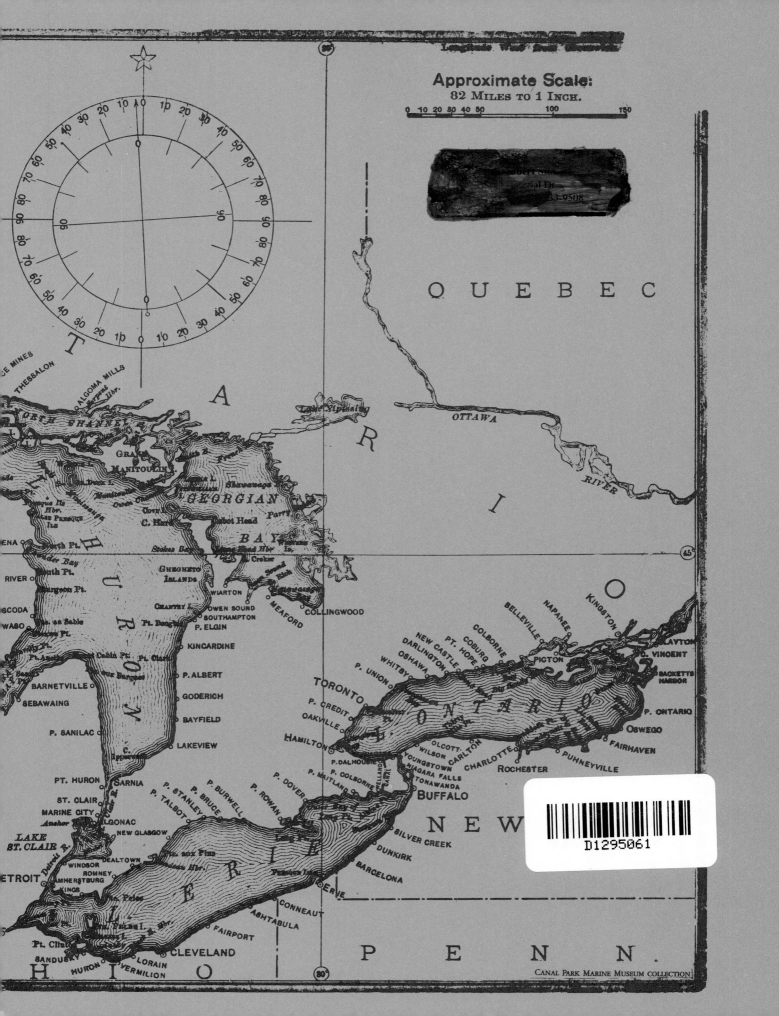

Approximate Scale:
82 MILES TO 1 INCH.

0 10 20 30 40 50   100   150

Q U E B E C

O N T A R I O

OTTAWA

RIVER

GEORGIAN BAY

LAKE HURON

LAKE ST. CLAIR

LAKE ERIE

LAKE ONTARIO

NORTH CHANNEL

GRAND MANITOULIN

TORONTO
HAMILTON
BUFFALO

KINGSTON
BELLEVILLE
NAPANEE
PICTON
ROCHESTER
OSWEGO
SACKETTS HARBOR

DETROIT
WINDSOR
CLEVELAND
SANDUSKY

COLLINGWOOD
OWEN SOUND
SOUTHAMPTON
KINCARDINE
GODERICH
BAYFIELD
SARNIA
PT. HURON

N E W

O H I O

P E N N.

Julius F. Wolff Jr.'s
Lake Superior Shipwrecks

Best wishes to Bob Stokes!

Julius F. Wolff Jr.

Julius F. Wolff Jr.'s
Lake Superior Shipwrecks

Dr. Julius F. Wolff Jr.

Thomas R. (Thom) Holden
Contributing Editor

Endorsed and Registered by
the Association for Great Lakes Maritime History
as Publication B2

Lake Superior Port Cities Inc.

First published in 1979 as *The Shipwrecks of Lake Superior*
by Lake Superior Marine Museum Association Inc.
Duluth, Minnesota

Second expanded edition published by
LAKE SUPERIOR PORT CITIES INC.
P.O. Box 16417
Duluth, Minnesota 55816-0417

DESIGN: Lynn Lynas
EDITING: Paul Hayden
TYPOGRAPHY: Stacy L. Winter
PHOTO RESEARCH: Thom Holden, C. Patrick Labadie
EDITORIAL ADVISORS: Donn Larson, James R. Marshall
PRINTING: BookCrafters

Printed in the United States of America

ISBN 0-942235-01-0 SOFTCOVER
ISBN 0-942235-02-9 HARDCOVER

10   9   8   7   6   5   4   3   2   1

Library of Congress Card Catalog Number: 89-062968

Table of Contents

To the memory of my father and mother
who taught me to love and respect Lake Superior

Foreword

The ships of Lake Superior have long fascinated me. It was probably due to my home influence, for my late mother was an office secretary for the James Pickands Company at Marquette, Michigan, and the Oliver Iron Mining Company at Duluth. At Marquette, she actually had an opportunity to meet many of the famous lake captains who came to the Pickands office, and both the Pickands and Oliver companies provided occasional lake trips aboard the ore ships for their employees. My mother had sailed many times. Then, too, as a youngster, she had witnessed the wreck of the steamer *Charles J. Kershaw* and the daring rescue of the crew by the U.S. Life-Saving Service at Marquette in September 1895. An enthralling story teller, she related many gripping tales of Lake Superior to her sons and daughter. These I still remember.

When I first entered Holy Rosary Parochial School at Duluth in 1923, the ships again figured. Every vessel entering the Duluth port passed in full view of the first grade classroom, and for a couple of days I bounced up every time a ship whistled. In fact, my first academic penalty came on the third day when my teacher sentenced me to stand at the window and watch ships until my legs were tired. I got the message. Ship watching was henceforth reserved for recess or out-of-school hours. I would often sit for hours on a bare rock knob overlooking Lake Superior, observing all kinds of ships coming and going. I frequently wondered how they fared as they moved northeast out of view. After I learned to read, I assiduously followed every shipwreck report.

This study, however, came about accidentally. When I became an upper teenager, my interests shifted to woods, forest and wildlife conservation, and for years I roamed the Minnesota north shore country. After World War II, my graduate education reinforced these interests in the natural resources conservation movement. After I began teaching at the University of Minnesota, Duluth, in 1949, I soon developed an official reason for continuing to roam the Minnesota coast of Lake Superior.

Then came the break. In January 1956, Dr. Maude Lind-quist, Head of the Department of History, University of Minnesota, Duluth, was the program director for the annual banquet of the St. Louis County Historical Society, the gala historical event of the year. Ten days before the event, her guest speaker from New York City was taken ill. In casting about for an emergency replacement, she hit upon the topic of shipwrecks on Minnesota's north shore. As I knew the north shore area, I was the logical substitute speaker. Accordingly, after a very hasty research effort, I discussed "Shipwrecks of Minnesota's North Shore" before the banquet guests. The accident list, incidentally, had been furnished by John Fritzen, Area Supervisor, Minnesota State Forest Service, an acknowledged north shore author in his own right. While I had intended this venture as a one-shot affair, a courtesy to the Department of History, I soon learned otherwise.

The late Captain Joseph E. Johnston, Editor, *Telescope,* bimonthly publication of the Great Lakes Maritime Institute (the Model Shipbuilders Guild), heard about the speech and wrote me, asking permission to publish it. As university people are constantly under pressure to publish, I gladly complied. Johnston presented the story serially and encouraged me to continue writing on Lake Superior ships, as very few people had hitherto done so. Next, Dr. Richard Sielaff, Chairman, Division of Social Sciences at the University of Minnesota, Duluth, took an interest in the subject and urged me to continue, as this topic had never been explored in University of Minnesota circles either. The following year the Graduate School of the University endorsed the project and allotted a small subsidy. I was in business as a shipwreck researcher.

My initial investigation of a handful of ships lost on the north shore has expanded into an inquiry into the permanent loss of more than 350 vessels with more than 1,000 other accidents examined. Upward of 1,000 persons have lost their lives in shipwrecks on this lake. Property loss has run into millions of dollars.

Dr. Julius F. Wolff Jr.
May 1990

ix

Acknowledgments

No research can ever really be accomplished by an individual working alone. It must be the end result of a great deal of cooperation from a number of individuals and institutions. This manuscript would not be as complete as it now is without the interest, concern, time and encouragement many have given over the decades involved.

I am indebted to a host of people for research assistance. The late John E. Keast of Marquette, Michigan, formerly a researcher with the Marquette County Historical Society, gave invaluable information in the early stages. He possessed phenomenal knowledge of Lake Superior shipping. Personnel of the Marquette County Historical Society were of immense help, as their Longyear Research Library contains newspaper files dating back to the 1840s. At Duluth, both the Public Library and St. Louis County Historical Society staffs were extremely generous in making research material available, while the library staff of the University of Minnesota, Duluth, and the Northeast Minnesota Historical Center were outstandingly cooperative in obtaining items which were not readily available. Area help also was provided by the Douglas County Historical Society, Superior, Wisconsin, and the Lake County Historical Society, Two Harbors, Minnesota. Librarians of the Superior Public Library in Wisconsin discovered early Duluth newspapers in a forgotten corner of their archives, and these were highly useful, as Duluth had pretty much lost its first 20 years of newspaper history in a library fire about 1889.

The Duluth office of the United States Coast Guard furnished valuable documents, as did the Duluth Area Office of the U.S. Army Corps of Engineers. The late Ralph Knowlton, civilian administrator with the Corps, made special efforts to assist. More recently, I have received significant help from C. Patrick Labadie, Director, Corps of Engineers' Canal Park Marine Museum, Duluth, who is a well-known Great Lakes scholar, formerly having been an associate editor of *Telescope* and currently Contributing Editor of *The Nor'Easter,* bimonthly Journal of the Lake Superior Marine Museum Association which originally published this manuscript. The late Captain Frank Hamilton likewise contributed hard-to-get information, as has Thomas R. Holden, the current Isle Royale shipwreck scholar. D.M. (Mac) Frimodig, formerly with the Michigan Department of Natural Resources, Marquette, and Bernard J. Gestel with the National Park Service, Grand Marais, Minnesota, formerly with the Service at Grand Marais and Isle Royale, Michigan, also furnished choice items from files on Michigan waters.

Most of my previous periodical publications have come through the guidance of the late Janet Coe Sanborn as Editor, *Inland Seas,* Quarterly Journal of the Great Lakes Historical Society. For more than 20 years she patiently steered my approaches to historical writing. I am eternally grateful for her repeated use of my Lake Superior studies and for her innumerable pointers in literary improvement.

To enumerate all who have helped would be impossible. Over the years I have interviewed active and retired captains and crewmen, countless coastal residents, divers, dock workers, fishermen and Coast Guard and Corps of Engineers personnel. Two of Lake Superior's most colorful hard hat divers, the late Captain Horace Thompson and Paul Flynn, gave priceless reports of their decades-long underwater experiences. Moreover, a retired Coast Guardsman, the late John F. Soldenski, related fascinating accounts of the early Life-Saving Service in which he served on the eastern Lake. The list could go on and on.

Members of my own field crew deserve special mention for their efforts in our past beachcombing trips on the Michigan coast: Peter Prusak of Spooner, Wisconsin; Paul Prusak of Fairbanks, Alaska; Bruce Schoenberg of Cromwell, Minnesota; Thomas Schoenberg of Santa Barbara, California; John F. Wolff of Seattle, Washington; and Scott E. Wolff of Duluth. In 1977 and 1978, Sean Bradley, Randy Lally and Eric Campbell of Duluth were my beach rovers. Likewise, the reliable help of my one-time student assistant, now Colonel Thomas Kubiak, USAF (Ret.), O'Fallon, Illinois, should be especially acknowledged.

During the beachcombing trips of the early 1980s, my crew included Thomas J. Dungan of St. Paul, Minnesota; Curt Sinkiewicz and James Pigman of Duluth, Minnesota; and Thomas J. Turk of Las Vegas, Nevada. In my rare lecture appearance of the late 1980s, my projectionist and driver was Tod M. Dungan, also of Duluth. I am indebted to these young men for invaluable assistance in some of the rugged beach country of Lake Superior where my deteriorating physical condition would not permit me to go unaccompanied.

In this revised and expanded edition I owe special thanks to two members of the Great Lakes historical research community, C. Patrick Labadie and Thomas R. Holden, both of the professional staff of the Corps of Engineers' Canal Park Marine Museum, Duluth. Pat and Thom have painstakingly examined hundreds of photographs of vessels involved in difficulties on Lake Superior and selected the best from the Lake Superior Marine Museum Association and Corps of Engineers archives as well as their personal collections. Thom, an acknowledged scholar on Isle Royale shipwrecks, author of numerous articles for *The Nor'Easter, Telescope,* the Wisconsin Marine Historical Society's journal, *Soundings,* and regional magazines and newspapers, and the book *Above and Below: A History of Lighthouses and Shipwrecks of Isle Royale,* has examined records of Lake Superior marine casualties meticulously for the 1970s and 1980s, chronicling a wide variety of shipping mishaps. Since even a minor mishap to a modern ship can cost many times that of a total loss for a wooden vessel, he has, as contributing editor to this revised manuscript, carefully included these accidents for the record in the last two chapters of this volume and others throughout the manuscript. I am especially grateful for the help of these two scholars in preparing this second edition. Without their aid, the publication of this revision would have been impossible during the four years of my recent illness.

Additional thanks must be extended to Donn Larson of Westmoreland, Larson & Webster Inc., Duluth, who is a longtime boater with an interest in maritime history, and James R. Marshall, publisher of *Lake Superior Magazine*, who is also intimately familiar with the waters of Lake Superior, for their dedicated review of the text and layout of this new volume.

This study strives to enumerate the permanent loss of all sizable ships on Lake Superior. Hundreds of significant accidents are also reported, since many of these have been designated erroneously by other writers as total losses. The general area of destruction will be designated, if known, while dimensions of the vessel involved are often included as a guide to identification for future historians, underwater archaeologists and scuba divers. Far more information is available on some wrecks than on others.

Dimensions listed for the ships are derived mainly from the United States Treasury Department and Department of Commerce publication, *Merchant Vessels of the United State,* from Beeson's *Inland Marine Directory,* Lloyd's *Register of Shipping,* Dominion of Canada, Department of Transport *Casualties to Vessels Resulting in Total Loss on the Great Lakes* and, in later years, *Greenwood's Guide to Great Lakes Shipping.*

Invaluable for this investigation has been the pioneer wreck list compiled by Homer Wells of the Corps of Engineers, Duluth, *History of Accidents, Casualties and Wrecks on Lake Superior,* a 91-page typewritten report prepared in 1938. Wells identified a majority of the mishaps.

In the interest of brevity, the following analysis concentrates on those incidents where physical damage exceeded $1,000 or a life was lost. Heavy use has been made of newspaper files from the Lake Superior area, of annual reports of the United States Life-Saving Service and Coast Guard, of Lighthouse Service annals and of miscellaneous shipping items recorded in the United States National Archives. Every effort has been made to cross reference particular incidents, as innumerable contradictions and some obvious errors have appeared. Personal narratives also have had to be checked carefully against existing records, especially if these were recollections. And in some instances, the scholar still is left wondering if what was reported actually was what had happened.

Photographic Acknowledgments

For the pictures in this volume and the original I owe thanks to many people. First, I am deeply indebted to Kenneth J. Moran, Photographer, University of Minnesota, Duluth, for his professional expertise as well as his patience and cooperation in reproducing several hundred prints from negatives, slides or prints of diverse forms and shapes, many in a poor state of preservation. The pictures came from a variety of sources; A.R. Inman of the famed Inman Towing Company of Duluth donated dozens for my personal collection 30 years ago. LCDR Edward J. Geissler, USCG (Ret.) contributed more than a hundred when he left active duty. Pat Labadie and Thom Holden of the Canal Park Marine Museum, Duluth, were generous in providing numerous negatives or prints from their personal collections as well as from the Museum's archives. The picture collection of the Great Lakes Historical Society has been the origin of a number of items, particularly since the late Captain H.C. Inches had allowed Pat Labadie to reproduce a great many of their photographs. The Milwaukee Public Library likewise was most cooperative. At Duluth, the St. Louis County Historical Society permitted copying of their extensive holdings now on file in the Northeast Minnesota Historical Center at the University of Minnesota, Duluth. Also, two of Duluth's professional photographers with an affinity for the maritime scene, Wesley R. Harkins of Harkins Marine Photography and Tim Slattery of Harbor Reflections Photography, made several original images available from their extensive holdings. Photographs in the collection of the late Arvid Morken, Superior, Wisconsin, were also made available.

Private collectors from around the nation were very helpful. The late John E. Keast of Marquette, Michigan, provided a number of unusual views, as did the late Judge William E. Scott of Two Harbors, Minnesota, and the Rev. Edward J. Dowling, S.J., of the University of Detroit. Laurence E. Burke of Buffalo and the late Captain Frank Hamilton of Kelleys Island, Ohio, offered some rare contributions, as did the late Edward N. Middleton of Kansas City, Missouri, and Mrs. Janice H. Gerred of Lansing, Michigan. And I must not forget the photographic work of my two beach party crewmen in 1977 and 1978, Sean Bradley and Randy Lally of Duluth, who were my backup cameramen. To these and all the others who have furnished pictures over the years I am deeply grateful.

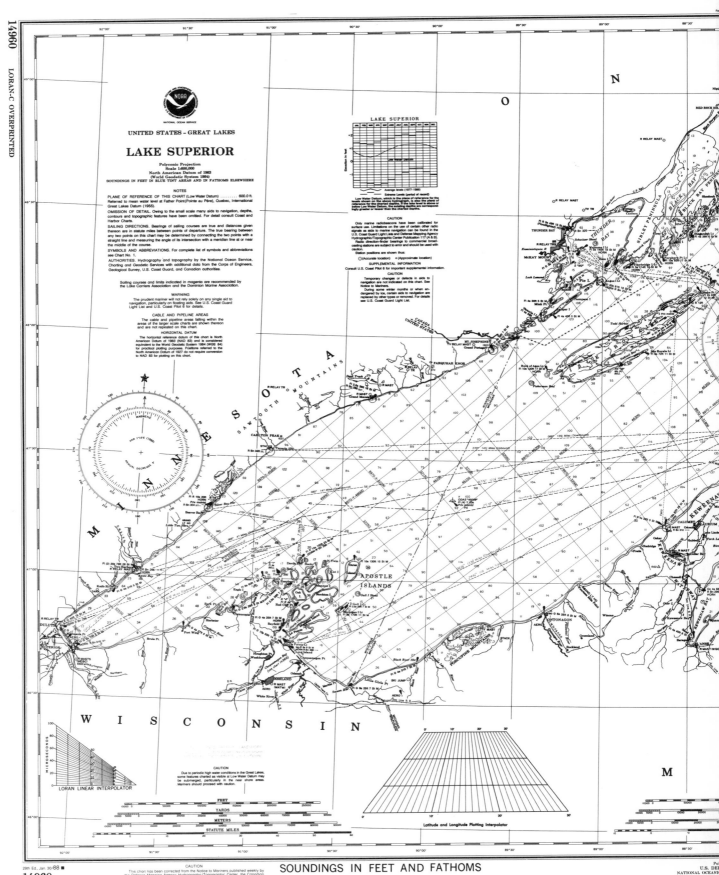

UNITED STATES - GREAT LAKES

LAKE SUPERIOR

Polyconic Projection
Scale 1:600,000
North American Datum of 1983
(World Geodetic System 1984)
SOUNDINGS IN FEET IN BLUE TINT AREAS AND IN FATHOMS ELSEWHERE

LAKE SUPERIOR

SOUNDINGS IN FEET AND FATHOMS

Nautical Chart Catalog No. 4, Panels A, B, C

LORAN-C
GENERAL EXPLANATION

LORAN-C FREQUENCY 100kHz
PULSE REPETITION INTERVAL
8970 .... 89,700 Microseconds
STATION TYPE DESIGNATORS: (Not individual station letter designators).
M .... Master
W .... Secondary
X .... Secondary
Y .... Secondary
Z .... Secondary

EXAMPLE: 8970-Y

RATES ON THIS CHART
8970-X   8970-Y

The Loran-C lines of position overprinted on this chart have been prepared for use with ground wave signals and are presently compensated only for theoretical propagation delays which have not yet been verified by observed data. Mariners are cautioned not to rely entirely on the lattices in inshore waters. Skywave corrections are not provided.

LORAN LINEAR INTERPOLATOR

MICROSECONDS

FEET
YARDS
METERS
STATUTE MILES

FEET
YARDS
METERS
STATUTE MILES

A R I O

O

TIP TOP MOUNTAIN
2120

MICHIPICOTEN I.

BARE SUMMIT

MOUNTAIN ASH HILL

BRULE HILL

Cape Chaillon

GRANGOUBIER HILL

BALD HEAD

MONTREAL HILL

MAMAINSE HILL

WHITEFISH   BAY

SAULT STE. MARIE

HURON MOUNTAINS

MARQUETTE

NEGAUNEE

MUNISING

C H I G A N

NOTE A
Navigation regulations are published in Chapter 2, U.S. Coast Pilot 6. Additions or revisions to Chapter 2 are published in the Notices to Mariners. Information concerning the regulations may be obtained at the Office of the Commander, 9th Coast Guard District in Cleveland, Ohio, or at the Office of the District Engineer, Corps of Engineers in Detroit, Michigan.
Refer to charted regulation section numbers.

NOAA VHF-FM WEATHER BROADCASTS
The National Weather Service stations listed below provide continuous marine weather broadcasts. The range of reception is variable, but for most stations is usually 20 to 40 miles from the antenna site.

Duluth, Mn.	KIG-64	162.55 (Chan. WX-1)
Marquette, Mi.	KIG-66	162.44 (Chan. WX-2)
Sault Ste. Marie, Mi.	KIG-74	162.55 (Chan. WX-1)

RADAR REFLECTORS
Radar reflectors have been placed on many floating aids to navigation. Individual radar reflector identification on these aids has been omitted from this chart.

POLLUTION REPORTS
Report all spills of oil and hazardous substances to the National Response Center via 800-424-8802 (toll free), or to the nearest U.S. Coast Guard facility if telephone communication is impossible (33 CFR 153).

FEET
YARDS
METERS
STATUTE MILES

FATHOMS
FEET
METERS

(Lake Superior)

SOUNDINGS IN FEET & FATHOMS · SCALE 1:600,000

14960
LORAN-C OVERPRINTED

D.C.
MMERCE
C ADMINISTRATION
VICE

DMA STOCK NO. 14XCO14960

Julius F. Wolff Jr.'s
Lake Superior Shipwrecks

*O*nly a part of what was observed in the past was remembered by those who observed it; only a part of what was remembered was recorded; only a part of what was recorded has survived; only a part of what has survived has come to the historians' attention; only a part of what has their attention is credible; only a part of what is credible has been grasped; and only a part of what has been grasped can be expounded or narrated by the historian.

Louis Gotschalk
Understanding History

UNITED STATES & DOMINION
TRANSPORTATION COMPANY.

BOOTH LINE.

U. S. MAIL.

Passengers await boarding the America *at Tobin Harbor, Isle Royale, on one of her regular visits to the island's resort in 1906. The* America *sank in Washington Harbor in 1928.* GLEN MERRITT COLLECTION.

Opening of Soo Locks in 1855 ushered in economic growth for several Lake Superior towns. Propeller Cuyahoga, *built in 1856, was a pioneer Chicago and Lake Superior liner.* C. Patrick Labadie collection.

Chapter 1

The Ships Arrive on Lake Superior
Prior to 1870

Lake Superior has haunted sailors from the beginning. To be sure, it is not the most dangerous of the Great Lakes, as evidenced by the paucity of shipwrecks when compared to several of the others. Certainly, the weather is no more treacherous than that afflicting the rest. It was probably the wilderness nature of Lake Superior's shore which contributed to the aura of mystery and lessened the chances of survival, should one be stranded on its forest-shrouded coasts. Indeed, until the end of the 1800s, a large percentage of the shoreline remained completely wild, desolate and uninhabited. Winter's cold also hit Superior first and spring's warming breezes frequently came late, adding fear of death from exposure or freezing to the accepted risks of drowning. The coldness of Lake Superior's waters meant discomfort in any season.

While the Lake was explored in the seventeenth century by French adventurers and missionaries, the eventual build-up of the future United States would leave the area by-passed, a side show on the north flank. Hence, it was the mid-nineteenth century before Americans began to populate the Lake Superior country, and the lake became a major communication channel. Typically, initial shipping activities appeared as a trickle, growing to a torrent as the frontier developed and finally reaching flood proportions. As the number of ships and sailors multiplied, so did the number of accidents, until lake sailing became popularly regarded as a high-risk occupation. Actually, the expanding railroad industry was probably far more dangerous, but a shipwreck made more impact on the public mind. Hence, Lake Superior was and continues to be viewed as an ominous body of water.

1

Navigating this inland sea was no mean feat. Approximately 360 miles separate Duluth-Superior (Minnesota-Wisconsin) from Sault Ste. Marie (Michigan-Ontario). The north-south expanse runs more than 160 miles in some places. There are positions where a northeast or northwest gale can gain a 200-mile sweep. Some sections of the littoral were particularly vulnerable. In early spring, the stretch of Michigan coast from Whitefish Point to Munis-

mishaps at this time. In the eighteenth century, more and larger canoes coasted the shores of Lake Superior, and in the latter decades of the century diminutive wooden ships appeared. The French mineral explorer LaRonde reputedly built a small wooden craft for his work in the 1730s, while Canadian adventurers Baxter, Bostwick and Henry constructed a sloop and a barge for their investigations, also in the 1730s.

An 1819 manifest for furs shows the cargo of two canoes. RECORDS OF THE CHIPPEWA PORTAGE CO. IN BAYLISS PUBLIC LIBRARY, SAULT STE. MARIE, MICHIGAN.

ing was especially awesome, as were the waters around Grand Island. The approaches to Marquette were often troublesome. Later, Keweenaw Point received involuntary marine visitors nearly every year. Ultimately, Isle Royale had more than its share of ill-fated maritime callers, as did the channels contiguous to Thunder Bay, Ontario, on the north and the Bayfield Peninsula (Wisconsin) on the south. Aside from the catastrophic gale of November 27-29, 1905, the western lake has had a reasonably good safety record. The extreme eastern open lake, on the other hand, has seized many an unlucky vessel and crew. Then too, in Whitefish Bay and off Michigan's Whitefish Point were the recurrent dangers from the ships themselves, the fog-shrouded collisions.

To be sure, the American Indians and their predecessors of the Mississippian culture traversed Lake Superior for centuries before the coming of the European. This was very likely canoe travel, probably coasting, but some travel did involve navigation to the ancient copper mining sites of Isle Royale, no mean accomplishment for canoes. Seventeenth century French explorers and missionaries also utilized the canoe, but no record exists of

The Montreal-based merchants of the Northwest Company were likely the first to introduce a string of wooden schooners for the voyage across the lake from Sault Ste. Marie to Grand Portage, Minnesota. Primitive shipyards at Point-Aux-Pins, near Sault Ste. Marie, and at Fort William, Ontario (after 1803), turned out a number of these craft. Their names have been preserved for us: *De Peyster, Mackinac, Athabasca, Otter, Mink, Beaver, Invincible, Perseverance, Recovery I* and *Recovery II*. Despite the total lack of navigational aids, their pioneer skippers apparently had a good safety record in normal fur trade operations.[1]

The First Shipwrecks

Strangely enough, the first recorded shipwrecks and fatalities would occur as a result of a Canadian interfamily squabble — the feud between Lord Selkirk and the Northwesters. In August 1816, the Selkirk forces with tough De Meuron mercenary soldiers seized Fort William

2

and arrested key Northwest Company leaders who were there for the annual rendezvous. Selkirk sent the leading Northwesters by canoe to eastern Canada for trial, but one sail-equipped Montreal canoe commanded by De Meuron Lieutenant Fauche never got off Lake Superior, capsizing in rough seas off Parisienne Island northwest of the Soo, August 26, 1816. Of the 24 or more persons aboard, a number were drowned, 9 or 11, according to different Canadian sources, including Northwest Company bourgeois Kenneth MacKenzie, several soldiers and a half dozen Iroquois paddlers. The famed Northwester Dr. John McLoughlin had a close brush with death.

In the same sequence of events more tragedy would befall the Northwesters.[2] In November 1816, one of their leaders, de Rochblave, made a rash attempt to reach Fort William in the schooner *Invincible*, but a storm on the 13th and 14th over the eastern lake intervened. The *Invincible* was hurled ashore and dashed to pieces in the vicinity of Whitefish Point. Those aboard reached shore, but the firm little schooner was no more.[3]

After the Hudson's Bay Company and Northwest Company settled their differences by amalgamating in 1821, the new Hudson's Bay Company gradually abandoned sailing on Lake Superior. Their recently constructed schooner *Recovery* was eventually sent down the St. Marys Rapids to the lower lakes in 1828. For the next six years, only Montreal canoes, Mackinaw boats or the barges of various exploration parties plied the lake. Then in 1835, the American Fur Company assembled a sizable

schooner at Sault Ste. Marie, Michigan, from prefabricated materials.

The 78-foot, 112-ton *John Jacob Astor* was launched under command of Captain Charles Stannard. For nine years she plied Lake Superior's waters under command of either Charles Stannard or his brother, Benjamin. Though these early captains had only rudimentary charts compiled in the 1820s by British Royal Navy Lieutenant Bayfield to guide them and were without lighthouses or navigational beacons, they successfully brought trade goods and supplies to the scattered outposts, picking up furs for the return. The *John Jacob Astor* ultimately became the first documented American total loss shipwreck on Lake Superior. While anchored in the presumed shelter of Copper Harbor, Michigan, on September 21, 1844, during a major equinoctial storm, Captain Benjamin Stannard watched his faithful ship part her cables and go on the rocks, a shattered wreck, though the crew and troops from nearby Fort Wilkins managed to save most of the cargo.

Fortunately, Lake Superior was not left without transportation since the American Fur Company had constructed a 40-ton schooner, the *Siskawit*, at La Pointe in 1840. Sold to Captain James Bendry of Baraga, Michigan, this vessel filled the gap, as did a 54-foot, 60-ton schooner, *Algonquin*, portaged onto Lake Superior about 1839 and sailed by Captain Lewis W. Bancroft.[4]

The *Siskawit* had been a casualty herself, wrecking at Isle Royale October 2-3, 1840, while under command of Captain John Angus. The schooner visited American Fur

The first gravity ore dock was built at Marquette in 1859. MARQUETTE COUNTY HISTORICAL SOCIETY.

Company fishing stations along the Minnesota north shore and then proceeded to the Company station in Siskiwit Bay, Isle Royale, where she was to take on about 50 passengers to be transported to La Pointe for the winter. The *Siskawit* came to anchor just offshore from the station in about 33 feet of water. What had been a strong breeze turned into tremendous gusts of wind with rising seas. The *Siskawit* began dragging her anchor until Captain Angus felt she was going onto the rocks. He cut the chains and tried unsuccessfully to run her safely ashore. Instead, the *Siskawit* bounded over a reef, breaking her frames just aft of the main mast. She quickly filled with water and settled in for the winter. The crew, with the help of those on shore, managed to get nearly all of her cargo ashore, close to 200 barrels of fish. There were no casualties in the accident, and the survivors, as well as those on shore, were eventually transported to La Pointe by the rival *Algonquin,* undoubtedly at some embarrassment and expense to the Company. In June of the following year, the *John Jacob Astor* under Captain Charles Stannard was sent to raise the *Siskawit* and return her to La Pointe for repairs. He was obviously successful in his task; winter had been kind to the stranded vessel. Thus, the ship which was destined to become the first American vessel totally wrecked on the lake was the

Copper Harbor west to Ontonagon. Almost simultaneously, iron ore was discovered at Negaunee, a bare 10 miles inland from what is now Marquette. The wilderness of Lake Superior, hitherto broken only by Indian villages and scattered fur trade outposts, was soon the site of numerous copper and iron mining settlements. To supply these, a whole new shipping industry was necessary.

Vesselmen responded by portaging substantial ships across the mile-plus overland route around the rapids of the St. Marys River at Sault Ste. Marie, Michigan. Taken out of the river below the rapids on the Lake Huron side, a number of propellers and schooners were dragged on rollers by oxen, horses and men to a launching spot above the rapids. Prior to the opening of the Soo Canal in 1855, steam powered ships and schooners aggregating more than 3,000 tons were hauled to Lake Superior, beginning in 1839 with the schooner *Algonquin.* Among those brought over in 1845 were the schooners *Merchant, Swallow, Chippewa, Florence, Uncle Tom, Ocean* and *Fur Trader,* and the propeller *Independence.* The sailing vessels were small, from 20 to 110 tons, but the *Independence* reached 262 tons. Much larger ships were portaged to the upper lake in the next few years: the 280-ton steamer *Julia Palmer* in 1847, the 330-ton propeller *Manhattan* in 1850, the 460-ton propeller *Monticello* in 1851 and

An 1852 cargo manifest shows upbound merchandise and downbound copper typical in that era. RECORDS OF THE CHIPPEWA PORTAGE CO. IN BAYLISS PUBLIC LIBRARY, SAULT STE. MARIE, MICHIGAN.

salvor of the first documented American non-total loss shipwreck on Lake Superior.[5]

Meanwhile, the scattered American civilization was sharply augmented in the 1840s after announcement of copper discoveries by Michigan's State Geologist Dr. Douglass Houghton, who was drowned himself on October 13, 1845, in the capsizing of a Mackinaw boat. Within 10 years, miners by the thousands appeared from

the 500-ton steamer *Baltimore* in 1852. During 1853 came the sizable 100-ton schooner *George W. Ford* and the 355-ton propeller *Peninsula.* The 433-ton steamer *Sam Ward* also was dragged over in 1854. In addition, the 150-ton schooner *Napoleon* was converted to a propeller at the Soo in 1845. Bringing such substantial vessels over the Soo portage was costly, several thousand dollars in some cases, and required seven weeks in the case of the *Independence.* Commanding these ships were a number of doughty early navigators: Captains Averill, Bancroft, Brown, Halloran, McKay, Moore, Pope, Ripley, Wilson and Wood, to name a few. Tales of their exploits still astound sailors of the Big Lake.[6]

As one might suspect, there would be accidents — many minor, some serious. Narrow escapes were commonplace. On her last trip to Keweenaw in the fall of 1847, the 100-foot, 280-ton side-wheeler *Julia Palmer* encountered a ferocious gale and was tossed out of control for 14 days before coming to shelter in the Slate Islands on the north side of the lake. Her voyage from the Soo to Copper Harbor required 16 days. After this expe-

John Jacob Astor *wrecked near Fanny Hooe Creek in Copper Harbor, Michigan, on September 21, 1844. Her remains are inspected by author's friends in July 1978 at Fort Wilkins State Park.* AUTHOR'S PHOTO.

rience and several other narrow escapes, her owners retired her to the status of a "dock" on the west side of Whitefish Bay about 1848. She was the first of the powered vessels to end her career, though not in shipwreck as such.[7]

This was perhaps the first documented use of a Great Lakes vessel as a "dock" on Lake Superior, but certainly not the last. As recently as 1987, the ore carrier *Sewell Avery* was towed from long idleness in the Duluth-Superior Harbor to be sunk as the foundation for a new materials transfer dock just above the Canadian Soo.[8]

The Lake's first disappearance was also experienced in 1847. On June 11, 1847, the 80-ton schooner *Merchant* under Captain Robert Moore left the Soo for the Keweenaw Point area with 14 persons aboard. She was never heard from again, though the door to her companionway was found floating months later on the north shore of the lake. Five years after, a group of persons coasting the shore northwest of Grand Island reported seeing the top masts of a schooner about 30 feet below the surface. Reputedly, the observers would attempt salvage, although nothing is known of their efforts. Among the passengers aboard the ill-fated *Merchant* were representatives of mining companies bound for L'Anse, who allegedly carried $5,000 in

cash, a rich prize for salvors in those days. The unfortunate Captain Moore had broken his leg the day before sailing and had tried to induce Captain Brown of the schooner *Swallow* to take the voyage. Whether the captain's injury produced the schooner's loss will never be known.[9]

The tiny 40-ton schooner *Siskawit,* formerly of the American Fur Company, became the Lake's next victim. In November, 1849, the *Siskawit* had been loaded with supplies for the fledgling community of Marquette. Possibly because of weather, however, her captain bypassed Marquette on his run west and went to L'Anse, 80 miles to the northwest, where the ship was laid up for the winter, her Marquette cargo with her. The Marquette pioneers were in dire want. Accordingly, two of their number, Captain Sam Moody and James Broadbent, snowshoed over to L'Anse, took possession of the schooner by force, and sailed for Marquette on Christmas Eve. Fortuitously, they arrived at Marquette on Christmas Day, unloading the badly needed supplies in temperatures of 15 degrees below zero. Then, since the waterfront at Marquette was completely exposed in those days, they tried to run the ship into the shelter of the Chocolay River but missed the channel and stranded. The unfortunate *Siskawit* was destroyed on the beach by the rampaging waters. Her crew escaped.[10]

The 1850s

Increased demands for shipping capacity brought new vessels to Lake Superior. Portaged over in 1850, the 330-ton propeller *Manhattan* had a capacity of 3,000 barrels, making her the most spacious freight ship on the lake, while the passenger-freight propeller *Monticello,* which arrived in 1851, was a close second with a capacity of 2,500 barrels. Oddly enough, with only four steam-powered vessels on the entire lake, these two would meet in collision off Parisienne Island on August 4, 1851, the *Manhattan* sinking in shallow water near the Endress Dock without casualties. As the two ships belonged to rival owners, the *Manhattan* to Spaulding and Bacon and the *Monticello* to S. McKnight & Company, there was some talk that the collision was not an accident. However, as the *Monticello* assisted in the salvage operations on the *Manhattan,* the sinking was probably not the result of barratry but perhaps a consequence of a pioneer sailors' game of "chicken." The *Manhattan* was raised and repaired, reportedly at a cost of $10,000, being out of commission for two months.[11]

Fate was less kind to the *Monticello.* Coming out of Ontonagon on the night of September 25, 1851, with a large roster of passengers and a heavy cargo of copper, she headed to the east, ramming some floating object, perhaps a large pine trunk. Though disengaged without difficulty, she was discovered to be leaking shortly afterward. Then a savage storm arose. As the water gained ominously, her crew threw overboard the valuable deck cargo of large chunks of mass copper. Still, the water gained. In desperation, Captain Jack Wilson beached his ship on the cliff-lined shore. Maneuvering the ship's boats up and down a hawser, the *Monticello*'s people succeeded in getting everybody to shore, though the rescued still had a long unpleasant hike to Eagle River. The following July, a testimonial was held for Captain Wilson at Eagle River with the grateful survivors presenting him a pair of silver goblets for his prowess in saving those aboard. The stranding of the *Monticello* could have been a major calamity. The *Monticello* was a goner, though her engines were salvaged and placed in a new 555-ton propeller, *Mineral Rock,* which was built in 1856 at Buffalo.[12]

Each year's operation took a toll of the original vessels brought to Lake Superior. In late November, 1847, the schooner *Chippewa* under Captain Clarke stranded at Eagle River trying to put one Judge Bacon ashore. Her crew suffered the arduous ordeal of a trip on forest trails all the way back to Milwaukee on foot. Whether the ship was destroyed in the accident or whether she was retired and scrapped, we do not know.[13] Similarly, the schooner *Swallow* was reported aground in the St. Marys River at the Soo in July, 1852, and this may have finished her career.[14]

The checkered experiences of the propeller *Independence* are better reported. Reputedly rebuilt by Jacob Banta for Averill of Chicago, and intended for the European grain trade, the 118-foot, 262-ton *Independence* proved too slow at 4-8 mph, and too heavy on fuel consumption for an Atlantic crossing. Hence, she was acquired by S. McKnight & Company for their Lake Superior routes. On her very first trip to La Pointe in 1845 she had been badgered unmercifully by storms, and weather continually bedeviled her. Stranding damage in late 1850 kept her out of commission during a good part of 1851; another grounding in a gale near Bad River on October 7, 1852, kept her beached there through the winter of 1852-53. Captain John McKay and his son worked most of the following summer repairing her and, with the help of numerous Indians, took her off and over to La Pointe for refitting.

Her end has been described frequently; in fact, so many stories are told that it is difficult to separate fact from fiction. However, the early record indicates that the *Independence* left the Soo on the night of November 22, 1853, with a heavy cargo of freight for Ontonagon and La Pointe, Captain McKay in command. When only a mile from dock, her boiler burst, blowing three-fourths of the ship to pieces and sinking her in 18 feet of water. Miraculously, only four persons were killed: Chief Engineer George Sisson, Levi Sischoe and his brother who was working as a fireman, and a passenger, David Martin of Montreal. Many passengers and crew survived by clinging to wreckage, including the bales of hay upbound for

the horses at the mining camps. The *Independence* was a total loss, her remains being removed some 40 years later when the channel was deepened. One of her propellers was recovered by the U.S. Army Corps of Engineers

Schooner George W. Ford *(front) is pictured at Ontonagon, Michigan, with propeller* Quincy *in 1860s view. Ontonagon was an important source of copper. The* Ford *was lost at Eagle River in 1870.* ONTONAGON COUNTY HISTORICAL SOCIETY COLLECTION.

while dredging in the area of her loss in 1933 and subsequently put on display in Sault Ste. Marie, Michigan. Portions of her hull were also brought ashore. Over the years a number of canes, letter openers, checker boards and other souvenirs were fashioned from her planking. Samples of the ship's structural remains finally were recognized as valuable historical artifacts and are now being preserved in the maritime museum at Whitefish Point.[15]

Shipping losses would be offset by the addition of new tonnage via portaging overland at the Soo. Thus the aforementioned propeller *Peninsula* and the side-wheeler *Sam Ward* entered service on Lake Superior. The 154-foot, 355-ton *Peninsula* lasted only a year, breaking a shaft and drifting on the rocks November 15, 1854, at Eagle River where the waves quickly took her apart. There was no loss of life.[16] With the opening of the initial Soo Canal in 1855, of course, ships from the lower lakes moved into the Lake Superior trade at will.

The steamer *Superior,* however, accounted for one of the most tragic wrecks in Lake Superior history. Under Captain Hiram J. Jones, a veteran master, the 184-foot, 646-ton wooden side-wheeler was proceeding west of Whitefish Point on October 29, 1856, when a northerly gale developed. Captain Jones ran for the shelter of Grand Island. The *Superior* almost made it.

Approaching the Pictured Rocks, the *Superior* suddenly lost her rudder. Then her stack went overboard. She fell into the trough of the seas causing her cargo to shift. She began to list and was leaking badly. Knowing his ship would be driven ashore, Jones ordered the bow anchors dropped so the vessel would float onto the beach stern first. But the chains parted and the *Superior* crashed into the rocks broadside just west of the Cascade at Pictured Rocks. She disintegrated in 15 minutes. Perhaps 18 badly bedraggled survivors managed to struggle to the rocks on

LAKE SUPERIOR!

1858.   1858.

McKnight's Lake Superior Line

FROM CLEVELAND AND DETROIT
TO
Mackinac, Saut Ste. Marie, Marquette

PORTAGE LAKE, COPPER HARBOR,

EAGLE HARBOR, EAGLE RIVER, ONTONAGON,

La Pointe, Bayfield, and Superior City.

The New and Splendid Upper Cabin, Low Pressure, Fast Sailing Steamer

ILLINOIS!

JOHN FRASER, MASTER.

WILL MAKE SEVEN GRAND

PLEASURE EXCURSIONS

DURING THE SEASON OF 1858.

Leaving Cleveland, O., and Detroit, Mich., as follows:

LEAVES CLEVELAND	LEAVES DETROIT
THURSDAY, July 1st, ... 8 o'clock, P. M.	FRIDAY, July 2d, ...10 o'clock, A. M.
MONDAY, July 12th	TUESDAY, July 13th, ...
THURSDAY, July 22d, .	FRIDAY, July 23d, ...
MONDAY, August 2d, ...	TUESDAY, August 3d, ...
THURSDAY, August 12th,	FRIDAY, August 13th, ...
MONDAY, August 23d, ...	TUESDAY, August 24th.
THURSDAY, Sept. 2d, ...	FRIDAY, September 3d,

HUSSEY & McBRIDE, Cleveland,
G. O. WILLIAMS & Co., Detroit.

L. L. McKNIGHT, General Agent, Detroit,

Office over G. O. Williams & Co., foot of First Street.

The proud steamboat Illinois *became the first ship to transit the new Soo Locks when she came up from Detroit on June 18, 1855.* C. PATRICK LABADIE COLLECTION.

debris and crawl from the reach of the waves. There, they watched Captain Jones, swimming valiantly in his buffalo coat, drown at the base of a cliff and eight crewmen, hanging on to the paddle wheels, drop one-by-one to their deaths. Fortunately, First Mate Davis and Chief Engineer Stephen Callahan were among the survivors.

They and several companions made their way in a patched-up lifeboat to the home of a trader named Powell near the present location of Munising. As the lifeboat could not accommodate all, some of the castaways had to trudge through snow along the shoreline to reach the trader's home. They suffered terribly from exposure, and two died from exhaustion. A few days later, Engineer Callahan and three others rowed the 40 miles to Marquette where the propeller *General Taylor,* under Captain Ryder, happened to be in port. Captain Ryder brought the *Taylor* down to Munising to pick up survivors and retrieve the body of Captain Jones for burial in Detroit. Only four crewmen and 12 passengers remained of the 66 or more aboard, making this the worst loss of life from a single accident in the whole period of Lake Superior sailing.[17]

A ship's fire on November 13, 1856, produced another fatality when the brand new 183-foot, 843-ton propeller *B.L. Webb* burned in Waiska Bay. Only one life was lost, but supplies badly needed in Marquette were consumed in the blaze. The vessel had been built in Detroit with keel laying on July 10 and launching on September 27, 1856, for the Detroit & Lake Superior Iron Co. The ship was salvaged and the hull towed by the *Mineral Rock* to Detroit, arriving there on July 6, 1857. Her hull was subsequently completely rebuilt into the propeller *Marquette* in the fall of 1859. This vessel was eventually converted to a schooner in 1870 and later reduced to a barge in 1880, finally going off the registry in 1888, presumably abandoned.[18]

During 1857, a typical ship owner's horror occurred on the lake. With the vicissitudes of Great Lakes navigation, shipping companies could expect to lose vessels. Indeed, a steam ship lasting 10 years was "old." Very likely at least three years of use were necessary to recover the investment, even with insurance. Imagine, then, the consternation of Hanna, Garretson and Company of Cleveland when they learned that their fine new propeller *City of Superior,* launched only a few months earlier on July 18, had run ashore at Copper Harbor on November 10 and broken up the following day. The *City of Superior* had been built in Cleveland by the esteemed shipbuilders Lafrinier and Stevenson. She was large at 190 feet and 700 tons, and fast, making about 15 mph. Under Captain John Spalding, she had completed five trips from Cleveland to Superior City at the west end of the lake and was on her sixth when disaster struck. Coming into Copper Harbor in a snowstorm, Spalding misjudged his distance from the lighthouse and ran full speed onto the beach near the light. The steamer *Michigan,* which happened to be in port, tried to drag the *City of Superior* off her rocky perch, but had to give up after breaking three hawsers. The *Superior's* personnel were then removed and a rising storm tore her to pieces that night. She was a financial casualty of $50,000, with insurance coverage of only $32,000.[19]

The Panic of 1857 slowed the shipping industry on

Lake Superior. Few major accidents occurred during the late '50s, though minor storm damage struck most of the steamers and propellers working the lake: included were the *Planet, Illinois, North Star, General Taylor, Lady*

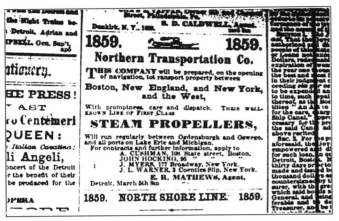

Northern Transportation Company ran 20 modern passenger and freight steamers from Lake Ontario through the upper lakes. DETROIT FREE PRESS, APR. 15, 1859.

Elgin, Ontonagon and *Mineral Rock.* A few schooners also encountered trouble, among them the U.S. Lighthouse Board's *Lamplighter,* which stranded at Isle Royale and again at Whitefish Point in 1857.[20]

Downbound from Marquette with a load of 280 tons of iron ore in June 1858, the propeller *Indiana* began leaking and foundered off Crisp Point with no loss of life, a $14,000 item.[21]

This may have proven the last ever heard of the *Indiana* except for its discovery in 118 feet of water by sport divers in 1975. Subsequent films of the vessel underwater showed her ancient machinery to be virtually intact and historically significant, particularly if it could be salvaged intact and properly curated. The Smithsonian Institution in cooperation with the U.S. Army Corps of Engineers, Michigan Department of State, U.S. Navy and representatives of various Great Lakes maritime institutions together orchestrated salvage efforts in the summer of 1979. Divers recovered the *Indiana*'s steam engine and portions of its wooden gallows, her boiler, the steering quadrant and rudder, preheater, throttle mechanism and the screw propeller with three of its four blades still intact. These artifacts are massive: the propeller weighs about 10 tons and was manufactured by Spang & Co. of Pittsburgh, the steering quadrant is 16 feet long and weighs 1.5 tons, the boiler is 13 feet tall weighing 3 tons and the 5-ton engine is more than 18 feet tall. The artifacts, said to be the earliest marine steam plant in existence which was manufactured in North America, were painstakingly restored over many months for display at the Smithsonian's National Museum of History and Technology.[22]

On September 1, 1859, the veteran 149-foot, 319-ton *Manhattan,* one of the early propellers on the lake, struck and broke up at Grand Marais, Michigan. No lives were lost and some of her cargo was saved. Owned by Harvey of Marquette and Redingler of Cleveland, she had been insured for $7,500. A salvager named Everett recovered her engine, boiler, anchors, chains, rigging and furniture.[23]

Only a week later, north of Marquette, a yacht cruise proved fatal. The 85-ton yacht *Dream,* under Captain G. Wooton of Elyria, Ohio, encountered rough weather two or three miles from Partridge Island and a mile off shore, after a cruise to Sauks Head. The yacht capsized, drowning the captain and a Mrs. Toms. Seven survivors escaped in a small boat. Crewmen of the propeller *Montgomery* recovered the *Dream* and brought her to Marquette. An outing had regrettably miscarried.[24]

The 1860s

The decade of the 1860s was ushered in by two serious steamer mishaps. In a fog on the night of May 28, 1860, the 237-foot, 861-ton side-wheeler *Arctic* under Captain F.S. Miller slammed aground in the Huron Islands. Fortunately, the crew and passengers were able to jump from the bow to shore as rising seas destroyed the wooden ship in two hours the following morning. Built in 1851 at Newport, Michigan, she had been sold in 1855 to the Clements interests and ran in opposition to the Ward steamers. She was a reported loss of $34,000.[25]

The lake drew second blood on September 10, 1860, when a storm caught the new 158-foot, 422-ton Ward Line side-wheeler *Gazelle* as she attempted to enter Eagle Harbor. Driven on the rocks, the two-year-old wooden craft was quickly shattered though her people escaped safely. She was a $33,000 liability.[26]

As might have been expected, the impact of the Civil War brought feverish shipping activity to the Marquette and Keweenaw areas. Iron and copper were two vital wartime commodities. After an initial lull in 1861 because of political uncertainties, shipments of iron ore, the big tonnage item on Lake Superior, virtually skyrocketed, reaching the unprecedented high of 243,127 tons in 1864. By comparison in 1855, when the Michigan State Locks opened at the Soo, just 1,449 tons of iron ore were shipped to the lower lakes.[27]

Despite the boom in cargoes, serious accidents were few. The first fatal collision on the lake occurred on August 9, 1862. The 141-foot, 323-ton schooner *Oriole* under Captain Daniel McAdams had left Marquette at 8 p.m., Friday, August 8, bound for Erie, Pennsylvania, with 501 tons of iron ore in her hold. There were 13 persons aboard, the captain having brought his wife and mother-in-law as passengers. Shortly after departure, the schooner encountered a blinding fog. Since Captain McAdams could still see his masthead signal lights from the deck, he kept right on going. Three men joined the mate on watch after midnight. About 3 a.m. on the 9th, a steamer charged out of the mist, struck the schooner on her starboard quarter and literally cut the vessel in two. Only one person survived; Cook Andrew P. Fleming of Sodus, New York, found himself cast from his bunk into the water. Grabbing a piece of wreckage, he floated for several hours; when day broke and the fog began to lift, he spotted the detached stern of his ship nearby, climbed back aboard and lowered the ship's undamaged yawl. The yawl had no oars and Fleming could only float around on the lake for the next day and a half. He was picked up by Captain Clifford of the brig *Globe* and brought to Marquette on August 11. Meanwhile, as the weather cleared, Captain McLeod of the schooner *Plover* found the remains of the *Oriole*, including portions of her sides, masts and deck, eight miles due north of Pictured Rocks. The hull had been completely severed; sails and rigging floated nearby, but there was no sign of life. Ten crewmen and two passengers had died with their ship.

The new side-wheel steamer Sunbeam *was sunk by an unusual midsummer storm on August 27, 1863. Only one person survived.* GREAT LAKES HISTORICAL SOCIETY COLLECTION.

In Marquette, Cook Fleming discovered that his schooner had been downed by the crack steamer *Illinois* under Captain Ryder. As the ships had separated immediately after impact in the whiteout, Ryder was unaware that he had sunk the other. Thinking the schooner was not badly damaged, and with considerable bow injury to his own vessel, he had continued to Marquette. It would appear that in the blinding mists of a summer fog the *Oriole* had unwittingly crossed the bow of the approaching *Illinois*. At that, Mr. Fleming was lucky to have been a survivor. Not long after landing in the water, he heard the whistle of another steamer closing rapidly. This was the fast *Seabird*, which was following the *Illinois*. Fortunately, the *Seabird* missed the debris which would save Fleming.[28]

Several times in Lake Superior history, late August has produced unusually heavy storms which wreaked havoc on unwary shipping. This was the story of the Civil War period's most costly tragedy on the lake. The trim new side-wheeler *Sunbeam* of the Chicago-based Goodrich Line had just been assigned to western Lake Superior in midsummer 1863, running from Superior City to the Keweenaw Point area. A 398-ton passenger and freight steamer, she had been launched in July 1861 by the reputable builders Bates & Son of Manitowoc, Wisconsin. Her original name had been *Victor*. As the *Victor*, she had been built with an unusual propulsion system consisting of twin propellers mounted on her sides. The unique scheme, patented by Captain Harry D. Whittaker, proved a failure and she was returned to the Bates shipyard in Manitowoc for rebuilding as a conventional side-wheeler, operating as such in her second season. Though a wood burner, she was reasonably fast, making 11 mph. Captain Dougall, with several years of Lake Superior experience, was in command with Chief Engineer Thomas Healy, formerly of Marquette. After a few hours stop at Superior City on August 26, the *Sunbeam* left for the Keweenaw in good weather, arriving at Ontonagon the next day. Taking on freight and passengers, she cleared Ontonagon about 6 p.m. for Portage Lake on what appeared to be a routine summer voyage.

But trouble arose shortly after dark in the form of an unexpected northerly gale. Throughout the night, she struggled on toward the east, being sighted the next morning off Eagle River by the crew of the steamer *Michigan*, also in bad shape. Fearing that he could not round Keweenaw Point safely, Dougall turned back, apparently intending to run for the shelter of La Pointe in the Apostle Islands. Then the engine quit and sails had to be set. By this time, however, the ship was out of control, listing badly and beginning to sink. Despite the deplorable situation, Dougall had maintained good order. Two lifeboats were launched and most of the passengers and crew were placed aboard them. When the *Sunbeam* began to break up, her people abandoned her about 15 miles off the Keweenaw coast. At the last minute, Wheelsman Charles Fregeau gave up his seat in the lifeboat to make room for the ship's chambermaid who had been left behind inadvertently. Jumping on a piece of the hurricane deck which broke away as the ship settled, Fregeau grabbed ropes from the signal mast on the pilothouse and lashed himself to his raft. When articles of cargo bobbed up while the hull dove for the bottom, Fregeau succeeded in seizing a five gallon keg of port wine which he also tied to his precarious perch. This "nourishment" may have kept him alive, as he floated watersoaked for more than 30 hours before being tossed ashore on the Keweenaw Peninsula, about 20 miles west of Eagle River. Yet, he was more fortunate than his shipmates, since both lifeboats capsized, drowning everybody aboard.

Fregeau landed on a narrow rock beach just out of reach of the waves; here he remained for another day and a half, waiting for the seas to subside. He had begun to crawl and stagger along the beach toward the Keweenaw Portage when a party of coasting explorers found him and brought him down to Portage Lake and Houghton. He turned out to be the sole survivor. The *Sunbeam* was no more. Between 25 and 35 lives had been lost, and a brand new steamer worth $40,000 had gone to the bottom.[29]

The same gale nearly claimed another victim. The steamer *Michigan* was carried over the rocks of dreaded

the schooners *Fannie Bissel* and *David De Kalb* ashore at the same port in August; the schooner *George Goble,* storm mangled in the eastern lake during August; and the schooner *Jesse H. Farwell,* stranded and sunk in the Sault River, also in August.[32]

The booming cargo year of 1864 saw a number of lesser difficulties, but as far as can be ascertained, only one permanent loss on the lake. June blasts stranded and sank the

The steamer Cleveland *is pictured at busy Marquette, Michigan, docks in 1860s. She was damaged in an unfortunate stranding at Eagle Harbor in May 1863, but afterwards repaired.* C. PATRICK LABADIE COLLECTION.

Saw Tooth Reef, off Eagle River, without striking and managed to ride out the storm.

Further to the east, at Waiska Bay, the steamer *Cleveland* lost her new skipper, Captain Rattray, who was swept to his death off the pilothouse ladder. Lake Superior sailors would long remember the tempest of late August 1863.[30]

Late fall of 1863 witnessed two other casualties southeast of Marquette. The lumber firm of Wetmore and Company had a small saw mill at Au Train River. A young Nova Scotia immigrant, Richard Ross, skippered a small, four-ton sail boat which hauled food and supplies to the mill site. On November 26, 1863, Ross and a Frenchman named LeClaire left Marquette with a cargo of two tons of corn meal, 50 bushels of potatoes and four bales of hay. They failed to arrive. Another supply boat, two weeks later, discovered the Ross boat capsized and smashed on the rocks six miles northwest of Au Train, but no trace was found of the two sailors. The nameless sailboat and the two crewmen had succumbed to the lake.[31]

Bad weather during the year had caused damage to several other vessels, with expensive repair bills accruing to the steamer *Cleveland,* stranded at Eagle Harbor in May;

steamer *Illinois* at Eagle River and also grounded the propeller *Lac La Belle* there. They were both retrieved. A rugged November saw the 361-ton schooner *George Foote* and the 365-ton schooner *Queen City* go on the rocks near Marquette, substantially beaten. The *Queen City* was all through, laying her bones on the Chocolay shore, a $10,000 loss. To the east, the hard luck steamer *City of Cleveland* lay on the beach at the mouth of Big Two-Hearted River. Abandoned and initially reported a complete wreck costing more than $35,000, salvagers reclaimed her remaining hull and reduced it to a barge by May 1866.[33]

On August 17, 1865, fire seized its first victim on western Lake Superior. En route to Superior, Wisconsin, the 179-foot, 689-ton side-wheeler *Traveller* had just docked at Eagle Harbor, Michigan, when she was discovered burning. Fire-fighting efforts were to no avail; all aboard escaped easily, and the baggage, ship's records, furniture and even some of the freight were saved; damage of $48,000 was entailed.[34]

Despite a remarkable upsurge in the iron ore trade which continued after the Civil War, shippers were spared the loss of a single additional vessel during 1865, 1866 and 1867. Only a collision of the propeller *Lady Franklin* with some nameless ship in Waiska Bay produced a moderate repair bill in 1865. Less serious damage was sustained by the schooners *Harriet Ross* and *Saginaw* in strandings at Eagle Harbor during June 1866. A single accident in May 1868 was worthy of note. Downbound from Marquette with a cargo of pig iron, the 252-ton schooner *Oneida Chief* ran ashore at Au Sable Point, a total loss of $35,000. She belonged to the Fitzgerald interests of Port Huron, Michigan.[35]

A different story unfolded in 1869, with 16 ships involved in mishaps of consequence, five totally destroyed and 12 fatalities. On June 12, fire scored again, this time at Marquette where the 185-foot, 637-ton propeller *Queen of the Lakes* was taking on a load of pig iron at the Cleveland dock. Just as her whistle signaled her departure, fire was discovered near the boiler on the main deck, well aft. Fire control attempts by the crew failed and the ship was soon a mass of flames. The tug *Joe D. Dudley,* owned by Peter White of Marquette, pulled her away from the dock in time to keep the flames from spreading ashore, and she slowly drifted to the sand beach near the Rolling Mill dock, where she burned for 40 hours. Flames lit the entire waterfront, an eerie sight visible for miles. Belonging to C.G. Evans and Company of Buffalo, she was worth more than $40,000 and her cargo still more, though salvage operations were conducted on her for several years.[36]

Also in June, the 185-ton schooner *North Star* was capsized by a squall on the eastern lake. She was righted with only moderate repairs necessary; two of her crew were drowned in the incident.[37] The following July 17, the 160-foot, 287-ton schooner *Grey Eagle,* en route from Chicago to Marquette, crashed aground near Whitefish Point, a $22,000 item. September brought news that the 297-ton bark *Nucleus,* already a participant in two mishaps earlier in the year, had sprung a leak when outbound from Marquette with ore and had gone to the bottom. Her crew escaped.[38] October would add the 204-ton schooner *Maumee Valley* to the toll, the vessel being severely mauled in a stranding at Marquette. She remained at Marquette for repairs until the next spring.

The storms of November 1869, nevertheless, were the worst yet experienced on the lake, the sailing ships bearing the brunt of the blasts. The first accident well illustrates the lonely, utterly desolate south shoreline which bounded sailors on their 140-mile run from Marquette to the Soo. On November 4, the 426-ton schooner *W.W. Arnold* cleared Marquette about 4 p.m. with 550 tons of iron ore bound for her home port of Cleveland. Under Captain Beardsley, the *Arnold* carried a crew of eight and two passengers. Three or four hours after she sailed, a frightful northwesterly gale with snow raked eastern Lake Superior. Lighthouse keeper Ashman at Whitefish Point Light reported the most terrific storm in his recollection, and it blew for 24 hours.

The *Arnold* failed to arrive at the Soo. Days later, when this news was communicated back to Marquette, concern was felt for the vessel, especially since the captain was well-known in Marquette and Munising; also, one passenger, Willie H. Boyes, had been a clerk at the post office in Marquette, hence an acquaintance of many townspeople. Initially, vesselmen could hardly believe her lost. She was a stout, seaworthy craft only six years old, built at Buffalo, rated A-1 and valued at $19,000. Captain Beardsley was a highly competent master. But as days went by and incoming ships reported no sign of the *Arnold,* the outlook was ominous. Of course, Marquette people were aware that there was virtually no civilization between Munising and Whitefish Point, nor on the eastern Canadian shore. It might have been possible for the ship to be ashore someplace where it would take the crew days to walk out. Yet, sailors well knew that any unfortunate ship trapped in the breakers of the south shore in that kind of tempest would stand little chance of survival without help from shore, and there was no one in that country to give such aid. November ran out with no word on the *Arnold.*

Finally, on December 7, an Indian mail carrier reached Munising with dreadful news. He had observed the shattered hull of a dark-colored vessel hurled on the beach at the mouth of the Big Two-Hearted River, about 25 miles west of Whitefish Point. Wreckage was everywhere, but ice and snow covered everything. The mail carrier reported that he had talked to an Indian trapper who had walked the beach at the Two-Hearted River four days after the storm; the trapper had counted 10 bodies at the water's edge. Four Munising men, David Sang, J.S. Wood, J.T. McCullam and A.S. Perinier, left the next day for the site, reaching the location after four days of intermittent coasting and snowshoeing along the shore. Stopping with trapper David Blucher at Grand Marais, they confirmed that the November 4 storm had been terrible at that spot. The water in Grand Marais harbor had been raised four feet by wind blasting in from the lake. The mail carrier's report was confirmed. The shattered hull lay dismasted off the mouth of the Two-Hearted River, the main mast in the river mouth and miscellaneous wreckage plastered over the 50-foot cliffs which rise some 50 yards south of the lake. But no bodies remained. One of the searchers did find the ship's nameboard, *W.W. Arnold.*

Subsequently, with an early spring and the snow mostly gone in the first week of April 1870, parties from both Munising and the Soo visited the scene. The schooner had struck off the river mouth, torn her bottom out and disintegrated. Those aboard had no chance in the roaring surf. Pieces of the wreck were scattered all the way to Whitefish Point, and a body, presumed to be that of the captain, was found and buried four miles east of the hull. Salvors for the insurance companies did recover some ropes, anchors and chains. Investigators surmised that a broken foremast had caused the accident. The mast was found snapped off 20 feet above the deck, and there were signs that the boom had been chopped away. As the sails had been carried close reefed on the main mast, found near the hull, the loss of the foremast simply put the ship at the mercy of the northwesterly gale, and she had been tossed ashore to her demise. Thus ended the

Marquette Harbor with 480 tons of iron ore in her hold, she broke loose in a storm on December 4 and was shattered on the shore south of the Cleveland dock. Built in 1856 and owned by R.K. Winslow of Cleveland, she was adjudged a complete wreck of $25,000.[41]

Word also arrived that the vile November weather had caused trouble at Copper Harbor, where the 129-foot, 227-ton schooner *Jura,* laden with railroad iron for Duluth,

Old Hanna Line propeller Comet *served the Lake Superior trades from 1857 until her loss by collision on August 26, 1875.* C. PATRICK LABADIE COLLECTION.

saga of the *W.W. Arnold,* whose loss had undoubtedly attracted more attention in the eastern lake than any accident up to that time.[39]

Two weeks after the gale which ravaged the *Arnold,* Marquette was bedeviled by another. The incoming schooner *Bermuda* was cast aground at Shot Point, while four vessels riding in the supposed safety of the harbor suffered injury. At daylight on November 19, only nine miles short of Marquette Harbor, the 394-ton schooner *Bermuda* was pinned on the rocks with four feet of water in her hold. Her crew reached shore, and her captain walked the beach to Marquette to report her situation. Owned by William Stewart of Detroit, she was under charter to Captain E.B. Ward with a cargo of merchandise for Marquette, where she was to have taken on a cargo of iron ore. Originally feared broken in two and a ruin, the *Bermuda* was salvaged the following July and taken to Detroit for repair. Built at Oswego, New York, in 1869, she was valued at $12,000, but destruction of her cargo made for a casualty of $25,000.[40] Four ships moored in Marquette Harbor fouled each other, the *DeSoto, Athenian, Jane Bell* and *Clara Parker,* all requiring repair work in varying degrees. The 411-ton bark *DeSoto* fared worse in another accident two weeks later. Moored in

had stranded and sunk. She was raised, unloaded, taken to Detroit for repairs and sailed back to Copper Harbor the following spring. She had stranded on November 10, 1869, and completed her voyage to Duluth, June 19, 1870.[42]

The rugged seas around Grand Island claimed another victim in the same November blasts. The 233-ton schooner *Eveline Bates,* en route from Cleveland to Marquette with a cargo of supplies, piled into Grand Island and was badly holed. Salvors got her off, but not before damages of $33,000 had been incurred. Rebuilt, she would again strand off Grand Island the following May.[43]

For purposes of study, the year 1869 might be considered the end of the development period of Lake Superior shipping. By this time more than 1,500 vessel passages were being recorded annually at the St. Marys Falls Canal, with tonnage carried exceeding a half million short tons. The casualty list indicates approximately 25 ships lost and 146 fatalities, but these records are admittedly inexact. Iron ore, pig iron, copper, some grain and lumber were carried east, with coal and general freight coming west. The major port areas included Marquette and the towns of the Keweenaw Peninsula; the Head-of-the-Lakes communities of Duluth and Superior would just start to come into their own in 1869.

[1] Dr. Grace Lee Nute has presented the most succinct account of pre-American shipping on Lake Superior in her fascinating book, *Lake Superior* (New York, Bobbs-Merrill, 1944), pp. 116-119. Numerous American and Canadian sources have fragmentary descriptions of these early ships, including the following: Alexander MacKenzie, *Voyages from Montreal on River St. Laurence through the Continent of North America, 1789 and 1793* (London, T. Codell, Jr. and W. Davis, et al, 1801) pp. xxxix and xl; Elliott Coues, *Manuscript Journals of Alexander Henry and David Thompson, 1799-1814* (New York, Francis P. Harper, 1897), p. 221; Daniel W. Harmon, *A Journal of Voyages and Travels in the Interior of North America* (New York, Allerton Book Co., 1905), p. 13; American boundary commissioner Major Joseph Delafield made shipping observations in *The Unfortified Boundary,* edited by Robert McElroy and Thomas Riggs (New York, privately published, 1943) Book 10, p. 381, and Book 11, p. 400; Canadian boundary commissioner Dr. John J. Bigsby had similar comments in *The Shoe and Canoe II* (London, Chapman & Hall, 1850), p. 234.

[2] The disaster to the Selkirk canoe is well documented. See "Diary of Nicholas Garry" in *Proceedings of the Royal Society of Canada,* Second Series (Ottawa, James Hope & Son, 1900), pp. 78, 113. Garry had just completed an ocean voyage with Dr. John McLoughlin, one of the survivors. Also, George Bryce, *The Remarkable History of Hudson's Bay Company* (New York, Burt Franklin, 1904, 1968 reprint), p. 244; and Marjorie W. Campbell, *McGillivray, Lord of the Northwest* (Toronto, Irwin & Co., 1962), p. 244.

[3] The stranding of the *Invincible* was noted by trader Jean Baptiste Perrault, in "Narrative of Jean Baptiste Perrault," John S. Fox, ed. in *Michigan Pioneer and Historical Collections,* Vol. 37, 1909-1910, p. 615; also, Gordon C. Davidson, *The Northwest Company* (New York, Russell and Russell, 1918, reissued 1967), p. 214.

[4] George W. Thayer, a surveyor's assistant to Michigan State Geologist Dr. Douglass Houghton, confirmed the position of the wreck off Fort Wilkins in 1845. See "From Vermont to Lake Superior" in *Michigan Pioneer and Historical Collections,* Vol. 30, 1905, p. 564. A fine contemporary account of the *Astor* is presented in Mac Frimodig, *Shipwrecks Off Keweenaw* (Lansing, Michigan Department of Natural Resources, 1974), pp. 3-5.

[5] Thom Holden, "Fall of 1840, the *Siskawit* Stranding" in *Nordic Diver,* Superior, Wisc., July-August 1974, pp. 8-9.

[6] The early fleet on Lake Superior is well described by William L. Bancroft, "Memoirs of Captain Samuel Ward," in *Michigan Pioneer and Historical Collections,* Vol. 21, 1892, pp. 336-367. See also Nute, *op.cit.,* p. 121.

[7] Rev. J.A. Ten Broek, "Old Keweenaw" in *Michigan Pioneer and Historical Collections,* Vol. 30, 1905, pp. 139-149. Rev. Ten Broek graphically depicts the terrible trip of the little side-wheeler; luckily, she was a good floater and drifter.

[8] *The Nor'easter,* Journal of the Lake Superior Marine Museum Association, Duluth, Minn., Vol. 12, No. 3, May-June 1987, p. 6.

[9] "Autobiography of Captain John G. Parker" in *Michigan Pioneer and Historical Collections,* Vol. 30, 1905, pp. 582-585; *Lake Superior Journal,* Aug. 8, 1852.

[10] John Keast, "Early Navigation on Lake Superior." Unpublished manuscript in Marquette County Historical Society, Marquette, Mich., Oct. 20, 1942. Mr. Keast, formerly associated with the Marquette County Historical Society, was a student of Lake Superior shipping for over 50 years.

[11] *Lake Superior Journal,* Aug. 13, 1851, and Dec. 1, 1851; Keast, *op.cit.*

[12] *Lake Superior Journal,* Dec. 12, 1851, and July 21, 1852; a recently discovered diary of a passenger on the *Monticello* was extracted as "Wreck of the Monticello" in *Inland Seas,* Vol. 24, No. 1, Spring 1968, p. 34; W.R. Williams, "Colonel McKnight's Lake Superior Line," in *Inland Seas,* Vol. 16, No. 2, Summer 1960, pp. 138-144; William M. Lytle and Forrest R. Holdcamper, *Merchant Steam Vessels of the United States, 1790-1868,* C. Bradford Mitchel, ed., (Staten Island, New York, The Steamship Historical Society of America, 1975), pp. 145, 149.

[13] "Autobiography of Captain John G. Parker", *op.cit.,* p. 584. A schooner *Chippewa* was still sailing in 1860, but whether this was the same ship is uncertain.

[14] *Lake Superior Journal,* July 7, 1852.

[15] *Lake Superior Journal,* Oct. 20, 1852, Sept. 24, 1853, and Jan. 2, 1854. "Soo Park's Propeller Recalls Story of Steamer *Independence* " in Lake Carriers' Association, *The Bulletin,* July 1953, pp. 17-19. Also Lewis Marvill, "First Trip by Steam to Lake Superior" in *Michigan Pioneer and Historical Collections,* Vol. 4, 1881, pp. 67-69. The *Independence* is reputed to be the first steam vessel to enter Prince Arthur's Landing, which later evolved into the present port of Thunder Bay, Ont. Thomas Farnquist, one of Lake Superior's outstanding scuba men, has preserved some of her timbers and iron work in Sault Ste. Marie, Michigan. Some of these artifacts are now exhibited at the Whitefish Point Lighthouse museum.

[16] W.R. Williams, *op.cit.,* p. 140.

[17] *Lake Superior Journal,* Nov. 8, 1856; *Chicago Democratic Press,* Nov. 15, 1856; *New York Daily Times,* Nov. 26, 1856, has the story of a survivor, Joseph W. Dennis. C.M. Shields, son of survivor James Shields, later prepared a manuscript, "An Account by My Father of Shipwreck," a copy of which is on file in the Peter White Public Library, Marquette, Mich. The Shields recollections, apparently written some years later, contain some discrepancies from earlier published reports. The *Lake Superior Mining Journal,* Dec. 12, 1868, has further information.

[18] *Lake Superior Journal,* Nov. 27, 1856; Lytle and Holdcamper, *op. cit.,* p. 16; Document of Enrollment, Detroit, Oct. 24, 1856; *Cleveland Evening Herald,* Sept. 16, 1856; *Detroit Free Press,* Sept. 28, 1856 and July 7, 1857; *Cleveland Plain Dealer,* Nov. 18, 1856. As the schooner *Marquette,* this vessel stranded in November 1872 west of Grand Island.

[19] *Detroit Daily Free Press,* Nov. 17, 1857; Richard J. Wright, "A History of Shipbuilding in Cleveland" in *Inland Seas,* Vol. 13, No. 1, Spring 1957, pp. 29-37.

[20] Homer Wells, *History of Accidents, Casualties, and Wrecks on Lake Superior* (Duluth, Corps of Engineers, U.S. Army, 1938), 90-page unpublished typewritten manuscript, p. 3.

[21] Wells, *ibid,* p. 3. Scuba divers discovered the *Indiana* intact in 118 feet of water north of Crisp Point in the early 1970s. Her capstan and anchor have been on display in the *Valley Camp* Museum at Sault Ste. Marie, Mich.

22 *Houghton Daily Mining Gazette,* July 30, 1979; *Duluth News Tribune,* Aug. 7, 1979; Thom Holden, "One Cylinder Steam Engine Target of Recovery Teams" in *Superior Evening Telegram,* Aug. 7, 1979; *Escanaba Daily Press,* Aug. 8, 1979; *Pontiac Oakland Press,* Aug. 9, 1979; *Sault Ste. Marie* (Mich.) *Evening News,* Aug. 9, 1979 *Cleveland Plain Dealer,* Sept. 24, 1979; *"Indiana"* in American Bureau of Shipping, *Surveyor,* Vol. 14, No. 3, August 1980, p. 20. Author's transcript of exhibit labels on the *Indiana* machinery displayed in Smithsonian Institution, Dec. 1982.

23 *Lake Superior Journal,* Sept. 14, 1859; Document of Enrollment, Cleveland, March 13, 1847.

24 *Ibid.*

25 *Superior Chronicle,* June 9, 1860; *Lake Superior News,* Aug. 9, 1884. Writing to the editor of the *News,* Captain Barton Atkins of Elmira, New York, reported his recollections of sailing Lake Superior in the 1860s. He supplied interesting details on these two wrecks of 1860.

26 *Superior Chronicle,* Sept. 15, 1860; also *Lake Superior News,* Aug. 9, 1884.

27 Ralph D. Williams, "Commerce of the Great Lakes" in Charles Moore, ed., *Saint Marys Falls Canal Semicentennial 1905* (Detroit, Semicentennial Commission, 1907), p.193.

28 *Lake Superior News and Journal,* Aug. 15, 1862.

29 *Lake Superior News and Journal,* Sept. 4, 1863. Edward N. Middleton Collection notes housed in U.S. Army Corps of Engineers' Canal Park Visitor Center, Duluth, Minn. John A. Bardon, "Wreck of the Propeller Sunbeam," unpublished manuscript in files of the St. Louis County Historical Society, Duluth, Minn., based on interviews years later with Wheelsman Charles Fregeau who resided in Superior, Wisc. There are some differences in details with earlier published material. Fregeau's name had been anglicized to Frazier in many accounts. Lost in this accident were two prominent political leaders, the Hon. Abner Sherman, Michigan State Representative from Ontonagon, and Augustus Coburn, brother of the U.S. Representative from Indiana. Sherman had been one of the Lincoln electors from Michigan in 1860.

30 *Lake Superior News and Journal,* Sept. 4, 1863.

31 *Lake Superior News and Journal,* Dec. 18, 1863.

32 National Archives, Microcopy T-729, *Marine Casualties on the Great Lakes, 1863-1873* (Record Group 26, Records of the U.S. Coast Guard). Pages unnumbered.

33 Wells, *op.cit.* pp. 5-6; National Archives, *Microcopy T-729;* Lytle and Holdcamper, *op. cit.,* p. 37.

34 *Superior Gazette,* Aug. 26, 1865.

35 National Archives, *Microcopy T-729.*

36 *Duluth Weekly Minnesotian,* July 3, 1869; *Marquette Mining Journal,* Oct. 31, 1874 (notes on salvage operations).

37 Wells, *op. cit.* p.7.

38 National Archives, *Microcopy T-729.*

39 The *Arnold* disappearance occupied the Marquette newspapers for months. *Marquette Mining Journal,* Nov. 20, 27, Dec. 18, 25, 1869; Jan. 1, 1870; April 9, 25, 1870; May 14, 1870.

40 *Marquette Mining Journal,* Nov. 20, 1869, July 23, 1870.

41 *Marquette Mining Journal,* Nov. 20, Dec. 11, 18, 1869, May 14, 1870.

42 *Marquette Mining Journal,* Nov. 20, 1869; *Duluth Weekly Minnesotian,* June 25, 1870.

43 National Archives, *Microcopy T-729.*

The opening of the port of Duluth was one of the most significant events of the 1870s era on Lake Superior. The iron steamer India *is pictured with two schooners in this 1874 view.* CANAL PARK MARINE MUSEUM COLLECTION.

Chapter 2

The Booming Seventies
1870-1879

Events of the 1870s completely revamped Lake Superior shipping. The Lake Superior and Mississippi Railroad was completed to Duluth during the summer of 1870 and produce from agricultural Minnesota and the Great Plains began moving eastward across Lake Superior. A considerable volume of shipping would be attracted to the western lake for the first time. The Riel Rebellion of 1870 in western Canada also impressed upon Canadians the need to link the eastern provinces with the western country or face the threat of sacrificing the western provinces to expansionist American interests. Accordingly, the community now known as Thunder Bay, formerly Prince Arthur's Landing and later Port Arthur and Fort William, became a bastion for railroad development

and Canadian shipping on the northern shore of Lake Superior. For 12 years, while the Canadian Pacific Railroad was under construction, a large amount of Canadian freight was routed through Duluth for railroad transfer to the Red River, where river boats conveyed it to Winnipeg. The development in the 1870s of a fabulous silver mine at Silver Islet near Thunder Bay also spurred shipping on the north shore, as a good deal of prospecting was carried on. Lumber from northern Wisconsin gained access to Lake Superior in 1877 when the Wisconsin Central Railroad reached the western south shore of the lake at Ashland, Wisconsin. Iron ore production continued to make modest gains on the Marquette Range, while the increase in other commerce was hardly short of phenomenal. The 1879 figure for wheat shipments was 50 times that of 1870; the totals for other grains multiplied three-fold; coal commerce had jumped sixfold and lumber more than thirty-fold.[1] Despite the two-year setback in many economic activities caused by the panic of 1873, the Lake Superior shipping boom was on.

To accommodate pyramiding freight demands, vessel passages at the Soo in 1879 would nearly double those of 1870 and more ships meant more accidents. During the 1870s, approximately 25 vessels sailed their last with 81 fatalities. As many ships were lost as hitherto had been destroyed in more than 80 years of Canadian-American sailing on Lake Superior.

1870

Schooners took the brunt of beatings in 1870. May weather brought considerable damage to the 233-ton schooner *Evaline Bates* in a second scrape at Grand Island and to the 292-ton schooner *Southwest* which went ashore at Vermilion Point. The schooner *Africa,* a little 186-tonner, was temporarily sunk in a striking at the Soo during August as was the 682-ton propeller *Onton-agon* in the St. Marys River above the Canal. Two per-manent losses were recorded in summertime accidents. The 17-year-old veteran *George W. Ford* struck and went to pieces on a reef at Eagle Harbor. This 100-ton schooner was owned by Captain John G. Parker. Captain Parker was one of the pioneer masters on the lake. He had portaged the *Ford* around the rapids at the Soo in 1853, nursing her through all kinds of weather in innumerable voyages to diverse ports. He was not aboard at the time of the mishap.[2]

Also, a schooner, *Mary M. Scott,* sank near Grand Island on November 2. There continues to be some con-fusion as to this vessel's full identity. The available liter-ature refers to a *G.W. Scott,* a *Marien Scott* and a *May Scott,* all apparently in reference to the same 361-ton vessel becoming a total loss at or near Grand Island.[3]

As usual, autumn did worse mischief. An October gale drove the 394-ton schooner *Bermuda,* fresh out of the shipyard after her ordeal on Shot Point in the fall of 1869, onto the rocks of Grand Island where she was declared to be a total loss with costs running more than $25,000. Laden with iron ore, she held fast to her shallow water berth although lake waves and ice did not destroy her. To the surprise of vessel men, a group of enterprising Cana-dian salvors came along to tackle her 13 years later. The attempt was unsuccessful. The schooner is still in Mur-ray Bay in 40 feet of water.[4]

November added to the Grand Island toll with the sizable 412-ton schooner *Dreadnaught* tossed aground and initially abandoned. She was apparently salvaged, but losses exceeded $13,000.[5] November blasts caught the

schooner *S.B. Pomeroy* in the eastern lake; her injuries were slight but she lost two crewmen overboard.[6] The schooner *William Shupe* apparently came away from a November 15 grounding among the Apostle Islands vir-

Two-year-old scow-schooner Cháska *was wrecked at Ontonagon in the summer of 1871. She was the first commercial ship built at Duluth.* CANAL PARK MARINE MUSEUM COLLECTION.

tually unscathed. She was reported carrying 445 tons of coal headed to the Northern Pacific Railway dock in Su-perior when she grounded in the channel between Sand Island and the mainland. The *Shupe* was drawing nine and a half feet of water where channel depths were but eight feet. She was released after lightering part of her cargo overboard.[7] The final casualty of 1870 involved the 426-ton schooner *A.H. Moss,* which needed moderate repairs after a grounding at Eagle Harbor.[8]

1871

The shipping season of 1871 opened more favorably. Minor losses were sustained in harbor sinkings from leaks to the schooners *H.C. Winslow* at Marquette and *Stranger* at Superior. August brought an accident of importance to Duluth sailors. On August 28, the 72-foot, 50-ton scow-

built at Milan, Ohio, by Merry and Gay, having roamed the lakes for 15 years, a fair life for an early schooner. She was a liability in excess of $28,000.[10]

Altogether, 1871 brought good sailing with only slight repairs being needed by the steamer *Cleveland* which suffered a mechanical breakdown in September, the bark *Gen. Franz Siegel* which grounded at Vermilion Point and

Before excavation of the Duluth Ship Canal in 1871, the port's docks were all on the open lakeshore. NORTHEAST MINNESOTA HISTORICAL CENTER.

schooner *Chaska,* was caught by a sudden northwesterly blow and dashed ashore while hauling stone for the Ontonagon breakwater. Only her rigging could be saved. Her crew escaped, but the loss of $3,500 was a severe setback to her owners, the Merritt family from Oneota, Duluth. This pioneer Head-of-the-Lakes family, then active in western Lake Superior sailing, built the *Chaska* in 1869 as the first vessel constructed at a Duluth shipyard. The Merritt family would later become famous in Minnesota iron ore exploration and development.[9]

A gale in eastern Lake Superior was awaiting the 390-ton schooner *Plover,* which left Duluth on October 7 after loading 18,000 bushels of grain. Her cargo was being shipped by J.L. Dumont of Duluth to J.D. Sawyer of Buffalo. Caught in high seas, she was driven ashore, stranded and sunk near Whitefish Point on October 12. Word of the accident reached the Soo and it was relayed to the lower lakes that the *Plover* had gone down with all hands. However, Captain Jones and his eight man crew had taken a small boat to safety, reaching the Soo two days later. Owned by R.K. Winslow of Cleveland, she had been

the propeller *City of Madison* which stranded at Grand Traverse Bay.

1872

The story for 1872 would be much different regarding casualties. This proved to be an excellent year for most freight tonnage, but to their sorrow, mariners would be active until late November. Early season accidents were minor. The propeller *Union* stranded in June with negligible injury at Laughing Whitefish Point near Marquette. On July 11 the Canadian side-wheeler *Manitoba* hooked on a rock near Michipicoten Island. The *Manitoba* incident was more scary than destructive. She remained pinned on an uncharted rock for two days until another Canadian side-wheeler, *Cumberland,* came along, took off her 75 passengers and pulled her free. The *Manitoba* had to be beached and taken to Detroit for repairs. An August fire seared the tug *F.L. Danforth* at Duluth.

Things got much worse in autumn. An unusually rugged equinoctial gale riled central and eastern Lake Superior, blowing for 14 hours at Marquette. Caught at the Rolling Mill Dock in Marquette's partially protected harbor,

Propeller Northern Light *is pictured here with brig* Commerce *in an 1872 view of the port of Duluth along the Lake Superior shoreline.* CANAL PARK MARINE MUSEUM COLLECTION.

the schooners *A.H. Moss* and *E.C. Roberts* had to be scuttled on September 18 to prevent their being beaten to pieces, as they were in the process of discharging coal cargoes and could not be quickly moved. Salvage and rebuilding costs exceeded $10,000.[11] This weather giant caught the brand new schooner *Maple Leaf* off Isle Royale, whipping her on the rocks and stripping off her masts and cabin. She had been launched the previous June by R.D. Pike of Bayfield. Originally reported a goner, she was taken off and rebuilt, serving another nine years before laying her bones in the western lake. Her crew escaped on a scow.[12]

Things seemed to calm down in October, losses being slight. The scow-schooner *You Tell,* owned by L.H. Tenney of Duluth, hit the rocks off Isle Royale's Washington Harbor on September 26 and proved unsalvageable, but she was of low value. She had been hauling a load of hay from Prince Arthur's Landing, now Thunder Bay, to Ashland. Minimal refitting was needed by the schooner *Middlesex* which developed a leak at Marquette, the propeller *Cuyahoga* after hitting bottom at Eagle Harbor, the Canadian schooner 204-net-ton *Lillie Pratt* which struck at the Soo and the propeller *St. Paul* which suffered a mechanical breakdown off Whitefish Point.

Then came *the* November with two of the worst storms ever to afflict shipping on Lake Superior. The first monstrous nor'easter unquestionably shaped the destiny of the port of Duluth. Although the Duluth side of St. Louis Bay was accessible, after a fashion, from the natural harbor entry at Superior and the original Duluth Ship Canal that had been cut through Minnesota Point in 1871, an extensive port installation had been constructed on the open lake, below 3rd and 4th Avenues East in Duluth. Here a breakwater, grain elevator, wharves and warehouses were placed, complete with railroad trackage. The rampaging waves on November 12-13, cast spray 100 feet high, demolished part of the breakwater and hurled four vessels, presumably in the safety of the breakwater, on the beach of Minnesota Point. Stuck hard with varying degrees of damage were the schooners *Alice Craig, Sweetheart* and *Francis Palms* and the propeller *St. Paul.* A dare-devil tug captain named Martin Wheeler ran the big harbor tug *Bob Anderson* through the Duluth entry at the height of the storm to prevent her joining the casualties. The schooner *Craig* would not be salvaged and rebuilt for five years. After this experience Duluthians realized that the future port of Duluth had best be inside the shelter of Minnesota Point.[13]

Ward Line propeller St. Paul *was torn from the Lake Superior & Mississippi Railway dock at Duluth in a November 1872 storm which destroyed the new outer harbor breakwater.* CANAL PARK MARINE MUSEUM COLLECTION.

Roaring eastward, the winds drove the schooner *Exile* stern-first over the bar at Chocolay River, Marquette, into the comparative safety of the river, but were less considerate of the 131-foot, 323-ton schooner *Marquette* under Captain Young, pitching her hard ashore on the mainland west of Grand Island. At first thought only lightly injured, she proved impossible to retrieve. The ensuing winter was harsh with ice lasting into the next May. Salvors could only glean odds and ends; her anchors, capstan, chains.[14]

No final loss figure was reported, though she must have been worth $15,000 to her owner, E.B. Ward.

Worse was to follow 10 days later when a horrendous gale swooped down on Marquette, moving gradually eastward. The little schooner *Libby* was wrenched from the Cleveland Dock and hammered to bits on the rocks below the Northwestern Hotel on November 24. The weather was immediately reinforced by more sinister blasts. Meanwhile, the 400-ton schooner-barges *Jupiter* and *Saturn* were loading iron ore in Marquette. They cleared port on the morning of November 27 in tow of the wooden side-wheel steamer *John A. Dix* under Captain Joseph Waltman. At the same time, moving into the eastern lake downbound from Duluth with grain were the 400-ton schooner *W.O. Brown* and the 354-ton schooner *Charles C. Griswold*. About 5 p.m. on November 27, the *Dix* and her tows were engulfed by enormous seas off Vermilion Point. In half an hour the *Jupiter* broke her towline and an hour later the *Saturn* broke hers. The *Dix* had to run for the shelter of Whitefish Point to save herself. Her decks were quickly covered with a foot of ice, as intense sub-zero temperatures accompanied the winds. The luckless schooner-barges were cast ashore; the *Saturn* three miles west of Whitefish Point and the *Jupiter* 12 miles further west of Vermilion Point. Apparently, both struck bottom, then were dragged by the undertow to deeper water, since only masts were visible. Their entire crews of 14 men and one woman were dead, either drowned or victims of exposure.

The two grain carriers fared no better. The *Griswold* must have been overwhelmed with all hands in southern Whitefish Bay, as masts protruding from deeper water off Gros Cap are presumed to have been hers. The unlucky *W.O. Brown* was literally captured by the "hurricane" and nearly thrown out of the lake in a little bay near Point Maimanse, disintegrating in the shallows with her main mast actually crashing down on the shore. Captain R.L. Manning, First Mate John Hansen and Seaman Henry Edward were washed overboard and drowned when the foremast went over the side, while Second Mate George Manning, hitherto half frozen while on watch, drowned in his bunk. Two more were washed away, until only seamen John Ring, Malcolm McCloud and Jugan Alberts remained. They clung to the hulk for two more hours and then made a rush to the nearby beach by leaping from rock to rock.

Ring, McCloud and Alberts made it, but their troubles were only beginning. On the heels of the storm came a cold wave seldom seen in the Lake Superior basin during November. For several days after the fateful November 28 when both the *Brown* and the *Griswold* met their end, sub-zero temperatures blanketed the eastern lake. The intense cold froze the St. Marys River and the Canal, trapping many ships above the Soo. Only an uncanny knowledge of survival techniques kept the three castaways alive.

The cabin of the shattered *Brown* was cast ashore intact. After finding no shelter in the snow-covered forest, the three sailors returned to the cabin perched on beach rocks and ingeniously started a fire, without matches. They simply fired blank cartridges from a revolver into a woolen shirt that had remained dry in the cabin. With copious wood supplies at hand, they maintained sufficient warmth in the cabin to keep themselves from freezing. But, they were weakened by having eaten nothing for 30 hours. There was ample wheat from the wreck, but the men couldn't stomach it raw. By boiling the wheat for hours, however, they were able to make a kind of porridge that kept them from starving. When the lake finally calmed, they were able to make a raft from wreckage and retrieve the ship's yawl, hanging on rocks a short distance out. With canvas from the ruined sails, they gradually patched the little boat so that on December 7, ten days after the tragedy, they were able to start paddling along the Canadian shore southeastward in search of help.

After 25 miles of frigid coasting, they struck Batchawana Bay, finding a small logging camp there. The lumberjacks took them in, fed them and nursed them back to health, as the three were pretty well exhausted. At Christmas, an Indian guided them cross-country to Sault Ste. Marie where the local citizens clothed them. Canal Superintendent Carleton and others took them to a railhead on the Lower Peninsula across the Straits of Mackinac. Jugan Alberts, who provided newspapers an account of the disaster and the survivals, reached his home in Freeport, Illinois, in the fourth week of January, nearly two months after his ship should have taken him to Chicago. Thus ended the most unusual rescue story in the annals of Lake Superior sailing.[15]

The luxurious propeller Peerless *was built for the Chicago and Duluth route in 1872 to handle increasing traffic in passengers and package freight.* CANAL PARK MARINE MUSEUM COLLECTION.

Contradictory figures have appeared concerning the human and financial losses in this quadruple catastrophe. The human casualty toll seemingly should be: seven on the *Jupiter*, eight on the *Saturn*, six on the *Brown* and

The handsome schooner Cambridge *was dashed to pieces on the rocks near Marquette in the summer of 1873.* University of Michigan Transportation Library collection.

eight on the *Griswold.* Minimum monetary losses would include: $12,000 for the *Jupiter,* $13,000 for the *Saturn,* $24,000 for the *Brown* and $27,000 for the *Griswold.*[16]

Narrow escapes were myriad. The new 210-foot iron steamer *Japan* had a close call, losing her deck load of flour before reaching safety at the Soo. The schooner *Golden Rule* was stripped of her sails and iced up, several of her crew being badly frozen. So many ships were trapped by ice on the lake side of the Soo Canal that the iron steamer *China* broke her way to open water and sailed back to Marquette with more than 400 seaman aboard. These sailors then made the overland trek to the Straits of Mackinac where they were picked up by boat.

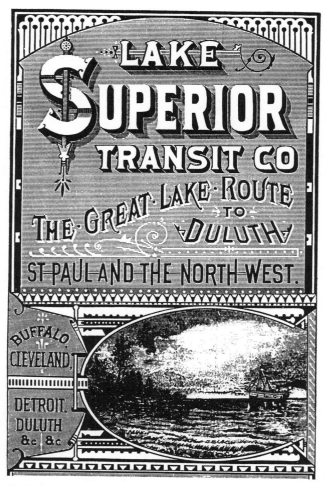

The largest companies advertised through service from Buffalo to the Head of the Lakes. INSTITUTE FOR GREAT LAKES RESEARCH COLLECTION.

Most ships took some battering, but the most important damage seemed sustained by the propeller *Atlantic,* the iron propeller *India* with a machinery breakdown at Eagle Harbor and the tow tug *Tempest* which lost a scow carrying machinery worth more than $4,500. The tempestuous November of 1872 would always be remembered. So widespread had been the early freeze that the

new Keweenaw Waterway, just opened in 1870, was sealed tight, locking several ships therein, while far to the south at Detroit, six inches of ice plugged the St. Clair River.

As is frequently the case, out of a miserable catastrophe emerges some good. The schooner-barges *Jupiter* and *Saturn* belonged to the highly regarded Captain Eber Ward of Detroit, the *Charles C. Griswold* to Chesebrough & Company of Detroit and the *W.O. Brown* to William Doyle of Chicago. All four schooners were insured; likewise, it is highly possible that the dead officers and crewmen carried personal life insurance policies. At any rate, it is interesting to note that, after shipping men had expressed the opinion that some lives might have been saved if professional lifesavers had been present, the Board of Lakes Underwriters began an immediate exchange with the Secretary of the Treasury, then responsible for the fledgling U.S. Life-Saving Service. On March 24, 1873, less than four months after the accidents, Secretary of the Treasury Richardson instructed a Board of Life-Saving officers to survey Lake Superior for prospective sites of lifesaving stations. The Life-Saving Board's report, filed on January 21, 1874, was communicated to Congress and in an Act of June 20, 1874, Congress authorized the establishment of four lifesaving stations on eastern Lake Superior. The specific locations were chosen by Captain J.H. Merryman of the U.S. Revenue Marine in September 1874. The stations were constructed in 1875 and became fully operational in 1876 at Vermilion Point, Crisp Point, Two-Hearted River and Muskallonge Lake which was also known as Deer Park.[17]

1873

While traffic demands held up rather well despite the onset of the financial panic, shipping accidents were halved. During July, the bark *Massillon* suffered slight injury in a stranding at Whitefish Point and the brig *Mechanic* needed a few repairs after a leak caused her to settle at Marquette. A sprightly August gale, nevertheless, lambasted the 162-foot, 445-ton schooner *Cambridge,* putting her on the rocks near Marquette. Though she had withstood the Duluth gale of mid-November 1872 and the disaster of November 27-28, 1872, in the eastern lake, ultimately being frozen in above the canal, this stranding was the end of the line. With cargo she was valued in excess of $33,000.[18] Apparently she was outbound from Marquette to Cleveland with iron ore at the time of the mishap.

Tough August weather also necessitated moderate repairs for the bark *Acorn* which began leaking near Marquette. Yet, a late September blow produced another "sailed her last." Leaving Marquette on September 24, with 432 tons of iron ore consigned to the Elk Rapids Iron Company of Michigan, the 553-ton propeller *Union* under

Captain D.L. Stearns ran head on into the northerly gusts. She was driven ashore at Point Au Sable about September 25. The waves quickly broke her up, though salvors picked off some articles of value. Her crew was safe. Built in Manitowoc, Wisconsin, in 1861, she was owned by Mark English of Green Bay and was worth more than $18,000.[19]

October brought most of the bad news this year. Exceedingly rough water on the eastern lake caused the crew of Eber Ward's 889-ton propeller *Annie L. Craig* to jettison 200 barrels of flour costing more than $5,000 in a successful effort to keep the ship afloat. The raging seas caught the 372-ton schooner *Athenian* in Waiska Bay and deposited her hard aground. Originally reported a total loss valued at $32,000, she was raised the following spring by Captain Robinson of Buffalo, the marine inspector for Inland Union Insurance Company, and towed to Detroit for rebuilding.[20] A mechanical breakdown on the steamer *Metropolis* northwest of Marquette was relatively insignificant, but a similar incident aboard the brand new 741-ton steam barge *Geneva* proved terribly costly. The *Geneva* was just out of the shipyard in the spring of 1873, one of an innovative series of bulk freight vessels originating with the *R.J. Hackett* in 1869, which had pilot house forward and engines in the stern, leaving the entire intermediate hull space available for unobstructed loading and unloading of iron ore, coal, grain, or lumber. Downbound from Duluth under Captain George McKay with 33,000 bushels of wheat and towing the barge *Genoa*, she lost a coupling on the shaft, her propeller dropped down, tearing planking and the inrushing water swamped the pumps, though her crew tried valiantly for 20 hours to save her. About 15 miles off Caribou Island on October 23, Captain McKay ordered the vessel abandoned and her people boarded the *Genoa* which was picked up later by the steam barge *Nahant* and towed to the Soo. The *Geneva* slid to the bottom, a probable loss of $125,000. She was owned by the Hanna Company of Cleveland.

Two more strandings rounded out the year; the schooner *Pelican* at Grand Island and the schooner *John L. Gross* at Eagle Harbor, but damage supposedly was only moderate. The *Gross*, laden with 400 tons of coal, could not be salvaged after her November stranding.[21]

1874

Reduced economic activity after the Panic of 1873 was reflected in one-third fewer vessel passages at the Soo Canal. Down also were casualties for 1874. Four casualties were negligible, although four other ships were destroyed. Few repairs were needed by the schooner *Sweetheart* after some mauling by rough water and by the schooner *Harvest Home* after striking in Waiska Bay. Minor mechanical replacements were needed for the steam barge

Jarvis Lord whose engine went dead off Whitefish Point and for the propeller *City of Duluth* which suffered a breakdown off Portage.[22] The 144-foot, 369-ton schooner *F. Morrell,* however, crashed into a reef at Grand Island. There she ended her days, a liability of $23,000.[23]

Three autumn mishaps in the western end of the lake further clouded the record, and one was fatal. On September 9, the 112-ton schooner *D.R. Owen* was whipped aground at Bad River and abandoned by her crew. Owned in Sheboygan, Wisconsin, she was insured for $3,000 by the Northwestern National Insurance Company. An attempted salvage was successful.[24]

Little side-wheel freighter Lotta Bernard *served Head of the Lakes communities for several years before her 1874 foundering.* CANAL PARK MARINE MUSEUM COLLECTION.

The most sinister event of the year was the early morning foundering of the 125-foot, 190-ton side-wheeler *Lotta Bernard* when northeast of Encampment Island and about six miles off shore, roughly 40 miles from Duluth. One passenger and a deck hand were drowned in the October 29 accident, while the cook died of exposure. The *Lotta Bernard* was built in Port Clinton, Ohio, in 1869 and brought to Duluth in 1870 by Major L.H. Tenney who named her for his partner's daughter and his own son. In 1872, she was sold to Edmund Ingalls of Duluth who operated her at the time of the disaster. Of shallow draft with a clear forward deck for cargo, she was a convenient craft for entering the new ports on both north and south shores of the western lake, handling general cargo as well as lumber, timber and stone. Though a stout little ship, she was dreadfully slow, about four mph. Her critics predicted that a sweeping northeaster would sometime catch up with and overwhelm her. Though her owners took exception, her critics were right. In her five seasons of service at the Head of the Lakes, the *Lotta Bernard* had been in frequent scrapes, but she bravely carried on.

In late October 1874, she was on the north shore run from Canadian lakehead to Duluth. Under Captain Michael Norris, she left Silver Islet at 5:30 p.m., October 27, reaching Pigeon River at midnight where she hove to. At

6 a.m., October 28, with the wind briskly from the northeast but no real heavy weather threatening, Captain Norris sailed for Duluth, 150 miles away. All day and into the night the little side-wheeler plodded along, making excellent time with a trailing sea. Yet, in late afternoon and evening, a gale blew up, giant waves steadily coming over the stern. They systematically took their toll, smashing bulwarks and cabin, until only the smoke stack remained intact. Fortunately, two boats held to their davits. Water began to build up below decks and the pumps were started. Gradually, however, the water gained. Crew discipline was excellent. Some of the men were in water up to their waists, but remained at their posts. The 13 crew members and two passengers bailed furiously. As a last resort, Captain Norris ordered the bow anchor thrown out in a final attempt to bring the bow into the wind.

About 12:30 a.m., October 29, the ship began to settle and the captain reluctantly had the two boats launched into the swirling snow and rampaging waves. The small boat with eight in it capsized immediately, though six survivors succeeded in regaining the derelict where the yawl was in process of being put over. Passenger Willie Blanchard and deck hand James Hansen tried to cling to the overturned boat and were swept away. Thirteen persons were now in the badly over-loaded yawl. Figuring he was off Encampment Island, Captain Norris edged the boat toward shore, but he had to avoid the trough. Desperately, they rowed and bailed, as the little craft had a hard time to avoid swamping. With only a tin pan for bailing, the crew quickly applied hats and boots.

Daybreak found them six miles from land. As the hours passed, they worked toward shore until by noon they were just off the mouth of Silver Creek several miles west of Encampment. They made a run for the beach, but swamped in the breakers. Fortunately, a high wave threw them well up on the gravel. They were alive, barely, half naked, starved and benumbed with cold. Realizing they had to find help immediately on the wilderness coast, the survivors split into two groups. The captain took nine with him and First Mate Calverly brought the two cooks with him. Shortly, the captain's group came upon an Indian encampment. The Indians took them in, revived and fed them. The other group was not as fortunate. They wandered for another day, the second cook succumbing to exposure while Indians searched for them. Luckily, Mate Calverly did recover the yawl on the shore to the west, not too badly damaged. The whole group then rowed to Agate Bay where they encountered two fishermen who made them comfortable, housed and fed them. On Sunday, November 1, the castaways were sufficiently recuperated to row into Duluth, arriving about 3 p.m. Three men had died, yet 12 had been saved by a combination of careful seamanship, superhuman endurance and a copious sprinkling of luck in their discovering generous and hospitable Indians and fishermen. The *Lotta Bernard* was worth $20,000 and insured for $10,000. Lost with her was a cargo of 200 sacks of flour, 60 kegs of fish and a horse.[25]

The weather gods had one more blast to level at Duluth and the western lake during 1874. A southwesterly storm with winds from 24-40 miles an hour hit unexpectedly on November 7, leveling some buildings in the community. Ripped from her berth at Vaughn's mill dock,

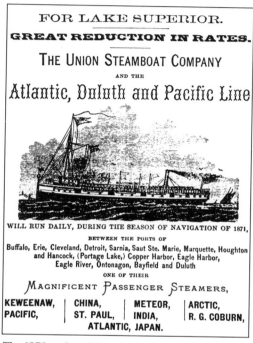

The 1870s ushered in whole fleets of modern ships, many built specifically for Lake Superior service. UNIVERSITY OF DETROIT MARINE COLLECTION.

the little 19-ton tug *J.C. Keyes* was thrown on the beach and severely damaged. She was worth $1,800 to her owner, James Chapman. The *Keyes* was finally declared abandoned in 1880.[26]

1875

A slight improvement in economic conditions brought more ships to the lake in 1875. Indeed, vessel passages at the Soo slightly exceeded those for 1872, yet remained considerably below those for 1873. Steamships now surpassed sailing craft in the locks by well over two to one.[27] The accident list was slightly longer than in the previous year.

The worst collision fatalities since the 1862 crash of the *Oriole* and *Illinois* occurred in late August. Having cleared Duluth on August 23 for Buffalo, with stops at intermediate points on Lake Superior, the 744-ton propeller *Comet* under Captain Francis Dugat (also Dugot or Dugart by various sources) was making good time after leaving Munising. She rounded Whitefish Point by 8 p.m. on August 26 and headed on the usual southeast course to Point Iroquois. The lookout reported a vessel ahead. This turned out to be the steam barge *Havana* and her consort which were passed without incident. Only five minutes later, however, the lookout spotted a white light in

ly the whole below deck crew had gone down with their ship. The *Manitoba* returned to the Soo with the rescued. The *Comet* carried a mixed cargo including 500 tons of pig iron, some copper ore and 70 tons of Montana silver ore which had been loaded at Duluth and was consigned to Philadelphia. Belonging to the Hanna Company of Cleveland, the *Comet* and her cargo were valued at more than $95,000 and 11 lives were lost.[28]

The big liner Manitoba *ran afoul of the* Comet *on August 26, 1875, in Whitefish Bay. She survived, but the* Comet *did not.* C. PATRICK LABADIE COLLECTION.

the hazy dusk right on their course, and 15 minutes thereafter a red light. The captain altered course a half point to port, heading SE½ S. Moments later appeared the green light of the approaching vessel. To his horror the captain realized he had swung across the bows of an oncoming steamer. He blew one blast on his whistle which went unanswered. Frantically ordering a hard turn to starboard, Captain Dugat saw the speeding Canadian sidewheeler *Manitoba* bear down on him; seconds later came the crash.

The *Manitoba* struck the *Comet* on the port bow, about 20 feet from the stem, cutting in deeply. Immediately the *Comet* began to settle stern first, sinking in 10 minutes roughly seven miles southeast of Whitefish Point. The *Manitoba* halted at once, lowered her boats and picked up 10 survivors including the *Comet*'s captain, two mates, two wheelsmen, two deck hands, one lookout, a fireman and a porter. First Engineer Bogy and near-

During October, what apparently was a sideswipe collision in the Portage Lake Ship Canal between the steamer *Keweenaw* and the schooner *Southwest* cost the steamship a sidewheel, not too serious a repair bill. But, a formidable snowstorm on October 30 caught the propeller *Sparta* and the barge *Sumatra* off Stannard Rock. For self-preservation the crew of the *Sparta* was forced to cut the towline and limp into Marquette for shelter, while the *Sumatra* used her sails and was given a hundred-mile ride to the shallows off Big Two-Hearted River where she went ashore not too much the worse for wear.[29]

On a lovely Saturday, November 20, the *Jay C. Morse* towed the 384-ton Winslow schooner *Chenango* out of Marquette harbor about 2:30 p.m., bound for the furnace at Onota near present-day Christmas, Michigan, loaded with iron ore. As luck would have it, at 6 p.m. a violent mixture of fog and snow stormed in, enveloping both vessels. To save himself, the *Morse* captain cut the towline, leaving the schooner on her own. As a last resort, the *Chenango*'s captain tried the western passage at Grand Island, but crashed onto the Wood Island reef, where the ship was quickly reduced to wreckage. Her 10-man crew

The decade of the 1870s brought introduction of several big new bulk freight steamers for the Lake Superior iron ore and grain trades. This early view of Marquette shows two such craft with their schooner "consorts." MARQUETTE COUNTY HISTORICAL SOCIETY COLLECTION.

spent a miserable night aboard the desolate wreck before being rescued the following day. No lives were lost, but a $16,000 loss was incurred.[30]

Elsewhere, moderate damage was suffered when the propeller *Pacific* stranded at Point Iroquois and slashing seas roughed up the propeller *Winslow* and the schooner *J.F. Card*. An end-of-season tragedy at Grand Marais, Minnesota, however, ended four lives and a diminutive trading schooner. With favorable weather the 60-foot, 12-ton schooner *Stranger*, owned by P.E. Bradshaw & Company of Superior, continued to operate in the late season coasting trade. Under command of Captain Isaac Clark, the *Stranger* left Duluth on December 11 with supplies for Grand Marais. With Clark were crewmen George Coburn, Joe Cadotte and Jimmy LaFave. In their haste to leave, the crew neglected to carry an anchor, even though Captain Alfred Merritt, later of *Seven Iron Men* fame, had offered the anchor off his small schooner, *Handy*, which had already been laid up. Presumably, the *Stranger* would not need an anchor in Grand Marais harbor which was sheltered from northwest winds. At any rate, the *Stranger* reached Grand Marais by December 12 without incident.

Before she could unload, however, a storm arose and Captain Clark tried to move the ship around the point to a more sheltered section of the harbor. She struck on the rocks and became unmanageable. Waves poured over her and she capsized. George Coburn was swept overboard and drowned; the other three, desperately swinging axes, cut loose the masts and the rigging, and the schooner righted. Yet, with an off-land wind and without an anchor, she began drifting toward the open lake.

Seeing her plight, a group of Grand Marais men, Sam Howenstein, Jack Scott, John Morrison, Sam Zimmerman, Sam Paul and another named LaPlante, made a death-defying attempt to reach the schooner with a fishing boat. They did get alongside, but the schooner crew were too weakened by exposure to grasp lines thrown to them and the sea was too rough to permit boarding. Reluctantly, the rescuers had to give up and pull for shore which they reached four miles from their point of departure in an exhausted condition. The *Stranger* drifted into the open lake with the remaining crew still aboard. They were never seen again. With sub-zero temperatures and an offshore gale, there was little chance of survival in a small dismasted ship between Grand Marais and the Keweenaw, 80 miles away. The missing anchor proved to be terribly important.[31]

Captain Edward Carus, the Lake Michigan shipwreck researcher, recorded a Canadian steamer *Algerian* as being lost at Split Rock, Lake Superior, in 1875 with seven crewmen, but a search of Lake Superior sources discloses no such wreck. It is more likely his reference is to an occurrence at Split Rock in the St. Lawrence River.[32]

1876

The navigation year of 1876 was a good one. Registered tonnage passing through the Soo Canal exceeded the 1873 peak. Still, the number of mishaps decreased. One horrible tragedy occurred, a December stranding brought a scare at Marquette and there were four lesser incidents. Throughout the history of Lake Superior sailing, disciplined crews capable of handling panicking passengers generally have been the rule. Yet, in one instance, ship's discipline broke with consequent heavy loss of life. In 1876, Captain Eber Ward of Detroit operated the 316-ton, steam barge *St. Clair* on the run from Duluth to Houghton, in competition with the propellers *Manistee* and *Mary Groh*. Constructed at Algonac, Michigan, in 1866, the *St. Clair* had worked in the lumber trade from Saginaw to Lake Erie and from the east coast ports of Lake Michigan to Chicago. Eventually, she was sent up to Lake Superior as an iron ore carrier operating between Marquette and the iron furnaces at Onota near Munising. In 1876, her deck was housed in to accommodate 15 cabin passengers and five in steerage, her gross tonnage increasing from 266 to 316 tons.

The *St. Clair*'s fatal voyage began when she left Duluth on the night of July 7, stopping at Bayfield, Ashland and Ontonagon. She carried a mixed cargo including flour, feed, grain, cattle, sheep and hogs. At 11:55 p.m., July 8, she pulled out of Ontonagon where she had picked up a number of additional passengers and headed northeast. Weather had been warm and pleasant with southerly winds. Most of the 16 passengers and 15 crewmen had retired while Captain Robert Rhynas stood watch with one lookout and Thomas Fortier at the wheel.

In calm water the ship made good time. By 1:35 a.m. she was off Fourteen Mile Point, 12 miles northeast of Ontonagon, and about 10 miles off shore. Stopping in the engine room before going off-shift, Chief Engineer Daniel J. Stringer thought he smelled smoke coming from the bulkhead between the engine room and the main hold. He investigated and discovered a raging fire in the hold. The alarm was given at once. The crew tried to fight the flames with a hose and a steam line, but neither water nor steam had any effect. Within minutes the fire had raced through the cabins to the hurricane deck where, leaping wildly, it consumed the big yawl which was capable of carrying all on board. At the same time, Captain Rhynas headed the ship toward shore. The flames gained, spreading virtually from stem to stern.

In this dire predicament the master remembered that in the cargo hold, ahead of the flames, was a sizable metallic lifeboat en route to the steamer *Northerner* at Houghton. All aboard were ordered to put on life jackets. With great difficulty the metal boat was retrieved and launched with the steamer still under way. As it dropped over the side, the metal boat knocked Captain Rhynas into the water, though he was able to crawl into the boat and bring it alongside the flaming hulk as he assisted 12 passengers into their places. Then another passenger jumped from an upper deck and capsized the lifeboat. With the captain again in the water, chaos emerged, and other passengers and crew leaped into the boat, panic-stricken, fighting each other for positions in the little craft which rolled over and over.

When the lifeboat was finally righted, only three persons remained therein, Captain Rhynas, Chief Engineer Stringer and passenger J.B. Sutphin, later Mayor of Duluth. Bailing out the boat, they began paddling about picking up those still alive, but these unfortunates quickly died from exposure and their bodies were cast overboard. Riding a hatch cover were Wheelsman Fortier, a second wheelsman and Mate Thomas C. Boothman. They were brought into the boat. The search continued, though no more survivors were encountered. Therefore, Captain Rhynas headed the lifeboat to shore. As there was only one oar, seats of the lifeboat had to be used for paddles, and it took seven hours for the bedraggled group to reach a fisherman's home near Portage Entry. The second wheelsman died on the way in to shore and was put in the water, while J.B. Sutphin seemingly had a heart seizure but was revived by Engineer Stringer. The fishermen dried out the castaways, fed them, provided dry clothes and took them in a mackinaw boat to Portage Entry on the afternoon of July 9. Captain Rhynas at once procured the tug *Bob Anderson* and rushed back to the scene of the disaster. The tug retrieved 14 bodies, though it is

thought that 25 or 26 died. Since Purser Shackleton was among the dead, and his books destroyed, no one could be sure how many persons were aboard the *St. Clair* on that dreadful night.

The origin of the fire was thought to have been in the oil lamp used by wood passers in the hold. While there was no oil in the cargo, sufficient other inflammables were present. One rumor said that the *St. Clair* formerly had hauled oil on the Lower Lakes and was saturated, though this the owners denied. At any rate, the rapidity with which the ship was engulfed by flames had mightily shocked those aboard and undoubtedly contributed to

Steam barge Ira Chaffee *was driven ashore near the Chocolay River in the severe snowstorm of December 8, 1876.* C. PATRICK LABADIE COLLECTION.

the unbalanced mentality of many that caused such a loss of life. Only five persons came back from the 31 or more aboard. Prominent citizens from the Lake Superior area who died included Judge Edwards and a mining associate, Neil Leitch of Marquette, mining captain Thomas B. Mellen of Ishpeming, sawmill manager David Lawrence of Ontonagon, an attorney named Beardsley of Ontonagon, a timber cruiser for the Northern Pacific Railroad at Duluth named M. Stewart, L.D. "Waterman" Collins of Duluth and Mrs. Shea of Ishpeming.

At the investigation held by inspectors of the U.S. Steamboat Inspection Service, the officers concurred that the oil lamp used by the wood passers was a probable cause of the conflagration. Conduct of the ship's officers was commended. In fact, had it not been for the coolness and courage of Captain Rhynas, together with the knowledge of first aid for exposure exhibited by Engineer Stringer, it is possible that there would have been no survivors. The ship herself was of low value, insurable for only $16,000 and rated B-1.[33]

During most of the remaining season, there were two strandings with light to moderate damage and one significant schooner mishap, together with fire loss to a lesser tug. The propeller *Nahant* grounded at Waiska Bay with little injury, though somewhat more serious were the schooner *Constitution*'s bills after going ashore at Whitefish Point. The tug *Chasset,* burning at Portage Entry was a $4,000 item; yet, the stranding of the schooner *H. Taylor* at Eagle Harbor could have been a finale, as a loss of $14,000 was reported. Details are lacking.[34]

An expected quick weekend trip by a party of Marquette men, however, might have produced another Upper Peninsula tragedy. At 10 a.m. on a pleasant December 8, the Marquette group sailed on the little 128-foot, 194-ton propeller *Ira Chaffee* for a jaunt to the iron furnace at Onota near Munising, a trip of less than 40 miles. But weather in December on Lake Superior can change with the flick of an eye. Without warning, a raging snowstorm blew up. That night the *Ira Chaffee* did not return. The following morning, search parties left Marquette to scour the beach toward Munising. They dragged dories with them. The searchers didn't have to go far. A few miles to the southeast, beyond Chocolay, lay the *Ira Chaffee* hard aground, badly iced up but intact. Using dories, the rescue party took off the 12 weekend trippers who were thoroughly scared but not much the worse for a harrowing experience. The *Chaffee* rested for a time in a mass of snow and ice but was eventually taken off and reconditioned.[35]

1877

Sailing performance this year was unusual in that most of the serious troubles occurred in May, June and July. The propeller *Pacific* gave insurance men a scare late in May by piling into Traverse Island in Keweenaw Bay so hard that 100 feet of her lay on rocks. The propellers *Manistee* and *St. Louis* pulled hard but couldn't take her off; whereupon her freight was removed and waterfront talk spoke of her as a wreck. Nevertheless, the tug *Winslow* came to Lake Superior, freed the *Pacific* and towed her back to Detroit for rebuilding at a cost of $10,000.[36]

In June trouble struck off Whitefish Point with a collision between the propeller *City of New York* and schooner *America,* the propeller being beached near Vermilion

Point. She was pumped out and repairs to the two were moderate. The schooner *W.B. Ogden* was another victim of the eastern lake, grounding at Whitefish Point on June 19. She was retrieved at a cost of $5,000.[37]

Luxurious passenger steamers boasted cuisine as good as the country's finest hotels. INSTITUTE FOR GREAT LAKES RESEARCH COLLECTION.

Late July, oddly enough, brought the year's worst accident in a broad daylight stranding. The 204-foot, 418-ton wooden side-wheeler *Cumberland* of the Canadian Northern Railroad had been a frequent visitor at Duluth, bringing freight for reshipment to Manitoba. Under Captain J.G. Parsons, she had been in Duluth harbor in late June, had cleared on July 1 for eastern Ontario ports and was due back in late July. After a stop at the Canadian Lakehead, the *Cumberland* was proceeding July 24 toward Duluth, her master taking the route around the west end of Isle Royale. To his dismay, he stranded hard on Rock of Ages reef roughly seven miles from Isle Royale, a reef which was not marked on Canadian charts. The *Cumberland* stuck hard. Canadian tugs from Thunder Bay, a tug from Duluth and a salvage unit from the Detroit Wrecking Company worked hard on her for two weeks, but in the end her crew was removed and she was abandoned. Rough weather badgered the derelict and an early September storm broke her to pieces. Her wreckage still lies strewn below Rock of Ages Reef and in Grace Harbor where some of her bow structure drifted. Built in 1871 at a cost of $101,000 and named for Fred W. Cumberland, general manager of the Northern Railroad, she was probably worth about $50,000 at her demise, and insured for $34,000. She had taken quite a beating in her seven years of operation. While the ship was a total loss, there was considerable salvage of furnishings and equipment from the vessel before she went to the bottom. These items were later sold at auction.[38]

1878

Sailors could be justly proud of their performance on Lake Superior in 1878. Despite a record number of vessel passages at the Soo and an excellent volume of freight traffic, ship losses were minimal and material damage was rather insignificant. There was one fatality.

The little schooner *Phantom* appears to have become

Canadian side-wheeler Cumberland *went to pieces after stranding on Isle Royale's remote Rock of Ages Reef in July 1877.* CANAL PARK MARINE MUSEUM COLLECTION.

A ship fire at Houghton caused the only other sizable financial casualty of the year when the little iron side-wheeler *Ivanhoe* burned. For several years she had operated between Houghton and L'Anse. Rebuilding cost $16,000.[39] Other mishaps included a stranding of the Wieland Brothers schooner *Charley* at Grand Marais, Michigan, and storm damage to the steamer *Keweenaw* and schooner *C. Hinckley*. Additionally, the propeller *City of Fremont* was forced to dump part of her cargo in riding out a gale. Losses were moderate.[40]

What might have been a fatal disaster, ended favorably on October 27 when the small passenger steamer *St. Marie* of Marquette was nearly blown out of the lake near Crisp Point. The 30 passengers and four crewmen were able to wade ashore and walk to a lifesaving station, while the vessel was salvaged little the worse for wear.[41] This vessel is sometimes identified as *St. Mary* .

The small schooner *Josephine,* owned by Captain Brown and reported carrying flour, sugar and other groceries, went aground near Michigan Island in the Apostle Islands group early in November. Most of her cargo was saved, but local press accounts initially declared the vessel a total loss. No record of salvage subsequently appeared.[42]

the season's only total loss when she wrecked on June 1 and was apparently demolished during the following 24 hours. The *Phantom,* owned by Percy Beaser of Ashland, wrecked at the mouth of the Bad River as she attempted to leave the river after delivering a cargo of lumber to be used in assembling a log raft there. As she started out the river mouth in a strong northeast wind, she bottomed on a sand bar which tore out her centerboard. She began leaking and her anchor was let go, but the chain broke and she was quickly driven ashore, "a perfect wreck." No record of salvage has come to light although her rigging and tackle were surely recovered.[43]

On June 20, off the Huron Islands, the 357-ton schooner *Exile*, en route from Cleveland to L'Anse, struck a blustery squall and lost portions of her rigging, one of her crew going overboard. Injury to the ship was nominal. Otherwise, only limited repairs were needed by the tug *Ontario*, fire damaged at Marquette, the barge *Trempe* which grounded at Whitefish Point, the schooner *D. Wagstaff* after a buffeting on the eastern lake and the propeller *City of Fremont* which struck bottom near Whitefish Point.[44]

The tug *Fred & Will* became the season's final total loss

on October 14 in the Apostle Islands. Fire broke out while the tug was running in the channel about a mile off shore between Sand Island and the mainland while en route to Outer island. Captain McLaren thought the fire started in the starboard coal bunker where a hot coal may have landed. It spread quickly, fanned by a strong northwest breeze. The tug was immediately turned toward shore, but as flames spread into the wheelhouse, the wheelsman was forced to run for his life, leaving the tug on its own. Despite efforts to work the tiller manually, the tug turned toward the open lake only to fetch up on a reef about a quarter mile from shore. Her three crewmen swam ashore, hiking 16 miles before reaching a lumber camp. They then moved on to Red Cliff and from there were taken into Bayfield. The tug was a total loss although it is possible her machinery was retrieved. She was valued at $3,500, but insured for only $1,500. Her owners subsequently purchased a replacement tug, the *Siskiwit,* noted below.[45] Despite small losses such as this, the season's performance was phenomenal.

1879

The season of 1879 was another excellent one for shipping people. For the first time, vessel passages at the Soo exceeded 3,000 and most categories of freight were on the increase. The accident pattern was more normal; 11 ships in difficulties and three probably lost, although all were low value items. On June 21, the large 209-ton towing tug *Satellite* with five schooners on line was proceeding west of Whitefish Point upbound to Duluth. Apparently, her propeller hooked a floating log, smashing in her stern planking. She started leaking so rapidly that she foundered before she could be run ashore. Her crew escaped. She was worth $16,000.[46]

Dense fog on July 19 brought the second casualty some miles to the west. Captain George Wilson was guiding the little schooner *Annie Coleman* toward Marquette when he lost his bearings and went hard aground near Grand Marais. Realizing his hopeless position, the captain took his crew ashore and hiked the beach and adjoining forest for more than 70 miles to Marquette. Caught on the exposed shore, the little schooner became a total wreck. While her value was not reported, she undoubtedly was a liability of $10,000 or thereabouts. She may be the derelict whose remains still rest at the mouth of the Hurricane River west of Grand Marais.[47]

At unspecified times during the season there were the usual strandings and reports of topside weather damage. A tug *Antelope* went ashore and sank at some undisclosed location, possibly near Marquette, a $6,000 item. The propellers *Manistee* and *City of Duluth* were both badly abused by rugged seas west of Portage Lake Ship Canal,

being disabled and needing moderate repairs. The schooners *Monticello* and *Reindeer* hit shore in the same area, slightly broken. Off Marquette, the 187-foot, 924-ton propeller *Arizona* of the Anchor Line suffered some beating.[48] On November 20, the frigid northerly blasts in Whitefish Bay caught the 133-foot, 269-ton schooner *Laura Bell,* badly icing her sails and rigging so that she went out of control and fetched up on the shoals of Waiska Bay. Her crew suffered frost-bite and exposure but managed to make the beach and hike to the Soo the following day. At the time, she was presumed a complete ruin, yet, she must have been taken off, as this seems to be the same vessel wrecked four years later near Marquette.[49]

Proud little tug Siskiwit *connected Duluth with ports along the Minnesota north shore for many years, although she barely survived a disabling December 1879 storm.* CANAL PARK MARINE MUSEUM COLLECTION.

A late season adventure on the Minnesota north shore produced some anxious days for families of tugboatmen and fishermen, an extremely grim experience for two tug crews and their passengers, and an icy death for one of the unfortunate hitchhiking fishermen. The Duluth fishing firm of Cooley, Hector and McLean used a small tug, the *Siskiwit,* in picking up the catch and supplying their scattered fishermen along the north shore. As December provided pleasant sailing weather, Captain Archie McLaren took the *Siskiwit* out of Duluth harbor on December 12 on a routine pickup run to Grand Marais, Minnesota. While working along the shore, however, perhaps near Good Harbor Bay a few miles southwest of Grand Marais, the *Siskiwit* hit a reef, badly damaging her propeller. Captain McLaren and his two-man crew succeeded in nursing her into Grand Marais harbor for a sheltered anchorage, then caught a sailboat back to Duluth where they reported their ill fortune. With calm seas still holding, Captain McLaren prevailed upon Captain Martin Wheeler of the 45-foot, 14-ton tug *Amethyst* to undertake a recovery expedition. Captain Wheeler already had earned himself the reputation of a daredevil tugboatman by racing the tug *Bob Anderson* through the Duluth Ship Canal to safety at the height of the violent gale on November 13, 1872. On December 20, therefore, the *Amethyst,* with the *Siskiwit* crew aboard, headed back to Grand Marais, arriving the next day. After visiting the fishing camps and picking up five fishermen who wished to winter in Duluth, Captain Wheeler hitched up a tow and at 10:30 p.m. on December 21 cleared Grand Marais for Duluth. Aboard the *Siskiwit,* then in tow, were Captain McLaren, Engineer Robert Thompson and Clerk Charles Hector. Captain Wheeler had his Engineer Charles McManus on the *Amethyst,* a Grand Marais passenger, H. Mayhew and five fishermen; Robert Sanborn, Charles Winters, Ned Smith, George Harris and Mike Laundrigan.

Early progress was good. Yet, when the tugs were only a few hours out of Grand Marais, a sharp southeaster arose which was soon blowing a gale. Captain McLaren got up steam on the *Siskiwit* and even with the broken propeller was able to push the tow along. About 8 a.m. on December 22, however, as the two little craft were approximately off the Manitou River, 70 miles northeast of Duluth, the towline broke and the *Siskiwit,* having lost her rudder in the earlier stranding, fell into the trough. For three hours the two struggled on. Finally, the *Siskiwit* began leaking so badly that Captain McLaren whistled for help. At considerable risk to the *Amethyst,* Captain Wheeler brought her alongside the foundering *Siskiwit* and took off the crew, abandoning the *Siskiwit* to the lake. She later blew ashore not far west of Manitou. Eleven persons were now aboard the *Amethyst,* which took a terrific beating from the seas. Soon she was leaking badly. As a last resort, Captain Wheeler ran her ashore near Belmore

Bay, about 13½ miles northeast of Beaver Bay, managing to hit a decent piece of beach. As the tug struck, all aboard leaped into the icy surf. All except fisherman George Harris succeeded in staggering ashore. He may have been injured by the collapsing smoke stack.

The survivors were in a desperate position with their clothes frozen stiff. In addition, a tremendous snow was falling. Still, the men had woods know-how. Building fires and crude shelters, they managed to dry themselves and also to retrieve food from the *Amethyst* which had been pushed into shallow water. A deluge of snow continued. The next day, the bedraggled party started a 52-hour trek covering the 13 odd miles to Beaver Bay. Fisherman Laundrigan froze his feet and had to be left in a shelter on the way, but the remaining exhausted group reached the village where the Wieland family gave them shelter. A young Wieland with a dog team went out and brought in the disabled Laundrigan. After several days rest, Captain McLaren and Charles Winters took a small boat to Duluth and tug owners Hector and McLean returned by boat to help at Beaver Bay. The Duluth families were relieved to learn that all except the unfortunate Harris were alive. Over the next few weeks, the party would be brought back to Duluth by small boat, though the disabled Laundrigan did not arrive until January 28. Even the two tugs were salvaged the next year and sailed for many more seasons. Undoubtedly, it was the woodsability of the castaways which enabled them to endure their harrowing adventure, together with the presence of generous and helpful settlers at Beaver Bay. Only the unfortunate George Harris had died in what otherwise might have been a "lost with all hands" disaster.[50]

The Lifesaving Station at Two-Hearted River was one of four constructed in 1875 as a direct result of the terrible 1872 tragedies on the eastern lake. BRADLEY-LALLY PHOTO COURTESY OF MS. IONA PROUE, NEWBERRY, MICHIGAN.

[1] "Statement of Commerce Through the St. Marys Falls Canal For Each Calendar Year Since 1870" in *Blue Book of American Shipping* (Cleveland, Marine Review Publishing Co., 1901), p. 266.

[2] "Autobiography of Captain John G. Parker" in *Michigan Pioneer and Historical Collections,* Vol. 30, 1905, pp. 582-585; *Marquette Mining Journal,* Aug. 27, 1870.

[3] There is a good deal of confusion in the records regarding the *Scott* wreck. *National Archives, Microcopy T-729, Marine Casualties on the Great Lakes, 1863-1873* (Record Group 26, Records of the U.S. Coast Guard), lists a schooner *G.W. Scott* stranding at Grand Island in August 1870, with nominal damage; *Marquette Mining Journal* Nov. 11, 1887, in its list of all Grand Island total losses, notes a schooner *Marien Scott; Munising News,* Oct. 21, 1921, cites a schooner *May Scott* sunk there in 1871. The Munising story described removal of the hulk by the Coast Guard. It appears we can be sure that a schooner named *Scott* was lost at Grand Island, but the exact name is unclear. Also, *Milwaukee Sentinel,* Nov. 9, 12, 1870.

[4] National Archives, *Microcopy T-729; Toronto Globe,* Nov. 2, 1882.

[5] National Archives, *Microcopy T-729;* Homer Wells, *History of Accidents, Casualties, and Wrecks on Lake Superior* (Duluth, Corps of Engineers, U.S. Army, 1938), 90 pp. unpublished typewritten manuscript, p. 8; *Marquette Journal,* Nov. 11, 1887, does not include the *Dreadnaught* among permanent losses.

[6] National Archives, *Microcopy T-729;* Wells, *op. cit.,* p. 8.

[7] Thom Holden, *Apostle Islands Shipwreck Survey List, 1870-1940,* (Bayfield, Wisconsin, Apostle Islands National Lakeshore, National Park Service, 1985), p. 94; *Bayfield County Press,* Nov. 26, 1870.

[8] Wells, *op. cit.,* p. 8.

[9] *Duluth Minnesotian,* May 21, 1870, Sept. 16, 1871; *Superior Times,* Sept. 23, 1871.

[10] *Duluth Minnesotian,* Oct. 7, 28, 1871; Wells, *op. cit.,* p. 8; National Archives, *Microcopy T-729.*

[11] *Marquette Mining Journal,* Sept. 21, 1872; National Archives, *Microcopy T-729.*

[12] *Duluth Minnesotian,* July 6, 1872; *Marquette Mining Journal,* Oct. 26, 1872.

[13] The havoc at Duluth is well described in *Duluth Minnesotian,* Nov. 16, 23, 1872. A fine account is presented by Steven J. Wright as "The Forgotten November Storm" in *The Nor'easter,* Vol. 12, No. 5, September-October 1987, pp. 1-3. Details of damage to the breakwall at the outer harbor are given in Senate Executive Document No. 21, 42nd Congress, 3rd Session, "Government Works in Harbor of Du Luth," pp. 1-6, a report to Congress from the Secretary of War based on on-site reports by representatives of the Chicago District of the Corps of Engineers within whose district Duluth Harbor developments were at the time. Numerous details on that terrible month on the eastern lake are presented in *Marquette Mining Journal,* Nov. 9, 16, 23, 30, 1872.

[14] *Marquette Mining Journal,* Nov. 20, 30, 1872, April 26, 1973.

[15] Good summaries of the quadruple wrecks appeared in *Marquette Mining Journal,* Dec. 7, 21, 1872. Several letters concerning the *Brown* wreck and the fascinating trek to safety by the three survivors were reprinted in *Duluth Minnesotian,* Jan. 18, 25, 1873, and Feb. 8, 1873. The interview with crewman Jugan Alberts (reprinted from the *Chicago Tribune,* Jan. 30, 1873) appeared in the Feb. 8 issue.

[16] Wells, *op. cit.,* p. 9.

[17] Dr. Julius F. Wolff Jr., "The Coast Guard Comes to Lake Superior, 1874-1875" in *Inland Seas,* Vol. 21, No. 1, Spring, 1965, pp. 14-21.

[18] Wells, *op. cit.,* p. 10; National Archives, *Microcopy T-729.*

[19] *Marquette Mining Journal,* Oct. 4, 1873; Wells, *op. cit.,* p. 10.

[20] National Archives, *Microcopy T-729; Marquette Mining Journal,* June 13, 1874.

[21] *Duluth Minnesotian,* Nov. 1, 15, 1873; *Superior Times,* Nov. 1, 1873; Wells, *op. cit.,* p. 10; National Archives, *Microcopy T-729; Duluth Daily Tribune,* Oct. 27, 30, 1873.

[22] Wells, *op. cit.,* p. 10.

[23] Wells, *op. cit.,* p. 10; *Marquette Mining Journal,* Nov. 11, 1887.

[24] *Marquette Mining Journal,* Sept. 26, 1874. The *D.R. Owen* may have been taken off as a schooner of that name was lost off Manistee, Michigan, in 1878.

[25] *Daily Minnesotian,* Nov. 30, Dec. 14, 1872, April 25, 1874, May 23, 1874, Oct. 31, 1874, Nov. 7, 1874; *Superior Times,* Nov. 7, 1874; *Marquette Mining Journal,* Nov. 7, 1874.

[26] *Duluth Minnesotian,* Nov. 14, 1874; William M. Lytle and Forrest R. Holdcamper, *Merchant Steam Vessels of the United States, 1790-1868,* C. Bradford Mitchell, ed., (Staten Island, New York, The Steamship Historical Society of America, 1975), p. 104.

[27] *Blue Book of American Shipping, op. cit.*

[28] *Marquette Mining Journal,* Aug. 28, Sept. 4, 1875; *Duluth Minnesotian-Herald,* Sept. 11, 1875; *Annual Report, U.S. Life-Saving Service, 1876,* p. 130.

[29] *Marquette Mining Journal,* Nov. 6, 1875.

[30] *Marquette Mining Journal,* Nov. 27, 1875; Wells, *op. cit.,* p. 11. The *Chenango* had been built as a bark in 1862.

[31] *Duluth Minnesotian-Herald,* Dec. 25, 1875; *Duluth Weekly Tribune,* Dec. 23, 1875; *Annual Report, U.S. Life-Saving Service, 1876,* p. 129.

[32] Captain Edward Carus, "100 Years of Disasters on the Great Lakes," in *Manitowoc Herald-News,* Nov. 19, 1931.

[33] *Duluth Minnesotian-Herald,* July 15, 1876; *Houghton Gazette Extra,* July 9, 1876; *Marquette Mining Journal,* July 15, 1876.

[34] Wells, *op. cit.,* p. 11.

[35] *Marquette Mining Journal,* Dec. 9, 1876.

[36] *Duluth Weekly Tribune,* May 25, 1877; *Duluth Minnesotian-Herald,* May 26, 1877; Wells, *op. cit.,* p. 11.

[37] *Duluth Minnesotian-Herald,* June 30, 1877; Wells, *op. cit., p. 11.*

[38] Thom Holden, *Above and Below* (Houghton, Michigan, Isle Royale Natural History Association, 1985), pp. 36-37; Thom Holden, "Reef of the Three C's: Part I, Wreck of the *Cumberland*," in *The Nor'Easter*, Vol. 2, No. 4, July-August 1977, pp. 1, 4-6; Larry Murphy and Thom Holden, "Shipwrecks of Isle Royale: The Historical Record," in *Submerged Cultural Resources Study: Isle Royale National Park*, Daniel J. Lenihan, ed., (Santa Fe, New Mexico, Submerged Cultural Resources Unit, National Park Service, 1987). pp. 65-71; Larry Murphy, Daniel Lenihan, and C. Patrick Labadie, "Shipwrecks of Isle Royale: The Archeological Record" in Lenihan, ed., *ibid.*, pp. 220-253; *Duluth Weekly Tribune*, Aug. 3, 1877; *Duluth Minnesotian-Herald*, Aug. 4, 11, 1877, Sept. 8, 1877. Despite good documentation, there appears some confusion in the popular literature over the exact wreck date, July 23 or 24.

[39] *Duluth Minnesotian*, June 8, 1872; Wells, *op. cit.*, p. 11.

[40] Wells, *op. cit.*, p. 11.

[41] *Annual Report, U.S. Life-Saving Service, 1878*, p. 75.

[42] Holden, *Apostle Islands Shipwreck Survey*, *op. cit.*, p. 52; *Bayfield County Press*, Nov. 14, 1877.

[43] Holden, *ibid*, p. 86; *Ashland Weekly Press*, June 8, 1878; *Bayfield County Press*, June 12, 1878.

[44] *Annual Report, U.S. Life-Saving Service, 1878*, p. 190.

[45] Holden, *Apostle Islands Shipwreck Survey*, *op. cit.*, p. 39-40; *Bayfield County Press*, Oct. 19, 1878, Nov. 13, 20, 1878; *Lake Superior News (Duluth)*, Oct. 17, 24, 1878; *Superior Times*, Nov. 19, 23, 1878; Lytle and Holdcamper, *op. cit.*, pp. 76, 262.

[46] *Marquette Mining Journal*, June 28, 1879. This may be the hulk of a small steam vessel which has bothered net fishermen just east of the Big Two-Hearted River, not too far off the beach.

[47] *Marquette Mining Journal*, Nov. 29, 1878.

[48] Wells, *op. cit.*, p. 12.

[49] *Marquette Mining Journal*, Nov. 29, 1879.

[50] *Annual Report, U.S. Life-Saving Service, 1880*, p. 231; *Duluth Weekly Tribune*, Dec. 26, 1879, Jan. 2, 30, 1880; John A. Bardon, "Early Pioneering Along the North Shore," an interview with Engineer Charles McManus of the *Amethyst* some years after the incident. Unpublished manuscript in files of St. Louis County Historical Society. There are some differences in details from earlier newspaper accounts.

The 1880s were a time of unprecedented growth in the Lake Superior region, with new facilities and new ships for grain, iron ore, passengers and package freight. CANAL PARK MARINE MUSEUM COLLECTION.

Chapter 3

The Momentous Eighties
1880-1889

The 1880s saw phenomenal expansion in the Lake Superior area. Widespread railroad development was pushed at Marquette, Houghton, Ashland, Duluth, Two Harbors and Thunder Bay, Ontario. With additional railroads came a flood of commerce from the hinterland. Existing communities were mushrooming and new ones were being established. Duluth's population leaped four-fold. While the flow of iron ore from the Marquette Range steadily increased in volume, so did copper from the Keweenaw Peninsula country, and two new iron mining ranges appeared, the Gogebic in the western Upper Peninsula and the Vermilion in northeastern Minnesota. Iron ore traffic jumped seven-fold. Large scale lumbering operations moved steadily westward with an enormous upsurge in the Ashland-Bayfield and Duluth-Superior regions. Lumber cargoes increased by nine times during the decade. Grain from the Prairie Provinces of western Canada now joined an already substantial quantity of wheat from western Minnesota and the American Great Plains. Grain shipments evidenced a six-fold upturn. More than 9,500 vessel passages were recorded at the Soo in 1889, three times those of 1879, while the registered ship tonnage increased four and a half times, indicating a shift to larger and larger vessels.[1] The wooden schooner continued in use, though often reduced to tow-barge status. Wooden steam barges or straight decked freighters were still produced in numbers by American shipyards. Many of these new ships approached the 300-

33

foot range. More iron and, after 1886, steel vessels started to come out of American shipyards, though American Great Lakes shipping people continued to debate the future of steel hulls on the Lakes. Several new British-built Canadian passenger-package freight ships already were of steel hulls.

As expected, the number of accidents multiplied. More than 50 ships fell to the clutches of the lake with approximately 120 dead. Less serious mishaps were myriad.

1880

Seldom have shore dwellers been able to watch the drama of shipwreck and rescue while they basked in midsummer sunshine, but this was the situation at Marquette on August 1, 1880. The day seemed long since past when diminutive sailing ships manned by a two-man crew carried freight along the Lake Superior coast. Yet, on that August Sunday, telescope-equipped Marquette residents observed such a tiny craft as it struggled to make headway only two miles off the port. Exceedingly high southwesterly winds were racing over the town to kick up a furious sea east of the breakwater. As Marquette residents watched shortly before noon, they were horrified to see the little vessel suddenly heel over and disappear. Minutes later, an incoming propeller unexpectedly veered off course and hove to where the schooner had vanished. Rumors quickly spread through Marquette and a crowd gathered in the dock area, since several well known young men of the community had been on a pleasure sailing jaunt off the coast. Perhaps they had met with disaster. As the propeller resumed course and approached the harbor an hour or so later, she was observed towing a small yawl with two occupants. When the freight ship docked and the yawl was beached, however, out stepped Captain W.H. Daniels and his 15-year-old crewman, Willie Annear. Their 50-foot schooner *Tom Boy*, laden with 2,043 kegs of blasting powder, had capsized from a leak after the two had labored for five hours on the pumps in an effort to save her. The captain and his one-man crew had abandoned ship only five minutes before the end. The freighter had come along in the nick of time. The *Tom Boy* was of low value, worth about $7,000, including her cargo. Captain Daniels related that this was his ninth experience with a shipwreck. He was apparently somewhat of a daredevil sailor, willing to use a small ship to handle dangerous commodities from which most masters shied.[2]

The following month, another minute freighter met her fate. As the Detroit, Munising and Marquette Railroad inched northwestward toward Marquette, the construction camps were supplied by a small sailing yacht picturesquely named *Starlight*. Under Captain Elmo Lamong, the *Starlight* departed from Marquette on September 28, with

provisions for railroad workers at various locations on the route from Munising. She arrived without incident at the Sucker Bay camp and delivered a portion of her cargo. Then it appears that Captain Lamong and his four crewmen decided to celebrate their successful voyage before completing the remaining 20-mile run. Well through the night, they toasted good fortune, enjoying the glow of alcoholic reverie. With daylight approaching, however, Captain Lamong decided to set sail, despite protests of construction camp officials who recognized an approaching storm. When no supply ship reached Munising the following day, a railroad contractor named Hendrie organized a search party. At Au Train, the would-be rescuers found only floating masts and sails, and cargo scattered along the shore. Three weeks later, the body of Captain Lamong floated onto the Au Train beach. His watch had stopped at 7 o'clock, grim evidence that the *Starlight* had not lasted long on that gale-tossed morning of September 29. All five aboard perished.[3]

Light to moderate losses were reported at far-flung points during the rest of the season, the propeller *Quebec* jettisoning cargo off Grand Marais, Michigan, the tug *W.B. Castle* disabled from a leak off Whitefish Point, the schooner *Annie M. Peterson* aground west of Whitefish Point, the schooners *I.N. Foster* and *John B. Wilbor* gale-wracked near Duluth and the schooner *Anna Maria* stranded near Portage. With the exception of the *Starlight* catastrophe, this was not a bad year.

1881

Only five accidents were reported in 1881, but four involved the temporary or permanent loss of a vessel. On May 10, the little lumber schooner *Charley,* belonging to the Wielands of Beaver Bay, was trapped at the dock in

Canadian propeller City of Winnipeg *was destroyed by an 1881 midsummer fire in Duluth.* AUTHOR'S COLLECTION.

that community by a sudden northeaster. She was badly beaten, initially adjudged damaged beyond repair. Seemingly, efforts to rebuild her were undertaken, though it has not been ascertained whether or not she ever sailed again.[4]

July brought a fatal ship fire to Duluth Harbor. At 2 a.m., July 19, the 200-foot, 889-ton propeller *City of Winnipeg* arrived in Duluth and immediately tied up at the Northern Pacific dock where stevedores commenced unloading. Captain Joseph Kennedy and most of the passengers and crew went to bed. Shortly after, fire was discovered near the engine. The flames spread rapidly. Purser J.R.

forth, where she burned to the water's edge and sank. The *City of Winnipeg* had been built at Gibraltar, Michigan, in 1870 as the *Annie L. Craig* and originally operated by E.B. Ward of Detroit. She was later sold to the Canada Lake Superior Transit Company. After 1878, she ran in the Collingwood-Lake Superior Line. Lost in the blaze were 13 fine horses en route to western Canada and a substantial quantity of bonded Canadian whisky. Possibly for the

The Soo Locks were enlarged between 1874 and 1881, enabling the canal to move more and larger ships. UNIVERSITY OF DETROIT MARINE COLLECTION.

Crawford and Steward Robert Burns raced through the cabins and quarters rousing passengers and crewmen. All 18 passengers and most of the crew safely crossed to the dock. Yet, the rampaging blaze cut off a number of crewmen in the forward quarters. Pantryman Henry Burns, First Porter William Harvey and Waiter Ed Aliston dove through a window into the water and swam to safety. Waiter J. Branscombe, a messboy named Harvey and another unnamed messboy, who was working his passage, either suffocated or burned in their rooms or drowned trying to escape. Fireman Joe Smith entered the hold in an effort to combat the flames and was never seen again. Thus, four of the crew died in the presumed safety of Duluth Harbor, and a ship worth $40,000 was completely destroyed.

Dock personnel cut the *City of Winnipeg* loose as the flames mounted, and she drifted across the Bay to Minnesota Point, finally being pushed into shallow water near the blast furnace by the tugs *Eliza Williams* and *F.L. Dan-*

latter, the burned out hulk was quickly purchased for $2,000 by one Lake Superior Fish Company of Prince Arthur's Landing (now Thunder Bay), but salvage operations were very disappointing. Negligible quantities of whisky or of anything valuable were recovered. Of course, it is highly possible that any remaining cargo was pilfered by area residents who got there first.[5]

Another Canadian ship, the 347-ton schooner *Mary Merritt,* ran into bad luck in American waters on September 7. The *Merritt* was loading timber off the beach at Hurricane River when she was driven ashore there by rising wind. Under Captain Neil Murray, the *Merritt* was heavily laden with 160 pieces of squared timber ultimately destined for the European market. Captain Freeman of the tug *Jim Hays* went to her assistance as seas moderated, but the schooner had to be abandoned and her five crewmen brought to Marquette. Thought injured beyond repair, the *Merritt* was salvaged and towed to Detroit by the wrecking tug *Winslow.* Launched in 1865 at St. Catherine's, Ontario, the *Merritt* was rebuilt at Detroit, switched to American registry as the *Dot* and bought first by Captain S.B. Grummond and then by A.C. Smith. Renovated, she was valued at $7,000. She will figure in another accident two years later.[6]

The most costly mishap of the year involved the new American steam barge *Middlesex,* a 190-foot, 568-ton bulk carrier. The *Middlesex* had discharged a load of coal at Marquette on November 17 and left for L'Anse the same evening. Arriving early the following morning, she went to the pier of the Hebard and Thurber Lumber Company near Pequaming. There, she burst into flames which could not be controlled and burned to the water's edge before going down. She was a casualty of $65,000. However, much of her hull was still sound. Hence, salvors raised her the following spring, and she was towed to the Lower Lakes for reconstruction as a barge.[7]

The propeller *Asia* completed the mishap roster for the season, needing light repairs after a collision with an unidentified vessel near Duluth.

1882

The brisk navigation season of 1882 brought grief to 12 ships, yet the three which joined the ranks of the vanquished were relatively minor items. Attempting to enter the Portage Canal on August 28, the schooner *Nellie McGilvray* hit the pier and sank in the channel. Attempts to raise her failed, and the 427-ton *McGilvray* had to be dynamited in October as a menace to navigation. Built by Williams in 1870 at Black Rock, New York, she was valued at less than $4,000.[8]

In the second week of October, the whole of central and eastern Lake Superior was severely riled by a giant storm. Caught off Keweenaw Point, the propeller *D.M. Wilson* was pummeled miserably, losing her consort, the schooner *Frank Perew,* and forced to run to Marquette for refueling. Putting out again, the *Wilson* recovered the barge miles from where the line broke and both proceeded safely. Not as fortunate was the small lumber camp supply steamer *Grace,* which suffered an engine breakdown and was driven by easterly winds for 25 miles, clear across Whitefish Bay. Crewman Robert Holmes drowned trying to swim ashore. Another crewman, Thomas S. Stonehouse of the Soo, reached the beach but dropped dead from exertion. The remaining crew got off safely. The little craft was worth only $3,000.[9]

In the last week of November, another little coastal vessel reached the end of the line, the schooner *Maple Leaf* under Captain Larson being pitched aground near the mouth of Iron River. Built in 1872 at Bayfield for R.D. Pike, she was adjudged a ruin, a financial casualty of $3,000 with her cargo of lumber and fish. Though re-

covery efforts were slated for spring, she vanished from the records.[10]

A rash of relatively insignificant difficulties afflicted sailors throughout the year. The scow *Pearl* was grounded at Whitefish Point, and the propeller *Ontario* dumped cargo off the same place when trapped by rough seas. The schooners *General Sigel* and *Eclipse* both hit bottom at Au Sable Point. The schooner *Southwest* was leaking and settled in shallow water at Grand Island. At Lighthouse Point, probably Marquette, the schooner-barge *G.H. Ely* was ashore, while the steam barge *V. Swain* was bounced around off the same port. The steam barge *Huron City* got hung up in Eagle Harbor, and the tug *Siskiwit* was beached at Lester River near Duluth. Aside from the two fatalities on the *Grace,* this was another rather safe season.[11]

1883

Sailing would not be as pleasant in 1883. Not only was there a reduction in the demand for ships on Lake Superior, the first in nine years, but more vessels were in trouble, two of the accidents being serious tragedies. At least five became total losses.

St. Lawrence River steamer Spartan *was chartered by the Canadian Pacific Railway for the Port Arthur run, and nearly ended her career on Caribou Island in 1883.* UNIVERSITY OF DETROIT MARINE COLLECTION.

June weather put the iron side-wheeler *Spartan* aground on Caribou Island. When early attempts to release her failed, she was abandoned to the underwriters. Subsequent salvage undertakings apparently were successful. No costs were reported.[12]

Thick fog on July 4 victimized a sizable steam barge of the iron ore trade. Downbound from Marquette under Captain Everett with a cargo of ore, the 200-foot, 645-ton *Mary Jarecki* strayed off course and plowed at good speed into the Au Sable Reef, hitting so hard that she was out three feet at the bow. Her captain arranged for the tug *Mystic* to come from the Soo for initial salvage attempts, yet the *Jarecki*'s hull had been too badly holed. She had to be abandoned as a wreck, a casualty of $28,000. Constructed at Toledo in 1871, she had been rebuilt in 1880 and was classed A-2. A storm on September 24 added further significant damage. The wrecking tug *Williams* also worked on her in the summer of 1884 without result.[13]

The following August 25 recorded a mishap in the same general area, somewhat to the north and east of Au Sable Reef. Eastbound in tow of the steam barge *M. M. Drake* was the 347-ton schooner *Dot*. This was the former *Mary Merritt* as rebuilt and renamed after her casualty near Hurricane River two years before. When off Grand Marais, Michigan, the *Dot* began leaking and started to settle. The *Drake* maneuvered to take off her crew before she went down, a reported $15,000 liability to her new owner, A.C. Smith.[14]

Iron-hulled Nellie Cotton *lies beached at Duluth after enduring a September 1883 storm.* C. PATRICK LABADIE COLLECTION.

A wicked early blow on September 6 brought widespread difficulties. Caught near the outer breakwater at Duluth, the iron tug *Nellie Cotton* was slapped ashore and badly beaten. She had to be taken to the Duluth dry dock for repairs of $5,000, substantial for a tug. Things were worse at Marquette. Hurled ashore, the schooner *Sumatra* remained solidly aground until October 1 when Captain McCoy was able to drag her off for a long tow to dry-dock at Port Huron, a bill in excess of $6,500.[15] In less fortunate circumstances was the 133-foot, 269-ton coal laden schooner *Laura Bell* which struck at Laughing Whitefish (Long) Point near Marquette about September 9. One of her crew was drowned, and she initially was recorded as a total loss of $17,400. It is doubtful salvors were later able to reclaim her.[16]

Mid-November brought western Lake Superior's first major disappearance. The 184-foot, 677-ton wooden propeller *Manistee* had become a veritable institution in the western lake, as had her veteran master, Captain John McKay of Buffalo. Built by E.M. Peck at Cleveland in 1867, she first sailed on Lake Michigan for the Engelmann interests of Milwaukee. She was acquired by the Duluth

Lake Transportation Company in 1873 after the major shipping firms refused to send their larger ships to Duluth in the wake of the port's misfortune in the devastating November gale of the year before. Thus Col. Culver,

Manistee *was a south shore favorite until her disappearance in November 1883.* CANAL PARK MARINE MUSEUM COLLECTION.

W.R. Stone and George C. Stone of Duluth hastily organized a shipping company to link Duluth with the Michigan cities of the Keweenaw and Marquette. They obtained the *Manistee,* which had been trapped in the northern Lake Michigan ice pack for several weeks during the winter of 1872-73. The *Manistee* was sold in 1876 to the Leopold and Austrian interests of Chicago, the Lake Superior and South Shore Line. For the next seven years she was a Duluth link to important Lower Lakes shipping which terminated at Houghton. Captain McKay had been on the western lake for years, having commanded several other vessels before taking over the *Manistee.*

On her final voyage, the *Manistee* cleared Duluth for Keweenaw ports on November 10. Not far out, she encountered violent winds and snow, and Captain McKay wisely ran to Bayfield for shelter. To his disgust, however, he found himself weather-bound for six days while the gale roared and the snow flew. Some of his seven passengers transferred to the larger propeller *City of Duluth* which also lay in Bayfield. At length, the captain determined to sail. On November 16, the *Manistee* left Bayfield for eternity. As luck would have it, the weather cleared a day or so later.

When the ship did not appear at Ontonagon, the owner sent search tugs from Keweenaw port towns. Some 45 miles northeast of Ontonagon, the tug *Maytham* of Houghton, discovered a floating bucket, some floating charcoal and a piece of the pilothouse. Stencilled on the bucket was, ''Manistee.'' During the last week of November, two westbound ships, the *V. Swain* and the *Osceola,* each passed through wreckage off Ontonagon. In fact, the *Osceola* halted to retrieve some of the flotsam; a few barrels of flour, some sash and furniture and a piece of a bulwark. The *Manistee* had carried 1,550 barrels of flour.

Word also came from Eagle Harbor, Michigan, that debris came ashore eight miles north of there on the beach at Agate Harbor which contained five tubs of butter marked "Diamond Match Co., Ontonagon," a barrel marked "Manistee," some pulley blocks and heavy timbers. At Eagle River, the lake yielded an empty life boat, 20 barrels of flour and parts of the hull. Assorted flotsam was also reported coming ashore at Sand Bay, Isle Royale, Caribou Island and Mamainse Point. Yet, not a single body was recovered.

The following spring, wreckage appeared at Union Bay near Ontonagon in which was found the *Manistee*'s gold pilothouse eagle and her steering wheel, which was lashed into position. Perhaps her people had tried to abandon ship. A year and a half later came more dire evidence. On May 24, 1885, a beachcombing resident of Ashland, Wisconsin, Augustus Archambault, discovered a bottle floating at the mouth of nearby Fish Creek. In the bottle was a note which said, "This is of the *Manistee*, in a fearful storm. May not see morning. Ever yours to the world, John McKay, Cap." Two Ashland men who were quite familiar with Captain McKay's signature, C.J. Higgins, agent for the Wisconsin Central Railroad, and J. Bowen, collector for the port of Ashland, affirmed that the note was genuine while others, including the captain's brother, felt it was a cruel hoax. Fish dealer Alphonse LeBel of Ashland also reported that one of his fishermen had taken a large trout in November 1884 in the stomach of which was a silver spoon engraved "Manistee."

Thus, the *Manistee* had vanished on her route from Bayfield to Ontonagon, probably foundering somewhere east of the Apostles, perhaps off Ontonagon. Lost with the *Manistee* were her entire complement and passengers, from 23 to 35 souls. No one was sure just how many persons were aboard. She entailed a financial liability in excess of $60,000. To this day, the *Manistee* remains one of the unsolved mysteries of western Lake Superior. For the sailor, however, the answer was simple. She was an old ship, 16 years old, and the ruthless lake just tore her to pieces. She was out when she should have been in.[17]

The same violent storm which finished the *Manistee* caused more trouble east of Munising. The 680-ton schooner *Wabash*, in tow of the tug *Samson*, broke her line and drifted into the Pictured Rocks where the waves soon tore her to pieces. The next day, her crew got off safely in calmer seas, but the ship disintegrated, a financial casualty of $15,000.[18]

Ill fortune continued. Construction of the Canadian Pacific Railroad was in full swing along the eastern shore of Lake Superior. Provisions were being supplied from Port Arthur. On December 13, the Canadian steam barge *Kincardine* left the Canadian Lakehead with the American schooner *Mary Ann Hulbert* in tow. Both were laden with cargo for a railroad contractor named Burke at Michipicoten. Besides her crew of five, the *Hulbert* car-

ried 15 passengers, probably railroad construction workers. About 10 p.m., when the two were off St. Ignace Island, a violent storm arose. The *Hulbert* began to leak and settle. Though the crew of the schooner could be heard calling for help, those aboard the steam barge were powerless to assist in the mountainous waves. Suddenly, the schooner gave a wild lurch and went under. Only then, when the sinking tow threatened to drag down the steam barge, did the *Kincardine*'s captain order the towline cut. Taking 20 men with her, the *Mary Ann Hulbert* became the most fatal schooner foundering in the history of Lake Superior. She was an old two-master of 82 tons (old measure), owned by the O'Malley Brothers of Ontonagon and worth about $2,000. Newspaper comment considered her too old and unseaworthy. She never should have been carrying men on Lake Superior in December.[19]

The *Kincardine* did not fare much better a little later in the season. When working the Canadian east shore in December, she became ice cut and sank at McKay's Harbor. This 12-year-old 184-ton ship was at first regarded as a hopeless wreck, a $10,000 loss. But the salvage team of LeMay and Sons successfully raised her the following spring and brought her to Duluth for rebuilding.[20]

Elsewhere during 1883, ship difficulties were generally minimal. The schooner *Cecelia* was a $7,600 casualty, enduring storm damage and having to dump cargo in the eastern lake, while the schooners *George Sherman* and *King Sisters* suffered little in groundings at Grand Island and Marquette, respectively. Slight repairs were needed by the propeller *J.R. Whiting* in a mechanical breakdown off Whitefish Point. These fared far better than the others in what had been a rugged navigation season.[21]

1884

Vessel men of the 1880s long remembered 1884. A new record was set for ship passages at the Soo while overall freight increased by one-fourth over the previous year. Accidents skyrocketed, with the unprecedented total of 33 ships getting in difficulties of various kinds. Of these, five were definite goners and eight others possibly "totaled," though ingenious salvors cut the final toll. Nine men made their last voyage.

Spring was tough. Ice remained through April and well into May at the west end of the lake, the first arrival at Duluth being the steamer *Jay Gould* on May 9. Rough weather was a continual hazard. Attempting to land supplies for the Canadian Pacific Railroad at Michipicoten, two Canadian propellers came to grief on a reef in Michipicoten Bay. Early in the month, the propeller *Argyle* stranded, but the tug *Porter* managed to get her off with relatively minor cost. Not as fortunate was the 173-ton propeller *J.S. Seaverns*. Formerly the American side-wheel tug

John P. Ward, she had been sold to Walter Ross of Port Arthur in January 1884. She was on her first trip with miscellaneous cargo, a substantial quantity of general merchandise for the Canadian Pacific Railway, and saw mill machinery for Graham, Horne and Company when she hit the rocks near Michipicoten and holed herself. Sliding over the reef, her master attempted to beach her, but she foundered on May 12 in deep water. Since the *Seaverns*

to the efforts of salvors as her final demise is reported some years later in the same general area. No damage figures were reported.[25]

Another Canadian mishap came in late June. The 318-ton propeller *Georgian* of Graham's Lake Superior Line was eastbound from Port Arthur on June 26 when she piled into a reef off Peninsula on Ontario's northeast shore. With her stern on the bottom in 40 feet of water,

Duluth's inner harbor was dredged in the early 1880s and the first grain elevators were erected on Rice's Point. CANAL PARK MARINE MUSEUM COLLECTION.

had just been extensively rebuilt, she was a substantial loss in excess of $32,500.[22]

Wild winds took an additional toll later in the month. Caught on May 27 off the mouth of the Bad River where she was rafting logs, the small side-wheel steamer *Ozaukee* was catapulted ashore and broken up. Salvors picked off her engines and machinery, but the ship was through. She belonged to the Union Mill Company of Ashland, being used to raft logs on Chequamegon Bay.[23] At the same time, the schooner *Three Brothers* was driven aground off the Porcupine Mountains to the east. With a heavy cargo of stone for St. Paul's Church in Milwaukee, the ship seemed permanently stuck, abandoned by her crew and surrendered to the underwriters by her owners. However, the wrecking tug *Winslow* of Detroit was rushed to Lake Superior. Assisted by lighters, she unloaded part of the stone cargo and retrieved the *Three Brothers* from her rocky roost. A salvage and repair bill of $8,500 was incurred.[24] Near Marquette, it was the 164-foot, 384-ton schooner *Guiding Star* hard ashore. Though deserted by her crew, she must have responded

but her bow out, she presented a ticklish salvage problem. Rescue measures were initiated immediately, and with the aid of a diver named Quinn, the *Georgian* was raised and brought to the Soo. After preliminary refurbishing, she was able to sail to Owen Sound for permanent repairs in mid-August. Her cargo of oats was ruined. Her total liability, though unstated, must have reached $10,000 or more.[26]

July brought more grief for Canadian sailors. At an unspecified location along the Canadian north shore, the small 317-ton schooner *Sir C.T. Van Straubenzie* was solidly aground. Captain Ganning of Detroit came to her assistance, retrieved her and towed her all the way to Collingwood for rebuilding. Worth approximately $14,000, the salvage bill must have run half that amount.[27] In July embarrassment also came to the United States Revenue Marine. Their fine revenue cutter *Fessenden* hit an uncharted rock in Prentiss Bay and settled to the bottom in shallow water. Help was quickly at hand. She was soon brought up, but an expense of $5,000 resulted.[28]

Fog resulted in a fatal collision late in July. Downbound

from Marquette on the evening of July 27, the new 178-foot, 891-ton wooden steam barge *J.M. Osborne* under Captain Thomas Wilford was groping her way through the dense mists, towing the barges *George W. Davis* and *Thomas Gawn*. Methodically, Captain Wilford was sounding his whistle, three blasts at a time. Suddenly, when the *Osborne* was approximately three and a half miles northwest of Whitefish Point, another steamer answered too close for comfort. Moments later loomed the bow of a large steel passenger steamer on collision course with the *Osborne*'s starboard side. The oncoming ship was the sleek new Canadian passenger vessel *Alberta* of the Canadian Pacific Railroad fleet. Then came the crash, the *Alberta* striking the *Osborne* on the starboard side between the main and mizzen masts and close to the boilers.

Though the wooden vessel was almost cut in two, she remained wedged to the *Alberta* while most of her people crossed to the steel ship. A passenger on the *Alberta*, a cook named O'Connor who was en route to join the Canadian propeller *Argyle* at Port Arthur, jumped aboard the *Osborne* and assisted a number of passengers and crew to safety. O'Connor was in the act of trying to bring the badly scalded fire-hold crew to the deck when the entangled ships unexpectedly parted and the *Osborne*, with 1,000 tons of iron ore in her hold, dove for the bottom, taking the heroic cook and three of her crew to their deaths. The *Alberta*, only slightly injured, returned to the Soo with the survivors. Built in 1882 at Marine City, the *Osborne* was rated A-1 and valued at $65,000. Her owners, George F. Cleveland and the Cleveland Iron Mining Company, filed a liability suit for $91,237.50 against the *Alberta*. Already, the *Alberta* had had a narrow escape in a sideswipe with her sister ship *Athabasca*, and before the *Osborne* incident had a minor scrape with the steamer *Pacific*. She undoubtedly was going too fast for safety in that fog — 12 mph. She had checked down after the *Osborne*'s whistle sounded, otherwise she might have cut the steam barge completely in two with heavy loss of life. The two barges were untouched. They were picked up by a passing steam barge and towed into the Soo.[29]

A stranding on August 4 at Au Sable Point caused relatively little injury to the schooner *Mystic*, but a boiler explosion on the 69-foot tug *Pacific* took two, and possibly three, lives on August 20. The Union Mill Company's tug *Pacific* was lying near the Miller and Ritchie Mill in Ashland when her boiler suddenly let go, killing her captain and engineer and perhaps a third crewman. The 19-year-old tug was valued at $5,000. Since an official damage report of $3,000 was given, it is probable that the vessel was reconditioned.[30]

Typically nasty early September weather east of Keweenaw Point drew blood on the 458-ton Canadian schooner *W.R. Taylor* of Picton, Ontario. Under Captain H. Buckley and laden with a cargo of rails en route from Buffalo to the Canadian Lakehead for the Canadian Pacific Rail-

road, she was blown into Huron Bay where she settled in 14 feet of water. Though abandoned to the underwriters, she obviously was raised, as only a moderate loss is listed.[31]

October gales brought bad luck *en masse*. Early in the month, the diminutive sailing yacht *Golden Rule* out of Ashland was found capsized off Ontonagon with her two crewmen missing and presumed drowned. A couple of weeks later, the rowdy seas whipped the 300-ton Canadian schooner *Lady Dufferin* into the shallows off Caribou Island. Her crew reached shore safely, though the vessel was abandoned. The wrecking tug *International* worked on her unsuccessfully through early November. The following spring, the *International* and the tug *Charlton* returned, but there is no direct confirmation that their efforts were crowned with success, and the *Lady Dufferin* could have laid her bones on Caribou Island. However, it is most probabie that she was recovered since a schooner of the same name and similar dimension was reported lost on Georgian Bay in 1886. She was worth $8,000.[32]

Late October brought worse news. The 231-foot, 1,502-ton iron steamer *Scotia*, built in Buffalo in 1873, had just changed owners in mid-October and was on her way upbound light to Duluth. With Captain Bogart in command, she encountered tempestuous winds and blinding snow east of Keweenaw Point. To the horror of all aboard, at about 5 a.m. on October 24, she plowed into the tip of Keweenaw Point some miles east of Copper Harbor. She was on so hard that her twin screws powered by 600 horsepower engines could not back her off. Some of her crew went aboard the steamer *Nyack* which gave assistance, and the rest made shore safely. Before wrecking tugs could arrive, the rampaging waves broke her in two, a total loss. Constructed at a cost of $170,000 for Holt & Ensign's Commercial Line of Buffalo, she was one of four identical package freighters. Reputedly, she was still worth $100,000, having been purchased only 10 days before by a syndicate of P.P. Pratt, F.L. Danforth and James Ash. Theirs must have been a bad investment, as newspapers listed only $60,000 in insurance. Two years later, a salvage group under a wrecking master Johnson with a diver named Dwyer, burned off her remaining upper works and retrieved both boilers and engines, together with 150 tons of scrap metal. Owners of the wreck then were listed as Thomas Maytham, M.M. Drake and Wiener & Son of Buffalo. The recoveries of the salvors may have reduced the net liability to $80,000, still bad enough for those days. Nearly 90 years later, scuba divers brought up one of her propellers for display at Michigan's Fort Wilkins State Park in Copper Harbor.[33]

A trio of difficulties hit Waiska Bay in the last week of October with schooners *Negaunee* and *White Star* aground with the tug *Winslow*. Aggregate repairs amounted to a little more than $8,000.

November brought widespread miseries. A powerful

40

The 1880s brought a whole new breed of larger, more efficient freighters for grain and iron ore trades. WALLACE MORSE, CANAL PARK MARINE MUSEUM COLLECTION.

norther at Marquette on November 17 left the 162-foot, 497-ton schooner *Harvey Bissell* pitched well up on the beach at the mouth of Carp River. Early attempts to relieve her were to no avail and her owners, the Murphy interests of Detroit, turned her over to the underwriters who retrieved her intact the next spring. Her official loss figure of $20,000 undoubtedly was too high.[34] Four days later, the storm gods whaled the 181-foot, 869-ton steam barge *Morley* as she sailed into the eastern lake downbound from Duluth with grain. The raging waters finally deposited her well into shoal water at Lonesome Point east of Grand Marais, Michigan. Her crew reached safety, but rescue tugs could do nothing with the ship. For months she was regarded as a complete ruin. Despite her open exposure to northerly gales, her hull held together over the winter and Captain S.A. Murphy with the tug *A.J. Smith* succeeded in releasing her the next May 14. Taken first to Marquette, she was discovered to be leaking badly, whereupon she was towed to Detroit for rebuilding and eventual renaming. Captain Murphy supposedly received $10,000 for his services, while reconstruction costs likely exceeded $20,000. Her cargo of 36,000 bushels of wheat insured by the Continental Insurance Company was wiped out. When one considers the salvage charges, rebuilding expenses and the loss of insured cargo, her casualty figure of $76,000 may not be excessive for a wooden ship which was recovered.[35]

Off Keweenaw Point on November 23, the lake won another contest. The 225-ton Canadian steam barge *Erin* had the 316-ton schooner-barge *Mary Battle* in tow. The line broke and the *Mary Battle* was pitched aground on the Keweenaw Peninsula five miles from Eagle River. Meanwhile, the *Erin* failed to find shelter and ended up on the shoals at Gull Rock off the tip of Keweenaw Point. Both crews escaped. The *Mary Battle,* built in 1872 and owned by John Battle of St. Catherine's, Ontario, at first was adjudged a total loss worth $10,000, but persistent salvage crews finally picked her off on October 16, 1885, for rebuilding. The steam barge *Erin,* launched in 1881 by Shickluna and valued at $30,000, was retrieved within a month by the tugs *Gladiator* and *A.J. Smith* and taken to Lac La Belle where she was left for the winter. She was towed to Port Arthur the following June for unloading and then taken to Owen Sound for complete repair. This salvage exploit must have been worth some thousands of dollars, though the *Erin*'s costs were not reported.[36]

In the Apostle Islands on November 24, the two-year-old 68-foot, 47-ton tug *N. Boutin* foundered off Washburn, Wisconsin. She was recovered.[37] At the same time Canadian sailors took another beating with the 180-foot, 889-ton wooden propeller *City of Owen Sound* ashore and in bad shape at Michipicoten. A sister ship of the ill-fated *City of Winnipeg,* she had been built in 1875 and valued with cargo at $55,000. Happily for her owners, the dire original dispatches proved untrue, and wreckers

released her the following June 13 for a trip to the shipyard at Owen Sound. Her final liability was slightly less than $12,000.[38]

Nine other ships had mishaps at undisclosed times during the year. The scow-schooner *J. Bigler,* a 150-foot, 351-ton craft, foundered off Portage Entry about 40 miles north of Marquette to the tune of $13,500. She was en route from Nipigon to Chicago when rough weather caught her in early September. All crewmen were saved, but details are lacking. Moderately battered in groundings were the propeller *City of Duluth* at Copper Harbor and the schooner *E.A. Mayes* at Grand Island. Only light repairs were needed by the propeller *Pacific,* the schooner-barge *Mears* and the schooner *John Martin,* all ashore at Whitefish Point, and the steam barge *S.C. Baldwin* at Ashland. Gale wracked to the extent of more than $8,000 were the propeller *Wocoken* and the schooner *Richard Winslow.* Indeed, the *Wocoken* twice felt the wrath of slashing winds. In number of accidents, this was the worst season experienced to date.[39]

1885

Freight volume showed another healthy increase in the season of 1885, but the number of accidents was substantially reduced. Still, more ships were definitely destroyed, and there was one catastrophic disaster. A pair of tug fires in mid-May inaugurated the casualty roster with the new 65-foot tug *Cora A. Sheldon* losing her upper works at Houghton and requiring several thousand dollars in reconstruction.[40] Flames on May 17 caught the tug *Carrington* between L'Anse and Baraga as she was towing a raft of logs. The steam yacht *Eva Wadsworth* picked off the crew as the *Carrington* burned to the water's edge. Owned by Nester and Company, she was worth $6,000.[41]

Heavily laden with coal for Duluth-Superior Harbor, the 232-foot bulk freighter *Egyptian* went hard aground near Raspberry Island off the Bayfield Peninsula on May 20. Salvage was effected by both lightering cargo and simply dumping some over the side into 16 feet of water. Tugs *N. Boutin* and *Mollie Spencer* released the *Egyptian,* which proceeded to Duluth for repairs, despite leaking badly. Part of her coal cargo was recovered by the *T.H. Camp* soon afterward.[42]

On July 27 a small steam vessel met her end, the 91-ton *Isle Royale* succumbing to a leak when off Susie Island southwest of her island namesake. Passengers and crew escaped to the island. The unfortunate little ship was built at Port Huron in 1879 as the *Agnes* and was brought to Duluth only the year before her demise. She was owned by Cooley, LaVaque & Company who valued her at $12,000.[43]

Fire scored again on September 11, the victim being the

138-foot, 710-ton Canadian propeller *Prussia* of the Western Express Line which was consumed off Raspberry Island near Bayfield while en route from Fort William to Duluth. The fire was believed to have started in her after

North shore packet Isle Royale *succumbed to heavy seas near Susie Islands.* AUTHOR'S COLLECTION.

end beneath the ship's boilers, but first noticed when flames broke through the boat deck around the stack. Sand Island Lightkeeper Lederlee rescued 11 persons, including one woman, after spotting the *Prussia* when about 10 miles northwest of his station. All passengers and crew had managed to get away, though destruction of ship and cargo was complete. As the *Prussia* was of Canadian registry, no financial loss is recorded in American documents. However, the 12-year-old vessel must have been worth at least $40,000 to her St. Catherine's, Ontario, owners.[44]

Next, two schooners joined the list of the vanquished. Downbound from Two Harbors with 1,800 tons of iron ore, the new schooner-barge *F.W. Wheeler* was proceeding routinely in tow of the steam barge *Kittie M. Forbes* when the schooner began to leak. About seven miles off Grand Marais, Michigan, on September 29, her crew realized the situation was hopeless. Their ship was settling. They took to their yawl as the schooner dove for the bottom. Just two years old, she was a financial liability of $40,000. The following week her wreckage littered the beach at Grand Marais, but there was no clue as to what sank her. This situation was most unusual, for new wooden ships have almost never succumbed to leakage in good weather.[45]

Another weird incident occurred at Duluth on October 10. Propelled by a good wind, the 198-foot, 694-ton schooner *Guido Pfister* approached the old Duluth Ship Canal off which a tug waited to take her through. A tug crewman, however, muffed the line tossed from the schooner and the *Pfister* kept right on coming, missed

the canal entrance and smashed hard aground alongside the south pier. Her crew jumped safely to the pier as their ship ripped her bottom out. With her coal cargo, she was an item of $28,000. Most of her coal was retrieved by enterprising Captain Alexander McDougall of Duluth with the aid of a centrifugal pump, possibly a first in salvage techniques for Lake Superior. Still, residents of Minnesota Point managed to liberate a sizable quantity for their own needs. Virtually all of the *Pfister*'s shattered hull was finally removed in 1898 prior to the reconstruction of the Duluth Harbor entry. A major rehabilitation of the Duluth Ship Canal was undertaken by the U.S. Army Corps of Engineers in 1985-87. During work along the south pier, portions of the *Pfister*'s hull were recovered along with a small sample of her coal cargo. This material is now in the collection of the Corps of Engineer's Canal Park Visitor Center and Marine Museum in Duluth.[46]

High seas in late October caused minor damage to the wooden propeller *Starrucca*. A tragic explosion aboard the 175-foot Canadian propeller *Myles* in Duluth Harbor on October 28 took two lives. Chief Engineer Thomas Hickey and Assistant Engineer William Rooney were killed in the blast which wrecked their engine room but did not sink the ship.[47]

The first week of November brought one of the most ghastly catastrophes in the history of Lake Superior sailing. The 262-foot, 1,773-net-ton propeller *Algoma* of the Canadian Pacific Railroad was one of the finest steel passenger ships on the Great Lakes. She was brand new, having been built in Scotland by Aitken and Mansell at Kelvinhaugh-on-Clyde in 1883. Her engine was constructed by the renowned John Rowan of Govan, Scotland. Along with her fleetmates *Alberta* and *Athabasca*, she was the pride of the Canadian merchant marine on the lakes. On November 5, the *Algoma* left Owen Sound for Port Arthur. The following evening, as the ship headed northwest from Whitefish Point, she encountered worsening weather: rain, sleet, heavy snow and a violent gale from the northeast. She still made excellent time, about 16 mph. About 4 a.m. on November 7, Captain John Steed Moore, sensing that he was running ahead of schedule, ordered the auxiliary sails taken down, the engine checked down and the ship turned to the open lake. However, he was much closer to Isle Royale than he realized and at least two miles south of his expected course.

As the *Algoma* turned, she struck at the stern on Greenstone Rock, off what is now known as Mott Island, at the northeastern end of Isle Royale. The pummeling surf drove her further on the rocks and proceeded to punish her unmercifully. The ship had stranded about 4:20 a.m.; by 6 a.m. she had broken in two and the towering seas systematically ripped to pieces her whole hull and superstructure forward of the boilers. Passengers and crewmen were swept overboard to death in the icy waters. Captain Moore behaved heroically, herding survivors to the stern which remained on the reef, until he was crushed and trapped by the collapsing cabin. Despite his injuries, he retained command, leading the desperate band in prayer through the dismal day and terrifying night which followed. Apparently, their prayers were answered; the seas subsided, a mate and two men succeeded in reaching shore. With the aid of a life line, they towed a makeshift raft from ship to shore, transferring 11 more bedraggled castaways.

The following summer, Captain F.I. Merriman raised the *Algoma*'s main engine and picked up 13 lesser engines, together with 200 tons of scrap. The *Algoma* engine later was sleeved to reduce piston diameter and thus better accommodate higher pressure steam before being placed in the new propeller *Manitoba* built at Owen Sound in 1889. Later scrap collectors visited the site in 1903 and 1905. Captain H. Brooks with the steamer *J.C. Suit* took 150 tons of scrap steel in the spring of 1903,

Steel steamer Algoma *was built in Scotland for the Canadian Pacific Railway in 1883.* GREAT LAKES HISTORICAL SOCIETY COLLECTION.

These 14 were all that remained of a total of 51 or more who had been aboard the *Algoma*. Fortunately, Isle Royale fishermen found the miserable group and gave them shelter and food, saving them from death by exposure. The next morning, at the request of Captain Moore, the fishermen took their boat north to the vessel lane and flagged down a passing passenger steamer which turned out to be the *Athabasca*. Captain Foote of the *Athabasca* hove to and picked up the *Algoma*'s people, taking them to Port Arthur where their dreadful experience was reported. Purser Alex McKenzie of the *Algoma* was among the dead and his records were destroyed; hence, the exact death toll is unknown, reports ranging from 37 to 48 — some stories listed 15 survivors. The ship undoubtedly was worth in excess of $345,000. A court of inquiry appointed by the Canadian Minister of Marine tried Captain Moore and found him guilty of negligence due to his faulty navigation. He was suspended for a year, although in view of his exemplary behavior after the crash, three months of the sentence were remitted.

while Captain Wanless of Duluth gathered more in the spring of 1905. Various hard hat divers and more recently, sport divers, have recovered a number of artifacts from this wreck. However, the *Algoma* is protected under various archaeology and cultural resource laws of the National Park Service and no further artifact retrieval is permissible. The tragedy of the *Algoma* was the worst financial loss of the 19th century and the second worst fatality list for a single ship mishap in the entire history of Lake Superior shipping.[48]

From 1981 through 1986 the National Park Service's Submerged Cultural Resources Unit, consisting of underwater archaeologists, assisted by photographers, illustrators and a cadre of volunteer historians and sport divers, conducted a thorough inventory of the shipwreck resources of Isle Royale National Park. The *Cumberland* wreck of 1877, mentioned earlier, along with the *Algoma* and eight other wrecks were investigated *in situ* and in archives of the United States and Canada. While a large amount of information was gathered on each wreck, a couple of especially noteworthy things stand out about the *Algoma*. One is that the ship is not broken up like any of the other steel-hulled wrecks around the island or almost anywhere on the Lakes. Instead of being ripped and

Proud Algoma *blundered onto Isle Royale's rugged south shore in a tragic 1885 snowstorm.* GREAT LAKES HISTORICAL SOCIETY COLLECTION.

torn apart, it is in large part simply disassembled due primarily to rivet failure. Structural elements seem to be relatively intact, just not attached to other components.[49]

Another intriguing aspect of the *Algoma* loss and the subject of much intense searching by sport divers has been the whereabouts of her bow section, fully two-thirds or more of the ship. Historic photographs clearly show the stern section only days after the incident. The bow had broken away within hours after the incident occurred. The fact that 13 engines were reported as recovered in 1886, that is, the main propelling engine and a dozen auxiliaries, indicates that salvors of that period had access to both the stern and all or most of the "missing" forward section. It appears that the search has been for an intact bow section while the archeological record now indicates the bow very likely came apart during the wrecking process and subsequent storms, leaving it in scattered pieces. At least one sizable bulkhead, almost unmistakably from the forward end, was located among the several debris fields. Also located was a portion of the deck of the bow. Thus, it is not likely that an intact forward section actually exists, rather that additional elements of the bow will be located and identified.[50]

The *Algoma*'s loss was not the end of problems for 1885. On November 11 the new wooden propeller *Kittie M. Forbes* hit a shoal in the Apostle Islands. Salvage men freed her, but the bill for renovation was $17,000, plenty for a vessel only two years old costing $65,000.[51]

December tripping brought more grief. On December 23 in decent visibility, the 85-foot, 91-ton steam packet *Mary Martini* struck Brule Point northeast of Grand Marais, Minnesota. This was her end. Brought to the Head

of the Lakes in the summer of 1883 by L.F. Johnson and James Bardon, she had served as a ferry between Superior and Duluth. Then she was sold to Captain Joseph Lloyd of Duluth for north shore passenger service which she was in at the time of her final mishap. The tug *T.H. Camp* brought the *Martini*'s passengers and crew to Duluth the following week, along with 3,500 pounds of fish. Local vessel men blamed faulty navigation for the sinking of the little two-decker which was a ship of historic significance, being the first hull from the famous F.W. Wheeler shipyard at Bay City, Michigan.[52]

Passenger steamer Mary Martini *was in the fish collection trade when she was wrecked at Grand Marais, Minnesota, in November 1885.* ST. LOUIS COUNTY HISTORICAL SOCIETY COLLECTION.

A number of lesser scrapes bothered sailors throughout the year with strandings afflicting the propeller *Egyptian* at Eagle Harbor, the schooner *S.V.R. Watson* at the Huron Islands and the schooner *Sandusky* at Whitefish Point. More serious injury occurred to the propeller *Wallula* in the eastern lake with storm damage of $6,900, while the schooner *Favorite,* which sank from a leak at Bayfield, had a $5,500 charge. Two fires cost several thousand dollars, the tug *Thomas Quayle* burning at Ontonagon and the new 268-foot propeller *City of Rome* at Duluth Harbor. High seas caused minor repairs to be required by the propeller *Tacoma,* while the collision-sinking in shallow water of the schooner *H.M. Scove* brought expenses of $3,000. All of these were annoying to marine men, but miniscule compared to the *Algoma* incident.[53]

1886

Despite a phenomenal jump of one-third in vessel passages and tonnage at the Soo during this year, the casualty roster was moderate. Salvage operations on the *Algoma* resulted in the loss of the tug *George Hand* near Little Schooner Island Reef in Siskiwit Bay, Isle Royale, during early August. She was worth only $1,500. Lightkeeper

John H. Malone of the Isle Royale Light on Menagerie Island made the following entries in his log of 1886 pertaining to the *Algoma* and *George Hand:*

June 28: *We found four life preservers on the beach abreast of our station belonging to the ill-fated steamer* Algoma. *They are damaged from washing along the Island. Also found a couple of small pieces of a piano — some wire mattras* [sic] *frames and one pillow.*

August 5: *The wrecking tug* George Hand *of Algonac passed the station up the Bay after a crib that laid there for blocking for the boilers of the* Algoma. *Captain Manyman Waecker said he has the machinery all out of her and said he will finish in a few days.*

August 10: *We discovered a tug on the Schooner Island Reef almost a wreck. I found her to be the* George Hand *of Algonac, Michigan, the tug that was wrecking the steamer* Algoma *at Rock Harbor. Full particulars of how she got on there are not known yet. We have had very thick smoky weather here lately. She is laying in about four feet of water on her starboard side and about five hundred yards from the Little Schooner Island Rocks. She is listed starboard and full of water. She is surrounded with very shole water. The foggy weather on the ninth prevented us from seeing the main shore.*

August 12: *Wrecking party are at work raising the machinery of tug* George Hand.[54]

It can be said, then, that the wreck of the *Algoma* contributed to the wreck of the wrecking tug *George Hand,* which had been built in 1868 at Buffalo and purchased in 1884 by Calvin Curry and Albert Gilbert. The *Hand* was chartered to the salvage firm of Merriman & Fowler at the time of loss. Despite the tug's loss, salvage efforts continued on the *Algoma* with the schooner *L.L. Lamb* delivering her engines and boilers to Owen Sound late in August. Considerable effort has been made to locate the tug's remains during the mid-1980s, but without success.[55]

On August 27, in dense fog and smoke, the coastal propeller *A. Booth* of the A. Booth and Sons Fish Company hit a submerged reef only a mile and a half from Grand Portage. After the 14 persons aboard were removed by the tug *T.H. Camp,* the *Booth* slid off into deep water. Built at Chicago in 1882 by J. Parker Smith, she was one of the fastest boats on the lakes, valued at $14,000 and insured for $10,000. The veteran salvor Captain S. Murphy of Detroit was originally hired to raise the *Booth,* but may have run into trouble due to her odd position on the bottom, her bow being considerably below the stern. At any rate, salvor J.Q. Falcon succeeded in bringing her up the next year and towing her to Grand Marais, Minnesota, a final liability of $7,000.[56]

Three days of blinding fog on the eastern lake left the propeller *E.B. Hale* and schooner-barge *Fayette Brown* solidly in the clutches of Pancake Shoal northeast of Whitefish Point on August 30. Iron ore worth several thousand dollars had to be jettisoned before they could float free, though the ships suffered little.[57] At the Soo on September 12, the propeller *Escanaba* and the schooner-barge *T.L. Parker* had a stranding and colliding experience, sustaining little injury. The *Escanaba* had started leaking in high seas while downbound with ore from Ashland and was drawing too much water as she entered the river above the locks. She thus stranded and the *Parker* rammed into her.[58]

Accidents would get worse. On October 19, the little steam yacht *Lizzie Sutton,* which had been the ferry boat between Houghton and Hancock, caught fire and burned to the water's edge east of Portage. The steamer *St. Marie* came along in time to rescue the whole crew. The *Sutton* was listed at only $1,500.[59]

A vicious northwester on October 20 brought death. The 138-foot, 330-ton schooner-barge *Eureka,* under Captain Cartwright, had cleared Marquette with iron ore early that day as one of three barges in tow of the steamer *Prentice.* That night, in gale-riled darkness, the *Eureka* broke her line and disappeared. The following morning, Captain Smith of the upbound propeller *Winslow* spotted three feet of main mast and the bow of a white yawl protruding from the lake about six miles off Vermilion Point. As Captain Smith pulled up for a closer look, he noted the U.S. Lifesaving Service from Vermilion Point scouring the area. The sunken vessel apparently was a fore-and-aft schooner with no top masts; the foremast had broken off, possibly a cause of foundering; a davit halyard still held the yawl. Hence, the crew had not abandoned ship. Captain Cartwright and his five crewmen were gone forever, and the *Eureka* was a $10,000 liability for owner D.C. Whitney of Detroit. The sinking or stranding of a breakaway schooner would become a common accident pattern on Lake Superior.[60]

On the same day at Edward Island on the Canadian north shore, the little steamer *A. Neff* went awry on the rocks off Porphyry Island near the entrance to Black Bay. Her crew reached Port Arthur after being rescued from the island by the tug *Mary Ann* returning from Silver Islet. The *A. Neff* was one of several vessels which had earned their keep in the railroad and mining supply business, but had recently been used primarily as a passenger and excursion vessel around Port Arthur and Fort William following completion of the Canadian Pacific Railway. One of her owners, R.E. Mitchell, viewed the wreck soon after the incident and proclaimed her a total loss estimated at $6,500. Yet her hull was raised and rebuilt as the 74-ton steamer *Butcher's Maid.*[61]

Another blow on November 10 brought a close call to the steam propeller *St. Marie* which was whipped ashore near Deer Park. Her captain wisely ordered his ship scuttled to prevent her pounding to pieces in the shallows. Lifesavers from the Deer Park Station took off her crew, their baggage and the ship's furnishings. When the seas calmed, salvors retrieved the ship which had suffered only nominal injury.[62]

The third week of November brought one of the most violent weather monsters ever to bedevil western and

as well as articles of clothing were all recovered and preserved despite being on the bottom of Lake Superior for nearly a century. While untrained, excellent paraprofessional underwater archaeological techniques were employed with numerous drawings and photographs of artifacts taken *in situ* and as recovered and as later restored. An excellent body of information was thus built from what might otherwise have become simply another plundered

The schooner Lucerne *was in the ore trade out of Ashland for years before her loss with all hands in 1886.* MILWAUKEE PUBLIC LIBRARY, HERMAN G. RUNGE COLLECTION.

central Lake Superior. The waters thrashed for three days. Driven by hurricane-like northeast winds, heavy sleet and blinding snow engulfed Michigan's Upper Peninsula. Putting unsuspectingly out from Ashland was the 227-foot steam barge *Raleigh* with the 195-foot, 728-ton schooner *Lucerne* in tow, both heavily laden with iron ore. Caught by the tempest, the schooner was overwhelmed a short distance out of the harbor, foundering off Chequamegon Point and taking her complement of 10 men with her. The *Raleigh*'s crew had many anxious moments until their ship found shelter. The *Lucerne* was owned by Corrigan and Mack of Cleveland, worth $33,000. Her 10-man death toll was one of the worst for a schooner sinking on Lake Superior. During the 1970s, a group of sport divers under the direction of the late LaMonte Florentz conducted extensive excavation and salvage work on the wreck of the *Lucerne*. Their discoveries and recoveries were remarkable considering this was an all-volunteer effort. Artifacts both large and small ranging from a few coins and a clay pipe to wooden paint buckets and a wooden ship's knee

shipwreck. A handful of the artifacts are in the collection of the U.S. Army Corps of Engineers' Canal Park Visitor Center and Marine Museum in Duluth while the bulk are being kept at the Apostle Islands National Lakeshore in Bayfield, Wisconsin, near the site of the *Lucerne*'s loss.[63]

The storm rolled on. Actually, the disturbance on Lake Superior was part of a gigantic snow and gale pattern which covered the Midwest. Indeed, sailors on Lake Michigan fared far worse than those on the Upper Lake. St. Paul received more than 13 inches of snow and a temperature of 15 above; Des Moines was lambasted as was Chicago. Telegraph lines to Milwaukee came down, as did those north of Detroit. At Marquette, high winds began early on the morning of November 17. By early afternoon, raging seas overtopped the breakwater, ripped off the plank surface and hurled the wooden lighthouse tower into the lake. Blinding snow added to the deteriorating situation. Many of Marquette's citizens gathered along the waterfront to watch the dreaded performance. About 2 p.m., their hearts figuratively went to their mouths when out of the snow loomed a schooner with all sails reefed, heading on a collision course for the breakwater. Disaster appeared imminent. Yet, out popped the little 28-ton tug *F.W. Gillett,* Captain John Frink at the

Schooner Florida *dragged her anchors and drove ashore at Whetstone Creek in Marquette Harbor.* BLAMEY COLLECTION.

wheel. Breasting the turbulent harbor water, the *Gillett* pulled alongside the sailing ship, which proved to be the schooner *Eliza Gerlach,* a line was put aboard and adroitly the *Gillett* led the schooner around the breakwater into a comparatively sheltered portion of the port. Only minutes later, another schooner raced out of the snow blanket. This was the two-masted, 299-ton *Florida,* heavily laden with coal. Too late, Captain F.A. Goodell realized his proximity to the shore, and though the anchors were dropped, the *Florida* smashed into the beach near the mouth of Whetstone Creek and started beating herself to fragments against the docks. Again, it was Captain Frink and the tug *Gillett* to the rescue. At tremendous risk to his own vessel, Frink brought the tug alongside the stricken schooner, and six of the *Florida*'s crew leaped to safety on the tug's deck. The *Florida*'s crippled mate, Andrew Peterson, couldn't make it, being crushed between the ships and dying on the docks several hours later. The *Florida* was ground to ruin as outrageously high waves wrought havoc in the supposedly protected harbor. Water rose so high that it engulfed the Rolling Mills Dock, throwing large quantities of lumber and shingles into the maelstrom.

As bad as was the havoc during the day and night of November 17, the following morning would bring far greater excitement. As daylight broke on November 18, shore dwellers southeast of Marquette spotted the outlines of two snow- and ice-encrusted vessels trapped in vicious surf off the mouth of the Chocolay River, about 400 yards off shore. Through rifts in the snowfall, the two were also visible in fleeting glimpses from downtown Marquette. Marquette villagers quickly assembled teams and wagons and began hauling a large yawl boat the several miles to the wreck site. Sailors from the sunken *Florida* volunteered to man the yawl, but repeated launchings brought only failure. The surf was much too high. Next, Marquette residents remembered that a Civil War mortar was available at the local powder factory. This was dragged to the mouth of the Chocolay since the Marquette men were determined to shoot a line aboard the two wrecks and take the men off via breeches-buoy or bosun's chair. The first shot with a 24-pound projectile, however, was far short; at the second shot, the old mortar, which was probably overloaded with powder, exploded into useless pieces. Fortunately, no one was injured.

Darkness now was approaching and the future looked mighty bleak for those trapped on the two ships which proved to be the 209-foot, 1,190-ton steam barge *Robert Wallace* and her barge, the 217-foot, 1,088-ton four-masted *David Wallace,* the two downbound from Duluth with 104,000 bushels of wheat. Under Captain Frank H. Brown of the *Robert Wallace* and Captain Henry Wallace of the *David Wallace,* the two had been well east of Marquette, perhaps northwest of Grand Marais, when the gale prompted Captain Brown to turn west in search of shelter. The walls of snow precluded sighting the shoreline, while the absence of the Marquette breakwater lighthouse, wrecked earlier, at Marquette, permitted the two to sail right past the port in the darkness. For that matter, so terribly confused was the *Robert Wallace*'s master, that when he first spotted the lights of Marquette after the stranding, he thought he was off Michipicoten Island 100 miles to the northeast. The stranding itself had been quite a shock when the steamer narrowly escaped being run down by her barge. Luckily, both ended up aground with their bows toward the seas and the forward cabins intact. The crews had shelter, but all they could do was wait for rescue and hope that their new ships would hold together. The *Robert Wallace* was only four years old and the *David Wallace* but two. Both vessels were built at Cleveland.

Meanwhile, Captain John Frink, learning that the tug *Jay C. Morse* failed in an attempt to approach the ships from the lake side, realized that local rescue was all but impossible. In desperation, he telegraphed the U.S. Lifesaving Service at the Portage Station more than 110 miles away. In such a dreadful gale his request was a long shot, but it paid off. The message had to be delivered to Captain Albert Ocha at the station by the tug *James W. Croze.*

One man died as the Florida *was smashed against the docks in Marquette Harbor.* JOHN E. KEAST COLLECTION.

The lifeboat and equipment then had to be loaded aboard the tug for the six-mile run into Houghton. At the same time, Manager Hornby of the Marquette, Houghton, and Ontonagon Railroad ordered a special train made available and the track cleared. Purely by chance, daredevil engineer Henry Jackson and No. 39, a fast engine, were both in Houghton awaiting a run south. Volunteers placed the lifeboat and equipment on two flat cars and the lifesavers entered a coach. At 8 p.m., Engineer Jackson pulled out into the ravaging snow storm. The normal time for the trip from Houghton to Marquette was nine and a half hours. Jackson made it in three hours and ten minutes, despite two feet of snow in the Ishpeming area. At Marquette, the Detroit, Mackinac and Marquette Railroad had another special waiting to take the lifesavers a few miles closer to Chocolay, after which wagons and sleighs brought the rescue group and a number of local people to the wreck sites. At 1 a.m. on November 19, the lifesaving party had arrived.

The bulk freighter Robert Wallace *and her consort,* David Wallace, *lost their way in blinding snow during the November 1886 gale.* JOHN E. KEAST COLLECTION.

Captain Ocha first fired a line over the *Robert Wallace,* but the crew couldn't reach it in the darkness and waves. He then launched the lifeboat into the enormous surf, succeeded in crossing the treacherous reefs, though in crossing he had his rudder, which had already been damaged during handling, become disabled. For safety's sake, Ocha returned to the beach where he and his crew worked the remainder of the night repairing their craft by the light of giant bonfires. The lifesavers attempted to fire another line aboard the *Robert Wallace,* but failed again. At daybreak, Ocha launched again, crashed through the mountainous seas and in three trips took all 24 men off the two vessels. The shipwrecked sailors were taken to the bonfire-strewn beach where food and drink donated by Marquette merchants awaited. Some of the men had not eaten in two days. The lifesaving endeavor had

spanned more than 110 miles and, with a similar experience the following year, ranks as the longest overland rescue trek in the history of Lake Superior navigation.

Salvors went to work as soon as the seas subsided. On November 21, the *Robert Wallace* was further damaged by a fire originating in a coal stove used by crewmen in the forward cabins. Her whole forward upper works burned off. Feverishly throwing the wheat cargo overboard, salvors pulled the *Robert Wallace* off the beach and brought her into Marquette Harbor on November 28, where salvage of the remainder of her cargo continued. The recovered wheat was sent to Milwaukee in boxcars. It took nearly two weeks for Marquette tug captains Benham and Gillett to release the *David Wallace* and drag her into the harbor for reclamation of as much wheat as possible. The *Robert Wallace* was valued at $80,000 and the *David Wallace* at $50,000. Initial estimates of necessary repairs amounted to more than $25,000 for the steamer and $8,000 for the barge, the heaviest loss being in the cargo, most of which was ruined. The final liability figures reported by the U.S. Lifesaving Service were $75,000 on the *Robert Wallace* and $59,000 on the *David Wallace.* Both ships were owned by David Wallace of Lorain, Ohio.[64]

The lake toll continued. On November 26, the towing tug *Niagara* cleared Marquette with a string of iron ore-laden schooners. Rugged seas off Grand Island broke the line on the 139-foot, 314-ton schooner *Republic* which crashed into Williams Island west of Grand Island. Marine men feared that this was the end of the line for her, as, loaded with 496 tons of hard ore, she stuck firmly. Her crew made shore. Salvors succeeded in retrieving the old *Republic,* built in 1854 at Clayton, New York, by the shipbuilder Oades. She had been reconstructed in 1870 and 1880. She was owned by H. Esselstyn of Detroit at the time of her difficulties. Her value was unstated, though she was probably worth in the vicinity of $10,000. She sailed for many more years.[65]

1887

Shippers in 1887 had an unusual year. While the number of ship passages was the highest to date, the safety record improved. Indeed, for the first four months of sailing, only one insignificant stranding was reported, the steamer *Argonaut* aground northwest of Crisp Point on June 2. A fatal foundering marred the pattern for September, followed by a whole series of troublesome incidents for the last six weeks of sailing. Downbound from Ashland with iron ore in tow of the steamer *Australasia* was the 205-foot, 765-ton schooner-barge *Niagara.* In the eastern lake a sudden gale struck. The towline parted and the *Niagara* was on her own. Captain Clements ordered the sails set, but slashing winds tore her canvas to ribbons. Early on September 7, the *Niagara* was off Vermilion Point, several miles from shore. Then she fell into the trough, her spars collapsed and she capsized, lying on her starboard side. Clements herded his crew into the yawl and attempted to pull for safety as the schooner slid below. The tossing waters overturned their lifeboat and all perished. The *Niagara* had been constructed at Tonawanda, New York, in 1873 and rebuilt in 1883. At the time of her sinking she was owned by James Corrigan of Cleveland, worth $30,000. There is some dispute as to the total casualties, either nine or 10. At first, Captain Clement's family was said to be on board as passengers, though they showed up safely in Detroit. But for a quirk of luck, the fatalities could have been much larger.[66]

A tragic fire on Chequamegon Bay took the lives of two crewmen as a 90-foot, 84-ton side-wheeler only four years old was lost. The *City of Ashland* caught fire and burned before foundering three miles northeast of Washburn on August 8 while towing a log raft from Bad River to Ashland. Four crewmen escaped the quickly spreading flames. There was no mention of salvage on this vessel in the regional press over the half century following the incident. The relatively shallow nature of the bay may yet permit her discovery, particularly her walking beam engine.[67]

While it is difficult in many instances to keep track of the many casualties involving yachts, small craft and tugs, one such occurrence of interest has recently come to light. En route from Jarvis Island, northeast of Victoria Island, to Port Arthur on the night of October 14 was the *Nettie,* an 11-ton steam yacht under command of Captain McKinnon. Gale force winds kept several freighters in port but caught the *Nettie* out when she should have been in, even though her destination was relatively close. She succumbed to the storm taking six souls down with her. The tug *Salty Jack* searched in vain for survivors throughout Thunder Bay and the Welcome Islands. However, it was the fish tug *Three Brothers* which picked up some oars and a rudder floating between Mutton and Welcome Islands, presumed to have been from the little *Nettie* which had served not only as a yacht, but frequently chartered as a supply vessel to the various island mines, including the one on Jarvis Island.[68]

Wild weather lambasted Marquette later in October, bringing three-fold difficulties. Striving to reach Marquette harbor on the afternoon of October 23, the 140-foot, 323-ton coal-carrying schooner *George Sherman* under Captain Nelson Gifford succumbed to the norther, being driven well onto the shoals of Shot Point, 12 miles short of her goal. Her crew stayed aboard until the masts fell, then launched the yawl and breasted the surf to shore, though Gifford was hurt in the landing. As they pulled themselves together on the beach, they watched as another, much larger schooner impaled herself on the rocks of Shot Point farther out. They could not make out her name.

The *Sherman* crew next hiked the woods in the direction of a railroad that Gifford knew was there, found the tracks and flagged down an ore train which brought them into Marquette. There, they promptly reported the wreck of the unidentified schooner. This time Marquette people telegraphed immediately for the Portage Lake Ship Canal lifesavers, and Captain Ocha brought his crew and lifeboat down from Houghton on a night express. Arriving in Marquette about 10:30 p.m., Ocha, after consultation with local vessel men, decided to have the tug *A.C. Adams* tow the surfboat through the tossing seas to Shot Point. The gale having switched from northwest to southwest, the *Adams'* master dropped the surfboat a safe distance from the reefs, and Ocha took his oar-propelled lifeboat to the derelict. He learned she was the 190-foot, 649-ton *Alva Bradley* of Cleveland, another coal carrier. The schooner was pounding heavily on the rocks, threat-

Coal-laden barge Plymouth *was lightered by horse-drawn sleighs during the winter of 1887.* JOHN E. KEAST COLLECTION.

ening to go to pieces at any time. Hence, Ocha took the 10-man schooner crew into the lifeboat and started out to where the tug should have been. However, through a mistake in signals, the *Adams* had returned to Marquette. Since the survivors already were suffering from exposure, Ocha deemed it wiser to go back aboard the *Bradley* and remain under cover until daylight when he took the surfboat into the beach and landed the survivors. A beach party had stood vigil and kept bonfires going through the night. After warming the schooner crew, those already on shore took them through the woods to a waiting train.

Meanwhile, the lifesavers relaunched, were picked up by the tug *Adams* which had returned for them and were towed back to Marquette. On the way back the temperature dropped sharply, the lifeboat took considerable water, and the lifesavers were frozen to their seats. Their clothing had to be cut away to free them when they reached Marquette. The *Sherman* was done for, badly mangled in the surf. She had been built by Quayle and Martin at Cleveland in 1862 and valued at only $9,000 in 1887. The *Bradley* also had been built by Quayle and Martin at Cleveland in 1870 and had been rebuilt. Salvors worked feverishly to release her before later storms could do further damage. She was taken off before mid-November and towed by the steamer *Sarah E. Sheldon* to the Soo for transfer to a Lower Lakes shipyard. Salvage and repair costs were more than half her value, probably about $20,000.[69]

To add to the excitement on that October 23 at Marquette, another shipwreck occurred on the northeastern outskirts of the community. The 213-foot, 777-ton schooner-barge *Plymouth* in tow of the steamer *Chauncy Hurlbut,* parted her line as the two sought shelter in Marquette Harbor. The *Plymouth* was driven on the rocks of Presque Isle with her coal cargo. Badly iced over, she presented a depressing spectacle although the outcome was fortuitous. Captain Rivard held his crew aboard until the worst of the blow was past, then launched his yawl for the shore, only a stone's throw away. All were safe. Salvors had to abandon immediate recovery efforts because of the ship's exposed position, but the early formation of ice protected the hull from the ravages of winter gales. Her coal cargo was taken off in sleighs and the lightened vessel, after spring breakup the next year, was finally floated off her rocky perch by the Reid salvors and brought into Marquette Harbor. She sailed for many years afterward. In fact, her recorded liability of $30,000 undoubtedly is excessive, perhaps initially set when total loss seemed imminent.[70]

That same vicious afternoon produced another potential tragedy near Deer Park, east of Grand Marais, Michigan. There, the 96-foot, 75-ton steamer *Laketon* was landing supplies for lumbermen at a small wooden wharf as high winds and snow blew up. Rather than run for Grand Marais Harbor, the *Laketon*'s master decided to ride out the blasts at anchor about three-quarters of a mile off shore. During the night, the anchor chains parted and the *Laketon* drifted toward the deadly breakers. The Deer Park lifesaving unit had anticipated this situation, and Captain Henry Cleary launched the surfboat at once, crashed through the tossing surf and plucked off the seven-man crew. The combers were now so high that Cleary backed the surfboat clear to the beach to avoid being dumped. When the storm subsided, the lifesavers picked off the remainder of the freight and other articles of value, then refloated the little coaster and towed her with the surfboat to the Deer Park wharf. She had suffered damages of $2,000.[71]

Though the news would not be known for two weeks,

a Canadian schooner went to the bottom on October 28. The 273-net-ton *Bessie Barwick* of Hamilton, Ontario, foundered at Pilot Harbor, Michipicoten Island. Her crew got to land and were sheltered by fishermen, but it was November 12 before they were able to reach the Soo by small boat. No financial loss was disclosed.[72]

While en route from Bayfield to Siskiwit Bay along the Wisconsin shoreline of Lake Superior, the two-masted schooner *Alice Craig,* formerly the United States Revenue cutter *John B. Floyd,* was driven ashore near Bark Point in a November 18 gale. There was no loss of life, but Captain Thomas H. Bunker, master of the *Craig* for the previous 18 years, took the brunt of blame for the accident. The 29-year-old 62-foot vessel was a total loss, although she was stripped of her rigging and other fittings soon after the incident. Curiously, her rudder washed ashore in Eagle Bay more than 20 years after the wreck, showing its distinctive copper fastenings, reflective of her initial role in government service.[73]

The third week of November brought the worst dispatches — a wreck a day for four consecutive days. On November 15, a wind-blasted snowstorm 10 miles east of Grand Marais left the 218-foot, 1,313-ton *Starrucca* of Lake Superior Transit Company stranded firmly. Two of her crew reached land and alerted the Deer Park lifesavers who removed the 21 persons remaining aboard. The *Starrucca* was en route from Buffalo to Duluth with a cargo

Steam barge Pacific *was once a popular passenger liner.* C. Patrick Labadie collection.

of general merchandise when her compass went awry in the whiteout. The seas proceeded to punish her so viciously that she proved unrecoverable, although portions of her cargo and equipment were retrieved. Built by the Union Dry Dock Company of Buffalo in 1874, this wooden steamer lasted only 13 years. She was worth $65,000 and her cargo another $50,000. Approximately $35,000 in cargo and equipment was recovered, making this an $80,000 incident, a big sum for the 1880s.[74]

The next night the Deer Park crew was busy again. Skies were threatening on November 16 when the 191-foot, 482-ton steam barge *Pacific* pulled from the Cook and Wilson Lumber dock at Deer Park about 7:00 p.m. Laden with lumber for Michigan City, the *Pacific* stuck on the outer bar as she headed for the open lake. Seeing her predicament, the lifesavers rowed to her in a matter of minutes, but the *Pacific*'s captain considered his ship in no danger. In fact, he thought he could work her over the sand bar when the seas grew a little higher. The lifesavers ran a hawser from the ship to the dock before returning to their quarters. About 10 p.m. another snow storm began; by midnight a gale was blowing. The *Pacific* was hurled broadside to the waves and disabled. Thoroughly concerned for his crew of 14 and a woman passenger, the *Pacific*'s captain sounded the distress whistle. This time, however, the lifesavers were a half hour in approaching the helpless steam barge. Still, they successfully removed the whole complement by 4 a.m. on November 17.

All that day, battering waves worked on the *Pacific* until by midafternoon only her after cabin remained on deck. Then, the *Pacific*'s master recalled that he had left his dog in the cabin. Would the lifesavers make another rescue? They did, and the dog was brought ashore. The following day the lifesavers made a number of trips to the derelict, picking off whatever was movable. But, by the afternoon of November 19 the ship had completely disintegrated, her debris cluttering the shore east of Deer Park. A loss of $32,000 was registered. The *Pacific* was an older ship, launched in 1864, and rebuilt in 1872, 1881 and 1887. She was owned by the Cook and Wilson Lumber interests of Detroit.[75]

The day of November 17 was long remembered by Marquette harbor people. But for the grace of God, the downtown area could have been a shambles. Events started in the early morning when the 187-foot, 929-ton propeller *Arizona* of the Anchor Line was tossed about off Big Bay Point northwest of Marquette while en route from Marquette to Portage. Her manifest was interesting. Besides a number of carboys containing acid, she carried 1,100 barrels of cement, 900 barrels of oil, 1,100 boxes of candles, a quantity of tar paper and some iron-working machinery for Alexander McDougall's new whaleback shipyard at Duluth. Captain George Graser turned back for Marquette. As the vessel rolled and pitched, however, a carboy of acid broke, filling the below decks area with choking fumes. Perhaps six miles off the harbor, fire broke out. The ship was soon a torch. With his whistle blowing distress signals, Graser rounded the end of the breakwater and entered the harbor.

He had to think fast. First, he must save his crew, yet, at the same time, prevent a harbor conflagration. He may have known that in 1868 a good deal of Marquette waterfront had been burned out. The captain and his wheelsman stuck to their posts, brushed the breakwater onto which all jumped to safety. Before leaving, Graser must have lashed the wheel.

The *Arizona* headed right up the harbor into an unoccupied slip near the Marquette waterworks and burned to the water's edge, a 24-hour bonfire. Hardly a stone's throw away was the Burt dock, towering with stacks of

Arizona burned for nearly 24 hours, threatening Marquette's waterfront with total destruction. JOHN E. KEAST COLLECTION.

white pine lumber. To the west and southwest lay wooden docks and wharves. The wind must have been right and the blaze did not spread. The Marquette city fire department, augmented by the tug *Gillett,* battled the flames for hours. Finally, a firefighter, A.J. Freeman of Marquette, daringly used an ax to cut holes in her hull planking and scuttle her. She continued to smolder the next day.

The *Arizona* had been built in Cleveland in 1865 for the Anchor Line, but was under charter to the Lake Superior Transit Company at the time of her destruction. She was worth $90,000, and her cargo in excess of $60,000, making this a $150,000 liability. Salvors later raised the lower portion of the propeller's hull which was rebuilt as a steam barge which continued to sail for many years. Still, the whole harbor as well as the city of Marquette could have taken a terrible scorching in this episode.[76]

And trouble was not over! The same rugged winds continued for another day and plastered the 268-net-ton Canadian schooner *Richard Morwood* of St. Catherine's, Ontario, against the cliffs of Grand Island on November 19. Because of threatening seas the crew remained on board for two days before escaping to a nearby cliff. Captain McPherson had saved his people, but his ship at the outset was deemed a ruin with a valuable cargo of 2,500 barrels of oil consigned to Port Arthur. But Marquette salvage men quickly went to work, recovering the oil which belonged to the Standard Oil Company. By June 1888, the oil had been saved. Then in July 1889, the schooner herself was dragged off, brought to Marquette and pumped out before being towed to Port Huron for rebuilding. When wrecked, the *Morwood* was an $8,000 item. She was 31 years old, launched at Port Dover, Ontario by the shipbuilder Waterbury in 1856 and reconstructed in 1874. This time $15,000 was spent on her re-furbishment and her name was changed to *E.B. Palmer*.[77]

1888

Fewer ships were using the lake in the 1888 navigation season, even though the tonnage hauled showed a slight increase. Happily, there was a dramatic decrease in accidents, only five consequential mishaps being reported. On May 30, the 314-ton Canadian schooner *Maggie McRae* foundered 10 miles off Thunder Cape. The *McRae* was one of two schooner-barges in tow of the steam barge *Bruno,* all heavily laden with grain bound for Montreal. Trailing behind the *McRae* was the *Laura.* The trio got into an ice pack which damaged both the *Bruno* and *McRae,* the latter severely ice cut. Her crew scrambled aboard the *Bruno* and returned to port for repairs. The crew had escaped, but a $35,000 financial casualty was incurred by the Mathews interests of Toronto, including approximately $12,500 for her 25,000-bushel cargo of wheat.[78]

In attempting to enter the north portal of Portage Lake Ship Canal on September 26, the 900-ton Canadian steam barge *Myles* struck the pier and went aground. With the aid of the Portage Station lifesaving crew she was refloated easily, repairs amounting to $2,000.[79] Continued rough water three days later brought a sinking, the 517-ton schooner-barge *Brandon,* tow of the tug *James A. Walker,* going to the bottom 40 miles southwest of Isle Royale. Along with the schooners *Regina* and *Jennie,* the *Brandon* was proceeding as part of the *Walker*'s tow when she began to leak and settle. The crew successfully abandoned her before she joined the undersea fleet. The financial liability was not disclosed.[80]

Keweenaw Point was the scene of another mishap on October 19, as the American schooner *Reed Case,* under Captain Green, struck the shore five miles north of the Portage Station. The 137-foot, 330-ton *Case,* en route light from Duluth to Portage, rammed the east pier in attempting to enter the canal during the gale and was driven four miles to the northeast where she anchored in a badly exposed position. The lifesavers lookout spotted her, and the Portage crew reached the schooner after a two-hour row. But Captain Green did not wish to abandon ship, and the lifesavers merely brought the steward ashore to wire for a tug and then brought him back to the ship at 2 a.m. Afterward, a violent gale arose. Neither tug nor lifesavers saw the schooner's yawl lowered, which soon capsized. The lifesaving crew waded into the surf, rescuing two of the three occupants. Captain Charles L. Green of Chicago had drowned. The lifesavers revived the two around a bonfire. The lifesaving crew then managed to cut through the treacherous surf and take off the remaining members of the schooner's complement. One man

had died, but seven were safe. As the waves subsided, the tug *A.C. Adams* got a line on the *Case* and nearly got her to the Ship Canal, when the water-filled schooner suddenly rolled on her beam ends and went to pieces only a quarter mile short of the canal entrance and safety. She was worth $8,000.[81]

Another October mishap saw the Canadian steamer *City of Montreal* crashing aground at Michipicoten Island while towing the *Keewatin.* The schooner *Keewatin* did not hit. Under Captain Redfern, the *City of Montreal* was laden with 475 tons of building stone from Verte Island bound for Chicago. A crew of 11 men and two women survived the ordeal in two small boats, drifting for three days before being rescued by the *W.B. Hall.* The vessel was well insured at $9,500 on a value of about $12,000. Her owner, A. Campbell of Colbourne, Ontario, had only acquired her in 1886.[82]

1889

A sharp spurt in vessel activity during 1889 sent the accident list rising, but not a life would be lost. Ice in the western lake broke up early and the first victims of spring weather appeared on April 23. High winds and a heavy slushy snow forced the steamer *Australasia* and the schooner *George* into shelter among the Apostle Islands. Visibility was extremely limited. In trying to negotiate the south passage between Madeline Island and Michigan Island, the two vessels ran aground. Captain Reid ordered the vessels scuttled. This maneuver succeeded in saving the vessels, although not terribly damaged. The *George* had bottom damage and the steamer lost her rudder shoe and damaged her propeller wheel. Both crews were safe, and despite initial fears of total destruction, the two were quickly relieved by salvors with a bill of $12,000. The *Australasia* was released on April 30 and went to Cleveland after temporary repairs. The tug *Sea Gull* worked on the *George* which was released on May 17 and taken to Bayfield for temporary repairs before the *Emerald* towed her into Ashland to await a larger tug for the downlakes tow and dry-docking.[83]

Especially thick fog over the entire lake on June 19 brought grief to six ships in widely scattered locations. A stranding occurred on the Minnesota north shore six miles northeast of Two Harbors, the new 256-foot, 1,610-ton wooden steam barge *City of Cleveland,* with the schooner *John Martin* in tow, nearly running ashore. Salvors soon had them off, but costs undoubtedly ran into several thousand dollars. This episode cost Captain James Lawless his command. The *City of Cleveland* was a Bradley ship. Captain Bradley didn't carry insurance, claiming that he hired the best captains and bought the finest ships. Therefore, no insurance was needed. Obviously,

Captain Bradley was more than displeased by the professional performance of Captain Lawless in this fog.[84]

On the same day west of Whitefish Point, a much more serious event was unfolding. The two-year-old steel steamer *Charles J. Sheffield* was struck broadside by the Northern Steamship Company's new steel *North Star,* the first major collision encounter of the novel metallic giants just beginning to come off the ways of Great Lakes ship-

Captain Henderson. Both ships ended up fast on the shoals. The *Adams* suffered only a broken propeller, but the *Monterey,* with 575 tons of iron ore in her hold, was seriously injured and abandoned as a $7,000 loss. Still, wreckers later reclaimed her. Although 23 years old, she was rebuilt and was still sailing 14 years later.[86]

Fog scored again at 4 a.m. on July 13 when the 233-foot, 1,536-ton wooden steamer *James Pickands* side-

City of Cleveland *was badly damaged in her 1889 stranding, but survived for many more years.* St. Louis County Historical Society collection.

yards. Captain Thorn of the *North Star,* sensing that he had mortally wounded the 260-foot, 1,700-ton *Sheffield,* held his bow in the gaping hole until Captain Allen and all 18 men in the *Sheffield's* crew had crossed to the *North Star.* As the latter backed off, the *Sheffield* rolled over and plunged to the bottom of the lake, becoming a $175,000 liability and the second highest to that date in Lake Superior history. Indeed, the cost of losing a steel ship henceforth would far outrun that of a wooden equivalent. Despite the poor visibility, both steamers were traveling at a fair rate of speed when contact occurred. The *Sheffield* belonged to Harvey Brown of Cleveland.[85]

The same fog blanket brought another incident not far away, at Sandy Island, 15 miles northeast of Whitefish Point. Captain J.H. Gillette in the tug *A.C. Adams* was towing the 127-foot, 309-ton schooner *Monterey* under

swiped the wooden steam barge *Smith Moore,* a 223-foot, 1,191-ton ship. Visibility was so bad that Captain Clint Ennis of the *Pickands* did not see the *Moore* until the latter was only 75 yards away, about 10 miles off Grand Island. In the whiteout the two vessels separated immediately, and Captain Ennis, thinking injuries to the two only superficial, continued on to Marquette where he reported the contact. The *Smith Moore,* laden with 1,753 tons of iron ore, nevertheless had fared far worse, taking water badly. As fog began to lift, the steam barge *M.M. Drake* spotted her plight, came alongside and picked off her three passengers and 15-man crew. The *Drake's* captain then put a line aboard the stricken *Moore* and began to inch his way toward Munising. For six hours, the *Moore* remained afloat as the two worked their way toward safety. Finally, only 300 feet from the bar at the mouth of the harbor, the *Smith Moore* dove to the bottom in 105 feet of water, blowing off her upper works as she went under.

Captain John Morrison reported the vessel worth more than $80,000 to her owner Harvey Brown of Cleveland.

City of Cleveland *wreck attracted excursion boats up the shore from Duluth.* CANAL PARK MARINE MUSEUM COLLECTION.

Several days later, Captain Morrison was at the Soo on his way back to Cleveland when Captain Ennis and the *Pickands* locked through. Morrison boarded the *Pickands* and a vehement argument took place over which ship was at fault. There is no record as to which captain won.[87]

On August 10 a fire struck the 185-foot, 1,009-ton wooden freighter *Chauncey Hurlbut* at Superior. Her upper works were lost to the gnawing flames. Her hull remained intact, nonetheless, rebuilding cost $20,000.[88]

On October 1, the 194-foot, 727-ton schooner-barge *Zach Chandler* was anchored outside Deer Park, awaiting her turn at the lumber wharves. A wicked norther arose. Her towing steamer, the *Huron City,* tried to pull her into safe water but suffered a machinery breakdown. The *Chandler* then dragged her anchors and went onto the shoals where her master, Captain Rafferty, slipped the anchors and allowed the ship to slide up on the beach about a mile and a half east of Deer Park. The Deer Park lifesavers responded to the lookout's call, though the *Chandler* crew had simply to lay down a ladder to dry land. In fact, the Lifesaving Service put up a tent for the *Chandler* crew on the shore while salvors attempted to free the ship. As the storm died down, the lifesaving men removed all portable stores and equipment from the schooner and stored them at the station. Repeated salvage attempts failed until the *Chandler* was finally pulled off the next season with damages of $4,000. She would sail another two years before leaving her remains within two miles of the same spot.[89]

September spelled the end of the 65-foot *Tourist,* which burned in two successive fires. Built at Bayfield by F.L. Maynard in 1888, the *Tourist* spent her entire brief career working the Chequamegon Bay area hauling pas-

sengers, freight and fish to earn her keep. An early morning fire broke out aboard the vessel on September 6 while she was docked in Bayfield. It was thought to have been entirely extinguished, when, but a few hours later, she was ablaze again. The *Tourist* was cut loose from the dock and allowed to drift until burning to the water's edge. No clear record of her final disposition has come to light nor have any records of salvage attempt. It is presumed she was a total loss.[90]

A wild northwester with snow squalls on October 5 caused a weird happening at the north entrance to the Portage Lake Ship Canal. The 178-foot, 590-ton wooden steam barge *Bessemer* with the 152-foot, 472-ton schooner-barge *Schuylkill* in tow, had departed Ashland at 11 a.m. on October 3. Both were loaded with iron ore. Good weather gave way to a vicious storm which stopped the ships when they were off Eagle Harbor early on October 5. They were tossed about unmercifully. The *Bessemer* began to leak freely, leaving a trail of iron ore-stained water like a wake of blood. Captain Hurlbut realized he had to find shelter somewhere or go down. With difficulty, the ships were turned and course set for the Portage Lake Ship Canal, the two arriving off Portage about 8 a.m. Now a horrendous realization came to Captain Hurlbut. The heavy ore loads, together with the sizable

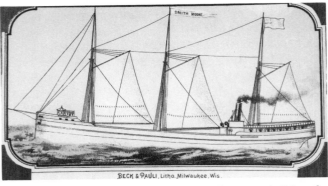

After a collision on the Lake, Smith Moore *almost made it to safety before sinking behind Grand Island.* MARQUETTE COUNTY HISTORICAL SOCIETY COLLECTION.

leakage, caused the ships to draw more water than there was depth in the canal. If they attempted to enter, they would strand; on the other hand, if they stayed outside, they would founder, probably with all hands. Captain Hurlbut decided to take his chances on grounding. As the *Bessemer* approached within 500 feet of the canal piers, she hit bottom and swung broadside to the channel. The *Schuylkill* also struck, spun broadside and smashed into the *Bessemer.* The two began to break up. Gigantic rollers pushed the disintegrating vessels against the canal pier, and all 14 crewmen from the steamer and five of the schooner's crew leaped to safety. Three schoonermen trapped on the bow were rescued by the Portage lifesavers who reached the scene within half an hour. Two hours later, both ships were completely demolished. The Portage Lake Ship Canal was solidly blocked and could not be satisfactorily cleared until September of the next year when remains of the two hulks were finally dynamited. For wooden ships, the losses were considerable, $39,100 for the *Bessemer* and $20,000 for the *Schuylkill*, with expenses of channel clearing adding another $7,000.

Still another disaster was narrowly averted that same evening when the gale-badgered schooner-barge *Minnehaha*, which had broken away from the steamer *Hiawatha*, made a dash for the canal. Lifesavers warned her off before she crashed into the wreckage and her anchors held outside. Though she had four feet of water in her hold, her steam pumps took care of this, while the lifesavers maintained an all night vigil. Winds subsided during the night, and the *Hiawatha* appeared the following morning to pick up the large four-master.[91]

Duluth's Captain Alexander McDougall built dozens of the novel steel whaleback ships between 1888 and 1896. CANAL PARK MARINE MUSEUM COLLECTION.

1 *Blue Book of American Shipping* (Cleveland, Marine Review Publishing Co., 1901), p. 266.

2 *Marquette Mining Journal,* Aug. 7, 1880.

3 *Marquette Mining Journal,* Oct. 2, 9, 30, 1880.

4 Homer Wells, *History of Accidents, Casualties, and Wrecks on Lake Superior* (Duluth, Minnesota, Corps of Engineers, U.S. Army, 1938), 90 pp. unpublished typewritten manuscript, p. 11; *Lake Superior News,* Apr. 27, 1882.

5 *Lake Superior News,* July 21, Sept. 22, 1881; *Marquette Mining Journal,* July 30, 1881.

6 *Marquette Mining Journal,* Sept. 10, 1881.

7 *Marquette Mining Journal,* Nov. 19, 1881.

8 *Lake Superior News,* Oct. 26, 1882; Wells, *op. cit.,* p. 14.

9 *Marquette Mining Journal,* Oct. 21, 1882; *Annual Report, U.S. Lifesaving Service, 1883,* p. 363.

10 *Lake Superior News,* Dec. 7, 1882, May 10, 1883.

11 Wells, *op. cit.,* pp. 13-14.

12 *Lake Superior News,* June 28, July 5, 1883.

13 *Marquette Mining Journal,* July 14, 1883, July 4, 1884; *Log of Au Sable Lighthouse Keeper,* July 4, Sept. 25, 1883, in files of Bernard J. Gestel, Grand Marais, Minnesota.

14 *Marquette Mining Journal,* Sept. 1, 1883; Wells, *op. cit.,* p. 14.

15 *Marquette Mining Journal,* Oct. 6, 1883; Wells, *op. cit.,* p. 14.

16 *Marquette Mining Journal,* Sept. 15, 1883, Dec. 4, 1886, Nov. 11, 1886; Wells, *op. cit.,* p. 14. *Merchant Vessels of the United States* continues to list this ship through 1888; however, she is included among total losses by the *Mining Journal* in 1886 and 1887.

17 *Marquette Mining Journal,* Apr. 19, 1873, Nov. 24, 1883, June 9, 1884; *Duluth Minnesotian,* Sept. 13, 1873, Apr. 22, 1876; *Lake Superior News,* Nov. 22, 29, 1883, June 21, 1884, May 30, June 27, 1885; *Superior Times,* Nov. 24, Dec. 8, 29, 1883; *Bayfield County Press,* Nov. 24, Dec. 1, 15, 1883, May 22, 1897, Nov. 22, 1902, Nov. 3, 1905; Thom Holden, *Apostle Islands Shipwreck Survey List, 1870-1940,* (Bayfield, Wisconsin, Apostle Islands National Lakeshore, National Park Service, 1985), p. 61; James M. Keller, *The "Unholy" Apostles: Tales of Chequamegon Shipwrecks,* (Bayfield, Wisconsin, Apostle Islands Press, 1984), pp. 27-32; Frederick Stonehouse, *Went Missing,* (Au Train, Michigan, Avery Color Studios, 1984), pp. 13-25.

18 *Marquette Mining Journal,* Nov. 24, 1883; *Wells, op. cit.,* p. 14.

19 *Toronto Globe,* Dec. 17, 1883; *Lake Superior News,* Dec. 20, 1883; *Superior Times,* Dec. 22, 1883.

20 *Lake Superior News,* Jan. 31, Apr. 24, July 5, 1884.

21 Wells, *op. cit.,* p. 14.

22 *Lake Superior News,* May 17, July 19, Aug. 16, 1884; *Marquette Mining Journal,* July 9, 23, Aug. 16, 1884; *Toronto Globe,* May 20, 24, 27, 1884; Ronald H. Wrigley, *Northern Superior Shipwrecks,* 198 pp., unpublished manuscript, ca. 1979, p. 106. Copy in author's collection. This is one of few works by an independent researcher covering the Canadian north shore of Lake Superior which uses mainly Canadian source materials.

23 *Lake Superior News,* May 31, 1884; *Marquette Mining Journal,* June 4, 1884; *Bayfield County Press,* May 31, 1884; Wells, *op. cit.,* p. 14; Holden, *Apostle Island Shipwreck Survey, op. cit.,* p. 84.

24 *Marquette Mining Journal,* June 5, 9, 11, 1884 Wells, *op. cit.,* p. 15.

25 *Marquette Mining Journal,* June 14, 1884.

26 *Marquette Mining Journal,* July 9, 10, Aug. 16, Oct. 18, 1884.

27 *Marquette Mining Journal,* July 28, 1884.

28 *Marquette Mining Journal,* July 12, 1884.

29 *Marquette Mining Journal,* July 30, Aug. 1, 2, 4, 11, 1884; *Lake Superior News,* Aug. 1, 1884.

30 *Lake Superior News,* Aug. 23, 1884; *Marquette Mining Journal,* Aug. 23, 1884.

31 *Lake Superior News,* Sept. 13, 1884.

32 *Lake Superior News,* Nov. 1, 15, 1884, June 27, 1885; J.B. Mansfield, *History of the Great Lakes,* (Chicago, J.H. Beers, 1899) Vol. 2, p. 846.

33 *Marquette Mining Journal,* Oct. 18, 25, 29, 1884, Aug. 11, 1886; *Lake Superior News,* Nov. 1, 1884; Wells, *op. cit.,* p. 15.

34 *Marquette Mining Journal,* Nov. 18, Dec. 9, 1884; Wells, *op. cit.,* p. 15.

35 *Lake Superior News,* Nov. 22, 29, 1884, May 16, 1885 *Marquette Mining Journal,* Nov. 26, 28, Dec. 3, 1884; Wells, *op. cit.*

36 *Lake Superior News,* Nov. 29, Dec. 6, 20, 1884, June 6, 1885; *Marquette Mining Journal,* Nov. 25, Dec. 3, 1884, Oct. 17, 1885.

37 *Lake Superior News,* Nov. 29, 1884.

38 *Lake Superior News,* Nov. 29, 1884, June 20, 1885.

39 Wells, *op. cit.,* p. 15.

40 *Lake Superior News,* May 23, 1885; Wells, *op. cit.,* p. 16.

41 *Marquette Mining Journal,* May 18, 1885; Wells, *op. cit.,* p. 16.

42 *Bayfield County Press,* May 23, 30, 1885. Holden, *Apostle Island Shipwreck Survey, op. cit.,* p. 30.

43 *Lake Superior News,* May 10, 1884; *Marquette Mining Journal,* July 29, 1885; *Superior Times,* Aug. 1, 1885; Wells, *op. cit.,* p. 15.

44 *Marquette Mining Journal,* Sept. 16, 1885; Dominion of Canada, Department of Transport, *Casualties to Vessels Resulting in Total Loss on the Great Lakes, From 1870 to Date,* p. 21; *Ashland Weekly news,* Sept. 23, 1885; *Bayfield County Press,* Sept. 19, Dec. 12, 1885, Oct. 16,

1903; *Washburn Bee*, Sept. 9, 1885; Holden, *Apostle Island Shipwreck Survey, op. cit.*, pp. 91-92.

[45] *Marquette Mining Journal*, Oct. 3, 6, 1885; Wells, *op. cit.*, p. 16.

[46] *Superior Times*, Oct. 17, 1885; *Duluth Evening Herald*, May 20, 1899 (the recollections of Duluth Lighthouse Keeper Jefferson who witnessed the wreck); Wells, *op. cit.*, p. 16.

[47] *Superior Times*, Oct. 31, 1885.

[48] *Marine Protest, Dominion of Canada, Province of Ontario, District of Thunder Bay, John Malcolm Munro, Notary Public, by John S. Moore, Master*, Nov. 9, 1885; letter of First Mate Joseph Buckley Hastings to Miss McKenzie, sister of Alex McKenzie, Purser, Nov. 18, 1885; extracts of newspaper clippings collected by Judge W.E. Smith, Nov., 1885 (all of above in files of D.M. Frimodig, Marquette County Historical Society); *Marquette Mining Journal*, Nov. 10-11, 1885, Sept. 13, 1886; W.R. Williams, "Shipwrecks at Isle Royale" in *Inland Seas*, Vol. 12, No.4, Winter, 1956, p. 253; *Annual Report of the U.S. Lifesaving Service, 1886*, p. 427. The U.S. Lifesaving Service said 48 died. Larry Murphy and Thom Holden, "Shipwrecks of Isle Royale: The Historical Record" in *Submerged Cultural Resources Study: Isle Royale National Park*, Daniel J. Lenihan, ed., (Santa Fe, New Mexico, Submerged Cultural Resources Unit, National Park Service, 1987), pp. 80-103; Larry Murphy, Daniel Lenihan, and C. Patrick Labadie, "Shipwrecks of Isle Royale: The Archaeological Record" in Lenihan, ed., *ibid.*, pp. 254-258; Thom Holden, *Above and Below* (Houghton, Michigan, Isle Royale Natural History Association, 1985), pp. 4-9.

[49] Murphy and Holden, *op. cit.*, p. 254; Holden, *Above and Below, op. cit.*, p. 9.

[50] Murphy and Holden, *ibid.*, p. 100; Murphy, Lenihan and Labadie, *op. cit.*, pp. 256-57; *Cleveland Herald*, Nov. 30, 1883; Ann Z. Russell and Yvonne Nissen, "The Elusive Algoma Bow" in *Lake Superior Port Cities Magazine*, Vol. 8, No. 1, Winter 1985-86, pp. 10-15, and subsequent clarifying editorial in *Lake Superior Port Cities Magazine*, Vol. 8, No 2., March-April 1986, p. 7.

[51] *Marquette Mining Journal*, Nov. 13, 1885; Wells, *op. cit.*, p. 16.

[52] *Lake Superior News*, Aug. 30, 1883; *Superior Times*, Jan. 2, 1886; George C. Mason, "A List of Hulls Built by F.W. Wheeler & Co., Bay City, Michigan" in *Inland Seas*, Vol. 1, No. 4, 1945, p. 54.

[53] Wells, *op. cit.*, p. 16.

[54] Holden, *Above and Below, op. cit.*, pp. 7, 9. Original log of the Isle Royale Lighthouse on Menagerie Island is in the historical collection of Isle Royale National Park housed at park headquarters on Mott Island.

[55] *Marquette Mining Journal*, Aug. 12, Sept. 13, 1886.

[56] *Marquette Mining Journal*, Sept. 15, 1886; *Marquette Mining Journal*, Aug. 31, 1886.

[57] *Marquette Mining Journal*, Aug. 31, 1886.

[58] *Marquette Mining Journal*, Sept. 15, 1886.

[59] *Marquette Mining Journal*, Oct. 23, 1886; Wells, *op. cit.*, p. 17.

[60] *Marquette Mining Journal*, Oct. 23, 30, 1886; *Annual Report, U.S. Lifesaving Service, 1887*, p. 432.

[61] *Marquette Mining Journal*, Oct. 30, 1886; Wells, *op. cit.*, p. 17. Wells puts the loss at $8.500. Wrigley, *op. cit.*, pp. 29-30.

[62] *Annual Report, U.S. Lifesaving Service, 1887*, pp. 150-151.

[63] *Marquette Mining Journal*, Nov. 22, 1886, Feb. 9, 1887; *Bayfield County Press*, Nov. 27, 1886, Jan. 29, Feb. 19, June 18, July 30, 1887, May 11, 1889, June 11, 1892; *Ashland Weekly News*, Nov. 24, 1886, Dec. 1, 1886; *Duluth Daily Tribune*, Nov. 20, 21, 1886; *Annual Report, U.S. Lifesaving Service, 1887*, p. 432; Holden, *Apostle Islands Shipwreck Survey, op. cit.*, pp. 56-58. The sample of *Lucerne* artifacts on display at the marine museum in Duluth shows an assortment of artifact materials unlike most other shipwreck exhibits including fabrics, rubber, leather, horse hair, wood, china, glass and even food, demonstrating what can be done when artifacts are skillfully recovered and preserved as well as what Lake Superior can do in its own preservation role.

[64] *Marquette Mining Journal*, Nov. 18-20, 22, 29-30, Dec. 1, 8, 11, 16, 1886; *Annual Report, U.S. Lifesaving Service, 1887*, pp. 162-166, pp. 316-317. The *Wallace* story probably was the best reported shipwreck incident in Lake Superior area journalism history.

[65] *Marquette Mining Journal*, Dec. 1, 4, 6, 1886.

[66] *Marquette Mining Journal*, Sept. 9-11, Oct. 21, 1887; *Annual Report, U.S. Lifesaving Service, 1888*, p. 431.

[67] *Ashland Weekly News*, Aug. 10, 24, 1887; *Bayfield County Press*, Aug. 13, Sept. 3, 1887, Mar. 3, 1888; *Washburn Bee*, Aug. 13, 1887; Holden, *Apostle Islands Shipwreck Survey, op. cit.*, pp. 5-6.

[68] Wrigley, *op. cit.*, pp. 1-2.

[69] *Marquette Mining Journal*, Oct. 24-28, Nov. 1, 15, 1887; *Annual Report, U.S. Lifesaving Service, 1888*, pp. 145-146.

[70] *Marquette Mining Journal*, Oct. 24, Nov. 8, 1887.

[71] *Marquette Mining Journal*, Nov. 25, 1887; *Annual Report, U.S. Lifesaving Service, 1888*, p. 139.

[72] *Marquette Mining Journal*, Nov. 14, 1887.

[73] *Bayfield County Press*, Nov. 26, 1887, July 9, 1909; Holden, *Apostle Island Shipwreck Survey, op. cit.*, p. 27.

[74] *Marquette Mining Journal*, Nov. 18, 19, 1887; Wells, *op. cit.*, p. 17; *Annual Report, U.S. Lifesaving Service, 1889*, p. 331. For some reason the Lifesaving Service was a year late in publishing notes on this rescue.

[75] *Marquette Mining Journal*, Nov. 21, 25, 27, 1887; *Annual Report, U.S. Lifesaving Service, 1888*, p. 183; Wells, *op. cit.*, p. 17.

[76] *Marquette Mining Journal*, Nov. 18, 19, 1887; Wells, *op. cit.*, p. 17.

[77] *Marquette Mining Journal*, Nov. 23, 28, Dec. 1, 1887, June 30, July 12, 15, 1889.

[78] Dominion of Canada, Department of Transport, *op. cit.*, p. 25; Wrigley, *op. cit.*, pp. 2-3.

[79] *Annual Report, U.S. Lifesaving Service, 1889,* p. 330.

[80] *Marquette Mining Journal,* Oct. 3, 1888; Dominion of Canada, Department of Transport, *op. cit.,* p. 25.

[81] *Marquette Mining Journal,* Oct. 3, 1888; *Annual Report, U.S. Lifesaving Service, 1889,* pp. 23-27.

[82] *Marquette Mining Journal,* Oct. 25, 1888; Wrigley, *op. cit.,* p. 109.

[83] *Bayfield County Press,* Apr. 27, May 4, 11, 25, 1889; *Duluth Evening Herald,* Apr. 26, 27, May 1, 4, 8, 9, 15, 22, 28, June 1, 8, 1889; *Duluth Weekly Herald,* May 15, 1889; *Marquette Mining Journal,* Apr. 29, 1889; Wells, *op. cit.,* p. 18; Holden, *Apostle Islands Shipwreck Survey, op. cit.,* pp. 7-8.

[84] *Marquette Mining Journal,* June 20, July 13, 1889.

[85] *Marquette Mining Journal,* June 20, 21, July 30, 1889; Wells, *op. cit.,* p. 18.

[86] *Marquette Mining Journal,* June 21, 25, 28, 1889; Wells, *op. cit.,* p. 18.

[87] *Marquette Mining Journal,* July 15, 16, 19, 1889; Wells, *op. cit.,* p. 18.

[88] Wells, *op. cit.,* p. 18.

[89] *Annual Report, U.S. Lifesaving Service, 1890,* pp. 162-163, 390; *Marquette Mining Journal,* Oct. 3, 1889.

[90] *Ashland Daily News,* Sept. 7, 1889; *Ashland Weekly Press,* Sept. 14, 1889; *Bayfield County Press,* Sept. 7, 1889, Jan. 18, 1890; Holden, *Apostle Islands Shipwreck Survey, op. cit.,* p. 104.

[91] *Marquette Mining Journal,* Oct. 7, 1889; *Annual Report, U.S. Lifesaving Service, 1890,* pp. 168-169, 390.

The Minnesota iron ore mines began shipping enormous quantities of ore during the 1890s from Two Harbors, Duluth and Superior. The Industrial Revolution created insatiable demands for the ore which resulted in new docks, new steel ships and much prosperity for the region. CANAL PARK MARINE MUSEUM COLLECTION.

Chapter 4

The Dynamic Nineties
1890-1899

The 1890s produced another bonanza for Lake Superior shipping people. The number of ships traversing the lake doubled, while their registered tonnage tripled and total freight jumped three and a half times. Population in the lake area continued its spectacular growth. Duluth's population nearly doubled in the period. On the water, the technical revolution in Great Lakes shipbuilding was clearly manifest. The steel monsters came off the ways in increasing numbers. Despite the fears of some sailors and vessel builders who questioned steel as a hull material, the 500-footer would be a reality by the turn of the century. The giant ship-operating corporation had also come into existence.

Despite the enormous upsurge in activity, the accident toll did not rise proportionally. As many as 60 ships may have succumbed, though the death list stood at only 71, a sharp reduction from the previous decade. Of course, the U.S. Life-Saving Service accomplished some seemingly impossible rescues. Actually, the mishap pattern was quite similar to that of the '80s, with more frequent incidents in the western waters of Lake Superior.

1890

An early navigation season brought trouble in April. At 6 p.m., April 29, the 244-foot, 1,506-ton wooden steamer *Continental* was towing the 264-foot, 1,676-ton schooner-barge *Magnetic* off Big Point, five miles west

61

of the St. Marys Falls Canal. Both were downbound with iron ore from Marquette. Suddenly, an oil tank exploded beneath the forward deck of the *Continental,* and her upper works took fire. The steamer halted quickly, but the *Magnetic* could not stop and crashed into the *Continental.* Unexpectedly, the barge got the worst of this encounter. The *Magnetic* was apparently holed in the crash and taking water, so the barge captain directed his ship toward

though losses were not significant: $3,500 for the *Viking* and $5,000 for the *Olympia.* Lifesavers assisted in salvage operations in both cases.[2] A minor mechanical breakdown on June 4 afflicted the little steamer *Hunter* of Booth Packing Company near Duluth, and a nasty fire at Ashland on July 4 stripped the forward upper works of the wooden steamer *Iron King.* She was a $20,000 repair bill.[3] On August 21 the pleasure yacht *Cruiser* found-

Corps of Engineers specialists developed plans for a new 1,000-foot Poe Lock at Sault Ste. Marie in the early 1890s. CANAL PARK MARINE MUSEUM COLLECTION.

shore where she foundered in 25 feet of water. Her crew was safe. Meanwhile, the crew of the *Continental* doused the fire, and Captain Rattray was able to proceed with the *Magnetic*'s people. Both ships were owned by the Republic Iron Company of Cleveland. The *Magnetic,* built in 1882, was valued at $50,000. Loaded with 1,692 tons of iron ore, she presented a serious salvage problem as the ore had to be mucked out before she could be raised. The cost of salvage was estimated to run from $15,000 to $30,000, a significant amount for a wooden ship.[1]

The next four months provided relatively smooth sailing. June fogs caused minor inconvenience, the steamer *Viking* and the schooner *Michigan* grounding near Eagle River on June 3, while the brand new Gilchrist steamer *Olympia* struck near the tip of Whitefish Point on June 28. Portions of their iron ore cargoes had to be jettisoned,

ered at Chapel Rock, the financial loss undisclosed.

A particularly vicious west-southwest gale raked central Lake Superior on September 12-13. There were casualties. Caught off Keweenaw Point with three barges in tow, the steamer *Charles Hebard* was having tough going. In the midst of the blow on September 12 the 318-ton barge *Ben Brink* broke the line and was hurled into the shallows of the Keweenaw near the Calumet water works. Though enduring a rugged working over by the pounding surf, the two-year-old *Brink* held together and was salvageable. Her six-man crew, however, apparently was lost trying to reach shore. Aside from pulling into Copper Harbor to inform the lighthouse keeper of the missing *Brink,* the *Hebard* could do nothing to help. She continued on to Ashland with the two remaining barges. The *Brink* tragedy later became an argument for the establishment of an additional lifesaving station along the Keweenaw Peninsula at Eagle Harbor.[4]

More grief was in store that same day. The 199-foot, 910-ton schooner-barge *Comrade* had departed Ashland with 1,600 tons of iron ore in tow of the 235-foot, 1,373-ton wooden steamer *Columbia*. At 6 p.m. on September 12, when the two were off the Keweenaw, waves became so violent that Captain Gunderson of the *Columbia* felt he had to drop his tow in order to save his own vessel. The *Columbia* gradually edged her way toward shelter behind Keweenaw Point. Captain Gunderson had kept the *Comrade* in sight until about 9 p.m., and he presumed that the *Comrade*'s master, Captain Peterson, a veteran schooner man, would ride out the storm, perhaps sailing to the eastern lake. Winds subsided during the night and the *Columbia* returned to pick up the *Comrade*. Though she combed the waters between the Keweenaw and Isle Royale, the *Columbia* could find no trace of the barge. The *Comrade* had vanished. A day or two later Captain Maloy of the steamer *Winslow* encountered scattered wreckage 25 miles west of the Portage Lake Ship Canal, finding fragments of fore and aft cabins, railings and spars. The seven-year-old *Comrade* and her eight crewmen were gone. Owned by J.C. Gilchrist of Cleveland, she was valued at $35,000.[5]

Difficulties were minimal for the remainder of the year. The steamer *Hiram R. Dixon* stranded lightly off Grand Portage on October 3. Fires damaged three tugs at the Head of the Lakes, the 62-foot tug *Cora B.* burning in Duluth on October 30, the 66-foot ferry *Free Trade* at Superior on November 1, and the 69-foot tug *James Bardon No. 7* up the St. Louis River at Fond du Lac on November 10. The total cost for all three incidents was estimated at $10,500. It appears that the *Free Trade* and *James Bardon No. 7* were not rebuilt.[6]

1891

This season opened on a somber note. On May 3, the 172-foot, 600-ton schooner *Atlanta,* laden with coal, was proceeding westward off Deer Park in tow of the steamer *Wilhelm*. About 7 p.m. a blustery northwester set in. For four hours the *Wilhelm* bucked the seas, getting nowhere. The *Wilhelm*'s captain decided to return to Whitefish Point for shelter, but the tow-line snapped and the *Atlanta* was on her own. Captain James L. Knowlton of Saginaw, Michigan, ordered the sails set, but the foreboom snapped and the foresail was slashed to ribbons. In a few minutes the *Atlanta* began leaking, became unmanageable and fell into the trough. Her crew stuck to the pumps all through the night until by 11 a.m. on May 4 it was obvious that the schooner would go down. The captain ordered the crew of six men and the woman cook into

the yawl and pulled away as the *Atlanta* went under about 20 miles northwest of Crisp Point.

The *Atlanta*'s little yawl drifted downwind toward the Michigan shore until 4 p.m. when it came abreast of Crisp Point. Captain Knowlton wanted to float the remaining 17 miles to Whitefish Bay where a safe landing might be made, but the exhausted crew implored him to try a landing at the Crisp Point Life-Saving Station. As they approached the breakers at Crisp Point, a sailor crabbed his oar and was flipped overboard. The others dragged him back into the boat, but the lifeboat had been drawn into the breakers, was capsized and three of the occupants drowned. The remaining four hung to the swamped craft which rolled over again. At this point the lifesaving crew, which had been at supper, was alerted by a coastal resident. The lifesaving lookout had not recognized the approaching yawl, thinking it a large pine trunk. Lead by Captain Small, the lifesavers in their cork life jackets dashed into the breakers and rescued two of the half dead occupants who, though unconscious when brought to shore, responded to the lifesavers' resuscitation efforts. Five of the *Atlanta* crew had died, including the cook. Lifesavers from the Crisp Point Station recovered the body of Captain Knowlton 18 days later, while the Vermilion Point crew found that of another crewman on July 20. The unfortunate lifesaving lookout was summarily discharged for his failure to spot the yawl in time to prevent the capsizing. The virtually new *Atlanta* was worth $37,000.[7]

Off the Superior Entry on June 2, a scow-schooner met her end. The 147-foot, 230-ton *Mayflower* with a cargo of sandstone from Portage Entry was approaching the Superior Harbor when Captain Zirbest ordered her sails lowered, perhaps prematurely. In moderate seas driven by a northwesterly wind, the cargo shifted and she capsized. The tug *Cora A. Sheldon* raced to assist and her crew saved three of the *Mayflower* sailors. The unfortunate Captain Zirbest, however, could not hold onto the line tossed and drowned. Out of Escanaba, Michigan, he had been a Pacific Ocean sailor. The *Mayflower* was a $9,000 casualty.[8]

The usual summer fogs brought a string of groundings. The steamer *Idaho,* out of Buffalo under Captain Chatterton, went ashore nine miles east of Ontonagon on June 8. The steamer *Empire State* of Buffalo stranded July 17 on Au Sable Reef about 65 miles east of Marquette. Captain Green ordered 10 crewmen to take all 24 passengers to shore the following day since weather continued threatening. After five days aground, the *Empire State* was successfully released. Salvage and repair costs for the two wooden vessels were moderate, $10,500 for the *Idaho* and $13,000 for the *Empire State*. All passengers and crew were safe.[9] Little injury accrued to the steamer *Marina* which struck at Two Harbors on August 1, to the bark *Constitution* aground at Portage Entry on September 25, or to the schooner *Mabel Wilson* which had run afoul of the shoals west of Crisp Point on September 21.[10]

Few details have surfaced surrounding the loss of the towing tug *Rambler* on August 24. The vessel burned to the water's edge in the vicinity of Red Cliff just outside Bayfield. Period accounts speculated that the vessel had been deliberately burned in an attempt to gain $5,000 in insurance, her owners reported as having used the tug as collateral against outstanding loans. The attempt to recover from the underwriters apparently failed. The 57-foot, 42-ton tug built by Union Dry Dock at Buffalo in 1873 was simply a total loss with no recorded attempts of salvage, although area residents probably retrieved some items.[11]

The propeller Winslow *was in the Lake Superior trades for almost 30 years when she burned in 1891.* UNIVERSITY OF DETROIT MARINE COLLECTION.

Late in September, schooner owners whose ships were on the lake were quite concerned. An unknown schooner was thought to have sunk west of Whitefish Point. The captain of the steamer *John W. Moore,* a brand new steel ship, had spotted a schooner obviously in distress northwest of Vermilion Point. Before the *Moore* could approach to offer assistance, the schooner vanished in the high seas. The *Moore's* master had witnessed the last moments of the 174-foot, 525-ton schooner *Frank Perew,* a coal carrier en route to Marquette. She had been in tow of the steamer *N.K. Fairbank.* Off Grand Marais, Michigan, the two had been trapped by violent winds and tried to turn back for shelter in Whitefish Bay, but the tow-line snapped. Captain Marky of the *Perew* made a run for it. However, the tempestuous seas swept away the hatch covers and stove in the cabins. At 9 a.m. on September 29, the seven-person crew took to the yawl just before the schooner went to the bottom some 15 miles northwest of Vermilion Point. Knowing the treacherous surf west of Whitefish Point, Captain Marky guided the yawl around the point, but was prevented from landing on the lee side by the northwesterly gale. The seas took him a dozen or so miles to the southeast off Parisienne Island. The exhausted crew, which had already traveled 30 tortuous miles in the open boat, attempted in desperation to slip through the

surf at Parisienne. The results were typical. The ship's lifeboat capsized and only seaman Charles Larabie reached the beach alive where fishermen found him. They also recovered the bodies of his drowned shipmates: Captain Marky, Stewardess Mary Ann McKay and four sailors. Until Larabie was brought to the Soo some days later, it was thought that the whole crew had gone down with the *Perew.* The *Perew* was a financial loss of $16,000.[12]

A spectacular ship fire on October 3 had the harbor of Duluth in an uproar. The 220-foot, 1,050-ton wooden steamer *Winslow* lay at the St. Paul and Duluth Railroad dock unloading after grounding at Lakeside on the east edge of Duluth the day before. A small fire was detected in her wood bunker, and Captain Chris Mason directed his crew in a routine fire control operation. The blaze made headway, whereupon the City of Duluth fire department was called. Alas, the hydrants were too far for the available hose supply, and it appears that no pumps were available to take water directly from the bay. The old wooden passenger packet, built by Peck and Masters at Cleveland in 1863, was soon a mass of flames. Harbor master Miller ordered tugs to push her across the bay, away from the docks and warehouses, onto the mud flats off Minnesota Point. There, she burned to the water's edge, a $55,000 casualty. In her cargo were 200 barrels of brown sugar. The aroma of burning sugar, drifting landward, attracted bears from the forest then only a couple of miles from the port area. Several of the animals were seen in downtown Duluth the following day, apparently seeking the source of that delectable odor. In late August 1892, Captain Inman raised the burned out hull, though it apparently was too badly damaged for rebuilding. The *Winslow* was owned by the Erie and Western Transportation Company and running in the Lake Superior Transit Line at the time of the fire.[13]

Late October witnessed a sinking on the Canadian north shore east of Thunder Bay. The 387-net-ton steam barge *Sovereign* had the 137-foot schooner *Sligo* in tow when the grain-laden steamer was simply overpowered by the rugged seas southwest, by some accounts southeast, of Lamb Island, grounding near a small island thereafter known as Sovereign Island. The *Sovereign* apparently sailed about 10 miles further to the south before foundering, Captain Trudeau apparently convinced damage was slight. Her crew escaped to the barge before the steamer slipped away. The vessel was a probable liability of $20,000 to her Canadian owners. The *Sligo* also had a tough time before riding out the gale, about October 25.[14]

Things were tough all over in November. On November 14, the year-old 262-foot, 1,729-ton steel steamer *Parks Foster* cleared the Soo and rounded Whitefish Point just in time to meet a rocking southwester which drove her clear to the northeastern corner of the lake and deposited her ashore at Dog River near Heron Bay. She remained stuck for 55 hours while her crew worked to release the ship. She finally got clear, not too seriously hurt, and began to retrace her route to the Soo. Arriving in lower Whitefish Bay, the *Foster*'s captain was hailed by the new 276-foot steel steamer *Brazil*. Aboard the *Brazil* was the entire crew of the wooden steamer *Samuel Mather* which had been struck and sunk by the *Brazil* at 2 a.m., November 22, eight miles north of Point Iroquois. The *Brazil* hit the *Mather* on the starboard side near the aft hatch.

age floating in at Whitefish Point. Vesselmen were ready to concede that Lake Superior had claimed the *Pelican* when on November 26 the bedraggled *Pelican* appeared at the Soo. This is one of the very few instances where a break-away schooner-barge arrived safely after being so long overdue.[16]

Losses were generally minimal, but the season closed with the demise of two tugs: the 45-foot *Courier* burn-

The October blaze left little of the old steamer Winslow *despite efforts by several tugs with fire pumps.* AUTHOR'S COLLECTION.

Loaded with 58,000 bushels of wheat consigned from Duluth to Buffalo, the 246-foot, 1,576-ton wooden ship was 25 minutes going under, allowing time for her crew to take to the boats and pull away, although the crewmen lost all their personal possessions. The *Foster* took the *Mather* crew to the Soo while the *Brazil* proceeded with her load of coal to Duluth where it was discovered that she had broken three frames and a stringer in the encounter. Launched at Cleveland in 1887, the *Mather* was owned by Pickands, Mather & Company and valued in excess of $50,000. With the wheat cargo destroyed, this incident must have cost in excess of $110,000. The *Parks Foster* also had a shipyard bill of $15,000 from her own ordeal.[15]

About the same time, the R.T. Winslow Company of Cleveland had cause for great worry. Their 18-year-old 813-ton schooner *Pelican* had left Two Harbors on November 17 in tow of the steamer *Wocoken* under Captain Muller. Three days later the *Wocoken* was observed by the steamer *Rosedale* off Isle Royale alone and flying distress signals. About the same time, the *Pelican* was sighted off Copper Harbor by the steamer *Germanic*, gale-damaged and minus her topsail. On November 22 the *Wocoken* crept into the Soo the worse for wear, Captain Muller reporting the schooner's loss in a gale on November 18. He had been unable to find her. Now came reports of wreck-

ing at Superior on November 27 and the *May Corgan* foundering on December 7. The *Corgan* incident lacks considerable detail. It is known that the tug, used in commercial fishing and passenger service around the Bayfield Peninsula, was under tow of the larger tug *T.H. Camp* when she began leaking in foul weather near Sand Island. Little could be done to save the vessel. She was reported to have foundered in 30 feet of water with the possibility of being raised, although no record of salvage was noted during the next several years. She had been owned by Booth Packing Company, but was reported as having been sold shortly before the incident. A second account gives the location as being off Bark Point, Wisconsin. She was reported a loss of $10,000.[17]

1892

Shipping began and ended in a "blaze of excitement" this year. On April 30 the 152-foot, 310-ton wooden steamer *Yosemite* was towing her consorts, *Ryan* and *Grey Oak,* off Emerson in Whitefish Bay when she was discovered to be on fire. Her crew escaped with the clothes on their backs, and their steamer burned to the water's edge. The schooners were safe. While her value was not disclosed, the *Yosemite* must have been appraised at $20,000 or more.[18]

Mishaps to small vessels dotted the summer months, the towing tug *Keystone* losing her wheel May 13 near Bayfield, the tug *F.L. Danforth* burning at Duluth-Superior Harbor on June 21, the tug *A.C. Adams* injured in a collision at Superior on June 26 and the 88-foot, 39-ton steam yacht *Nautilus* seared by fire on August 14 at Bark Bay, Wisconsin. The 58-foot, 29-ton *Danforth* was a total loss casualty valued at $6,000. Built in 1867 at Buffalo, she had served the Duluth waterfront for more than 20 years. For the others, rebuilding costs were light.[19]

The mysterious loss of the new steamer Western Reserve *shocked the marine industry in 1892.* University of Detroit Marine Collection.

On the morning of August 31, however, the Great Lakes shipbuilding world received a terrific shock. A patrolling lifesaver came upon exhausted Wheelsman Harry Stewart of the steel steamer *Western Reserve* crawling on the beach near the Deer Park Life-Saving Station. Stewart gasped out a story of bitter tragedy on arrival at the station. The magnificent new bulk carrier had cracked in two about 35 miles northwest of Deer Park, off the Au Sable Banks, going down in 10 minutes, about 9 p.m. the

previous evening. While a well trained crew had launched two lifeboats and placed all 21 crewmen and six passengers in them, both had capsized in moderately rough seas. All except Wheelsman Stewart were drowned. The *Western Reserve* was less than two years old. She already held cargo records for wheat and iron ore. She was a product of the Globe Shipbuilding Company of Cleveland, launched October 20, 1890, at 301 feet in length and of 2,392 gross tons. Her owner, Captain Peter G. Minch of Cleveland, was delighted with her performance. Indeed, so highly did Captain Minch rate this vessel that he, his wife, two children and two relatives had joined the crew for the run to Two Harbors where they would load ore. Her top officers were veterans: Captain Albert Myers and Chief Engineer W.H. Seaman.

The *Western Reserve* had cleared the Soo in late afternoon, August 30. As she approached Whitefish Point, Captain Myers noted that a sharp westerly wind was kicking up a substantial sea. Accordingly, he hove to, behind the point for a while. Yet, no major storm was brewing and conditions seemed stable. Myers resumed the trip toward the northwest. For several hours sailing was normal, though the *Western Reserve,* being light, did labor in the seas. About 9 p.m. a crash was heard; the main mast had broken half way up and fallen to the deck. Across the deck ahead of the boiler house stretched a widening crack that extended down the sides of the hull. The *Western Reserve* had broken in two. Wheelsman Stewart recalled jumping the gap as he raced for the stern. Although the ship settled quickly, good discipline prevailed, and all 27 aboard were placed in the two lifeboats which pulled away just in time. The *Reserve* went down in 10 minutes with her propeller still swinging. One of the lifeboats capsized soon after launching and only two survivors were pulled into the remaining yawl which already held 17 persons. Moreover, the yawl contained no flares or lanterns with which to attract passing vessels. All the survivors could do was pray and bail as they drifted before the wind toward the Michigan coast. The wind, however, had swung northerly, creating vicious breakers all along the shore. About 7 a.m., the yawl hit the breakers and sank stern first. Grabbing a life preserver, which he put on in the water, Wheelsman Stewart struck out for the shore more than a mile away. After two grueling hours, he alone made it to shore some miles west of Deer Park. He was on the sands working his way toward the station when the lifesaver found him. A continued beach patrol turned up no other survivors but did recover the bodies of 16 more unfortunates, including four members of the Minch family. The ship herself was valued at more than $200,000, making this the second most costly loss in this century of Lake Superior navigation.[20]

The demise of the *Western Reserve,* followed by that of her sister ship, *W.H. Gilcher,* in northern Lake Michigan two months later under similar circumstances, set off months of worried discussion among naval architects and shipbuilders. As a result, stronger steel was specified along with improvements in methods of construction. Consequently, the Great Lakes shipbuilding industry so well rectified previous deficiencies that a complete hull failure of the *Western Reserve* type was not again documented until November 29, 1966, in the *Daniel J. Morrell* disaster on Lake Huron. There have been other instances in more recent years where structural materials failed due to weakness in design, materials, or due to stress of weather.

The same rough weather brought another mishap near Marquette on August 31, as the 163-foot, 384-ton schooner-barge *Guiding Star* broke the line of the steamer *Toledo* and struck on Big Bay Point. This apparently was her end. Built at Marine City in 1867, she would have been 25 years old at that time. While no value was denoted, she likely was a casualty of $10,000.[21]

The next two weeks brought four more incidents. The steamer *Edward S. Pease* developed a bad leak at Marquette. Fortunately, one of the U.S. Life-Savers, who had been stationed at Marquette just the year before, was able to don diving gear and make necessary repairs on September 5. The following day at Siskiwit Bay, Wisconsin, the 74-foot, 52-ton tug *John A. Paige* suffered a fire while on a log rafting job. Captain Cronk believed the fire started below in the engine room while the five-man crew slept and the tug lay at anchor for the night awaiting daylight to assemble its raft. This incident ended her service.

On September 10, the 282-foot wooden bulk carrier *Neshoto* drove hard on the rocks at Union Bay near Keweenaw Point. Off course in fog while under command of Captain Humphrey, she ran on so hard that she ripped 15 feet out of her forward bottom, necessitating a $10,000 repair job. She had to jettison 1,200 tons of coal before being refloated.[22]

A most unusual collision on September 16 sank another wooden steamer. Downbound with iron ore from Marquette was the steamer *Vienna* under Captain J.W. Nicholson with the schooner *Mattie C. Bell* in tow. Off Whitefish Point, she encountered the upbound steamer *Nipigon* with the schooners *Melbourne* and *Delaware*. As they approached, the 191-foot, 626-ton *Nipigon* suddenly sheered and struck the 191-foot, 1,006-ton *Vienna* on the port side. Both steamers immediately dropped their tows, and the *Nipigon* tried to tow the mortally wounded *Vienna* to shore. A mile from the beach, however, the ore-laden *Vienna* dove into rather deep water. Owned by M.A. Hanna and Company, she was a liability of $50,000. One could not explain why the *Nipigon* failed to obey her helm.[23]

During autumn, difficulties popped up with unpleasant regularity. A nasty fire at Duluth on October 1 necessitated extensive rebuilding of the brand new 42-foot, 12-ton tug *John H. Jeffrey Jr.* Late in the month, wild winds took their toll. Serious concern was felt in Mar-

quette on October 28 when a tug reported she had lost the lighter *J.W. Fee* about 12 miles north of town in a gale and snowstorm. On board the lighter were 10 men and lumber camp supplies for Big Bay. Knowing dangerous

The Vienna *took a load of ore with her to the bottom after a fatal collision in September 1892.* MARQUETTE COUNTY HISTORICAL SOCIETY COLLECTION.

shoals lay in that area, the Marquette-based lifesavers hauled their surfboat four miles along the shore, then sent most of their number through swamps, over rocky ridges and along coastline cliffs until at daylight the following morning they discovered the missing lighter safely near the beach with the 10 men ashore. What might have been a fatal disaster turned out to be nothing more than a routine salvage operation with minimal cost. The lifesavers, however, had experienced a completely miserable hike, in the dark at that.[24]

The same storm claimed a victim over at Deer Park. As the lookout of the lifesaving station scanned the horizon at daylight, he was astounded to see a three-masted schooner about nine miles distant, headed west but being driven eastward and southward toward deadly breakers. He was observing the 194-foot, 727-ton lumber schooner *Zach Chandler* which had broken loose from the towing steamer *John Mitchell* the evening before. On his own when the towline snapped, Captain T.H. Skinner raised the *Chandler*'s sails, but these were torn away one by one. The 25-year-old vessel labored, hopelessly waterlogged, with much of her deck load gone over the side. All the *Chandler* crew could do was hang on and hope. Their ship, which had been 25 miles northeast of Deer Park when the line separated, was now only a few miles north of certain destruction. The lookout alerted Captain Frahm who called his crew, procured a wagon and horses to haul the surfboat and beach apparatus and started eastward along the beach while the disabled schooner was swept east of the lifesaving station. About three miles east of Deer Park the *Chandler* struck. Abreast of her, 300 yards away on the beach, were the lifesavers, ready to fire the lifeline. Just as the schooner was about to hit, her yawl was seen to dart free with five persons in it. The little craft made it safely to the beach. Before the lifesavers could fire their gun, however, the schooner's three masts went overboard and, within 10 minutes, the ship had completely disintegrated, filling the water with her own debris together with thousands of pieces of lumber from the cargo. The lifesavers saw the three remaining crew, who happened to be the captain, first mate and a seaman named Frank Richter, launch a makeshift raft which immediately was surrounded by the thrashing flotsam. Instead of moving toward the beach, the raft began drifting parallel to the shore, as wave after wave dashed over the survivors. Seaman Richter was washed off and drowned. The lifesavers followed for half a mile along the beach until they hit a shallower stretch where, with lines around their waists, they waded into the churning, wreckage strewn waters, snatched the two remaining sailors from their perch and carried them safely to shore. One man had died and the *Zach Chandler*'s days were over. She was a liability of $23,500. Sailor Richter's body was recovered on November 5 and buried by the lifesavers.[25]

The weather gods scored twice on November 7. The 410-ton schooner-barge *G.M. Neelon* broke her line from the steam barge *L.S. Tilley* and crashed into the reefs at Gull Rock off Keweenaw Point. No lives were lost, but the *Neelon* was presumably a goner. One of her name boards was found on the coast of Isle Royale weeks later. The schooner *John Wesley* also drifted into the shoals at Rock River, Sucker Bay, east of Marquette. In neither stranding was the financial loss reported. The 20-year-old 302-ton *Wesley* probably involved a several thousand-dollar salvage operation while the 19-year-old *Neelon* was likely a $10,000 liability.[26]

Still, there was more grief. While lying in Duluth Harbor on November 28, the 149-foot wooden steamer *Hiram R. Dixon* blew a steam pipe, killing two of her crew.

The final casualty of the year was the result of an extremely odd series of incidents. About December 7, the 220-foot, 1,391-ton wooden steamer *Northerner* stranded at the tip of Keweenaw Point. After dumping 2,000 barrels of oil, much of which floated to the Whitefish Point country during the winter, the crew worked her clear and nursed her into L'Anse. As she lay at dock in L'Anse on December 11, someone aboard dropped a kerosene lamp and the ship was soon a mass of flames. Fire spread to the dock and a warehouse. Most strangely, Captain Peter McKinnon tried to prevent the local firemen

from combating the blaze. Word quickly spread that the ship had been burned by the crew and Captain McKinnon was immediately relieved by Captain John McCullough. Eventually the *Northerner* was scuttled to halt the fire. Apparently, she was a $50,000 loss. In her cargo were 400 tons of iron beams which likely were retrieved. This was her second bad fire in six years. She had been badly gutted at Kelley Island, Lake Erie, on November 13, 1886, although rebuilt in 1887. She had been launched in 1871 at Marine City, Michigan, belonging to the Rochester Transportation Company. She was under charter to Eber Ward for Ward's Detroit and Lake Superior Line at the time of the second fire.[27]

1893

The great Panic of 1893 did not appreciably affect Lake Superior sailing. There were fewer ships and tonnage was off less than five percent from the previous year, but ship passages at the Soo remained 25 percent higher than the best year of the '80s. Difficulties increased slightly. But nothing too startling occurred during the first five months

With her hull pierced by floating ice, the A. Everett *was beached to prevent her sinking.* AUTHOR'S COLLECTION.

of the season. A dense fog in the eastern lake on May 14 caused the lumber hooker *Nipigon* and her two schooner-barges, *Delaware* and *Melbourne,* to pile into the sands of Vermilion Point. With the aid of tugs and the U.S. Life-Savers, all three were quickly refloated with a combined cost of only $3,100.[28]

The next day, ice caused trouble for the steamer *A. Everett*. Ice-cut and leaking, she was run ashore a few miles from Two Harbors, a $10,000 job for the salvors and repair men. Fire claimed the 54-foot, 20-ton tug *George P. Savage* in St. Louis Bay on June 1. On August 17 the wooden steamer *N.K. Fairbank* banged into the reefs at Point Iroquois with a $20,000 rebuilding fee. The *Fairbank* suddenly began to leak badly. Her captain didn't have much choice: sink or intentionally go aground. He went aground. At Duluth Harbor on August 20 came a collision between the 80-foot steamer *Lucille* and the yacht *Ellida*. Property loss was negligible, but one person drowned.[29]

British-built Rosedale *was five years old when she ran on the beach at Knife River, July 6, 1893.* CANAL PARK MARINE MUSEUM COLLECTION.

Fog, darkness and magnetic deviation of the compass combined to put the steel package freighter *Rosedale* well ashore just south of Knife River along the Minnesota north shore. Despite blinding fog and known problems with the compass in that area, the *Rosedale*'s master had his ship moving along at a brisk 11 miles per hour at the time of the incident on July 6. The ship was upbound light, en route from Kingston to Duluth for 60-65,000 bushels of grain. The *Rosedale* went so far ashore that fully 40 feet of her keel was resting above the shore and her stern unsupported in the water. There was no chance she could get her 600-horsepower engine to simply back her off. Two Inman tugs were called up from Duluth, the *Bob Anderson* and either the *M.D. Carrington* or *Buffalo*. The 256-foot, 750-horsepower propeller *J. Emory Owen* also got into the act. The wreck and the salvage process became so interesting that a special excursion train visited the site as well as excursion voyages aboard the 153-foot *Ossifrage* and the 90-foot *Nautilus* from Duluth. Salvage involved use of marine jacks, heavy oak timbers, a lighter and the tugs and propeller. The combined effort resulted in release of the *Rosedale* on the night of July 9. She

came immediately to Duluth-Superior Harbor under her own power for dry-docking on the 10th. Built in 1888 for Thomas Marks and Company of Port Arthur, the *Rosedale* was owned at the time by Captain Samuel Crangle and J.H.G. Hagerty of Toronto. Damage to the 246-foot, 1,507-ton vessel was more extensive than anticipated. She had 30 broken frames and about 30 plates needing renewal before leaving dry-dock on the 22nd with a $6,500 repair bill plus undisclosed salvage costs.[30]

What could have been a major fire aboard the 227-foot, 1,680-ton wooden bulk freighter *Gogebic* was contained by her crew and local fire fighters resulting in only about $700 in damage to the vessel. The *Gogebic* was docked on July 20 at the St. Paul & Western Dock in Superior along Connor's Point when a lantern was overturned in her forward end. As the blaze grew, local fire fighters assisted the crew, but the ship had to be cut from her moorings to protect overhead cranes from damage. Still, Captain W.D. Neal insisted a single line be kept to tether his ship to the dock until the blaze was extinguished. The *Gogebic* was owned by Mills Transportation Company of Marysville, Michigan, and valued at $90,000.[31]

A unique mishap on August 23 saw the schooner *Charles P. Minch* slamming into a log raft with one of the timbers piercing her hull. She soon had seven feet of water in the hold, and Captain Kaufman feared her limestone cargo might sink her. Accordingly, he ran the vessel ashore at Vermilion Point where lifesavers obtained a tug and a steam pump. Costs amounted to only $2,000.[32]

The tempo picked up in September. Blinded by thick weather on September 14, the 166-foot, 523-ton lumber schooner *James Mowatt* slid into the Keweenaw reefs 10 miles north of the Portage Lake Ship Canal station. Lifesavers worked with the wrecking outfit in lightering the cargo and putting steam pumps aboard. The schooner was taken off within a week and brought into Hancock, Michigan. En route from Washburn, Wisconsin, to Benton Harbor, Michigan, under Captain Becker with a valuable lumber cargo, the ship was found to have suffered substantially. Her loss figure of $22,875 was rather high for a schooner that was not destroyed.[33]

At Duluth Harbor on September 17 came a minor collision between the wooden steamer *George G. Hadley* and the steel steamer *Codorus,* the steel vessel getting the worst of it to the tune of $4,000. A harbor fire at Duluth on September 27 raked the tug *Edward Fiske,* a $1,000 item. Flames at Tahquamenon Bay consumed the 81-foot, 68-ton steamer *Mystic* on the same day, a $9,000 liability. Still another fire blasted the 49-foot, 16-ton tug *Maggie Carroll* on September 28 at Superior with costs of $2,000. On October 7 the schooner *Dundee* suffered slight weather damage northwest of Two-Hearted River, and high seas on October 14 slapped the wooden steamer *Charles J. Kershaw* ashore in Waiska Bay. Rebuilding amounted to $5,000.[34]

Vessel men knew that the blow of October 14 had claimed some ship, but the vessel's identity would not be verified for several days. The steamer *Jay Gould* reported large quantities of wreckage floating west of Whitefish Point on October 15. The following day, the steamer *Sitka* reported finding five survivors of the schooner *Annie Sherwood* in a yawl seven miles southeast of Caribou Island. In such pitiful condition was the *Sherwood* crew that they were unable to climb the ladder to the *Sitka* without help. Captain Louis Guthrie of Chicago and Seaman James Cousins had died of exposure and injuries. Survivors told how the 184-foot, 622-ton schooner *Sherwood,* downbound from Washburn, Wisconsin, to Chicago with lumber, waterlogged off Caribou Island and had to be abandoned. She presumably went to the bottom, filling the lake with wreckage. The unseasonable cold wrought havoc on the soaked occupants of the yawl, most of whom were snatched from death by the timely arrival of the *Sitka.* Though the steamer *White and Friant,* ostensibly the tow vessel, had reported the schooner sunk, the shipping community was in for a surprise. A week later the Canadian steamer *Telegraph* discovered the derelict *Sherwood* badly battered, but intact, three miles above Otter Head on the Ontario east shore, with one dead crewman still aboard. She had traveled 70 miles north from the position where abandoned. Two were dead, and a probable property loss in excess of $30,000 sustained.[35]

Another schooner fell to the clutches of the lake on October 25. En route to Marquette with 1,333 tons of coal for the James Pickands Company, the 203-foot, 790-ton schooner *George* under Captain C.C. Roberts hit the biting blasts of a northerly storm on October 24. Captain Roberts tried to take cover at Grand Island, but the gale intended otherwise. The *George* broke her gaff, and the foresail split; then the mizzen ripped to pieces. Out of control, the schooner crashed into the Pictured Rocks and began to disintegrate as waves poured over her deck. The captain wasted no time in putting eight men, a girl and the ship's dog into the yawl and pulling for Grand Island. They made it on October 25 by a dexterous piece of small boat handling. There they obtained shelter and were able to send for the Marquette lifesavers who came down with their lifeboat in tow of the tug *C.E. Benham* the next day. As the seas subsided, Captain Henry Cleary of the lifesavers was able to inspect the *George,* but she was a sad wreck; hatch covers gone, decks battered, seams open and water in the hold. He and his crew were able to strip her of equipment worth about $5,000 which was held for the owner, Miles B. Fox of Sandusky, Ohio. Ship and cargo were a casualty of $28,250.[36]

Heavy weather on November 3 caught the steamer *Superior* and her consort, *M.R. Warner,* downbound from Duluth-Superior Harbor and approaching the Apostle Islands. The towline was cut or parted, leaving the 199-foot, 699-ton *Warner* on her own. She ran aground off

the western end of Sand Island in attempting to reach shelter. Her cargo of squared timber was half gone, her starboard quarter heavily damaged and her back broken. Her crew, however, survived. A wrecking party from Sault

TOUR OF THE GREAT LAKES ON THE FLOATING PALACES OF THE

Northern Steamship Co.

A new steamer and two sailings weekly to CHICAGO and MILWAUKEE, in addition to the Duluth service, will be added this season, which opens early in June

Take it in visiting the Pan-American Exposition

For printed matter, giving particulars, address
W. M. LOWRIE, Gen. Pass. Agent, Buffalo

Northern Steamship Company ships called weekly at Soo, Houghton and Duluth docks. INSTITUTE FOR GREAT LAKES RESEARCH COLLECTION.

Ste. Marie was assembled, including tugs *Smith* and *Simpson* and schooner-barge *Austin,* to attempt recovery of both the *Warner* and her remaining cargo. Some 250,000 feet of lumber were recovered within the first 10 days of salvage and taken to the Soo, but the *Warner* remained on the bottom with grim prospects of successful salvage. The schooner *Monterey* was added to the salvor's arsenal near the end of November. Plagued by bad weather, salvage efforts were abandoned and the *Warner* broke up in the surf. There were no additional reports of salvage.[37]

The usual rugged November gales also put the new steel steamer *Centurion* aground at Waiska Bay on November 13 with an $8,000 repair list. Then on November 28 came an unusual personal tragedy. About two miles off the Portage Lake Ship Canal, Captain Thomas Rawley of the steam barge *James H. Shrigley* was directing a turnabout of his ship which was bound for Ashland. During the turn, a giant wave raked the *Shrigley,* lifted the captain from the icy deck and hurled him to certain death in the icy waters. Portage lifesavers patrolled the beaches in hope that he might have made shore, but this was not to be. This was one of the very few occasions where a ship's captain was lost by going overboard in heavy seas.[38]

While not a shipwreck *per se,* the loss of the side-wheel passenger and freight steamer *Emerald* is noteworthy of inclusion here. The exact year of her demise is unclear from available records although it would appear she was abandoned between 1893 and 1903. She was last known to have sailed in 1893. Afterwards, she was allowed to settle to the bottom in Ashland Harbor near a dock in about 15 feet of water. Some salvage is known to have occurred during 1917. Salvage done at that time or earlier involved removing the boiler, walking beam engine and additional machinery for scrap metal needed in the war effort. It is not clear if her bottom was then moved to another site or simply became buried in the silt.[39]

1894

The volume of shipping picked up substantially during 1894. Despite the increase in sailing, the number of accidents was cut in half. Two collisions marred the record in the third week of May: the tug *C.E. Benham* striking the barge *Aberdeen* at Marquette on May 19 and the steamer *Pacific* hitting the schooner *H.B. Richards* in the Portage Lake Ship Canal on May 20. Property damage was slight in both cases, but a crewman of the *Benham* was killed when the tug's smoke stack collapsed. The *Pacific* sank in shallow water after the crash.[40]

On August 7 a spectacular fire 20 miles off Ontonagon claimed the 218-foot, 1,070-ton wooden steamer *Roanoke.* Fortunately, the lake was calm. When her captain realized the crew could not control the rampaging flames, he ordered the boats lowered and all escaped the burning hulk. Before long, the steamer *George Spencer* came by and picked up the castaways. The *Roanoke* was a $54,860 casualty, including cargo.[41] The very next day another fire required $1,000 in repairs to the steamer *Alva* at Washburn, Wisconsin. However, most excitement of the entire month came from an innocent excursion trip from Houghton to Isle Royale on August 26. There were 45 persons aboard the 69-foot, 58-ton tug *Valerie.* The crossing to Isle Royale was pleasant, but a minor storm caught the little ship on the way back, and she was pitched on Gratiot Reef along the Keweenaw Peninsula about 12 miles northeast of the Portage Lake Ship Canal. Lifesavers and tugs quickly came to the rescue bringing

all aboard safely ashore. The tug was refloated on September 6 with minimal cost. Nevertheless, her Michigan passengers had a scare which would last them all their lives.[42]

Residents of the western Lake Superior country long remembered September 1894. A series of catastrophic forest fires seared large tracts in northern Minnesota and upper Wisconsin. For days a blue haze obscured the lake. On September 22 the smoke clouds caused a major disaster as the 233-foot, 1,536-ton wooden steamer *James Pickands* under Captain Beach got off course and ran hard on Sawtooth Reef at Eagle River. En route from Duluth to South Chicago with iron ore, she stuck tight. As a precaution, Captain Beach took his 15-man crew to shore in the ship's boat, a fortunate move. A roaring equinoctial gale raced across the Keweenaw three days later and broke the *Pickands* to pieces. The Portage lifesavers picked off the crew's baggage, but this relatively new ore carrier was a ruin. She had been built in Cleveland by Thomas Quayle and Son in 1886, a twin stacker. With cargo she was a loss of $88,200, plenty for an ore carrier.[43]

A sudden norther at Deer Park on October 13 trapped the lumber carrier *George L. Colwell* and the schooner-barge *D.P. Dobbins* at the wharf. The *Colwell* tried to pull away but struck a sand bar and lost her rudder, drifting back against the wharf where she pounded miserably. Her crew jumped to safety on the wharf, whereupon the steamer drifted away to the beach where the waves gave her a rugged beating. The schooner also began to pound and her crew went over the side to the wharf. She, too, broke free, struck the beach and was worked over by the seas. The Deer Park lifesavers recovered the crew's personal effects and assisted salvors in removing both vessels nine days later. The crews had a long walk along the beach to the Soo. In both cases salvage and repair costs exceeded half the value of the vessel.[44]

A strange ship fire closed the season. The steamer *Kittie M. Forbes* was in dry dock at Superior. Through carelessness, a pile of oily rags had been left in a compartment of her forecastle. These ignited spontaneously and the *Forbes* suffered fire damage amounting to several thousand dollars, a bad break for a ship supposedly in the safety of the dry dock.[45]

1895

Expanding commerce in 1895 brought a slight increase in accidents. However, six of the ships involved were completely destroyed and nine lives were lost. Aside from a minor stranding of the new 328-foot steel steamer *I.W. Nicholas* in May at Caribou Island, sailing was safe until September. A collision occurred in the Duluth Ship Canal on September 1 between the tugs *Medina* and *Pathfinder.* The *Pathfinder* sank and Fireman Jacob Wasser drowned.

The incident illustrates the fiercely competitive, devil-may-care attitude of harbor tugboat masters. The tug *Medina* of the Singer Towing Company and the tug *Pathfinder* of the Inman Line were lying off the Duluth Ship Canal awaiting business as the large 266-foot steel steamer *Joliet* approached. While the steamer nosed her way toward the piers, the two tugs raced up, one on either side forward, and the tug captains proceeded to bargain with

squarely on the starboard quarter, rolling her over and sinking her immediately. As the tugs hit, Fireman McAllister of the *Pathfinder* jumped on board the *Medina,* but the *Pathfinder*'s captain, engineer and cook were catapulted into the water. Fortunately, they were able to grasp life buoys thrown from the *Joliet* and were saved. Fireman Wasser went down with his tug. Though the *Pathfinder* was raised and rehabilitated at a cost of only

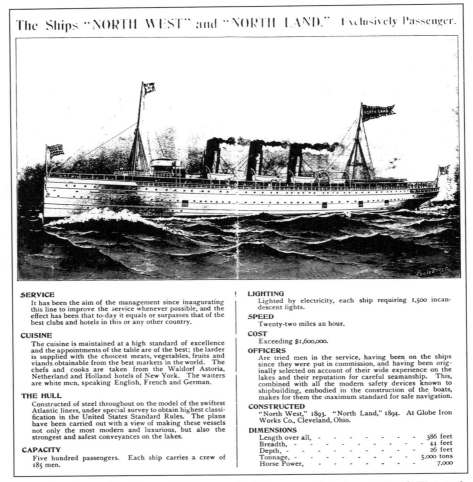

The Ships "NORTH WEST" and "NORTH LAND." Exclusively Passenger.

SERVICE
It has been the aim of the management since inaugurating this line to improve the service whenever possible, and the effect has been that to-day it equals or surpasses that of the best clubs and hotels in this or any other country.

CUISINE
The cuisine is maintained at a high standard of excellence and the appointments of the table are of the best; the larder is supplied with the choicest meats, vegetables, fruits and viands obtainable from the best markets in the world. The chefs and cooks are taken from the Waldorf Astoria, Netherland and Holland hotels of New York. The waiters are white men, speaking English, French and German.

THE HULL
Constructed of steel throughout on the model of the swiftest Atlantic liners, under special survey to obtain highest classification in the United States Standard Rules. The plans have been carried out with a view of making these vessels not only the most modern and luxurious, but also the strongest and safest conveyances on the lakes.

CAPACITY
Five hundred passengers. Each ship carries a crew of 185 men.

LIGHTING
Lighted by electricity, each ship requiring 1,500 incandescent lights.

SPEED
Twenty-two miles an hour.

COST
Exceeding $1,600,000.

OFFICERS
Are tried men in the service, having been on the ships since they were put in commission, and having been originally selected on account of their wide experience on the lakes and their reputation for careful seamanship. This, combined with all the modern safety devices known to shipbuilding, embodied in the construction of the boats, makes for them the maximum standard for safe navigation.

CONSTRUCTED
"North West," 1893. "North Land," 1894. At Globe Iron Works Co., Cleveland, Ohio.

DIMENSIONS
Length over all,	386 feet
Breadth,	44 feet
Depth,	26 feet
Tonnage,	5,000 tons
Horse Power,	7,000

James J. Hill's Northern Steamship Company built the ocean-style steamers North West *and* North Land *in the early 1890s. They were the finest and fastest liners on the lakes.* CANAL PARK MARINE MUSEUM COLLECTION.

the *Joliet*'s master over docking service fees. Suddenly, Captain Brown of the *Pathfinder,* on the *Joliet*'s port bow, decided he would be in a better operating position if he were on the starboard bow of the big ship. He either did not know or had forgotten that the *Medina* was already there. As the ships entered the canal, Brown ordered full steam ahead, and the *Pathfinder* zoomed forward across the *Joliet*'s bow, narrowly clearing the big steel vessel which was making nine miles an hour, only to be struck by the *Medina* which already occupied the starboard side. The 56-ton *Medina* hit the 38-ton *Pathfinder*

$4,000, the U.S. steamboat inspectors took a dim view of the whole performance and revoked the licenses of both Captain Brown and Captain Ditzel of the *Medina* for a hazardous maneuver that had taken a life.[46]

On September 7, the steamer *Samuel F. Hodge* hooked herself on a sunken crib in Duluth Harbor, a $2,500 repair job. Late September storms also caused multiple troubles. A wild gale which had brought heavy snow to the central Rockies and northern Great Plains swept south of Duluth but raked northern Wisconsin, Michigan's Upper Peninsula and ravaged eastern Lake Superior. Caught in its ruthless path were the 180-foot steel steamer *Viking* and the schooner-barges *W.K. Moore* and *A.W. Comstock* which had cleared Duluth at 2 p.m., September 21. When east of Keweenaw Point, their grain cargoes shifted. The *Viking* and *Moore* had a narrow escape, but the 200-foot, 806-ton *A.W. Comstock,* only three months old, capsized and went to the bottom off Stannard Rock on the evening of September 23. Captain William McArthur and his seven-man crew launched their yawl, but spent a nerve-wracking three hours trying to stay afloat. Their companion ships could do nothing for them. Fortunately, the brand new 352-foot steel steamer *John J. McWilliams* of the Mitchell fleet came along in the nick of time. Spotting the bobbing lifeboat, the *McWilliams'* crew got a line to her and brought all eight survivors aboard, including the battered Captain McArthur, who had suffered three broken ribs and a smashed leg. The *Comstock* was worth $45,000 and her 51,500 bushel wheat cargo somewhat more. She had been completed the previous June at Algonac, Michigan.[47]

The weather in the last week of September was atrocious. Bucking high seas on September 26, the 236-foot, 1,535-ton steamer *Montana* ducked between the piers at the northern end of the Portage Lake Ship Canal. She struck a submerged object which holed her wooden hull in a supposedly clear channel. As tugs sought to release her, she settled to the bottom. She was easily patched and pumped out in the safety of the canal with a bill of $8,000, though her cargo of flour was a $24,000 loss. The "snag" was quite embarrassing to the local office of the U.S. Army Corps of Engineers. The Corps had been in the process of installing a boiler for a foghorn on the west pier at Portage when the storm forced a halt to the work. The boiler presumably had been left in a secure position on the pier, but unexpectedly high seas washed it over the side and into the vessel channel where the *Montana* had encountered it.[48]

Vicious winds and heavy rain clipped five ships in 48 hours at scattered positions in central Lake Superior on September 28-29. Minor injury was sustained by the 298-foot wooden steamer *City of Paris* which ran aground at Copper Harbor, September 28. That afternoon, a fatal stranding was the lot of the 165-foot, 401-ton schooner-barge *Elma* which broke the towline from the steamer *P.H. Birckhead.* The *Birckhead* had three barges in tow as she headed westward from Whitefish Point: the *Elma, Commodore* and *Chester B. Jones.* The seas got rough and the *Birckhead's* master tried to return to Whitefish Bay. When the lines parted, the *Birckhead* was able to regain only the *Elma.* The two others eventually made safety. Pushing westward, the *Birckhead* had almost reached the shelter of Grand Island when the line let go again. This time the *Elma* went out of control, lost her rudder and was pitched aground at Miner's Castle east of Munising, a dangerous, cliff-strewn spot for a shipwreck. A sailor,

George M. Johnson, tried to carry a line ashore with the ship's yawl. He reached the base of a cliff, but there the yawl was smashed to bits. He lost the line and barely escaped by climbing the rocky wall to a small cave part way to the top. Another sailor, Rudolph Yak, tried to swim ashore with a line but was drowned. The ship held together that first night and Johnson was safe but uncomfortable in his roost. Johnson worked his way down to the water's edge the next day and grabbed another line floated ashore from the wreck. By dexterous manipulation of lines, Johnson brought ashore the remaining crew along with Captain Thurston, his wife and three-year-old child. They had to spend another chilly, foodless night in the cave-like depression on the cliffs until the following day when a nearby lighthouse keeper sighted them and rowed over in a large dory. The lightkeeper took the bedraggled survivors a short distance down the shore to where the *Birckhead* had anchored in her search for the schooner. The *Elma* was beaten to pieces. Built in 1873, she probably was a liability of $10,000 or more.[49]

Lifesavers struggled to get the 13-man crew from the wrecked steamer Kershaw *in an 1895 gale.* JOHN E. KEAST COLLECTION.

On the wicked, rain-swept morning of September 29, a spectacular drama was being enacted at Marquette. The 223-foot, 1,324-ton wooden steamer *Charles J. Kershaw* was struggling to reach the protection of the Marquette breakwater with the schooner-barges *Henry A. Kent* and *Moonlight* in tow. A steam pipe burst and the disabled *Kershaw* and her barges were swept southeastward toward the dreaded Chocolay Reef. Missing the reef, the barges went nearly high and dry on the beach, but the ill-fated *Kershaw* was impaled between giant boulders where she was pounded miserably. At 2:45 a.m., a patrolling surfman from the Marquette lifesaving station spotted the trouble and gave the alarm. For the next four hours Captain Henry Cleary and his lifesavers labored, dragging a surfboat through the brush, swamp and sand to the beach opposite the wreck. They launched by 7 a.m., working their way through furious surf to come alongside the stricken *Kershaw*. Nine sailors slid down a line from the derelict into the lifeboat. This was all that Cleary deemed advisable to take in the tempestuous seas. Leaving four crewmen on the hulk, Cleary nursed the lifeboat back to shore where a beach party cared for the rescued. Lifesaver Greenwald was painfully injured in the landing.

Salvage of Kershaw*'s two consorts was a Herculean task. Both schooners were high on the Chocolay beach.* JOHN E. KEAST COLLECTION.

Cleary took a volunteer, Nelson Coty, from the shore workers and started out once more. This time, as the lifeboat approached the disintegrating *Kershaw,* three immense waves crashed down on the little craft, capsizing it, smashing a hole in its hull and disabling two more lifesavers. All hung onto the boat and floated to shore in their cork life jackets where the beach party fished them out.

With four *Kershaw* sailors still to be rescued, Cleary returned to his station for another lifeboat. He also obtained three Marquette citizens, Frank Coutre, William Parker and an engineer named Collins, to row in place of the incapacitated lifesavers. After an exhausting row against the northeast gale, the lifeboat came alongside the *Kershaw* where Captain Pringle and three men had taken refuge in a yawl when the steamer broke up. Taking the four aboard, Cleary guided the lifeboat back to the beach by the use of a drag, and a safe landing was made with the aid of the beach party. All 13 *Kershaw* crewmen were safe in a rescue viewed by thousands of Marquette citizens. The *Kershaw* was a ruin, a liability of $45,000. Salvage of the *Moonlight* and *Kent* was a major story of the day, taking most of the next year to accomplish.[50]

After a four-week lull, rough autumn weather returned. Downbound from Duluth with 26,000 barrels of flour and 600 tons of copper ingots she had picked up at Keweenaw ports, the new 360-foot steel giant *Centurion* of the Hopkins Steamship Company ran hard upon the middle reef of Hog Island, Isle Royale, in the midst of the gale on October 28. Working desperately to lighten their two-year-old ship, her crew threw overboard flour valued at $40,000 and copper worth $100,000. Seeing the dire

straits of the *Centurion,* the captain of the spanking new 351-foot steel steamer *Penobscot* halted to lend a hand and succeeded in pulling the *Centurion* off her rocky perch. Repairs to the *Centurion,* valued at about $200,000, must have run into several thousand dollars. Salvors, under the direction of Captain Inman of Duluth, rushed to the scene in an effort to recover the valuable cargo.[51]

More than a week later came another thrilling tale. The 272-foot, 1,927-ton wooden steamer *Missoula* was eastbound from Duluth on November 1 when she broke her shaft 30 miles west of Whitefish Point. Driven by the westerly blasts, she drifted for a day before foundering about 15 miles northeast of Whitefish Point on November 2 following a wild ride of more than 30 miles. Her crew escaped in the yawl. Then the wind switched more than 90 degrees to the south, and the lifeboat had another unpleasant trip of 30 miles before coming to rest on Lizard Island. Five of her crew then procured a sailboat, probably from fishermen, and managed to reach the Soo on November 8, a week after their ship went down. All were safe, but the *Missoula* was a loss of $90,000, and with her went a 75,000-bushel wheat cargo worth almost as much.[52]

The Moonlight *and* Henry A. Kent *were not refloated until the spring of 1896, and then only at enormous cost.* WISCONSIN MARINE HISTORICAL SOCIETY COLLECTION, MILWAUKEE PUBLIC LIBRARY.

Three weeks later, the lake scored again at Pictured Rocks. Outbound from Marquette where she had loaded 325,000 board feet of lumber at the Dead River mill, the little 142-foot, 290-ton steam barge *Michael Groh,* under command of Captain Michael Groh, suffered an engine breakdown just east of Grand Island. The northerly winds drove her steadily southward until she struck at Pictured Rocks near where the *Elma* had hit two months before. Though she had grounded on the night of November 22, the seas were not overly formidable. Her crew was able to reach shore in small boats. Salvors, under Captain John H. Gillett of Marquette, began lightering the lumber immediately, utilizing the diminutive schooner *Criss*

Grover belonging to Captain Daniels. While a good deal of the cargo was saved, about 140,000 board feet, a major storm on the night of November 30 tore the *Groh* to pieces, a casualty of $9,000.[53]

The following week came a tragic sequel to the *Kershaw* accident in late September. The Inman Line of Duluth had stationed the tugs *Pearl B. Campbell, W.B. Castle* and *Corona* at Marquette to assist in salvage of the *Henry A. Kent* and *Moonlight* at Chocolay. Initial efforts to release the two schooners were unsuccessful. The tugs were ordered back to Duluth in the first week of December, leaving shortly before midnight on December 6 in good weather. But off the Huron Islands, the three encountered a roaring tempest with snow and sleet. They began to ice up. The *Castle* under Captain Rattray was towing the *Corona* with the *Campbell* bringing up the rear. As the *Castle* struggled to reach the lee of the Huron Islands for shelter, her crew heard distress whistles from the *Campbell* and, moments later, through a rift in the snow veil, a sailor on the *Castle* spied the bow of the *Campbell* high in the air. She was seen no more. The 55-foot, 22-ton *Campbell* apparently had filled and sunk stern-first with only time for a distress signal, taking to a watery grave Captain McGillivray and the six-man crew, all Duluthians. The *Campbell* had been built in Saugatuck, Michigan, in 1883, probably worth about $6,000.[54]

A small Canadian propeller, the 75-foot, 113-ton *Kakabeka,* was lost off Sand Island on December 12, although little has been found to describe the accident. Canadian sources indicate strongly that the loss was on the north shore as the *Kakabeka* frequently called at Silver Islet. It is believed that she parted her mooring lines at Silver Islet where she was in regular service for the winter and then was blown some distance to the tiny rock island where she met her end. The wandering *Kakabeka* was soon found by the tugs *Mockingbird* and *Georgina* under command of captains Malone and Morin, respectively. Salvage hopes dimmed quickly as the vessel was beaten to pieces. The *Kakabeka* had been built in 1885 at Toronto for Thomas Marks and Company, apparently as a ferry operating between Port Arthur and Fort William, later being used as a harbor excursion vessel and also ferrying passengers to and from Silver Islet.[55]

Also in December, the 150-foot, 397-ton schooner *R.J. Carney* was reported stranded at Sheldrake in Whitefish Bay, but details are lacking.

1896

Despite a modest increase in tonnage, the sailing season of 1896 proved to be the safest in eight years. At that, four ships succumbed, but not a life was lost. During the first half of the season, only two minor incidents were report-ed. The steamer *Omaha* went aground east of Devil's Island on May 12 and the steamer *Norseman* was crippled by a mechanical mishap on August 11 six miles north of the Portage Lake Ship Canal. Repairs were minimal.

Crisp Point lifesavers risked everything to save eight men and the cook from the sunken Phineas S. Marsh *in the summer of 1896.* WISCONSIN MARINE HISTORICAL SOCIETY COLLECTION, MILWAUKEE PUBLIC LIBRARY.

A sudden northwester on the night of August 25, nevertheless, sank a schooner and brought a classic rescue by the U.S. Life-Saving Service at Crisp Point. Eastbound from Portage Entry to Buffalo under Captain Somerville with a cargo of stone, the 177-foot, 543-ton schooner *Phineas S. Marsh* was taking a mauling. She began to leak. In the stormy darkness the vessel gradually worked her way eastward until 1 a.m. when she was perhaps five miles west of Crisp Point and a half mile off shore. Water was gaining in the hold and the ship could founder momentarily. In desperation, Captain Somerville sent the crew of nine into the rigging and burned distress flares. These were spotted immediately by the lookout at the Crisp Point station and the keeper ordered the lifeboat launched. After an exhausting, two-hour row, part of it in the trough of the seas, the lifeboat reached the sinking schooner. Just then, the schooner lurched and sank in 22 feet of water, eight of her crew hanging on to the rigging, though the woman cook had been pitched into a mass of wreckage. At grave risk to the lifeboat, the lifesaving captain crashed his way through the tossing flotsam and picked up the woman. At this point, a sailor panicked and jumped from the rigging into the lifeboat, almost capsizing it. Thereupon, the lifeboat skipper resolved to take the *Marsh* crew ashore, three at a time, since the masts seemed stable and there was little danger of their going over. He instructed the sailors to hold tight and, in three trips to the beach, took off the whole crew. Meanwhile, the lifesaving crew from Two-Hearted River station had arrived and functioned as beach party, taking the rescued to that station for shelter and dry clothing. Two days later, after the waves had subsided, the lifesavers stripped the wreck of everything worth saving, but the *Marsh* had sailed her last, a liability of $24,500.[56]

September passed with only a minor stranding of the steamer *Harvey H. Brown* at Round Island on the 13th, and most of October was ideal. The whaleback steamer *A.D. Thompson* went aground near Red Cliff, west of Bayfield, on October 5. The 265-foot, 1,399-ton bulk carrier required a substantial portion of her ore cargo to be jettisoned before refloating. Otherwise, there was no significant damage reported.[57]

Still, the weather gods could not behave indefinitely, and on October 29 the most horrendous gale and rain in over a decade slammed into western Lake Superior, growing worse as the day progressed. Fifty-mile-an-hour winds ripped down electric wires and Duluth was blacked out. The lake was churned white with foam. Innocently sailing into these blasts were the 250-foot wooden steamer *Hesper* and the 200-foot, 627-ton schooner-barge *Samuel P. Ely,* having left Duluth at 11 a.m. The grain-laden *Hesper* was to tow the *Ely* to Two Harbors for a load of iron ore. After hours of bucking the raucous seas, the two reached the shelter of the Two Harbors breakwater, but then the towline either broke or was dropped prematurely, and the *Ely* was whipped out of control, crashing into a contractor's scow in the harbor and impaling herself on the west breakwater where she began to break up. Her crew and two men off the scow took refuge in her rigging. Dangerous waves within the harbor prevented the *Hesper* from assisting her barge. Accordingly, Superintendent John Owens of the Duluth and Iron Range Railroad, at whose docks the *Ely* was to load, telegraphed for the U.S. Life-Saving crew from Duluth, sending a special train to pick them up. The lifesavers started for the railroad, but found their route blocked by debris. In the meantime, the railroad itself was cut by washouts and wreckage.

Informed of the situation, Superintendent Owens realized that a local rescue would be needed. He instructed his railroad personnel to build bonfires along the harbor front. Then Captain Joe Cox of the railroad tug *Ella G. Stone* procured a sailboat belonging to a fisherman named Strand. Towing the sailboat, Cox took the *Stone* as close to the derelict as he dared, letting the sailboat, commanded by Strand, drift down on lines until it was alongside the *Ely.* Four sailors dropped from the wreck into the sailboat, and the *Stone* towed it to shore. Twice more Captain Cox repeated the operation until all 11 from the *Ely* had been brought to safety. Word of the rescue was telegraphed to Duluth in time to recall the lifesaving crew which was still struggling to drag a lifeboat to an unobstructed portion of the railroad. The *Ely* broke up and sank alongside the breakwater. When a new breakwater was constructed years later, it was built right over the wreck. While her value was undisclosed, the 27-year-old *Samuel P. Ely* likely was valued at more than $15,000.[58]

Although details of the incident would not be known until mid-November, the crew of the 177-foot, 806-ton Canadian steamer *Acadia* suffered a dismal experience beginning on November 5 while carrying 25,000 bushels of grain loaded at the Canadian Lakehead. Their 30-year-old wooden ship was hurled on the rocks near the mouth of Michipicoten River and badly battered. Fortunately, the crew was able to reach shore where they had to camp in the forest. Captain Clifford and four men eventually located fishermen and borrowed a sailboat with which they sailed to the Soo and reported their predicament. The Canadian steamer *L.S. Tilley* retrieved the involuntary campers, but their steamer reportedly was damaged beyond repair, a casualty item probably in excess of $15,000, perhaps as much as $25,000. This accident illustrated the primitive communications still existing in the 1890s. The *Acadia* had been a shattered wreck for 12 days before the whereabouts of her crew was known to the shipping community.[59]

Old lifesaving station at Crisp Point saw many years of service. MRS. JANICE GERRED COLLECTION.

The U.S. Life-Saver's lookout at the Portage Lake Ship Canal Station knew something was awry on the night of November 21 for far out on the western horizon was a bright glare. The lookout called his captain who ordered the lifeboat manned. Seas were moderate and there was no need to wait for a tug. Out went the lifesavers. What the lookout had spotted was the blazing demise of the 202-foot, 944-ton wooden lumber hooker *B.W. Arnold* downbound with cargo from Duluth and having the schooner *James Mowatt* in tow. Off Ontonagon, the *Arnold's* deck load had taken fire, perhaps from smokestack sparks. For hours the crew fought the blaze to no avail. Finally, realizing his ship was doomed, Captain Neal had the yawl launched and the whole crew climbed aboard the *Mowatt* and sailed for Portage. En route, they met the lifesaving crew. The lifesavers continued to row the 20 miles out to the blazing hulk, but could only watch. She finally drifted into the shallows off the Salmon Trout River, seven miles from the ship canal, where she burned to the water's edge. She had been built in 1885 at Bay City, was owned by the Mills Transportation Company of Marysville, Michigan, and valued at $45,000.[60]

Vile weather and intense cold brought several close calls at the end of November, but no losses. The big wooden Canadian passenger steamer *Monarch* under Captain Edward Robertson negotiated the Duluth Ship Canal with extreme difficulty in the mountainous seas of November 26. Effects of the cold wave were visible on November 29 when the wooden steamer *Iosco* under Captain F.A. Bailey crept into the port of Duluth weighted down by 150 tons of ice on her superstructure. The wooden steamer *Fayette Brown* became ice-cut in the central lake and had to sneak into Lac La Belle for emergency repairs, while the schooner *Hattie* broke her tow and ended up with a slight stranding at Grand Marais, Michigan. In addition, the 134-foot, 392-ton schooner *City of the Straits* burned at the Mercer dock in Ontonagon. Loss for the 30-year-old vessel was not revealed. All personnel escaped.

1897

Not a life was taken in a shipwreck for the second year in a row, although a healthy rise in tonnage was accompanied by a greater number of mishaps. Actually, fewer ships were on the lake this year, the increasing presence of the new steel giants with their larger carrying capacities making itself felt. Early difficulties were minor. The 60-foot, 30-ton steamer *Henry F. Brower* went down in shallow water at Duluth after colliding with the barge *D.H. Keyes* on June 30. The tug *J.W. Eviston* suffered fire damage on July 20. Vessel men were thanking their lucky stars, however, on July 27 when in a dense fog off Manitou Island, two large steel steamers met nearly bows on, the downbound 343-foot *Selwyn Eddy* striking the 330-foot *Mariposa*. The ships were throttled down at the time of contact. The *Eddy* was able to continue to the Soo, and the *Mariposa* ran for Marquette with a large hole in the bow. Repair costs for the two were estimated in excess of $40,000, but things would have been far worse if the ships had been moving faster.[61] Two days later, another steel newcomer, the brand new 424-foot steamer *Robert Fulton*, endured a $3,000 plate bender when brushing a Duluth-Superior railroad bridge. On August 13 a more substantial fire caused a $10,000 rebuilding job for the upper works of the steamer *George W. Roby* at Marquette.[62]

The equinoctial storm period in September brought the year's first sinking. The 195-foot, 772-ton schooner-barge *Henry A. Kent* was in tow of the 252-foot steamer *J.C. Gilchrist* off Stannard Rock in the midst of a terrific blow. The *Kent* began taking water. About 11:45 p.m., Captain Sullivan of the *Kent* signaled to his tow steamer that his ship was settling. Dropping his tow, Captain William

Blattner of the *Gilchrist* brought his sizable wooden steamer around the foundering barge three times before he was able to lap the schooner's stern about 15 feet. Those aboard the *Kent,* including three children, were quickly transferred to the *Gilchrist* on lines. Within an hour the rescue was completed, and 15 minutes later the tired old *Kent* slid to the bottom in the early hours of September 18. Built in 1873 at Detroit, she was 24 years

A popular Chicago and Lake Superior line was the L.M. & L.S.T. Company, with four fine ships.
INSTITUTE FOR GREAT LAKES RESEARCH COLLECTION.

old and valued at $22,000. She had spent the winter of 1895-96 stranded at Marquette after the *Kershaw* incident. Needless to say, Captain Blattner won high praise in shipping circles for ingenious handling of a large wooden freighter under such adverse conditions.[63]

In early October came another loss of a schooner-barge. When off Michigan Island on October 7, the 187-foot, 523-ton schooner *Antelope* was proceeding coal-laden to Ashland in tow of the steamer *Hiram W. Sibley.* The *Antelope* carried 1,000 tons of coal loaded in Sandusky, Ohio, at the Pennsylvania Coal Dock. The lake was choppy, but there was no storm and the two were mak-

The 308-foot steel whaleback Thomas Wilson, *invention of Alexander McDougall, a Duluth captain. She sank on June 7, 1902.* MINNESOTA HISTORICAL SOCIETY COLLECTION.

ing 11 or 12 miles per hour. Suddenly, the *Antelope* began to leak badly. As her pumps couldn't handle the water, the *Sibley* proceeded to take off the schooner's crew in the nick of time. The aged *Antelope* succumbed to the lake, reportedly foundering in 360 feet of water. She had been built at Newport, Michigan, in 1861 and at age 36 was one of the lake's genuine old-timers. She formerly had been a steamer. Vessel men surmised that the speed with which the tow was proceeding simply put too much strain on the old hull in choppy seas, opening her seams. Flotsam from the schooner was sighted soon after her demise by another schooner, *Gawn,* off Michigan Island, including the *Antelope*'s cabin. She was a liability of $14,000.[64]

Later in the month, two of the larger wooden towing vessels fell victims to fire. Off Two Harbors on October 12, the 67-foot, 32-ton tug *Comet* burned, though her crew escaped. On October 30 at Superior, the 71-foot, 57-ton tug *Commodore Jack Barry* went up in flames, again with no lives lost. The two were among the newer tugs on Lake Superior, the *Comet* constructed at Muskegon, Michigan, in 1881, and the *Barry* launched at Saugatuck, Michigan, in 1885. Each was a casualty of $5,000.[65]

November weather was easy on sailors until the end of the month. A leakage problem for the barge *G.H. Warmington* at Marquette on November 17 required nominal repairs. Storm conditions on November 26, however, put the new, 178-foot wooden lumber hooker *H.E. Runnels* aground at Point Abbaye. Bound westward with a coal cargo, she had to be lightered before being pulled off and taken to the safety of Portage Entry, a $5,000 salvage job.[66]

The seas grew wilder as the month ran out. Caught in a violent gale and blinding snowstorm northwest of Whitefish Point on the night of November 30, the 180-foot wooden steamer *H.B. Tuttle* had to drop her barge, the 190-foot, 626-ton schooner *Joseph Paige* under Captain Rose. Loaded with iron ore from Marquette, the *Paige* made a run for shelter in Whitefish Bay. Captain Rose ordered the sails raised, but these quickly froze, the schooner becoming unmanageable, and at 3:30 a.m., December 1, she struck about one mile east of Vermilion Point. A riotous surf soon broke her apart. Despite the wild night, the Life-Saving Service beach patrol was out. Indeed, a surfman from Vermilion Point had spotted the *Paige* in dangerous waters and had tried to warn her off with a Coston flare, but the ship was out of control. The surfman alerted his captain who ordered the Vermilion Point crew to the beach. Dragging their equipment in a sleigh, they soon reached the wreck site. Repeatedly, they tried to shoot a lifeline in the darkness, but the derelict was too far out. Waiting for daylight, they tried more shots, but failed. In the meantime, the keeper had telephoned the Crisp Point crew, eight miles to the west, and five surfmen from that station responded. The raging northwester had piled up a 20-foot bank of ice along the

shore. Finally, when it was apparent that a lifeline rescue was impossible, the combined lifesaving crews wrestled a surfboat over the ice mound and at 9:15 a.m. launched into the roaring surf. After a bitter row, they reached the disintegrating schooner and plucked a woman and three men, all half frozen, from the hulk, rushing these survivors back to the beach. In the landing the surfboat was damaged. Therefore, the lifesavers had to manhandle another boat over the ice barrier before they could breast the breakers to get alongside the wreck and pick off the remaining three crewmen who were badly beaten by exposure. They, too, were delivered safely to the beach. The *Paige* crew was taken to the Vermilion Point station where their ice-encrusted clothing had to be cut from their bodies. All survived. A week later, the lifesavers helped strip the *Paige* of rigging and anything else usable, but she had sailed her last, a loss with cargo of $19,500. The *Paige* rescue stands as one of the most difficult in U.S. Life-Saving Service history on Lake Superior.[67]

1898

The shipping industry set a new tonnage record for the lake in 1898. Unfortunately, the ships also set a high mark for accidents, 35 vessels encountering difficulties, 10 joining the ranks of total losses. Spring troubles were plentiful. On April 27 the 242-foot, 1,425-ton wooden steamer *Servia* was downbound from Duluth with a cargo of corn towing the schooner *Frank D. Ewen*. West of Whitefish Point, Captain Fred Ahlstrom sighted the crippled steamer *Argonaut,* and took her in tow also. In late afternoon, when the ships were approximately 15 miles northwest of Whitefish Point, fire was discovered in the forward works of the *Servia*. Her crew fought the blaze for hours with pumps and extinguishers, but still the flames made headway. About 7 p.m. the steel Canadian Pacific passenger steamer *Alberta* hove into sight and, under Captain McAllister, came alongside and put a crew of her own firefighters aboard the *Servia*. For six more hours the sailors of both ships battled the conflagration unsuccessfully. Finally, about 3 a.m., with seas getting rougher and a storm approaching, they realized that the *Servia* was doomed. The *Alberta* took the *Servia*'s crew off as leaping flames enveloped the ship. She burned to the water's edge, going under about 6 a.m. April 28. Captain McAllister then towed both the *Ewen* and *Argonaut* to Waiska Bay, where a tug picked them up for the run to the Soo. The *Servia* had been built at West Bay City, Michigan, in 1883 as Hull No. 41 of the F.W. Wheeler Company. Owned by Hawgood and Avery of Cleveland, she was valued with cargo in excess of $92,400.[68]

Fire struck again the following week, crippling the schooner *Mautenee* at Lake Linden off the Portage Lake

Ship Canal. She undoubtedly was an expensive repair bill, though costs were not stated. On May 18 another good Samaritan got in trouble. The new 301-foot steel steamer *Vega* was upbound with coal for Duluth. Off Stannard Rock, her master spotted the 280-foot wooden steamer *Bulgaria* with the barge *Amazon* dead in the water. The *Bulgaria* had lost her propeller. The *Vega* took the *Bulgaria* and barge in tow and headed westward. West of Keweenaw, a northerly blow pushed the ships farther south than they should have been and, in the dark blustery night of May 18, the *Vega* and *Bulgaria* piled up on Gull Island Reef in the Apostles. The Singer tugs *Superior* and *Zenith* rushed from Duluth to assist the beleaguered steamers. Within two days, the ships were released. The *Vega* was towed to Superior and a date with the shipyard. The *Bulgaria* and *Amazon* were taken first to Bayfield and then to Ashland. The neighborly *Vega* needed a $20,000 repair, though the *Bulgaria* had only a $3,000 tab. Salvors had to jettison 600 tons of coal from the *Vega* before she would come free.[69]

Salvagers patched up the Tecumseh *and raised her from the bottom of Marquette Harbor.* BLAMEY COLLECTION.

The 200-foot Canadian steamer *Tecumseh* was afflicted at Marquette. Almost in the middle of the lower harbor, she punched a hole in her wooden hull on an uncharted rock and settled to the bottom. In the protected waters salvors soon had her up, but the endeavor must have required several thousand dollars.

Next came a bad one at Duluth. On the night of June 2 the 68-foot iron tug *Record* of the Inman Line was trying to assist the 424-foot steel steamer *Robert Fulton* in Duluth Harbor. Inadvertently, the *Record* swung across the bow of the ponderous *Fulton*, which rolled her over in an instant, drowning Captain John H. Bricquelet, Engineer George Briggs and Steward Elmer Cook of the *Record*. A Duluth policeman, pounding his beat along the waterfront, witnessed the accident which occurred just inside the Duluth Ship Canal and began throwing planks from the shore toward the spot. The *Record*'s fireman, Al Davidson, grabbed one of these and became the sole survivor. Constructed in 1884 by the Globe Iron Works of Cleveland, the *Record* was one of the strongest tugs at the Duluth port, though she had a penchant for trouble. Sunk in shallow water, she was quickly repaired after being raised at a cost of $7,000. But she had taken the lives of three crewmen. The body of one crewman was found on July 23 a mile and a half from the hull, but that of Captain Bricquelet was not recovered until September 8, two miles east of Port Wing, Wisconsin, 37 miles from the place of drowning.[70]

Another Duluth Harbor collision on June 7 saw the 295-foot wooden steamer *Amazonas* settling in shallow water after being hit by the 340-foot steel steamer *Pathfinder,* but repairs were minor.

On August 16, when about three miles east of Lester Park, Duluth, the 51-foot, 23-ton wooden tug *R. F. Goodman* took fire and went to the bottom. A product of Buffalo, New York, shipyards in 1882, she belonged to the Thompson Brothers of Duluth, being mastered by Captain W.F. Thompson. Her crew was safe, though she was a $4,500 casualty.[71] Another fatal collision occurred nine days later at the entrance to the Tower Bay slip in Superior Harbor. The 61-foot tug *George Emerson* of the C.S. Barker Company struck and sank the Witt Company's 34-foot tug *Lyric*. A crewman of the *Lyric* was lost. This tug may have been damaged beyond repair, a probable several thousand dollar item.[72]

September brought grief to nine ships. On September 7, as the steamer *Garden City* struggled to reach the piers of the Portage Lake Ship Canal, she swung too far leeward in the darkness and her two consorts, the schooner-barges *James C. King* and *Wenona,* missed the canal and ran aground. The Portage lifesavers came to their assistance immediately and all crews were safe. The following morning a tug pulled the *King* off unscathed. The unfortunate *Wenona*, however, ran so far up on the beach that she proved to be irretrievable, a $9,000 liability. There was a pathetic note here. The 41-year-old *Wenona* represented the savings of 27 years for Captain H.F. Davis and his wife. They remained aboard for three weeks after the stranding in the vain hope that she might be recovered. This was not to be. Launched in 1857, she was one of the veterans of the lake.[73]

The fall of 1898 was bad for forest fires in the Lake Superior country. Blankets of smoke and rough winds combined to give mariners a bad time from September 18 to 23. Six vessels stranded in this five-day period. Groping her way to Portage on September 18, the aged 137-foot, 292-ton schooner *Southwest* found herself on the reefs of the Huron Islands. Captain Gibson and the seven-man crew reached safety in the yawl as their vessel went down. Though her value is not recorded, she must have been worth about $10,000. She was built in 1866 at Ogdensburg, New York.[74] On the same day west of Keweenaw Point, the lumber steamer *Kalkaska* was finding hard going with the schooner-barges *J. H. Mead* and *Mediator* in tow. The towline parted, and the unfortunate schooners were hurled on the Keweenaw Peninsula one mile west of the mouth of the Gratiot River, about 14 miles north of the lifesaving station on the Portage Lake Ship Canal. Lifesavers located them. Their crews, however, had already reached the beach. Salvors went to work and had both off within a week. The schooner *Mead* did not suffer too severely, but the 127-foot, 257-ton *Mediator* was discovered to be battered beyond renovation. Her age was against her, too, as she had been constructed at Clayton, New York, in 1862. Hence, she was abandoned, a loss of only $3,700 with cargo.[75]

Worse things were in store for the Keweenaw the next day, on September 19. Driven ashore at Eagle River six miles northeast of the schooners *Mead* and *Mediator* was the 252-foot, 1,471-ton wooden steamer *Colorado*. Loaded with 1,500 tons of flour, she stuck firmly. For three days the U.S. Life-Savers from Portage assisted salvage tugs and lighters in removing 600 tons of flour. On September 23, however, the lake kicked up again. The *Colorado's* crew was taken off and, before the day was out, the 31-year-old steamer had been beaten to pieces by the crashing surf on Sawtooth Reef. This is the same area where the *James Pickands* had broken up four years before. The *Colorado* had been built at Buffalo in 1867. She was worth $60,000 and her lost cargo another $30,000, making this wreck a $90,000 liability.[76]

The same weather conditions caused the new 291-foot wooden steamer *Uganda* to go ashore near Whitefish Point on September 19, but only nominal repairs were required here. The September 23 gale which crushed the old *Colorado,* harassed the 201-foot lumber hooker *W. H. Sawyer* which had departed Duluth on September 22 with the schooner-barges *C. E. Redfern* and *A. C. Tuxbury* in tow. All had lumber cargoes. The *Sawyer* finally went ashore at Sand Island with little injury. Another burst of winds put the lumber schooner *Annie M. Peterson* aground on a reef at the Huron Islands about September 27. She was a tow of the lumber hooker *Charles Hebard* along with the schooner *Wilson*. Indeed, this was the same reef where the schooner *Southwest* had sunk only the week before. Not far out of Skanee where she had loaded, the *Peterson* was quickly pulled off. She was little damaged and able to rejoin her tow, reaching the Soo Locks on October 2.[77]

The participant in the last September incident was not as lucky. The 181-foot, 579-ton lumber steamer *Toledo* with the barge *Shawnee* in tow was plodding along eastward toward the Portage Lake Ship Canal when she began leaking rapidly. She waterlogged about 25 miles south-

west of Portage, whereupon, her crew boarded the *Shawnee* and sailed to Portage where they procured the steamer *D. F. Rose* to tow the *Toledo* to shelter. Within 500 feet of the Portage piers, the low riding *Toledo* touched bottom. With the aid of a tug and lighter, her crew, assisted by the U.S. Life-Savers, went to work removing the lumber cargo. They had managed to save about $2,000 worth of lumber, when a strong sea arose and the ship had to be evacuated. Angry waves completely demolished the 36-year-old *Toledo* during the night and following day while lying in the vessel channel. She was a menace to navigation. Hence, Captain W.H. Singer, the Duluth salvor, was hired by the U.S. Army Corps of Engineers to dynamite her hulk a few weeks later. Her remains were even more completely removed by the Whitney Brothers under another contract with the Corps of Engineers in 1902.[78]

Bad luck continued to dog shipping during October. A collision in Duluth Harbor on October 4 caused inconsequential damage to the steamers *Monarch* and *Mahoning*. However, a stranding wrought havoc with the 92-foot, 103-ton schooner *John Jewett* in Grace Harbor, Isle Royale, on October 7. She had been built in 1866 at Vermilion, Ohio. Her value was not recorded.[79] At Copper Harbor on October 16, the 212-foot wooden steamer *Jesse H. Farwell* hung up on the rocks, but Captain Singer soon had her off. Shipyard work of $5,000 was required.

Turbulent seas on the central lake then grabbed two more victims. The 257-foot, 1,773-ton wooden steamer *Henry Chisholm* of the M.A. Bradley fleet had departed Duluth on October 16 with the schooner *John Martin* as consort. The *Chisholm* was a powerful towing vessel of 1,707 horsepower and held her own in a wild gale which enveloped the two vessels. On October 17, Captain James Lawless of the *Martin* decided in the interest of safety for his own vessel to drop the towline and run for shelter on his own. The *Chisholm* slogged along for two more days before the storm subsided. Captain P.H. Smith then began looking for his wandering consort. He doubled back along the Keweenaw and put into Ashland to refuel before heading northward along the Minnesota coast. Approaching Washington Harbor, Isle Royale, from the south, the *Chisholm* ran up onto Rock of Ages Reef. Captain Smith and his 15-man crew abandoned ship by lifeboat and succeeded in reaching Washington Island not far distant. Captain Singer was hastily summoned from Keweenaw Point, but help came too late. The *Chisholm,* badly damaged from the initial impact, broke up, a total loss. With her cargo of 92,000 bushels of barley, the financial casualty must have approached $150,000, a truly costly mishap.

The 220-foot, 938-ton *Martin* was more fortunate. She was picked up by the steel steamer *Roman* off Copper Harbor and towed to safety.

The *Chisholm* was a product of Cleveland shipyards in 1880. Twin Scotch boilers had replaced her originals in 1896. These relatively new boilers were recovered in the summer of 1901 by Captain England working off the little steamer *H.A. Root* of Duluth. The *Chisholm*'s engine was also located, but, lying in more than 100 feet of water, had to be left.

Sport divers exploring the *Chisholm* wreck site today find two shipwrecks, the other being the 1877 wreck of the side-wheeler *Cumberland*. Both vessels apparently wrecked on the same portion of the reef, and their remains fell together on the bottom. They are quite distinguishable by the massive size of the *Chisholm*'s structural timbers, while the *Cumberland* is rather lightly framed and planked on the diagonal. The *Chisholm*'s massive two-cylinder steam engine miraculously rests upright on the bottom and in perfect condition.[80]

Heavily laden Arthur Orr *was blown into rocks at the Baptism River in the gale of November 21, 1898.* AUTHOR'S COLLECTION.

The 54-foot, 29-ton tug *Rebel*, owned by Whitney Brothers of Superior, furnished the final incident of the month. Towing a scow to Pork Bay on the Minnesota north shore, the *Rebel* was overtaken by a storm off Two Harbors. She started taking water. Realizing their vessel would sink, Captain Roselle Coburn and his crew went aboard the scow before the tug went under. After some drifting around in the open lake, they were located by the wooden steamer *City of London* and towed to Duluth. The 27-year-old tug was valued at about $2,500.[81]

Two wind-driven snowstorms punctuated November sailing, each taking a toll. A biting gale of short duration on November 21-22 put three steamers in precarious positions. On the south side of Mott Island, Isle Royale, the 183-foot, 980-ton wooden steamer *Osceola* was driven ashore. Captain J.C. McLeod took his crew ashore where they remained for 13 hours. When the seas subsided, the crew returned to their endangered steamer undertaking the task of jettisoning 2,000 barrels of salt. For a day and a half they toiled. Thus lightened, the *Osceola* was able to get afloat under her own power.[82]

At the same time, the howling northeaster deposited two more vessels on the Minnesota north shore: the steel

286-foot, 2,329-ton package freighter *Arthur Orr* at the mouth of Baptism River and the wooden 291-foot, 1,972-ton steamer *Tampa* on the reef at the south side of the present day harbor of Silver Bay. Captain Green of the *Orr* held his crew aboard, as the ship was only in a few feet of water a stone's throw from land. As the *Tampa* was in danger of sliding off and sinking, Captain Leonard launched his boats and rowed to Beaver Bay when the waves had subsided. Both captains spoke of being overwhelmed by winds which might have gusted to 100 miles an hour. Green reported that his steering gear had failed completely. Valuable cargoes were carried: the *Tampa* with 2,700 tons of coal and the *Orr* with a combination of 2,200 tons of flour out of Duluth, 500 tons of copper from the Keweenaw, plus a deck load of shingles.

With the ships lying only eight miles apart, salvage captains B.B. Inman and W.H. Singer of Duluth took personal charge of operations. The *Orr*, on a gravel bottom, was floated rather easily, a salvage and repair cost of $10,000. The eight-year-old *Tampa* was a different story. Her wooden hull had taken a bad beating; hence, her bill was $50,000, probably more than half her worth. Yet, she was to sail for many additional years.[83]

Package freighter Harlem *was salvaged from Menagerie Island at Isle Royale after spending the winter stranded there.* STEAMSHIP HISTORICAL SOCIETY OF AMERICA COLLECTION.

Only three days afterward came another nasty blow. At Duluth the only problem was a harbor collision between the steamers *Jas. L. Colgate* and *Globe* with negligible damage on November 25. The next day, double trouble hit in the central lake. Near Munising, the steamer *Escanaba* went aground but managed to get free after her crew dumped a thousand barrels of salt overboard.

A far worse situation existed at Isle Royale. Caught in the throes of a wicked northwesterly snowstorm, the 288-foot, 2,299-ton steel package freighter *Harlem* wandered into dangerous waters and struck on rock pinnacles within sight of the Isle Royale Light on Menagerie Island about 1 a.m. on November 27. As the waves flattened a bit, her crew took to the lifeboats and reached a small island near the lighthouse. Owned by Western Transit Company, this fine 10-year-old ship, one of the fastest on the lakes, was thought to be a total loss of more than $200,000. To the surprise of all, she remained intact through the winter and was salvaged the next fall by Captain W.H. Harrow of the Thompson Towing and Wrecking Associates of Port Huron in an amazing operation. Taken to shipyards, first at Port Huron and later Toledo, she was rebuilt as a coarse freighter. The reclamation operation, nevertheless, was not an economic success and caused grave financial difficulties for Mr. Thompson, who invested more than $167,000 in the effort, probably more than she was worth as a 10-year-old package carrier.[84]

The season's finale was a harbor fire at Duluth on December 23 when fire badly singed the 114-foot wooden tug *W.B. Castle* of the Inman Line, necessitating more than $1,000 in rebuilding costs. Despite the astounding number of ships in trouble, only four lives were lost during the season and all of these in tug sinkings right in the Duluth-Superior Harbor.

1899

Shippers had a spectacular year in 1899. Another phenomenal increase appeared in total tonnage, surpassing the previous record by nearly one-fifth. About 15 percent more ships were on the lake. At the same time, the number of ships in trouble was drastically reduced. Still, six vessels were lost and nine men died.

An extremely grim experience marked the early season. Westbound on May 13, 20 miles north of Grand Marais, Michigan, was the 180-foot wooden steamer *A. Folsom* with the schooner-barges *Mary B. Mitchell* and *Nelson* in tow. Suddenly, they were hemmed in by a 50 mile-an-hour gale with snow and freezing sleet. They began to ice up. Realizing his peril, the *Folsom*'s master tried to return to Whitefish Bay, but the towline parted, and the three were on their own. The *Folsom* and *Mitchell* rode it out, as they were relatively new vessels. The 33-year-old *Nelson,* laden with 1,300 tons of coal consigned to Hancock on the Portage Lake Ship Canal, couldn't stand the stress. Water began rising in her hold.

Captain Haganey steered for shore, but the 164-foot, 767-ton *Nelson* was in her death throes. About 2:30 p.m., the captain perceived that she could founder momentarily. Accordingly, he ordered his crew, his wife and child

into the yawl, while he stayed aboard to assist in lowering away. He jumped for the yawl and missed, just as the schooner threw her stern in the air and dove for the bottom with the yawl still attached to the davits, drowning

Veteran schooner Nelson *(at right) broke from towing steamer and foundered with seven of the eight people on board in May 1899.* CANAL PARK MARINE MUSEUM COLLECTION.

all seven persons in it. So rapidly did the *Nelson* go under that she popped her cabin off. Floundering in the icy water, Captain Haganey spotted the cabin, reached it and dragged himself on top. He hung on for hours, half dead from grief and shock, while the northwester drove the improvised raft for 18 frigid miles before depositing it on the beach not far from the Deer Park Life-Saving Station. He was the only survivor of the eight who had been aboard. Though once a crack schooner, the *Nelson* was a liability of slightly more than $10,000 to her owners, the Mitchell Transportation Company of Bay City.[85]

In the days before an excellent road system connected the small, shallow-draft ports on the north and south shores with railroads or major highways, a number of small packet ships provided passenger and cargo service to the scattered pioneer populations. One of these was the 100-foot, 198-ton steamer *R.G. Stewart,* a ferry on the Niagara River before being rebuilt and brought to Duluth in 1882. Outbound from Ontonagon on June 3, on a run from Hancock to Duluth with her owner, Captain Cornelius O. Flynn, in command, the *Stewart* entered a blinding fog. About midnight, she slid onto the sands off Michigan Island, 20 miles from Bayfield. The following morning, Captain Flynn used the kedge anchor and pushed his boilers hard in an effort to back her off. They had backed the boat about 150 feet toward deeper water when fire was discovered around the smoke stack over the engine and boiler rooms. Despite desperate efforts of the crew to combat the flames, the little ship was soon ablaze from stem to stern.

Captain Flynn first ordered the cargo of cattle driven overboard, since the shore was close at hand. Next, the dozen persons aboard began entering the lifeboat which was already moored alongside from the kedging operation. Wheelsman George McKenna became excited and jumped from the upper deck to the gunwale of the lifeboat, capsizing it and dumping all 12 into the numbing water. Six tried to swim to the nearby beach, but only five reached it. Wheelsman McKenna went under and, although a fellow crewman quickly brought him to the surface and dragged him ashore, he could not be resuscitat-

A harbor collision on June 13 at Duluth-Superior saw the lumber steamer *Adella Shores* hitting a scow towed by the tug *Ella G. Stone* with slight injury to the *Shores*. However, a fire off the Minnesota north shore destroyed a veteran tug on July 29. The 100-foot, 118-ton *Bob Anderson,* built at Cleveland in 1862, was rafting logs for Duncan, Brewer and Company out of Grand Marais, Minnesota. During the night, her master, Captain Cox, found

Detroit's Grummond Company performed many of the 1890s' most challenging salvage jobs. BEESON'S MARINE DIRECTORY, 1891.

ed. The other six righted the lifeboat and crawled back in. For a while they had a warm time of it, since there was no ax or knife in the boat with which to cut the line securing it to the blazing hulk. Finally, the line burned through and the lifeboat was brought to land. Only the unfortunate wheelsman had died.

The little *Stewart* was worth just $8,000. Remains of the *Stewart* were discovered in the summer of 1983 by the family serving as volunteer lightkeepers for the National Park Service at Michigan Island. Subsequent investigation by volunteer sport divers revealed no immediate evidence of her machinery or substantial structural members of her hull.[86]

her afire, the blaze already cutting off the crew from the water valves and the yawl. Luckily, the night was calm, and a shore party, perceiving the predicament, came to the rescue by canoe. The tug *Mystic,* also at the site, towed the flaming *Anderson* into shallow water where she burned and sank. A 200-horsepower vessel, she was one of the more powerful tugs at the Head of the Lakes and one of the oldest. Because of her age, she was a liability of only $6,000 to her owners, the Inman Line of Duluth.[87]

A summer snowstorm along the Canadian north shore, not an uncommon occurrence on the lake despite what the calendar would seem to indicate, claimed another old-timer on August 10. Feeling her way on a run from

Sarnia to Nipigon where she expected to load pulpwood, the 181-foot, 1,338-ton wooden Canadian steamer *Ontario* grounded on Battle Island and proved irretrievable. Her crew escaped with little difficulty, working their way to the island's lighthouse, and her barges avoided the beach. Owned by Captain John Cornwalt of Sombra, Ontario, she was valued at $15,000, having been built in 1874 at Chatham, Ontario. The ship's boilers are still on Battle Island, marking the disaster.[88]

The fog on western Lake Superior the night of August 19 brought an unpleasant surprise to Captain L.D. Gibson of the three-year-old 352-foot, 3,502-ton steamer *Penobscot*. On several occasions ships' compasses have gone awry in fog off Knife Island, 20 miles northeast of Duluth. Imagine the consternation of Captain Gibson when, supposedly in safe water and on course, his steel giant was crashing over a reef and slamming through boulders before coming to rest with her stern nearly on shore in the sheltered bay to the landward side of Knife Island. Captain B.B. Inman of Duluth and his tugs quickly floated her, but the *Penobscot* had a $20,000 trip to the shipyard.[89]

Miscellaneous minor troubles afflicted sailors during September. A fire on September 2 at Ashland caused more than $1,000 damage to Booth's 60-foot wooden steamer *R.W. Currie*. A harbor crash occurred in Duluth on September 7 resulting in the shallow water sinking of the wooden steamer *Peerless* which had hit the barge *Stewart*. It took $8,000 to float and refurbish the 27-year-old *Peerless*. On September 28 off Bayfield, the wooden steamer *City of Traverse* lost her rudder and had to be towed in.

Another harbor collision on October 8 saw the unlucky 68-foot iron tug *Record* tipped, drowning a crewman. The *Record* was towing the inbound 320-foot steel steamer *James B. Neilson* of the Bessemer Fleet in the Duluth Harbor when the steamer suddenly put on a burst of speed, overtook the tug and rolled her over. Four crewmen leaped to safety on a life raft as the *Record* sank, but Fireman Harry Ellis, asleep in his bunk, was drowned. The *Record* was raised, again at a cost of several thousand dollars, and the body of the lost fireman recovered.[90]

Rough weather on October 24 proved the end for the unusual little schooner *Criss Grover*. This 90-foot, 133-ton vessel had been built in Lorain, Ohio, in 1878 and operated out of Marquette for years by the doughty Captain Daniels. She carried dynamite to the mining towns, a commodity that most masters wouldn't touch. After a sinking in Marquette Harbor in 1898, she had been repaired by Captain Gibson. He was sailing her from Bay Mills to Duluth to pick up a lumber cargo when a gale drove the ship onto a reef near Split Rock where she broke up, a $2,000 loss.[91]

The 1890s closed with one of the most unusual survival stories in Lake Superior annals. The iron ore ships were running late and, during the second week of December, the 256-foot, 1,169-ton steel whaleback barge *115* was moving eastward in tow of the 277-foot whaleback steamer *Colgate Hoyt*. Both were heavily laden with ore. The two steamed unwittingly into a gigantic storm which heavily blasted northern Michigan and the eastern lake for four days. Striving to avoid the worst of the northerly gales and snow, the *Hoyt*'s master followed the Canadian north shore. But, when he was 10 miles off the Pic Islands on December 13, the towline broke, and the *115* was loose. Failing to recover the tow in the snowstorm and running short of coal, the *Hoyt* steered for the Soo where her master reported the incident. It was believed that the barge had gone down, since the *Hoyt* crew had observed her pumps spewing red water, indicating leakage in the cargo hold. No other ship had sighted her after the breakaway. As the snowstorm had passed, however, variable winds tossed the *115* indiscriminately around northeastern Lake Superior for five days, before strong southerly blasts pitched her aground on Pic Island, December 18.

Captain Arthur Boyce and his crew fashioned a makeshift raft and reached the Ontario mainland near Pic River. Then followed two days of wandering in the snow-covered forest until the survivors struck the Canadian Pacific Railroad and made their way to a remote station named Middleton from which Captain Boyce wired the report of survival to the owners, Pickands, Mather and Company. The group was suffering badly from exposure and hunger. The nine crewmen had existed for nine days on two days' rations. Whaleback barge *115* was smashed beyond recovery by the surf at Pic Island, becoming a liability of $80,000. She was a relatively new steel ship, built at Superior, Wisconsin, in 1891.

Substantial underwater archaeological work has been done on the *115* by a group of dedicated Canadian sport divers working in cooperation with the Ministry of Citizenship and Culture's regional archaeologist in Thunder Bay and Save Ontario Shipwrecks' local chapter.[92]

1 *Marquette Mining Journal,* April 30, May 8, 17, 1890.

2 *Annual Report, U.S. Life-Saving Service, 1890,* pp. 340, 349.

3 Homer Wells, *History of Accidents, Casualties, and Wrecks on Lake Superior,* (Duluth, Corps of Engineers, U.S. Army, 1938), 90 pp., typewritten, p. 18.

4 *Duluth Daily Tribune,* Sept. 17-18, 1890; *Marquette Mining Journal,* Sept. 14, 1890.

5 *Duluth Daily Tribune,* Sept. 16-18, 1890; *Marquette Mining Journal,* Sept. 16-18, 1890.

6 Wells, *op. cit.,* p. 19.

7 *Marquette Mining Journal,* May 7, 9, 1891; *Annual Report, U.S. Life-Saving Service, 1891,* pp. 63-66, 249.

8 *Superior Daily Call,* June 3, 1891; *Annual Report, U.S. Life-Saving Service, 1891,* p. 249. In the late 1970s two sport divers reported finding large pieces of cut sandstone off Minnesota Point, possibly the cargo of the *Mayflower,* lost when she turned turtle. No evidence of hull structure was reported.

9 *Annual Report, U.S. Life-Saving Service, 1891,* p. 158; *ibid,* 1892, p. 184; Frederick Stonehouse, *Munising Shipwrecks,* (Au Train, Michigan, Avery Color Studios, 1983), p. 30.

10 *Annual Report, U.S. Life-Saving Service, 1892,* pp. 64, 184; Wells, *op. cit.,* p. 19.

11 *Duluth Daily News,* June 16, 1892; Thom Holden, *Apostle Islands Shipwreck Survey List, 1870-1940,* (Bayfield, Wisconsin, Apostle Islands National Lakeshore, National Park Service, 1985), p. 93.

12 *Duluth Daily Tribune,* Oct. 1-3, 1891; *Marquette Mining Journal,* Oct. 1, 3, 1891; *Annual Report, U.S. Life-Saving Service, 1892,* p. 279.

13 *Duluth Daily Tribune,* Oct. 3-4, 1891, Aug. 21, 1892; Alan W. Miller, "*Winslow:* Gone, But Not Forgotten" in *The Nor'Easter,* Journal of the Lake Superior Marine Museum Association of Duluth, Vol 13, No. 1, January-February 1988, pp. 1-4.

14 *Duluth Daily Tribune,* Oct. 28, 1891; Dominion of Canada, Department of Transport, *Casualties to Vessels Resulting in Total Loss on the Great Lakes, From 1870 to date,* p. 28; Ronald H. Wrigley, *Northern Superior Shipwrecks,* typewritten manuscript, 198 pages, *ca.* 1975, pp. 31-32.

15 *Duluth Daily Tribune,* Nov. 23, 1891; *Marquette Mining Journal,* Nov. 23, 1891; Weather Bureau, U.S. Department of Agriculture, *Wreck Chart of the Great Lakes, 1886-1891.* The Weather Bureau figure of $176,000 loss on the *Mather* undoubtedly is too high.

16 *Duluth Daily Tribune,* Nov. 21, 23, 27, 1891.

17 *Duluth Daily Tribune,* Nov. 29, 1891; Wells, *op. cit.,* p. 19; *Ashland Weekly Press,* Dec. 12, 1891 *Bayfield County Press,* Dec. 12, 1891; Holden, *op. cit.,* pp. 22-23; James M. Keller, *The "Unholy" Apostles: Tales of Chequamegon Shipwrecks,* (Bayfield, Wisconsin, Apostle Islands Press, 1985), pp. 49-50. A variety of spellings for the *May Corgan* have appeared including *Mary Cargan* and *May Corrigan.* Unfortunately, the vessel did not appear in *Merchant Vessels of the United States* during the several years prior to her loss, although it seems she should have been registered.

18 *Marquette Mining Journal,* May 2, 1892.

19 *Ashland Press,* May 14, 1892; Holden, *op. cit.,* p. 54; Wells, *op. cit.,* p. 20.

20 *Duluth Daily Tribune,* Sept. 2, 5, 1892; *Marquette Mining Journal,* Sept. 2-3, 5, 7, 1892; "Sworn Statement of H.W. Stewart" in *Marine Review,* Vol. VI, No. 11, Sept. 15, 1892, p. 7; *Annual Report, U.S. Life-Saving Service, 1893,* pp. 79, 133-134, 322.

21 *Marquette Mining Journal,* Sept. 1, 1892.

22 *Bayfield County Press,* Sept. 10, 1892; *Lake Superior Review & Weekly Tribune* (Duluth), Sept. 9, 1892; Holden, *op. cit.,* p. 85. There is some oral history indicating the *John A. Paige* may actually have sunk in Squaw Bay just to the east of Siskiwit Bay. A tug is reported sunk in Squaw Bay with its machinery exposed as if it had burned. *Duluth Daily Tribune,* Sept. 9, 15-16, 1892; *Marquette Mining Journal,* Sept. 15-17, 1892; Wells, *op. cit.,* p. 20.

23 *Marquette Mining Journal,* Sept. 19, 1892; Wells, *op. cit.,* p. 20.

24 *Annual Report, U.S. Life-Saving Service, 1893,* p. 89; Wells, *op. cit.,* p. 20.

25 *Duluth Daily Tribune,* Oct. 30-31, 1892; *Marquette Mining Journal,* Oct. 31, 1892; *Annual Report, U.S. Life-Saving Service, 1893,* pp. 25-28, 91, 142, 230-231.

26 *Duluth Daily Tribune,* Nov. 14, 1892; *Marquette Mining Journal,* Nov. 2, 1892.

27 *Marquette Mining Journal,* Dec. 12, 14, 16, 1892; *Annual Report, U.S. Life-Saving Service, 1893,* p. 137.

28 *Annual Report, U.S. Life-Saving Service, 1893,* p. 122.

29 *Duluth News-Tribune,* Aug. 18, 1893; Wells, *op. cit.,* pp. 20-21; *Annual Report, U.S. Life-Saving Service, 1894,* pp. 86, 268.

30 *Buffalo Morning Express,* July 8-11, 16, 22, 1893; *Duluth Daily Commonwealth,* July 7, 10, 1893; *Duluth Evening Herald,* July 7-8, 1893; *Duluth News-Tribune,* July 8-9, 11, 1893; *Duluth Weekly Herald,* July 12, 1893; *The Scanner,* Journal of the Toronto Marine Historical Society, March 1977, midsummer 1982 and April 1983.

31 *Duluth Evening Herald,* July 21, 1893; *Duluth News-Tribune,* July 21, 1893.

32 *Annual Report, U.S. Life-Saving Service, 1894,* pp. 86, 268.

33 *Annual Report, U.S. Life-Saving Service, 1894,* p. 95.

34 Wells, *op. cit.,* p. 21.

35 *Duluth News-Tribune,* Oct. 16-19, 1893; *Annual Report, U.S. Life-Saving Service, 1894,* p. 373.

36 *Marquette Mining Journal,* Oct. 26, 28, 1893; *Annual Report, U.S. Life-Saving Service, 1894,* pp. 109, 268; Stonehouse, *op. cit.,* p. 31, states that wreckage in this location and visible in 10 feet of water may be the *George.*

37 *Duluth Evening Herald,* November 4, 6, 1893; *Duluth News-Tribune,* November 5, 14, 29, 1893; Holden, *op. cit.,* pp. 105-106; Keller, *op. cit.,* pp. 51-53.

38 *Marquette Mining Journal,* Nov. 29, Dec. 1, 1893; Wells, *op. cit.,* p. 22.

39 *Bayfield County Press,* Aug. 10, 1917; Guy M. Burnham, *The Lake Superior Country in History and in Story* (Ashland, Wisconsin, *Ashland Daily Press,* 1930), pp. 358-365 Holden, *op. cit.,* p. 32-34; Keller, *op. cit.,* pp. 143-45; William Lytle and Forrest Holdcamper, *Merchant Steam Vessels of the United States, 1790-1868,* (Staten Island, New York, The Steamship Historical Society of America, 1975) p. 63; Herman G. Runge Collection vessel history files, Wisconsin Marine Historical Society, Milwaukee Public Library.

40 *Annual Report, U.S. Life-Saving Service, 1894,* p. 366; Wells, *op. cit.,* p. 22.

41 *Duluth News-Tribune,* Aug. 9, 1894.

42 *Annual Report, U.S. Life-Saving Service, 1895,* pp. 91, 306; Wells, *op. cit.,* p. 22.

43 *Duluth News-Tribune,* Sept. 26-27, 1894; *Annual Report, U.S. Life-Saving Service, 1895,* pp. 100, 306; Wells, *op. cit.,* p. 22.

44 *Duluth News-Tribune,* Oct. 16, 1894; *Annual Report, U.S. Life-Saving Service, 1895,* pp. 113, 306; Wells, *op. cit.,* p. 22.

45 *Duluth News-Tribune,* Oct. 28, 1894; Wells, *op. cit.,* p. 22.

46 *Duluth News-Tribune,* Oct. 16, 1895; *Annual Report, U.S. Life-Saving Service, 1896,* pp. 29-32, 331; Wells, *op. cit.,* p. 23.

47 *Duluth News-Tribune,* Sept. 25, 1895; *Detroit Journal,* Sept. 24, 1895.

48 *Annual Report, U.S. Life-Saving Service, 1896,* pp. 87, 330; E.N. Jennison, "Reminiscences of the Keweenaw Waterway" in *Inland Seas,* Vol. IX, No. 2, p. 144, Summer, 1953; Wells, *op. cit.,* p. 23.

49 *Duluth News-Tribune,* Oct. 2, 1895; *Annual Report, U.S. Life-Saving Service, 1896,* pp. 88, 331; Wells, *op. cit.,* p. 23.

50 *Marquette Mining Journal,* Oct. 5, 1895; *Annual Report, U.S. Life-Saving Service, 1896,* pp. 88, 331; Wells, *op. cit.,* p. 23.

51 *Duluth News-Tribune,* Nov. 9, 1895; Wells, *op. cit.,* p. 24.

52 *Duluth News-Tribune,* Nov. 9, 1895; Wells, *op. cit.,* p. 24.

53 *Marquette Mining Journal,* Nov. 23, 25, 29, Dec. 2, 1895.

54 *L'Anse Sentinel,* Dec. 14, 1895; *Annual Report, U.S. Life-Saving Service, 1896,* p. 426.

55 Loss of the *Kakabeka* has been variously reported by usually reliable sources, apparently erroneously. Wrigley *op. cit.,* p. 4-6, relates the account cited here based on Canadian source materials. Errors of location appear in Holden, *op. cit.,* p. 53, John M. Mills, *Canadian Coastal and Inland Steam Vessels, 1809-1930,* (Providence, Rhode Island, The Steamship Historical Society of America, 1979), p. 64, and in the handwritten notes of Herman G. Runge in the Wisconsin Marine Historical Society collection at Milwaukee Public Library. Each of the latter attributes the location to the Sand Island in the Apostle Islands archipelago. The casualty date, too, varies between December 12 and 19, 1895.

56 *Annual Report, U.S. Life-Saving Service, 1897,* pp. 91-92.

57 *Bayfield County Press,* Oct. 10, 1896; Holden, *op. cit.,* p. 103.

58 *Duluth News-Tribune* Oct. 30-31, 1896; an undated clipping, presumably from the *Two Harbors Chronicle,* also credits two other residents of that city, Captain Malcolm McEachern and James McDonald, with figuring prominently in the rescue, in *Vol. 1, Files of Lake County Historical Society, Judge Scott collection;* Wells, *op. cit.,* p. 24.

59 *Duluth News-Tribune,* Nov. 17-18, 1896; Wrigley, *op. cit.,* pp. 110-111.

60 *Duluth News-Tribune,* Nov. 23, 1896; *Annual Report, U.S. Life-Saving Service, 1897,* pp. 136, 332.

61 *Duluth News-Tribune,* July 28, 1897; Wells, *op. cit.,* p. 24.

62 *Duluth News-Tribune,* July 29, 1897; Wells, *op. cit.,* p. 25.

63 "Captain William Blattner of Vermilion, Ohio, A Steamboat Man of Nerve" in *Marine Review,* Sept. 23, 1897, reprinted in *Inland Seas,* Vol. 13, No. 4, p. 315, Winter, 1957.

64 *Duluth News-Tribune,* Oct. 8-10, 1897; Harvey C. Beeson, *Inland Marine Directory, 1898,* p. 147; Holden, *op. cit.,* p. 2; Keller, *op. cit.,* pp. 55-57.

65 Beeson, *op. cit.,* 1898; Wells, *op. cit.,* p. 25.

66 *Duluth News-Tribune,* Dec. 1, 1897; Wells, *op. cit.,* p. 25.

67 *Annual Report, U.S. Life-Saving Service, 1898,* pp. 126-127, 290-291.

68 *Duluth News-Tribune,* April 29, 1898; Wells, *op. cit.,* p. 25.

69 *Duluth News-Tribune,* May 18, 20-21, 23, 1898; Wells, *op. cit.,* p. 25.

70 *Duluth News-Tribune,* June 3, Sept. 9, 1898; *Annual Report, U.S. Life-Saving Service, 1898,* pp. 40, 292; Wells, *op. cit.,* p. 26.

71 *Duluth News-Tribune,* Aug. 17, 1898.

72 *Duluth News-Tribune,* Aug. 25, 1898; Wells, *op. cit.,* p. 26. The *Lyric* disappears from the roll in *Merchant Vessels of the United States* after this incident.

73 *Duluth News-Tribune,* Sept. 28, 1898; *Annual Report, U.S. Life-Saving Service, 1899,* pp. 94, 316-317.

74 *Duluth News-Tribune,* Sept. 22, 1898; Beeson, *op. cit., 1899,* p. 134.

75 *Duluth News-Tribune,* Sept. 19, 24, 1898; *Annual Report, U.S. Life-Saving Service, 1899,* pp. 98, 316-317.

76 *Duluth News-Tribune,* Sept. 20-21, 23-24, 1898; *Annual Report, U.S. Life-Saving Service, 1899,* pp. 98, 316.

77 *Duluth News-Tribune,* Sept. 20, 24, 30, 1898; *Marquette Mining Journal,* Sept. 29, Oct. 2, 1898.

78 *Duluth News-Tribune,* Oct. 4, 22, 1898; *Annual Report, U.S. Life-Saving Service, 1899,* pp. 102, 318.

79 Beeson, *op. cit., 1899,* p. 134.

80 *Duluth News-Tribune,* Oct. 22, 1898, Aug. 2, 1901; Beeson, *op. cit., 1899,* p. 134; Toni Carrell, *Shipwrecks of Isle Royale National Park: Thematic Group Nomination to*

the National Register of Historic Places, (Santa Fe, New Mexico, Submerged Cultural Resources Unit, National Park Service, 1983, 172-page typewritten manuscript), pp. 21, 23, 26, 121-133; Thom Holden, *Above and Below* (Houghton, Michigan, Isle Royale Natural History Association, 1985), pp. 38-41; Thom Holden, "Reef of the Three C's: Part II, Wreck of the *Henry Chisholm*" in *The Nor'Easter, op. cit.,* Vol. 3, No. 2, March-April 1978, pp. 1-3, 5; Larry Murphy and Thom Holden, "Shipwrecks of Isle Royale: The Historical Record," in *Submerged Cultural Resources Study: Isle Royale National Park,* Daniel J. Lenihan, ed., (Santa Fe, New Mexico, Submerged Cultural Resources Unit, National Park Service, 1987), pp. 72-79; Larry Murphy, Daniel Lenihan and C. Patrick Labadie, "Shipwrecks of Isle Royale: The Archeological Record" in Lenihan, ed., *ibid.,* pp. 220-253. Reference to the name of one small steamer used in salvage on the *Chisholm* has commonly appeared in two forms, both in the literature and on photographs of the vessel, the variations being *Joseph C. Suit* and *J.C. Suit.* They are the same vessel.

[81] *Duluth News-Tribune,* Oct. 25, 1898; Wells, *op. cit.,* p. 26.

[82] *Duluth News-Tribune,* Nov. 25, 1898.

[83] *Duluth News-Tribune,* Nov. 24-25, Dec. 1, 1898; Wells, *op. cit.,* p. 27.

[84] *Duluth News-Tribune,* Nov. 29, Dec. 1, 1898; *Houghton Daily Mining Gazette,* Sept. 29, Oct. 4, 12, 1899; *Marquette Mining Journal,* Oct. 26, 28, 1899; Beeson, *op. cit.,* 1900, p. 175. Salvors went to work on the *Harlem* on June 11, 1899, and the ship came off Sept. 27, being towed to Port Huron the following week. Captain Washington Harrow used the tug *M.F. Merrick* and steambarge *Snook.* Another item attracting salvors at the *Harlem* site was 100 tons of chrome steel billets which had been jettisoned. Insurance underwriters supposedly paid $225,000 for ship and cargo.

[85] *Duluth News-Tribune,* May 15, 16, 1899; *Annual Report, U.S. Life-Saving Service, 1899,* p. 179; Beeson, *op. cit.,* 1900, p. 139.

[86] *Ashland Daily News,* June 6, 8, 1899; *Bayfield County Press,* May 6, June 10, 1899; *Duluth Evening Herald,* June 7, 1899; *Duluth News-Tribune,* June 6-7, 1899; *Duluth Weekly News Tribune,* June 10, 17, 1899; Holden, *Apostle Islands Shipwreck Survey List, op. cit.,* p. 99-102; Keller, *op. cit.,* pp. 59-62; *The Nor'Easter, op. cit.,* Vol. 8, No. 6, November-December 1983, p. 8; Wells, *op. cit.,* p. 27.

[87] *Duluth News-Tribune,* Aug. 2, 1899; Beeson, *op. cit., 1900,* p. 110; Wells, *op. cit.,* p. 27.

[88] *Duluth News-Tribune,* Aug. 12, 1899; Beeson, *op. cit., 1900,* p. 110; Wrigley, *op. cit.,* pp. 32-33.

[89] *Duluth News-Tribune,* Aug. 21, 1899; Wells, *op. cit.,* p. 27.

[90] *Annual Report, U.S. Life-Saving Service, 1900,* pp. 30-31, 278; Wells, *op. cit.,* p. 28.

[91] *Marquette Mining Journal,* Nov. 4, 1899; Beeson, *op. cit.,* 1900, p. 110. Variations of this vessel's name appear in the literature, particularly as *Chris Grover.* The spelling used here, *Criss Grover,* is as listed in various editions of *Merchant Vessels of the United States.*

[92] *Duluth News-Tribune,* Dec. 18, 23, 27, 1899.

John B. Cowle *was nearly cut in two by the upbound* Isaac M. Scott, *14 men going down with her.* UNIVERSITY OF DETROIT MARINE COLLECTION.

Chapter 5

The Wild 1900s
1900-1909

The initial decade of the twentieth century saw a fantastic expansion in Lake Superior shipping. Total tonnage nearly tripled over the previous decade. Substantial population growth continued in the western lake area. Traffic sources were plentiful. Lumbering was at its peak. Iron mines poured forth an increasing volume of ore. A flourishing grain trade continued. And the multifarious needs of expanding cities, towns and farms stimulated package freight. The rapid evolution in American steel shipbuilding persisted until, before the decade was out, the standard 600-footer had appeared, the epitome of lakers for the next half century. Dozens of steel giants had emerged from the shipyards as steel hulls replaced wooden hulled ships. Multi-million dollar shipping corporations pre-empted the field.

Fortunately, the number of accidents did not rise in proportion to the expanded volume of traffic. Still, there were plenty of casualties. A total of 338 vessels were in substantial trouble and the death toll soared to 251 individuals. This was the worst decennial record in Lake Superior sailing history. Eight ships went down with their entire crews and another drowned 22 of 23 crewmen. Material damage skyrocketed, too. A new steel freighter cost three to four times as much as her wooden counterpart. A minor plate-bender mishap for a steel steamer could easily bring higher repair costs than incurred by complete destruction of a wooden schooner.

For the first five years of the decade, the mishap roll was only moderately longer than that for the last five years of the nineties. Beginning with 1905, however, each

89

year was bad. And the 1905 performance was a ship owner's nightmare to say nothing of the impact on hundreds of individual sailors and their families.

1900

A winter ship's fire inaugurated the loss column for the twentieth century. On January 28, a blaze devoured the 66-foot, 36-ton wooden tug *E.P. Ferry* in Duluth Harbor, a $4,000 liability to her owner, George R. King of Duluth.

Ice held up the regular navigation season until April 24 at Duluth. Indeed, the ice pack off Whitefish Point on April 30 brought a close call to the 478-foot steel steamer *John W. Gates* and the 283-foot steel *Mariska* which banged into each other because neither could maneuver. The spanking new *Gates,* on her maiden trip out of Lorain, Ohio, needed a $10,000 shipyard visit, and the *Mariska* needed touching up to the tune of $2,500. At that, without the ice drastically reducing speed, the result of the collision might have been far worse.[1]

The first week in May struck two from the vessel roster. While downbound on May 2 with iron ore from Two Harbors to Conneaut in tow of the wooden steamer *M.M. Drake,* the 189-foot, 698-ton schooner-barge *R. Hallaran* began leaking badly on the east side of Keweenaw Point. Off Stannard Rock, it was obvious the schooner was settling. The *Drake* removed the eight-man crew, and the *Hallaran* soon foundered. Owned by Corrigan, McKinney and Company of Cleveland, she was worth $12,000.[2]

Fire claimed another victim the very next day, May 3, at Superior with the 59-foot, 28-ton wooden tug *Josie Davidson* becoming a complete ruin. She was valued in excess of $2,500.[3]

Things went smoothly for the remainder of the spring and throughout most of the summer, aside from a harbor collision at Duluth on June 10 between the steamers *Brazil* and *W.H. Gratwick* with negligible damage.

Troubles began to pick up in the fall. On September 20 a blaze at Superior did extensive harm to the relatively new 69-foot, 70-ton wooden tug *Superior,* resulting in a several thousand dollar restoration job for her owner, Captain J. Hanson.

Also September 20, a far more serious drama was being enacted 50 miles east of Port Arthur on Bachand Island at the mouth of Nipigon Strait. The 193-foot, 1,113-ton Canadian steamer *St. Andrew* was hugging the Canadian north shore at night in rough seas while traveling light to Port Arthur from Jackfish Bay where she had discharged her coal cargo. In darkness, with her compass slightly awry, she crashed into Bachand Island, running so high on a rock ledge that three of her crew were able to jump to land. As the remainder prepared to abandon ship carrying supplies of food and clothing for a possi-

ble extended ordeal, a giant wave struck the *St. Andrew* causing her to slide partially backward off the reef and list sharply. Rampaging seas carried away her pilot house, boiler house and cabin as 13 bedraggled crewmen hung onto her bulwarks. A courageous seaman, Assistant Cook George Gallagher, swam to shore at daybreak carrying a line. With the aid of the three already ashore, he rigged a hawser, and the remaining 12 came hand over hand to safety. A fisherman on the little islet found them and alerted the tug *Georgina* which took the crew back to civilization. While Captain Featherstonehaugh and the crew survived not much the worse for wear, the *St. Andrew* slid off the reef into deep water and was lost, a casualty of more than $30,000. She had been built by Louis Shikluna at St. Catharine's, Ontario, in 1885 as the *W.B. Hall* and later rebuilt as the *St. Andrew.* She was owned at the time by James Playfair and Company.[4]

The Canadian bulk freighter St. Andrew *ended her days on a lonely island in Nipigon Bay.* C. PATRICK LABADIE COLLECTION.

Another September mishap involved the Bradley steamer *City of Cleveland* which lost her propeller and had to be towed into Marquette along with her barge, *Adriatic.* The schooner *James G. Blaine* also sustained minor collision injury in the Keweenaw Waterway.

The only incident of consequence in October resembled a chain reaction automobile pileup. On October 30, as the wooden steamer *Iron King* was docking at Missabe Dock No. 1 in West Duluth, her engineer misconstrued a signal from the bridge and gave her too much power. The *King* surged ahead and slammed into the already docked steamer *City of Genoa,* which in turn rammed the steamer *Oglebay.* Bouncing off the *Genoa,* the *Iron King* crashed into the dock and knocked an ore spout down. No one was hurt, but the *King's* lunge caused $10,000 damage to the ships and the dock.[5]

The situation in November was different. Weather brought grief all over the lake on the 8th. At Good Harbor Bay, near Grand Marais, Minnesota, the little 112-foot schooner *Stafford* parted her anchor chains and went into the shallows, but was relatively unscathed. Across the lake at Eagle Harbor, a more sinister experience seemed impending. The new wooden 288-foot, 2,037-ton schooner *Abyssinia* of Captain James Davidson had broken the line of the steamer *Orinoco* and was being pushed toward the reefs off Eagle Harbor. Captain Colman of the *Abyssinia* ordered the anchors down. They dragged at first, but caught at the last moment. The powerful 90-foot, 126-ton steel tug *S.C. Schenck* was able to approach

A.C. Keating broke her line from the 268-foot wooden steamer *New York* about 20 miles west of Whitefish Point on November 8. Desperately short of bunker coal, the *New York* had to run for the Soo to refuel before attempting to recover her consort. Meanwhile, the westerly tempest took over. The ill-fated *Keating* was driven eastward more than 35 miles before being driven ashore near Coppermine Point on the Canadian side. There, she was sys-

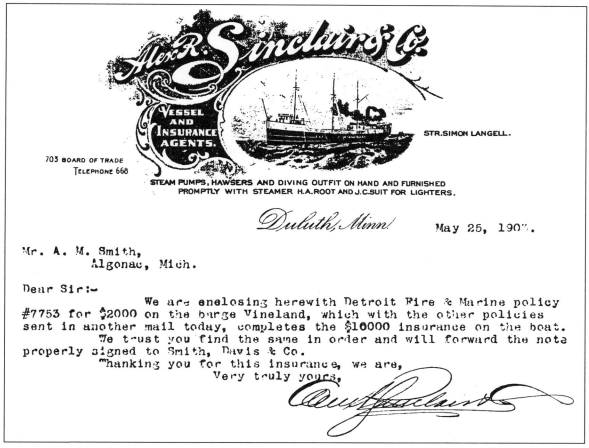

Duluth's Alex Sinclair was typical of scores of independent vessel owners in the era before large corporations. HENRY R. BARKHAUSEN COLLECTION.

her on November 10 and drag her out of danger. The U.S. Life-Saving Service from Portage had removed the crew as a precaution. As the lake calmed down, the steamer *Orinoco* returned and picked up her barge for the haul to Buffalo. The *Abyssinia* was an asset of $125,000 or more with her cargo of wheat. She needed repairs of $8,000 after this brush with disaster.[6] At the same time, the small 178-foot, 770-ton Canadian steamer *Arabian* went aground eight miles west of Whitefish Point. The U.S. Life-Saving Service, probably from Vermilion Point, took off her crew. After the seas subsided, she was found pretty much intact and still seaworthy.

One of the vessels trapped in that early November gale did not fare so well. The 138-foot, 326-ton schooner-barge

tematically demolished by the waves. Her crew reached land safely and was picked up by the *New York* about November 11 when she returned to search for the schooner. The property of Thomas Currie of Port Huron, the *Keating,* built in 1874, was adjudged a liability of $12,000.[7]

Mid-November brought the last trip for a veteran of the A. Booth & Company fishing fleet, the 64-foot, 58-ton tug *T.H. Camp,* launched in 1876 at Cape Vincent, New York. The *Camp* was en route from Ashland via Bayfield with a deck load of nearly 20 tons of supplies for the W.T. Gardner logging camp on the northern tip of Madeline Island when she foundered on November 15. She had slowed down and nearly stopped to take a sailboat in tow when the incident took place, either from her deck load shifting or as the stern wake closed quickly, pouring water onto her deck. In either event, she settled rather quickly by the stern. The *Camp*'s crew successfully abandoned her for the sailboat they had intended to assist before she went to the bottom. The *Camp* was listed at only $3,500.[8]

Also near the Apostle Islands, the 175-foot lumber hooker *Lizzie Madden* had fared better on November 18. Approaching Ashland with the schooner-barges *Mautenee* and *Noquebay* in tow, the *Madden* was discovered to be on fire. Captain M.J. Madden directed fire fighting efforts which finally extinguished the flames, despite a second outbreak. It took $2,000 to make the *Madden* ship-shape again, but the 13-year-old steamer was fortunate. Many other ships had succumbed to fire on the open water.[9]

Two other events blotted the record on November 18. An unidentified schooner reportedly sank off Munising with the tug *J.W. Ward* picking up the crew. Perhaps this was a shallow water settling. It is not reported in major casualty listings. To the east near Deer Park, a woeful incident unfolded. While not technically a shipwreck, this marine casualty cost five lives. That evening, the large 117-foot tug *Andrew J. Smith* had a line on a lighter which was beached about 15 miles east of Grand Marais while a crew of woodsmen unloaded a cargo of railroad iron. A rugged northwester blew up about 11:30 p.m., and the tug captain, desirous of getting both tug and lighter out of that dangerously exposed position, pulled the lighter off the sands and started for Grand Marais. Unknown to the tug captain, 11 woodsmen, through a mistake in signals, remained aboard the shelterless barge. Rising seas poured into the open hatches of the hapless craft, taking her cargo remnants and five of the work crew into the lake. As the tug approached Grand Marais, her captain finally discerned the surviving lumberjacks aboard the half-sinking lighter and whistled for assistance. The Grand Marais lifesavers rowed out into the storm and rescued the rest of the work crew, who were suffering from cold and exposure. The following spring, bodies of the dead appeared to the east on the beach near Big Two-Hearted River. While not a life had been sacrificed in actual shipwreck this season, five men had drowned because of a tug captain's almost incredible mistake.[10]

1901

Increasing tonnage during 1901 brought more sailings and more mishaps — more severe ones, unfortunately, as nine ships fell victim to the lake, with a death toll of 38. Ice retarded early navigation. Coastal steamers in early May faced a big backlog of freight and passengers.

The 153-foot, 500-ton wooden *Bon Voyage* had been acquired in February for Captain W.H. Singer's White Line Transportation Company. She was a trim little packet, built at Saugatuck, Michigan, in 1891 and ideal for shallow harbor work. The *Bon Voyage* cleared Duluth on May 9 for communities along the Keweenaw, laden with freight and carrying 20 passengers in addition to her 20-man crew.

About 9 p.m. the following day, the *Bon Voyage* was observed to be on fire as she approached the western entrance of Portage Lake Ship Canal. Her master, Captain John P. Foley, steered for the beach, but she grounded 1,000 feet off shore and burned to the water's edge at Redridge, eight miles southwest of the Canal. The flames cut off the ship's lifeboats from passengers and crew who congregated in the forward end of the vessel, with the exception of five women from the Altman family of Duluth who had inadvertently been locked in a stern dining room. Captain Foley distributed life jackets, and these enabled 35 of the 40 aboard to reach shore where they were quickly picked up by tugs and the Portage lifesavers who raced to the scene.

The Altman women tried to escape their fiery tomb by walking the ship's rubbing strake, but slipped off into the icy water. Only a 15-year-old girl survived by clutching a piece of wreckage until picked up by a tug.

The blaze had originated with an overheated pipe, spreading so quickly through the wooden hull and superstructure that the crew was powerless to halt the flames. Some confusion must have prevailed, as the ship's officers failed to provide for the safety of the Altmans, a fact which was bitterly condemned by Keweenaw residents.

The Portage lifesavers, after a difficult series of patrols in inclement weather, finally recovered the bodies of the four women. The women were Hebrew, and their co-religionists on the Keweenaw were extremely grateful for the lifesavers' endeavors. As a result, the Hebrews of Hancock had substantial gold medals prepared for Captain McCormick and each of his lifesaving crew, these being presented in October with appropriate ceremonies. As far as is known, this is the only instance in the Lake Superior country where a religious group has conferred a lifesaving award. The *Bon Voyage* with cargo was worth $30,000, though insured for only $13,000. She had been brought to Duluth by the Howard Transportation Company before being sold to Captain Singer.[11]

Two other mishaps in May were rather inconsequential: the steamer *Bon Ami* hitting a rock at Split Rock on May 18 and the tug *Zenith* striking a dock at Duluth on May 21.

Some unusually vicious winds on June 29 and 30, however, brought fatalities. Duluth was raked by tornadic blasts which did little injury to shipping there, but in the central lake it was another story. Caught by the maelstrom as she steamed toward Fort William with lumber for MacKenzie and Mann of the Canadian Northern Railway, the 154-foot, 472-ton wooden lumber hooker *Preston* started taking water and soon water-logged some distance off the Canadian north shore. The 262-foot steel Canadian Pacific Railroad passenger steamer *Athabasca,* under Captain McDougall, recognized the *Preston*'s plight, but to attempt the launching of a lifeboat was suicidal. Therefore, Captain McDougall brought his big ship as close as he dared, put a lifeline aboard the *Preston* by rocket and in a daring four-hour maneuver took off the 13 crewmen and Captain W.J. Harlow. There was only one fatality, Wheelsman William Eckert of Algonac, Michigan, who was inadvertently crushed against the ship's side. The *Preston* was left to sink.

Two days later, however, she was picked up by a tug 20 miles off Heron Bay in the northeastern corner of the lake and brought in to Port Caldwell before being transferred to Port Arthur. An examination by a marine surveyor disclosed such extensive damage that her owners put her up for public auction and her captain, W.J. Harlow, bid her in for $18,000, although it took nearly $20,000 to reconstruct her. She was a capacious little hooker for her length, able to carry a million board feet of lumber.[12]

On the evening of June 29, the 65-foot, 48-ton salvage tug *Fern* was anchored over the 1898 wreck of the steamer *Colorado* on the reef at Eagle River where Captain Arthur Heminger of Algonac, Michigan, and his four-man crew were retrieving scrap iron. Despite ominous skies and rising seas, Captain Heminger apparently felt secure, and the five-man crew, including the diver, stayed aboard as darkness descended. Her anchors held, but at daylight only a mast protruding out of 20 feet of water marked the *Fern*'s resting place. When calm returned, another diver searched the sunken hull, but found no trace of the crew. Her lifeboats were gone, however. It may have been that Heminger changed his mind, tried to launch a boat and he and his men were swept into the open lake and eternity.

Two days later, as the Portage lifesavers patrolled the beach looking for bodies, they came across evidence of another disaster, only a mile from the *Fern* wreck site. The hull of the little schooner-yacht *Marguerite* lay bottom up on the beach. She had taken two Houghton men, Will Brandon and A. Hull, to Isle Royale on an agate hunt before being caught by the tempest. Initially, the agate hunters were given up for dead, but good fortune had smiled on them. They clung to their capsized craft until the new 322-foot steel steamer *Yuma* came along. The big ship hove to, and *Yuma* crewmen dragged the Houghton men aboard. Brandon and Hull were landed safely in Two Harbors when the ore carrier docked.[13]

The stormy conditions of June 29 and 30 were no time for a ship fire, though that was the fate of the 251-foot, 1,702-ton wooden steamer *Avon.* Having mastered the torturous waves on a run from Duluth to Buffalo with flour and general merchandise, the *Avon* had almost reached the Soo locks when, off Pointe Aux Pins, she was found to be on fire. The steamers *Manitoba* and *Victory*

stood by, and tugs rushed to push her into shallow water where the flames did their dirty job before she went under. The 24-year-old vessel, belonging to the Union Transit Company of Buffalo, was recovered and rebuilt with slightly less capacity. Rebuilding costs supposedly exceeded $30,000.[14]

A slight scrape between the steamer *W.E. Reis* and barge *Maia* on July 5 off Two Harbors was inconsequential. The 150-foot U.S. Lighthouse Tender *Marigold* ran into difficulty in the early morning hours of July 22 when she ran onto a sand bar near the Chequamegon Point Lighthouse, breaking off a couple of blades on her propeller. She was able to release herself, moving into port at much reduced speed.[15]

A September gale took the powerful steel steamer Hudson *in 1901 not far from Eagle Harbor.* MILWAUKEE PUBLIC LIBRARY COLLECTION.

A thick fog on Whitefish Bay the morning of July 29 brought fatal results as the Northern Steamship Company's 300-foot steel steamer *Northern Queen* missed the 340-foot steel steamship *Pathfinder* but sliced into her barge, the steel whaleback *Sagamore* of the Pickands-Mather Company. Hit on the starboard side near the after turret, the ore laden *Sagamore* slipped to the bottom in 72 feet of water off Point Iroquois, taking Captain Joiner of Henderson, New York, and two other men with her. She was a $90,000 casualty. Built at the Head of the Lakes in 1892, the 308-foot, 1,601-ton *Sagamore* was the second whaleback barge to meet her end within a year. Poor visibility brought grief to another whaleback barge on the same day, the *131,* which stranded when downbound with ore in tow of the steamer *German.* Duluth salvor Captain Kidd and the tugs *General* and *S.C. Schenck* had her off in a couple days, costs being minimal.[16]

Dirty weather at the end of August bedeviled two lumber carriers. Off Sand Island, the ancient 39-year-old 160-foot schooner-barge *Oneonta* sprang a bad leak, and her towing steamer, the 135-foot *Alvin A. Turner,* coaxed her across the lake to Two Harbors where she sank to her bulwarks with only her cargo keeping her afloat. Little injury resulted.

Another hooker, the 205-foot, 781-ton wooden steamer *Eliza H. Strong,* a two-year-old 510-horsepower vessel, took such a terrible mauling 16 miles southeast of Stannard Rock that her crew abandoned her, climbing aboard one of her barges. When seen by the 268-foot wooden steamer *New York,* which was big enough to breast the storm, the *Strong* was gradually breaking up and rolling fiercely, having lost her deck load and become

trophe was substantiated. At 10 a.m. on September 16 the keepers at Eagle River Light had observed a sizable twin-stacked steamer dead in the water, listing badly. The unidentified steamer suddenly rolled over and sank stern first as they watched. Another steamer was seen in the area and, as no yawl boats were sighted, the keepers first thought a passing steamer may have picked up the crew. Unfortunately, this was not the case. As the lake quieted,

Nineteen-year-old M.M. Drake *was the victim of an October 1901 storm which also claimed her consort.* C. PATRICK LABADIE COLLECTION.

badly waterlogged. Fortuitously, a tug out of Munising located the derelict and managed to get a line aboard and drag her into that harbor before the lake claimed her. A sizable reconstruction job costing $15,000 was necessary. More than two weeks later, her wreckage and deck load were pitched ashore at Grand Marais, Michigan, setting off an erroneous report that another ship had gone down.[17] The same tough sailing also smashed a scow at Houghton and a lighter at Marquette, low value items.

A whooping pre-equinoctial gale ravaged the central and eastern lake for several days beginning on September 16. Shipping came to a standstill. Telegraph and telephone wires were downed along the Keweenaw country. Unconfirmed rumors filtered into Houghton that a large ship had gone down off Eagle Harbor while debris cluttered the beaches at Grand Marais, Michigan. For a while, as no new information came in, the sinking story was discounted. Yet, by September 19, when communications were restored to the Keweenaw, the ugly fact of a major catas-

fishing boats put out and sighted wreckage all the way from Eagle River to Copper Harbor, a stretch of 25 miles. The black and yellow posts seen in the debris, as well as the observers' description, seemed to indicate the victim was the package freighter *Hudson* of the Western Transit Line, which had cleared Duluth on September 15 with a cargo of 69,000 bushels of wheat and 22,500 bushels of flax. They were correct. On September 21, a cabin and a yawl boat came ashore near Eagle River and 75 miles to the east, near Stannard Rock, a pilothouse was picked up by the steamer *J.C. Ford.* Still in the pilothouse was the body of Wheelsman Sherman G. Brooks wearing a life preserver stenciled "S.S. *Hudson*." The entire crew of 24 had gone down with their ship.

The *Hudson* was a 288-foot, 2,294-ton steel vessel built in 1888 at Wyandotte and one of the fastest ships on the lakes. Her master was Captain Angus J. McDonald, and Moses Trouton was her chief engineer. Most of her crew was from the Buffalo area. The ship was worth about

$200,000 and the grain another $95,000, making this one of the most expensive accidents to date. Insurance of $211,000 was carried. Quantities of wreckage were tossed up for days along the Keweenaw coast — yawls, hatch covers, a cabin, spars, a good deal of flour. Still, nothing to indicate the cause of the sinking. Shipping men presumed that her grain cargo shifted, but an engine breakdown might also have contributed to or caused the loss.

The ship which the lighthouse keepers had seen near the foundering *Hudson* proved to be the 263-foot wooden steamer *John M. Nicol* of the Union Transit company out of Buffalo under Captain McLean. Captain McLean revealed that he had approached as close as he dared to the *Hudson,* but could see only four persons on deck. Therefore, he concluded that her crew wasn't too worried about their predicament and, with his own ship taking a battering, he had better pull away. Indeed, the *Nicol* had to be dry-docked for extensive weather damage repairs. Since there was apparently no attempt to launch lifeboats, vessel men supposed that most of the *Hudson* crew may have been in the hold trying to trim the shifted grain cargo and were trapped when the ship rolled over. This supposition is reinforced by the fact that despite an intensive water and shoreline search of three months by the Western Transit Company, only seven bodies were recovered, some well down the east side of Keweenaw Point. Why the *Hudson* succumbed when many other less substantial ships came through remains one of the mysteries of the lake.[18]

While the *Hudson* story was being unraveled, a fine wooden steamer was being taken by fire to the west on September 20. The 282-foot, 1,848-ton *Fedora,* owned by Captain W. Brown of Cleveland, was en route light from Duluth to Ashland when a lamp exploded in the engine room while the vessel was between Red Cliff and Basswood Island near Bayfield. She was going full throttle, and the fire got out of control quickly, forcing the engineer to abandon his post before any effective fire fighting effort could begin. Captain F.A. Fink beached her near Chicago Creek while going an estimated 12 miles per hour, allowing himself, his crew and two passengers to escape in the lifeboats. The 12-year-old *Fedora* was a $90,000 loss.[19] Her boilers and machinery were salvaged, and her hull now rests in just 10 feet of water.[20]

Cantankerous Lake Superior made a bid for more lives on September 24 near Two Islands on the Minnesota north shore. A scow carrying 12 men in tow of the tug *Annie L. Smith* suddenly settled, but Captain Eli Jacques of the *Smith* rescued all. The next day in Portage Lake Ship Canal, the schooner *Paisley* needed minor repairs when a steel rail in her cargo pierced her wooden hull.

More wild water on October 2, nevertheless, produced a unique situation, a double sinking — both towing steamer and barge. Taking a wicked pasting off Vermilion Point, the 19-year-old 201-foot, 1,102-ton wooden steamer *M.M.*

Drake was pushing along with her 27-year-old 213-foot, 1,056-ton schooner-barge *Michigan* in tow. Suddenly, Captain John Arthur Jr. of the *Michigan* signaled that the schooner was filling. Captain J.W. Nicholson of the *Drake* dropped the towline, maneuvered alongside the stricken *Michigan* and took off her crew. But a towering wave drove the ships together, the *Drake* losing her smokestack and having her cabin bashed in. Then the *Drake* lost headway and began to take water. Captain Nicholson flew distress signals. Fortunately, two strong steel ships, the 300-foot *Northern Wave* and the new 406-foot *Crescent City,* were nearby and steamed to the rescue. The *Northern Wave* took off four of those aboard the *Drake* and the *Crescent City,* the rest. However, when the survivors were counted at the Soo, it was found that Harry Brown, cook of the *Michigan,* was missing. He had either gone overboard or had remained with the *Drake* when she took the final plunge. The *Drake* was a liability of $35,000, the older *Michigan,* $19,000. Both belonged to Captain James Corrigan of Cleveland.[21]

High winds and a snowstorm on October 19 brought hard work and a lot of excitement for the Crisp Point lifesavers. To the west of Crisp Point, lifesavers sighted a substantial schooner heading for destruction in the surf. They launched and, after a miserable row, pulled alongside the 204-foot, 649-ton lumber schooner *Montgomery* which was a water-logged, deserted derelict, her crew taken off earlier by the towing steamer *Leland* when the schooner became unmanageable. Lifesavers boarded her, but were unable to release her anchors. There was nothing else they could do but watch her pile into the sands three miles west of Crisp Point where the raging surf soon did its work. The 45-year-old *Montgomery* was done for, broken in two and beaten to pieces, a loss with cargo of $17,000. Lifesavers from both Crisp Point and Two-Hearted River assisted in stripping the hulk as the storm died. They stacked what they could recover of the lumber cargo on the beach for reclamation.[22]

The remainder of the season was relatively uneventful with but one exception. A Portage Lake Ship Canal collision on October 21 between the schooner-barge *B.W. Parker,* tow of the steamer *A.A. Parker* and the schooner *Peshtigo* resulted in a shipyard bill of $8,000 for the *Peshtigo.*

Several days of truly nasty gales and snow in mid-November caused widespread difficulties, mostly minor, though one particularly dangerous. The schooner *Connelly Brothers,* which had gone ashore at Sand Point, Munising, on November 12, was released virtually unharmed, while the 122-foot, 183-ton scow *D.H. Keyes,* which broke away from the tug *Mystic,* found a resting place on Fourteen Mile Point near Ontonagon. She was badly broken and adjudged a $5,000 casualty.

So boisterous were the seas on November 15 north of Marquette that the brand new 461-foot, 5,054-ton steel steamer *Harvard,* a 1,800-horsepower vessel, was unable to hold her barges. Whaleback barge *127* was retrieved by the tug *S.C. Schenck* and brought to Marquette, but the giant steel barge *John Smeaton,* a two-year-old 458-foot,

Big barge Mary N. Bourke *went on to survive the Carp River beaching in the spring of 1902.* GREAT LAKES HISTORICAL SOCIETY

5,049-ton ship, was hurled on the rocks east of the Rock River near Au Train, southeast of Marquette. The Marquette lifesavers went to the scene. However, the nine-man *Smeaton* crew was quite safe. Their ship, one of the largest barges on the lakes, nestled in four feet of water after slamming over rocks and boulders for hundreds of yards. Her owners, the Pittsburgh Steamship Company, were anxious for a while about regaining their $200,000 investment, as their ship seemed to defy salvage efforts. Finally, the famed father-son salvage team, captains James and Tom Reid of Sarnia, was brought to the scene in late November. By the ingenious application of compressed air, the Reid crew had her off in three days for a trip to the shipyard at Superior and a $50,000 rebuilding job. The Reids also received a fine fee, one rumor saying 40 percent of the ship's value.[23]

A fire at Ashland on November 19 required a $15,000 renovation effort on the 88-foot, 94-ton steel tug *Keystone.* Also, a small patching job on the lumber hooker *Adella Shores* had her afloat on December 3 and at dock in West Superior. She had taken a log through her hull in Duluth Harbor.[24]

1902

One of the earliest navigation seasons in years greeted mariners in 1902, presaging another new record for total tonnage, 25 percent ahead of 1901. Needless to say, some April difficulties occurred. The Grand Marais lifesavers received a workout from April 9 to 11 with the steel steamer *Crescent City* and her consort, whaleback barge *130,* astride Au Sable Reef, but the two came off with sur-

prisingly little injury. The 64-foot, 48-ton passenger and towing tug *Fashion* had some problems in Ashland Harbor when she dropped her propeller and damaged her shaft in mid-April, but was soon back in service.[25]

Most early season excitement came in a rowdy northeast snowstorm at Marquette on April 26 when the lumber steamer *Schoolcraft* struggled with her consorts to reach the sanctuary of the breakwater. The steamer and the schooner-barge *George Nester* made it. The towline broke, however, leaving the 219-foot, 920-ton schooner-barge *Mary N. Bourke* at the mercy of the seas which hurled her on the rocks at the mouth of Carp River in Marquette. Alerted at 4:25 a.m., the Marquette lifesavers rowed through the surf and brought to safety the *Bourke*'s crew of eight. Although it was feared at first that the *Bourke* had broken in two, a wrecking company released her in a few days with steam pumps controlling her leaks. She was able to reload her lumber cargo and continue to the east a week later with an $8,000 repair charge.[26]

At Stoney Point, 17 miles northeast of Duluth, the 291-foot wooden steamer *Tampa* and her 290-foot schooner-barge *Aurora* were on the shore April 29 due to compass deviation, a familiar problem in that area. Again, several days of effort by wreckers got them free, the *Aurora* in good shape and the *Tampa* in need of $10,000 in shipyard work. She had just been rebuilt in 1899 after her smashing on the reef at Silver Bay in 1898.[27]

A fluke mishap off Duluth on the evening of May 2 brought the year's first fatality when scow *No. 20* suddenly flipped over while dumping mud a mile off Minnesota Point, drowning one of her crewmen. Lifesavers searched for the missing man to no avail. Then on May 13, Captain Pasque ran the 47-foot tug *Eliza* onto a reef on the east side of Sand Island while picking up fish, damaging her propeller and losing her rudder.[28] The rest of the month was tame, the steel coastal steamer *America* bouncing off a pier at Duluth and the steel ore carrier *Wawatam* tearing a rudder at Marquette, both slight repair items. A master's embarrassment and modest bottom renovation was the lot of the new 430-foot steel steamer *Mataafa* which slid up on Knife Island Reef in a June 2 fog, compass error once again the culprit.

The relatively safe performance in the first two months of sailing was marred on June 7 by an unprecedented event, a collision off the Duluth Ship Canal in which two ships were sunk and nine men drowned. On a clear, calm late spring morning the 288-foot, 2,073-ton wooden steamer *George G. Hadley* approached the Duluth Ship Canal inbound, as the 308-foot, 1,713-ton steel whaleback steamer *Thomas Wilson* came through the canal outbound. Less than a half mile off the pierhead, the *Hadley* was hailed by the tug *Annie L. Smith* and instructed to enter the Superior Harbor for discharge of her coal cargo, as the Duluth coal docks were full. Captain Mike Fitzgerald of the *Hadley,* who was on the starboard side of his vessel talking to the tug captain, immediately ordered a left turn, since he had little turning room for the run to Superior. He failed to notice the *Wilson* bearing down on him. He apparently had changed course before blowing the required whistle signals. Hence, Captain Cameron of the *Wilson* was in a quandary. If he continued on course, he may or may not avoid the *Hadley*. If he swung to port, there was a chance of stranding. Therefore, he ordered a starboard turn to deep water, the same direction as the *Hadley*'s maneuver. The turning arcs of the ships intersected and the *Hadley* struck the *Wilson* a wicked blow just forward of the after hatch, the wooden prow cutting sharply into the whaleback's steel hull. While the *Hadley* recoiled from the impact, dead in the water, the *Wilson* rolled sharply to port, righted, skidded along a few more yards, quickly settling at the bow and finally tossed her stern high in the air while diving for the bottom with her propeller still spinning. All of this occurred within three minutes after the crash. As their ship began to founder, the *Wilson* crew raced top-side, frantically trying to launch lifeboats and life rafts. But there was no time. All leaped overboard or went into the water as the steamer went under, nine men being dragged down. Eleven others grasped life preservers thrown from the *Hadley* or clutched pieces of debris and were rescued by the *Hadley* and the tug *Annie L. Smith*. The U.S. Life-Saving lookout had witnessed the collision at 10:27 a.m., had sounded the alarm and the lifesavers put out in the surfboat, reaching the site a mile away in only 13 minutes. But no more survivors could be found.

After bringing the *Wilson*'s people aboard, the *Hadley* tried to resume her trip to Superior. But Captain Mike Fitzgerald learned she was leaking badly. Personally taking the wheel, he nursed her toward the sandy beach just south of the Duluth Ship Canal where she settled to the bottom with her deck houses above water and everybody safe. Salvors labored for two weeks in inclement weather before delivering the *Hadley* to the shipyard in Superior.

Divers investigating the *Wilson* hull discovered she had broken in two when she hit the floor of the lake. Also, her iron ore cargo would cause serious problems in raising her. She still lies where she sank, a mecca for scuba divers, though the hard-hat divers did blast off her stack and pilothouse to remove a menace to navigation.

The financial ramifications were sizable, salvors billing the *Hadley* for $14,000 to raise her; shipyard costs added another $20,000 for her repairs. The *Wilson* was a total loss of $207,000.

The Duluth inspectors of the U.S. Steamboat Inspection Service, after holding hearings on the disaster, took disciplinary action against the two captains, Captain Fitzgerald suffering revocation of license for his faulty turn and Captain Cameron receiving a 60-day suspension for failing to reduce speed and sound adequate warning signals. The 73-year-old Fitzgerald, captain for 40 years

without a significant mishap, was later allowed to take a new examination for restoration of master's papers, in view of his excellent record.[29]

Most of the summer passed serenely. The new passenger steamer *Iroquois* endured an inconvenient but innocuous stranding July 2 at Tiger Island on the Port Arthur run, and the 24-year-old 75-foot, 40-ton wooden steamer *Northern Belle* sank on the open lake August 10, her worth not reported. Another harbor death at Duluth occurred on September 1 as the 67-foot, 64-ton iron tug *M.D. Carrington* capsized while trying to tow the 405-foot steel steamer *James Watt*. Her engineer was drowned, his body being recovered by Duluth lifesavers. The tug was raised. Fire on September 8 at Duluth did light damage to the little ferry steamer *Belle*, while a moderate storm on September 11 left the schooner-barge *John B. Wilbor* aground at the Portage Lake Ship Canal and sent the steamer *City of Rome* to the beach in Bete Grise Bay with a bad leak. Salvage costs for the two aggregated $6,000.[30]

The George G. Hadley *barely made it to shallow water before sinking following a collision with the* Wilson. ST. LOUIS COUNTY HISTORICAL SOCIETY COLLECTION.

Autumn was something else! Ten ships came to grief, five were destroyed and 21 men sailed their last. Wild seas caught the 430-foot, 4,951-ton steel steamer *Maunaloa* and her 292-foot, 1,310-ton whaleback barge *129* about 30 miles northwest of Vermilion Point. Both had ore cargoes. The towing hawser separated in high waves, and the *Maunaloa* maneuvered to regain her barge. Rough water slapped the two together, the port anchor of the steamer raking the side of the *129*. The barge took water rapidly, but the *Maunaloa* successfully removed Captain Bailey and the crew as the *129* went to the bottom, an $80,000 liability. She was an 1893 product of Captain Alexander McDougall's American Steel Barge Company in Superior, Wisconsin.[31]

Vermilion Point was the location of a noted rescue on October 24. The diminutive 72-foot, 39-ton schooner *W.T. Chappell* of Port Huron was having a miserable time as she worked her way eastward with a cargo of wood. The Vermilion Point lifesavers were watching her about 1 p.m. in a violent westerly gale four and a half miles northeast of Vermilion Point. She suddenly went down as they watched. The keeper ordered out the lifeboat and after two hours of launching and rowing, the lifesavers approached the site of the sinking. The main mast of the schooner still stood, and clinging to it were Captain Jones and his solitary crewman. The keeper brought the lifeboat up to the precarious perch by delicate boat-handling so that the two sailors could be taken aboard. By now the waves were so high that a return to base was out of the question for the lifesavers. They rowed eight miles to Whitefish Point, swung into the sheltered waters and landed at the lighthouse dock, taking shelter with the rescued sailors for the night in the lighthouse quarters. The miniature schooner was a liability of less than a thousand dollars, but two men had been saved in another classic lifesaving endeavor.[32]

The Canadian Bannockburn *vanished on Lake Superior carrying a crew of 20. Her fate was never determined.* UNIVERSITY OF DETROIT MARINE COLLECTION.

In the narrow confines of the Portage Lake Ship Canal on October 26, the wooden steamer *George Spencer* scraped the schooner-barge *Pennington,* towed by the steamer *John Eddy,* with the *Spencer* only slightly the worse for wear. The seeming jinx on the 68-foot, 59-ton iron tug *Record* struck again early in the morning of November 7, the tug being rammed and sunk by the 414-foot steel steamer *Bransford* of the Hawgood fleet which mysteriously refused to obey her helm. All five of the tugboat crew were taken from the water alive, though badly scalded. Fireman McAllister of the *Record* died eight days later. A $7,000 expenditure raised and reconditioned the *Record* once again. The tug had been lying off the Great Northern docks in Superior when run down by the large steel ore carrier.[33]

Hardly two hours out of Duluth, the 209-foot, 1,189-ton wooden steamer *Robert Wallace* suffered an unusual mishap on November 17 which proved to be her last. Lad-

en with iron ore and having the 218-foot schooner-barge *Ashland* in tow, the *Wallace* ripped out her stern post and stern pipe about 13 miles southeast of Two Harbors. Captain J.W. Nicholson had felt a heavy vibration through the ship about 11 p.m.; minutes later, the second mate brought word that water was pouring into the stern. As the seas were calm, the captain ordered the crew into the yawl for a short jaunt to the *Ashland,* and the 20-year-old *Wallace* slid beneath the waves about midnight. The *Ashland* burned distress flares which were answered by the railroad tug *Edna G* of Two Harbors which brought the barge safely to that port. As the *Wallace* went under, her pilothouse popped free so gently that the lanterns on her Texas house were still burning when found by Captain Howard of the steamer *Argo* the following morning. Owned by Corrigan, McKinney and Company of Cleveland, the *Robert Wallace* was worth $40,000 and insured for $25,000.[34]

Only four days afterward came a happening which still has sailors and marine historians guessing. The 245-foot, 1,620-ton Canadian steamer *Bannockburn* of the Montreal Transportation Company was British-built, only nine years old, actually designed for ocean work. She cleared Port Arthur on November 21 under Captain George Wood of Port Dalhousie, Ontario, with 85,000 bushels of wheat consigned to Midland. She had run aground while leaving the harbor, but got off with no apparent injury. That night and for several days, a terrific storm riled central Lake Superior. Two Canadian ships, the passenger steamer *Huronic* and the canaller *Algonquin,* reported sighting the *Bannockburn* during the night, the latter about 60 miles southeast of Passage Island and northeast of Keweenaw Point. That is the extent of positive information. The *Bannockburn* did not arrive at the Soo on November 22, nor did she ever show.

Four days after her last sighting, the American steamer *Frank Rockefeller* discovered unidentified wreckage off Stannard Rock, but the seas were too high to permit recovery of the flotsam. Rumors were abroad that the *Bannockburn* was stranded on the eastern or northern Canadian shores. The tugs *Boynton* and *Favorite* from the Soo, however, scoured these areas with no result. Ten days after her sailing, the *Bannockburn* was given up for lost with the 20 men aboard her. In the second week of December, fragments of wreckage began appearing on the beaches of Grand Marais, Michigan, and Captain Ben Trudell of the lifesaving station brought in a life jacket stenciled "*Bannockburn,*" which seemed to have been around a body.

To this day, no clue exists as to what sank this fine ocean-going vessel, although numerous theories have been advanced. Some think she may have hit Superior Shoal, though she would have been well off course to have done so. Another theory stresses hull failure, with her engines being driven through her bottom. Still another holds that a ship's hull plate found in the Canadian Soo locks was the *Bannockburn*'s and that leakage ultimately got the better of her. Hardly another shipwreck, with the notable exception of the *Edmund Fitzgerald,* has attracted the speculation accorded the *Bannockburn.* Lake Superior alone knows. She was a liability of around $200,000 including cargo.[35]

A howling gale trapped a late season lumber tow on November 29 and the morning of November 30. The 184-foot, 763-ton wooden lumber steamer *Charles Hebard,* with the schooner-barges *Aloha, J.A. Francomb* and *G.H. Warmington,* was northwest of Whitefish Point when the lines separated and the quartet of vessels were each on their own. The barges reached the comparative safety of the Canadian east shore the following morning. The *Hebard* was not as fortunate, though, being driven on the rocks at Point Mamainse, Ontario, where she was pummeled frightfully. When viewed by the horrified crew of the *Francomb* which sailed along the shore after daylight, the *Hebard* was showing only her pilothouse and smokestack in the slashing surf, and even these had disappeared by 8:30 a.m. as her debris littered the shoreline. Hailing the passing steamer *Ossifrage,* en route from Michipicoten to the Soo, the *Francomb*'s captain put his wife aboard the steamer with instructions to take the news of the calamity to the Soo. Indeed, Captain George Ryan and his crew of 13 must be dead.

Actually, the outcome was far more favorable. The *Hebard* had gone on in the dark of night close to the shoreline cabin of a settler named Oscar Carlson, the only habitation for 15 miles. At daybreak, despite the tossing combers, mates Correll and Jackson had taken a yawl to land with a line. While they suffered cuts and bruises in landing and climbing the rocky littoral, they reached solid land. Then, with the aid of Carlson and his sons, they rigged a "bosun's chair," taking off the remaining 12, including the woman cook, Jennie Barnes. Captain Ryan, the last to leave the ship, had the most miserable trip of all, the lines tangling and dunking him in the icy waters before he was pulled out. The Carlsons took the castaways into their home, warmed, dried and fed them, very likely saving the crew from death by exposure on a cold, inhospitable portion of the Lake Superior coast. The *Hebard* was one of the newer lumber hookers, built at Detroit in 1888 and owned by Holland and Graves of Buffalo. She had a price tag of $40,000.[36]

1903

A traffic drop was evident in shipping for the first time in 10 years, the 1903 totals slightly below the peak of 1902. The list of difficulties was likewise shorter, although eight joined the ghost fleet. A late April snowstorm on Minnesota's north shore produced the first ac-

cident of the season. The 153-foot, 198-ton wooden steamer *Belle P. Cross* crashed ashore just south of the mouth of Gooseberry River. The *Cross,* loaded with railroad ties and timber, was en route from Two Islands to

Lumber hooker Charles Hebard *was dashed to pieces on rocks at Mamainse, Ontario.* MILWAUKEE PUBLIC LIBRARY COLLECTION.

Duluth when the gale and snow got the better of her. The crew made land, only a stone's throw away, as the rollers systematically tore the 34-year-old steamer apart. She belonged to the Clow and Nicholson Transportation Company of Duluth, under charter to the Coolidge Supply Company of Minneapolis. She had just been rebuilt after a fire in 1901. Salvors went to her immediately and gleaned what they could, recovering her boilers, engine, pumps, anchors and chains, but the April 29 stranding had made her a $12,000 liability.[37]

Insurance men winced at what a simple grounding of a new steel freighter might cost them after the 380-foot, 4,037-ton *George B. Leonard* sliced into Vidal Shoal near the Soo on May 4. This powerful 1,800-horsepower vessel, less than a year old, was in no danger. Captain Loftus and his crew were safe, but taking her off and rehabilitating the hull cost a hefty $27,000.[38]

On May 9 near Grand Marais, Michigan, the lifesavers prevented a serious incident by rowing out to the waterlogged schooner *Lizzie A. Law* off Au Sable Point and removing her exhausted, exposure-beaten crew. The lifesavers repaired the schooner's broken-down steam pump and cleared the water from her hold, then brought the crew back on board. Her anchor chains held in the moderately rough water until a steamer was able to tow her to the lee of Grand Island. Injury to the schooner and her coal cargo was light. Yet, without the availability of lifesavers, the *Law* might have suffered the fate of others in that dangerous section of the lake.[39]

Foggy conditions in Duluth-Superior Harbor on May 18 contributed to a fatal mishap. As the 69-foot, 57-ton wooden tug *Edward Gillen* was working near the Superior Entry about 7 a.m., she was run down and nearly cut

A.A. Parker *opened her seams and went down four miles off Grand Marais, Michigan.* C. PATRICK LABADIE COLLECTION.

in two by the Pittsburgh Steamship Company's large 430-foot steel steamer *Maunaloa* under Captain C.H. Cummings. Captain William Hutchins and most of the tug crew were picked up, though J. Landercook, the cook, drowned. Badly battered as she was, the *Gillen* was retrieved and rebuilt at a cost of $6,000.[40]

Sailing business was rather routine throughout most of the summer. The coastal packet *Bon Ami* received little injury in a south shore grounding on July 4. A severe leak at Two Harbors on July 25 caused the 29-year-old wooden steamer *V. Swain* to settle with accompanying raising and renovation expenditures of $12,000. The 254-foot composite ship *E.M. Peck* hit the sands off Whitefish Point on August 6, needing nominal repairs. A fire in Quebec Harbor at Michipicoten Island on August 18 ended the career of the 30-year-old 149-foot, 329-ton wooden steamer *Hiram R. Dixon,* formerly of the Booth Packing Company fleet. She must have been worth $20,000 to her new Canadian owner, William Robinson.[41]

The violent storms which badger mariners in the third week of each September were on schedule again this year. For three days, from September 17 through 19, the lake was riled horribly. The treacherous waters claimed two ships and nearly caught a third. Sailing from Ashland into the gale were the 270-foot wooden steamer *Volunteer* and her consort, the 206-foot, 777-ton *Moonlight.* They didn't get very far out of Ashland. Off Michigan Island, the 29-year-old *Moonlight* began taking water rapidly. After the *Volunteer* removed her crew, the *Moonlight* slid to the bottom about 12 miles off Michigan Island carrying 1,400 tons of iron ore, a liability of more than $12,000. She was owned by J.C. Gilchrist of Cleveland.[42]

The following day, September 18, and somewhat to the northeast, the 191-foot wooden lumber hooker *H.D. Coffinberry* was meanly tossed about with her schooner-barge, the 32-year-old 182-foot, 580-ton *Angus Smith,* faring worse. She was leaking. Ever so slowly the steamer inched her tow toward the Portage Lake Ship Canal which they neared on the early morning of September 19. Fearing that his water-logged barge, drawing more water than she should, might be grounded off the entry, the *Coffinberry*'s captain signaled for the Portage lifesavers. They rushed to the scene, assisted in getting the barge into the piers and in pumping her out. The operation required several thousand dollars but saved the schooner and her valuable lumber cargo from the clutches of the lake.[43]

Fighting her way through the same mid-September gale downbound with iron ore from Superior was the 247-foot, 1,660-ton wooden steamer *A.A. Parker,* formerly the *Kasota.* East of Keweenaw Point, Captain White of the *Parker* found a roaring southwester. The steamer began to pitch and roll miserably, straining her seams. Water began coming in. The captain set course for Whitefish Point, but before long it was obvious the ship would never last. About noon on September 19, when they were 10 miles off Grand Marais, Captain White ordered the ship to head toward shore and sounded distress signals. The lifesaving lookout sighted her, noting the puffs of steam from the stacks even though he couldn't hear a sound with the howling winds blowing away from him. He knew the vessel was in trouble. He called Captain Ben Trudell who ordered the surfboat launched. With the wind behind them, the lifesaving crew was alongside the *Parker,* now four miles off shore, in 50 minutes. One look at her told Captain Trudell that she could founder momentarily. There was little time. Realizing that he could not carry her entire crew of 17 in such seas, he instructed the crew to launch their own yawl, placing nine men in that and taking the remainder in his own boat. Now came the excruciating task of rowing against the seas. They labored for three hours and still were three-quarters of a mile from the harbor, whereupon the tug *E.M.B.A.* came out and brought in the ship's yawl to Grand Marais. The lifesavers stuck it out for another half mile when, nearly exhausted, they were taken in tow by the tug *J.W. Westcott* and hauled in. Not long after she was abandoned, the *Parker* slipped under, bow first, a $75,000 casualty. The 20-year-old vessel belonged to J.C. Gilchrist of Cleveland.[44]

Another brand new steel steamer had a return date with the shipyard on October 3. The year-old 468-foot *D.G. Kerr* slammed into the entry pier of the Duluth Ship Canal, necessitating a $20,000 repair job.

The second two weeks of October, nevertheless, brought worse luck, four ships joining the vanquished. Two of these also belonged to the Gilchrist fleet. The 235-foot, 1,343-ton wooden steamer *Marquette* under Captain Charles Caughell cleared Ashland with more than

2,000 tons of iron ore on October 14. Emerging from Chequamegon Bay in a calm sea, she began leaking at the head. Damage control efforts were too little, too late for the 22-year-old hull. She began to take water so fast that

The 12-year-old William F. Sauber *foundered before reaching safety.* GREAT LAKES HISTORICAL SOCIETY COLLECTION.

the pumps could not handle it. She plunged to the bottom approximately five miles off Michigan Island, going down head first, popping off her hatch covers as she sank, twisting and breaking the hull just aft of the forward cabins. The crew took to the lifeboats and rowed to Madeline Island where they were picked up over the next couple of days by a passing steamer and small boats. Her wreckage drifted over to the Michigan coast at Black River a few days later, prompting reports of another wreck. The *Marquette* was valued at $40,000 by her owner J.C. Gilchrist.[45]

Only a week later, a tempest with heavy snow assaulted the eastern lake. Caught off Grand Marais, Michigan, the Alger-Smith Company's 209-foot lumber hooker *Gettysburg* with the schooner-barges *Buffalo* and *Saveland* in tow was forced to make a dash for that harbor of refuge. The *Gettysburg* and *Buffalo* slipped through the Grand Marais piers. When the *Saveland* came up to the pierhead, however, the line snapped. Captain McDermott dropped his anchors but they dragged, and the *Saveland* was swept eastward into an old pile dike where she was impaled. The Grand Marais lifesavers pushed a surfboat around the dike in a daring rescue endeavor and took off the seven-man crew. Salvors quickly went to work on the 195-foot, 689-ton *Saveland,* but she was too badly battered, eventually breaking up, a $15,000 loss. Built in Milwaukee, she was 30 years old.[46]

The weather blasts scored a double on October 26. Downbound from Ashland with iron ore, the 291-foot, 2,053-ton wooden steamer *William F. Sauber* sailed into a nasty storm off Keweenaw Point. Seas were terrible all day long on October 25. Abreast of Manitou Island, the *Sauber* started to leak. As the hours went by, the water in her hold kept rising and Captain W.E. Morse flew dis-

tress signals. Coming on the scene was the large 371-foot steel steamer *Yale* under Captain Jackson. Positioning his more powerful ship windward of the stricken *Sauber,* Jackson escorted the settling wooden vessel toward the safety of Whitefish Bay. The two steamers crept toward shelter for the remainder of the day and into the night. The gap was closing.

By 11 p.m., with sanctuary only a few miles away, it was evident that the *Sauber* probably couldn't make it. Captain Jackson brought the *Yale* as close alongside as he dared, and with a line and yawl the *Sauber* crew began abandoning ship, a four-hour process. Oiler Frank Robinson apparently was crushed between the yawl and the *Yale,* losing his hold on a line and dropping to his death in the frigid water. Still clinging to the hope that his ship might make those few miles to Whitefish Point, Captain Morse declined a seat in the lifeboat and remained aboard the *Sauber.* Shortly afterward, the icy waters touched her red hot boilers and she blew up, disappearing immediately. The captain was heard calling from the wreckage, and a line was tossed to him, but, weakened by the ordeal, he could not hang on to it. The *Yale* brought the 15 survivors to the Soo. A fairly new wooden vessel, built at West Bay city in 1891, she was worth $80,000 to her owner, W.D. Becker of Cleveland.[47]

The big Manhattan *was burned to a worthless hulk in October 1903.* MILWAUKEE PUBLIC LIBRARY COLLECTION.

Another vessel also perished at the threshold of safety on October 26. The 252-foot, 1,545-ton wooden steamer *Manhattan* downbound with wheat from Duluth-Superior was enduring such a mauling east of Keweenaw Point that her captain turned south and headed for the lee of Grand Island. He reached the protection of the island all right, but his wheel chains suddenly broke and the *Manhattan* piled on a reef. Then fire broke out. The ship was soon sheathed in flames. The crew hastily took to the boats, seeking the safety of Grand Island. After the upper works burned off, the *Manhattan* floated free and was driven by the winds on Sand Point near Munising where she remained a burned-out ruined hulk. Wreckers recovered some equipment a year and a half later, though the *Manhattan* was done for. With the cargo of 76,000 bushels of wheat insured for $65,000 and the ship herself a $50,000 item, this disaster aggregated more than $115,000. Again, the *Manhattan* belonged to the Gilchrist fleet, the seventh unit to be lost that year. Happily for J.C. Gilchrist, all of his fleet carried insurance during 1903, the first time in several years. After these strokes of ill luck, one might suppose that Mr. Gilchrist was a firm believer in insurance.[48]

November was mild with only one ship canal incident at Duluth on the docket. As the steamer *John Harper* towed the schooner-barge *Thomas Gawn* in through the Duluth Ship Canal on November 9, the schooner suddenly sheered and struck the south pier, rupturing her hull. Tugs quickly shoved her into shallow water at the Osbourne dock where she settled in shallow water. Repair costs were slightly more than $3,000, but a bitter, two-year legal battle resulted over responsibility, the federal Circuit Court finally awarding the whole amount to barge owner O.M. Sicken of Marine City from the J.C. Gilchrist Company, owners of the steamer.[49]

J.T. Hutchinson *was brand new when she nearly ended her career at Eagle River Reef in 1903.* CANAL PARK MARINE MUSEUM COLLECTION.

A snowstorm on November 29 was followed by mean seas. The combination brought gray hair to Great Lakes vessel underwriters. Befuddled in the snow, the virtually new 346-foot, 3,734-ton steamer *J.T. Hutchinson* slammed into an uncharted rock a half mile off shore, five miles west of Eagle River on Keweenaw Point. Downbound from Duluth under Captain John Smith with 187,000 bushels of flax aboard, she at first appeared an insurance liability in excess of $400,000, which would have made her the most expensive Lake Superior accident to date. Marine surveyor Joseph Kidd and salvors were rushed to the site, discovering the two-year-old ship to be in a perilous position, caught on rocks amidships, the hold half full of water and dangerously exposed to raging seas. In the storm which stranded her, the waves had not been unduly high. Three days afterward, nevertheless, such a rugged gale blew up that the U.S. Life-Savers felt compelled to remove the crew as a safety precaution. Two days thereafter, still another storm drove the salvors away. Hopes were sagging.

Fortunately, when the salvors returned after the blow of December 4, they found the *Hutchinson* floating at anchor, released from her rocky cradle. Powerful pumps held down leakage and the salvage tugs *Favorite* and *M.F. Merrick* guided the battered steamer all the way to Buffalo, the trip requiring about 10 days. Including salvage fees, rebuilding charges and cargo destruction, she was an insurance liability of $220,000, bad enough to be sure, yet much better than one of $400,000. For that matter, the *Hutchinson* case was a tip-off to the insurance industry that with larger ships and cargoes on the lakes, insurance liabilities of the future would greatly exceed anything of past experience.[50]

The season's finale saw the little 124-foot, 383-ton coastal steamer *C.W. Moore* getting hung up at Sucker River on the Minnesota north shore. The tug *S.C. Schenck* had her afloat in two days. Two more days in a Duluth shipyard made her ready to resume her schedule to Grand Marais.[51] In those days, with an entire north shore coastal population depending on water transportation, it was important that these little coastal packets sail until the ice closed them down.

1904

For the first time in more than 30 years, Lake Superior witnessed a second consecutive drop in tonnage, nearly 10 percent below that of 1903. The total of ships in difficulty was about the same, yet most troubles were of the nuisance type. Of the five vessels leaving the rolls, only one was of more than modest value.

Fog in western Lake Superior waters on June 4 brought a nerve-wracking experience for some women guests aboard the 130-foot, 276-ton towing steamer *Niagara* of the Perry Wrecking Company, Sault Ste. Marie. Between the whiteout and the "compass devils," the *Niagara* slid securely onto the reef at Knife Island, listed heavily and began to pound in the high swells. The women were in cabins on the high side of the ship, with doors opening outward; hence, they were trapped for a while as the ship seemed to be breaking up. Meanwhile, the ship lay undetected by the citizens of Knife River. From his position on the elevated right-of-way, the telegrapher for the Duluth and Iron Range Railroad could hear distress whistles and ultimately made out the *Niagara*'s masts above the surface fog. He telegraphed the superintendent's office at Two Harbors eight miles away. From there, the railroad's tug *Edna G* rushed down the shore from her berth near the ore docks. In the meantime, the women had been liberated by the ship's crew. All 13 persons aboard were transferred to the *Edna G,* fortuitously it turned out, as that night a grinding surf shattered the 32-year-old *Niagara,* a $12,000 casualty. Wreckers got only her engine and various odds and ends.[52]

A grounding at Grand Portage on June 18 only slightly ruffled the 135-foot coaster *Mabel Bradshaw.* A light collision in the Duluth Harbor on July 19 between the spanking new 420-foot steel steamer *Edwin F. Holmes* and the 165-foot steel coastal steamer *America* did surprisingly little harm to the *America.* She made preliminary repairs and loaded materials and workmen to finish the job on the run. A stubborn fire at Ashland on August 4 necessitated a $15,000 rebuilding project for the 80-foot, 136-ton steamer *Lucille.* A foundering on September 2 at Two Harbors ended the career of the 39-foot, 11-ton schooner *Lewie,* a curiosity at the Head of the Lakes for about 20 years.

A series of groundings in September brought insignificant vessel damages. The steel steamer *Choctaw* struck Manitou Island on September 7, the lumber hooker *Homer Warren* went on the shore near Sucker River on September 10 and the 266-foot wooden steamer *C.C. Hand* went on the shoals off the northeast end of Madeline Island, opposite Michigan Island on September 14. The 265-foot *Hand* was released by the tug *E.G. Crosby,* but only after a crew of 20 ore trimmers lightered part of her 2,000 tons of ore directly into the lake. She was the former *R.E. Schuck,* built in 1890 at Cleveland.[53]

Thick weather brought double trouble in the eastern lake on October 4. Downbound with grain, the new 256-foot steel canaller *Ottawa* of the Canada Atlantic Company plowed head on into the Midland Navigation Company's new 249-foot steel *Midland Queen* off Caribou Island. Both vessels remained afloat, though the *Midland Queen* had to limp to port for a substantial date with the shipyard, perhaps in excess of $10,000.[54]

Things were much worse on that same October day 50 miles to the southwest. Plodding along serenely with a load of iron ore taken on at Marquette, the 272-foot, 1,740-ton wooden steamer *Sitka* suddenly found herself hooked hard on Au Sable Reef, a mile from shore. As luck would have it, she was only 100 feet from safe water. The Grand Marais lifesavers responded to Captain Johnson's distress signals, finding ship and crew in no danger. After

putting a surfman ashore to call for a tug, the lifesaving captain decided to stand by the *Sitka* through the night. Perhaps he sensed a change in the weather. This proved a wise decision, as 5 a.m. brought a rising gale.

The rafting tug Niagara *broke her back on Knife Island.* C. PATRICK LABADIE COLLECTION.

The *Sitka* crew was removed and landed at the sand beach near Au Sable Light. The *Sitka* was doomed. With the vicious waves pounding her on the reef, she soon disintegrated. The wreckers coming to her assistance could only strip her with the aid of the lifesavers. The *Sitka* was built at the West Bay City shipyards in 1887 and owned by J.C. Gilchrist of Cleveland. The 17-year-old vessel was valued at $53,225 with cargo.[55]

While the *Sitka* was being ground to bits, excitement was rife in the harbor at Grand Marais. Under Captain Lewis, the 134-foot, 224-ton wooden steamer *Hunter* of the Booth Packing Company had first stranded, then caught fire. The 27-year-old Philadelphia-built fish packet was completely consumed, a $10,000 liability. There were no injuries in this October incident.[56]

On October 13, the 297-foot bulk freighter *City of Glasgow* grounded off La Pointe on Madeline Island while headed toward Ashland to pick up her consort. The *Glasgow* had already loaded 2,981 tons of ore at Superior. Tugs *B.B. Inman* and *E.G. Crosby* released her on the 16th after 300 tons of ore were jettisoned into the lake. She apparently was unscathed as she proceeded to Ashland for her barge and then headed directly down the lake.[57]

During the remainder of October only a string of minor difficulties in the Keweenaw Waterway bothered sailors. The schooner-barge *Jeremiah Godfrey* banged a pier and grounded on October 11. The schooner-barges *Delaware* and *Jenness* were involved in a rear-end collision on October 27. The new 332-foot steel steamer *G.A. Flagg* stranded on October 31.

November was almost a quiet, pleasant surprise. The wooden steamer *William H. Gratwick* caught a log in her rudder on November 8 and needed repair. The final significant casualty of the season occurred five days later. In late afternoon on November 13, the 198-foot, 683-ton schooner-barge *W.S. Crosthwaite,* tow of the steamer *E.M. Saunders,* was lying at anchor in Whitefish Bay under the lee of the Point. Taking advantage of a lull in the trip, several of the crew were doing their laundry in the forecastle which was heated by a small stove. Then the crew was called to dinner. While they were eating, the stove must have overheated, and a fire broke out. It was all but over when the flames hit the heavily tarred deck. The crew jumped into the yawl with only the clothes they wore at mess, and their ship was a $9,000 torch. Constructed at Saginaw in 1873, she probably was well dried out, hence, the speedy conflagration. Voicing sailors' superstitions, however, some schooner men had a different explanation. She was a Gilchrist vessel and carried a yawl salvaged from the recently wrecked *Sitka* and oars from the ill-fated *Waverly,* two other Gilchrist units which had met their end. Sailors considered it extremely bad luck to take on board equipment from a ship which had been lost.[58]

1905

The shipping business rebounded amazingly in 1905 with tonnage up more than 40 percent from the preceding year. On the negative side, though, the number of ships in trouble quadrupled, 21 making their last voyage, by far the worst single year's record in Lake Superior history. Rough weather and fog in May, a killer gale in late summer, weeks ahead of the expected blows, vicious late October seas and a November weather monster in the western lake which is still the worst ever experienced, combined to take their toll along with the usual fires and collisions.

Ice conditions, even on Lake Erie, were bad well into May. Those ships venturing out in April were able to get through after a fashion. Nevertheless, the lake experienced a northwester at the end of April which heavily windrowed ice in Whitefish Bay and caused unexpected devilment. Lead ships were hung up and rammed by the vessel following, either another steamer or their own consorts.

By May 4, 14 steamers and barges had been involved as they tried to follow narrow channels through the ice pack. All were steel. The steamer *Mariposa* was hit by the steamer *Admiral,* the steamer *Lafayette* by her whaleback barge consort *134,* the steamer *Douglass Houghton* by her barge *Sidney G. Thomas* and the steamer *Maritana* by her barge *John A. Roebling.* Other entanglements included the steamer *William R. Linn* being struck by her barge *James Nasmyth,* the steamer *Sir William Siemens* by her barge *John Smeaton* and the steamer *Empire City* run down by the steamer *R.L. Ireland.* Collectively, the shipyards must have had a good many thousand dollars

in business, the *Roebling* alone being a $10,000 item and the *Empire City* probably more. The slow speeds in the ice undoubtedly prevented sinkings.[59]

The most newsworthy event in the western lake came on May 3 when the 250-foot, 2,105-ton wooden steamer *Hesper* was caught in the throes of a 60-mile-an-hour northeaster. She was driven well off her intended course and hurled on a reef which now marks the southwest

Hesper *succumbed to a violent spring storm in 1905.* MILWAUKEE PUBLIC LIBRARY COLLECTION.

edge of Silver Bay Harbor. After enduring a pounding for some time, the steamer was lifted over the reef by a giant wave, only to founder and break up in 42 feet of water. Captain E.H. Heaton and the 15-man crew remained aboard as long as there was any hope of saving their vessel. Moments before she broke up, they launched two lifeboats and pulled away. The boat commanded by the mate reached the lee of a large rock and protected waters, being swept safely to the mainland. Captain Heaton's boat slipped behind the shelter of a small island until the waves subsided. Both arrived at Beaver Bay where villagers made the crew comfortable. Then Captain Heaton and the chief engineer walked overland to the Alger Smith logging railroad, flagged a train and were taken to the junction with the Duluth and Iron Range Railroad where they caught another train to Two Harbors.

At Two Harbors they reported the wreck of the *Hesper* and notified their vessel agent, G.A. Tomlinson of Duluth, who arranged for the tug *B.B. Inman* to bring the shipwrecked crew to Duluth. The *Hesper* was totally destroyed, a loss of $80,000. Captain John Tuttle of London Salvage Associates visited the site four days later and discovered complete desolation. The cabin and spars had gone over the side, her stack fallen and the deck blown off. Debris was scattered for five miles along the shore.

There was a touchy side to this incident. For 15 years following her launching in 1890, she had been an M.A. Bradley ship; accordingly, she had sailed without insurance. With the death of Captain Bradley, the *Hesper* was turned over to C.E. Grover and stockholders to be managed by Hutchinson and Company of Cleveland. The new owners immediately insured her for $50,000 only to lose her two weeks later. Naturally, eyebrows would be raised in maritime circles. Mindful of this, Captain Heaton and his crew refused to discuss the experience with the press. Yet, evidence seems quite conclusive that a turbulent Lake Superior, not skullduggery, was the reason for the *Hesper*'s demise.[60]

The lake bid for another substantial wooden ship on May 6, the 288-foot *William P. Rend* striking hard on the east side of Manitou Island. Salvage master Captain C.C. Sinclair and the wrecking tug *Favorite* went to work on her, but it was 10 days before the *Rend* was refloated for a $15,000 visit to a Chicago shipyard. She was a vessel continuously in difficulties. As the former *George G. Hadley*, she had been involved in the fatal collision with the whaleback steamer *Thomas Wilson* at Duluth in June 1902.[61]

Fog brought a lopsided confrontation on May 16 some 30 miles east of Manitou Island as the 461-foot, 5,054-ton steel *Harvard* of the Pittsburgh Steamship Company slashed into the port side of the 281-foot, 2,134-ton composite steamer *Thomas W. Palmer* owned by former Senator Thomas W. Palmer and William Livingstone of Detroit. Realizing he had mortally wounded the smaller ship, the *Harvard*'s master adroitly held his bow in the gashed *Palmer* until her 19-man crew had crossed safely to his vessel. As the two separated, the *Palmer*, almost cut in two, dropped to the bottom of the lake. Built in 1889, she was insured for $100,000.

June fog continued to plague sailors. Poor visibility on June 9 left the 301-foot wooden steamer *City of Genoa* under Captain Pierre Bouille on the shoals at Sand Island. Two days later, wreckers had this Gilchrist ship off with little injury.

The same unsettled conditions saw the new 380-foot steel steamer *George B. Leonard* stuck at Point Iroquois, but again with little damage. In the early morning fog of June 13, however, a sideswipe collision occurred in Whitefish Bay. The spanking new 504-foot, 6,272-ton steel *Sylvania* of the Duluth Steamship Company, downbound with ore, raked the port side of the 413-foot, 4,321-ton steel *Sir Henry Bessemer* of the Pittsburgh Steamship Company, upbound light. Though the contact was glancing, the *Sylvania* ripped a gash 175 feet long in the *Bessemer*, fortunately above the waterline, but still necessitating a $40,000 replacement of plates. The *Sylvania*, which lost a port anchor and damaged shell plating, also had a $10,000 bill.[62]

A suddenly terminated sailing outing on June 26 caused anxiety for the Knights of Pythias and guests from the Keweenaw Point area aboard the 78-foot wooden steamer *Plow Boy*. A half mile west of Eagle Harbor, the little vessel impaled herself on an uncharted rock, abruptly halting the excursion. Fortuitously, the lake was calm and the 115-foot towing steamer *Howard* was able to approach and take off all passengers, while the *Plow Boy* herself came off relatively unscathed. Nevertheless, for a while there were some anxious people aboard her, especially those who knew that they were encumbered on one of the most dangerous coasts of the entire lake. Had Lake Superior been growling, a terrible tragedy might have resulted.[63]

Sailing was rather tame during July. A brush collision on July 16 in fog 12 miles north of the Portage Upper Entry between the 284-foot wooden steamer *Neshoto* and the 320-foot whaleback *James B. Neilson* was the only incident. Neither vessel required much repair.

August brought more problems and a foundering. Riding along behind the 277-foot wooden steamer *Caledonia* on the morning of August 17, the 229-foot, 980-ton schooner-barge *John M. Hutchinson* started to take water rapidly. Off Fourteen Mile Point near Ontonagon, the *Hutchinson* began to settle, and the *Caledonia* removed the barge crew before the 32-year-old schooner slid under. Belonging to Captain James Corrigan of Cleveland, she was a $10,000 item.[64]

Fire at Port Arthur on August 20 seared the Canadian excursion steamer *Gordon* to the extent of $20,000. Just a few days later on August 23, the steel steamer *H.B. Hawgood* banged a bridge at Duluth, receiving only minor damage. Not quite a week later, on August 29, the large steel passenger steamer *Tionesta* slammed into a dock, also at Duluth and again with minimal damage to herself.

Steel steamer Sevona *was dashed to pieces on a reef off Sand Island in the September gale.* C. PATRICK LABADIE COLLECTION.

Ship captains who left the lake's ports at the end of August or on September 1, however, were to endure a truly nightmarish experience. A killer fall storm struck several weeks ahead of schedule. It proved to be a storm which could sink modern wooden ships and drive powerful steel vessels to shelter. To be sure, the U.S. Weather Bureau had ordered storm warnings raised on September 1, but captains could not remember when a blow on that date was anything more than inconvenient on the western lake. Indeed, one would have to recall the *Sunbeam* dis-

Steel Steamers crowd into the Missabe ore docks in Duluth for cargoes of red iron ore about 1908. CANAL PARK MARINE MUSEUM COLLECTION.

aster of August 27, 1863, as the only real precedent. Consequently, the lake was full of ships. This time the weather forecasters were correct. Winds of more than 40 miles an hour and blinding rain pummelled the western lake for more than two days, beginning on the night of September 1, with turbulence over the entire lake carrying on for an additional two days. The full brunt of the gale seemed to be borne along the south shore, although the waters adjoining the north shore did not escape. Small craft, too, suffered.

The sloop *Lua* was among the first to go on September 1. Captain Wesley Boutin had planned for christening ceremonies to take place on the 4th, but the boat was wrecked near Bayfield before the event took place, a disappointment for a young Iowa lady, Lua Hoxie, her namesake.[65]

The first indications that all was not well with the lake's fleet east of Duluth came on September 2 when the 468-foot, 5,531-ton steel steamer *D.M. Clemson* limped into Two Harbors, badly listing, with railings down and two hatch covers gone. She had taken water through the top, her cargo had shifted and she had precious little freeboard remaining. This powerful, 1,800-horsepower vessel, just two years out of the Superior shipyards, had been bested by the elements. Captain Samuel Chamberlin ran in desperation for Two Harbors, reaching the protection of the breakwaters in time to prevent sinking.

At Duluth on September 4, the stalwart 300-foot steamer *North Wind* was slapped by the seas against a pier of the Duluth Ship Canal, but managed to limp into her berth at the Northern Pacific slip before settling to the bottom. Injury to the ship was moderate, but fears of cargo damage approaching $100,000 were expressed. Even the large Canadian passenger liner *Huronic* reported being tossed around like a feather.[66]

Over the next several days came more and more verification of genuine tragedy. On September 3 off Knife Island, just a short distance out of Duluth, the 308-foot steel whaleback steamer *Samuel Mather* was engulfed by a giant wave which took Watchman John Lindquist of Cleveland overboard to his death. From the Apostle Islands archipelago came reports that a large steel freighter had broken up on Sand Island Reef and that a sizable barge had sunk off Outer Island. Wreckage appearing off Keweenaw Bay and to the northeast of the Huron Islands indicated that at least one, and possibly two, ships had disappeared there. A collision between a steel steamer and a Canadian tug was reported near the Soo. All reports were true. Five ships were no more.

The first of these, apparently, was the 372-foot, 3,166-ton steel steamer *Sevona* under Captain D.S. MacDonald of the McBrier interests in Erie, Pennsylvania. Leaving Superior with about 6,000 tons of ore at 6:03 p.m. on September 1, the *Sevona* had taken such a mauling when just past Outer Island that Captain MacDonald turned back

to seek refuge among the Apostles. Confused by the drenching rain and mist, the captain plowed onto Sand Island Reef shortly after 5:15 a.m. on September 2. His ship quickly began breaking apart as it pounded unmer-

Salvors strip Sevona's *stern. Nothing else remained above the surface. Seven men had lost their lives.* CANAL PARK MARINE MUSEUM COLLECTION.

cifully. The break at No. 4 hatch rapidly widened so that the captain and six crewmen in the forward section were cut off from the 16 persons in the stern. Through a megaphone, Captain MacDonald ordered the two lifeboats lowered, but held in the lee of the vessel until a more opportune moment for boarding appeared. Everyone remained aboard for six tense hours. Finally, at about 11 a.m., when the stern cabins began to disintegrate, Chief Engineer William Phillipi put the after personnel in the lifeboats. He commanded one and deck hand Charles Scouller was in charge of the other when they pulled away. In the roaring wind and seas the people in the lifeboats could not arouse the forward crew who had taken refuge under the turtle deck. After a torturous ride, both boats reached land, the Scouller craft on Sand Island and Chief Phillipi's boat on the Wisconsin mainland outside of Bayfield. Those marooned in the forepeak were not so fortunate. Early in the afternoon, as the bow section began breaking up, Captain MacDonald and his men were observed by the Sand Island lightkeeper to leave the ship on rafts made of hatch covers. These shattered in the surf off Sand Island and all seven men were drowned. The surviving castaways were aided by fishermen on Sand Island or by homesteaders and lumberjacks on the mainland. With the aid of lumberman "Nap" Rabideaux, Chief Engineer Phillipi finally arrived at Bayfield to report the disaster. The tug *Harrow* was sent out, but all that remained above water was the *Sevona*'s shattered stern still on the reef. Captain MacDonald and the whole forward crew were dead and a fine, 15-year-old steel steamship valued at more than $220,000 was no more.

Salvors soon went to work on the *Sevona*'s stern, including the highly touted Reids of Sarnia, but she was irretrievable. Reid had purchased the wreck for $5,000.

They did recover her engine, boilers, tons of hull plating and a few other items of value. Sightseers, though, were probably the first to claim portions of the wreck as mementos of the disaster, traveling there on the *Skater.* There was one extremely discordant note to the *Sevona* incident. Whereas a number of local settlers were most hospitable to the shipwrecked crew, several others were not as charitable. Three Bayfield area men were arrested for robbing the bodies of the dead when they came ashore.

In recent years, the *Sevona* site has been a mecca for scuba divers and a number of interesting artifacts were recovered, most going into private collections. The *Sevona* is a most unusual shipwreck in that she has been picked at and over for decades by both private and commercial interests as well as the government. Reid's salvage efforts went on during 1906 and again in 1907 and 1908. The U.S. Army Corps of Engineers dynamited the wreck in late June and early July 1909 as a menace to navigation. Duluth diver J.B. Wanless worked the wreck over in 1917 for scrap metal, removing at least 180 tons and perhaps as much as 1,000 tons.[67] Perhaps no other steel shipwreck on Lake Superior has seen such extensive salvage activity and not been brought to the surface. Few, too, could claim the variety of extensive post depositional impacts that this wreck has undergone.

Five crewmen were lost when 338-foot schooner-barge Pretoria *sank less than a mile off Outer Island.* CANAL PARK MARINE MUSEUM COLLECTION.

That same dire September 2, another ship was in mortal trouble not many miles to the east. The 338-foot, 2,790-ton wooden schooner-barge *Pretoria* had left Superior the previous day in tow of the 263-foot wooden steamer *Venezuela,* which had loaded at Two Harbors. Both were heavily laden with iron ore. In the violent waves of that night, when the two were about 30 miles northeast of Outer Island, the steering gear of the barge let go. The steamer then tried to take the *Pretoria* into the shelter of Outer Island, but the towline parted under

inordinate strain. The *Venezuela* could not find her tow in the darkness and riotous seas. Her master thus elected to run for shelter at Ashland where he reported the missing barge.

Meanwhile, the situation went from bad to worse aboard the *Pretoria.*

Captain Charles Smart ordered the sails raised, but these were quickly blown to ribbons. He ordered the anchors dropped. They dragged. Waves poured over her decks, penetrating the hatch coamings. Some hatch covers came off. Water in the hold rose ominously. The crew labored at the pumps for hours. Suddenly, when the schooner was only four-fifths of a mile northeast of Outer Island, the *Pretoria* skidded over a reef, the pumps quit and it was over. The covering board gave way, the deck began to float off and Smart and his nine-man crew scrambled for the lifeboat as the *Pretoria* went down on an even keel with her masts still showing in 52 feet of water. Then came the familiar story of a ship's lifeboat approaching a windswept shore in heavy surf. The *Pretoria*'s boat capsized and five of the 10 occupants drowned. The remaining five hung onto the boat and floated ashore where they were picked up by Keeper John Irvine of Outer Island Light. After the storm subsided, they were taken off the island by the steamer *Venezuela* which had returned to hunt for her consort.

The *Pretoria* was a new wooden vessel, built in 1900 at West Bay City by Captain James Davidson and worth $60,000. Reputedly, she was the first ship that Captain Davidson ever lost. Lying in relatively shallow water, she also has been a rendezvous for sport divers. Her bell was found some years ago by Coast Guards four miles from the site of sinking, confirming the report that the deck had separated from the ship as she went under. Captain John Pasque accomplished the only formal salvage on record, recovering a 1,200-pound steam pump from the wreck in 52 feet of water along with one of the ship's masts, nearly 100 feet long and two feet in diameter at the base.[68]

Still, the grim harvest of this early fall blow increased. During the miserable night of September 2, or perhaps the next day, two more vessels met their ends. On Sunday, September 3, the passenger steamer *Juniata* encountered a mass of wreckage 10 miles east of Portage Entry. The next day, the Michigan coast was littered with debris for 50 miles from the Huron Mountain Club 30 miles northwest of Marquette clear down into Keeweenaw Bay at L'Anse. There were hatch covers, broken bulwarks, parts of cabins and a yawl boat. A nameboard with "*Olive*" on it was recovered, indicating the possibility that the four-masted schooner-barge *Olive Jeanette* may have been involved. This was clearly established by subsequent discovery of an oar and a chair with the full name, "*Olive Jeanette.*"

Better evidence that the towing steamer of the *Jeanette,* the steamer *Iosco,* was involved appeared with the discovery of life rings marked "*Iosco.*" Yet, with some miscellaneous wreckage was a basket marked "*Gilchrist*" leading to a belief that the steamer *J.C. Gilchrist* might have perished. Gradually, the picture cleared. The steamer *J.C. Gilchrist* showed up intact at Duluth early on the morning of September 5. Later that day, the keeper of Huron Islands Light completed a 20-mile row from his station to Pequaming to report that he had watched a schooner sink about four miles north of the light on the

seas were rough, and the new steel steamer was taking her licks, but Captain Massey thought the *Iosco* and *Jeanette* were doing well enough, too, slogging along under control. Then something must have caused Captain Gonyaw to turn back. Perhaps he was seeking shelter in the Keweenaw Waterway. The ships must have fought a slowly losing battle, since the bodies wore life preservers but no shoes, indicating that the sailors knew they were in a tight

Iosco **and her barge,** Olive Jeanette, *were victims of the September gale.* MARINE HISTORICAL SOCIETY OF DETROIT COLLECTION.

afternoon of September 3. The grimmest testimony of all began to show on September 5 when bodies came ashore from Keweenaw Bay all the way east to the Huron Mountain Club. The remains were identified as crewmen of the 291-foot, 2,051-ton wooden steamer *Iosco* and her consort, the 242-foot, 1,271-ton *Olive Jeanette*.

The two had departed Duluth on August 30 laden with iron ore for Toledo and Sandusky, the *Iosco* under the command of Captain Nelson Gonyaw and the *Olive Jeanette* under Captain McGreavy, both veteran masters. The vessels were middle-aged, as wooden ships go, out of the West Bay City shipyards, the *Jeanette* built in 1890 and the *Iosco* in 1891. Presumably, they were staunch, seaworthy ore carriers. They had been sighted during daylight on September 2 a good 20 miles east of the Huron Islands by Captain Massey of the 416-foot steel steamer *Martin Mullen,* a year-old 1,500-horsepower unit. The

spot and might not make it. Probably, the steamer went first; the Huron Island lightkeeper saw no steamer in sight when he observed the waterlogged schooner make her dive. And extensive patches of wreckage had been seen northeast of Keweenaw Bay at noon on September 3, while it was afternoon when the keeper watched the foundering. Whatever the cause, this twin disappearance remains one of the major mysteries of the lake.

The ships belonged to the Hawgood Company of Cleveland. Captain Smith of the company hurriedly came to Marquette and coordinated the search for bodies. By September 14, 15 bodies had been recovered, eight by volunteers from the Huron Mountain Club who patrolled 25 miles of beach and the remainder near L'Anse in Keweenaw Bay. Another body would appear near L'Anse the following June. A disagreeable incident appeared in the hunt for bodies, also. While most shore dwellers were wonderfully cooperative, there was still the ghoul. Homesteader J.J. Behrendt, one of the searchers, discovered signs that a body had been dragged off the beach into the forest. Following the trail, he picked up underwear with the initials, "N.G.," probably Nelson Gonyaw. Evidently, some conscienceless person or persons had come across the drowned captain's body, had removed the $800 that Captain Gonyaw customarily carried on his person and had then hidden the body in the woods to conceal the crime. The grave of Captain Gonyaw was never found, even though the captain's brother came from lower Michigan to carry on the hunt. Five of the dead were never identified. These sailors were buried in the Park Cemetery at Marquette. The *Iosco* was worth in excess of $65,000 and the *Jeanette* possibly half that amount.[69]

Two episodes near the Soo rounded out this devastating September storm experience. A slight platebender, which could have been serious, occurred on September 3 as the steel steamer *George Stephenson* was blown off her course at Point Aux Pins and grounded. Her steel consort, *John A. Roebling,* kept right on coming and banged into her.

The veteran V.H. Ketchum *burned off Parisienne Island in September 1905.* IRV SCHULTZ COLLECTION.

The event of September 5 was far more serious. Just out of the Soo, the little Canadian fishing tug *Shamrock* unexpectedly cut across the bow of the 354-foot steel steamer *W.C. Richardson* under Captain Thomas Wilford. The tug sank immediately following the collision, drowning her captain and engineer who were in their bunks. Oddly enough, a deck hand was wheeling the *Shamrock* at the time. He apparently underestimated the speed of the big steel carrier. No financial loss was reported, and it is probable that the tug was raised, as she is not included in the list of Canadian losses.[70]

The 31-year-old 233-foot, 1,806-ton wooden steam freighter *V.H. Ketchum* ended her days at Parisienne

Island on September 16. Fire broke out in the after cabins, and the captain beached her off the island in 23 feet of water. As the crew lowered a lifeboat, however, the boat capsized. Mate Andrew Johnson tried to rescue the cook, Mrs. B. Ames, but she panicked and dragged him down, the only two fatalities. The aged *Ketchum,* which had been the first ship of the Pickands-Mather fleet, was owned by the Seither Transit Company of Cleveland at the end, a $12,000 casualty.

A stranding at Grand Island on September 18 brought modest injury to the steel Pittsburgher *Maritana*. A nasty mess developed in the Keweenaw Waterway on September 22 when the 196-foot lumber hooker *C.F. Curtis* of the Tonawanda Iron and Steel Company was towing the schooner-barges *Nelson C. Holland* and *Scotia* past Houghton. As they were going through the Portage Lake bridge, the schooners sheered out of control, both striking the center pier and wrecking the bridge. While the *Scotia* remained afloat, the 187-foot, 564-ton *Holland* necessitated an immediate, weeks-long salvage job. Salvage master H.W. Baker constructed the largest cofferdam ever used on Lake Superior in his efforts. Captain Baker at length brought her up on November 17. No estimates of cost were given, but the *Holland* job must have consumed many thousands of dollars. Rehabilitating the drawbridge very probably took a larger sum. This was undoubtedly a terribly expensive mishap for the ship's owners or their insurance underwriters.[71]

This troublesome September was rounded out on the 25th by a fire in Ashland Harbor. The 182-foot, 614-ton schooner-barge *Melvin S. Bacon* had been loaded with ore and was waiting to be picked up by her towing steamer, the new steel *E.N. Saunders,* when she started leaking. Tugs pushed her into a shallow section of the harbor, preparatory to repair work the next day. That night, however, she took fire. Though she had settled to the bottom in 18 feet of water, Captain Henry Elbe and the mate, who had stayed aboard, narrowly escaped with their lives as the 31-year-old schooner burned to the water's edge. She was a liability of about $10,000 to her Gilchrist owners. Still, battered as she was, salvors apparently got her up and rebuilt her since she is listed as sailing for many years thereafter, though registered out of Port Huron.[72]

The wooden sailing fleet took an additional beating in October. The veteran lumber schooner *Noquebay* was intentionally grounded in 12 feet of water at Presque Isle Bay on Stockton Island after catching fire on October 5 while in tow of the *Lizzie Madden.* The fire was discovered when the two were about 20 miles outside the Apostle Islands, apparently starting near the donkey boiler up forward. It appears that her crew managed to jettison part of her lumber cargo even as she burned. The 205-foot, 684-ton schooner-barge was built at Trenton, Michigan, in 1872 and owned by T.F. Madden of Bay City. At the time of her loss she was valued at $7,000. Captain Cornelius

O. Flynn of Duluth succeeded in salvaging about 175,000 feet of lumber plus the ship's anchors. The venerable *Noquebay* sailed no more.[73]

Wild blasts east of Keweenaw Point on October 20-21 knocked three more vessels from the ranks of the schooner hookers. Winds howled 65 miles an hour as the 185-foot wooden lumber steamer *L.L. Barth* tried to reach shelter with her tows, the 170-foot, 611-ton schooner *Nirvana* under Captain Hudson and the 176-foot, 610-ton schooner *Galatea* commanded by Captain Carr. This was a mammoth northwesterly storm which spread heavy snow and destruction all over the Midwest. Though the schooner-barges were light, the towlines still parted off Grand Marais, Michigan. On their own, the schooners almost reached safety. The *Nirvana* crashed into the west pier at Grand Marais and started to go down. The *Galatea* hauled onto the beach 300 feet west of the piers, her bow 20 feet out of water. In a daring lifeboat maneuver, Captain Benjamin Trudell and the Grand Marais lifesavers removed the seven-man crew from the stern of the stricken *Nirvana,* which had split in two. The *Galatea* was so far ashore that her people were safe. The *Nirvana* became a shattered wreck. A series of salvors over the next two years attempted to retrieve the *Galatea,* but she also left her bones west of the Grand Marais pierhead. Each vessel was valued at $15,000 by the Hines Lumber Company of Chicago. These were not particularly old lumber schooners, both produced at West Bay City shipyards, the *Galatea* in 1882 and the *Nirvana* in 1890.[74]

Fighting the same fearsome gale and snowstorm was the 256-foot steambarge *F.A. Meyer* with her tows, the 198-foot, 935-ton schooner *Alta* and the 178-foot, 593-ton schooner *Olga.* All three were heavily laden with lumber from Duluth. The *Meyer*'s captain may have been seeking refuge behind Grand Island since he was somewhat south of the usual course. Again, the towlines separated. The larger *Alta* was pitched high on a reef at Grand Island, her back broken. The *Olga* endured the enervating experience of being dismasted and having her deckload go over the side. At the last moment her anchors caught to prevent her from being ground to pieces along the Pictured Rocks east of Munising. The crews of the two survived. Captain A.C. Louden of the *Olga* prevented a fatality by diving into the churning water and rescuing one of his sailors who had gone overboard. The *Olga* would be refurbished with new masts, rigging and a rudder, probably at the expense of a thousand dollars or so. The ill-starred *Alta* was through, whipped more than a hundred yards across a reef and boulders, with a large rock piercing her hull. Despite efforts of the illustrious Reids of Sarnia, she went to pieces, a $10,000 loss.[75]

Disasters and deaths were wholesale on the Lower Lakes in this October tumult, but the last to feel the wrath of the weather gods on Lake Superior was the 197-foot, 774-ton wooden steamer *Oregon* towing the 189-foot schooner *Samuel H. Foster.* En route light to Pequaming, the *Oregon,* under Captain Frank Elliott, was slapped into four feet of water adjacent to the shore five miles northwest of Marquette on October 20. The *Foster* did not strand. In such a position her crew was safe, and salvage tugs finally freed her a week later. The *Oregon* had to be dragged 500 feet over a rocky bottom to deep water, entailing a $15,000 shipyard bill in the process. Both steamer and consort belonged to J.A. Calbick of Chicago.[76]

The first three weeks of November were pretty much routine. Vessel gossip during the first two weeks concerned the 366-foot, 2,759-ton steamer *Frank Rockefeller,* one of the largest whalebacks. In a blinding snowstorm on November 2, the *Rockefeller* plowed far into the shallows of Rainbow Cove on the western end of Isle Royale. Her steel barge, the 375-foot, 3,474-ton *Maida,* crashed into her. Under Captain P.A. Peterson, the *Rockefeller* had left Duluth on November 2 with 4,900 tons of iron ore and the *Maida* carrying 5,763 tons. Hence, when at virtually full speed and with the mate conning the ship, the *Rockefeller* hit the rocks of Isle Royale, and her larger, heavier barge kept right on coming. In the end, the substantial whaleback steamer had a crushed stern besides a ravaged bottom. Captain Peterson and the crew convinced one of the island's many fishermen to take them into Port Arthur. There, Captain Peterson notified Pittsburgh Steamship Company of events. Since the *Rockefeller,* worth more than $225,000 and one of the prize whalebacks in the 112-unit Pittsburgh fleet, was in a badly exposed position and deteriorating weather was expected any day, the salvage reaction was fast and furious. The wrecker *Favorite* and barge *Rescue* were rushed to the scene as well as the big steel tug *S.C. Schenck* with a lighter. The 330-foot steel steamer *Maritana* was detached from normal ore carrying duty and made a type of "transfer barge" as well as towing steamer. For more than a week, day and night, the frantic rescue effort was pursued. At length, after the ore cargo had been placed aboard the *Maritana,* the *Rockefeller* was pulled off her rocky berth and towed by the *Maritana* to Two Harbors where preliminary damage estimates were made. The loss report of $9,000 undoubtedly was only part of the story, perhaps just covering the visible injury to the stern. Very likely the shipyard bill was several times this amount, to say nothing of the costs of the extensive salvage fleet.[77]

The 213-foot wooden barge *Moravia* suffered a sideswipe on November 4 in the Keweenaw Waterway and needed help from the lifesavers and some minor fixing. Nearby at Portage Lake on November 8, the diminutive 88-foot, 87-ton schooner *Abbie* suddenly foundered. She was of nominal value. Then on November 20, the 238-foot wooden steamer *Portage* grounded off Grand Marais, Michigan. In moderate seas the lifesavers pulled out to her and spent the night helping the crew jettison cargo. More than 400 tons of salt went over the side, after which a tug freed the ship and brought her to the safety of Grand Marais Harbor. Little injury to the *Portage* resulted, but cargo worth more than $2,400 was gone.[78]

Vessel men were hardly prepared for what would happen in the last 10 days of the month. The shipping business was brisk, and masters were trying to complete as many trips as possible before winter forced a shutdown. Just the same, November gales are to be expected and can be deadly. Hence, when storm warnings were raised for the western lake on November 23, most captains stayed in port, a wise decision. A tumultuous northeaster with torrents of rain splashed the western lake country on the 23rd, changing to heavy, slushy snow. Winds of 60 miles an hour blasted Duluth on the 24th. The waves were frightful. It seems that the only ship caught on the western lake was the 255-foot wooden steamer *Charlemagne Tower Jr.* of the Gilchrist fleet, a downbound iron ore carrier. She barely crept into the Keweenaw Waterway, where, after surveying his battered vessel, with bulwarks ripped off, the aft cabin stove in, numerous straps broken and a strained hull, her captain ruefully told newsmen that never again would he be out when he should be in.

Monkshaven *wrecked on Angus Island.* EDWARD N. MIDDLETON COLLECTION.

Decent weather returned on the weekend of the 25th and 26th, continuing through part of the 27th. Accordingly, ships by the dozens steamed out on the lake in the end-of-season rush, particularly since big storms usually have been followed by periods of relative calm. Then the weather gods threw their most wicked curve. In a phenomenon probably never before nor afterward recorded in American weather annals, rather accurately maintained since the 1870s, a far more violent gale and snowstorm blasted the Lake Superior Country just three days after an admittedly wild tumult. The weather forecast on the morning of the 27th was a call for fair and cold. Disconcerting storm signals were hoisted since

heavy snow was falling over northern North Dakota behind which was an enormous cold wave. Of course, this might possibly miss Lake Superior. It didn't.

Snow began to fall at Duluth about 6 p.m., November 27. Within an hour, the winds were rushing 44 miles an hour. As the night wore on, winds grew stronger and stronger until 70 miles an hour was officially registered at 5:40 a.m. The tempest raged at higher than 60 miles an hour for more than 12 hours. One official report said 79 miles an hour was reached. Clouds of snow cascaded down. The whole western lake was enveloped, including the Canadian lakehead. St. Paul was being plastered and the snow was heading toward Chicago. Indeed, on the morning of the 28th, Duluth weather forecaster H.W. Richardson no longer could get data on the magnitude of the storm mass. Telegraph and telephone communications with the Weather Bureau headquarters in Chicago were out. Train and street car traffic was paralyzed in the Upper Midwest. Downed telephone and telegraph poles blocked streets and roads, while areas of Duluth near lake level were flooded.[79]

As bad as things were on land, this experience was sheer hell for sailors. Snow cut all visibility. Waves seemed to run higher than pilothouses or smokestacks. Even new 1,800-horsepower, 478-foot steel ships were stopped cold when fully loaded. Some days elapsed before the full story was known. When the toll was tallied, 18 ships were discovered to be disabled or destroyed by stranding, one had foundered with all hands and nearly a dozen others suffered various degrees of injuries to hulls or superstructures. All except two had come to grief west of Keweenaw Point. Five of the mishaps had fatalities. In lakes history, this is called the "*Mataafa* Blow," in memory of a major steel carrier wrecked at the Duluth pierhead.

The first victim apparently was Canadian, the 249-foot, 1,425-ton steel turret steamer *Monkshaven* of the Algoma Central Line. British-built in 1882, she had 22 years on the ocean before being brought to Lake Superior in 1904. She was overwhelmed on the night of November 27 less than 15 miles from the safety of the Thunder Bay ports and pitched bow first to the edge of Angus Island, about a mile or so southeast of Pie Island. Her bow was virtually on the shore which allowed her crew to easily reach solid ground. This was extremely fortunate since she was receiving a terrible pounding. Her hull was officially declared a ruin. However, salvors managed to take her off the next year.[80]

A hapless scow-barge was the first sacrifice to the storm gods on the Minnesota north shore. The 305-ton scow *George Herbert* was in tow of the 55-foot tug *F.W. Gillett* of Duluth en route on the afternoon of November 27 to Two Islands, 78 miles northeast of Duluth. Owned by L.R. Martin of Duluth, the *Herbert* was under charter to the M.H. Coolidge Company taking supplies to the lumber camps at Two Islands. Vile weather struck the north shore earlier than at Duluth. Accordingly, the tug and scow with towline still attached anchored in the lee of Two Islands, the only protection for miles. Both vessels had their anchors down. For 10 hours, they hugged the

Gale winds drove the 406-foot Crescent City *onto shoreline rocks.* AUTHOR'S COLLECTION.

meager shelter of the islands. Nevertheless, about 1 a.m. on November 28, the lines snapped and the ill-fated scow was catapulted onto the rock-strewn shore. As the *Herbert* hit, Captain Charles Johnson and lumber camp clerk William Hicks leaped to rocks and scrambled up the low cliffs. Three other crewmen refused to jump and perished when the three-year-old scow was splintered to kindling in a matter of minutes. The two survivors found a settler's cabin where they were hospitably received. They began hunting for their shipmates at first light, but unsuccessfully. They then hiked the shore southwestward to Thomasville, the site of another accident, where they caught a tug for Duluth. Three Duluthians had died and a property liability of $5,000 was incurred.[81]

As the ill-starred *George Herbert* was in her death throes, scarcely five miles closer to Duluth two other ships were approaching disaster. The 231-foot, 1,360-ton wooden steamer *George Spencer* and her schooner-barge, the 209-foot, 893-ton *Amboy,* were lost in the snow and completely overpowered by the seas. The *Spencer's* officers knew they were someplace near the north shore as the compass was spinning wildly. Yet, with only a 625-horsepower engine, they couldn't pull away. In a few moments, both vessels skidded to a halt on a gravel beach, probably the only decent landing spot for miles. They were off Thomasville, perhaps three miles northeast of the Manitou River. To be sure, the surf was furious and the ships were pounded savagely, but neither the 21-year-old steamer nor 31-year-old barge showed signs of disintegrating immediately. The crews stuck to their vessels until daybreak.

Meanwhile, local fishermen and lumberjacks hastened to the spot, attracted by the steamer's distress whistle.

Captain Frank Conlin of the *Spencer* and Captain Fred Watson of the *Amboy* realized their ships could not withstand the onslaught indefinitely and ordered lines tied to life buoys and planks thrown over on the shore side. The shore party waded into the surf and retrieved the lines which were made fast to trees. Then Watchman James Gibson of the *Amboy* came hand-over-hand across 50 yards of boiling lake and instructed the fishermen in rigging a chair buoy. With lines attached to both ships, 22 more men and one woman were removed from the beleaguered vessels by breeches buoy. The Thomasville settlers brought the castaways into their homes to warm, feed and revive them. Not a life was lost.

The next day, the 66-foot tug *Crosby* arrived from Duluth and picked up the crews. Marine surveyors quickly appraised both ships. In the opinion of Captain Cornelius O. Flynn, the *Amboy* had made her last run, with her back broken and considerably shattered. The *Spencer,* however, had fared better. She could be taken off after her cargo was removed. The *Amboy* was left to break up and the *Spencer,* after the Whitney Brothers had retrieved her coal cargo, recovered to sail additional years. The *Amboy* was a $10,000 loss. The *Spencer* a $30,000 salvage and rebuilding operation.[82]

The powerful steel steamers fared even worse. The 406-foot, 4,213-ton *Crescent City,* a 1,600-horsepower vessel only eight years old, was enveloped by snow and seas west of Devil's Island while heading for Two Harbors. Captain Rice ordered the anchors dropped before 1 a.m. on the 28th and the ship headed into the wind at full throttle. She wouldn't come around. For three hours, with anchors down and engines churning their best, she was steadily pushed for 20 miles past her destination and virtually docked against a low cliff a mile west of the Duluth Pumping Station at Lakewood. Slapped into only a few feet of water with towering waves slamming her broadside, she broke in two. Noting that the land was deck level, Captain Rice ordered a ladder slung ashore and the whole crew crossed safely. There was a problem finding shelter along that stretch of then sparsely inhabited suburban Duluth, but the crewmen eventually reached the Duluth Pumping Station or scattered homes. The chief engineer and second mate actually hiked seven or more miles in the blizzard to downtown Duluth and the Pittsburgh Steamship Company headquarters to report the plight of their ship. About six months later, salvors took her off for a $100,000 reconstruction job.[83]

Within 90 minutes after the *Crescent City* struck, four more vessels of the same Pittsburgh Steamship Company came to grief within 15 miles of each other on the north shore. Inching her way westward toward Duluth in the early morning hours of November 28 was the 478-foot, 5,910-ton steel steamer *William Edenborn* with the 436-foot, 5,039-ton steel barge *Madeira* in tow. Despite her 1,800 horsepower, Captain Talbot could not hold this splendid five-year-old creation of West Bay City ship-builders on course. About 3 a.m., the towline parted and both ships were on their own. Though all visibility was blotted out in the snow-filled darkness, the captain may

The Lafayette *and her barge* Manila *were blown right up into the trees along the Minnesota north shore.* CANAL PARK MARINE MUSEUM COLLECTION.

have suspected he was uncomfortably close to the north shore. Accordingly, he planned to drop anchor after he had worked his way upwind. By this time, all genuine sense of direction was lost. At 4:40 a.m. he ordered full speed ahead. Just 20 minutes later, however, instead of being in deeper water, the giant *Edenborn* was sliding over rocks and gravel, pushing her bow well into the shoreline forest. Partly on land and partly in the lake, the steamer soon cracked amidships. Yet, she was so far ashore that 24 of 25 in her crew were safe. As the *Edenborn* began cracking, her hatch covers began falling into the hold. When the stern crew made their way forward, a giant wave caught three and pitched them into an open hatch. Third Assistant Engineer Johnson was killed in the fall. The other two caught on the shelf-piece and were pulled out. Captain Talbot discovered that he had crashed aground at the mouth of the Split Rock River, approximately 45 miles northeast of Duluth. Later in the day, he contacted local fisherman Octave Iverson who hiked for 12 hours in the raging snow to reach Two Harbors and report the fate of the *Edenborn* to Pittsburgh Steamship Company officials. In no danger in the forepeak of the ship, the crew remained aboard, reasonably comfortable, until the tug *Edna G* came to their relief the next day. Months later, the *Edenborn* was retrieved for reconstruction, another $100,000 item.[84]

The lot of the barge *Madeira* was grotesquely different. For two hours after the line let go, she drifted shoreward, though Captain John Dissette had no idea where they were. Suddenly, about 5:30 a.m. on November 28, came a crash which sent shudders through the steel vessel. To

their horror, the crewmen discovered their vessel being battered broadside against the base of a cliff stretching as high as their masts. The *Madeira* was breaking apart. In a desperate but heroic move, Seaman Fred Benson leaped from his ship as the barge rose against the cliff on a high wave, seized a small rock on the cliff face and worked his way to the top like a human squirrel. Attaching a small rock to the coil of line he carried with him, Benson dropped the weighted line to the sinking bow and three more crewmen came up the line to the top. Repeating the technique, he put his rope on the sinking stern, drew up a stronger hawser and five more climbed to safety. Unfortunately, Mate James Morrow went overboard and was drowned. Wading through deep snow, the beleaguered crewmen first found a fisherman's cabin and then a logging camp where they were revived and dried out before being picked up at Split Rock River two days later. They discovered that the ill-fated *Madeira* had hammered herself to pieces at the base of Gold Rock, the first large promontory northeast of modern Split Rock Lighthouse, sinking in two parts. Her debris still litters the bottom there, providing a popular attraction for today's sport divers. The crewmen suffered severely from exposure and frostbite, but all recovered. Even the body of Mate Morrow was recovered and brought to Two Harbors on the tug *Edna G*. The *Madeira,* a five-year-old creation of Chicago shipbuilders, had become a $175,000 liability.[85]

At almost the same moment the *Edenborn* and *Madeira* were losing their battle to the elements, two other units of the same fleet were in an identical predicament. The 454-foot, 5,113-ton steel steamer *Lafayette* with the 436-foot, 5,039-ton barge *Manila* were firmly in the grip of the horrendous northeaster, driven far off their course to West Superior. The 1,800-horsepower steamer was helpless. Surrounded by walls of snow, Captain Dell P. Wright had no idea where he was until breakers were heard off the starboard bow. A few minutes later, the *Lafayette* was sent broadside into large rocks about 50 feet off shore from a high bluff on the mainland, opposite the north end of Encampment Island, six miles northeast of Two Harbors. The spot has since been named Lafayette Bluff. With no time to drop anchors, the barge *Manila* came right on, ramming the stern of the steamer and permitting four *Lafayette* crewmen to jump aboard the barge.

The *Manila* came to rest astern of the steamer and abutting the shore where trees overhung her side. The *Lafayette* broke in two in just three minutes, her stern remaining about 50 feet off shore and separated from land by a vicious surf. The bow section actually swung against a lower offshoot of a high, receding cliff. Captain George Balfour and the barge crew, together with the four *Lafayette* crewmen, immediately climbed the trees to land and raced to the beleaguered *Lafayette*. The steamer's second engineer grabbed a large nut from the engine room and found a stout rope to which he tied the nut.

Braving the elements on deck, he cast the weighted line ashore where Captain Balfour pulled it from a tree. The shore crewmen then dragged a stronger hawser across and made it fast to a tree. Those trapped on the founder-

The Lafayette *was turned into scrap metal by enormous seas, with only her stern salvaged.* CANAL PARK MARINE MUSEUM COLLECTION.

ing stern were then able to come hand over hand to safety — all but Fireman Patrick Wade who slipped off the line and perished. Those on the bow, with Captain Wright the last to leave, were able to jump to the rocks, then scale the rocky bluff. Most suffered miserably, building fires in the snowy forest and trying to find shelter from the shrieking winds and piercing cold. As the seas subsided the following day, they were able to climb back aboard the *Manila* where there was heat and food. They had been able to find a fisherman who volunteered to hike the six miles to Two Harbors where Superintendent Owens of the Duluth and Iron Range Railroad dispatched the tug *Edna G.* The tug, however, could not venture into the shallow water on the morning of the 29th and had to return to Two Harbors to pick up dories with which all of both crews remaining on the *Manila* were brought to Two Harbors. Many of the survivors had to be hospitalized for severely frostbitten hands and feet. Only the fireman was lost, but the five-year-old *Lafayette* was a $300,000 casualty. Just 150 feet of the *Lafayette*'s stern with the engine and boilers intact was retrieved more than nine months later. The barge *Manila* was refloated without difficulty, although she sustained injuries requiring shipyard work in excess of $10,000.[86]

Later in the morning of the tempestuous November 28, a more gruesome event was unfolding some miles northeast of Outer Island on the open lake. The day before, two grain steamers had departed Duluth. The first was one of the early steel-hulled vessels, the 262-foot, 1,753-ton *Ira H. Owen*, a twin-stacker built in 1887 with a meager 750 horsepower, under the command of Captain Joseph Hulligan. The other was the new, three-year-old 380-foot, 4,310-ton *Harold B. Nye*, boasting 1,450 horsepower.

Three days later, the bedraggled *Nye* staggered into Two Harbors, storm damaged, badly down at the bow and barely afloat. Her weary master reported that two days before, at the peak of the gale on November 28, he had observed a two-stacked steamer northwest of Outer Island blowing distress signals. The disabled steamer vanished behind a snow cloud. Some two hours later, as the snow halted, the *Nye*'s captain could see no sign of the other ship. As the *Nye* was in such desperate straits herself, any attempt to steer toward the other vessel was out of the question. The *Nye*'s captain thought she had gone down. This opinion was confirmed two days later when the captain of the steamer *Sir William Siemens*, M.K. Chamberlain, reported encountering wreckage 12 miles east of Michigan Island bearing life-rings marked "*Ira H. Owen.*" Captain Hulligan and his crew of 18 were gone.

The vanishing of the *Owen* remains a mystery to this day. Her cargo of 116,000 bushels of barley was not a heavy load, and the ship apparently was sound, having just been inspected in Duluth Harbor by Captain J.J. Keith, the manager of National Steamship Company, her owners. Despite the catastrophic gale, she was the only steel ship to founder in this horrendous storm. The testimony of Captain Alva Kellar of the *Nye* that the *Owen* was asking for assistance indicates that Captain Hulligan knew he was in trouble. Perhaps her cargo of barley had shifted or she suffered from some overwhelming stress of the weather.[87]

Ira H. Owen *disappeared with 19 crewmen off Outer Island.* GREAT LAKES HISTORICAL SOCIETY COLLECTION.

November 28 saw the worst two hours in the history of shipping in the port of Duluth. Three major ships were involved in calamity. Not long after noon, the year-old 363-foot, 3,887-ton steel steamer *R.W. England*, under Captain Richard England, approached the Duluth Ship Canal in the tempest. Seeing he would miss the canal, Captain England attempted to turn back to the open lake. The shrieking winds caught him and only minutes later, at 12:40 p.m., the *England* was pitched aground two and a half miles south of the Canal, just north of the Oatka recreation center. Actually, the giant combers put her so high up on the beach, stern first, that she was reasonably safe. A Minnesota Point resident, Fred J. Cosford, wit-

Wind and waves drove the Mataafa *into the pierhead at Duluth during the height of the storm.* KENNETH E. THRO COLLECTION.

nessed the stranding and ran nearly a mile in the fierce snow and blowing sand to reach the Duluth Life-Saving Station. Captain McLennan and the lifesavers responded, putting a line on the *England* and taking off those crewmen who wished to leave. Most stayed aboard. As the lake calmed, three days later, tugs dragged the *England* into deep water for a trip to the shipyard. Rehabilitation charges ran to $70,000 on a ship worth $230,000. Lake Superior had really roughed her up.[88]

Within the next half hour, a larger, much more powerful steel ship felt the lake's wrath at the mouth of the Duluth Ship Canal. The 478-foot, 5,904-ton *Isaac L. Ellwood,* only five years out of the West Bay City shipyards and boasting 1,800 horsepower, was trying to enter. Loaded with iron ore, she left the Duluth harbor the previous day, Captain C.H. Cummings being instructed to pick up the barge *Bryn Mawr* at Two Harbors. Between the snow and mountainous waves, he could not make out the entrance at Two Harbors and tried anchoring in the open water to await better weather. The lake gave the *Ellwood* a real dusting, masses of water pouring over her, ripping off hatch tarpaulins, loosening hatch covers. She started taking water.

In a delicate maneuver, Captain Cummings turned back to Duluth and reached the canal at 1:08 p.m. He charged right in and down the canal toward safety, despite the blanket of snow. But, the seas caught the big ship and sent her veering into the north pier where she ripped out plates, then ricocheted off only to hit the south pier where more plates were knocked loose. Spectators lining the piers in Canal Park cheered the *Ellwood* as she made it through. Happily, tugs were waiting just inside the harbor. Seeing her sideswipe the piers, the tug captains

pulled quickly on the *Ellwood* and pushed her into the shallows where she settled to the bottom just off the Duluth Boat Club in 22 feet of water with her deck houses above the waves and everybody safe. Her raising and rebuilding cost $50,000.[89]

As the *England* and the *Ellwood* were fighting to avert disaster, another in the same predicament was the 430-foot, 4,840-ton steamer *Mataafa* with the 366-foot, 3,422-ton barge *James Nasmyth* in tow. Under Captain R.F. Humble, the *Mataafa* had cleared the Duluth pierhead with her barge about 3:30 p.m., November 27. Despite the ominous forecast, the weather appeared decent. For sure it was cold, but the lake was relatively calm. About 7:30 p.m., when the ships were off Two Harbors, the maelstrom exploded. Despite her respectable 1,400-horsepower engine, the *Mataafa* made virtually no headway towing her consort over the next 10 hours. The two took a horrible battering. Captain Humble turned across the trough and commenced the return to Duluth at about 8:30 a.m., November 28, only by dexterous maneuvering. The seas were ferocious and visibility virtually zero. They inched their way southwest over the next several hours, occasionally swinging to windward to avoid a possible stranding. After noon, the snow let up a bit and Captain Humble could make out the north shore. Approaching

Enormous seas swept over the wrecked Mataafa *for hours as she lay beached.* CANAL PARK MARINE MUSEUM COLLECTION.

within a few miles of the canal, Humble realized that the monstrous waves precluded his dragging a tow through the Duluth Entry. Accordingly, he signaled the *Nasmyth* to let go her anchors and ordered the towline dropped within two miles of the harbor entry. The anchors caught. The captain then ordered the *Mataafa* full steam ahead for the final run to safety. Yet, just as he approached the entrance at 2:15 p.m., a giant wave hit, lifting the stern so high that the bow struck bottom, sending the *Mataafa* careening into the north pierhead. Another wave struck and the ship was pushed perpendicular to the pier, battering her midships against the concrete pierhead. Her engine seemingly had gone dead; perhaps it was the buckets on her wheel having been sheered off when her rudder became disabled. Another wave slammed into the immobilized vessel, whirled her over 180 degrees and tossed her aground about 100 feet north of the north pier and 600 feet off the beach. Comber after comber struck sledge hammer blows, shortly breaking her amidships.

As the *Mataafa* touched bottom, 12 of her crew were

broke and the sailors could not find the others in the seas. Any attempt to launch a lifeboat would have been suicidal. As the night wore on, it was obvious that nothing could be done to rescue those aboard, even though 10,000 Duluthians lined the beach lighted by giant bonfires. About midnight, the now exhausted lifesavers were sent back to their station to get a few hours rest.

Aboard the *Mataafa,* the 15 remaining crewmen col-

The Mataafa *lay a twisted wreck on the Duluth shore until salvors refloated her in June 1906.* EVELYN ABERNETHY PHOTO.

aft and 12 forward. Directed by their second mate, who had been aft supervising the dropping of the towline, four crewmen made a dash for the bow. Three made it while a fourth, after nearly going overboard, returned to join eight others of the stern crew on the open deck near the smokestack. These unfortunates either were washed overboard or succumbed to exposure, the temperature being not far from zero with the winds in excess of 60 miles an hour. Fifteen sailors took refuge in the forepeak.

Meanwhile, the U.S. Life-Saving Service crew was still out on Minnesota Point rescuing the crew of the *R.W. England.* A tug picked them up and rushed them to the *Mataafa* site. With darkness approaching, the lifesavers quickly put several lines aboard the ship. One froze and

lected all of the ship's lamps in the forepeak; these were lighted for heat. The captain instructed the mates and wheelsmen to keep the men on their feet and moving, even though all were exhausted. As the temperature dropped, the captain got a fire started in a bathtub dragged to the windlass room after breaking up a bathroom for wood. The fire kept all from freezing to death. With the wind and seas dropping somewhat at daybreak, the lifesavers returned with the surfboat. In a death-defying launch through still mountainous surf, they quickly reached the *Mataafa* and in two trips removed the 15 crewmen left alive.

Before leaving his ship, Captain Humble had worked his way aft only to discover four of his dead crew frozen in the iced-up top deck. Five others were missing and presumed dead. Battered as she was, the *Mataafa* was taken off six months later by the renowned Reids of Sarnia. She was rebuilt the following year at a cost in excess of $100,000 to resume a Great Lakes career that would span another 60 years. The *Mataafa* affair, viewed by thousands of Duluthians, has undoubtedly been one of the most famous of Lake Superior shipwrecks.[90]

latter two sporting 2,300 and 2,000 horsepower respectively. Also present were the 93-foot steel tug *Edna G.* from Two Harbors and the 115-foot wooden tug *Gladiator* of Duluth, two of the strongest tugs at the Head of the Lakes, together with the older 66-foot wooden tug *E.G. Crosby.* The flotilla struggled unsuccessfully for 12 long days. On December 10, the $450,000 *Corey* was finally pulled off by the steamers *Houghton* and *Marina*

The famous Reid Wrecking Company operated some of the Great Lakes' most powerful tugs. GREEN'S MARINE DIRECTORY, 1915.

While the Pittsburgh Steamship Company fleet was taking this shellacking on the north shore, another event was unfolding on the south shore. In seeking the protection of the Apostle Islands on that dismal November 28, the three-month-old, 558-foot, 6,363-ton steel *William E. Corey,* flagship of the fleet, slammed into Gull Island Reef, lodging tight in a horribly vulnerable position. Captain F.A. Bailey held his crew aboard. This brand new vessel withstood the devastating combers, but took terrific punishment. What followed the storm became one of Lake Superior's most sensational salvage efforts. With President Harry Coulby of the Pittsburgh Steamship Company rushing from the New York headquarters to Duluth in order to personally take charge, a rescue fleet of four regular ore carriers, three tugs and necessary lighters was hurriedly assembled. Two older carriers, the 282-foot *Manola* and 292-foot *Marina,* each with a respectable 1,200 horsepower, were detailed to the salvage crew along with two newer, far more powerful vessels, the 456-foot *Douglass Houghton* and the 413-foot *Sir William Siemens,* the

and sent to the shipyard for a $100,000 overhaul. During the effort, both the *Sir William Siemens* and *Edna G.* struck bottom, needing modest shipyard attention. Still, a prize ore carrier, one of the newest on the lakes, had been lifted from the lake's grasp, her entire crew safe. There may be another explanation for this unprecedented salvage operation. The *Corey* was named for the president of the parent United States Steel Corporation.[91]

The ill luck of the Pittsburghers continued. The 413-foot steel steamer *Coralia* with the 376-foot steel barge *Maia* in tow struck hard near the shore on the east side of Keweenaw Point at Point Abbaye. Wreckers had only modest difficulty floating both vessels into deep water with little injury.[92]

To the west of the Keweenaw, the two-year-old 416-foot, 4,764-ton steel steamer *Western Star* came to rest well up on the shore at Fourteen Mile Point near Ontonagon. She had been blown 125 miles off her course for Fort William. In this case the beach was favorable and the little 217-foot steamer *Viking* was able to drag her off with only a $20,000 repair charge.[93]

Narrow escapes and cases of substantial topside weather damage were myriad. The 414-foot steel steamer *Bransford* straddled a reef off Isle Royale at the height of the storm on November 28. The *Bransford,* however, was swept free by a giant wave. Then, under Captain "Doc" Balfour, she fought her way more than 175 miles to Duluth with 27 plates punctured and 50 frames cracked. An investment of $15,000 was needed to make her seaworthy again.[94]

Somewhere off Copper Harbor, the giant 452-foot steel barge *Constitution* was wrenched loose from her 459-foot steel towing steamer, *Victory.* The *Victory* was forced to backtrack all the way to Two Harbors, while the *Constitution,* with crippled steering gear, had a terrifying 130-mile ride in the trough of the sea all the way southwest to the Porcupine Mountain area of the Keweenaw. There, she was captured by the diminutive 124-foot, 383-ton wooden steam packet *C.W. Moore* of the Booth Fisheries Company which safely coaxed her into Chequamegon Bay. The Booth people subsequently asked $10,000 for their rescue services.

Many of the new steel steamers were battered in various degrees, including Hawgood's new 420-foot *Umbria,* Tomlinson's 356-foot *Yosemite,* the 416-foot *Perry G. Walker* and the 323-foot *E.C. Pope.* The 414-foot *Angeline* slogged her way into the Soo days late with her captain reporting seas higher than the smokestack.

Topside weather damage on the open lake struck Pittsburgh Steamship's 330-foot *Mariposa* and the three-year-old 380-foot *Harold B. Nye,* while the 245-foot Canadian package freighter *Rosemount* stranded in Thunder Bay and another package freighter, the 255-foot *S.C. Reynolds,* was slightly damaged while doing more damage to the grain elevator where she was docked in Duluth Harbor.[95]

Perhaps the most unnerving adventure of all was that of the little 189-foot, 765-ton lumber hooker *Arizona,* substantially rebuilt following her disastrous fire at Marquette in 1887. Under Captain Walter D. Neal, she approached the Duluth pierhead in the early hours of November 28. A wild, cyclonic gust caught her and spun her wildly when just a quarter of a mile from the Duluth Ship Canal. Fortunately, when she came around, her bow was pointed directly up the middle of the entry and Captain Neal drove her through with all the might her 558-horsepower engine could generate. Her master gratefully admitted later that she had made it purely by luck.[96]

Mariners were glad to conclude the 1905 season. More than two million dollars had been lost to shipping companies or their underwriters, while the death toll stood at 78. Indeed, this had been an awesome year. Fully 30 vessels had been directly involved in marine casualties during this single three-day storm ranging from dockside havoc to topside weather damage and mechanical failures on the open lake to foundering with all hands. This is virtually one percent of all known marine casualties on Lake Superior and two percent of all significant Lake Superior casualties. There has been no storm before nor since that caused such widespread plundering of Lake Superior shipping.[97]

1906

Vessel men were greeted by another banner year in 1906 with a tonnage increase of 15 percent over the record set in 1905. Sailing was far safer. To be sure, 40 ships were in miscellaneous scrapes, but only two tugs and six steamers joined the vanquished. Most situations were of the nuisance variety involving only little vessel damage.

A pair of collisions on May 17 were minor platebenders. The steamers *Joseph G. Butler Jr.* and *Myron* collided in Duluth Harbor. Likewise, the steamers *Troy* and *James Gayley* collided in Whitefish Bay. Poor visibility on May 25 brought another set of simultaneous, but well separated incidents. The five-year-old 346-foot, 3,748-ton steel steamer *Uranus* of the Gilchrist fleet plowed unsuspectingly into a reef off Eagle River. The tug *S.C. Schenck* and lighter *Rescue* raced to her assistance and had her afloat on the afternoon of May 28 after removing 2,000 tons of the iron ore cargo. It took $10,000 to patch her up.[98]

Near the Soo, blind navigating brought a weird collision. Unwittingly, the new 436-foot, 4,901-ton steel steamer *Howard L. Shaw* cut between the steamer *Coralia* and her consort, the *Maia.* The *Shaw* encountered the steel towline which passed over her bow and proceeded to "decapitate" her as she passed beneath. Sliced off were the top of her pilothouse, the masts, smokestack and anything protruding above the top of the deck house. If any crewmen were top-side, they must have hurriedly hit the deck, since there were no fatalities. Again, the shipyard had several thousand dollars worth of business.[99]

A fire on May 30 concluded the monthly trouble list when the 20-year-old 79-ton wooden steamer *Kaministiquia* was badly damaged at Port Arthur, a liability of several thousand dollars.[100]

June was calm. The steamer *Merida* and barge *Antrim* had a brush collision in Duluth Harbor on June 17. The 34-year-old wooden 156-foot steamer *Robert Holland* settled in shallow water on June 25, also in Duluth Harbor. Both were largely insignificant matters.

The year-old Duluth-based 66-foot wooden tug *Alfred W.* met a reef a half mile southeast of Pie Island about 1 a.m. on June 27 while Captain Frank Frechette Jr. was running in dense fog. The crew made it ashore when the lifeboat floated to the surface. The nine men were later picked up by the *Kaministiquia.* The badly listing and damaged tug, however, slipped into deep water, becoming a total loss of $14,000. The *Alfred W.* was owned by

Duluth-Superior Wrecking Company.[101]

July continued in the same vein with the only difficulty involving the brand new 549-foot, 6,996-ton steel steamer *Charles Weston,* which needed $10,000 in bottom work after hooking a reef off Keweenaw Point on July 26.

August contributed two more mishaps, one highly expensive. The 398-foot, 3,655-ton steel steamer *Troy* rammed the Interstate Bridge connecting Duluth and Superior on August 11. The steamer suffered only nominal injury, but the bridge, a significant railroad and vehicular link between the two towns, was dumped into the harbor, necessitating a drawn out salvage and rebuilding operation which ran more than $125,000. Land communication was disrupted for weeks.[102]

A summer fog on August 21 brought serious embarrassment to Captain A.G. Tappan of the 430-foot, 5,002-ton steel steamer *Frank H. Peavey.* In fog and heavy rain, the *Peavey,* en route light to Two Harbors, ran well up on the beach at Castle Danger, about 12 miles northeast of her destination. Second Mate Elmer Farquhar and Wheelsman Earl Moore hiked to Two Harbors during the early morning, and the tug *Edna G* sailed to her relief. Two days of pulling brought her off for a $15,000 trip to the shipyard in Superior.[103]

A wrecker's life was dull in September, too. On September 5, the little 33-year-old 52-net-ton wooden steamer *A. Seaman,* a Canadian vessel, sank at Michipicoten Island. The *Seaman* was a loss of several thousand dollars. Nine days later, the steamer *Tempest* touched bottom near Tahquamenon on the eastern lake with only slight injury.

The *Panama was beached and damaged beyond repair near Ontonagon.* C. PATRICK LABADIE COLLECTION.

Things were not as rosy in October. A slashing 50 mph gale with snow and sleet riled the lake west of Keweenaw Point on October 8, bringing grief to three schooner-barges in the vicinity of the Portage Lake Ship Canal. Breaking away from their towing steamer, the 189-foot barges *Wayne* and *Samuel H. Foster* ran ashore southwest of the canal, the *Wayne* at Redridge and the *Foster* at Misery Bay. The crews reached shore safely, and the ves-

sels presumably were salvageable, though the *Wayne* was not removed until July of the following year, while the *Foster* disappears from the register, possibly damaged beyond repair. Financial losses were not stated.[104]

The October 8 plight of the *Pasadena* was more tragic. In tow of the 283-foot, 2,453-ton wooden steamer *Gladstone,* the 259-foot, 2,076-ton wooden barge *Pasadena* swung too far to the northeast as the *Gladstone* tried to bring her into the safety of the Keweenaw Waterway. Seeing that he might collide with the east pier, the *Pasadena*'s master ordered the towline cut and the anchors dropped. They dragged, and the *Pasadena* smashed into the pierhead and quickly began going to pieces. Eight of her crew with life preservers made shore on floating wreckage. Two others, however, were either drowned or killed by the deadly flotsam. The Portage Canal lifesavers under Captain McCormick had spotted the trouble and quickly started for the mouth of the ship canal only to have the gale drive them back on the first try. Setting out again, they reached the canal entrance only to have their tiller give way, and the lifeboat itself was hurled on the beach near where the *Pasadena* survivors had already landed. Crewmen of ships anchored in the shelter of the waterway's Lily Pond assisted the *Pasadena* crew in reaching the lifesaving station. Under Captain Sullivan, the *Pasadena* had been en route to Superior with a coal cargo. She was a $42,000 casualty.[105]

A trio of collisions marked the remaining days of October with negligible results. The new steel steamers *Sinaloa* and *Francis L. Robbins* came together in Duluth Harbor on October 15. The steamer *Kensington* and whaleback barge *134* also collided in Duluth Harbor on October 23. The beleaguered steamer *Troy* and barge *Chieftain* had a brief encounter at Portage on October 28.

Those rough waters of October 28 also caused the destruction of the 139-foot, 330-ton lighter *Elgin* along the Minnesota north shore at the very mouth of Grand Marais Harbor, entailing a liability of $5,500. Carrying a load of coal and hay, the *Elgin* was in tow of the tug *Crosby* under Captain John Shea when she began to leak off Cross River. For 30 miles Captain Shea had the crew working the pumps as the water gained steadily. As the two tried to enter Grand Marais, the *Elgin* hit bottom and stuck, the waves quickly bringing her to ruin. She formerly had been the Canadian schooner *Elgin* launched at St. Catharines, Ontario, in 1874. Because of her age and condition, she was worth only $5,500 with cargo.[106]

Adverse weather in the third week of November brought a string of mishaps. The 205-foot, 1,101-ton wooden Canadian steamer *Strathmore* was downbound with 31,000 bushels of wheat from Fort William to Kingston on November 14 when the gale drove her on the rocks at the northwest point of Michipicoten Island. Captain Patrick Sullivan's crew manned the pumps until rising waters put out her fires. Thereupon the 13-man crew launched the yawl and fortuitously rode through the breakers to the island. They found shelter at Michipicoten Lighthouse. Two days later, the tug *Boynton* picked them up and took them to the Soo. The *Strathmore* went down, battered beyond recovery, a probable loss of $25,000 or more to her owner, George Plunkett of Cobourg, Ontario. She was formerly the American *Gordon Campbell*. She has been visited in recent years by sport divers who recovered her anchors which are now displayed in the park at the Canadian Soo.[107]

The northern and western lake was severely badgered by wind and snow on November 17, bringing a sinking and two strandings to Thunder Bay. Striving to reach shelter in the 50 mph gusts and pelting snow, the 255-foot, 1,175-ton steel steamer *Theano* of the Algoma Central Line was pushed off course into Trowbridge Island. She then swung broadside to the rocky shore, crushing in her side. The 20-man crew under Captain George Pearson remained aboard two hours in a desperate effort to save her. With water pouring in faster than the pumps could handle it, they wisely launched two lifeboats and pulled away. Moments later, the icy waters touched her red hot boilers and she blew up, sliding off the ledge into the depths. One lifeboat was soon picked up by the passing steamer *Iroquois,* but the second had to fight its way for 20 miles to Port Arthur with 10 men exposed to the bitter cold for nearly half a day. Built at Newcastle in Great Britain and only 16 years old, the *Theano* undoubtedly was valued in excess of $125,000.[108]

The same blow drove the American steamer *Philip Minch* and the Canadian steamer *Strathcona* onto the shore of Thunder Bay with little damage. Nevertheless, far to the southwest at Two Harbors, the seas sent the big 416-foot steamer *H.C. Frick* smashing into the breakwater for a $5,000 plate renewal job.

Vicious winds continued. The 275-foot, 2,044-ton wooden steamer *Panama* of the Davidson Steamship Company took such a beating off Ontonagon on November 21 that she began to leak badly. Rather than risk a foundering, Captain Jones beached her at Mineral Point, 14 miles west of Ontonagon. The crew reached shore and camped in the woods. Her barge *Matanzas* was safe, anchored a distance out, where she was picked up by the fishing tug *The Tramp* and towed into Ontonagon. The 18-year-old *Panama,* however, did not fare as well. The pounding of the waves broke her in two and so badly shattered her that she was irretrievable, a financial casualty with her coal cargo of $40,000. She formerly had been the steamer *John Craig.* Sport divers have visited her remains in recent years only to find her hull badly mangled by subsequent storms and ice, as well as by commercial salvors who recovered her engine and boilers.[109]

Storms struck sporadically over the next three weeks. The wooden steamer *Pere Marquette No. 5* went aground in the Keweenaw Waterway on November 25. Then on November 27, the steamer *Turret Crown* slid ashore near Grand Marais, Michigan. Neither incident amounted to much. The tossing waters on December 3, however, slapped the 300-foot steel steamer *Northern Queen* on Point Abbaye, and she was a $12,000 rehabilitation item.[110]

The next day, December 4, at Brule Bay south of Michipicoten, the 183-foot, 980-ton wooden steamer *Golspie*, owned by R.O. and A.B. McKay of Hamilton, Ontario, ended her days, stranded hard and broken. She was downbound from Fort William on December 2 with 38,650 bushels of oats, barley and general cargo when a storm set in as the ship closed to within 10 miles of Passage Island. The ship was brought about and run for shelter on the north shore, trying first at Battle Island where shifting winds caused them to move on to Nipigon Straits to anchor.

The *Golspie* was under way again the next day, still in a freshening wind. The course was set to run north of Michipicoten Island and along the coastline toward the Soo. Once again the storm kicked up, this time getting the better of the *Golspie* as she was being damaged badly by the stress of weather. Captain Harry Boult turned her toward Michipicoten Harbor, but was forced to head into Brule Bay where she ran up on the gravel beach broadside. The storms had won out. She was previously the American steamer *Osceola*, built in 1882. Her value was not reported, but the 183-foot, 1,122-ton vessel must have been worth $20,000 or more. There was no loss of life although several of her crew suffered crippling injuries from cold and frostbite as they walked toward shelter over the next few days after the accident.[111]

The Canadian passenger steamer Monarch *wrecked in a blinding 1906 snow storm.* C. PATRICK LABADIE COLLECTION.

Thick snow off Thunder Cape on the night of December 6 caused a far more costly accident. The 240-foot, 2,017-ton wooden passenger-package freight steamer *Monarch* of the Northern Navigation Company was hauling mostly grain and a few passengers in the off-season. On the outbound course from Port Arthur with Captain

Edward Robertson in command, the *Monarch* somehow strayed too far to the south when threading the needle between Passage Island and Blake's Point at the northeastern tip of Isle Royale and slammed into the palisades just

The Monarch *blundered into rock bluffs in darkness and snow just west of Blake's Point on Isle Royale.* MILWAUKEE PUBLIC LIBRARY COLLECTION.

west of Blake's Point. She hit so hard that her wooden hull accordioned amidships, her bow butted up against the ice covered bluff.

Captain Robertson ordered the lifeboat put in the water and pulled forward where the entire crew and a handful of passengers assembled in the cold. Although some crew members were able to get into the boat, they were unsuccessful in getting out on the icy shore and they returned to the *Monarch*.

The vessel was in danger of breaking apart, so a second plan was worked out involving J.D. McCallum, the younger brother of the ship's first mate, who was working off his passage down to Sarnia as a lookout. The young McCallum volunteered to go overboard and down the ladder which was usually used at the locks to get crewmen back aboard. Then McCallum and the ladder, to which a line had been fastened, were swung pendulum-fashion until he was confident he could leap safely ashore. Luck was with him. He scrambled up the bluff, used his lifeline to pull across a stout hawser and fastened that to a tree. The crew began one by one to cross ashore hand over hand on the line. About half the crew had made it when the stern broke away and settled. In a moment of confusion, Watchman J. Jacques apparently grabbed a short or unsecured line and fell into the lake, drowning. The rest of the crew continued across the line, except Captain Robertson who spent the first night aboard. On the second day, he was persuaded to come ashore with the rest of the 30-man crew. Bonfires were lit and a truly meager amount of food was consumed. Still no rescuers were in sight. Part of the crew went to explore

for fishermen's cabins where there would be shelter and possibly food while others stayed at the main camp.

The crew had an uncomfortable 36-hour wait for help. Thick fog persisted for a whole day following the snow, making the wrecked *Monarch* invisible from the steamer lanes. During the second night, the fog lifted and the Passage Island Lighthouse keeper, who had climbed his tower after midnight to have a look around, spotted a glow in the sky over Blake's Point. He sent his assistant over the next morning to investigate. Finding the bedraggled, frozen crew, he took Purser Beaumont with him and rowed out to the shipping channel where they could flag down a steamer to carry the news back to port. That night, they flagged down the downbound *Edmonton* which returned to Port Arthur. The *James Whalen* and *Laura Grace* quickly set out for Blake's Point. They were hampered somewhat in picking up the crew by thick shore ice, but eventually rescued everyone.

The *Monarch* mishap was difficult to explain. The compass may have gone somewhat awry, but more likely the taffrail log iced up and the distance run was misjudged. With her 85,000-bushel grain cargo, the *Monarch* undoubtedly was a liability in excess of $150,000, though the exact figure was not reported. The following July 4 at Port Arthur, the heroic young J.D. McCallum was given the Royal Humane Society Medal by the Canadian Board of Trade for his dramatic role in rescuing his shipmates. The *Monarch*'s remains were purchased in the fall of 1908 by Reid Wrecking Company of Port Huron and Sarnia; salvage began immediately after work was concluded on the *Sevona*. Fourteen men worked on the wreck for 25 days using two barges, a tug and two divers. Their work was apparently thorough as Captain Reid stated:

"We took everything of value out of the wreck, having found conditions such that we were able to make a very complete job of it. We have the boilers, engines, dynamos, chains, windlasses, etc. loaded on the barge ready to be taken to Sarnia."

The barge Captain Reid referred to was the *Bennington,* which foundered October 5, 1908, on Lake Superior. The *Monarch*'s engine, at least, was not on this barge and did successfully make it to the Reid yard. It was not, however, reused and was destroyed some years later to reduce it to scrap metal.[112]

The cold weather on December 6 made a bid for another major wooden ship when ice pierced the hull of the 298-foot ore carrier *John Harper* of the Gilchrist fleet. She managed to reach the Keweenaw Waterway and the Lily Pond where the leaks were halted and she was pumped out. Had a harbor of refuge not been available, she could have been in a serious predicament.

The following day, December 7, did leave the three-year-old 416-foot, 4,470-ton steel steamer *R.L. Ireland* in a horrible position astride Gull Island Reef with the seas getting a full sweep at her. One of the Gilchrist line, her owners rushed the 416-foot steel steamer *Joseph C. Gilchrist* and the Reid wrecker *Manistique* to her assistance. Several of the *Ireland*'s crew reached Bayfield in a yawl. The rest of the crew was taken off when the winds worsened and the temperature dove to 20 degrees below zero. However, four days later, the wreckers pulled her loose and the crew went back aboard when the tug *E.G. Crosby* began to tow her to Superior. The lake would not leave the *Ireland* alone. Yet another wild storm hit, breaking the towline. Once again the crew had to abandon ship, this time transferring to the tug *Crosby*. One man was lost overboard in the transfer and drowned. Eventually, the *Crosby* brought the *Ireland* to port for a salvage and rebuilding operation aggregating $90,000. The *Manistique* fought the gale head-on for 23 hours before reaching her base at Port Arthur. For a while, fears were felt for her safety.[113]

A postseason mishap at Ontonagon saw the 52-foot tug *Adventurer* apparently break her moorings and strand, a total loss. No one was aboard at the time. Damage for this December 16 incident was not reported.

1907

Shippers reaped another all-time high in tonnage during 1907, and the total operation was safer, with 34 units reporting difficulties and only six ships overwhelmed. Three incidents alone accounted for the 34 lives lost.

Sailing got under way in early April and ice caused trouble in harbors, narrow passageways and Whitefish Bay. Most situations were trivial. The excursion steamer *Mascotte* sank at her dock in Hancock when ice pierced the hull on April 1. The steel steamers *Harvey D. Goulder* and *Anna C. Minch* came together in Duluth Harbor on April 12. The ice pack in Whitefish Bay caused the steel *Joseph G. Butler Jr.* to slam into the steel *William A. Paine* on April 25. The *Paine* needed the most attention, about $8,000 worth of shipyard work. The very next day, the steel *Joseph C. Gilchrist* rammed the stern of the *John Sherwin*. Ice in the Portage Lake Ship Canal persisted through the month, sinking the 69-foot wooden tug *Buffalo* of the Great Lakes Towing Company and the 298-foot wooden steamer *Alex Nimick* on April 29. The *Nimick* was raised immediately. The *Buffalo,* sunk in 48 feet of water off High Point in the Keweenaw Waterway, was a tough proposition, even for the wrecker *Favorite.* After several months of effort, she was abandoned as a total loss of $4,000. She was 20 years old.[114]

The next three months were reasonably normal. The Pittsburgh fleet's 296-foot steel steamer *Saxon* slid into the reefs off Caribou Island in fog on May 14. Initially, there was some doubt of her salvageability, but she proved to be resting on a relatively smooth bottom and was taken off with repair charges of $20,000. In a har-

bor maneuver on May 29, the steamer *William A. Paine* smacked a dock at Two Harbors, requiring light repairs.

A spectacular fire on the night of June 26 claimed the 26-year-old wooden Canadian steamer *Batchawana* off Coppermine Point. Downbound with iron ore from Fort William to the Algoma Steel Company at Sault Ste. Marie, Ontario, the 209-foot, 674-net-ton vessel somehow took fire and soon was enveloped in flames. The crew took to the lifeboats and was saved, but their ship had made her last trip. She had previously been the American steamer *R.A. Packer* of the Lehigh Valley Line. Insurance coverage amounted to $28,000 on the vessel although probably worth more than $35,000.[115]

The fogs of July brought the usual minor strandings and collisions. The steamer *J.Q. Riddle* pushed herself into the sands of Whitefish Bay on July 10. The steel steamers *Saxona* and *City of Bangor* brushed in the mists of Whitefish Bay on July 13 resulting in $15,000 damage. The 300-foot steel freighter *North Wind* needed a little attention after slamming into a dock at Duluth on July 27. The schooner *B.B. Buckhout* went ashore at Crisp Point that same day.

A senseless catastrophe in Duluth Harbor on the evening of August 10 took six lives. A 62-foot wooden tug was towing a mud scow off 12th Avenue West as a group of stevedores was trying to cross the harbor in a badly overloaded rowboat. For reasons hard to ascertain, the rowboat cut between the tug and her tow, was caught by the scow and capsized. Six men drowned and several narrowly escaped death.[116]

Six men died when the Alex Nimick *wrecked near Vermilion Point on September 20, 1907.* C. PATRICK LABADIE COLLECTION.

The steel steamer *Northern King* banged the pier at Superior on August 11 and had to be touched up, while a port fire ravaged the tug *Tempest* in Duluth on August 13.

The lake east of Duluth was badly riled by a 40 mph gale on August 23 which caught the 31-year-old 76-foot, 52-ton wooden tug *E.T. Carrington* about 18 miles out.

The pounding waves opened her seams, and she started to take water rapidly. At an opportune moment, the 430-foot steel steamer *Frederick B. Wells* came along and offered assistance. A line from the tug was put aboard the steamer, and Captain Frechette and the *Carrington* crew went aboard the big carrier. The *Wells* then tried to tow the settling tug to Duluth Harbor, but the tug's towing cleat tore out and down she went. The *Carrington* had been built as a side-wheeler at Bangor, Michigan, in 1876, being rebuilt at Duluth in 1900. She had previously served as an excursion steamer at Duluth and was valued at $3,000 by her owner, Captain Walter Lloyd of Duluth.[117]

Cyprus was only on her second trip when she rolled over and sank on October 11, 1907. One of her 23 men survived. AUTHOR'S PHOTO.

Sailing in September took on a more serious note. A destructive fire in Marquette Harbor raked the 32-year-old 238-foot wooden steamer *Portage* on the 16th, necessitating rebuilding efforts of $10,000, perhaps one-third of her worth.

This year the usually devastating equinoctial northwester was right on time, harassing the entire eastern lake on September 21 and 22. The storm gods scored. After lying behind the protection of Whitefish Point on the night of September 20, Captain John Randall of the 298-foot, 1,968-ton wooden steamer *Alex Nimick* decided that the worst was not going to materialize and headed to the west in a deceptively light southwester. Only a few hours later, however, a blustering northwest gale set in. The seventeen-year-old *Nimick*, with a respectable 1,200 horsepower, was stopped cold. She was taking such a beating that Captain Randall abandoned hope of reaching the shelter of Grand Island and turned about for a return to Whitefish Point. He couldn't make it. The *Nimick* began leaking off Crisp Point. Captain Randall blew distress signals which were recognized by Captain James Scott of the Crisp Point lifesavers, who ordered the surfboat launched. The *Nimick* continued to the east, but giant waves stove in her bow and port gangways, and water rose so rapidly that her fires were put out. She crashed aground

about 6:40 p.m., a mile and a half west of Vermilion Point, disintegrating within minutes.

Launching with grave difficulty, the Crisp Point lifesaving crew scoured the shore for 18 miles all the way to Whitefish Point, but in the darkness they could not find the ravaged hulk whose lights had been extinguished. The *Nimick*'s first mate, Gordon Tobin, had launched the stern yawl, and this little lifeboat survived the hideous surf to bring 10 of the crew to the beach at the Vermilion Point Life-Saving Station where they were sheltered by the lifesavers who were patrolling the beach at the request of the Crisp Point Station captain.

Those in the forward portion of the *Nimick* were not so lucky. Their yawl had been smashed before it could be launched. Of the six men forward, including Captain Randall, only the chief engineer would reach the beach alive with the aid of a life jacket. The other five were killed or drowned in the mass of tossing debris. The cook had been washed overboard earlier and drowned. Six men had died and a $70,000 financial liability incurred. The *Nimick* was owned by J.C. Gilchrist of Cleveland.[118]

The same violent September winds sent the 308-foot steel whaleback steamer *James B. Colgate* and her consort, whaleback barge *133,* scurrying for the shelter of Grand Island. They reached protected waters, but the steamer stranded and her barge smashed into her, sending both to dry-dock for thousands of dollars worth of refurbishing.

This October was a rough one, too. An incident in the Duluth-Superior Harbor on the 2nd inaugurated the mischief when the new 504-foot, 5,841-ton steel *Hoover & Mason,* a 2,000-horsepower ship, clipped the north pier of the Northern Pacific Railroad bridge spanning the harbor. The vessel needed $5,000 in repairs, but the pier went to the bottom, a very costly rebuilding operation.

Then came the shocking event of October 11, the capsizing of the two-month-old 420-foot, 4,900-ton steel steamer *Cyprus,* a Lackawanna Transportation Company vessel managed by Pickands Mather & Company. Perhaps no foundering since that of the *Western Reserve* in 1892 surprised the marine world more. The *Cyprus* had been launched the previous August 17 at Lorain, Ohio, and was on her second trip, having loaded 7,400 tons of iron ore at the Allouez docks in Superior, which she left at 8 a.m. on October 10. A moderate northerly storm began blowing east of the Keweenaw. Still, when observed by Captain Smith of the 504-foot steel steamer *Charles O. Jenkins* at 10 a.m., October 11, the *Cyprus* was pushing right along about 10 miles off Stannard Rock. Later in the day, she was observed by Captain Harbottle of the Pittsburgher *George Stephenson* and seemed to be doing well.

That evening, about 7 p.m., as the *Cyprus* was headed east about 18 miles north of Deer Park, Michigan, and roughly 35 miles west of Whitefish Point, the steamer listed sharply to port, taking water in the hatches. Crewmen put on life jackets, but Captain F.B. Huyck did not order the boats lowered since the engines were functioning perfectly and the weather was not really alarming. He expected they would be safe in three or four hours. Some minutes later, however, the *Cyprus* rolled over on her port side and sank instantly. Four men forward, two mates, a watchman and a wheelsman slashed loose a life raft as the ship dove to the bottom. They clung to this precarious float for seven dreadful hours as the wind slowly drove them toward the Michigan coast. When they struck the malevolent south shore surf, however, it was the usual story. Over and over rolled the life raft until only one man remained, Second Mate Charles J. Pitz. As the raft touched the sandy beach, Pitz had sufficient strength to crawl out of reach of the waves before he collapsed in the darkness.

Some time later, a patrolling lifesaver discovered his unconscious form and carried him to the Deer Park Life-Saving Station where, after more hours, he was revived and told what had happened. When first brought in, he could only gasp out the name of the ship and report the crew gone. From information furnished by Second Mate Pitz, vessel men deduced that the *Cyprus,* equipped with new Mulholland hatches, but no tarpaulins, had taken water seepage around the hatch covers which were not water tight. A sufficient quantity of water mixing with the natural iron ore caused the cargo to shift as the vessel rolled, and the *Cyprus* capsized. She was an official loss of $280,000 and 22 men went down with her. Lifesavers maintained a beach patrol for many days after the sinking, 20 life-jacketed bodies being recovered, that of Captain Huyck some 10 miles east of where Pitz had come ashore. The crew apparently had died of exposure in the frigid water. An aftermath of the *Cyprus* disaster was the requirement of tarpaulined hatches on Lake Superior at certain times of the year.[119]

In the same moderate blow of October 12, the 193-foot, 908-ton steel pulpwood steamer *John B. Ketchum 2nd* ran ashore on Copper Island, southeast of Nipigon Bay on the Canadian north shore. She was quickly retrieved, but needed several thousand dollars worth of bottom plates at the shipyard.[120]

A pioneer steel ship, the 312-foot, 2,368-ton steel steamer *Spokane,* made an unfortunate run on October 28. The first steel-hulled American laker, the *Spokane* was en route west to Duluth with a coal cargo when, in a snow-bearing gale, she was tossed on Gull Island Reef near Manitou Island off Keweenaw Point. Captain John McArthur and his 18-man crew took the ship's lifeboat to Manitou Island Lighthouse where they found temporary shelter. As the seas quieted, Captain McArthur sailed the lifeboat to the mainland and reached the Delaware Mine where he telegraphed for help. Before the wrecker *Favorite* could pull the *Spokane* to deep water, however, another storm broke her in two. While her crew was safe, the *Spokane* was in sad condition. The following May,

she was taken off by the Reids of Sarnia and towed to Detroit. There she was discovered to be so badly shattered that her owners, Wilson Transit Company, apparently ordered her scrapped, a $50,000 casualty only 21 years old. From the record, nevertheless, it seems that another operator purchased the hull and rebuilt her, as she was registered out of Port Huron three years later.[121]

The old steamer Cormorant *was burned to the water's edge in October 1907.* C. PATRICK LABADIE COLLECTION.

Another old-timer bade farewell on October 30. The 218-foot, 977-ton wooden lumber hooker *Cormorant* of the Edward Hines Lumber Company caught fire off the north side of Basswood Island in the Apostles. Her master beached her, and she burned to the waterline, exposing her machinery. Her crew rowed to nearby Red Cliff for help. Built by I. Laffrinier at Cleveland in 1873, this steam barge had put in 34 years on the lakes. She was a $19,000 item. The burned-out hulk was purchased by wrecker J.B. Wanless of Duluth who patched her up enough to tow her to Bayfield where she arrived on November 17. Her engine, boilers and miscellaneous items were quickly removed. Her remains were then towed to Duluth by the tug *E.G. Crosby,* arriving on December 6. Final disposition of the *Cormorant*'s remains is unknown. Her bottom was solid and may have been rebuilt into an unregistered barge.[122]

The remainder of the season was quiet. The steel steamer *Harvey D. Goulder* banged a bridge at Duluth on November 2, and the wooden steamer *Louisiana* managed to strike bottom in the Keweenaw Waterway. Both ships needed only modest renovation.

1908

Ship owners received a rude jolt in the navigation season of 1908. The Panic of 1907 had resulted in a severe contraction of business activity, and tonnage on Lake Superior dropped 30 percent, the sharpest curtailment since the Panic of 1893. Still, the year was fruitful by the standards of the early 1900s. Ships ran until early December, and most of the accidents were insignificant. An end-of-season catastrophe, however, did leave a blight on this year.

An inequitable collision occurred in Duluth Harbor on May 3 when the 346-foot steel steamer *J.T. Hutchinson* whacked the 67-foot wooden tug *J.L. Williams.* The *Williams* remained afloat, but needed some $1,800 worth

with little injury. The steel steamer *Salt Lake City* banged a scow in Duluth waters on June 24.

Fog along the Minnesota north shore brought mostly embarrassment to one master on July 28, but a sizable dry-dock bill for the second. A few miles northeast of Two Harbors, the new 558-foot Pittsburgher *George W. Perkins* slid ashore at Stewart River. She had to be dry-docked for nominal repairs, but her captain undoubtedly had

Old Chauncy Hurlbut *was wrecked beyond repair at Vermilion Point.* MILWAUKEE PUBLIC LIBRARY COLLECTION.

of rebuilding before returning to service. Incidents in the Keweenaw Waterway included the May 11 stranding of the big new 504-foot steamer *John Stanton* of the Hutchinson fleet. She required $5,000 in bottom plates. The steel steamer *Samuel Mitchell* grounded at Houghton Point on May 18, and the barge *Chickamauga* slammed into her, another $7,000 in business for the shipyards.

Lifesavers at Grand Marais, Michigan, were called to the beach 20 miles to the west where a small Lighthouse Service sailboat had been blown ashore on June 12. In the little craft, the *L.H.E.,* was a solitary occupant dead of exposure, probably a victim of a substantial blow on June 7. The lone sailor was unidentified, but he probably was a crewman from the Grand Island Light Station.

A fender-bender in Superior Harbor on June 18 saw the steel steamers *Leonard C. Hanna* and *Socapa* scraping

some difficulty explaining a several mile error in navigational reckoning.

Circumstances were more severe at Passage Island, northeast of Isle Royale. The brand new 530-foot steel steamer *Daniel B. Meacham* of the Frontier Steamship Company at Tonawanda, New York, rammed a reef and punctured her hull while en route to Port Arthur with 9,000 tons of coal. She had just been launched a few weeks before. As she lay wide open to possible ravages of the lake, the Canadian Towing and Wrecking Company went to work on her, with salvager Captain Kidd of Duluth observing. They took her off quickly for a $40,000 trip to the shipyard. Captain Deringer of the *Meacham* was replaced.[123]

Two more trouble-laden situations rounded out the month as the 540-foot steel *Augustus B. Wolvin* grounded in the Portage River on July 30 and the steamer *Scranton* and Standard Oil's tankerbarge *S.O.Co.No.86* brushed in the same waterway on July 31. Only slight injury was involved.

Mid-August brought several items. The tug *Tom Dowling* took fire at Ashland on the 17th and was badly singed. The next day at Duluth, the tug *Sarah Smith* suffered a similar fate. Both were reconstructed with the expenditure of several thousand dollars in each case. Far to the east, also on August 17, the 253-foot steel Canadian steamer *Neepawah* was pitched aground at Otter Head. After a difficult salvage effort requiring more than 10 days, the *Nepeewah* was released by the Reids of Sarnia and towed to Ecorse, Michigan, for shipyard work aggregating $28,000.[124]

September was more turbulent, as usual. The 382-foot steamer *Buffalo* of the Western Transit Line sliced into the 585-foot steel *William B. Kerr* of the Tonawanda Steamship Company on September 1 at Elevator B in Duluth Harbor. Neither sank, but both headed for the dry dock, the *Buffalo* needing $15,000 in reconstruction charges and the *Kerr,* $10,000.[125]

Wild weather east of Keweenaw Point on September 5-6 brought a pair of losses. En route from Port Arthur to the Soo in tow of a tug on September 5, the Reid Company's wrecking barge, the 250-ton *Bennington,* suddenly foundered, drowning her crew of two.

That same night, the venerable 34-year-old 185-foot, 1,009-ton wooden steamer *Chauncy Hurlbut* sailed her last. Downbound from Lake Linden to Toledo with a cargo of copper sand, the schooner *Clint* in tow, the aged *Hurlbut* began leaking from the pounding she was taking. Rather than risk foundering, her captain ran her ashore in the early hours of September 6, a half mile northwest of the Vermilion Point Life-Saving Station. A patrolling lifesaver spotted her at daybreak. Captain Carpenter of the lifesavers ordered the surfboat launched and, despite the treacherous waves, the lifesavers removed the *Hurlbut*'s full crew of 14 persons in two trips. As the storm subsided, the lifesavers also were able to save the personal belongings of the crew. The Revenue Cutter *Tuscarora,* which happened by shortly afterward, attempted to retrieve the *Hurlbut,* but she was too badly broken. Because of her age, she was worth only $17,000 with cargo.[126] The same winds left the wooden steamer *Robert L. Fryer* aground at Traverse Bay, but she did not suffer much damage.

Another minimal incident took place near Gay, Michigan, on September 20 when the 266-foot steel steamer *J.H. Wade* touched bottom as she was attempting to land a 2,600-ton coal cargo for the Mohawk Mine. Damage was inconsequential.

Not so on September 27. Forest fires were plaguing the coasts of Lake Superior, and the lake was shrouded with dense bluish smoke and haze. Attempting to push through,

despite limited visibility, was the 284-foot, 2,255-ton wooden steamer *Neshoto* laden with iron ore out of Superior. She plowed into the shallows two and a half miles northeast of Crisp Point. The lifesaving patrol discovered her, and the lifesavers pulled out in the surfboat. As the seas were not too rough at the time, they proceeded to assist the crew in attempting to back her off. She was stuck too hard. As they labored to free her, the wind rose and the surf began to pound. To the discouragement of all, the *Neshoto* swung broadside to the waves and began to break up. The lifesavers took the 16-man crew to the safety of the station as the 19-year-old *Neshoto* disintegrated, a $65,000 casualty for the J.C. Gilchrist Company.[127]

The smoke-fog combination scored again the following day at Parisienne Island when the 270-foot steel steamer *Frontenac* crashed hard aground. Salvors were able to relieve her six days later for a $20,000 date with the dry-dock facilities.

Another unequal confrontation occurred in Duluth Harbor on October 14. Just off the Elevator B slip, the 430-foot steel steamer *Mataafa* of the Pittsburgh Steamship Company fleet rammed the 308-foot wooden steamer *Sacramento* of the Davidson Company. Struck amidships and badly holed, the *Sacramento* was run into the shallows where she settled to the bottom. As would be expected, the *Mataafa* was largely unscathed, but the salvors had to tussle with the coal-laden *Sacramento* for several weeks before she could be taken to the shipyard for a $15,000 reconstruction undertaking.[128]

The Neshoto *broke up quickly on the beach at Crisp Point.* MRS. JANICE JERRED COLLECTION.

Tempestuous seas east of Keweenaw Point October 19-22 sent a veteran schooner-barge to the ship graveyard and came close to grabbing another schooner plus a steel steamer. Upbound off the Huron Islands when the gale hit was the 203-foot, 982-ton wooden steamer *Edward L. Hines* with her coal-laden consorts, the 196-foot, 747-ton schooner-barge *Lizzie A. Law* and the 175-foot, 618-ton schooner-barge *Selden E. Marvin.* The *Hines'* 505-

horsepower engine could make no headway against the rugged winds and, before long, the towlines parted. Propelled by easterly blasts, both barges crashed into Traverse Island. Sixteen men and one woman reached shore in the ships' lifeboats. The 33-year-old *Law* would sail no more, being beaten to pieces by the waves over the next few days. Salvors, however, were able to extricate the *Marvin*. While no financial figures were reported, the *Law* very likely was worth about $8,000.[129]

Caught in the same general area on October 22, the Lackawanna Transportation Company's 260-foot steel steamer *Scranton* was deposited on the rocks of Point Abbaye, east of Portage. Her bottom absorbed a $15,000 pounding before wrecking crews released her.[130] With poor visibility and moderate seas continuing on October 24, the brand new 530-foot, 6,971-ton steamer *Daniel B. Meacham* slammed into a reef approximately 12 miles northeast of the Portage Lake Ship Canal. It was her second incident of the season. Downbound from Superior with iron ore for Ashtabula, she was firmly aground. The Portage Lake Ship Canal lifesavers went to her in their motor lifeboat and, since the seas were rising, took off her crew as a precaution. The Canadian salvage tug *James Whalen* was summoned from Port Arthur. The lifesavers put the *Meacham* crew back aboard as calmer weather returned, and the *Whalen* had her off in two days for a run to the shipyard where an $85,000 rebuilding job was necessary on a ship launched only four months before at a cost of $385,000. Captain Hassen, who had replaced Captain Deringer after the Passage Island incident, was master of the *Meacham* in the second stranding. His luck appeared no better than his predecessor's.[131]

The big new D.M. Clemson *left no witnesses behind when she foundered.* UNIVERSITY OF DETROIT MARINE COLLECTION.

November seemed to produce moderately tranquil sailing up until the last week when gales and snow raked the entire lake. The sledge hammer weather blast struck on the night of November 30 when blizzard conditions and 50 mph winds lambasted the area west of Whitefish

Point, leaving an all-time mystery of Lake Superior. The new 468-foot, 5,531-ton steel steamer *D.M. Clemson* of the Provident Steamship Company simply vanished with her 24-man crew. The *Clemson* was a Duluth-owned vessel belonging to the Wolvin interests. She had been built in Superior in 1903. She was powerful for her size at 1,800 horsepower. Her officers, Captain Samuel R. Chamberlain, First Mate W.E. McLeod and Chief Engineer J.J. McCoy, were all Duluth men as were several of her crew.

She had a creditable five-year career, although the killer storm of September 1-2, 1905, almost claimed her when she crept into Two Harbors, badly listing, nearly awash with hatch covers gone. Ill luck had dogged her in October 1908, when she first struck a pier at Ashtabula, cracking 10 plates on October 20 and then, after temporary repairs, she grounded at Point Pelee in forest fire smoke on October 23. Taken off, she still made two routine voyages to Lake Superior for iron ore, departing Duluth on November 9 and Two Harbors on November 20.

On her last run, she left Lorain, Ohio, with a cargo of coal for Superior and winter layup, locking through the Soo at 9:30 a.m., November 30. She proceeded up the St. Marys River and through Whitefish Bay in company with the recently launched 432-foot, 5,069 steel steamer *J.J.H. Brown* under Captain F.D. Chamberlain. At Whitefish Point they separated, the *Brown* taking a northerly course under cover of the Canadian shoreline and the *Clemson* the more direct route to Manitou Island. Crewmen of the *Brown* were the last to see the *Clemson*. Not long after they parted, the *Brown*'s master reported encountering the most vicious snowstorm he had ever seen in his long career. For 12 hours, the *Brown,* a respectable 1,500-horsepower ship, just drifted with the seas, arriving at the Head of the Lakes more than a day late, somewhat the worse for wear.

As the storm mass moved eastward and vessel traffic was resumed, officers of the steamers *Turret Court* and *Wasaga* reaching the Soo on December 4 reported sighting wreckage off Crisp Point including the top of a pilothouse and hatch covers seemingly from a wooden ship. The first candidate for eternity was the 292-foot wooden steamer *Tampa,* which would have been in that vicinity on December 1. No consternation was felt for the *Clemson* since a large steamer was reported anchored in the shelter of Grand Island. Other ships sighted additional wreckage, but it did not seem to come from a steel ship. Also, the steamer *Northern Queen* of the Mutual Transit Line was missing.

Gradually, speculations were put aside. The *Tampa* showed up safe at Fort William on December 5. The steamer behind Grand Island was the *D.O. Mills.* The *Northern Queen* was safe in the Keweenaw Waterway. The only ship unaccounted for was the *D.M. Clemson.*

By December 9, wreckage was appearing on the south shore from Grand Marais to Whitefish Point. A water barrel and a life jacket with the name "*D.M. Clemson*" washed up at Crisp Point. A pilothouse came ashore near Vermilion Point. Hatch covers found near Whitefish Point matched those of another Provident Steamship Company vessel, *Frederick B. Wells.* The clincher came on December 15. A patrolling lifesaver sighted a body bobbing in the surf. The stencil on the life preserver said "*D.M. Clemson.*" As far as western Lake Superior records indicate, this body found at Crisp Point and one discovered farther to the east two weeks later seem to be the only remains of the *Clemson* crew to reach land. At least two members knew that disaster was imminent and managed to put on life jackets.

Naturally, the disappearance of the *Clemson* started sailors' imaginations working overtime. What had happened? This powerful ship had gone down, while weaker vessels made it. Had she capsized? Did she lose hatch covers and founder? Did she break in two? Had overworked boilers exploded? There were many possibilities. Her property loss of $330,000 was the worst for any American ship on Lake Superior up to this time. Indeed, she was the third largest vessel to succumb in the sailing history of the lake. That death toll of 24 was the most serious since 1901. There was a truly ironic note in this tragedy. Captain Sam Chamberlain was about to retire. He had promised his wife that this would be his last trip. It was.[132]

The season's finale was a repeat performance for the new 504-foot steel steamer *John Stanton.* Early in May, she had skinned herself in the Keweenaw Waterway. This time she caught bottom on December 6 near Point Iroquois. Wreckers pulled her to deep water three days later, but this time she took $12,000 in fixing.

1909

Vessel traffic rebounded amazingly in 1909. Tonnage shot upward nearly 40 percent over 1908's performance. Yet, the mishap total leaped only too proportionally: 46 vessels in trouble, 10 gone forever and two more extremely difficult salvage risks. Three ships were lost in the first two weeks of sailing, something never before experienced.

The toll jumped off on April 15 at Susie Island, on Minnesota's north shore to the west of Isle Royale, as the 45-foot wooden fishing tug *Fred B. Hall* sank at her dock from ice cuts. At first thought a goner, she was raised nearly two weeks later by salvor Captain Horace Thompson of Duluth from 75 feet of water, though the recovery and rebuilding costs came to $8,000.

Two 416-foot steel steamers came together in Duluth Harbor on April 29, the *R.E. Schuck* and *Perry G. Walker,* with combined repairs of approximately $10,000. The same day, far to the east in Whitefish Bay, an unhappy in-

cident was in the making. Arriving at the Soo, Captain Boyce of the Wolvin steamer *George W. Peavey* reported that he had seen a substantial steel steamer, close to 400 feet long with a red hull and white deck houses, sink in

The steel Aurania *was holed and sunk by ice fields in the spring of 1909.* CANAL PARK MARINE MUSEUM COLLECTION.

the ice pack off the lower end of Parisienne Island in Whitefish Bay. The *Peavey*'s captain was only too correct. The 352-foot, 3,218-ton steel *Aurania* of the Corrigan fleet had been bucking heavy seas and worsening pack ice in Whitefish Bay, which her 700-horsepower engine could not drive her through. Giving up hope of ramming her through the windrows, Captain Robert C. Pringle succeeded in turning her back toward the Soo. But massive chunks of ice had stove in her steel plates, and she started to take water rapidly. Realizing the vessel was doomed, Captain Pringle led the crew on foot over the ice, dragging the ship's yawls through a heavy fall of snow toward another vessel four miles distant. She proved to be the new 504-foot *J.H. Bartow.* The whole *Aurania* crew was taken aboard the *Bartow* whose 1,650-horsepower engine enabled them to make the Soo. Other ships were in the vicinity, but were immobilized and their officers could only watch as the *Aurania* dove to the bottom of Whitefish Bay at 10 a.m. on April 29. Built at Chicago in 1895, she was insured for $200,000. To this day, she is the only steel hulled ship sunk by Lake Superior ice, although several others have had close calls in more recent years.[133]

The whole lake was riled unmercifully by a gigantic gale and snowstorm over the next several days. Caught off the Huron Islands by this turbulence on April 30, the 180-foot wooden lumber hooker *Schoolcraft* lost her schooner-barge, the 207-foot, 790-ton *George Nester,* when the line parted. The ill-fated *Nester* was driven on the reefs at the Huron Islands and torn to bits, Captain George D. Bau and his six-man crew drowning as the U.S. Lighthouse Tender *Marigold* failed to get near enough in a desperate rescue attempt. The *Schoolcraft* crept into Baraga for shelter.[134]

Slightly to the east on that dismal May 1, the macabre lake reaped another. The 195-foot, 734-ton wooden lumber hooker *Adella Shores,* upbound to Duluth with a cargo of salt, had entered the lake on April 29, following the new 580-foot, 2,000-horsepower steel steamer *Daniel J. Morrell.* The powerful *Morrell,* one of the strongest vessels on the lakes, slashed her way through seas, snow and ice to the Head of the Lakes, where Cap-

board and marked life preservers were found along the beach by patrolling lifesavers. Nearly three weeks after the presumed foundering, another grotesque bit of evidence turned up, a piece of decking floating with an oar driven through it, an improvised raft. On the decking was a seaman's coat, the pocket of which contained a union card made out to Peter Olson, West Allis, Wisconsin. Perhaps one man had survived the immediate sinking, only

Adella Shores *went down with her whole crew in a spring snowstorm.* CANAL PARK MARINE MUSEUM COLLECTION.

tain Millen reported that the *Shores* had been following him in the eastern lake. The *Shores,* however, did not appear at Duluth on May 2 as scheduled. Her mere 500-horsepower engine could not cope with the northeasterly blasts, but something far more serious went wrong. What transpired is any sailor's guess.

The first inkling that a tragedy occurred came when normal lake traffic resumed and the wooden steamer *Simon Langell* found herself in a mass of wreckage north of Grand Island. As the *Langell*'s Captain Geel and Mate Spaulding viewed the gruesome flotsam on May 4, they recognized the paint scheme and skylight structure of the cabin remains as those of the *Adella Shores.* Not long afterward, north of Au Sable Light, the captain of the steamer *Gettysburg* reported more debris, including a pilot-house, yawl boat and cabin. Positive identification came on May 10 at Grand Marais, Michigan, as the *Shore*'s name-

to die of exposure or to be washed off later. Captain S. Holmes of Milwaukee and his 13-man crew had perished. The 15-year-old *Shores,* which had been built in Detroit for the Shores Lumber Company, was worth $30,000 to her owners, the Manx Transit Company of Cleveland.[135]

After this ominous beginning, sailing became more routine, the usual trivial items appearing. The steamer *Wasaga* suffered little on May 13 in a brush with Vidal Shoals. Off Marquette on May 16, the schooner *Arenac* waterlogged badly and had to be lashed to the schooner-barge *W.K. Moore* to keep her afloat while the towing steamer *Simon Langell* fought her way to shelter. The *Arenac* needed help from the Marquette lifesavers and some modest fixing before she could join the lumber-laden *Langell* and *Moore* on their way to Tonawanda, New York. The three-year-old 536-foot, 6,657-ton steel steamer *E.J. Earling* had the misfortune to hit hard on Madeline Island in thick fog on May 27. She was taken off right away, but needed 40 bottom plates replaced for the tidy sum of $25,000. The small fishing tug *Gloriana* burned at Grand Marais, Michigan, on May 29, her value unreported. Slight injuries were incurred by the steamer *Calumet* which touched bottom at Two Harbors on June 3 and by the steamer *America* which hit a rock at Burlington Point, Two Harbors, on July 9.

The fog one mile north of Whitefish Point on July 12, nevertheless, brought a dreadful calamity. The downbound steel steamer *John B. Cowle,* a 420-foot, 4,731-ton iron ore carrier, was struck and nearly cut in two by the upbound steel steamer *Isaac M. Scott,* a 504-foot, 6,372-ton vessel on her maiden trip. The *Cowle* sank in three minutes, taking 14 of her people down with her. Ten survived, three catching lines tossed from the *Scott* and the others being picked up by a lifeboat lowered from the passing steamer *Goodyear* or by small craft in the vicinity. With her cargo of 7,000 tons of iron ore, the *Cowle* was a financial liability in excess of $275,000, while the *Scott* also returned to the shipyard for reconstruction work costing $30,000.

As 14 men had drowned, the United States Steamboat Inspectors meeting at Marquette took a dim view of this incident. After holding hearings, they suspended Captain W.G. Rogers of the *Cowle* and Pilot Edward E. Carlton for 30 days, concluding they were going too fast for the prevailing conditions. Pilot F.W. Wertheimer of the *Scott,* however, was beached a year for excessive speed and failure to signal. The *Cowle* was owned by the Cowle Transit Company of Cleveland, commissioned in 1902. For the *Scott,* this fatal collision on her maiden trip had sinister forebodings. She vanished with all hands just four years later in the Great Storm of 1913.[136]

A flare of excitement occurred in Duluth Harbor on July 25 when the little gasoline launch *Halcyon* caught fire at dockside. The Duluth lifesavers dragged her away from the dock and other boats pushed her into shoal water where they extinguished the flames. The little pleasure craft required considerable reconstruction. At Two Harbors on July 28, the doughty steel tug *Edna G* took a whack from the new 520-foot *General Garretson,* needing some shipyard attention.

Dense fog off Keweenaw Point on the morning of August 9 snared an unsuspecting master. The 340-foot, 2,424-ton steel whaleback steamer *Pathfinder* got too close to the Keweenaw Peninsula's western shore and slammed into a reef at Eagle River, her 369-foot, 3,250-ton steel barge *Sagamore* striking the steamer and then stranding herself. The Portage lifesavers went to the scene in their motor lifeboat, but, since the seas were calm, did not remove the crews. The wrecking lighter *Reliance* was dispatched immediately from Duluth, as well as the 300-foot steel steamer *Corsica.* The two were refloated by August 11, after several thousand tons of iron ore were

lightered. Dry-dock bills amounted to $30,000 for the *Pathfinder* and $10,000 for the *Sagamore.*[137]

The same poor visibility on the eastern lake caused the big 532-foot steel steamer *William A. Hawgood* to slide

The Neshoto *lost her way in smoke from forest fires.* CANAL PARK MARINE MUSEUM COLLECTION.

into the sands northeast of Vermilion Point on August 9. She came off virtually unscathed. A near major disaster occurred in Whitefish Bay as foggy conditions persisted on August 13. Hanna Company's *Daniel J. Morrell* and the Pittsburgh Steamship Company's *Henry Phipps,* both 580-foot, 2,000-horsepower steel steamers, came together in a brush collision. Rehabilitation charges totaled $10,000 for the *Morrell* and $5,000 for the *Phipps.*[138] Late August saw one additional grounding in the extreme southeastern lake with the steel steamer *Brazil* on the rocky bottom at Vidal Shoal, necessitating modest shipyard treatment.

The first of three September ship fires struck on September 10 at Gargantua Harbor, when the 150-foot, 230-net-ton wooden tug *Columbus* burned at dock. There were no injuries. The 35-year-old vessel, owned by Joseph Ganley of the Soo, was probably worth about $10,000. Part of her hull is reported still visible in the harbor.[139] The unlucky *Pathfinder* and *Sagamore* were in another scrape on September 16, just west of the Soo. As they moved upbound, the *Sagamore* apparently started to sheer and sideswiped the downbound steel steamer *Maruba,* both needing several thousand dollars in new plates.

A pre-equinoctial gale in the central lake on September 17 gave a barge crew a 60-mile hair-raising ride and the Portage lifesavers a nasty 30-mile rescue run. The substantial 362-foot, 2,729-ton steel whaleback barge *Alexander Holley* was finally brought up at anchor only a short distance off the Eagle Harbor reefs after breaking loose from her steamer and being whipped along for hours by the rugged gale. The Portage lifesavers were alerted. The lifesavers requested a tug captain to tow their lifeboat to the scene, but he refused to go out in the heavy seas. The life-savers had but little choice and put out in their surfboat. They reached the endangered *Holley* after a battering five-hour ride. Fearing that the barge might drag her anchors

Little M.C. Neff *burned way up the St. Louis River in the fall of 1909.* C. PATRICK LABADIE COLLECTION.

and go on reefs, the lifesaving master brought the barge crewmen ashore at Eagle Harbor. In calmer seas of the next day, the lifesavers put the barge crew back on their vessel, and a tug towed the *Holley* out of danger.

On consecutive days, September 20 and 21, fire claimed two wooden ships on the lake. First consumed was the little 137-foot, 276-ton lumber hooker *M.C. Neff* which was lying in the St. Louis River along the Wisconsin shoreline after unloading a cargo of pilings for the modern Oliver rail and highway bridge. She subsequently burned to the water's edge, a loss to her owners, the Thompson and Lavaque Lumber Company, of $18,000. Sport divers have visited the *Neff*'s remains, recovering several artifacts in the 1960s and '70s, some of which are displayed at Fairlawn, the Superior-Douglas County Historical Museum in Superior.[140]

A most unusual conflagration occurred the next day at Torch Lake in the Keweenaw Waterway complex northeast of Houghton. Lightning struck the 206-foot, 1,096-ton wooden steamer *Samoa*, owned by Captain H.W. Baker of Detroit; she was destroyed. Her crew escaped. The *Samoa*'s value was not reported, though a 29-year-old wooden ship of that size probably was appraised at $25,000.[141]

The initial October incident was a bad one. In a premature, wild mid-October snowstorm, the lake tossed viciously for nearly four days. Winds of 65 mph were recorded, and snow fell on the north and south shores. The 308-foot, 1,713-ton steel whaleback steamer *John B. Trevor,* downbound with iron ore, was seized by the malevolent waves and, despite her 1,100 horsepower, deposited firmly on the rocks of Rainbow Cove, Isle Royale, on October 11. The persistent gale prevented her crew from abandoning ship and seeking help, but Captain James Connolly of the Hawgood Line's 432-foot steel steamer

S.S. Curry spotted the beleaguered *Trevor* and carried word to the Soo. A wrecking outfit was sent as the seas subsided, but salvors struggled with her for a month before abandoning their efforts. Initially given up as a complete wreck, worth something in excess of $150,000, the *Trevor* subsequently was raised by her builder, Captain Alexander McDougall, and her hull sold to a Canadian. She was rebuilt as the Canadian whaleback *Atikokan.*[142]

Fire picked off a Canadian tug at Dog Island on October 15. The 61-foot, 39-ton *Jim Pullar* went up in flames while on a coasting trip out of Port Arthur. Though her value was not disclosed, a 15-year-old vessel of her size would be only a few thousand dollar item. She was previously an American tug, built at Sault Ste. Marie, Michigan, and working out of Marquette.[143]

Another close call occurred in Whitefish Bay on October 19 when the whaleback barge *Alexander Holley* brushed the 429-foot, 4,795-ton steel steamer *Superior City* of the Pittsburgh Steamship Company. This was just another plate-bender, but a hair's breadth from tragedy.

The early part of November was remarkably free from trouble. Yet, in the last 18 days of the month and in the first week of December, a dozen different vessels were figuratively in the soup. November 13 was a singularly unlucky day, the start of a violent weather mass which tormented the lake with vicious winds and intermittently blinding snow for most of five days. In lower Whitefish Bay, just out of the Soo, two of the new steel giants struck hard. The two-year-old 540-foot, 5,750-ton *Ward Ames* slashed the three-year-old 549-foot, 6,996-ton *Charles Weston.* Realizing his ship was badly hurt, the *Weston*'s master made a course straight for the Canadian shore where she settled in shallow water. Captain Fleck's quick reaction saved his ship and crew, though the salvors had a workout, and the whole operation likely ran in excess of $20,000.[144]

On that snow-bedeviled morning just one hour after the *Ames-Weston* collision, another sizable steel steamer found herself in a deplorable position. Pushing through the snow blanket amidst tossing seas, Captain Charles Ainsworth suffered the misfortune of having his engine disabled and his ship being slapped on an uncharted ledge two miles northeast of Outer Island. The 363-foot, 3,934-ton *James H. Hoyt* of the Provident Steamship Company was an excellent candidate for destruction. First Mate William Chamberlain, son of Captain Sam Chamberlain of the ill-fated *Clemson,* launched a lifeboat with several of the crew and in a torturous 13-hour ride reached Bayfield to call for help. Three tugs and a lighter were dispatched and went to work. Still, after a disappointing week of lightering iron ore and pulling on the steamer, the salvors made no headway. The *Hoyt* was abandoned to the underwriters who brought the well-known Reids of Sarnia to the scene. The Reids employed both the large wrecking tug *Ottawa* and the wrecker *Manistique* in their efforts. The *Hoyt* eventually was retrieved, though salvage and repair expense ran $65,000.[145]

As the wild weather remained, November 15 and 16 were rueful days for sailors. At Superior the two-year-old 420-foot steel steamer *Odanah* rammed a pier when outbound and had to return to the harbor for temporary plate work. In the supposed safety of Bete Grise Bay, the 413-foot steel *Coralia* caught bottom and needed consider-

away from the settling *Ottawa* shortly before 10 a.m. on November 15, and a few minutes later the ship sank stern first in a long glide with her whistle blowing a mournful requiem.

Next followed what is probably the most outstanding exhibition of small boat seamanship in the annals of Lake Superior sailing. Bucking high seas and snow with only a hand compass and a small flashlight, during the next

Steel Bransford *spent a week on the rocks at Isle Royale in November 1909.* University of Detroit Marine Collection.

able hull renovation. Off Crisp Point, the 211-foot wooden schooner-barge *Paisley,* tow of the steamer *Orinoco,* lost a deck load of 300,000 board feet of lumber.

Nevertheless, by far the worst experience on November 15 was that of the 256-foot, 1,344-net-ton steel Canadian steamer *Ottawa* of the Canada-Atlantic Transportation Company. Outbound from Port Arthur with wheat on November 14 under Captain Alexander Birnie, the nine-year-old *Ottawa,* a package freighter, met rugged seas about 20 miles east of Passage Island. Her cargo shifted, and she began to take water. Captain Birnie had the crew in the hold all night trying to trim the wheat. Their efforts were to no avail. Realizing their worsening situation, Captain Birnie withdrew his men from the cargo hold and reluctantly ordered an "abandon ship." The lifeboat pulled

12 hours Captain Birnie guided the oar-powered lifeboat containing 18 men for more than 50 frigid miles toward Keweenaw Point and into the narrow entry of Copper Harbor where they landed safely. Those of the crew able to walk aroused the townspeople who took the suffering crewmen into their homes and revived them. Doctors were rushed from Keweenaw Point towns by train and sleigh to Copper Harbor to treat the castaways, many of whom were in poor shape from exposure. All recovered.

As they were brought to Calumet two days later for railroad transportation to their homes, Captain Birnie and his crew spoke of their adventure. He blamed their predicament on a shaft between the steering gear wheel and the steering engine which jammed, making the *Ottawa* unmanageable and allowing her to fall into the trough where repeated hammering of the waves caused the cargo to shift. This was the last voyage for Captain Birnie. He retired to a farm after his fortuitous survival. First Mate W.L. Moles, however, went on to be a captain. Naturally,

The steamer Lafayette, *a 454-footer, was just five years old when driven ashore and broken apart.* C. PATRICK LABADIE COLLECTION.

the *Ottawa,* sunk in deep water off Isle Royale, was a total loss which, with the wheat cargo, must have exceeded $200,000. Again, the expertise of her crew in handling an oared lifeboat remains one of the most phenomenal exhibitions in Lake Superior history.[146]

Indeed, that November 15 was bleak all over the lake. Leaving Duluth for Two Harbors was the little 50-foot motor vessel *City of Two Harbors,* one of the many little coastal packets operating in the west end of the lake. The northwester caught her off the north shore and drove her well aground on the south shore, 13 miles east of Superior. Her crew stayed aboard for the next 62 hours as she apparently was far enough up on the beach to avoid being beaten to pieces. Finally, two of her hardy crewmen swam the short distance to land and hiked in frozen clothes to Superior where they caught a street car and ultimately reached the Duluth lifesaving station to report the plight of their vessel. The lifesavers went out and removed the remaining crew. The boat was pulled free some days later, little the worse for wear.[147]

Also putting out from Duluth on November 15 was the 414-foot, 4,657-ton steel steamer *Bransford* of the Hawgood Line. Captain A.C. Winvig bucked the gale and the snowblanket for a whole day with the *Bransford*'s substantial 1,500-horsepower engine. As she was heavily laden with iron ore, progress was demoralizingly slow. The following evening just after dark, to Captain Winvig's consternation, since he had estimated his position at 11 miles south of Isle Royale, he felt his stalwart steel vessel crash into a reef whose rocky pinnacles ripped his hull. Hung up and listing, the *Bransford* had run on the rocks near the entrance to Siskiwit Bay, Isle Royale, not far from where she had struck four years earlier in the *Mataafa* Storm of 1905. Word was sent to Port Arthur, and the tug *James Whalen* responded, to be joined later by the

wrecker *Favorite* from the Soo. The crew was safe, but it took a week before the *Bransford* floated free. She was then towed to the Soo by the *Favorite.* Captain Winvig's miscalculation in the snow clouds required dry-dock work of $25,000.[148]

Another ship's crew had an unnerving experience on that same wild November 16. Bound light from Fort William to Ashland, the three-year-old 420-foot, 4,795-ton steel steamer *James S. Dunham* was approximately 15 miles northeast of her destination when she encountered violently turbulent waters. Though traveling in 35 feet of water and drawing only 17 feet, she began to crash against the bottom in every trough. Rather than risk tearing out her bottom in the few remaining miles, her captain ran her ashore at Marble Point near the mouth of the Bad River. For some hours, they were isolated in the snow cover. Then, as the weather cleared, the captain sighted a person on the beach. A note was sent ashore in a bottle which was retrieved from the surf. He hastened to Ashland to report the *Dunham*'s predicament. The tugs *Bayfield* and *Bennett* were quickly dispatched, and the *Dunham* was speedily refloated with minimum injury. There was one fatality, though. As the *Dunham* pitched furiously before reaching the shallows, her cook was thrown down a ladderway and killed. The new *Dunham* belonged to D. Sullivan and Company of Chicago.[149]

The *Hoyt* stranding produced an unfortunate sequel. The Reids of Sarnia had been summoned, and Captain J.F. Reid responded with the 151-foot wooden wrecking tug *Ottawa*. On the night of November 29, as she lay tethered to the *Hoyt* in Frog Bay off Oak Island, she somehow took fire. She was cut loose from the *Hoyt,* and the crew of nine took her lifeboats to safety. However, the powerful 28-year-old wrecker, one of Captain Jim Reid's favorites, had appeared at her last salvage job. With her specialized equipment, she was a loss of $50,000. She had been built by the Miller Brothers at Chicago in 1881 as the *Boscobel.* It was speculated at the time of loss that the fire started from spontaneous combustion in the 130 tons of bunker coal aboard the *Ottawa.* Her machinery and boilers were recovered in 1910 by Whitney Brothers of Superior using a scow and the tug *Maxwell.* Her bottom is believed to remain in Red Cliff Bay roughly parallel to that of the *H.D. Coffinberry.*[150]

The last troubled vessel of the 1909 season was the same *City of Two Harbors* which had been in tight circumstances on November 15. Coasting along the Minnesota north shore on December 5, she became disabled northeast of Beaver Bay. Fortunately for her crew, local fishermen were able to nurse her into shelter, and she avoided becoming an end-of-the-year victim of Lake Superior.

While not a cargo ship, Canadian dredge *No. 8* became the last incident of the season, being wrecked December 9 at East Hatten Island in Thunder Bay. The financial loss for the 415-ton dredge was not reported.

1 *Duluth News-Tribune,* Apr. 27, May 1, 1900; Homer Wells, *History of Accidents, Casualties, and Wrecks on Lake Superior* (Duluth, Corps of Engineers, U.S. Army, 1938), 90 pp., typewritten, p. 28.

2 *Duluth News-Tribune,* May 4, 1900; Harvey C. Beeson, *Inland Marine Directory,* 1901, pp. 152-53.

3 *Duluth News-Tribune,* May 6, 1900; Beeson, ibid.; Wells, *op. cit.,* p. 28.

4 *Duluth News-Tribune,* Oct. 3, 1900; *Penetang Herald,* Sept. 27, 1900, as reprinted in *The Great Lakes News,* Jan. 1931, p. 8; Ronald H. Wrigley, *Northern Superior Shipwrecks,* 198 pp., unpublished manuscript, ca. 1979, pp. 34-37; Beeson, *ibid.*

5 *Duluth News-Tribune,* Oct. 31, 1900; Wells, *op. cit.,* p. 28.

6 *Duluth News-Tribune,* Nov. 9-10, 1900; *Annual Report, U.S. Life-Saving Service, 1901,* pp. 276-77.

7 *Duluth News-Tribune,* Nov. 9, 12, 1900; Beeson, *op. cit.,* 1901, p. 153.

8 *Ashland Daily News,* Nov. 17, 1900; *Bayfield County Press,* Nov. 24, 1900; *Duluth News-Tribune,* Nov. 17, 1900; *Washburn News,* Nov. 23, 1900; Beeson, *op. cit.,* 1901, p. 152; Thom Holden, *Apostle Islands Shipwreck Survey List, 1870-1940* (Bayfield, Wisconsin, Apostle Islands National Lakeshore, National Park Service, 1985), p. 10; James M. Keller, *The "Unholy" Apostles: Tales of Chequamegon Shipwrecks* (Bayfield, Wisconsin, Apostle Islands Press, 1985), pp. 69-71.

9 *Duluth News-Tribune,* Nov. 20, 1900.

10 *Duluth News-Tribune,* May 3, 1901; *Annual Report, U.S. Life-Saving Service, 1901,* pp. 101-102, 173-174, 276-277.

11 *Duluth News-Tribune,* May 10-11, 15, 1901; Superior *Evening Telegram,* May 11, 1901; *Annual Report, U.S. Life-Saving Service, 1901,* pp. 136-137, 204, 375; Beeson, *op. cit.,* 1902, p. 128. An excellent account based on Keweenaw Point sources is found in Mac (D.M.) Frimodig, *Shipwrecks Off Keweenaw* (Lansing, Mich., Fort Wilkins Natural History Association and Michigan Department of Natural Resources, 1974), pp. 25-30.

12 *Duluth News-Tribune,* July 1, 3, Aug. 2-3, 5, 1901.

13 *Duluth News-Tribune,* July 2-3, 1901; *Annual Report, U.S. Life-Saving Service, 1902,* p. 362; Beeson, *op. cit.,* 1902, p. 128.

14 *Duluth News-Tribune,* July 1, 1901.

15 *Bayfield County Press,* July 27, 1901; Holden, *Apostle Islands Shipwreck Survey List, op. cit.,* p. 63.

16 *Duluth News-Tribune,* July 30-31, 1901; Beeson, *op. cit.,* 1902, p. 129.

17 *Duluth News-Tribune,* Sept. 1, 1901; Wells, *op. cit.,* p. 29.

18 *Duluth News-Tribune,* Sept. 17-22, 24, 26-27, 29, Oct. 3-4, 7, 12, Dec. 3, 15, 1901; *Annual Report, U.S. Life-Saving Service, 1902,* p. 239; Beeson, *op. cit.,* 1902, p. 129.

19 *Ashland Daily News,* Sept. 21, 1901; *Bayfield County Press,* Sept. 28, 1901, Aug. 10, 1917; *Duluth Evening Herald, Sept. 21, 24, 1901; Duluth News-Tribune,* Sept. 22, 25, Dec. 15, 1901; Beeson, *op. cit.,* 1902, p. 128;

Holden, *Apostle Islands Shipwreck Survey List, op. cit.,* p. 37-38; Keller, *op. cit.,* pp. 73-76, 151; Wells, *op. cit.,* p. 29;.

20 Elmer Engman, *Shipwreck Guide to Western Lake Superior* (Duluth, Inner Space Diving, 1976), pp. 36-38.

21 *Duluth News-Tribune,* Oct. 3-4, 1901; Dec. 15, 1901; *Annual Report, U.S. Life-Saving Service, 1902,* p. 90; Beeson, *op. cit.,* 1902, pp. 129-130.

22 *Duluth News-Tribune,* Oct. 22, 1901; *Annual Report, U.S. Life-Saving Service, 1902,* pp. 97, 304-305.

23 *Duluth News-Tribune,* Nov. 13-19, 27, Dec. 1-2, 7, 18, 1901. A detailed description of the *Smeaton* operation based on Captain Tom Reid's recollections is contained in Mary F. Doner, *The Salvager* (Minneapolis, Ross and Haines, 1955), pp. 72-75. Though the dates are incorrect, the Doner account is highly informative.

24 *Duluth News-Tribune,* Dec. 2, 4, 15, 1901; Wells, *op. cit.,* p. 29.

25 *Bayfield County Press,* Apr. 19, 1902; Holden, *Apostle Islands Shipwreck Survey List, op. cit.,* p. 35.

26 *Duluth News-Tribune,* Apr. 27, May 4, 1902; *Annual Report, U.S. Life-Saving Service, 1902,* pp. 152, 304-305.

27 *Duluth News-Tribune,* Apr. 29, May 4, 1902; Wells, *op. cit.,* p. 30.

28 *Bayfield County Press,* May 17, 1902; Holden, *Apostle Islands Shipwreck Survey List, op. cit.,* p. 31.

29 *Duluth News-Tribune,* June 8-14, 17-18, 20-22, 24, 27, 30, July 1, Aug. 14, 17, 19, 1902, Nov. 17, 1903; *Annual Report, U.S. Life-Saving Service, 1902,* pp. 36-38, 167, 306-307, 391. A more detailed description of the accident can be found in an article by the author, "Collision Off the Pierhead" in *Inland Seas,* Vol. 20, No. 1, Spring 1964, pp. 15-20.

30 *Duluth News-Tribune,* Sept. 2, 9, 12, 15, 1902; *Annual Report, U.S. Life-Saving Service, 1903,* pp. 80, 385; Wells, *op. cit.,* p. 31.

31 *Duluth News-Tribune,* Oct. 15, 1902.

32 *Annual Report, U.S. Life-Saving Service, 1903,* pp. 102, 189, 296.

33 *Duluth News-Tribune,* Nov. 8, 16, 30, 1902; *Annual Report, U.S. Life-Saving Service, 1903,* p. 387; Wells, *op. cit.,* p. 31.

34 *Duluth News-Tribune,* Nov. 19, 1902; Wells, *op. cit.,* p. 31.

35 *Duluth News-Tribune,* Nov. 27-30, Dec. 1-2, 13, 1902; a concise summary of the *Bannockburn* disappearance is found in Fred Landon, "Loss of the *Bannockburn*" in *Inland Seas,* Vol. 13, No. 4, Winter 1957, pp. 303-305.

36 *Duluth News-Tribune,* Dec. 2, 9, 1902; *Marquette Mining Journal,* Dec. 2, 1902; Wells, *op. cit.,* p. 31.

37 *Duluth News-Tribune,* May 1, 5, 1903; Wells, *op. cit.,* p. 31.

38 *Duluth News-Tribune,* May 9, 1903; Wells, *op. cit.,* p. 31.

39 *Annual Report, U.S. Life-Saving Service, 1903,* pp. 157, 304-305.

40 *Duluth News-Tribune,* May 19, 1903; Wells, *op. cit.,* p. 31.

[41] Dominion of Canada, Department of Transport, op. cit., p. 36; Wrigley, *Northern Superior Shipwrecks, op. cit.,* p. 111.

[42] *Duluth News-Tribune,* Sept. 20, Oct. 28, 1903; Holden, *Apostle Islands Shipwreck Survey List, op. cit.,* p. 68; Keller, *op. cit.,* pp. 77-83.

[43] *Duluth News-Tribune,* Sept. 20, 1903; *Annual Report, U.S. Life-Saving Service, 1904,* pp. 99, 296-297.

[44] *Duluth News-Tribune,* Sept. 20, 1903; *Annual Report, U.S. Life-Saving Service, 1904,* pp. 99, 296-297.

[45] *Duluth News-Tribune,* Oct. 16-17, 19, 1903; Holden, *Apostle Islands Shipwreck Survey List, op. cit.,* p. 66; Keller, *op. cit.,* pp. 85-89; Wells, *op. cit.,* p. 32.

[46] *Duluth News-Tribune,* Nov. 22, 1903; *Grand Marais Herald,* Nov. 14, 1903; *Annual Report, U.S. Life-Saving Service, 1904,* pp. 116, 296-297.

[47] *Duluth News-Tribune,* Oct. 27-28, 1903; *Annual Report, U.S. Life-Saving Service, 1904,* p. 384; Wells, *op. cit.,* p. 32.

[48] *Duluth News-Tribune,* Oct. 28, 1903; Wells, *op. cit.,* p. 32.

[49] *Duluth News-Tribune,* Nov. 10, 1903, Aug. 8, 1905.

[50] *Duluth News-Tribune,* Dec. 1-2, 4-6, 17, 1903; *Duluth Evening Herald,* Nov. 30, 1903; *Annual Report, U.S. Life-Saving Service, 1904,* pp. 127-128, 296-297.

[51] *Duluth News-Tribune,* Dec. 9-11, 13, 1903; Wells, *op. cit.,* p. 32.

[52] *Duluth News-Tribune,* June 3, 6-7, 1904; Beeson, *op. cit.,* 1905, p. 122.

[53] *Duluth Evening Herald,* Sept. 16, 1904; Holden, *Apostle Islands Shipwreck Survey List, op. cit.,* p. 43.

[54] *Duluth News-Tribune,* Oct. 6, 1904.

[55] *Duluth News-Tribune,* Oct. 5, 25, 1904; *Annual Report, U.S. Life-Saving Service, 1904,* pp. 95, 296-297; Beeson, *op. cit.,* 1905, p. 122; Wells, *op. cit.,* p. 33.

[56] *Duluth News-Tribune,* Oct. 6, 1904; *Annual Report, U.S. Life-Saving Service, 1904,* pp. 95, 296; Wells, *op. cit.,* p. 33.

[57] *Bayfield County Press,* Oct. 14, 21, 1904; *Duluth Evening Herald,* Oct. 14-15, 17, 1904; Holden, *Apostle Islands Shipwreck Survey List, op. cit.,* p. 41.

[58] *Duluth News-Tribune,* Nov. 15, 1904; Beeson, *op. cit.,* 1905, p. 122.

[59] *Duluth News-Tribune,* May 3-4, 7, 1905.

[60] *Duluth News-Tribune,* May 5-6, 8, June 2, 1905; Wells, *op. cit.,* p. 34. The *Hesper* now rests just inside the rubble mound breakwall at Cyprus Northshore Mining's dock at Silver Bay, Minnesota. The breakwall was built several decades after the loss and apparently the contractors were totally oblivious to the wreck.

[61] *Duluth News-Tribune,* May 7, 9, 13, 18, 1905; Wells, *op. cit.,* p. 34.

[62] *Duluth News-Tribune,* June 14, 1905; Wells, *op. cit.,* p. 34.

[63] *Duluth News-Tribune,* June 27, 1905.

[64] *Duluth News-Tribune,* Aug. 19, 1905.

[65] *Bayfield County Press,* Sept. 8, 1905; Holden, *Apostle Islands Shipwreck Survey List, op. cit.,* p. 55.

[66] *Duluth News-Tribune,* Sept. 3-5, 1905; Wells, *op. cit.,* p. 35.

[67] *Ashland Weekly News,* Sept. 6, 1905; *Bayfield County Press,* Sept. 8, 15, 29, Oct. 6, 25, 1905, May 11, Dec. 14, 1906, July 26, Oct. 4, 1907, May 29, June 5, July 3, 1908, July 2, 1909, Aug. 10, Oct. 12, 1917; *Duluth Evening Herald,* Sept. 14, 1905, Apr. 12, 1906; *Duluth News-Tribune* Sept. 4-6, 8, 12, 16, 26, Oct. 20, 25, 28, 1905; *Annual Report, U.S. Life-Saving Service, 1906,* p. 391; Engman, *op. cit.,* pp. 27-31; Holden, *Apostle Islands Shipwreck Survey List, op. cit.,* pp. 95-97; Keller, *op. cit.,* pp. 95-105, 107, 119, 147, 152; U.S. Army Corps of Engineers, *Chief of Engineers, Annual Report for 1909,* pp. 683 and 1,940; *ibid,* 1910, pp. 756 and 2,094.

[68] *Ashland Weekly News,* Sept 6, 1905; *Bayfield County Press,* Nov. 3, 1905, May 18, 1906; *Duluth News-Tribune,* Sept. 4-5, 9, 12-13, Nov. 3, 1905; *Annual Report, U.S. Life-Saving Service, 1906,* p. 390; "Pretoria's Bell Found," *Inland Seas,* Vol. 4, No. 3, p. 207; Fall 1948; Holden, *Apostle Islands Shipwreck Survey List, op. cit.,* pp. 88-89; Keller, *op. cit.,* pp. 107-112.

[69] *Duluth News-Tribune,* Sept. 5-6, 9-10, 15, 18, 1905; *Marquette Mining Journal,* Sept. 27, 1905; *Annual Report, U.S. Life-Saving Service, 1906,* p. 390.

[70] *Duluth News-Tribune,* Sept. 9, 1905.

[71] *Duluth News-Tribune,* Sept. 23, Nov. 18, 1905.

[72] *Duluth News-Tribune,* Sept. 26, 1905.

[73] *Bayfield County Press,* Oct. 13, 1905; *Duluth News-Tribune,* Oct. 22, 1905; Toni Carrell, *Submerged Cultural Resources Site Report:* Noquebay (Santa Fe, New Mexico, National Park Service, 1985), pp. 27-31; Holden, *Apostle Islands Shipwreck Survey List, op. cit.,* pp. 71-72; Keller, *op. cit.,* pp. 91-93; Ellen Maurer, "Rough sketch of an unidentified wooden vessel, possibly a barge, examined on August 17, 1982" in Kate Lidfors, Thom Holden, Ellen Maurer, *et. al., Report of a Two-Day Underwater Survey of Selected Historical Sites at Apostle Islands National Lakeshore with Considerations for Future Research* (Bayfield, Wisconsin, National Park Service, Apostle Islands National Lakeshore, 1982), unpublished manuscript. There appear two different spellings for this vessel's name, *Noquebay* and *Noque Bay,* the former apparently being the most preferred.

[74] *Duluth News-Tribune,* Oct. 20-22, 25, 31, Nov. 3, 1905, June 22, July 17, Aug. 15, 1907; *Annual Report, U.S. Life-Saving Service, 1906,* pp. 97, 238, 239.

[75] *Duluth News-Tribune,* Oct. 22-23, 30, Nov. 22, 27 1905.

[76] *Duluth News-Tribune,* Oct. 22-23, 27, 1905.

[77] *Duluth News-Tribune,* Nov. 5, 11, 13-14, 1905; Wells, *op. cit.,* p. 35.

[78] *Duluth News-Tribune,* Nov. 23, 1905; *Annual Report, U.S. Life-Saving Service, 1906,* pp. 106, 238-239.

[79] *Duluth News-Tribune,* Nov. 24-28, 1905. A detailed description of the gale beginning the evening of November 27 is presented by H.W. Richardson, local

forecaster, U.S. Weather Bureau, in the *Duluth Evening Herald,* Nov. 28, 1905.

80 *Duluth Evening Herald,* June 22, Aug. 11, Oct. 11, Nov. 21, 1906; *Duluth News-Tribune,* Dec. 2, 1905; *Marine Review,* Aug. 23, 30, Oct. 18, 1906; Dominion of Canada, Department of Transport, *op. cit.,* p. 39; W.R. Williams, "Shipwrecks at Isle Royale" in *Inland Seas,* Vol. 12, No. 4, Winter 1956, p. 254. There is still some debate in marine historical circles regarding the ultimate disposition of the *Monkshaven.* Captain James Reid is known to have arrived in June 1906 to begin salvage on the *Monkshaven.* He was reported as having the vessel afloat in early August only to have her wreck again in early October. It is not clear if he continued salvage then or resumed in 1907. Flotsam from an unidentified wreck, presumed old, was being seen in Thunder Bay in November 1906, possibly from the *Monkshaven.* Also, Reid's attention was diverted late in 1906 to salvage of the Interstate Bridge in Duluth-Superior Harbor, toppled earlier by the steamer *Troy,* and also refloating the *Ireland* wrecked in the Apostle Islands. Rev. Edward J. Dowling, dean of Great Lakes vessel historians, although not a shipwreck historian *per se,* indicates in his notes that the vessel foundered off Ste. Felicite, Quebec, on Aug. 23, 1914, without explanation of her intervening history. However, Dowling's reference is actually to a second and different vessel of the same name.

81 *Duluth News-Tribune,* Dec. 1, 1905; *Duluth Evening Herald,* Dec. 1, 1905; *Annual Report U.S. Life-Saving Service, 1906,* p. 391.

82 *Duluth Evening Herald,* Dec. 1-2, 1905; Wells, *op. cit.,* p. 36; *Duluth News-Tribune,* Dec. 20, 1905.

83 *Duluth News-Tribune,* Nov. 30, Dec. 24, 1905, May 1, 1906; Wells, *op. cit.,* p. 36.

84 *Duluth News-Tribune,* Nov. 30, Dec. 1, 21, 1905; *Duluth Evening Herald,* Dec. 1, 1905; *Annual Report, U.S. Life-Saving Service, 1906,* p. 391.

85 *Duluth News-Tribune,* Dec. 1, 1905; *Duluth Evening Herald,* Dec. 1, 1905; *Annual Report, U.S. Life-Saving Service, 1906,* p. 391.

86 *Duluth News-Tribune,* Dec. 1, 5, 1905, July 27, Sept. 1, 1906; *Duluth Evening Herald,* Nov. 30, Dec. 1, 1905; *Annual Report, U.S. Life-Saving Service, 1906,* p. 391; Wells, *op. cit.,* p. 35.

87 *Ashland Weekly News,* Dec. 6, 1905 *Duluth News-Tribune,* Dec. 2-4, 10, 1905; *Duluth Evening Herald,* Dec. 1, 1905; *Annual Report, U.S. Life-Saving Service, 1906,* p. 390; Holden, *Apostle Islands Shipwreck Survey List, op. cit.,* pp. 81-82; Keller, *op. cit.,* pp. 113-116.

88 *Duluth News-Tribune,* Nov. 29-30, Dec. 1-2, 1905; *Duluth Evening Herald,* Nov. 29, 1905; *Annual Report, U.S. Life-Saving Service, 1906,* pp. 109, 240-241; Wells, *op. cit.,* p. 35.

89 *Duluth News-Tribune,* Nov. 29, 1905; *Duluth Evening Herald,* Nov. 28, 1905; Wells, *op. cit.,* p. 36.

90 *Duluth News-Tribune,* Nov. 29, 1905, May 21, June 4, Aug. 4, 1906; *Annual Report, U.S. Life-Saving Service, 1906,* pp. 28-34, 109, 152, 240-241, 391; Wells, *op. cit.,* p. 35.

91 *Duluth News-Tribune,* Dec. 1-2, 9-11, 1905; Wells, *op. cit.,* p. 36.

92 *Duluth News-Tribune,* Dec. 2, 5, 8, 1905.

93 *Duluth News-Tribune,* Dec. 2-3, 1905, May 16, 1906;

Duluth Evening Herald, Dec. 2, 1905, Wells, *op. cit.,* p. 36. In May 1906, owner M.J. Cummings of the *Western Star* received a bill for $25,000 from owners of the steamer *Viking* for services rendered.

94 Thom Holden, "Shipwrecks of Siskiwit Bay, Isle Royale, Lake Superior" in Thomas Robert Holden, *Park Interpretation as an Environmental Communication Process with a Sample Interpretive Booklet Text on the Maritime Disaster History of Siskiwit Bay, Isle Royale, Lake Superior,* 195 pp., unpublished masters' thesis, University of Wisconsin, Madison, 1974, pp. 129-132.

95 Thom Holden, *Summary List of Shipwrecks and Marine Casualties on Lake Superior Resulting from the Storm of November 27-29, 1905,* three pp., unpublished manuscript, ca. 1980, pp. 1-3.

96 *Duluth News-Tribune,* Nov. 28-30, Dec. 1-2, 1905; Wells, *op. cit.,* pp. 35-36.

97 Holden, *Summary List, op. cit.,* pp. 1-3.

98 *Duluth News-Tribune,* May 29, 1906; Wells, *op. cit.,* p. 37.

99 *Duluth News-Tribune,* May 29, 1906.

100 Dominion of Canada, Department of Transport, *op. cit.,* p. 39.

101 *Duluth Evening Herald,* June 28, July 4, 1906; Wrigley, *Northern Superior Shipwrecks, op. cit.,* p. 6.

102 *Duluth News-Tribune,* Aug. 11, 1906; Wells, *op. cit.,* p. 37.

103 *Duluth News-Tribune,* Aug. 22, 1906; Wells, *op. cit.,* p. 38.

104 *Duluth News-Tribune,* Oct. 10, 1906, July 27, 1907.

105 *Annual Report, U.S. Life-Saving Service, 1907,* pp. 47-49, 104, 240-241, 397.

106 *Duluth Evening Herald,* Oct. 30, 1906.

107 *Duluth News-Tribune,* Nov. 11, 1906; Wrigley, *Northern Superior Shipwrecks, op. cit.,* pp. 111-112.

108 *Duluth News-Tribune,* Nov. 23, 1906; *Duluth Evening Herald,* Nov. 19, 1906; Dominion of Canada, Department of Transport, *op. cit.,* p. 40.

109 *Duluth News-Tribune,* Nov. 23, Dec. 5, 1906, July 21, 1907.

110 *Duluth News-Tribune,* Dec. 4, 1906.

111 *Duluth News-Tribune,* Dec. 8, 1906; Dominion of Canada, Department of Transport, *op. cit.,* p. 40; Ronald Wrigley, *Shipwrecked: Vessels That Met Tragedy on Northern Lake Superior* (Cobalt, Ontario, Highway Book Shop, 1985), pp. 15-19.

112 *Detroit Free Press,* Dec. 4, 1913; *Duluth News-Tribune,* Dec. 11, 1906, July 5, 1907; *Port Arthur Daily News,* Sept. 9, 17, Oct. 6, 1908; *Annual Report, U.S. Life-Saving Service, 1907,* p. 397; Thom Holden, *Above and Below* (Houghton, Michigan, Isle Royale Natural History Association, 1985), pp. 12-15; Larry Murphy and Thom Holden, "Shipwrecks of Isle Royale: The Historical Record" in *Submerged Cultural Resources Study: Isle Royale National Park,* Daniel J. Lenihan, ed. (Santa Fe, New Mexico, Submerged Cultural Resources Unit, National Park Service, 1987), pp. 104-118; Larry Murphy, Daniel Lenihan and C. Patrick Labadie, "Shipwrecks of Isle Royale: The Archeological Record" in Lenihan, ed., *ibid.,* pp. 259-275; Wrigley, *Shipwrecked, op. cit.,* pp. 20-26.

[113]*Duluth News-Tribune,* Dec. 8, 13, 15, 17, 19, 1906; *Annual Report, U.S. Life-Saving Service, 1907,* p. 397, Wells, *op. cit.,* p. 38-39.

[114]*Duluth News-Tribune,* Apr. 30, July 17, 1907; Wells, *op. cit.,* p. 39.

[115]*Duluth News-Tribune,* June 28, 1907; Dominion of Canada, Department of Transport, *op. cit.,* p. 41; Beeson, *op. cit., 1908,* p. 141.

[116]*Duluth News-Tribune,* Aug. 11, 1907; Wells, *op. cit.,* p. 40.

[117]*Duluth News-Tribune,* Aug. 25, 1907; Wells, *op. cit.,* p. 40; Beeson, *op. cit., 1908,* p. 141.

[118]*Duluth News-Tribune,* Sept. 22, 1907; *Annual Report, U.S. Life-Saving Service, 1908,* pp. 30-34, 79, 230-231; Beeson, *op. cit., 1908,* p. 141; Wells, *op. cit.,* p. 40.

[119]*Duluth News-Tribune,* Oct. 13-14, 16, 1907; *Duluth Evening Herald,* Oct. 14, 1907; *Annual Report, U.S. Life-Saving Service, 1908,* pp. 169, 176, 257, 381; Beeson, *op. cit., 1908,* p. 141; Wells, *op. cit.,* p. 41.

[120]*Duluth News-Tribune,* Oct. 13, 1907.

[121]*Duluth News-Tribune,* Oct. 30, Nov. 2, 1907, May 22, 1908; *Duluth Evening Herald,* Oct. 30, 1907; Wells, *op. cit.,* p. 41.

[122]*Bayfield County Press,* Nov. 1, 22, 1907, Aug. 10, 1917; *Duluth Evening Herald,* Oct. 31, 1907; *Duluth News-Tribune,* Oct. 31, Nov. 22, Dec. 7, 1907; Engman, *op. cit.,* pp. 32-33, 36; Holden, *Apostle Islands Shipwreck Survey List, op. cit.,* pp. 15-16, 24-25; Keller, *op. cit.,* pp. 136-137, 147-148; Wells, *op. cit.,* p. 41. There is some considerable confusion over the final disposition of the *Cormorant's* hull. There is some opinion, particularly that of Engman and Keller, noted above, that the remains are in Red Cliff Bay. However, since the vessel is known to have been towed into Duluth after salvage work on the Bayfield waterfront, it is believed the hull bottom in Red Cliff Bay is being confused with that of the *H.D. Coffinberry.* The *Coffinberry* was a similar steam barge only slightly smaller at 191 feet and 858 tons, built in 1874 and abandoned in the midteens on the north side of Red Cliff Bay, also known as Schooner Bay, following salvage of her engine and boiler. She had previously been abandoned and settled to the bottom at Ashland and was on the bottom for about five years prior to machinery salvage in 1917. Just when she was removed to Red Cliff Bay is uncertain.

[123]*Duluth News-Tribune,* July 30, Sept. 1, 1908; Wells, *op. cit.,* p. 42.

[124]*Duluth News-Tribune,* Sept. 1, 9, 1908.

[125]*Duluth News-Tribune,* Sept. 2-3, 1908; Wells, *op. cit.* p. 42.

[126]*Duluth News-Tribune,* Sept. 7, 9, 18, 1908; *Annual Report, U.S. Life-Saving Service, 1909,* pp. 100, 254; Wells, *op. cit.,* p. 42; Beeson, *op. cit., 1909,* p. 131.

[127]*Duluth News-Tribune,* Sept. 29, Oct. 1, 1908; *Annual Report, U.S. Life-Saving Service, 1909,* pp. 109, 254; Beeson, *op. cit., 1909,* p. 132; Wells, *op. cit.,* p. 43.

[128]*Duluth News-Tribune* Oct. 15, 23, 29, 1908; Wells, *op. cit.,* p. 43.

[129]*Duluth News-Tribune* Oct. 21-23, 25, 27, 1908; Beeson, *op. cit., 1909,* p. 131.

[130]*Duluth News-Tribune,* Oct. 23, 25, 1908; Wells, *op. cit.,* p. 43.

[131]*Duluth News-Tribune,* Oct. 25, 28, Nov. 7, 1908; *Annual Report, U.S. Life-Saving Service, 1909,* pp. 119, 254-255; Wells, *op. cit.,* p. 43.

[132]*Duluth News-Tribune,* Oct. 21, 25, Dec. 1, 5-12, 16-18, 29, 1908; *Annual Report, U.S. Life-Saving Service, 1909,* pp. 194, 374; Beeson, *op. cit., 1909,* p. 132; Wells, *op. cit.,* p. 43.

[133]*Duluth News-Tribune,* Apr. 30, May 2, 1909; Wells, *op. cit.,* p. 44.

[134]*Duluth News-Tribune,* May 2, 1909; *Annual Report, U.S. Life-Saving Service, 1909,* p. 374.

[135]*Duluth News-Tribune,* May 8-9, 11, 21, 1909; *Duluth Evening Herald,* May 8, 1909; *Annual Report, U.S. Life-Saving Service, 1909,* p. 374; Wells, *op. cit.,* p. 44.

[136]*Duluth News-Tribune,* July 13-14, 17, 25-26, Aug. 3, Nov. 10, 1909; *Duluth Evening Herald,* July 12, 17, 1909; *Annual Report, U.S. Life-Saving Service, 1910,* p. 213; Wells, *op. cit.,* p. 44.

[137]*Duluth News-Tribune,* Aug. 10, 12, 1909; *Annual Report, U.S. Life-Saving Service, 1910,* pp. 82, 152; Wells, *op. cit.,* p. 45.

[138]*Duluth News-Tribune,* Aug. 14, 1909; Wells, *op. cit.,* p. 45.

[139]Dominion of Canada, Department of Transport, *op. cit.,* p. 43; Wrigley, *Northern Superior Shipwrecks, op. cit.,* p. 118.

[140]*Duluth Herald,* Sept. 20, 1909; Wells, *op. cit.,* p. 45.

[141]*Duluth News-Tribune,* Sept. 22, 1909.

[142]*Duluth News-Tribune,* Oct. 14, 20, Nov. 2, 15, 1909; Wells, *op. cit.,* p. 45.

[143]Dominion of Canada, Department of Transport, *op. cit.,* p. 44.

[144]*Duluth News-Tribune,* Nov. 14, 16, 21, 1909.

[145]*Duluth News-Tribune,* Nov. 14-16, 19, 21, 24, 30, 1909; Wells, *op. cit.,* p. 45.

[146]*Duluth News-Tribune,* Nov. 17-18, 1909; Robert W. Thom, "The Sinking of the Ottawa" in *Inland Seas,* Vol. 9, No. 4, pp. 296-297, Winter 1953.

[147]*Duluth News-Tribune,* Nov. 20-21, 1909.

[148]*Duluth News-Tribune,* Nov. 19, 24, 1909; Wells, *op. cit.,* p. 45.

[149]*Duluth News-Tribune,* Nov. 18-19, 1909; *Annual Report, U.S. Life-Saving Service, 1910,* p. 213; Wells, *op. cit.,* p. 45.

[150]*Bayfield County Press,* Dec. 3, 1909, May 20, 1910, Sept. 8, 1911; *Duluth Evening Herald,* Nov. 30, 1909; *Duluth News-Tribune,* Nov. 30, 1909; Dominion of Canada, Department of Transport, *op. cit.,* p. 44; Engman, *op. cit.,* pp. 34-36; Holden, *Apostle Islands Shipwreck Survey List, op. cit.,* pp. 77-78; Keller, *op. cit.,* pp. 117-120; John M. Mills, *Canadian Coastal and Inland Steam Vessels, 1809-1930* (Providence, Rhode Island, The Steamship Historical Society of America, 1979), p. 89.

The L.C. Smith *hard aground near Two Harbors in June 1910, although it was finally pulled free.* CANAL PARK MARINE MUSEUM COLLECTION.

Chapter 6

The Feverish Era of World War I
1910-1919

The decade of World War I was dynamic on Lake Superior. The already substantial commerce of the previous 10 years exhibited an increase of 75 percent. Indeed, the peak of nearly 92 million tons logged at the Soo Locks in 1916 would be only barely exceeded in the boom year of 1929 and the record not truly broken until the first 111-million-ton accomplishment in 1941. The annual volumes were erratic, however.

Lake Superior sailing showed a big improvement in safety, the number of troubled ships noting a 40 percent drop from the record of 1900-1909. The figure for ships destroyed was more than cut in half, although the fatality list was only slightly below that of the preceding decade. Nine sinkings cost the lives of complete crews. The death toll would have been higher except for the amaz-ing exploits of Captain S.L. Goldish. Maneuvering the little *L. Goldish* into shallow waters where larger ships could not approach, the captain towed several disabled smaller craft to safety from certain fatal stranding and saved 29 persons from probable death, most of them in this decade.

1910

This was another gala year, a new high for Lake Superior tonnage. Following a mild winter, the lake was ice-free in early April, and the ships ventured forth. As usual, there were the customary minor difficulties. The coastal steamer *America* stranded at Victoria Island Light southwest of Thunder Bay on April 10. *Dredge No. 2* got hung up at Ontonagon on April 21. The 251-foot wooden steamer *Lycoming* went ashore on April 25 at Grand Marais, Michigan, with little injury. It was pretty much the same in May. Entering Duluth Harbor on May 1, the 168-foot wooden lumber hooker *James H. Prentice* slapped a pier and settled in shallow water. Typical mid-May seas put the tug *Circle* on a reef three miles from Eagle Harbor on May 17 and two days later slapped a pile-driver aground at Marquette.

Fog and rough water brought embarrassment to three vessels within two days at the end of the month. The 298-foot, 2,051-ton wooden steamer *City of Berlin* and her 290-foot, 2,236-ton wooden schooner-barge *Aurora* both found the shore at Split Rock on May 28. Salvors quickly freed them, but the bills exceeded $7,000. Across the lake, the 380-foot, 4,305-ton steel steamer *E.N. Saunders* found the reefs off Gull Rock near the tip of Keweenaw Point on May 30. Captain McCormick and the Portage lifesavers went to the rescue, but the *Saunders* was in no particular danger. Salvors soon had her off with a $5,000 repair charge. A brush collision in Duluth Harbor between the steamer *America* and wooden steamer *Frank L. Vance* on June 19 amounted to little.

Salvaged stern of the William C. Moreland *moves down the St. Marys River nearly two years after the freighter wrecked and broke up on Saw Tooth Reef in October 1910.* STEFFKE MEMORIAL MARITIME COLLECTION, WYANDOTTE, MICHIGAN.

There was a good deal of excitement at Two Harbors in the fog of June 23. About 6:30 a.m., Captain Hough was endeavoring to bring the 414-foot, 4,702-ton steel steamer *L.C. Smith* into the port. He was deceived by the fog horn whose signals seemed to place it two miles east of the lighthouse point. Steering in blindly on a mistaken bearing, the captain ran the *Smith* well up on the beach between Burlington Bay and Flood Bay. Her hull was pretty well raked. Then a nasty gale arose. Frantically, her owners ordered the 525-foot steel steamer *Lyman C. Smith* and the 370-foot *Horace S. Wilkinson* to pull on her, but the *L.C. Smith* held tight. Three days later, the 80-foot tug *America* and 514-foot, 2,000-horsepower steel steamer *John Dunn Jr.* pulled her loose for a $33,000 trip to the shipyard in Superior.[1]

Fog again was the culprit on July 26 as the 388-foot, 3,850-ton steel steamer *Zenith City* was proceeding outbound from Marquette with a cargo of iron ore. Getting too close to Au Sable Point, nine miles west of Grand Marais, she found Au Sable Reef. Salvage men quickly liberated her, but her misadventure cost $10,600.[2]

The handsome William C. Moreland *beneath the Huletts on the lower lakes before stranding and breaking up off Eagle River in October 1910.* UNIVERSITY OF DETROIT MARINE COLLECTION.

The only other summer casualty was a fire on August 21 at Port Arthur. While lying at dock in that port, the 24-year-old 109-foot wooden steamer *Kaministiquia* was consumed by flames. There were no injuries as the wooden vessel ended her days, an undisclosed liability for owner A.H. Wiley. An incident at Superior on October 15 was inconsequential when two of the big steel steamers bumped, the 530-foot *Josiah G. Munro* and the 504-foot *Peter White*.[3]

Fall brought a vastly different story on the night of October 18. The two-month-old 580-foot, 7,514-ton steel steamer *William C. Moreland* of the Jones and Laughlin Steel fleet had departed from Superior earlier that day laden with 11,000 tons of iron ore. She was commanded by Captain Claude Ennes, one of the company veterans. But forest fires were raging in the Lake Superior hinterland and the lake was blanketed with smoke. About 9 p.m., in smoke and fog, Captain Ennes got slightly off course and rammed Sawtooth Reef off Eagle River along the Keweenaw Peninsula. The big carrier hit so hard that she bounced over the first set of rocks and halted on a second reef, impaled on both bow and stern. Captain Ennes was able to take a ship's yawl to Eagle River to phone for help. Portage lifesavers made the 21-mile run just in case they were needed. They were. About noon on October 19, a howling northwesterly gale rose and the lifesavers removed the full 25-man crew.

The following day, with the lake more moderate, the lifesavers were in the process of putting the *Moreland* crew back on board when the giant ship snapped in two. Thereupon, the full crew was taken ashore. Another storm hit, and the *Moreland* was broken into three parts. Salvors converged on the derelict with the wrecking tugs *Favorite* of Port Huron and *Boynton* of the Soo, together with the *James Whalen* of Port Arthur, accompanied by the lighters *Empire* and *Imperial.* Captain Joseph Kidd of Duluth supervised these initial operations, along with Captain Hill, the shore captain for the Jones and Laughlin fleet. Then came another rugged blast of weather which drove the salvors away. The bow section of the *Moreland* twisted off and rolled over. The situation looked hopeless.

Finally, the highly esteemed salvor, Captain James R. Reid, was brought to the scene with the wreckers *Sarnia City* and *Manistique.* Even he struggled for weeks. The ardors of this job were too tough for the elderly Captain Reid. He suffered a paralytic stroke in late December. His son, Captain Tom Reid, carried on. After months of frustration, Captain Tom Reid finally took the *Moreland* off the initial reef, only to have her strand and break in two again. This time the bow section sank. At the end of August 1911, the Reid salvors finally dragged the 254-foot stern section into the Portage Lake Ship Canal, later towing her down to Sarnia.

Next came a dilemma. Captain Jim Reid had taken the job on a "no cure-no pay" basis. His company could not deliver a full ship to dry dock. Technically, he had nothing coming. However, the insurance agents, recognizing an almost impossible salvage accomplishment, gave the Reids the rescued stern. For a while this was small consolation, as less than half a ship was not particularly marketable. But ultimately things turned out favorably. During World War I, Canadian ship owners purchased the *Moreland*'s stern from the Reids and had a new forward section constructed at Superior. The two were joined together, and the old *Moreland* emerged as a new 580-footer named *Sir Trevor Dawson.* Under different names, American and Canadian, she sailed another 60 years. The *William C. Moreland* was an official loss of $445,000, the worst on Lake Superior to that date.[4]

As a gale belabored the ill-fated *Moreland* on October 23, Captain J.H. Sinclair took the 281-foot, 1,810-ton wooden steamer *Langham* into the shelter of Bete Grise Bay. Loaded with coal for Port Arthur, the *Langham* already had slogged through two days of battering waves, and Captain Sinclair did not want to take any chances off Keweenaw Point. Yet, as she rested at anchor in 120 feet of water, she caught fire. Flames kept the crew away from the anchors. Hence, all they could do was take to the yawls as their steamer burned to the water's edge. Owned by John I. Adams of Detroit, the 22-year-old *Langham* was reported as a casualty of $150,000, although this figure appears quite steep for a wooden steamer of that age.[5]

A brush collision at Point Iroquois on October 28 did little harm to the steamers *Manitou* and *Venezuela,* but a Duluth Harbor fire on the night of November 3 gutted the 42-foot wooden tug *John H. Jeffery Jr.* so that she sank alongside her dock. The dock building likewise was singed. The *Jeffery* was raised, rebuilt and returned to service at an expenditure of several thousand dollars.

Bulk freight canaller Dunelm *is still leaking water in a Port Arthur dry dock after being freed from Canoe Rocks in December 1910.* CANAL PARK MARINE MUSEUM COLLECTION.

A fire at Copper Harbor on November 6 was more serious. Captain W. A. Glass had brought the 244-foot, 1,745-ton wooden Canadian steamer *Wasaga* into the shelter of Copper Harbor to avoid the tempestuous seas off the Keweenaw. As she lay at anchor, flames were detected in the number one hold. The 32-year-old ship was blazing in a matter of minutes. Her crew took to the boats, rowing to another sheltered Canadian ship, the *Westmount,* which took them to Fort William after the waves died down outside. Loaded with harvesting machinery, radiators, barbed wire and miscellaneous freight, the *Wasaga* was the subject of almost immediate salvage efforts by Captain Joseph Croze of Houghton, a portion of the cargo being recovered within the protected waters of Copper Harbor. No insurance statistics were given, though an old wooden vessel of this type probably was valued at $20,000 and the lost cargo a good deal more.[6]

A more favorable experience for another Canadian vessel ended the season. Outbound from Port Arthur on the night of December 6, only a half hour before the seasonal expiration of marine insurance, the 250-foot, 2,319-ton steel steamer *Dunelm* of the Inland Lines ran into a gale and wild waters off Thunder Cape. Tossed off course, she ran into the Canoe Rocks Reef due west of the northeastern tip of Isle Royale where she hung up tight. The powerful 410-foot steel steamer *F.B. Squire* spotted the luckless *Dunelm* and stood by to take off the crew, if necessary, until tugs of the Canadian Towing and Wrecking Company arrived from the Canadian Lakehead. Salvors worked incessantly for two weeks, as not too many ships have escaped the clutches of Isle Royale reefs. The *Dunelm* finally came loose on December 21. She was taken into Duncan Bay for emergency patching and then on to Port Arthur for dry-docking and reconstruction. Undoubtedly, she was a repair bill of more than $10,000. Her bow anchors and a substantial length of chain remain on the bottom today, marking the wreck site.[7]

1911

The shipping season of 1911 was unusual. Tonnage slumped about 15 percent. The accident roster dropped far more. However, the most serious incidents occurred during the summer months, a departure from typical sailing years. Sailors were spared the customary plate-benders and time-wasters early in the navigation period, but when a mishap occurred, it was a shocker.

The wooden steamer Rappahannock *struggled mightily in a July 1910 storm with 75 mph winds before succumbing to Lake Superior on the Ontario shore.* AUTHOR'S COLLECTION.

Early in the morning of July 10, Captain John H. Massey was standing his watch in shirt sleeves on a warm summer night as his 420-foot, 4,468-ton steel steamer *John Mitchell* groped her way westward in fog off Vermilion Point. Coal-laden for Superior, the *Mitchell* also carried a number of passengers, including six women and a little boy. Captain Massey was suddenly horrified. Breaking from the whiteout at close range was the black hulk of a downbound freighter heading directly for the *Mitchell*. He had only time to blow a warning whistle when, with a grinding crash, the ghostly newcomer struck him on the port side. The black hulk proved to be the 354-foot, 3,781-ton steel steamer *William Henry Mack* of Cleveland, traveling light. As the vessels struck, the *Mitch-*

ell heeled sharply to port, dropping a spar over the *Mack*'s deck so that the two ships were temporarily locked together. Working with lightning speed, the two crews lashed a ladder between the two carriers, while the *Mitchell* crew also launched a yawl.

Within seven minutes, the *Mitchell* slid to the bottom of Lake Superior, but in that time 25 persons crossed over the ladder and six more took to the yawl. Only three of the *Mitchell*'s crew, Second Mate Archie Causely, Steward Al Clemens and Watchman George Austin, went down with the ship.

The occupants of the yawl had more horrors in store. The suction of the submerging steamer capsized the little boat, dumping three men and three women into the icy water. Fortunately, 16-year-old Fay Clemens, daughter of the drowned steward, apparently was an expert swimmer. Calming the five floundering souls, she called for a line from the *Mack*, attached it to the overturned lifeboat and directed the *Mack* crew in righting the yawl so that the occupants could be dragged back into it and saved. Luckily, the *Mack* was sailing without a load, otherwise, two ships may well have sunk with heavy loss of life, since the *Mack* had her lower bow shoved back 20 feet by the impact, creating a ragged hole 20 feet square. Three men had made their last trip, and the *Mitchell* was a property loss of $350,000, including cargo. While the *Mack*'s rehabilitation charges are not recorded, hers must have run in excess of $25,000. The *Mitchell* was virtually a new ship, built in 1907 at St. Clair, Michigan, and owned by C.W. Elphicke of Chicago.[8]

Two weeks later, on July 25, a rare 75 mph gale raked eastern Lake Superior, catching the 308-foot, 2,380-ton wooden steamer *Rappahannock* and her 342-foot, 2,722-ton wooden schooner-barge *Montezuma* on the open water. The *Rappahannock* began to leak badly. Though en route to Duluth with coal cargoes, the vessels were running close to the Ontario north shore for what relief they could get from the elements. Captain Scott of the *Impoco* observed the struggling duo and altered course to come within a mile of the *Rappahannock*, following along as close as he dared. Dropping his barge, Captain Rattray headed for the shelter of Jackfish Bay north of Slate Islands. He almost made safety. With water rising dangerously in the hold, the captain decided to run the ship ashore at Jackfish Point. After running her aground in shoal water, the crew took to the boats and easily got to the nearby shore. All were safe.

Captain Rattray later credited the *Impoco*'s considerable concern for his crew's safety for thus encouraging his own crew to stay with their stricken vessel as long as possible, probably preventing loss of life if they had abandoned ship on the open lake. But, the 16-year-old vessel settled in 80 feet of water. The financial liability was not listed. However, a large wooden freighter of this type and age, with cargo, undoubtedly was worth more than

$100,000 to her owner, Captain James Davidson. Another Davidson steamer, the *Sacramento,* put out from the Soo and retrieved the drifting *Montezuma.*

Ice and weather damage continue to ravage the *Rappahannock,* but it was cargo salvage efforts years later which devastated the hull. The hull was dynamited and a simple clam bucket rig was used to rip away the remaining deck to gain access to the coal in the hold. Despite

pilot for the Schreiber Channel, whose fee he thought was too high, Harkness instructed the captain to guide the big yacht in. However, she struck hard on McGarvey's Shoal on the northwest side of Copper Island, her keel rising five feet above the water. Harkness took a motor lifeboat to Rossport where he telegraphed his insurance company and then returned to his ship.

The insurance officials procured the Canadian Towing

The steel yacht Gunilda *was grounded upon McGarvey Shoal in Nipigon Bay near Rossport in 1911. She slipped into 300 feet of water when a salvage attempt was made.* OSCAR ANDERSON PHOTO, *LAKE SUPERIOR MAGAZINE* COLLECTION.

this, the *Rappahannock*'s remains are popular with sport divers. The wreck rests upright in 80 feet of water with its hull relatively intact heading directly in toward shore in a narrow little bay on the picturesque Canadian shore. Unfortunately, the wreck is sometimes obscured by effluent from a nearby paper mill.[9]

Late August saw the lake claim one of its most uncommon victims, a multi-millionaire's ocean-going yacht. William L. Harkness of New York City, one of the original investors in Standard Oil, had purchased the magnificent yacht *Gunilda,* nearly 200 feet long, constructed in 1897 at Leith, Scotland. In early August 1911, Harkness, his family and two guests joined Captain Alexander Corkum and the crew of 20 for an extended cruise of Lake Superior. He decided that he would like to visit the quaint fishing village of Rossport on the north shore, some hundred miles east of Port Arthur. Declining use of a local

and Wrecking Company from Port Arthur with the tug *James Whalen* and barge *Empire.* When the wreckers appeared, passengers and crew left the stranded vessel, a most fortunate move indeed, since, as the *Whalen* attempted to pull the *Gunilda* off the reef, she listed badly to starboard, took water through unbattened companionways, filled and slid backward, foundering in more than 200 feet of water on August 31. She was an insurance liability of $100,000, probably worth far more, though not the multi-millions alleged by some imaginative writers of sport divers' treasure hunting stories.

A salvage plan was put together as early as 1938 to bring the *Gunilda* to the surface, but problems with insurance forced abandonment of the plan before any equipment ever reached the wreck site. Later, well-known hard hat diver E.J. "Doc" Fowler visited the wreck with visions of salvage. Another diver from the Canadian Lakehead,

Dan Coglan, also attempted to reach the dangerously deep wreck. Neither made any real attempt at salvage. In 1967 and 1968, Ed Flatt of Rossport, Ontario, attempted to grapple for the wreck, only to have it slip from 240 feet

The little ferry Hattie Lloyd *was repaired after a September 1911 fire on the Superior waterfront.* C. PATRICK LABADIE COLLECTION.

to about 290 feet, putting it even further out of reach. The end result was recovery of some line and portions of the bowsprit and main mast, damaging the otherwise perfectly intact wreck. Still others have been fascinated by the prospects of salvaging this luxury yacht including Charles Zehnder, Fred Broennle and Charles King Hague. The lure cost Charles Hague his life and instilled a life-long ambition in Broennle who has at various times developed the technical knowledge and created the equipment to effect salvage only to have financial difficulties overcome actual salvage attempt. In 1989, a deep dive attempt on the *Gunilda* by Reg Barrett of Brampton, Ontario, cost him his life.[10]

September was mild, the only incidents involving a plate scraper at Duluth by the steel steamers *Minnetonka* and *Juniata* on September 3 and a harbor fire at Superior on September 29, after which the 68-foot ferry steamer *Hattie Lloyd* required several thousand dollars in restoration.

October, however, was ushered in by a gale in the western lake which actually sank a loaded lumber hooker, the 174-foot, 639-ton wooden steamer *A.L. Hopkins*. At that, the hand of the Lord was with the *Hopkins* crew, their survival being one of the luckiest on record. Under Captain Alfred Dixon, the 31-year-old hooker had loaded lumber at Bayfield, Wisconsin, with both hold and deck cargo, before sailing on the afternoon of October 3 into the face of a stiff wind. Captain Dixon, who also was part owner of the ship, envisioned no difficulties with an October blow. After all, lumber ships were hard to sink. This time, the captain was wrong.

After enduring eight hours of battering, the elderly *Hopkins*' seams began to open and water got deeper and deeper in the hold. Toward midnight, Captain Dixon

came to the grim conclusion that the *Hopkins* was settling. Accordingly, he ordered two sailors top-side to unlimber the lifeboat carried aft of the stack. Suddenly a giant wave engulfed the vessel, taking men, lifeboat and much of the deck load over the side. The remaining crew thought the men gone forever, and themselves goners too, as they had no further means of escape.

Meanwhile, the men washed overboard had an incredible experience. In going over, one had hung onto the lifeboat and climbed into it, as it floated right side up. The other grabbed a plank from the deck load and floated to the lifeboat into which he pulled himself. Apparently hemmed in by the mass of floating timber, the lifeboat remained close to the sinking steamer. After two hours, the half-frozen seamen guided the lifeboat back alongside their ship, where their fellow crewmen hauled them aboard. But not for long. Minutes later, Captain Dixon realized the ship would sink momentarily. Reluctantly, therefore, he ordered the whole crew into the lifeboat as the waterlogged *Hopkins* slowly submerged to the tip of her bow. Then came six frigid hours as the 15 survivors struggled to keep their boat afloat and upright. Without flares or lanterns, they could not attract the attention of two ships which passed nearby in the darkness.

The whole group was suffering badly from exposure with the temperature in the thirties and snow flurries adding to their misery. Fortuitously, as if in answer to prayers, at about 8 a.m. on October 4 out of the morning mists loomed the huge bulk of a giant steel steamer, the new 580-foot *Alva C. Dinkey* of the Pittsburgh Steamship Company. Crewmen of the *Dinkey* spotted the lifeboat, and Captain W.J. Hunt ordered a change of course, positioning the big freighter to the windward of the bobbing craft. The *Dinkey* crew dumped barrels of oil to quiet the waves. A line was thrown and the lifeboat brought alongside the rescue vessel. Despite the tossing seas, the 15 *Hopkins* survivors were brought aboard. Within minutes their water-soaked clothing was stripped from them, and they were placed in warm blankets in a heated cabin, mighty thankful to be alive. Buoyed by the lumber in her hold, the ill-fated *Hopkins* floated for some days after being abandoned with her bow barely visible, eventually going to the bottom about 16 miles northeast of Michigan Island. No financial figures were given, but she likely was worth more than $25,000 to her owners, the major one being Lawrence D. Brown of Chaumont, New York.[11]

A harbor fire at Port Arthur on October 8 ended the career of the 27-year-old 26-ton wooden tug *Gordon Gauthier*. She must have been a loss of several thousand dollars to her owners, the Lake Superior Tug Company, although the exact amount was unstated.[12] Rough weather on October 28 pushed the new 420-foot, 4,907-ton steel steamer *Odanah* against the Two Harbors breakwater. She went back to the shipyard for $5,000 in renovation work.

A freak snowstorm off Marquette on the night of October 31 claimed another of the lumber fleet. The 178-foot, 646-ton wooden steamer *D. Leuty* under Captain Sparling was upbound for Pequaming where she was to pick up a lumber cargo when she encountered an unusually thick snow squall off Marquette. The captain sought the shelter of Marquette Harbor, but in the heavy snow blanket was unable to detect the lighthouse. Moreover, the storm had come up so rapidly that the fog horn had not yet been put into operation. The *Leuty* reached Marquette all right, plowing into the rocks off Lighthouse Point between the two harbors. She was caught tight. Tugs could not budge her. Consequently, with a storm arising, Captain Cleary and the Marquette lifesavers took off the *Leuty* crew. The waves broke her in two. Salvors stripped her before she went completely to pieces nearly three weeks later. Her after cabin was saved and became a summer home on the shore of Lake Superior north of Marquette. She was owned by C.H. Prescott Jr. of Cleveland, operating through the Saginaw Bay Transportation Company. With much of her machinery removed, she must have been a net financial liability of $20,000.[13]

The final event of the season was a harbor collision at Duluth between the new steel steamers *Michigan* and *Leonard C. Hanna.* The 530-foot *Michigan,* upbound with a coal cargo, punched a hole in the bow of the 504-foot *Hanna,* outbound with iron ore. Though the *Michigan* emerged unscathed, the *Hanna* had to halt for temporary fixing. What might have been a serious mishap in the harbor channel, just upstream from the Interstate Bridge in Duluth-Superior Harbor, didn't amount to much after all.

1912

Ship owners were smiling this year. Tonnage zoomed upward more than 35 percent from the previous season, while troubles actually decreased. Only three ships were lost, though one was a costly mishap.

Navigation started out much like in 1911 with no difficulties of consequence until August. Then, the first casualty was a bad one that could have been even worse. In a dense fog at 1:35 a.m. on August 7, about 43 miles east of Manitou Island and 100 miles north of Marquette, two large steel steamers hit nearly head on, the downbound 454-foot, 5,124-ton *Rensselaer* of the Pittsburgh Steamship Company fleet and the upbound 416-foot, 4,777-ton *James Gayley* of the Mitchell fleet. Struck on the starboard side 65 feet from the bow, the *Gayley* went down in 16 minutes. Captain M.M. Stewart of the *Gayley* ordered his lifeboats launched, but Capt. C.D. Secord of the *Rensselaer* brought his ship alongside and had the two vessels lashed together. Twenty out of 24 passengers and crew aboard the *Gayley* crossed over to the *Rensselaer,*

though Mate A.H. Norton and three *Gayley* crewmen took a lifeboat to the barge *George H. Corliss,* consort of the *Rensselaer.* After all had been removed, the ships separated and the *Gayley* plunged to the bottom. Then, the

The 263-foot wooden steamer Culligan, *which foundered in September 1912 on the eastern lake, was formerly the* George T. Hope. AUTHOR'S COLLECTION.

Rensselaer began to take water at the bow. Captain Secord whistled for assistance. Within an hour, the new 479-foot *Stadacona* happened by and took off the *Gayley*'s people. The *Rensselaer* was then steered to Marquette with a collision blanket over the bow. Her collision bulkhead held, but she had four feet of water in her forepeak. After temporary repairs, she was able to resume the trip east, clearing downbound at the Soo on August 11.

In the blinding whiteout and driving rain the two captains did not see each other until the ships were in deadly close proximity, too late to take evasive action. After the crash, the amazing coolness of the two masters and crews prevented serious tragedy. The five women passengers on the *Gayley* escaped barefooted in their nightclothes. Not a life was lost, yet the nine-year-old *Gayley* with her coal cargo was an estimated property liability of $330,000. Had the ore-laden *Rensselaer* lost her collision bulkhead, she might have joined the *Gayley,* with possible fatalities.[14]

Another collision on September 1 off Whitefish Point saw the 525-foot steel steamer *William A. Rogers* unwittingly cut across the towline of the tug *Security* in thick fog. At the end of the line was Standard Oil's barge *S.O.Co.No.96* which proceeded to plow into the starboard bow of the *Rogers,* sending the larger vessel limping back to the Soo for emergency patching. Ultimately, the *Rogers* was a $20,000 dry-dock proposition. The oil barge escaped virtually unhurt.[15]

A 29-year-old wooden veteran of the lakes went to her rest on the bottom of Lake Superior on September 27. The 263-foot, 1,748-ton steamer *Culligan* had taken on a load of 2,100 tons of iron ore at Marquette from which she departed under Captain Henry Richardson at 11 p.m.,

September 26. For some days she had been leaking, however, her pumps had always taken care of the problem, hence her officers were not too concerned. Several hours east of Marquette, nevertheless, water began to rise alarmingly in the hold as she encountered moderate seas. Captain Richardson ordered her headed to Grand Island in an effort to beach her. She couldn't make it. Surging water forced the chief engineer to draw the fires, and shortly thereafter Captain Richardson ordered the 15-person crew into two lifeboats. They stood by the derelict for several hours until being picked up by the fishing tug *Columbia*. A short time later, the old *Culligan* dove for the depths, blowing her pilothouse high into the air and sending one spar skyward like a javelin. The survivors were brought to Marquette. Owned by John J. Boland of Buffalo, the *Culligan*, formerly the *George T. Hope*, was insured for $25,000 and her iron ore cargo was worth another $10,000.[16]

Although suffering bow damage, the Rensselaer *survived an August 1912 collision with* James Gayley, *which foundered east of Manitou Island after all crewmen were rescued.* AUTHOR'S COLLECTION.

Strandings were of little consequence this season. In a fog on July 5 the little 217-foot steel steamer *Viking* had run into rocks near Split Rock. While she was in no particular danger, salvage and repair charges did amount to $12,500. On October 7 the 30-year-old 287-foot iron steamer *Onoko* began to leak and was intentionally beached in the Apostle Islands. Patching cost little.

The barge *Imperial* was severely damaged on October 10 while unloading rock from the Verte Island quarry in Nipigon Bay at Red Rock, Ontario. A particularly massive boulder crashed through her side while being hoisted ashore, leaving a gaping hole. The still-laden *Imperial* listed, turned turtle and then dove to the bottom in about 70 feet of water. Salvage seemed possible at the time, but pressure to complete the stone delivery contract on schedule saw the *Imperial* simply abandoned. She was valued at $30,000 (Canadian). The 120-foot, 413-ton *Im-*

perial had been built at Fort William in 1902 and owned by Canadian Towing & Wrecking of Port Arthur.[17]

Repairs were in order for the steel steamer *Sonora* after she hit a dock at Duluth on October 19 and for the steamer *J.J.H. Brown,* which took a dusting from high waves on October 28. On November 8 it was the steel steamer *North Wind* in docking trouble at Superior with slight injury. A final stranding came on December 8 at Michipicoten with the rebuilt 312-foot steamer *Spokane* needing a few new plates.

A thrilling rescue west of Grand Marais, Michigan, near Point Au Sable marked the last two weeks of sailing. The little 84-foot, 73-ton coastal packet *South Shore,* under Captain Ora Endress, was proceeding westward from the Soo to Grand Marais on November 23 when overtaken by a surprise gale and snow storm. Tremendous seas made an approach to the Grand Marais pierhead impossible. Captain Endress decided to attempt riding out the storm in the open water. The *South Shore* took a terrific mauling all night long. The next day, she began to leak so badly that the captain headed her ashore. Distress signals on the whistle were drowned out by the roaring northwester, but the master raised a white flag which was spotted by the lifesaving lookout at the Grand Marais station. Despite ravaging breakers, the lifesaving crew reached the *South Shore* and took off the 13 persons aboard before the little ship went under. It was a close one, but all survived their terrifying experience. She was a financial casualty of between $7,000 and $10,000 to her owner, Emil Endress, of the Soo.[18]

1913

Traffic hit another peak in 1913. The accident toll was the worst in four years. More than 30 ships came to grief, the holocaust known as ''The Great Storm'' blasting a dozen and taking 46 lives in two days. This was not an early sailing season. Ice conditions in the eastern lake were still so bad during the first week of May that the Revenue cutter *Tuscarora,* under Captain Berry, was brought to Lake Superior for ice breaking. Apparently, the shipping companies didn't challenge the ice pack either, as only the steamer *W.H. Bunk* reported minor ice damage on May 3. Only one other incident was reported in the month of May. Two sizable steel steamers, the 480-foot *Stephen M. Clement* and the 514-foot *Fred G. Hartwell,* suffered a plate-bender in Duluth Harbor on May 14.

Fog followed by a whooping late spring gale ended the career of a lumber fleet veteran on June 6. Eastbound with 830,000 feet of lumber loaded at Duluth, the 187-foot, 689-ton wooden schooner-barge *Alleghany* was being towed by the 155-foot, 523-ton wooden lumber hooker *M.T. Greene.* The *Alleghany* stranded in the mists off Vermilion Point. Wisely, the Vermilion Point lifesavers removed her crew; on the heels of the fog came a wild June blow which tore the 40-year-old schooner to pieces. She had been launched in 1873 at Erie, Pennsylvania. She was valued at only $7,500 and owned by John Dunseith of Toledo.[19]

In more fog off Keweenaw Point about 5 a.m., June 15, came a terribly close call. As the small 220-foot, 1,043-ton

needed $10,000 in dry-dock fees. Delivering her coal at the Duluth-Superior harbor, the brand new *Snyder Jr.* also was assigned to the shipyard for $3,500 in 14 new plates and additional refurbishing. The *Spalding* was especially lucky to remain afloat after being whacked by a 590-footer under good speed.[20]

Foggy weather continued to cause difficulties in June. Modest injuries were sustained by the steel steamers *Choc-*

Festive ship launchings drew crowds at Duluth, Superior and Port Arthur shipyards during the wartime ship-building boom. HAROLD ANDRESEN COLLECTION, CANAL PARK MARINE MUSEUM.

steel steamer *Jesse Spalding* proceeded eastward with a cargo of iron ore from Duluth-Superior, she was suddenly side-swiped by one of the fast, new giants of the lakes, the 590-foot, 8,603-ton *William P. Snyder Jr.* of the Shenango fleet, a 2,500-horsepower vessel. The year-old *Snyder Jr.* came and went so fast that Captain L.A. Garu of the *Spalding* did not know what ship had hit him. He knew her to be a Shenango vessel, but thought she was the smaller 554-foot *Wilpen*. Both ships separated after the impact. As Captain Garu knew the *Spalding* had suffered shattered plates on the port bow and was making water, he had distress signals blown. The *Snyder Jr.* reported the collision by wireless and then began circling in the fog, but she could not locate the *Spalding*. There was some anxiety aboard the *Spalding*. However, her bulkheads held, and her crew jettisoned 200 tons of iron ore from the forward hold, raising her bow so that a canvas patch could be applied. Rather out of trim, she managed to reach the Soo where it was discovered that she

taw, which went aground at Point Iroquois on June 20, and *William G. Mather,* which stranded on a reef at Marquette. The steel steamer *Sonora* also clipped a bridge at Duluth on June 23 with slight consequence. Not as fortunate was the 549-foot steel steamer *Charles Weston,* which ended up hard ashore in Burlington Bay on June 27 while groping for the Two Harbors entrance. It took $25,000 to make her ship shape.

At Marquette on August 1, the 414-foot steel *Hurlbut W. Smith* steamed into shallow water, necessitating minor repairs. On August 17 the huge 590-foot *Colonel James M. Schoonmaker* brushed the 504-foot *Hoover & Mason* in Duluth Harbor, the smaller vessel needing $3,000 worth of fixing. In poor visibility on September 10, the 300-foot steel *Northern Queen* plowed well up on Rock of Ages Reef near the lighthouse, ripping her bottom. The Canadian tugs *James Whalen* and *J.T. Horne* along with the barge *Empire* raced to the scene and took her off in short order, but with a $22,500 rebuilding job to follow.[21] Still, had she remained on that reef a few days longer, a slashing gale with snow might have torn her to bits. As it was, the storm of September 20, with 48 mph winds at Duluth and 62 mph at Houghton, caught the whaleback barge *137* out of Two Harbors in tow of the steamer *Matoa* and washed Captain O.W. Holdbridge overboard to his death.

Two strandings of steel steamers in October amounted

excursion steamer *International* burned at her dock on November 2 in the White City area of the Keweenaw Waterway. The 24-year-old *International* was owned by M.J. Carroll of Houghton, possibly worth less than $10,000.[23] Indeed, the early November weather was really too good. Forest fires were still being reported in the vicinity of Marquette on November 1.

Then came the terrible second week of November.

The crew of the badly battered L.C. Waldo *nearly threaded the needle between Keweenaw Point and Manitou Island in November 1913, but the ship stranded and quickly broke her back. Shown here in another grounding with big wrecker* Favorite *working off her stern.* AUTHOR'S COLLECTION.

to little; the 532-foot *J.Q. Riddle* grounded at Superior on October 7 and the 260-foot *Lackawanna* sustained damage at Michipicoten Island on October 14. On October 20, another schooner sailed her last, the 251-foot, 1,762-ton wooden *Mary McLachlan* which struck the rocks at Black Bay on the Ontario north shore about 41 miles out of Port Arthur and broke up. She was owned by Colin McLachlan of Port Huron, very likely worth about $20,000 or more since she was only 20 years old, rather young for the typical wooden schooner-barge.[22] The Canadians may have salvaged this vessel for use along the north shore. A ship of this name and approximate size under Canadian registry was lost at Nipigon Bay in the early 1920s.

Things continued to be rather routine. The steel steamer *Coralia* needed some retouching after scraping the wooden schooner-barge *B.L. Pennington* at some undisclosed location, while the little 80-foot, 130-ton wooden

Head-of-the-Lakes residents were enjoying lovely Indian Summer weather on Thursday, November 6, with the mercury at 58 degrees F, when the 451-foot, 4,466-ton steel *L.C. Waldo* steamed from Duluth to Two Harbors to pick up a load of iron ore. Nevertheless, forecasters of the U.S. Weather Bureau recognized ominous signs of rain, snow and wind coming in from the northwest. Storm warnings were raised at Duluth at 10:00 a.m., November 7. The weathermen were correct. A 60 mph gale struck Duluth about 6 p.m., raging for several hours before diminishing to lesser blasts the next day. A sharp temperature drop saw the thermometer descending to 20 degrees above zero on November 8 accompanied by strong winds and local snows. Three coal bridges were blown down at the Boston coal dock in Duluth that day, but that was the extent of serious material damage there. South shore points reported snow. At Ashland, the Ashland and Superior Central high school football game had to be cancelled due to the snowstorm. The blustery winds persisted until Sunday, then dropped, only to be followed by another weather mass bringing more gales and snow, necessitating another storm warning at 9:30 p.m., November 9. Aside from delaying ships 10-15 hours in reaching Duluth, even the second wintry flush brought little more than inconvenience to western Lake Superior.

Not so in the central and eastern lake. Virtually hurricane-like conditions existed on the open lake for more than four days, with intermittent snows and wildly howling winds. The first to feel the might of this weather monster was the *L.C. Waldo* as she slogged her way eastward. Captain J.W. Duddleson had sailed from Two Harbors on Friday morning, December 7, before the storm warnings were raised. The ship had made good progress early in the day, but conditions grew worse as evening approached. Rain changed to slushy snow and rising seas.

At 11:45 p.m., as the *Waldo* was off Manitou Island, a gigantic wave rolled down from the stern, crushed the pilothouse and swept it overboard, along with the compass. Captain Duddleson, the mate and wheelsman narrowly escaped being tossed over the side. The ship's lighting system was knocked out. With a hand compass procured by the wheelsman from a lifeboat, the group retreated to the auxiliary wheel on the after deck house where, with the mate holding a lantern and the compass, the captain managed to turn the vessel and head for the passage between Manitou Island and the tip of Keweenaw Point. He hoped to reach the shelter of Bete Grise Bay.

They jockeyed the disabled steamer about for several hours and came close to reaching safety. However, the tumultuous seas pitched the battered *Waldo* upon the rocks of Gull Island, west of Manitou, and quickly broke her in two. Captain Duddleson herded his crew forward to the windlass room where, from shortly after 4 a.m. on November 8 until 7 a.m. on November 11, they would be virtual prisoners in an ice-encrusted tomb, saved from freezing by an improvised stove made from the captain's bathtub and subsisting on two cans of preserves for 23 people.

The plight of the *Waldo* went undetected for hours. Because of the frightful winds and blinding snow, few vessels were passing Manitou Island and those that did stayed well out in open water. Finally, late Saturday, along came Captain Mosher with the 407-foot, 4,563-ton steel steamer *George Stephenson* of the Pittsburgh Steamship Company. Through a rift in the snow, he sighted the hapless *Waldo,* noted the distress flag above her forward works and fought his way into the shelter of Keweenaw Point at Bete Grise Bay. Putting a boat over, he directed the first mate to find a telephone and notify the Eagle Harbor Life-Saving Station. After an arduous trip of many hours, the officer eventually reached a telephone at Delaware and contacted Captain Charles Tucker at Eagle Harbor. It was now late Sunday, November 9, and the gale was still roaring. As luck would have it, the power lifeboat at

Eagle Harbor was immobilized for engine repairs. Yet, Captain Tucker and his crew set out at midnight in the eight-horsepower surfboat for the torturous 28-mile run along the windy shore to Gull Rock. After three miserable hours with little progress, they were so badly iced up that they had to return. Working straight through the day and into the following night, the Eagle Harbor lifesavers repaired the big lifeboat, departing in still mountainous seas for the *Waldo* at midnight on November 10.

Meanwhile, Captain Mosher held the *Stephenson* in shelter until the following day. Before pulling out, he decided to check on the rescue progress. Sending the second mate ashore this time, he learned that the Eagle Harbor unit had been driven back. However, the officer had managed to telephone Captain Thomas H. McCormick of the Portage Canal Life-Saving Station, and this crew prepared to respond, though the *Waldo* lay a good 80 miles away. The Keweenaw Central Railroad offered a special train to take them to the Bete Grise area, but Captain McCormick decided to sail down the Keweenaw Waterway to Portage Entry where Captain Bert Nelson of the 99-foot, 500-horsepower tug *Daniel H. Hebard* would give him a tow along the southeast, or lee side, of Keweenaw Point. The canal crew reached a site opposite the wreck in the early morning hours and prepared to wait for daylight.

Just as they were about to undertake the extremely hazardous rescue, the Eagle Harbor lifeboat hove into sight. Joining forces, the two lifeboat crews put men aboard the ice-encrusted *Waldo*, assisted the imprisoned ship's crew in chopping their way to the deck and safely removed all 23 aboard to the two lifeboats, which brought them to the *Hebard* where warm quarters and food awaited. So perilous was this mission that every man aboard the two lifeboats received the U.S. Treasury Department's Gold Medal of Honor.

The unfortunate *Waldo* was initially regarded a total loss exceeding $227,500 by her owners, the Roby Transportation Company. The insurance companies, however, employed the Great Lakes Towing Company to retrieve their expensive charge. In the early days of May 1914, the wrecker *Favorite* refloated the *Waldo* and towed her to Portage Lake. She was then towed east for complete rebuilding. She sailed for another 44 years. Net salvage and rebuilding fees must have been considerably less than the original loss estimate. Captain Duddleson terminated a maritime career of 39 years after this close call and took employment at the Soo.[24]

While the *Waldo* was fighting her losing battle in the early morning hours of November 8, a second casualty was occurring in the central lake area. The 253-foot, 1,881-ton steel Canadian steamer *Turret Chief,* under Captain Thomas Paddington, had locked through the Soo at 5:00 a.m., November 7, and had rounded Whitefish Point for the northwest before storm warnings were up. Late that evening, when the ship was 110 miles along the course to Thunder Bay, she was simply engulfed by wind and snow. The storm simply took over. While Captain Paddington thought he was holding to deep water, the northern blasts had driven him 50 miles off course.

About 4:00 a.m., the crew felt two shocks as the steamer rolled over reefs, halting with her bow nearly against the cliffs, six miles east of Copper Harbor near Keweenaw Point. The crew dropped down on ropes from the bow to ice-covered rocks and picked their way to shore where they quickly built a hut of boughs and driftwood. Procuring food from the galley, they made themselves as comfortable as possible as the norther blew furiously Saturday and Sunday. Indian trappers found them on Monday morning and guided them to civilization. They arrived at Mandan about noon on November 11, three days after their vessel had struck. Property of the Merchant's Mutual Line of Ontario, the English-built *Turret Chief* was at first considered a complete ruin, but she was retrieved the following year for reconstruction. Her preliminary liability estimate of $80,000 is undoubtedly a bit too high.[25]

The third victim was also Canadian. Indeed, little can be told. The 250-foot, 1,452-ton steel freighter *Leafield* of the Algoma Central Steamship Company at Sault Ste. Marie, Ontario, had departed from the Soo for Fort William at 8:30 a.m., November 7, with a cargo of steel rails and track fastenings. She likewise met the weather nemesis. However, the British-built ocean steamer seemingly slogged her way through, and on November 9 had rounded Isle Royale on the last leg of her journey. Then something went awry off Angus Island.

Heavily laden with steel rails, the Benjamin Noble *vanished between Two Harbors and Duluth during a violent April 1914 storm. It is still lost.* UNIVERSITY OF DETROIT MARINE COLLECTION.

Through a gap in the clouds of snow, officers of the Canadian passenger steamer *Hamonic* got a glimpse of the *Leafield*. Captain Baird and his first officer reported that she seemed to crest a giant wave and then vanish. Some reports at the Canadian Lakehead alleged that she was aground at Angus Island, though the tug *J.T. Horne* made two fruitless trips to the area. The 21-year-old *Leafield* had simply disappeared, taking Captain Baker

and 17 men with her in one of the lake's strangest accidents. Some surmised that her cargo had shifted. As far as is known, her hull has never been located. With her valuable steel rails, she must have been worth $175,000.[26]

On Sunday evening, November 9, came the major tragedy of the Great Storm on Lake Superior. The 525-foot, 6,631-ton steel steamer *Henry B. Smith* of Hawgood's Acme line had locked through the Soo upbound at 2:30 a.m. on November 7, arriving at Marquette for an ore cargo well before the blow began. Though safe at dock while other vessels were being shattered on November 7, 8 and 9, the *Smith* suffered a loading delay and was not ready to sail until late Sunday afternoon, November 9. The lake was still rolling, but there seemed to be a lull in the wind, the velocity having dropped to 32 mph. The gale already had hit the Soo with winds more than 50 mph for 36 hours and should have blown itself out. But, this was no conventional storm. In taking his vessel out of the safety of Marquette Harbor, Captain James Owen sailed into eternity.

A number of people ashore or on ships in the port watched the *Smith* head out, some of the vessel men in perplexed wonderment. Lifesaving Captain Henry Cleary was heard to remark, "Captain Owen will soon be back." Indeed, even as onlookers watched her lights in the early evening darkness, the steamer, when only a few miles out, was seen to swing hard to port, as if to come around or to meet head-on some unsuspected blasts from the north. Then a snow squall blotted her out. The storm raged worse that Sunday night and Monday.

The *Henry B. Smith* never did reach the Soo, or any other port for that matter. With communications in the eastern lake pretty well demoralized, no concern for the giant *Smith* was felt for several days, though after she remained unreported by Wednesday, worries grew. Captain Murphy of the incoming steamer *Frontenac* reported at Marquette that one of his oilers had sighted a body floating in a life jacket on Wednesday, about 11 miles northeast of Marquette. Seas were too rough to permit recovery. Some of the wreckage drifting into the Presque Isle section of Marquette Harbor was presumed to have come from the *Waldo,* impaled 65 miles to the northwest. Nevertheless, on Friday land-looker Dan Johnston, beachcombing between Chocolay and Shot Point, found a pike pole and several oars marked *Henry B. Smith.* Wreckage of a deck house appeared in the vicinity of Shot Point. A life raft recovered southeast of Marquette carried a brass lock from the American Shipbuilding Company which had built the *Smith.*

By November 18, the weather had finally moderated so that fisherman William Powell of Munising was able to coast the south shore between Pictured Rocks and Grand Marais. He brought back a ladderway, two cabin doors, two screens for port and starboard lights, pillows and life jackets stenciled *Henry B. Smith.* By the next day, miscellaneous debris was littering the beaches from Sand River to Laughing Whitefish Point.

Two weeks after the *Smith* sailed, Captain Corliss of the steamer *Saxona* spotted a body floating 50 miles west of Whitefish Point. Heaving to, he ordered a boat lowered under command of First Mate J. MacDonald. The boat crew recovered a body in a life jacket identified as Henry B. Askin, second cook of the *Smith*. Askin was fully clothed. The following May at Michipicoten Island far to the northeast, two Indians found the life-jacketed body of Engineer John Gallagher of the *Smith*.

In early June, a mile south of Coppermine Point Light, roughly 40 miles from the Soo on the Canadian shore, a fisherman recovered a bottle with a note addressed to the Hawgood Company, Rockefeller Building, Cleveland. Frank Carlton, who discovered it, gave the message to Captain Batten of the steamer *Caribou* who brought it to the Soo. Though water-soaked and partially illegible, the note said that the *Smith* broke in two at Number 5 hatch, 12 miles east of Marquette. However, as the note was dated November 12 and the *Smith* had sailed on the 9th, presumably sinking that night, the authenticity of the find was doubted. A badly blurred ''O'' at the bottom of the sheet might have been Owen. Still, sailors figured that the *Smith* had broken in two, taking with her 30-year veteran Captain Owen and his 24-man crew. The ship was a financial loss in excess of $350,000.[27]

Leaving Duluth in blustery weather on Saturday, November 8, two ore carriers were destined for an utterly miserable trip down the storm-tossed lake. Their journeys culminated in disastrous strandings in lower Whitefish Bay near Point Iroquois where they should have been completely safe. The 346-foot, 3,734-ton *J.T. Hutchinson* of the Hutchinson Company and the 514-foot, 6,623-ton *Fred G. Hartwell* of the Tomlinson fleet both came to grief about two miles apart on either side of Point Iroquois Light. Neither engines nor anchors could restrain the unholy tempest from driving the two vessels hard aground, where they sank in shallow water on November 10. Fortunately, the crews were safe, though exhausted and half starved. Salvagers would have the two off within a week for repairs of $20,000 to the *Hutchinson* and $65,000 to the *Hartwell*.[28]

Any master caught in the open on the eastern lake during those terrible days, November 8 and 9, endured anxious moments. The powerful, 504-foot, 6,184-ton steel *Peter White* needed the full output of her 1,700-horsepower engines to pull her through off Marquette. Inspection in port revealed the need for more than $22,000 in rehabilitation work.

Not as fortunate was the 377-foot, 4,234-ton steel steamer *William Nottingham* of the U.S. Transportation Company at Cleveland. Downbound from the Canadian Lakehead with a cargo of grain, she successfully challenged the elements on November 8 and 9, only to be driven east of the vessel lanes at Whitefish Point and hurled onto the reef between South Sandy Island and Parisienne Island during the afternoon of November 10. She took a terrible beating. Her coal supply gave out, and the firemen were forced to use grain to keep up steam. In desperation, three of the crew volunteered to launch a lifeboat for help, but the ill-starred craft was crushed against the side of the steamer. Three volunteers, a wheelsman, an oiler and a deck hand were lost. The remaining crew stayed aboard for three torturous days.

Meanwhile, the U.S. Revenue Cutter *Tuscarora* was ordered from Milwaukee to Lake Superior to assist the *Waldo*. Bucking the gale, the *Tuscarora* did not reach the Whitefish Bay area until November 12. As her master, Captain Shea, learned that the *Waldo* crew already had been rescued, his ship then was available for other operations. Sighting the beleaguered *Nottingham* that afternoon, the *Tuscarora* stood by. The next day, with the seas increasing to menacing proportions, Captain Shea very daringly nosed his 178-foot cutter against the side of the grounded *Nottingham* and removed her remaining personnel, one by one. Salvors plucked the *Nottingham* off the reef four days later. She was brought into the Soo and later headed to dry dock. Her rebuilding cost $125,000, her grain cargo was ruined and three of her people had died.[29]

Nearly 100 ships took refuge in Whitefish Bay from November 8 through 11. Even in shelter, not all were safe. The Canadian steamers *Acadian* and *Huronic* both grounded for a time but emerged unscathed. The 321-foot passenger liner *Huronic* reached the Canadian Soo locks on November 9 looking more like a floating iceberg than a passenger vessel.

The 356-foot, 3,943-ton *A.E. Stewart* likewise was whipped aground for a while, but with her 1,800-horsepower engines managed to extricate herself. An eerie experience greeted the brand new 580-foot, 7,705-ton steel *James A. Farrell* of the Pittsburgh Steamship Company fleet. Though anchored in Whitefish Bay with her 1,880-horsepower engine working at peak, she lost both forward anchors and chains, having to beat a hasty retreat to the Soo.

One of the strangest incidents involving any ship occurred to the 283-foot, 1,864-ton wooden steamer *Major*. Upbound with a coal cargo, the *Major* locked through the Soo on Thursday, November 13, just in time to be a casualty at the tail end of the storm. When 30 miles west of Whitefish Point, she blew a steam pipe and apparently fell into the trough. She began leaking badly. Then her upper works were carried away by rampaging seas. At the critical moment, the new steel 504-foot, 6,364-ton *A.M. Byers* appeared. The *Byers'* crew put a line on the stricken *Major* and took off her whole complement, leaving the 24-year-old vessel a sinking derelict. Yet, she wouldn't go down. Who should show up at the Soo on November 16 in tow of the 504-foot steel *George*

G. Barnum but the *Major.* Her 1,900-ton coal cargo was sold, though her 24-year-old wooden hull was adjudged wrecked beyond repair, a financial loss of $15,000.[30]

This was the Great Storm of 1913 on Lake Superior, with 46 dead and property losses of more than a million dollars. The cost was bad enough, though happily not comparable to the dreadful toll on Lake Huron. Numerous ships had narrow escapes. Indeed, the casualty list might have been higher, except that by the second day of the blow, most masters realized that this was no ordinary fall storm and sought whatever cover afforded itself. Others maneuvered adroitly on open water. This early November storm was a shocker that Great Lakes sailors would never forget.

1914

This was not a good year for shippers. Tonnage on Lake Superior was down more than 30 percent from the 1913 peak. The mishap roll was also sharply reduced, though a tragic disappearance inaugurated the season and a horrendous multiple disaster concluded it. Four ships were involved and the death toll stood at 48. Most of the year's mix-ups were routine collisions or strandings, however, with one fire claiming an ancient wooden vessel.

The barge George E. Hartnell *was driven ashore in late June 1914 near the corner of the lake off Duluth as onlookers watched helplessly, but was handily salvaged the next day.* AUTHOR'S COLLECTION.

The Capitol Transportation Company's 239-foot, 1,481-ton steel steamer *Benjamin Noble* vanished within 20 miles of Duluth in the early morning hours of April 28. She was a stout little vessel, built in 1909 at Wyandotte, Michigan, by Great Lakes Engineering Company. A seven-hatch ship, she was specially constructed to handle steel rails. She was heavily loaded with more than 2,900 tons of rails consigned to the Great Northern Railroad at Superior on her fatal trip. Her master was 31-year-old Cap-

tain John Eisenhardt of Milwaukee. This was his first command, though he had held master's papers for more than six years and had previously been first mate on the steamers *Merida* and *John Sharples.*

The *Noble* had entered Lake Superior on April 25, encountering heavy fog over the eastern lake. The 209-foot, 1,007-ton wooden lumber steamer *Norwalk,* under Captain Frank Goodrow, tailed the *Noble* through April 26, finally passing her well west of Keweenaw Point in late afternoon of the 27th. The deeply laden *Noble* was only a few miles behind the *Norwalk* as the two vessels were engulfed on the night of the 27th and morning of April 28 by one of the wildest spring gales ever to afflict the western lake. Gusts of 64 mph were recorded at Duluth at 6:56 a.m. on the 28th. So mountainous were the waves that the light on the south pierhead at Duluth was extinguished and the fog horn rendered inoperable. Over at Superior, two coal dock trestles were blown down. The steamers *John Lambert* and *Minneapolis,* which had left Duluth as the storm began, were forced to return, their captains reporting difficulty in locating the Duluth Ship Canal with one light out.

The *Noble* apparently continued to follow the *Norwalk* until 3:00 a.m., April 28, at which time the two ships were off Knife Island, 17 miles from Duluth. Captain Millen of the powerful 580-foot, 2,000-horsepower *Daniel J. Morrell* reported that he was watching, from a distance at this hour, the lights of two small vessels at that point which were fighting the seas. As he watched, the lights of the sternward ship disappeared. Thinking that a rain or sleet squall had blotted them out, Captain Millen thought nothing more of the observation until two days later when he heard that the *Noble* was missing. At any rate, the *Norwalk* struggled into Duluth Harbor at 4:30 a.m.

The *Noble* never appeared. That afternoon, Patrolman Murray of the Duluth Police Department discovered her hatch covers on the beach of Minnesota Point about 30th Street South. The next day, her pilothouse was found well south on Minnesota Point by a tug captain, Fred Winters. Oars, spars, life belts, a life raft, clothing and other debris cluttered the beaches of Minnesota Point and the north shore at Duluth, some of it at Lester River, five miles from the harbor.

Years later, a retired fisherman at French River, 10 miles northeast of Duluth, disclosed that he had found a body in his nets a few days afterward. A recent immigrant, he had no desire for contacts with either dead men or government officials, and returned the body to the lake with no notice to lifesavers, sheriff or coroner. As far as the record is concerned, the whole crew of 20 men had gone down with their ship.

The *Noble* remains western Lake Superior's best held secret. Shipping people surmised at the time that she either lost hatch covers or suffered a cargo shift, although some Duluthians believe that she missed the canal, stranded and sank off Minnesota Point, the hull slipping into deep water. More probably, she met her end off Knife Island. Possibly she was overloaded. For that matter, Captain Eisenhardt, who had taken command of the *Noble* on April 23 at Conneaut just before she sailed, had confided to his sister in a letter posted at the Soo on April 25 that he feared for the stability of the ship due to her heavy load. Whatever the cause of the sinking, the *Benjamin Noble* has become the prize ghost ship of the western lake.

In 1987, the publisher of *Lake Superior Magazine,* James R. Marshall, offered a $1,000 reward for a chart recording and location of the wreck, believing that one of the many charter captains and other sports fishermen would pass over the wreck in pursuit of their quarry. Many interesting leads have developed, but, to date, none has proven to be the elusive *Benjamin Noble.*[31]

Dense fog returned on May 5, causing grief on both sides of the lake. At 3 a.m., the 586-foot, 7,210-ton steel steamer *George F. Baker* of the Pittsburgh fleet plowed into Sawtooth Reef off Eagle River, Keweenaw Point. Downbound from Ashland with 10,500 tons of iron ore, she was stuck hard. With seas calm, her 25-man crew was in no danger, and the wrecker *Favorite* soon had her free. The *Baker,* however, was a $50,000 salvage and dry-dock job.

On the north side of the lake, at Fisherman's Point, a mile east of Two Harbors, the 183-foot coastal steamer *America* ran ashore. The 470-foot steel Pittsburgher *General Orlando M. Poe* went to her assistance only to get hooked on the same rocky bottom. Salvage tugs quickly had them both off. Ironically, it took only $4,100 to fix the *America,* but the good Samaritan *Poe* had a $14,200 shipyard bill.[32] A docking accident at Superior on May 25 brought a $15,000 dry-dock trip to the 525-foot steel *William A. Rogers,* but this was the only other incident of a customarily turbulent month.

An unusual 50 mph gale on June 27 brought much excitement to the waterfront at Duluth-Superior. Approaching the Duluth pierhead in tremendous seas, the master of the 294-foot composite steamer *S.R. Kirby* decided to drop his 352-foot, 3,265-ton steel barge *George E. Hartnell* about two miles out and let her anchor rather than risk an accident in trying to bring her through the canal. The *Hartnell*'s anchors began to drag, and the substantial steel vessel was gradually pushed shoreward. Seeing her predicament, the captain of the 351-foot steel steamer *Harvey H. Brown* tried to get a line on the *Hartnell,* but the two ships smashed together, and the *Brown* had to beat a quick retreat to the harbor with moderate injuries. In the seeming safety of the harbor, the *Brown* brushed the 238-foot wooden lumber steamer *George H. Van Vleck,* adding more to her repair bill.

Meanwhile, word had gotten around downtown Duluth that the *Hartnell* was approaching disaster, and a large crowd gathered on the waterfront at South 1st Avenue East. These citizens surely had in mind the *Mataafa*

calamity nine years earlier. Shoreward came the helpless *Hartnell.* This time, however, the rampaging combers were kind, taking the barge well landward of the north pier and beaching her at the extreme northeast end of Minnesota Point. All aboard were safe. Tugs pulled the *Hartnell* to deep water the next day. Her dry-dock charges of $10,000 were actually less than those of her would-be rescuer, *Harvey H. Brown,* which had an $11,500 expense item from the collisions.

Over at the Superior Entry, there was additional excitement when the 430-foot steel steamer *Mataafa* slammed into a pier. The steel tugs *America* and *Harvey D. Goulder* managed to maneuver her back into the Superior Harbor for a run to the dry dock and $8,000 worth of repairs. This June blow had wrought its havoc, yet nothing too serious.[33]

Summer passed rather quietly. The 480-foot steel *John J. Boland* stranded at North Twin Island in the Apostles on July 1, needing $7,000 in fixing. On August 2 came a fire situation. Downbound from Duluth with a million feet of white pine lumber aboard and having the 142-foot, 513-ton steel barge *Foster W. Mitchell* in tow, the 238-foot, 1,020-ton wooden steamer *George H. Van Vleck,* formerly the *Portage,* was making respectable time until she was 35 miles northeast of Outer Island. Suddenly, a fire was discovered on board. She dropped her barge which was picked up by the steamer *Corvus.* Her crewmen had the fire under control, but not out, when along came the 532-foot steel *William C. Agnew* of the John Mitchell fleet. The *Agnew* towed the *Van Vleck* back to Duluth Harbor. There the *Van Vleck* crew continued to fight the fire, assisted by the tugs *Gillett* and *Tempest,* but the stubborn flames persisted until they had gutted the 39-year-old *Van Vleck.* She sank in the harbor, a burned-out wreck. Owned by the Cornplanter Oil Company of Toledo, with lost cargo, she was a liability in excess of $25,000. In fact, the *William C. Agnew* had placed a libel on her for $15,000. Despite her deplorable condition, she was raised and patched up, sailing in 1918, after which she disappeared from the register.[34]

The only other summer incident saw the 241-foot wooden steamer *Wyoming* grounding at Whitefish Point on August 24, her 211-foot wooden schooner-barge *Scotia* banging into her. Damage was inconsequential.

Autumn started out innocently enough. A blow on October 11 off Au Sable Point necessitated a $5,000 rebuilding job on the same 27-year-old *Wyoming.* A much wilder gale and snowstorm on November 18 pushed the large 540-foot steel *Edward A. Uhrig* aground in the supposed sanctuary of Bete Grise Bay, though her injuries proved trivial. The following day, 100 miles to the southeast, off Grand Marais, Michigan, this storm became a ruthless killer. On the afternoon of Wednesday, November 18, three vessels of the Hines Lumber Company fleet cleared Baraga, Michigan, with lumber cargoes for Tonawanda, New

York. They were the 197-foot, 691-ton wooden steamer *C.F. Curtis* under Captain J.P. Jennings and two schooner-barge tows, the 191-foot, 631-ton *Annie M. Peterson* and the 175-foot, 618-ton *Selden E. Marvin*. They were old

The iron steamer Onoko *foundered mysteriously in fair weather outbound from Duluth in mid-September 1915. Her upside-down hull was located in 1988.* C. PATRICK LABADIE COLLECTION.

wooden ships, the *Peterson* launched in 1874, the *Curtis* in 1881 and the *Marvin* in 1882. Also, the *Curtis* carried only 480 horsepower.

The following morning, this whooping northwesterly wind and blinding snow overtook them somewhere off Grand Marais. Lifesavers from that station could hear the bleating of a steamer's whistle to the north that afternoon and evening as Captain Jennings sought a harbor of refuge. The roaring tempest, however, drowned out the replies of the Grand Marais foghorn. Gradually, the sounds faded to the east.

The next morning, lifesavers came upon a mass of debris on the beach from four to nine miles east of Grand Marais, including mountains of lumber, pieces of shattered ships, upset yawl boats and bodies. A widespread search revealed that two of those aboard the *Curtis* and *Peterson* had reached shore alive, probably in the yawl boats. Seaman Edward Anderson of the *Curtis* had worked his way some miles westward along the beach only to lose his way in the snow and fall in deep water on the eastern edge of Grand Marais Harbor. First Mate William Kolpack of the *Peterson* had climbed a 20-foot sand bank south of the lake and had proceeded several hundred feet into the forest, almost reaching the lifesaving station's telephone line, before he succumbed. Altogether, 19 bodies were recovered between Grand Marais and Two-Hearted River, all from the *Curtis* and *Peterson*. Apparently, these two ships had been driven into shallow water and smashed to pieces east of Grand Marais, while the *Marvin* had sailed on, only to founder somewhere to the east.

It would seem that lifeboats of the *Curtis* and *Peterson* had been launched in good order as the women cooks of the *Curtis* had even put on their fur coats and jewelry. Probably, the ship's boats had been capsized in the wicked surf just off shore. Wreckage of the *Marvin* appeared between Two-Hearted River and Crisp Point, but no bodies. The Revenue Cutter *Mackinac* found a 40-foot piece of the *Marvin*'s hull with her name plate off Point Iroquois in southern Whitefish Bay on November 29. To this day, the exact cause of the triple sinking is unknown. All aboard, 28 persons, had perished. Indeed, this is the only instance on Lake Superior, perhaps in the history of the Great Lakes, where an entire lumber tow was wiped out by the storm gods.[35]

1915

The demand for shipping capacity made a tremendous comeback in 1915, it being the third best year on record. Despite the boom in navigation, safety showed fantastic improvement. Only 11 vessels had significant trouble and only three were lost. Adverse weather did not claim a single ship this season.

A fish tug, the 62-foot, 56-ton *Osprey*, was the first casualty, catching fire on April 13 off Stony Point, about 15 miles northeast of Duluth. Wisely, her master ran her ashore, and the three-man crew made their escape. The *Osprey* burned to the water's edge, a $10,000 liability to her owner, John Wanless of Duluth.[36]

The rest of the spring and early summer ran smoothly. Heavy fog on August 4 left the 525-foot, 6,617-ton steel *Harvey D. Goulder* aground on Keweenaw Point, but salvors had her off quickly, and hull refurbishment cost just $10,000. Another fog blanket on September 6 nearly caused a disaster off Whitefish Point when the 413-foot Pittsburgher *Clarence A. Black* brushed H.S. Wilkinson's 545-foot *John Dunn Jr.* The combined shipyard bills amounted to $12,000, yet this close call could have been so much worse.

About noon on September 14, a most unusual mishap occurred off Knife Island, 17 miles northeast of Duluth, a sinking definitely traceable to hull failure. The 287-foot, 2,164-ton *Onoko* was one of the oldest iron steamers on the lakes. At the time of her launching, she was one of the largest, indeed, a design prototype of the modern steel laker. During her 33 years of service, she was rumored to have earned her cost a dozen times over. Moreover, she had seldom been in trouble.

Under command of Captain William Dunn of Cleveland, the *Onoko* had cleared Duluth at 10:30 a.m., September 14, with a cargo of 100,000 bushels of wheat valued at $110,000 and consigned to the Capitol Elevator Company of Toledo. The lake was smooth. For more than an hour, the trip was routine. Suddenly, Chief Engineer Higgins was alarmed by a rush of water into the engine room. He started the bilge pumps, but before he could reach the ladderway, the water was waist deep. He climbed to the deck with some difficulty. There he was joined by the firemen who also had made their escape. Higgins alerted Captain Dunn who quickly appraised the situation and realized the vessel was doomed. It appeared that a plate may have dropped from the hull, allowing the entire stern to be flooded.

The captain ordered the ship abandoned. Taking time to pick up their belongings, the 16 crewmen and single passenger, together with the bulldog mascot, Rex, lowered the lifeboats and pulled to safety. The Standard Oil Company tanker *Renown* rushed up, her lifeboats slung over, halting just a thousand feet away. A few minutes later, an explosion was heard aboard the *Onoko,* and the old ship, already settling at the stern, threw her bow 80 feet in the air and actually turned end-over-end. The 287-foot ship stood on end in 200 feet of water, then settled on her deck, blowing her hatch covers off as she went down. The two lifeboats pulled up to the *Renown,* and the *Onoko* crew was taken aboard. Owned by Henry Steinbrenner of Cleveland, the *Onoko* was under charter to the G.A. Tomlinson Transportation Company of Duluth. Her wheat cargo was worth $110,000 and the ship another $50,000, making this incident a $160,000 liability.

The *Onoko* wreck was discovered by Jerry Eliason of Cloquet, Minnesota, and his diving partner for nine years, Kraig Smith of Rice Lake, Wisconsin. Their find of this historic vessel on April 10, 1988, was hardly blind luck. Rather, it was a combination of good but affordable equipment, excellent research, patience and perseverance. It is unfortunate that the *Onoko* rests upside-down in more than 200 feet of water, her cabins broken away or buried in the bottom and her hull broken just forward of the boiler room. Still, subsequent deep water dives and the excellent underwater photographs made by the discoverers will undoubtedly provide new insights into this historic vessel and the cause of her unexpected fair weather foundering.[37]

The fall of 1915 was relatively uneventful. On September 26 near Two Harbors, the veteran 46-year-old tug *F.W. Gillett* was intentionally run ashore to keep her from sinking after she began to leak. Rebuilding cost $2,000. The 512-foot *Peter Reiss* hit a dock at Superior on October 3, requiring $7,000 in new plates.

The most expensive mishap involved a fire. The 286-foot, 2,207-ton wooden steamer *Alfred P. Wright* had cleared Duluth for Cleveland on November 13 carrying 106,000 bushels of wheat. Recognizing rough weather approaching that night, Captain George E. Benham took her into the Portage Lake Ship Canal where he laid over a day at Lily Pond, waiting for the storm to pass. Thinking the worst was over, Captain Benham proceeded east

on November 15, but the *Wright* was tossed about so badly off the Huron Mountains that the master took her back to the Portage Canal. She was tied up to a pier there, off White City, when a fire broke out about midnight. The crew fought the flames unsuccessfully. Captain Benham ordered all lines except the head line cast off so that the ship could swing out into the water, away from the pier. For three exhausting hours, the *Wright* crew battled in vain. Chief Engineer Roy Hansen stuck to his donkey engine until flames drove him out of the engine room. By 3 a.m. the fire, which had originated near the coal bunkers, had spread to the whole ship. Captain Benham ordered the crew to jump to the pier where they watched as the 27-year-old *Wright* burned to the water's edge.

The following morning, Superintendent Banks of the Portage Lake Ship Canal came down with the Corps of Engineers' tug *Circle* and attempted to tow the hulk away from the vessel lanes, but she foundered near midchannel, causing a partially obstructed channel. She was an unqualified menace to navigation before she could be removed. The elderly *Wright* was a $40,000 item and the grain cargo was insured for $120,000, making this conflagration a substantial marine casualty.[38]

Three days later, two steel steamers, the 266-foot *Niagara* and 480-foot *B.F. Berry,* brushed in Duluth Harbor with minor injuries. The 446-foot *City of Bangor* required shipyard work of $7,000 after stranding at Isle Royale on December 1. Altogether, this had been an excellent year for shipping safety and not a single life had been lost due to shipwreck.

1916

This was a memorable year on Lake Superior. Spurred by the business boom caused by America's aid to the Allies in World War I, tonnage at the Soo soared to 91,888,219 tons, a record which would not be surpassed until 1929 and not substantially exceeded until 1941. Needless to say, the number of ships in trouble increased. Most of the casualties were minor, except for one in which a ship appeared to break in two, one collision and the capsizing of a tug and scow.

Difficulties began on April 27 with the 380-foot *John A. Donaldson* and the 480-foot *John J. Boland* coming together in Superior Harbor. Damage was minimal. The next day in fog off Whitefish Point, the 377-foot *William Nottingham* and the 525-foot *William A. Rogers* scraped, a potentially dangerous incident which ended with surprisingly little plate fixing. The 504-foot *Charles S. Hebard* and the 413-foot *Sir William Siemens* grazed each other with negligible results in Duluth Harbor on May 6.

The story was vastly different a couple days later on May 8. All of northeastern Minnesota and the whole western lake region was visited by a veritable northwest hurricane. Duluth clocked winds of 76 mph. Destruction on land was considerable. Indeed, Duluthians long remembered this day. The blasts fanned an out-of-control fire

The Alfred P. Wright *burned to the waterline after beaching in the Portage Ship Canal in November 1915.* NORTHEAST MINNESOTA HISTORICAL CENTER COLLECTION.

in the Alger-Smith Company lumber yards on Garfield Avenue, and 20 million feet of choice white pine lumber went up in smoke. Caught by the roaring gale off Eagle Harbor was the 294-foot, 2,388-ton composite steamer *S.R. Kirby* with the 352-foot, 3,265-ton steel barge *George E. Hartnell* in tow. They had cleared Ashland the night before in good weather. Captain David Girardin of Detroit was in command of the *Kirby,* one of the best known navigators on the Great Lakes and reputed for his ability to weather the worst of storms. He formerly had been master of the steamer *Harvey H. Brown* before she was sold for ocean service.

Very heavily loaded with iron ore, the *Kirby* and her barge were finding rough going. The *Kirby*'s 1,250-horsepower engine could make little headway in the gigantic waves. About 10 a.m., the 504-foot steel steamer *E.H. Utley* under Captain C.C. Balfour passed her, downbound. Captain Balfour thought the *Kirby* was in a bad way. He signalled her, asking if she needed assistance, but Captain Girardin did not reply. Still worried about the *Kirby,* Captain Balfour pushed his 1,650-horsepower vessel ahead slowly, keeping the *Kirby* in sight. About an hour later, when the *Utley* was two miles to the east, Captain Balfour was horrified to see the *Kirby* crest a giant wave, snap in two, and disappear. He immediately ordered the *Utley* put about and sped to the scene, but all the *Utley* crew could see was reddened water from the iron ore cargo and masses of debris. Realizing that the barge *Hartnell* was rapidly drifting toward the dreaded reefs off Eagle Harbor, Captain Balfour drove the *Utley* alongside the barge, put a line aboard and proceeded to tow the *Hartnell* to

the safety of Bete Grise Bay on the sheltered side of Keweenaw Point.

The captains of two other powerful steel freighters had also witnessed the catastrophe. Captain William Landon of the 532-foot, 1,800-horsepower *Harry A. Berwind* crisscrossed the sinking area and spotted two figures on a piece of wreckage. By hanging from the *Berwind*'s ladder, her first mate plucked the *Kirby*'s second mate, Joseph Mudray, from the precarious perch and got him aboard. The second castaway unfortunately slipped off and drowned moments before rescue. The giant 549-foot, 2,000-horsepower *Joseph Block* also challenged the seas for hours, and her crew lifted Fireman Otto S. Lindquist off another piece of debris. These were the only survivors.

Two days later, when the combers had subsided a bit, the Eagle Harbor Coast Guard lifeboat thoroughly swept the vicinity of the wreck. Hugging a piece of flotsam was ''Tige,'' Captain Girardin's bulldog mascot for the *Kirby.* Taking the dog into the lifeboat, the Coast Guardsmen brought him into Eagle Harbor. When landed, however, the terrified animal took off into the forest and had to be rounded up by the rescuers before he could be shipped back to the captain's widow in Detroit. Mate Mudray had observed the dog swimming by Captain Girardin's side until the exhausted captain went under. Coast Guardsmen patrolling the beaches on May 10 discovered the body of

The S.R. Kirby *(right), shown alongside the* Sachem, *foundered suddenly off Eagle Harbor in May 1916 during a frightful gale within sight of the* E.H. Utley. *Only three crewmen and a dog survived.* C. PATRICK LABADIE COLLECTION.

First Mate E.M. Douglass of Detroit at Agate Bay on Keweenaw Point, 20 miles from the point of the foundering. Most of the remaining crew apparently were trapped in the ship which went under in three minutes. Mate Mudray, who was on the bridge at the time, saw the *Kirby* buckle at Number 1 hatch, and it was all over.

The *Kirby* had been built in 1890 at Wyandotte, Michigan, a composite ship, with a hull of iron and wood. Only a handful of her type were constructed, but two of them were lost on Lake Superior. She was owned by the

The *G.J. Grammer (left)* suffered topside weather damage as seas boarded the vessel off Manitou Island in November 1916. UNIVERSITY OF DETROIT MARINE COLLECTION.

Northwestern Transportation Company of Detroit and valued at $100,000. Twenty men went down with her.

The *Kirby* disaster caused a good deal of comment in marine circles. Technical sources attributed her hull failure to poor loading and overloading. In those days there were no loading marks on American Great Lakes ships, such as the Plimsol marks on British ships. A ship could be loaded to whatever depth her master considered safe. It would appear, however, that some owners and masters took chances. The *Kirby*, allegedly, was loaded to a 19-foot depth, whereas 14 would have been a safe figure. When leaving Ashland, she supposedly had only two feet of freeboard, which would have put her awash in virtually anything except a dead calm. She was in no shape to face the hurricane she encountered. Editorial comment forecast ultimate federal loading regulations, and, interestingly enough, by October 1916, a lakes committee was working on a load marking formula.[39]

The fertile collision grounds of Whitefish Bay added to their roster of hulks in the dense fog of early morning on June 27. Off Parisienne Island, the upbound 478-foot, 6,025-ton steel *James J. Hill* of the Pittsburgh Steamship Company plowed into the 248-foot, 1,634-ton wooden steamer *Panther* of the Massey Steamship Company, Duluth. The results were what might have been expected. The big steel freighter plunged deeply into the wooden vessel amidships. Keeping his wits, however, the *Hill*'s captain held his bow in the stricken *Panther* until her crew clambered aboard the steel ship. Then, as the *Hill* backed away, the *Panther* quickly listed, heeled over and sank. No value figure was given, though a wooden ship of that size and age must have been worth about $30,000.[40]

Some narrow escapes occurred during July fogs. In the whiteout off Ontonagon on July 7, the 504-foot *Herbert K. Oakes* slapped the 416-foot *Martin Mullen*. The *Mullen* later received $12,000 in shipyard attention. On July 21, the 532-foot *R.L. Agassiz* struck a bridge at Duluth, inheriting a $7,000 bill. The 356-foot *Lupus* suffered little in banging a dock in Superior. The accident-prone *William Nottingham* had a truly close one off Whitefish Point on July 27 when she was dusted by the giant 604-foot steel Canadian carrier *W. Grant Morden*, probably the largest ship on the lakes at that time. The *Nottingham* was lucky to sail away for $11,000 in dry-dock work.

The rest of the season was somewhat tame. A fire at Port Arthur on August 30 seared the steamer *St. Ignace* with undisclosed costs. On the same day in Duluth Harbor, the 478-foot steamer *John W. Gates* banged the 504-foot *D.M. Philbin,* resulting in negligible damage.

Over at Ashland Harbor on October 14, a fatal incident marred the autumn record. The 66-foot, 56-ton wooden tug *Alfred W.* of Duluth was capsized by a scow with which she was working. One crewman was drowned, though the material loss was only $2,500.[41] The 430-foot *Frederick B. Wells* had suffered a $6,000 repair bill earlier in the month by striking a pier at Superior. The final item of the year was a minor rebuilding charge after heavy seas boarded the 418-foot *G.J. Grammer* off Manitou Island on November 24.

Aside from the sinking of the *Kirby* and the *Panther,* this had been a most favorable season for navigational safety.

1917

This was another boom year as America's war effort got under way. Close to 90 million tons of cargo were logged at the Soo. Formidable ice conditions at the onset of the season probably prevented the 1916 record from being surpassed. The number of vessels reporting difficulties rose considerably, but the vast majority of incidents continued to be trivial. Only two collisions were dangerous. Interestingly enough, all but two incidents involved new steel ships.

Ice gave mariners a bad time well through May. Indeed, steel ships were icebound off Marquette in the second week of May. Fogs reinforced the ice devils. There were problems. The 504-foot, 6,349-ton *William T. Roberts* went hard aground May 1 at Isle Royale, ending up with a $22,000 salvage and dry-dock fee. The next day, the 525-foot *Edward N. Saunders Jr.* reported ice-crushed plates off Michigan Island, requiring $3,000 in renovation. Then the 532-foot *N.F. Leopold* suffered $10,000 in ice injuries off Whitefish Point on May 3. An unequal collision came on May 7 off Whitefish Point with the big

580-foot *Daniel J. Morrell* bouncing off the little 260-foot *Vulcan.* Logically, the *Vulcan* endured the worse of minor damage.

Three days later, the soup-thick mists northeast of Whitefish Point caused two ships to stray far east of the vessel lanes and end up stranded on Corbeil Point. The victims were the 540-foot *C.H. McCullough* and the 281-foot *John Owen.* Salvage was simple, but the *Owen* endured $7,000 in bottom damage. Ice scored again in midmonth with the 300-foot *Northern Wave* getting $4,500 worth of plates ruined off Superior on May 13.

The William E. Corey, *which stranded in the big 1905 storm, raked Gros Cap Reef while maneuvering in heavy Whitefish Bay ice in May 1917.* McKenzie photo, Canal Park Marine Museum collection.

The 549-foot *Harry Coulby* needed slightly more in rehabilitation of her steel sides after bucking the ice pack in Whitefish Bay on May 16. That same day, proceeding under limited visibility around the north end of Isle Royale, the 380-foot *Monroe C. Smith* went astride Passage Island. Her salvage and dry-dock costs reached $8,000. Worst sufferer among the early season casualties was the 558-foot *William E. Corey* of the Pittsburgh fleet which smashed solidly into the Gros Cap Reef at the southeast end of Whitefish Bay. She cost her owners $25,000 for this escapade. Last of the nuisance incidents in May was a collision on May 30 in Duluth Harbor between the 554-foot *Wilpen* and the 479-foot *Stadacona,* the larger ship the worse for wear to the tune of $3,300.

June evidenced fewer troubles. The 413-foot *Sir William Siemens* slapped a pier at Duluth on June 1 with minimal injury. On June 13 in Duluth Harbor, the 428-foot *A.F. Harvey* wracked the 352-foot barge *Magna,* though the *Magna* escaped relatively unscathed.

Two collisions marked July operations. In typically dense fog off Whitefish Point on July 9, the 303-foot Canadian passenger steamer *Manitoba* slashed into the 346-foot, 3,720-ton American freighter *William S. Mack.* Fortunately, the *Mack* took water only gradually, and her master was able to run her ashore where she settled in 20 feet of water. As she had a 28-foot depth, her cabins were

above water and her crew was safe. Salvors patched her and pumped her out; she went to dry dock for $20,000 in repair charges. Yet, she could just as well have joined a number of other ships on the bottom in the same vicinity.[42] Two weeks afterward in Duluth Harbor, the 590-foot *Colonel James M. Schoonmaker* raked whaleback barge *137* and put herself in dry dock for $15,000 in new plates.

The only August mishap was an open lake sideswipe in the fog of August 24 as the 416-foot *Cetus* grazed the 525-foot *J.A. Campbell,* each sustaining wounded steel to the amount of $5,000. Once more, it could have been much worse.

The year's only fatalities came on September 17 when two lives were lost a few miles off the Duluth Ship Canal as the little packet *Viking* was struck by the scow *Ajax* towed by the 70-foot wooden tug *Charley Ferris.* This is a hard one to explain. At 2 a.m. on an unusually warm late summer morning, the 38-foot, gasoline-driven fish packet *Viking* was off Lester Park, five miles from the Duluth Ship Canal, inbound with a load of fish taken on at Knife River. Outbound in the same vicinity, with the scow *Ajax* in tow, was the tug *Charley Ferris* en route to Cross River, 80 miles up the north shore, for a load of gravel. Captain William Cook of the *Viking* apparently was coasting a little south of the north shore vessel lane and, as he passed the *Ferris,* decided to cut sharply across the tug's wake for a position closer to shore. With the Duluth-Superior Harbor lights in his face, it is possible that Captain Cook failed to see the *Ajax* at the end of the towline.

Coastal vessel L. Goldish *rescued the lone survivor from blazing Herring King in the Apostle Islands in November 1917.* Goldish family collection.

At any rate, he suddenly cut in back of the *Ferris* and was rammed on the port side by the oncoming scow. Cook was thrown overboard and drowned. The *Viking* flooded at once, drowning Engineer Samuel Fagel in the engine room. The *Ferris* put about immediately and towed the stricken *Viking* into Duluth Harbor. Two men had died and several thousand dollars damage was incurred in one of the lake's strangest collisions.[43]

The rest of the season was routine. The 580-foot *James A. Farrell* needed $5,000 in plate straightening after hitting a dock at Duluth on October 17. The 354-foot *P.P. Miller* stranded at Madeline Island on November 8, requiring a $15,000 salvage and repair effort. Five days afterward came a plate-scraper in Duluth Harbor between the brand new 580-foot *Homer D. Williams* and the 430-foot *Otto M. Reiss,* formerly the *Frederick B. Wells.* The year's final item came on November 26 when the 425-foot *Rufus P. Ranney* had a little plate work after slamming a dock at Port Arthur.

The Boutin Fish Company of Bayfield lost one of its small fleet, the *Herring King,* on November 29 when a gas line began leaking and resulted in an explosion and fire while operating off Sand Island. Had it not been for the coastal packet *L. Goldish* of Duluth, both persons aboard the fish tug would have been lost. The *Goldish* crew successfully rescued one of them by bravely maneuvering to within 30 feet of the blazing hull. The flaming *Herring King* drifted out toward the open lake, but was corralled by a local fisherman and towed back to Sand Island in the hope that some salvage, particularly of the engine, might be possible. The *Herring King* had apparently been built locally, probably at Bayfield or La Pointe, as the *Fish Hawk* and later lengthened, repowered and renamed.[44]

Thus ended an amazing season for safety, a prodigious tonnage hauled by the big ships and the only fatalities incurred by the smaller craft.

1918

Still another busy season greeted mariners, total tonnage coming to within five percent of 1917's excellent showing. Mishaps were slightly less, a pattern resembling the previous season. However, sailor's luck lasted only until six weeks before the Armistice. During the last 10 weeks of sailing, four vessels made their last trip, two with catastrophic loss of life and one with enormous property loss.

As in 1917, ice bedeviled the lake ships well into May. It would appear that some winter sailing was attempted in January since the steamer *Argus,* the former 408-foot steel *Hendrik Holden,* reported plates smashed by ice to the extent of $5,000 off Crisp Point on January 28.

The ice barriers remained far into May, being particularly destructive in the eastern lake. During the first 10 days in May, five steel carriers reported injury by the ice demons between Crisp and Whitefish points: the 444-foot *E.L. Pierce,* the 266-foot *Granville A. Richardson,* the 532-foot *J.J. Sullivan,* the 504-foot *A.A. Augustus* and the 444-foot *F.R. Hazard.* The *Pierce,* with $11,000 in dry-dock work and the *Hazard* with $10,000 were the top losers.

A plate-bender collision on May 19 at Whitefish Point brought minor renovation work to the 504-foot *D.M. Philbin,* hit by the 370-foot *Belgium.* The new 525-foot *Louis W. Hill* also needed a little straightening after banging a dock at Superior on May 26. Two Tomlinson ships brushed in the fog off Whitefish Point on May 31, the 532-foot *Chester A. Congdon* glancing off the 504-foot *George G. Barnum,* again with minimal damage.

Bulk freighter Chester A. Congdon, *formerly the* Salt Lake City, *became Lake Superior's most costly casualty when she stranded and broke apart near Isle Royale in November 1918.* HAROLD ANDRESEN COLLECTION, CANAL PARK MARINE MUSEUM.

Through the summer, only nuisance scrapes with docks or other ships bothered masters. On June 16 in Duluth Harbor, the 590-foot *William P. Snyder Jr.* was whacked by the 558-foot *George W. Perkins,* spending $5,000 at the shipyard. Contacts with docks cost little to the 581-foot *Shenango,* striking at Marquette, or the 414-foot *Angeline,* hitting at Superior. The 549-foot *Henry C. Frick* bumped the 405-foot *Empire City* in Duluth Harbor on August 5 with little damage. In the fog at Whitefish Point two days later, the 480-foot *John J. Boland* slipped into the shoals, emerging with little bottom trouble.

When autumn appeared, however, it was a different story. Rough weather on October 1 caught the 277-foot, 2,197-ton wooden steamer *Gale Staples* with a coal cargo off Au Sable Point, eight miles west of Grand Marais. Now in Canadian ownership, she formerly had been the American steamer *Caledonia.* Her 1,050-horsepower engine was insufficient to keep her off the reef. She stranded hard. The U.S. Coast Guard lifeboat quickly reached her, but since her captain had hopes of saving her, the Coast Guard at first removed only 11 of the crew and returned to Grand Marais to call for tugs. The gale got worse the following day, and the 30-year-old ship showed signs of breaking. Thereupon, the Coast Guard removed the other six crewmen. Miserable weather over the next week completed demolition of the *Staples.* With cargo, she became a $75,000 liability. She had served her new Canadian owners only a year.[45]

A land-based holocaust had marine repercussions on the night of October 12. Whipped by a 60 mph gale during the afternoon, a number of small brush and bog fires became a flaming inferno in Duluth's hinterlands, destroying numerous small towns, claiming hundreds of lives and leveling parts of the city itself. Embers from the flaming forest set many spot fires along the Duluth waterfront during that terrible night, consuming three wooden tugs, a dredge and six scows. The veteran tugs *Mentor,* built in 1868 at 29 tons, *Ella G. Stone* at 42 tons, formerly the *E.L. Mason* built in 1881, and *John H. Jeffery Jr.,* built in 1892 at 12 tons, were blackened wreckage as was the dredge *Duluth,* and scows *N. 1, N. 2, N. 3, N. 4, No. 1* and *No. 40.* The *Duluth* was of 142 tons and built in 1872 while *N. 1* was built in 1884 at 90 tons, the *N. 2* built in 1883 at 84 tons, the *N. 3* built in 1892 at 175 tons, the *N. 4* built in 1894 at 192 tons, the *No. 1* newly built in 1913 at 42 tons and the *No. 40* built in 1891 at 185 tons. Damage to the shipping community must have exceeded $20,000, though this was miniscule compared to the estimated $27 million loss on land. More than 400 dead were counted in the blackened towns, farms, cabins and along the roads as many of the fatalities were motorists trapped by the walls of flame.[46]

Underwriter's photo of the Chester A. Congdon *on Canoe Rocks Reef in November 1918 before completely breaking in two and settling to the bottom on either side of the reef.* CANAL PARK MARINE MUSEUM COLLECTION.

The accident tempo picked up. The 580-foot *Percival Roberts Jr.* needed a bit of patching after ramming a dock at Duluth on October 23. A gale on October 30 brought multiple troubles to the 260-foot, 1,759-ton steel steamer *Vulcan.* En route to Hancock with 3,200 tons of anthracite coal, she was first pushed aground at Point Abbaye. While stranded, she next lost her pilothouse to a small fire. The tug *Alabama* and lighter *Reliance* quickly went to work on her and nursed her into dock at Houghton where the coal cargo was unloaded. But, no

sooner was her coal removed than water pouring through her punctured bottom blew her tank tops and she settled to the bottom at dock in 36 feet of water. Salvage required construction of a coffer dam. Her misadventures cost her owners or underwriters upwards of $40,000.[47]

A marine insurance underwriter's nightmare was unfolding on the north side of the lake. Picking her way outbound from the Canadian Lakehead in rough weather and poor visibility on November 6 was the Tomlinson fleet's 532-foot, 6,530-ton *Chester A. Congdon* with a heavy grain cargo. She stranded tight on the Canoe Rocks off the northeastern tip of Isle Royale. As the weather moderated, the chief engineer was able to take a lifeboat into the Canadian Lakehead for help. Rescuers responded immediately and took off the remaining crew. Then the weather worsened. Before salvors could aid her, this fine ship, only 11 years old, broke up and became a complete ruin. With her expensive grain cargo, she became a financial casualty in excess of $1,000,000, the first million dollar shipping loss in Lake Superior history. She had been built in Chicago as the *Salt Lake City* and renamed in 1913.[48]

A collision in Superior Harbor on November 20 between the steamers *The Harvester* and *Charles W. Kotcher* sent the 420-foot *Kotcher* to dry dock for a $10,000 reconditioning job. A grounding off Gull Rock Light on November 27 brought light bottom injuries to the 416-foot *Taurus.*

Meanwhile, somewhere out of the Canadian Lakehead was emerging one of the most grotesque mysteries of the lake. Oddly enough, the victims were members of the French Navy. Rushed to completion and sailing from the Canadian Lakehead on November 24 for harbor clearing in post-Armistice France were the 143-foot steel minesweepers *Inkerman, Cerisoles* and *Sebastopol* under French naval Captain Leclerc. Leclerc in the *Sebastopol* took the lead, having on board a Lake Superior pilot. That night a rugged storm swept the eastern area of the lake, the ships becoming somewhat separated. The *Sebastopol* reached the Soo on November 26. The other two never arrived. Despite adverse weather, Captain Leclerc chartered the new 64-foot tug *Frank Weston* under the command of Captain Sam Shields, a veteran Soo tugman. They combed the Canadian east and north shores for days while the American Coast Guard swept the south shore. Two other tugs, *Bennett* and *Sarnia,* were also sent out in search. The *Bennett* searched along the Canadian shore from Fort William to Otter Head while the *Sarnia* covered the area around Isle Royale. Nothing was found. Two brand new minesweepers had simply vanished on the lake taking with them 76 officers and men of the French Navy and their two Canadian pilots.

Their resting place has never been located, though sailors' talk says they may have struck the dreaded Superior Shoal, torn out their bottoms and immediately submerged in hundreds of feet of water, trapping their entire personnel within them. Still other evidence indicates the two were overcome in high seas while rounding Keweenaw Point, perhaps the victim of their own armament which was mounted forward, causing them to be both top and bow heavy. Perhaps at some future date, deep-diving submersibles, manned or unmanned, might be able to verify the latter hypothesis. Almost no wreckage was ever identified as having come from the two vessels although an

$4,000 worth of planking and caulking after sinking from a leak on May 19 while docked for a cargo at Knife River.

The first major disaster of the year struck on May 26. The 306-foot, 2,607-ton steamer *Ferdinand Schlesinger,* one of the largest wooden vessels on the lake, was en route to Port Arthur under Captain Ole Dyrhess with 2,000 tons of coal. When 25 miles off Passage Island, she developed a substantial leak. Her pumps were quickly

The Assiniboia *rescued the entire crew of the foundering* Ferdinand Schlesinger *off Passage Island in May 1919.*
C. PATRICK LABADIE COLLECTION.

unpainted lifeboat and some new gray-painted lumber did come ashore about December 6 near Grand Marais, Michigan.[49]

1919

With the pressures of World War I behind, the shipping people of Lake Superior enjoyed a more relaxed season. Tonnage was off 20 percent and the number of accidents was halved. Still, the roster of ships totally destroyed was the worst in eight years.

The lake was free of ice early in April, but the cargo demand was light. This undoubtedly accounts for the absence of ''plate-benders'' usually seen in the ice packs. The 410-foot steel steamer *F.B. Squire* did require $25,000 in new bottom plates after striking at Passage Island on April 22, the only early season incident. The 298-foot wooden lumber hooker *C.W. Jacob* needed

overwhelmed, and she began to settle. Then, at precisely the right time, along came the Canadian passenger steamer *Assiniboia* to pick up her crew. All were safe. Nearly four years later, marine insurance companies paid $32,700 in coverage of the *Schlesinger,* though a 28-year-old wooden vessel of that size possibly was worth a good deal more.[50]

In the typically thick weather of June 13, another wooden ship came to grief on the northern lake. The 227-foot, 1,680-ton steamer *Gogebic* was beached near Flatland Island en route to load pulp logs at Cloud Bay well north of Grand Portage. Salvors retrieved her at a cost of $25,000, which very likely was more than half the value of a 32-year-old ship of that type. She was later rebuilt as the lighter *Green River* and eventually abandoned in Thunder Bay, where sport divers led by Scott McWilliam discovered her remains in the fall of 1979 off the Welcome Islands.

Still another veteran wooden steamer ended her days at Grand Marais, Minnesota, on July 6. The 30-year-old

97-foot, 168-ton *Liberty* caught fire in the harbor and was reduced to smoldering ruins. She was a $10,000 item.[51]

One of the strangest incidents in the history of the Duluth Ship Canal occurred at 4:40 a.m. on August 7. The 74-foot, 71-ton steel tug *James R. Sinclair* of the Great Lakes Towing Company was pulling the 352-foot, 3,259-ton steel barge *Alfred Krupp* outbound through the canal when suddenly the *Sinclair* careened and capsized, sinking about 300 feet from the western end. Captain Edmund O. La Joie, Engineer Emil Wagner and Fireman John Stephanson jumped clear and survived, being picked up by neighboring craft, but Fireman August Johnson drowned. Four days later, the *Sinclair* was raised by two giant dredges under the supervision of Captain Alec Cunning of the wrecker *Favorite* and found to be relatively undamaged. The tug's peculiar behavior was hard to explain. Steamboat inspectors first suspended Captain La Joie, but subsequently reinstated him after a hearing. Perhaps the *Sinclair* caught unexpected currents which caused her to sheer and put the wrong angle on the towline to the heavier barge, thus upsetting and tripping the lighter vessel. At any rate, one man had died right in the ship canal.[52]

Shipping problems in the early autumn were relatively minor. The steamer *Lake Stobi* needed some fixing after whacking a dock at Duluth on October 2. The 430-foot steamer *Otto M. Reiss* raked the bottom east of Devils Island on October 17 to the tune of $11,500. Wild seas ravaged the 504-foot steel *Hoover & Mason* on November 3 when east of Manitou Island, requiring $8,000 in shipyard efforts.

Then the roof figuratively fell in. The lake reaped four victims within three weeks and injured another. Altogether, 38 sailors lost their lives, and the toll would have been much higher except for two heroic rescues by the Coast Guard. Seldom has November weather on Lake Superior been so vile, one gale and snowstorm after another lambasting the area. By November 8, Duluth had already received half as much snow as during the entire winter of 1918-19.

The first of the ill-fated four to meet destiny apparently was the 281-foot, 2,127-ton *John Owen,* a 30-year-old composite ship commanded by Captain George E. Benham and belonging to the W.C. Richardson Company of Cleveland. Arriving in Duluth on November 7, the *Owen* had loaded grain over the weekend, then lay over a day awaiting weather, departing eastward at 10:25 a.m., Tuesday, November 11, presumably behind a giant storm that had belabored North Dakota and northern Minnesota for two days. The next day, the *Owen* was observed by the crew of the 420-foot steel steamer *Edwin N. Ohl* off Keweenaw Point. The 1,650-horsepower *Ohl* was holding her own, but the *Owen* was obviously having a hard time, although there were no distress signals. Whatever happened thereafter is conjecture.

Terrific seas bedeviled the whole of eastern Lake Superior. The 554-foot, 2,000-horsepower Shenango freighter *Wilpen* reported she had encountered wreckage east of Manitou Island on November 14, though the Eagle Harbor Coast Guard lifeboat, putting out the following day, could find no sign of the *Owen* in that vicinity. Meanwhile, the steamer *Westmount* reported that she had sighted debris south of Caribou Island, and the tugs *Iowa* and *Alabama* were ordered out of the Soo to check that area. Approximately 20 miles southeast of Caribou Island, they discovered extensive flotsam, including a white pilothouse with the *John Owen's* nameboard on it. The *Owen* had made her last trip, taking veteran Captain Benham and his 21-man crew to eternity. As far as is known, the bodies of only four were ever found, one the next spring at Crisp Point on the south shore and three more on Parisienne Island later in the summer. She was a financial liability of $90,000.[53]

The same blasts which sank the *Owen* gathered in another sacrifice at Grand Marais, Michigan, on the morning of November 14. Under Captain Hugh O'Hagan, the 178-foot, 889-ton wooden lumber hooker *H.E. Runnels* had struggled westward from Whitefish Point on November 13 with a cargo of coal for Lake Linden, Michigan. The storm became too tough. Accordingly, Captain O'Hagan took the ship into the harbor of Grand Marais for shelter. Early the following morning, the wind seemingly abating, the *Runnels* pulled out of Grand Marais for Portage. However, when hardly an hour out off Point Au Sable, she encountered a veritable hurricane with winds more than 60 mph and blinding snow. Wisely, Captain O'Hagan retraced his course for Grand Marais, approaching the harbor at 5:30 a.m. Entering the piers in darkness was too risky with the enormous sea and the snow. Therefore, the Coast Guard lookout was not surprised when the ship was seen to back into the seas to wait for daylight and another try at the entrance. There were no distress signals or indications of trouble. Yet, as the little vessel tried to hold against the waves, her steering gear became disabled. Within minutes, she was hurled ashore west of the west pier, broadside to the seas which pounded her unmercifully.

When the *Runnels* was first reported at 5:30 a.m., the ranking Coast Guardsman, Surfman A.E. Kristofferson, the Grand Marais Station keeper being seriously ill, went aboard Coast Guard cutter *438* which was lying in Grand Marais Harbor for shelter. Kristofferson intended to ask Captain G.R. O'Conner of the former subchaser for men to assist in an impending rescue, as the surfman realized the dangerous predicament the *Runnels* was in. To his happy surprise, the Grand Marais man discovered that on board the *438* as a guest was Keeper John Anderson of the Chicago Coast Guard Station, formerly a veteran station captain on this Michigan coast of Lake Superior. Anderson volunteered to take charge. As he and Kristofferson returned to the Grand Marais station, they observed the *Runnels* already aground and being badly beaten.

The rescuers had to move fast. Rushing the Lyle gun to the beach, the Coast Guardsmen quickly put a line across

Steam barge H.E. Runnels *was the object of a dramatic Coast Guard rescue effort off Grand Marais, Michigan, during a November 1919 storm.* AUTHOR'S COLLECTION.

the bow of the *Runnels* which her crew picked up and made fast to the wheelstand in the pilothouse. Nevertheless, with the temperature at 18 above zero, the line iced up and snarled, rendering operation of a breeches-buoy impossible. Thereupon Keeper Anderson ordered the Beebe-McLellan surfboat hauled to the beach and placed under the line. With painters securing the surfboat to the line on both bow and stern, he and his crew worked the surfboat out to the disabled steamer four times, taking off four men, then six, then five and, on the last trip, the chief engineer and the captain. So exhausting was the task that five of the regular Coast Guard crew collapsed and had to be replaced by four Grand Marais civilians and an oiler from the *438*. Keeper Anderson was washed off the surfboat three times, but each time managed to swim back. In a few hours, all 17 of the *Runnels* crew were safe, just in time, it turned out, as the steamer was completely beaten to pieces that afternoon. So hazardous was this rescue, with the enormous waves, driving snow and icy condition of the steamer, that Keeper John Anderson, seven Coast Guardsmen from the Grand Marais station, Oiler Joseph McShea of the cutter *438*, Joseph Graham, James McDonald and Ora Endress were awarded the Treasury Department Lifesaving Gold Medal of Honor the following year.[54] Owned by Myron Blodgett, the *Runnels* was a liability of $60,000.

The very next week, on November 22, another tragedy occurred on that same gale-wracked coast west of Whitefish Point. Outbound from Munising with lumber and having the 194-foot schooner-barge *Miztec* in tow, the 186-foot, 676-ton wooden lumber hooker *Myron* received

a terrific mauling from gigantic waves whipped up by a snow-laden northwesterly gale as she plodded eastward along the Michigan south shore as fast as her 700-horse-power engine could drive her. She began to leak badly. As she struggled along, barely making headway, Captain Kenneth McRae of the 420-foot steel ore carrier *Adriatic* noted her plight and brought his 1,500-horsepower vessel to the windward of the faltering hooker, literally running interference against the smashing waves. Off Vermilion Point, Captain Neal of the *Myron* dropped his tow, which proceeded to anchor safely, and, with the steel ship still as escort, strove to inch his way around Whitefish Point 10 miles distant. The Coast Guard lookout at Vermilion Point had observed the strange procession and alerted his station keeper who surmised that the smaller ship might not reach the sanctuary of Whitefish Bay. Accordingly, the keeper ordered the lifeboat launched despite the wild, roaring surf. With extreme difficulty, the Coast Guardsmen launched and began to pursue the settling *Myron*.

Lake Superior won. When the *Myron* was only a mile and a half northwest of Whitefish Point, water extinguished her fires, she slowed to a halt and within four minutes dove to the bottom. Most of her crew scrambled into two lifeboats which were immediately surrounded by a sea of tossing lumber. Captain McRae drove the *Adriatic* into the mass of debris twice in an effort to approach the beleaguered men in the boats, but the steel ship struck bottom in the relatively shallow water and, for the safety of his own ship and crew, the *Adriatic*'s master had to pull away, leaving the castaways.

Then Captain Lawrence J. Francis of the 520-foot, 2,000-horsepower steel *H.P. McIntosh* came along. He, too, drove his powerful vessel into the maelstrom of wreckage and actually got close enough for his crew to throw lines to the survivors, but the benumbed *Myron* crewmen had been too weakened by subfreezing temperatures to catch the lines. In danger of stranding any moment in the mountainous waves and consequent danger of complete destruction, Captain Francis also had to pull away, leaving the *Myron* crew to their fate.

Meanwhile, the Vermilion Point lifeboat approached the sinking site. The murderous mass of tossing flotsam precluded her entrance. The keeper immediately realized that no small wooden boat could last long in such debris. However, as the seething mass of wreckage was fast moving around Whitefish Point, the lifeboat master hoped that some survivors just might be swept down into Whitefish Bay. Rounding the point, he took the lifeboat 20 miles down into the bay, all the way to Parisienne Island. In the pitch black darkness and heavy seas, he found nothing. Finally, the exhausted Coast Guard crew had to pull into the Whitefish Point Light Station for shelter.

All 16 crewmen who abandoned the *Myron* died by drowning or freezing. Their rigid bodies, still buoyed by their life jackets, were recovered days later well down the

Michigan coast of Whitefish Bay near Salt Point. More fortunate was Captain Walter F. Neal who went down in the pilothouse of his ship. As the *Myron* sank, the pilothouse blew off. Captain Neal then climbed to the roof which served as his raft for the next 20 terrible hours while he was being blown more than 20 miles into Whitefish Bay near Parisienne Island. The next day, Captain W.C. Jordan of the upbound steamer *W.C. Franz* was scanning the lake with binoculars when he spotted a body on some wreckage. The body moved. Swinging four miles off course, he brought his ship to a halt, launched a lifeboat, as the lake was now more quiet, and the *Franz* crewmen rescued Captain Neal from the pilothouse roof. Neal was half dead from exposure, yet he recovered.

In initial press interviews, Captain Neal was quite vehement in his denunciation of the steel steamers which failed in the rescue attempts, especially the *McIntosh*. His remarks prompted an investigation of many months by U.S. marine inspectors Gooding and Hanson of Marquette who finally handed down a verdict revoking the licenses of Captain Francis and Captain McRae for ''failure to render aid and assistance.'' The verdict, however, was considered a gross injustice to the two captains by the marine community. They had tried — tried hard — even risking their own ships and crews in the treacherous shallows off Whitefish Point. Again, their decisions were hard, but a captain's loyalty must first be to his own ship and crew.

Available records do not disclose the outcome of the revocation verdict, but, in view of preceding and subsequent cases, it is probable that higher authority reversed the decision of land-based inspectors. Owned by Omer Blodgett of Duluth, the 34-year-old *Myron* was worth $45,000. She had been named for Captain Myron Blodgett, owner of the ill-fated *Runnels*.[55]

Still, the lake was not through. The 409-foot steamer *Argus* had a moderate repair bill after stranding at Marquette on November 24. On November 26 three miles east of Eagle River, high winds and snow scored again. The 286-foot, 2,320-ton steamer *Tioga* was pitched hard on a reef. The Eagle Harbor Coast Guard safely removed the crew, but the 34-year-old *Tioga* had made her last voyage, broken on the rocks with her hold full of water. Belonging to the Massey Steamship Company of Superior, Wisconsin, she was valued at $110,000; her 110,000-bushel grain cargo was listed at $250,000. This was the second ship of the Massey Company to be lost this season, the wooden *Ferdinand Schlesinger* having succumbed in late May. The *Tioga*'s wooden pilothouse did survive and has ever since been in private hands in Eagle River, Michigan, having had multiple uses over the years including a summer cabin, playhouse and craft shop.[56]

Thus ended the 1919 shipping season. To be sure, only 14 vessels had indicated significant troubles, but six were gone forever and 39 sailors had made their last trip.

Dozens of coastal steamers and naval fleet auxiliaries were turned out at local shipyards during World War I. CANAL PARK MARINE MUSEUM COLLECTION.

1 *Duluth News-Tribune,* June 24-27, 1910; Homer Wells, *History of Accidents, Casualties, and Wrecks on Lake Superior,* (Duluth, Minn., U.S. Army Corps of Engineers, 1938), p. 46.

2 *Annual Report, U.S. Life-Saving Service, 1911,* p. 128; Wells, *op. cit.,* p. 46.

3 Dominion of Canada, Department of Transport, *Casualties to Vessels Resulting in Total Loss on the Great Lakes, 1870-1957,* p. 45.

4 *Duluth News-Tribune,* Oct. 20-23, 31, Nov. 20, Dec. 7, 9, 1910; *Marquette Mining Journal,* Oct. 21, 24-25, 28-29, Nov. 1-3, 5, 12, 22, 24, 29, Dec. 5, 9, 15, 22-24, 29, 1910; July 6, 11, 13, 25, Aug. 2, 28-29, Sept. 2, 1911; *Annual Report, U.S. Life-Saving Service, 1911,* pp. 71, 130; Wells, *op. cit.,* p. 46.

5 *Duluth News-Tribune,* Oct. 25, 1910; *Marquette Mining Journal,* Oct. 25, Nov. 14, 1910.

6 *Duluth News-Tribune,* Nov. 8, 1910; *Marquette Mining Journal,* Nov. 8, 14, 1910.

7 *Duluth News-Tribune,* Dec. 12, 22, 1910. Thom Holden, "Home for Christmas: *Dunelm* Stranding" in *Nordic Diver,* Vol. 1, No. 4, Winter 1975, pp. 3, 6-7; Larry Murphy and Thom Holden, "Shipwrecks of Isle Royale: The Historical Record" in *Submerged Cultural Resources Study: Isle Royale National Park,* Daniel J. Lenihan, ed., (Santa Fe, New Mexico, Submerged Cultural Resources Unit, National Park Service, 1987), pp. 210-211; Larry Murphy, Daniel Lenihan and C. Patrick Labadie, "Shipwrecks of Isle Royale: The Archeological Record" in Lenihan, ed., *ibid.,* pp. 312-313, 325.

8 *Duluth Herald,* July 10-11, 1911; *Marquette Mining Journal,* July 11, 1911; Beeson, *Inland Marine Directory, 1912,* p. 95; Wells, *op. cit.,* p. 47.

9 *Duluth Herald,* July 27, 1911; *Marquette Mining Journal,* July 27, 1911; Beeson, *op. cit., 1912,* p. 95; Ryan W. Leblanc, Schreiber, Ontario, personal communication at wreck site and personal interview recorded August 31, 1988, by Thom Holden; Ronald Wrigley, *Shipwrecked: Vessels That Met Tragedy on Northern Lake Superior,* (Cobalt, Ontario, Highway Book Shop, 1985), pp. 37-39.

10 "$3,500,000 in Lake Superior: Finder's Keepers" in *Argosy,* December 1971, pp. 36-38; *Duluth Herald,* Sept. 1, 1911; *Duluth News-Tribune,* Sept. 21, 1980; *Houghton Daily Mining Gazette,* Sept. 20, 1980; *Marquette Mining Journal,* Aug. 31, Sept. 1, 1911; Beeson, *op. cit., 1912,* p. 94; Jerry Eliason, "Ships That No Longer Sail," 1983 reprint from *Lake Superior Port Cities* Magazine, pp. 29-34; James R. Marshall, "The Deep Dive" in James R. Marshall, ed., *Shipwrecks of Lake Superior* (Duluth, Minnesota, Lake Superior Port Cities, 1987), pp. 24-29; James R. Marshall, "Ships That No Longer Sail" in Marshall, ed. *ibid.,* pp. 39-41; Wrigley, *Shipwrecked, op. cit.,* pp. 41-51; Chuck Zehnder, "Lake Superior's Richest Wreck" in *Treasure World,* February-March 1972, pp. 23-25. The earlier Eliason article, ghost written by Marshall, and later Marshall article titled "Ships That No Longer Sail" are virtually identical, the latter receiving slight editing for republication.

11 *Bayfield County Press,* Oct. 6, 13, 20, 1911; *Duluth Herald,* Oct. 4, 6-7, 9-11, 13-14, 16, 18-21, 23, 1911; *Marquette Mining Journal,* Oct. 4, 10, 1911; Beeson, *op. cit., 1912,* p. 95; Thom Holden, *Apostle Islands Shipwreck Survey List, 1870-1940,* (Bayfield, Wisconsin, Apostle Islands National Lakeshore, National Park Service, 1985), pp. 48-49; James M. Keller, *The "Unholy" Apostles: Tales of Chequamegon Shipwrecks,* (Bayfield, Wisconsin, Apostle Islands Press, 1985), pp. 138-139.

12 Beeson, *op. cit., 1912,* p. 94; Dominion of Canada, Department of Transport, *op. cit.,* p. 47.

13 *Marquette Mining Journal,* Nov. 2, 5, 20, 1911; Beeson, *op. cit., 1912,* p. 95.

14 *Duluth News-Tribune,* Aug. 8, 1912; *Marquette Mining Journal,* Aug. 8-9, 1912; Wells, *op. cit.,* p. 48.

15 *Duluth News-Tribune,* Sept. 2-3, 1912; Wells, *op. cit.,* p. 48; Wrigley, *Shipwrecked, op. cit.,* pp. 52-56.

16 *Marquette Mining Journal,* Sept. 28, 30, 1912; Wells, *op. cit.,* p. 48.

17 Department of Marine and Fisheries, *List of Shipping, 1913,* p. 305, as *Sessional Paper 21-b,* (Ottawa, 1914) and *Report of the Wreck Commissioner: Inland Waters Wrecks,* p. 207, as *Sessional Paper 21* (Ottawa, 1914); Ronald H. Wrigley, *Northern Superior Shipwrecks,* 198 pp., unpublished manuscript, *ca.* 1979, pp. 52-53.

18 *Marquette Mining Journal,* Nov. 26-27, 29, Dec. 2, 1912; Wells, *op. cit.,* p. 49.

19 Beeson, *op. cit., 1914,* p. 172.

20 *Marquette Mining Journal,* June 16-17, 1913; Wells, *op. cit.,* p. 50.

21 *Marquette Mining Journal,* Sept. 11-12, 1913; Wells, *op. cit.,* p. 51.

22 Beeson, *op. cit., 1914,* p. 172.

23 Beeson, *op. cit., 1914,* pp. 8, 172.

24 "Three Strikes on the *Mohawk Deer*" in *Scanner: Journal of the Toronto Marine Historical Society,* Vol. 3, No. 2, November 1970, pp. 5-7; *Duluth News-Tribune,* Nov. 7-14, 16, 19, 1913; *Marquette Mining Journal,* Nov. 11-13, 22, 27, 1913, May 5, Sept. 24, 1914; Beeson, *op. cit.,* 1913, p. 170; Wells, *op. cit.,* p. 52. There has been much confusion regarding the number of persons aboard the *Waldo,* 27 to 29 mentioned in various places. However, the survivors list published in the *Marquette Mining Journal,* Nov. 13, 1913, gives 23 names, and *Merchant Vessels of the United States, 1915,* notes 23 aboard in the loss report, p. 423.

25 *Duluth News-Tribune,* Nov. 11-14, 30, 1913; *Marquette Mining Journal,* Nov. 13, 22, 26, Dec. 11, 1913, May 27, 1914; Beeson, *op. cit., 1914,* p. 170.

26 *Duluth News-Tribune,* Nov. 13, 21, 1913; *Marquette Mining Journal,* Nov. 13, 21-22, 1913; Beeson, *op. cit.,* 1914, p. 168; Wrigley, *Shipwrecked, op. cit.,* pp. 35-36. Wrigley's account states that it was Captain Foote aboard the *Hamonic.* Wrigley also adds another wrinkle in the history and disposition of the *Monkshaven* wreck of November 27, 1905, and subsequent salvage attempts by stating that that hulk was still visible, but on the opposite side of Angus Island from where the *Leafield* was last observed. It would appear that both vessels still remain on the bottom near Angus Island, although neither wreck has been reported in recent years.

27 *Duluth News-Tribune,* Nov. 14, 1913; *Marquette Mining Journal,* Nov. 14-15, 17-20, 22, 24-25, 1913, May 7, 20, June 4, 6, 1914; Beeson, *op. cit.,* 1914, p. 170; Wells, *op. cit.,* p. 52.

28 *Duluth News-Tribune,* Nov. 9, 11, 13, 17, 1913; Wells, *op. cit.,* p. 52-53.

29 *Duluth News-Tribune,* Nov. 12, 19, 1913; *Marquette Mining Journal,* Nov. 12, 14, 22, 1913; Wells, *op. cit.* p. 52.

30 *Duluth News-Tribune,* Nov. 15, 1913; *Marquette Mining Journal,* Nov. 17, 1913; Wells, *op. cit.,* p. 53.

31 James R. Marshall, ''The Hunt for the *Benjamin Noble''* in *Lake Superior Newsletter,* Vol. 1, No. 1, Fall 1987, pp. 1-3; *Duluth News-Tribune,* April 26-30, May 1-3, 5, 1914; *Marquette Mining Journal,* April 30, 1914; *Superior Evening Telegram,* April 29, 1914; Wells, *op. cit.,* p. 53.

32 *Duluth News-Tribune,* May 6, 1914; Wells, *op. cit.,* p. 53.

33 *Duluth News-Tribune,* June 28-29, 1914; Wells, *op. cit.,* p. 54.

34 *Duluth News-Tribune,* Aug. 3, 1914; Wells, *op. cit.,* p. 54.

35 *Marquette Mining Journal,* Nov. 21, 23-24, 28, 30, Dec. 1-3, 8, 18, 1914; Wells, *op. cit.,* p. 55; *Annual Report, U.S. Coast Guard, 1915,* p. 234.

36 *Duluth News-Tribune,* April 1, 1915; Wells, *op. cit.,* p. 55.; *Merchant Vessels of the United States, 1915,* p. 423.

37 *Duluth News-Tribune,* Sept. 14-17, 1915, June 7, 1988; ''Onoko Mystery'' in Lake Carriers' Association *Bulletin,*, November 1958, pp. 5-8; *Lake Superior Newsletter,* No. 3, Spring 1988, pp. 2-3; Jerry Eliason, personal interview recorded on Sept. 6, 1988, by Thom Holden; James R. Marshall, ed., ''Jerry Eliason finds the *Onoko* in 207 feet of Water'' in *Lake Superior Newsletter,* No. 4, Summer 1988, pp. 1-3, 8; Amy Timmer, ''The Search for the *Onoko''* in *Lake Superior Newsletter,* No. 3, Spring 1988, pp. 3-4; Wells, *op. cit.,* p. 55.

38 *Marquette Mining Journal,* Nov. 17, 19, 1915.

39 *Duluth News-Tribune,* May 9-10, Oct. 11, 1916; *Marquette Mining Journal,* May 10-12, 1916; *Detroit Free Press,* May 10, 1916; Wells, *op. cit.,* p. 56.

40 *Marquette Mining Journal,* June 28, 1916; Wells, *op. cit.,* p. 57.

41 *Ashland Daily Press,* Oct. 14, 16, 1916; *Duluth Herald,* Oct. 14, 17, 1916; Holden, *Apostle Islands Shipwreck Survey List, op. cit.,* p. 122.

42 *Marquette Journal,* July 10, 1917; Wells, *op. cit.,* p. 59.

43 *Duluth News-Tribune,* Sept. 17, 1917; Wells, *op. cit.,* p. 60; *Annual Report, U.S. Coast Guard, 1920,* p. 305.

44 *Bayfield County Press,* Nov. 30, 1917; *Duluth Herald,* Nov. 30, 1917; *Duluth News-Tribune,* Nov. 30, 1917; Harry Goldish, engineer on the *L. Goldish,* personal interviews by Thom Holden in Duluth on March 6, 15, 1984; Holden, *Apostle Islands Shipwreck Survey List, op. cit.,* pp. 45-47; Keller, *op. cit.,* pp. 121-123; Julius F. Wolff Jr., ''A Coastal Packet on Lake Superior'' in *Inland Seas,* Vol. 22, No. 3, Fall 1966, pp. 183-184.

45 *Annual Report, U.S. Coast Guard, 1920,* p. 358.

46 *Duluth News-Tribune,* Oct. 13-17, 1918; *Merchant Vessels of the United States, 1918,* pp. 124, 137, 359, 386, 388, 391; *Merchant Vessels of the United States, 1919,* pp. 449-450, 453. *Merchant Vessels* for the 1908 through 1917 editions lists the *Duluth* as a scow, while the 1919 edition which lists the loss shows the vessel as a dredge. It is possible this vessel was converted during the season of loss.

47 *Duluth News-Tribune,* Nov. 5, 9, 1918; *Marquette Mining Journal,* Nov. 2, 11-12, 1918; Wells, *op. cit.,* p. 62.

48 *Duluth News-Tribune,* Nov. 10, 1918; Thom Holden, *Above and Below* (Houghton, Michigan, Isle Royale Natural History Association, 1985), pp. 17-19; Lake Carriers' Association *Annual Report, 1918,* pp. 142-143; Murphy and Holden, *op. cit.,* pp. 169-174; Murphy, Lenihan, and Labadie, *op. cit.,* pp. 306-311; Wells, *op. cit.,* p. 63.

49 *Duluth News-Tribune,* Dec. 6, 1918; *Inland Seas,* Vol 29, No. 1, Spring 1973, pp. 74-75; *Marquette Mining Journal,* Dec. 5-7, 1918.

50 *Duluth News-Tribune,* May 27, 1919, Jan. 6, 1923; Wells, *op. cit.,* p. 64.

51 *Duluth News-Tribune,* July 8, 1919.

52 *Duluth News-Tribune,* Aug. 8, 10, 12, Oct. 1, 1919; Wells, *op. cit.,* p. 64.

53 *Duluth News-Tribune,* Nov. 8, 10-11, 15-16, 18, 1919; *Marquette Mining Journal,* Nov. 18, 1919; Wells, *op. cit.,* p. 65.

54 *Duluth News-Tribune,* Nov. 15-16, 1919; *Annual Report of the U.S. Coast Guard, 1920,* pp. 17-19, 65, 195; Wells, *op. cit.,* p. 65.

55 *Duluth News-Tribune,* Nov. 24-26, 1919; *Marquette Mining Journal,* Nov. 24-25, Dec. 2-4, 1919; Wells, *op. cit.,* p. 65.

56 *Marquette Mining Journal,* Nov. 29, Dec. 2, 1919.

Despite her powerful engines, the Robert Fulton *was damaged when she scraped piers at Two Harbors in a wild November 1920 storm.* UNIVERSITY OF DETROIT MARINE COLLECTION.

Chapter 7

The Fantastic Twenties
1920-1929

The Twenties on Lake Superior were truly phenomenal. This was peacetime, yet the total tonnage evidenced a seven percent increase over the hurried period of World War I. At the same time, the safety record improved dramatically. Troubled ships decreased by 30 percent, and total losses dropped by 25 percent. Fatalities plummeted from 236 in the previous decade to 106, the least since the 1890s. The intensity of shipping activities varied considerably from year to year, yet 1923 and the years 1925 through 1929 would be considered boom years. Still, the vicissitudes of Lake Superior sailing continued to exact a toll. Approximately 140 ships reported significant problems and 28 joined the ranks of the vanquished.

1920

The shipping business was good with tonnage bouncing upward about 15 percent over that of 1919 which had been a little slack. The first four months of navigation were

167

pretty much routine in terms of vessel safety. Ten ships were involved in "plate-bender" collisions or inconvenient strandings, though only two had much repair work.

The 504-foot steel steamer *Harry Yates* brushed the 83-foot steel tug *America* in Duluth-Superior Harbor April 26 with little consequence. On April 30, though, the brand new 251-foot steel *LaCrosse* ran hard aground on Parisienne Island. She needed $20,000 in bottom

UNITED STATES AND DOMINION TRANSPORTATION CO.

THE ONLY LINE MAKING A DAYLIGHT CIRCUIT OF BEAUTIFUL

ISLE ROYALE

US&DTCO

DULUTH	PORT ARTHUR
ISLE ROYALE	CORNUCOPIA
FT. WILLIAM	GRAND MARAIS

United States and Canadian Mails
Passenger and Freight Line

For full information apply to
L. P. HOGSTAD —or— L. D. ROSENHEIMER
Supt. DULUTH, MINN.   Traffic Manager. CHICAGO, ILL.

POOLE BROS. CHICAGO.

Booth's "United States and Dominion Transportation Co." kept packets on Lake Superior until after 1930. STEVE GORDON COLLECTION.

work. This was plenty for a vessel just launched the year before at Duluth. The 532-foot *Matthew Andrews* set herself against the Duluth pier on May 27. In poor visibility on June 1, the 416-foot *Cygnus* slid into the shoal water of Flood Bay just northeast of Two Harbors. Refurbishing cost $8,000. The fog on June 12 brought another close one at Whitefish Point as the 380-foot *B. Lyman Smith* and 444-foot *F.R. Hazard* grazed one another. Damages were not disclosed. In Duluth Harbor on July

23, the 420-foot steamer *William P. Cowan* was hit by the barge *Limit,* again with minimal results. On August 5, however, the 504-foot steel *William H. Wolf* was a $20,000 dry-dock item after slamming into the shoals off Devils Island.

Then came the shocker. About 9:30 p.m., August 20, in Whitefish Bay about four or five miles southeast of the Point, two powerful freighters came together in the dimming light. The 429-foot, 4,795-ton Pittsburgher *Superior City,* downbound with iron ore from Two Harbors, was struck aft of amidships on the port side by the 580-foot, 7,568-ton steamer *Willis L. King,* upbound light. Within two minutes, the icy waters pouring into the *Superior City*'s boiler room caused a towering explosion which blew the whole stern away, sinking the ore carrier immediately with a loss of 29 lives. Only four of her crew were saved, all of the survivals being little short of miraculous.

To this day there is no satisfactory explanation for this collision, other than confusion in passing signals by the ships' officers. Lookouts on the vessels reported each other when the ships were four or five miles apart, and routine passing signals were exchanged. Captain Edward Sawyer of the *Superior City* was sure that he repeatedly whistled a starboard course for passing the *King* on her port side, whereas Captain Herman Nelson of the *King* was equally adamant that the *Superior City* had called for a port course, to pass the *King* on her starboard. Both ships apparently continued sailing at a rather good clip, the *Superior City* with her 1,900 horsepower actually being more powerful than the much larger *King,* which boasted 1,800 horsepower. Evasive action was taken by both only at the last moment. The *Superior City* had swung across the *King*'s bow, exposing herself to the fatal blow.

Captain Sawyer had sounded the alarm a couple of minutes before the crash, and his crew poured on deck and raced to the stern for the boats. Unfortunately, at the precise moment the boilers let go, the whole crew was concentrated above them, literally sitting targets for eternity. When boats from the *King* and the passing steamer *J.J. Turner* were lowered and reached the sinking area, only four survivors could be found. Captain Sawyer was clinging to a life jacket which he never had time to put on. Second Mate G.H. Lehnt clung to the bottom of a capsized lifeboat. Wheelsman Peter Jacobson was dragged down with the ship, but fought his way back to the surface and simply swam about for 20 minutes until the *King*'s lifeboat located him. Boatswain Walter Richter had been in his bunk when the warning signal was sounded. He raced to the deck only lightly clad. His clothing was blown off by the force of the explosion, before he was dragged under by the ship's vortex. He managed to swim back to the surface where he grabbed a hatch cover which he rode as a raft until picked up by a boat from the *J.J. Turner.*

The accident was investigated by U.S. Steamboat Inspectors Gooding and Hanson of Marquette, and the case was litigated in the courts for months. Eventually, the officers of both ships were held partially responsible. The *King*'s badly smashed bow was a $30,000 repair job, while the *Superior City* was a $650,000 financial casualty and with her went the lives of 28 men and one woman, the worst loss of life in the history of the Pittsburgh Steamship Company.[1]

The difficulties of autumn were customary. The 414-foot steel *Sweden* needed several thousand dollars in rebuilding after a bout with high seas on September 29. A 55 mph gale on November 2 pitched the 425-foot steel *Robert Fulton* against a pier at Two Harbors, despite her 2,000 horsepower. New shell plating cost $2,500. Off Stannard Rock on November 9, the 376-foot *E.W. Oglebay* took a light mauling, while on November 12 off Whitefish Point the 380-foot *Francis L. Robbins* took a real dusting, sustaining $9,000 in storm damage.

The riotous waves and snow on the afternoon and evening of November 12 were responsible for another total loss alarm northeast of Whitefish Point. Great Lakes area newspapers of November 14 shrieked another disaster, the 416-foot, 4,682-ton steamer *Francis Widlar* of the Cleveland Steamship Company, a Becker unit, supposedly being sunk with all 33 aboard off Pancake Shoal. Happily, the report was untrue.

A whooping gale and snow storm had raked the length of Lake Superior beginning on November 9. Leaving Duluth at 3 a.m. on November 11, Captain Arthur Forbes of the *Widlar* hoped the blasts would stay ahead of him, but discovered to his dismay the next day that he was right in the midst of them. Seas were terrible off Whitefish Point. Hours overdue at the Soo, the *Widlar* was driven well to the east of her normal course and hurled onto Pancake Shoal during the night of November 12. Following a few miles behind the 1,500-horsepower *Widlar* was the 390-foot, 3,200-ton steel whaleback *John Ericsson*. With her lower profile and 2,000-horsepower engine, the *Ericsson* managed to remain a respectful distance from danger. Captain William Rorke of the *Ericsson* knew that the *Widlar* was in treacherous waters. Then, when her lights went out, apparently as she struck, Captain Rorke interpreted this as a sudden foundering and so reported at the Soo some hours later. The following day, the roaring tempest kept other vessels at a distance from Pancake Shoal, though in the afternoon, during a rift in the snow veil, the captain of the *Stadacona* thought he detected the *Widlar* still above water. The storm had downed telephone lines out of the Soo, making it impossible to call the Coast Guard at Vermilion Point or Crisp Point, while the raging seas and snow prevented the Vermilion Point lookout from detecting the wreck fully 25 miles away. Similarly, the lighthouse keepers at Whitefish Point were blinded.

The captain of the *Stadacona* had been correct. Though sustaining a terrific thrashing, the *Widlar* had remained intact on the rocks through the night of the 12th

and all through the day and night of the 13th. When help had not arrived on the morning of the 14th, the waves now subsiding a bit, Captain Forbes decided on a daring move. Taking five crewmen with him, he launched a lifeboat and rowed west through the still tossing waters to the vessel lanes where he flagged down the large 532-foot steel *William Livingstone*. The big freighter picked up the six survivors and rushed them to the Soo from where the tugs *Iowa* and *E.E. Ainsworth* were immediately dispatched. The tugs succeeded in approaching the wreck and removed the 27 remaining crewmen together with the ship's mascot, a dog named Tootsie. The castaways had been aground 63 hours. Thanks to the unusually competent lifeboat handling of Captain Forbes and his hand-picked crew, no lives were lost. Subsequently, the badly battered *Widlar* was taken off her rocky perch in a risky salvage operation by veteran Captain Tom Reid of Sarnia. Worth $600,000, she proved to be a $200,000 salvage and rebuilding project. Then, she was sold to a Canadian company and passed out of the American Great Lakes fleet.[2]

The schooner-barge Miztec *foundered off Whitefish Point when she separated from the steamer* Zillah *and barge* Peshtigo *in mid-May 1921.* AUTHOR'S COLLECTION.

The next week, a very costly mishap befell the 530-foot, 6,924-ton *J.H. Sheadle* of the Cleveland-Cliffs fleet. In backing away from the Presque Isle dock at Marquette on November 20, the *Sheadle* was swept onto a reef and badly holed, settling to the bottom in 21 feet of water. Heavily laden with iron ore, she was a difficult job for salvors. The wreckers managed to move her into the main harbor of Marquette, but rough weather prevented her being moved to the lower lakes for dry-docking until the following spring. For a simple harbor stranding, her salvage and repair bill was an enormous $150,000.[3]

The final incident of the season involved the 340-foot whaleback steamer *Pathfinder* which struck a rock on November 23 at Shaganash Island, about 10 miles northeast of Porphyry Island on the Canadian north shore. She was in no danger of being lost, but needed $5,000 in bottom work.

1921

As a consequence of the postwar depression, the Lake Superior shipping business in 1921 was the poorest it had been in 13 years, recording a drop in tonnage of nearly 40 percent from the previous season. Early sailing was negligible. Indeed, it was fortunate that few ships were on the lake in mid-May, since one of the worst spring gales and snow storms in decades riled the entire lake from May 14 to 16. Duluth received the first May snow in 14 years. The Soo received a terrible plastering, with howling winds and a 10-inch snowfall which brought traffic to a virtual halt.

The 57-year-old tug Howard *was lost to fire off Victoria Island in June 1921.* WISCONSIN MARINE HISTORICAL SOCIETY COLLECTION, MILWAUKEE PUBLIC LIBRARY.

Locking through the Soo on the night of May 13, the 202-foot wooden steamer *Zillah* with two schooner-barges in tow, the 194-foot, 777-ton *Miztec* and 201-foot, 633-ton *Peshtigo,* pushed northward in rough seas through Whitefish Bay and around Whitefish Point to the west. The *Zillah* and *Miztec* were loaded with salt for Duluth, while the *Peshtigo* was bound light for Munising. Not until he was 10 miles west of Whitefish Point did the *Zillah*'s master realize that he was in no ordinary spring blow. He had tackled a snow-laden hurricane. He tried in desperation to turn back for the shelter of Whitefish Point, but the towline broke in the darkness, and the two barges were on their own. Then, the towline between the barges snapped. As he watched from the *Peshtigo,* Captain Don Campbell saw the lights of the *Miztec* suddenly disappear. The *Miztec* had foundered. This was a particularly bit-

ter observation for Captain Campbell, since his brother, Robert, was first mate on the *Miztec.* Captain K. Pederson of the *Miztec,* his wife, Florence, who was ship's cook, and five crewmen went down with their ship.

The *Peshtigo* had a close call, too. Her rudder smashed, Captain Campbell rigged a sail to try for the shelter of the Point. However, the gale kept driving him shoreward east of Vermilion Point, with his anchors dragging. The Coast Guard at Vermilion Point smashed two surfboats in vain attempts to launch to his rescue. Finally, the anchors caught when the schooner was only a quarter mile from the breakers. When the storm began to subside on May 15, the *Zillah* retrieved her surviving barge and limped back to the Soo with knee-deep water in her engine room.

First word of the tragedy came from the Standard Oil tanker *Renown,* whose officers observed wreckage of the *Miztec* during the height of the storm on May 14, including her cabin with the body of a man on top of it. The *Renown* reached the Soo that afternoon. The Coast Guard put in a call for the cutter *Cook* under Captain Benjamin Trudell. After the snow ceased and winds dropped a bit, the *Cook* managed to find the site of sinking, marked by a standing spar. The *Miztec* lay in 36 feet of water, though different distances from Vermilion Point were reported in various dispatches: seven miles northeast; five miles northeast and three miles off shore; and finally nine miles northeast and 1½ miles offshore. Possibly, the schooner could have been sliding along the bottom as her salt cargo dissolved away after she went down. No bodies were recovered at the spot of sinking. Nevertheless, six days after the foundering, Indians on Maple Island along the Canadian shore east of Whitefish Point discovered the body of Mrs. Florence Pederson, the captain's wife and cook on the *Miztec.*

Strangely enough, the demise of the *Miztec* was near the very place where her towing steamer *Myron* met her end on November 22, 1919, when the *Miztec* rode out the storm before being rescued by the steamer *Argus.* Ironically, Captain Walter Neal, the sole survivor of the *Myron,* was riding as first mate on the *Zillah* when the *Miztec* went down. The *Miztec* was abandoned by her owners as a total loss. Since she was near the vessel lanes, the U.S. Army Corps of Engineers ordered her dynamited as a menace to navigation. However, when the U.S. Coast Guard Cutter *Morrill* arrived on Lake Superior several weeks later to do the job, no *Miztec* could be found. Apparently, as her salt cargo dissipated, she worked her way along the bottom to the northeast until she finally slid into deep water. While her value was not given, the *Miztec* probably was worth $10,000 to her owner, O.W. Blodgett of Duluth and Bay City.[4]

A thick fog on May 22 brought grief to the 421-foot steamer *Captain Thomas Wilson* which ran hard astride Gull Island Shoal in the Apostles. Tugs quickly pulled her free for a $40,000 trip to dry dock. Then on June 13 came the end of one of the most ancient vessels in western Lake Superior, as the 115-foot, 195-ton wooden tug *Howard* stranded and burned at Victoria Island southwest of Thunder Bay. She had been built in 1864 at Wilmington,

In mid-August 1921, the large Corps of Engineer's tug General C.B. Sears *assisted in refloating a derrick scow sunk in the Keweenaw Waterway.* U.S. ARMY CORPS OF ENGINEERS PHOTO.

Delaware. At the time of loss, she was worth only $10,000. Some tough sailing weather on August 5 saw the 585-foot *William J. Filbert* slapped against a pier at Duluth, accumulating $4,000 worth of injured plates. In the Duluth Harbor on the same day, the 340-foot passenger steamer *Octorara* brushed the 293-foot *Samuel Mitchell* with minor consequences to both. Over in the Keweenaw Waterway, derrick scow *No. 8* foundered about August 15 near the Upper Entry, but was partially refloated the next day by the tug *General C.B. Sears* and derrick scow *No. 7*.

A pair of fires at Port Arthur claimed two Canadian victims during the fall. The 161-foot, 511-ton wooden steamer *W.H. Ritchie*, formerly the *Stephen C. Hall*, a 41-year veteran of the lakes, was destroyed on September 27. This casualty was followed on November 13 by the 66-foot, 85-ton wooden *Sarnia*, a 20-year-old tug owned by Canadian Towing & Wrecking of Port Arthur. In neither case was the financial liability listed, though these undoubtedly were low-value vessels.

The last casualty of the year was also Canadian, but a 34-year-old tug with a romantic history. In her old age, the 63-foot, 49-ton *Arbutus* was a rumrunner, helping to relieve the thirst of Michigan's Upper Peninsula citizens along Keweenaw Point. She was captured by American authorities off the Keweenaw and impounded in the fall of 1920, being sent to Marquette where she lay on the beach for a number of months. Finally, the federal court decided to return her to the Canadian bank which held a mortgage on her, and she was purchased by Captain E.A. Fader of Fort William. He was taking her to the Soo when high seas sent her to the bottom about 10 miles north of

Grand Marais, Michigan. Her three-man crew escaped. The sinking occurred about November 24.[5]

1922

While traffic on Lake Superior in 1922 showed a marked increase over 1921, this navigation season still ranks as a dull year. Consequently, the number of ships in trouble was small, only nine. Yet, four of these were total losses, and 34 sailors and passengers lost their lives.

Double tragedy struck in the first two weeks of sailing. To this day, one of the strangest mysteries of Lake Superior is the disappearance, some time after April 19, of the steel Canadian lighthouse tender *Lambton*. On that date, the 13-year-old 108-foot, 323-ton buoy tender *Lambton* departed from the Canadian lighthouse station at the Soo with her crew and the lightkeepers for eastern Canadian lights, especially those on Caribou and Michipicoten Islands. Nineteen persons were probably aboard. The lake was rough and extensive ice fields roamed the eastern shore. Still, this should have presented no serious difficulty for the rugged little steel ship.

Several days elapsed as the vessel season got under way, and various ships reported at the Soo that the five eastern Canadian lighthouses were not yet lit. This was surprising indeed since the *Lambton* should have reached these by April 20 or 21. Then the Canadian steamer *Valcartier* reported encountering wreckage on April 23 about 25 miles southeast of Michipicoten Island. The U.S. Coast Guard cutter *Cook* was summoned to sweep eastern Lake Superior and locate the debris. Bucking ice fields, the *Cook* recovered the tell-tale evidence after a week-long search, radioing the Soo on April 30 via the Whitefish Point wireless station to report her grim discoveries. These included a piece of cabin with white woodwork and a window with a shutter, a bracket lamp with a nickel-plated match box and a door painted brown having a brass knob on the inside and a ring on the outside. Coast Guardsmen examining the flotsam discovered the trademark "H.L. Pieper, Montreal" on the lamp and the word, "Seythe," over the window frame. The single glass in the window was colored brown as was the shutter. Canadian Lighthouse Service personnel familiar with the *Lambton* ruefully agreed that the fragments were hers. This fine little ship and all aboard had succumbed to Lake Superior somewhere south of Michipicoten Island and east of Caribou Island.[6]

A second sinking occurred in the fog off Two Harbors at 5:10 a.m., May 3, when the 283-foot, 2,340-ton wooden barge *Harriet B.* was rammed and sunk by the 504-foot steamer *Quincy A. Shaw* of the M.A. Hanna Company. The *Harriet B.*, along with the barge *Crete*, was in tow of the 298-foot lumber hooker *C.W. Jacob*. They had arrived off Two Harbors at 1:10 a.m., but the *Jacob*'s captain wanted to wait for the fog to lift before taking his barges into Two Harbors for a load of pulpwood. Hence, the three ships were anchored serenely a mile off shore and three miles southwest of the breakwater light when the rapidly moving *Shaw* slipped out of the fog bank and smashed into the *Harriet B.* The barge went down in 20 minutes, allowing time for Captain Theodore Claussen

Noronic *was the largest Canadian passenger steamer on the Great Lakes.* CANAL PARK MARINE MUSEUM COLLECTION.

and his crew to abandon ship and proceed to the *Shaw*, later to be transferred to the *Jacob.* The *Harriet B.*'s wheelhouse washed ashore nearby. Her hull has never been located. The *Shaw* endured $6,000 in bow damage above the waterline, being repaired in Ashtabula the following week. Though the value of the *Harriet B.* was not reported, the 27-year-old barge undoubtedly was worth more than $25,000 to her owners, the Hammermill Pa-

per Company of Erie, Pennsylvania. She formerly had been the steamer *Shenango No. 2.*

Another near tragedy struck in mid-May when the *Glenfinnan* and *Midland King* met unexpectedly southeast of Passage Island on May 18. The 324-foot, 2,406-ton *Glenfinnan* of the Great Lake Transportation Company had cleared the Canadian Lakehead the day before, carrying grain to Port McNicoll, while the 366-foot, 3,965-ton *Midland King* of the Canada Steamship Lines fleet was up at the Soo that same afternoon bound for Fort William and Port Arthur. Details of the collision are meager, but it must have been little more than a plate bender as the *Glenfinnan* passed down through the locks early on the morning of the 19th while the *Midland King* was reported making repairs at Port Arthur on the same day.[7]

Summer sailing was surprisingly accident free, the only item involving the 377-foot steel steamer *William Nottingham* which banged a pier at Duluth on July 6 with little injury. A freak fire on September 13 destroyed the 47-foot, 11-ton wooden gas tug *Wood Island* of the Cleveland-Cliffs Iron Company. En route from Munising to Whitefish River with a tow of boomsticks southeast of Marquette, the *Wood Island* suffered a carburetor backfire when off Five Mile Point. Almost instantly, her engine became a mass of flame. Her three-man crew fought the flames unsuccessfully, remaining aboard until the fire approached the fuel tanks. They leaped into the yawl and pulled away in the nick of time, as the rear gasoline tank of the *Wood Island* blew up moments after they left, sending the twin-screw, 100-horsepower tug to the bottom. The 14-year-old vessel probably was valued in excess of $10,000. The crewmen were picked up by the tug *Grand Island,* also of the Cleveland-Cliffs fleet, which was assisted in the rescue by the tug *Munis* of the Munising Paper Company.[8]

The early fall was also relatively uneventful. The 525-foot *C.S. Robinson* ripped her bottom to the extent of $20,000 when striking at Devils Island on October 22. The 536-foot *E.J. Earling* took a mean mauling in a gale west of Whitefish Point on November 23, requiring $25,000 in shipyard attention for extraordinary storm damage.

The last weeks of sailing, however, were also marked by double tragedy. The night of November 30 was miserable over western and central Lake Superior with howling winds more than 60 mph and a thick blanket of wet, slushy snow. Struggling northwestward en route to Fort William with 1,800 tons of coal was the 230-foot, 1,264-ton steel Canadian steamer *Maplehurst,* formerly the *Cadillac* of the Cleveland-Cliffs fleet. As he was tossed about unmercifully southeast of Isle Royale, 29-year-old Captain George Menard, one of the youngest masters of the Canada Steamship Lines, decided to abandon his attempt to reach the Canadian Lakehead and sought shelter along the Keweenaw Peninsula. He passed Copper Harbor, thinking the entrance too shallow and dangerous, and fought his way 45 miles to the southwest, being three miles off the piers of the Portage Lake Ship Canal shortly after midnight. Then, with the pummeling of giant waves, the little steamer showed signs of breaking up.

About 1 a.m., the captain ordered flares lighted as a distress signal. Meanwhile, the lookout at the Portage Coast Guard station had been watching the little ship, half suspecting that she could not long withstand the tempest. The Coast Guard crew had already been alerted. When the flares were displayed, Captain Charles A. Tucker and his lifesaving crew boarded the motor lifeboat and were off. It took the lifeboat a good half hour to reach the steamer which now had been driven in mountainous seas to about four miles west of the canal and two miles off shore.

Aboard the stricken *Maplehurst,* Captain Menard had told his crew that they could leave if they wished, but he was going to stand by the ship. The Coast Guard lifeboat closed on the foundering ship, and Captain Tucker shouted through his megaphone to the crew on deck to jump for the lifeboat as he brought it close under the vessel's lee. To the Coast Guardsmen's consternation, the *Maplehurst's* people did not comply. With a superb job of small boat handling in an enormous sea, Captain Tucker made 10 passes alongside the floundering ship. Only 10 of the sailors jumped, nine being clutched to the safety of the lifeboat by the Coast Guard crew, although First Mate Henry J. Smith missed the boat and drowned.

Finally, a towering wave struck the *Maplehurst,* disabling her power plant, and her lights went out. In the snow and darkness, Captain Tucker was unable to find her again. Accordingly, he nursed the heavily loaded lifeboat back to the safety of the Ship Canal.

For the *Maplehurst,* it was the end. The roaring gale drove her into the shoals west of the Ship Canal piers and beat her to pieces, sinking her in 35 feet of water with only the tops of her derricks and smokestack showing. All nine men who stayed with their captain died. When the lake finally calmed, the Reid Towing and Wrecking Company with the tug *James Whalen* was rushed to the scene, but the *Maplehurst* was unsalvageable. Thirty years old at the time, the ship undoubtedly was a liability in excess of $75,000, and 11 Canadian sailors had gone to eternity with her. Captain Tucker and the Portage Station Coast Guard's crew had done their best, but the Coast Guard cannot compel a crew to leave their ship, even when she is in imminent peril.[9]

Another shocker came just two weeks later, about December 15. En route to the Soo from the Superior Paper Company logging camps on the eastern shores of the lake was the large 124-foot, 311-ton company tug *Reliance.* In addition to her crew of 14, she carried 20 lumberjacks heading to the Soo for the holidays, together with Captain John McPherson, Superintendent of Booth Fisheries, and Forester Fred Regan of the paper company. Despite

inclement weather and heavy snow, Captain A.D. Williams pushed on. But the storm was too much, and the *Reliance* was hurled on the rocks surrounding Lizard Island, some 70 miles northwest of the Soo, and completely disabled.

Poor visibility in dense forest fire smoke caused the steamer Luzon *to strand at Passage Island in October 1923.* UNIVERSITY OF DETROIT MARINE COLLECTION.

The survivors were in a desperate situation, for following the snow came a wicked cold wave. Duluth registered 18 degrees below zero. Fireman Bill Gow of the *Reliance* swam ashore through the icy waters dragging a line, and those remaining aboard were able to get to the island. Captain Williams and six men launched a lifeboat, fortuitously reaching the eastern mainland, only to have a frigid 16-mile hike through the forest to a railroad which they followed to a small station. There they were able to telegraph the Soo for help.

First reports to the outside world listed 27 passengers and crew as missing and feared lost. However, the tugs *Favorite* and *Gray* quickly put out from the Soo, discovering 23 in an improvised shelter on Lizard Island. They were safely removed. When help had not arrived earlier, Captain McPherson, Forester Regan and two passengers set out in a second lifeboat. This was discovered days later, smashed on the Canadian east shore with no clue as to the fate of the occupants. As far as Lake Superior records indicate, these four were lost. The *Reliance* apparently was recovered.[10]

1923

This was a phenomenal year. With reviving national business activity, tonnage on Lake Superior soared nearly 40 percent, coming within an eyelash of the previous record year of 1916. Yet, with revived shipping, the number of mishaps jumped also, the total nearly tripling that of the previous season. Fortunately, not a life would be lost. Only two ships made their last run, and most of the troubles were of the nuisance variety.

The month of May furnished 10 incidents, one fire and the rest collisions and strandings. A blaze at Hancock, Michigan, on May 12 consumed the 91-foot, 162-ton wooden steamer *Sailor Boy,* a 32-year-old vessel. Monetary loss was not reported. Minimal injury was sustained by the 504-foot steel *W.H. Becker* when striking bottom west of Eagle River on May 6, but on the same day, the 530-foot *Edwin E. Slick* needed $15,000 in shipyard attention after being hit in Whitefish Bay by the 549-foot *J. Leonard Replogle.* The 504-foot *Hoover & Mason* and the 580-foot *Thomas Walters* clashed in Duluth Harbor on May 8 with nominal repairs being in order. On May 11 in Whitefish Bay, the 530-foot *Arthur E. Newbold* and 356-foot *Lupus* came together, again with little damage. The 532-foot *R.L. Agassiz* required $10,000 in bottom work after grounding at Point Iroquois on May 12, and the 380-foot *Frank W. Hart* needed the same amount for new plating after smashing into a Duluth pier on May 20.

The Glenlyon *stranded and became a total loss on a reef near Menagerie Island while seeking shelter in early morning darkness of November 1, 1924.* UNIVERSITY OF DETROIT MARINE COLLECTION.

The summer was more quiet. The little 122-foot tug *Victoria* banged herself substantially on June 22 when slapping a pier at Duluth, but only minor plate-scraping resulted when the 401-foot *Queen City* and 585-foot *William J. Filbert* brushed at Two Harbors. A different story unfolded in the thick weather of July 23 in the southeast corner of Whitefish Bay where two of the giants tangled. The 588-foot *Horace S. Wilkinson,* moving along at a respectable clip, slammed into the 580-foot *William B. Schiller.* The *Schiller* remained afloat, but encountered a $135,000 dry-dock bill. The *Wilkinson* required $15,000 in bow repairs.

With the approach of autumn came an increase in difficulties. The 147-foot, 307-ton wooden passenger steamer *Rotarian* suffered a bad engine breakdown on September 27 at Grand Island which necessitated a $15,000

rebuilding effort. She had been an excursion steamer at Duluth, but was transferred to Chicago. She may have been en route to her new home port when the trouble occurred. The remainder of the month passed with only the 381-foot *Alfred H. Smith* reporting injury when she ripped her bottom slightly on some obstruction in the Portage Lake Ship Canal.

A plague of forest fires erupted on both north and south shores during the first three weeks of October. The smoke blanket, coupled with customary October fogs, brought grief to eight vessels. The 350-foot *North Lake* stranded on the Pine River Shoal October 3, being released with a $23,500 salvage and repair bill. In the poor visibility of October 7, the 346-foot *Luzon* hit hard on the rocks of Passage Island. She was a $60,000 item for the wreckers and shipyard, but there was a more tragic note here. In the excitement of grounding, her master, Captain James Buchanan, died of a stroke.

The impenetrable mists of October 10-11 brought double disaster in the Whitefish Bay area. Off Whitefish Point on the afternoon of October 11, the downbound 416-foot, 4,720-ton *Cetus* rammed and sank the upbound 238-foot, 1,945-ton Canadian steamer *Huronton.* Realizing he had mortally wounded the smaller ship, the *Cetus'* captain held his bow in the gaping hole until the *Huronton* crew had crawled over the side of the larger vessel. The *Huronton*'s captain even had time to save the ship's papers and the crew list as his ship remained afloat for 18 minutes. When the *Cetus* backed off, the *Huronton* plunged to the bottom, a loss undoubtedly over $100,000. She belonged to the A.E. Mathews Steamship Company.[11]

Farther to the south in Whitefish Bay that same day, October 11, the 354-foot *John McCartney Kennedy* whacked the 426-foot *Henry Steinbrenner* with rehabilitation work of $15,000 needed for the two. The smoke and fog remained for several days. The 440-foot *Denmark* got in too close to Whitefish Point and snagged some obstruction on October 13, though the expense was trivial. Suddenly, the smog cover was dissipated by a slashing gale and snow storm on October 19 which bid strongly for a sizable victim. The 530-foot, 6,751-ton *Samuel Mather* was pitched on Gull Rock off Keweenaw Point in a badly exposed position, taking a considerable battering. The 532-foot *D.O. Mills* stood by, but the *Mather* held together, and the Eagle Harbor lifesavers removed the crew on October 21. Wreckers rushed to her assistance and released her almost immediately. She was towed to Superior where dry-dock inspection disclosed 68 smashed plates and a bent rudder stock, a total item of some $75,000.[12]

The final incident of 1923 involved the 420-foot *W.G. Pollock* which hit some underwater object near Rock of Ages Lighthouse, Isle Royale, November 15, resulting in a repair bill of $22,000. Also during 1923, the 50-year-old tug *Cayuga,* a 58-foot, 27-ton craft, was sunk in the St. Marys River, a light financial loss.

1924

Tonnage demands showed a substantial drop this season, with far fewer safety problems. Most serious difficulties came early. Of all things, a January sinking inaugurated the wreck list. A group of Cornucopia, Wisconsin, commercial fishermen had decided to attempt deepwater net fishing through the winter along a 20-mile stretch of the south shore. They hired Captain Einar Miller, owner and captain of the 96-foot, 70-ton wooden steamer *Thomas Friant*, which had been in the small port freight business of western Lake Superior during 1923. On a bitterly cold January 6, Captain Miller had picked up the fishermen and was sailing about nine miles off Port Wing, Wisconsin, when ice cut through the 40-year-old hull. Gradually, water gained on the pumps, put out the fires, and the *Friant* began settling. Happily, though snow was falling, the lake was not too rough, and Captain Miller with eight men launched a small boat and rowed 12 miles to the town of Knife River on the north shore, 19 miles northeast of Duluth. The old wooden vessel was a loss of $10,000.[13]

Shortly after noon on May 17, a most unusual incident occurred at the Great Northern docks at Allouez, Superior Harbor. As the 504-foot, 5,841-ton *Hoover & Mason* pulled away from Dock No. 1 fully loaded with iron ore, she was struck amidships by the 504-foot, 6,361-ton *J.S. Ashley* which intended to pull into the berth being vacated. With a giant hole admitting tons of water, Captain A.H. Kuhns of the *Hoover & Mason* beached his ship in 20 feet of water, and the crew was safe. Then the fun began. While she lay on the bottom, the *Hoover & Mason*'s hull buckled, and it took the services of the famed wrecker *Favorite,* brought all the way from the Soo, to bring her up for the short trip to the Superior shipyard and rebuilding costs of $50,000. Captain J.C. Swinton of the *Ashley* blamed the accident on a mistake in signals. His ship escaped unscathed.[14]

The very next day, tragedy hit in the eastern lake. Upbound for a load of pulpwood with the 342-foot, 2,704-ton wooden barge *Chieftain* in tow, the 295-foot, 2,226-ton wooden steamer *Orinoco* encountered a vicious 60 mph wind and sub-freezing temperatures. She started leaking badly. Dropping his tow about 40 miles north of Whitefish Point, Captain Anthony Lawrence put 17 of his crew into the lifeboats off Montreal Island, while he, Chief Engineer Joseph Wirtz and Wheelsman Hugh Gordon remained aboard in a desperate effort to nurse the settling vessel ashore. As the crew in the lifeboats struggled to reach the island, they watched their ship plunge to the bottom. Only with a great deal of effort did most of the men in the lifeboats survive. They were picked up by Captain D.A. Williams of the tug *Gargantua* which happened to be towing logs in that vicinity. Two crewmen, William Ostrander and Clarence Clarkson, had died of exposure in the boats, victims of the unseasonable

cold, but 17 had survived, in part due to the largely unheralded heroism of the three who had perished with their ship. Fortunately, the barge *Chieftain* reached the lee of Montreal Island and safety. While the value of the

The ice-cut Thomas Friant *foundered between Port Wing and Two Harbors while fishing in January 1924.* C. Patrick Labadie collection.

Orinoco was not recorded, a wooden ship of that size, built in West Bay City in 1898, must have been worth more than $50,000. And five of her crew had died.[15]

Until late autumn, things would be relatively quiet. In thick weather off Parisienne Island on July 24, the 525-foot *Amasa Stone* and 587-foot *Merton E. Farr* clipped each other, resulting in combined damages of $10,000. The 346-foot *J.W. Ailes* ran aground at Rocky Island on August 22 and needed $20,000 in bottom plates. And on September 22, the package freighter *Superior,* a 381-foot vessel, suffered a $20,000 fire in her cargo when off Duluth.

Then, November 1, a roaring northeasterly storm scored a hit. Downbound from Fort William on October 30, en route to Port Colborne with wheat, was the 328-foot, 2,759-ton package freighter *Glenlyon* of the Great Lakes Navigation Company fleet of Midland. Captain William Taylor found an angry Lake Superior beyond Thunder Cape and returned to shelter off the Welcome Islands. When the lake quieted down the next evening, the *Glenlyon* got under way again. Then, when 15 miles east of Passage Island, she found the going too rough with 40 mph winds and rising seas. Captain Taylor turned back to seek shelter in Siskiwit Bay, Isle Royale. Off course just a few hundred feet, the *Glenlyon* ran well up on a reef off Menagerie Island which punctured her hull, flooding the engine room and stokehold. The wireless operator was able to get out a distress signal before power was lost. Two of her crew, First Mate Donald McLaughlin and Watchman Wilfred Roy, took one lifeboat to examine the hull for exterior damage, but were driven away from the wreck only to be picked up 23 hours later by Coast Guardsmen near the head of Siskiwit Bay.

Meanwhile, the Canadian steamers *Glensannox* and *Glenlinnie* also picked up the distress signal and altered course for Siskiwit Bay. Initially held at bay, the *Glenlinnie* was able to maneuver alongside and begin taking off the crew. They were quickly transferred to the *Glensannox* which had positioned herself to shelter the other two vessels. The tug *Strathmore* also set out from the Canadian Lakehead. Eventually, salvage crews removed 10,000 bushels of grain but were forced off the wreck by bad weather.

Badly wracked, but thought salvageable in the spring, the *Glenlyon* was left through the winter. Ice and subsequent storms pulled her around 180 degrees. She broke up on the reef by spring 1925, making salvage all but impossible. The *Glenlyon* was a financial casualty undoubtedly in excess of $150,000. Built in 1893 at West Bay City, she formerly had been the American steel freighter *William H. Gratwick,* and later the *Minnekahta* under both U.S. and Canadian registry.[16]

The final mishap of the year caused grave inconvenience to citizens traveling between Duluth and Superior. On November 21, the 587-foot *Merton E. Farr* of the Zenith Steamship Company slammed into the Interstate Bridge which served railroad, vehicle and pedestrian traffic between the two cities, dropping the span into the water. The ship was only slightly injured, but rebuilding the bridge was a far more expensive story.

1925

This year, the shipping business was good. Total tonnage exceeded the previous year by 10 percent. Yet, ship troubles were fewer with only seven vessels involved. However, one incident was fatal.

The 532-foot *J.J. Turner* ripped her bottom off Michigan Island in an early season stranding on April 23, requiring renovation work of $20,000. The 251-foot package freighter *King* crashed into a pier at Duluth on August 18, a $10,000 shipyard job. In autumn, the 380-foot *Monroe C. Smith* hit an obstruction off Gros Cap, needing slight attention, though on October 31 the 580-foot, 7,215-ton *Charles L. Hutchinson* literally hit double trouble. Striking on one reef three miles south of Manitou Island in the dark, she managed to pull off at daybreak, but disabled both her rudder and propeller. She was then driven northwestward by a wild southerly gale to become impaled on Manitou Island. There, the pounding seas threatened to break her up. Captain James H. Smith radioed for help, and the Eagle Harbor Coast Guard lifeboat soon reached the scene, preparing to evacuate the *Hutchinson*'s 33-man crew. Suddenly, however, the storm abated. The wrecker *Favorite* and tug *Illinois* reached the *Hutchinson* the next day, and she was taken off just a few

days afterward. So perilous was the *Hutchinson*'s predicament in that wild southwester that the steamer *W.C. Franz* and four other ships stood by until the danger had passed. At that, as she was being towed to Superior on November 4, a serious leak developed, and she almost foundered. Owned by the Hutchinson Company and managed by Pioneer Steamship Company, she formerly was the ill-fated *William C. Moreland* which had been rebuilt at Superior as the *Sir Trevor Dawson* in 1916. This episode cost her owners or insurers a tidy $75,000.[17]

The "blue-bird days" which made possible the salvage of the *Hutchinson* ended abruptly. A vicious northerly gale raked the eastern lake on November 5 and 6, with gusts at Whitefish Point estimated at from 50 to 80 mph. Frantically, the radio crackled as the 350-foot, 5,364-ton passenger steamer *Hamonic,* pride of the Northern Navigation Company, reported losing her propeller 20 miles west of Caribou Island and being at the mercy of the seas.

The saga of the *Hamonic* ended happily. The powerful 504-foot steel steamer *G.A. Tomlinson* stood by, while the 580-foot Pittsburgher *Richard Trimble* and tug *Iowa* raced up from the Soo. The *Trimble* got a line on the wallowing passenger vessel and towed her to safety, the salvage and repair costs not disclosed. Meanwhile, the *Tomlinson* herself sustained moderate storm damage.

Somewhat to the south on that miserable evening of November 5, two more humble vessels were having grave difficulties as they slogged ahead of that snow-laden weather monster. Downbound from Pigeon River with pulp wood for Muskegon was the 210-foot wooden steamer *Herman H. Hettler* with the 44-year-old 187-foot wooden barge *J.L. Crane* in tow on a 1,200-foot line. The deck loads of pulp logs were the first to go over the side. Nevertheless, as the evening wore on they were making progress before the 80 mph blasts which seemed to be trying to blow them out of the water. The barge had her sails set to help push them along.

Without warning at 10:30 p.m., when the ships were off Crisp Point, the lights of the *Crane* blacked out; almost immediately the towing post of the *Hettler* tore out, crashing down through a dining room, carrying away part of the main rail and damaging the stern. Vainly attempting to put about to rescue the *Crane*'s crew, the bedraggled *Hettler* was driven eastward, leaking badly. Finally, after signalling for help from the Crisp Point Coast Guard, the *Hettler,* with two feet of water in her fire hold, slipped around Whitefish Point to shelter. Captain Richard Briggs, five men and one woman aboard the *Crane* had gone down with their ship.

During the next two days, miscellaneous wreckage, including the *Crane*'s nameboard, appeared on the beach west of Whitefish Point. Four days after the disappearance, when the lake had calmed sufficiently, Coast Guardsmen probing the area located her hulk in 25 feet of water about one mile off the Crisp Point Station. Her mast had broken, and she had gone down by the head, her bow on the bottom but her stern rail barely visible. Though her owner, O.W. Blodgett of Duluth and Bay City, came to the Soo to personally coordinate the search, none of her people was ever found according to existing records. The *Crane* is another Lake Superior vessel to depart without adequate explanation. Her value was not stated, possibly about $10,000.[18]

On the 6th off Whitefish Point, the 371-foot *Robert J. Paisley* was mauled so badly that it took $25,000 to make her shipshape again. Literally speaking, this was the final blast of the 1925 navigation season.

1926

This was another good shipping year with tonnage showing a slight increase over 1925. Safety was another story. The number of troubled ships more than doubled, and six made their last voyage. The casualties started early. On May 14 the ancient, 46-year-old 18-net-ton wooden Canadian steamer *Beaverton* stranded in Black Bay while on a trip from French River. She was a ruin, an undisclosed property loss which very likely was small in view of her age.[19] Two days later, May 16, about 18 miles off Duluth, a small wooden vessel met her end. The 120-foot, gasoline driven *Firien* under Captain Chester Massey of Superior was undergoing a trial run on a Sunday evening after some rebuilding. Suddenly, she took fire and, with flames fed by the gasoline tank, she soon was a goner. Captain Massey and the three-man crew launched the yawl and were soon picked up by the tug *Edna G* out of Two Harbors under Captain H.F. Brower. The value of the eight-year-old *Firien* was not disclosed.[20] Another May incident saw the 525-foot, 6,617-ton steamer *Harvey D. Goulder* aground at Lakewood near Duluth on May 30. Damage was insignificant.

Summer brought two losses. Another diminutive wooden veteran ended her days on July 28 in Duluth Harbor. The 77-foot, 19-ton ferry steamer *Swansea* owned by Henry W. Reinhold of Duluth caught fire and became a $10,000 total loss. A northeast gale off Whitefish Point on August 28 claimed a much larger wooden victim. The 36-year-old 202-foot, 748-ton steamer *Zillah* was laboring in heavy seas four miles south of Whitefish Point when her cargo of stone shifted, and she slowly capsized. Her predicament was recognized by the Coast Guard lookout at Whitefish Point and by the crews of the steamers *Kenosha* and *William B. Schiller*. The Coast Guard lifeboat assisted the ship's boats to the *Schiller*, as the steamers stood by, and the entire crew was safe when the *Zillah* plunged to the bottom about 12:30 p.m. Owned by O.M. Blodgett of Bay City, she was worth $50,000.[21]

Difficulties persisted. The new steel 456-foot, 6,644-

ton *Charles C. West,* only a year old, plowed into the Gull Rock Reef on September 7 with a bill of $40,000. Four weeks later on October 4, the 380-foot *B. Lyman Smith* whacked the pier at Duluth, needing $15,000 in shipyard attention.

Badly listing to port, the Zillah *plunged to the bottom with a distress flag raised in August 1926.* AUTHOR'S COLLECTION.

A wild gale and snow storm on western Lake Superior on the night of October 31 pulled a mean Halloween trick on Captain Edgar Recor of the 286-foot, 2,329-ton steel *Thomas Maytham*. In blinding snow with only an 800-horsepower engine to resist the vicious northeaster, the *Maytham* was whipped ashore at Knife River. She came to rest broadside to the shore with her bow almost against the old Alger-Smith Railroad dock. Salvors had her off in two days, but she had sustained injuries of more than $50,000 with a lost rudder and shoe and a ravaged propeller together with bottom problems. She was in the shipyard at Superior for most of the following month, only to sail into more grief.[22]

A collision in Superior Harbor on November 13 saw the 586-foot *William H. Warner* coming together with the 478-foot *Isaac L. Ellwood,* with less than $10,000 in repairs needed by the two. A violent blast lasting several days over the central and eastern lake caused more devilment, stripping the 382-foot *P.E. Crowley* of her anchors as she lay in Whitefish Bay and hurling the 253-foot, 2,450-ton steel steamer *Cottonwood* ashore at Coppermine Point on November 15. Under Captain W.E. Smith, the *Cottonwood* was downbound with 2,000 tons of copper ore from Torch Lake on the Keweenaw Waterway to Toledo when a 65 mph gale overwhelmed her. The crew managed to reach shore and live in fishermen's shacks, while Mate D.H. Giddings located a fisherman with a gas launch at Batchawana Bay who took him to the Soo to report the mishap. The tug *Alabama* was sent out to the castaways on November 18. Salvors quickly followed with the wrecker *Favorite,* the lighter *Reliance* and the tug *Iowa*. Extremely violent weather in early December drove the salvors away, and the *Cottonwood*

An 800-horsepower engine was not enough to keep the steamer Thomas Maytham *off the beach at Knife River on Halloween night in 1926.*
Mrs. Allen Newhouse collection, Canal Park Marine Museum.

had to wait until the following year for reclamation. Her salvage and shipyard bill exceeded $100,000, very substantial for a small, eight-year-old steel ship.[23]

Wretched November blows persisted. A close call was registered by the 580-foot, 7,053-ton Pittsburgher *Peter A.B. Widener*. Whipped by high seas over Rock of Ages Reef, Isle Royale, she was stripped of her rudder. The rugged northeaster then drove her pell-mell to the southwest

3,994-ton steel steamer *City of Bangor* under Captain W.J. Mackin en route from Detroit to Duluth with a cargo of 220 automobiles, mostly Chryslers and Whippets. The seas grew too rough, and Captain Mackin turned back off Eagle River and Eagle Harbor intending to go into shelter under Keweenaw Point. But the buffeting was too much for the 30-year-old freighter. Her steam steering gear let go, and some of her deck load of automobiles went over

The steam-barge Zillah *foundered in 1926 when her cargo shifted in a late summer storm.* AUTHOR'S COLLECTION.

more than 100 miles without steerage until she was sighted on November 18 off Duluth and escorted to the safety of the harbor. Repair costs were modest, yet she was mighty fortunate to avoid the rocky shorelines which had beckoned so many others.

Howling winds on November 23 brought the demise of another wooden veteran. In seeking shelter at Grand Island, the 210-foot, 789-ton lumber steamer *Herman H. Hettler* ran aground and broke up, climaxing a 36-year career on the lakes. She formerly had been the *Walter Vail*. Owned by Wenonah Transportation Company of Chicago, she was a recorded $75,000 loss, a value which may have been a bit high for a ship of this age and construction.[24]

End-of-the-month blasts produced double trouble. A terrible gale and snow storm bedeviled the waters off Keweenaw Point on the afternoon and evening of November 30, continuing the following day. Encountering the turbulence just west of Copper Harbor was the 446-foot,

the side before she was pitched ashore a half dozen or so miles east of Copper Harbor, only two miles from Keweenaw Point. Her crew of 29 took the ship's lifeboats to the beach just a stone's throw away where they made themselves as comfortable as possible around bonfires. None of the crew was clothed for the ordeal ahead. However, the heavy snow continued, and the wrecked *City of Bangor* was invisible from the lake side. Hence, on December 1, the *Bangor* crew had to slog the snow-drifted miles through the woods toward Copper Harbor, many of the men suffering seriously from frostbite and exposure.[25]

Meanwhile, the same belligerent lake had caught the already ill-fated 286-foot *Thomas Maytham* off Keweenaw Point, as she sailed eastward with 120,000 bushels of wheat for Toledo. Captain Recor successfully negotiated the Point and put into shelter, but in the snow got in too close to the reefs off Point Isabelle where the *Maytham* went hard aground. Two *Maytham* crewmen took a yawl ashore and contacted fishermen with a gas launch, who took them to a telephone from which they were able to call Captain Anthony F. "Tony" Glaza and the Eagle Harbor Coast Guard. Captain Glaza came down through the snow on December 1 and took the remaining 24 crew-

The wooden steamer Herman H. Hettler *became a total loss in the November gales of 1926.* AUTHOR'S COLLECTION.

men off the *Maytham,* returning them to Eagle Harbor.

As Captain Glaza coasted down the shores of Keweenaw Point that afternoon, he spotted the crew of the *Bangor* walking the beach. His boat was already loaded, so he got in close enough to the beach to let the *Bangor* crew know he would be back for them as soon as possible. Putting the *Maytham* people ashore at Copper Harbor temporarily, Glaza went back and picked up part of the *Bangor* group and then assigned two of his Coast Guardsmen to guide the rest into Copper Harbor. After procuring shelter for the *Bangor* men with the Bergh family and Fred the Swede, a colorful local character, he took the *Maytham* party on to Eagle Harbor. When the Eagle Harbor lifeboat returned to Copper Harbor a couple of days later, a bitter cold wave froze the rescue craft in, and Coast Guardsmen and survivors had to go by sleigh to Calumet.

The *Bangor* proved to be shattered beyond recovery. Salvors, however, waited for the lake to freeze, then in March drove the 202 remaining automobiles through the woods and over the ice field into Copper Harbor where the vehicles waited until the road could be plowed from Copper Harbor to Phoenix and the cars driven to Calumet for rail shipment back to Detroit for reconditioning.

The exact financial liability for the *City of Bangor* incident was not listed. However, she lost 18 automobiles worth close to $15,000 and the ship itself must have been worth $200,000. She was cut down to the waterline two or three years afterwards and the remaining underwater portion removed for scrap during World War II by salvors undertaking similar operations on the *Altadoc* described below. Only a few remnants of the ship and salvage work

remain on the shoreline where she wrecked. She had belonged to the Nicholson Transit Company.[26]

1927

Vessel men were kept busy on Lake Superior during 1927, the tonnage being only slightly less than that of 1926. The number of accidents, however, increased considerably, and several more joined the undersea fleet. An early navigation season brought the usual minor collisions and strandings which persisted into the fall.

The 371-foot steamer *Cletus Schneider* brushed the 350-foot *J.E. Gorman* off Outer Island on April 16 with negligible injury. Ice pummeled the 525-foot *Joseph G. Butler Jr.* on April 19 off Welcome Island, and she needed $10,000 in plate work. A grounding on May 9 at the Huron Islands necessitated $5,000 in bottom repairs for the 201-foot lumber hooker *Charles H. Bradley.* On the same date at Port Arthur, fire claimed the venerable 27-year-old 89-foot, 107-ton steamer *Thomas Maitland,* undoubtedly a low value item. The most serious of early season incidents involved the 416-foot *Samuel H. Squire* on May 28. She struck some underwater obstruction off Manitou Island and required a $35,000 patching job on her bottom.

A harbor collision at Duluth on July 12 caused minor damage to the 587-foot *Merton E. Farr* and the 432-foot *J.J.H. Brown.* Another harbor incident, this time at Port Arthur on July 21, saw the 183-foot steel steamer *America* crush and sink the 51-foot, 37-ton *Violet G.* at the Booth dock. This was the end of the *Violet G.,* a several thousand-dollar casualty. Fire on August 31 destroyed the ancient 53-year-old steamer *E.D. Holton* near Houghton, a reported $18,000 loss. An early gale on September 7 drove the 381-foot package freighter *Ralph Budd* of the Great Lakes Transit line on the Pine River Reef, but salvors soon had her off with a $35,000 bill. More wild weather on September 18 tossed the 504-foot *Joseph Wood* about on the eastern lake resulting in $13,000 in storm damage.

The worst was to come. A storm on October 13 sank the 297-foot, 1,615-ton steel Canadian barge *Ontario* off Outer Island. Owned by the Newago Tug Line, she was hauling 1,100 tons of pulp from Thunder Bay to Ashland. The tug *Butterfield* also had another smaller barge in tow at the time, the *Michigan.* The *Ontario*'s crew of four escaped. Wreckage appearing at Fourteen Mile Point near Ontonagon in late October touched off speculation as to what sinking had occurred, since the foundering apparently had not been immediately reported. A few days later, however, the tug *Butterfield* disclosed the loss at Port Arthur. The value of the 37-year-old barge was not listed, but she must have been worth in excess of $25,000. The pulp alone was valued at $30,000.[27]

An especially massive blow over the eastern lake on November 12 shook up two of the newest steel carriers badly. The three-year-old 597-foot motor ship *Benson Ford,* a powerful, 3,300-horsepower ship, incurred $20,000 in

November 1926 closed with the stranding and loss of the City of Bangor, *although most of her cargo of automobiles was recovered.* AUTHOR'S COLLECTION.

shipyard costs, and the brand new 586-foot *George M. Humphrey* needed $30,000 to heal her wounds.

Vessel traffic ran late this year, exposing the carriers to what was probably the worst December gale, snow storm and cold wave in the history of Lake Superior sailing. A brush collision on December 2 off Point Iroquois caused little grief to the 444-foot *S.H. Robbins* and the 580-foot *Daniel J. Morrell.*

The tempest of December 7, 8 and 9 was something else, claiming five ships in three days, one with heavy loss of life. The entire lake was raked. Heavy snow on December 7 was accompanied by winds of 70 mph at Duluth and temperatures which plummeted to 19 degrees below zero. The ghastly weather mass moved east. Upbound light for Fort William on December 8, the 376-foot, 3,666-ton steamer *E.W. Oglebay* under Captain Hays was forced to seek shelter at Marquette. Her 1,285-horsepower engine proved insufficient, and the vessel was driven into shoal water at Shot Point, only 10 miles short of safety. Shore dwellers spotted her and notified the Coast Guard at Marquette. After a battle with shore ice, Captain T.E. Deegan brought the Coast Guard motor lifeboat alongside the beleaguered *Oglebay* and transferred her crew to the waiting tug *Columbia.* The battered *Oglebay* then caught fire and suffered additional injury. She initially was abandoned as a complete ruin, a casualty of $250,000, but, a year and a half later, salvors took her off.[28]

In those same fateful hours far to the north, two other ships were in a desperate way. The 365-foot, 3,815-ton

Canadian steamer *Altadoc* under Captain R.D. Simpson also was headed for the Canadian Lakehead when the blizzard intercepted her on the night of December 7. After hours of pounding, her rudder let go, and the howling gusts drove her southward toward Keweenaw Point. Happily, she carried a radio, and Captain Simpson sounded an SOS which was received by the American Coast Guard at Two Harbors. The Coast Guard Cutter *Crawford* got under way at once, though she was many hours distant. Meanwhile, the unfortunate *Altadoc* was pushed clear across the lake, until about 7 a.m. on the morning of December 8 when she slid high up into the shallows of Keweenaw Point east of Copper Harbor, only a stone's throw from the hulk of the *City of Bangor.*

As his antenna had been carried away after he sent the SOS, Captain Simpson was not sure his distress signal had been received. Hence, he quickly dispatched Engineer Roy Hardman and three crewmen to the nearby shore with instructions to hike to Copper Harbor and report their predicament. Hardman and his lifeboat crew reached the beach through the rollers and then had the miserable walk of more than a half dozen miles through the woods in sloshing snow to Copper Harbor. They accomplished their mission and then were carried to the hospital at Calumet by sleigh.

With the wreck of the *Altadoc* now pinpointed, the Coast Guard Cutter *Crawford* reached her and stood by, as did the steel freighter *F.B. Squire.* Shallow water prevented both from a close approach. When the seas moderated a bit, Captain C.T. Christenson of the *Crawford* decided to backtrack to Eagle Harbor, breaking ice for Captain Tony Glaza's lifeboat which had been frozen in. They then returned to the *Altadoc,* and the Eagle Harbor lifeboat transferred the remaining 21 of the *Altadoc*'s crew to the *Crawford* which landed them at the Coast Guard Station at Eagle Harbor. All were safe, but the *Altadoc* had suffered so severely that her sailing days were over. She likely was a liability of more than $250,000 to her Canadian owners, Paterson Steamship Company.

A year or two after the wreck, salvors cut her down to the waterline, leaving the underwater portion for final scrapping when prices skyrocketed during World War II. Copper Harbor resident Charlie Maki convinced the early salvors that he would buy the pilothouses off both the *City of Bangor* and *Altadoc.* However, when they cut away the *Bangor* pilothouse, they cut too much of the deck along with it. It was too heavy and crashed to the deck of the salvage scow, shattering. Learning from this experience, the salvors successfully lifted the *Altadoc* pilothouse off intact, delivering it to Copper Harbor. The old pilothouse served in various capacities over the years ranging from a storage shed to tourist rooms to a gift shop, before succumbing to fire in spring 1987.[29]

More unfortunate was the three-year-old 250-foot, 2,402-ton steel package freighter *Kamloops* of Canada

Steamship Lines. Upbound toward the Canadian Lakehead with a mixed general cargo, which included thousands of pairs of new shoes, imported paper-making machinery, building supplies and imported teas and candies, she had battered her torturous way across eastern Lake Superior following the Canadian steamers *Quedoc* and *Winnipeg*. She was still in sight of the *Winnipeg* on December 6 when a snow squall cut visibility. The *Quedoc* reached her Canadian Lakehead destination directly, loaded and was quickly downbound, while the *Winnipeg* was forced to shelter on the Canadian north shore. The *Kamloops* failed to arrive.

The *Kamloops* had carried no radio. Although radio was available, it was not required on lake freighters as it was on the passenger vessels then operating. Thus it was not uncommon for vessels to be out of contact and several days overdue in their end-of-season runs. Hence, an intensive search was not immediately undertaken. The search did not actually begin until the *Kamloops* and her crew were at least a week overdue.

The search undertaken began with her last reported position, just east of Isle Royale. The Isle Royale area was patrolled by tugs as were the Canadian shorelines to the northeast and southwest. The U.S. Coast Guard was alerted and Coast Guardsmen swept the Keweenaw Point and Manitou Island areas. After 10 days of fruitless hunting, most conceded on Christmas Day that the *Kamloops* was lost with Captain Bill Brian and his crew of 19. For five months, nothing new was heard or seen of the missing vessel. Then, when fisherman David Lind went out to retrieve his nets about May 26 off Twelve O'Clock Point midway down the northwest coast of Isle Royale, he discovered two bodies wearing *Kamloops* life jackets. The cutter *Crawford* was immediately dispatched and Captain Christenson retrieved the crewmen, carrying them to the Canadian Lakehead. As the shore ice melted, a large field of wreckage was discovered in a remote bay between Green and Hawk islands in Todd Harbor. Recovered life rings were marked *Kamloops*. As searchers worked the beach and nearby forest areas, they discovered a battered lifeboat, scattered remnants of cargo, wooden hatch covers and personal belongings of several crewmen, including the trunk of Captain Brian. Nearby were bodies of several more *Kamloops* sailors.

It appears that one lifeboat was launched under command of the first mate and may have successfully approached shore, although it probably capsized in the surf just off the icy beach. Most of the occupants drowned, while at least two died of exposure in the wild winds and sub-zero temperatures, the first mate and Assistant Steward Alice Bettridge. The mate's body was found from 300 to 400 feet on shore amidst a crude attempt to build a shelter, while Miss Bettridge's body was recovered on the shore.

Marine men speculated that the *Kamloops* may have struck a reef as she rounded the north side of Isle Royale,

then was propelled southwestward by the gale until she grounded on some reef or island off Twelve O'Clock Point, ultimately to slip off into deep water. Her presumed point of foundering was a good 20 miles south of the vessel lanes. It is regrettable that she carried no radio, as help might have been summoned in those hours when she was drifting to destruction. All 20 aboard died, and the new package freighter likely was a property loss of $200,000.

The *Kamloops* remained a missing vessel until located by a small group of sport divers from the Minneapolis-St. Paul area in August 1977 making a deliberate search for the vessel. The wreck was discovered off Kamloops Point, just to the east of Twelve O'Clock Point, after both hard hat and scuba divers had hunted for nearly 50 years. The wreck is deep at 170 feet to more than 250 feet, hard over on her starboard side, with the stern being the shallowest and closest to shore, surrounded by a field of spilled cargo. Exploration in the engine room revealed the remains of one or more crewmen, but more importantly, disclosed that the engine telegraph had been rung up and answered with "Finished with Engines." This, coupled with the facts that the smokestack is missing or at least not immediately nearby the wreck and that the *Kamloops* was known to have carried a substantial deck cargo, has given rise to another theory on her demise. It is possible that the *Kamloops* was heavily iced-up, perhaps listing, as she rounded Isle Royale and began her approach into Thunder Bay. Somewhere off the Sibley Peninsula, she may have rolled her stack off as guy wires parted and the ship became powerless before the prevailing storm. She could have been driven south until the sound of the surf crashing on the Isle Royale shore could be heard and the lifeboat launched. The remaining crew, about half the complement, remained with Captain Brian aboard their stricken vessel in a vain attempt to keep her off the beach. Undoubtedly, more will be learned about this wreck and the condition of the hull as underwater video and remote sensing techniques become more affordable to the sport diving community. An attempt to survey the wreck using the submersible *Johnson Sea Link II* was aborted in 1986 when film showed too much debris and rigging to risk entangling the submersible. A partial hull survey was done by the National Park Service in cooperation with *National Geographic* Magazine, but the video showed little beyond what was already known. Little significant hull damage was recorded. The ship's hull, rudder and propeller are intact and apparently undamaged.[30]

Still, the December 1927 storm gods were not through, claiming two more Canadian vessels at widely separated points. To the west of Thunder Cape at Hare Island, the 349-foot, 3,396-ton *Martian* was stranded hard, a scant 15 miles from Port Arthur, though her value was not cited. Apparently, all escaped.[31]

Far to the southeast in Whitefish Bay, the 252-foot, 1,866-ton *Lambton,* only six years old, was slammed ashore. Captain Andrew Livingstone and his crew took a boat to shore and sought refuge in the forest, although two men were reported lost in the operation. Meanwhile, passing ships sighted the derelict and notified the U.S.

The canaller Kamloops *foundered off Isle Royale's north shore in December 1927.* CANAL PARK MARINE MUSEUM COLLECTION.

Coast Guard. Two tugs picked up the Coast Guard crew at Whitefish Point and transported them to the wreck site on Parisienne Island. Yet, when the U.S. Coast Guard lifeboat approached the *Lambton,* they discovered her abandoned. Checking the nearby beach, the Coast Guardsmen discovered the tracks of the survivors leading into the woods. Salvors went to work on the *Lambton* the next year, though she was so badly mauled that her engines were pulled out of her after she was taken off, and she spent her last days as a barge. She belonged to the Mathews Line, a loss of $150,000.[32]

1928

While the 1928 shipping season witnessed another tonnage boom, the number of troubled ships declined sharply. Two old-timers were lost, but most other accidents were trivial.

A Whitefish Point collision on May 8 caused only insignificant damage to the 504-foot *Charles S. Hebard* which brushed the Canadian *Lavaldoc.* Rough weather on May 21, however, sank the 35-year-old 199-foot, 712-ton wooden barge *Mingoe* at the Huron Islands. Built in 1893 at Marine City, Michigan, she belonged to the Mingoe Transportation Company of Michigan City, Indiana. Her value was not stated, but she probably was worth $10,000.[33]

The lake claimed another veteran early on the morning of June 7. The 183-foot, 937-ton steel coastal steamer *America* of the Booth Fisheries' U.S. & Dominion Transportation Company had been a familiar sight for years along the Minnesota north shore, providing passenger, mail and freight service from Duluth to Port Arthur and Fort William, now Thunder Bay, before development of the current highway system. Shortly after leaving the Washington Club dock at the head of Washington Harbor, Isle Royale, about 3 a.m., with Mate John Wick conning the ship, the *America* struck a rock pinnacle and began to take water. Mate Wick tried to run her ashore on a nearby gravel beach, but she hooked a rocky ledge and slid down gradually over the next 90 minutes into deep water. Good discipline prevailed. The 30-man crew and 15 passengers, including six women, launched five lifeboats and easily made Washington Island just a short distance away. The only casualty was a dog that had been tethered in the stern.

Perhaps no other shipwreck on Lake Superior so personally touched the people populating western Lake Superior as did this one. The Fort William *Daily Times Journal* carried a most fitting epitaph:

The unfortunate loss of the steamer America *has, for a time at least, removed from the run between Fort William and Duluth, a boat that has served the public at the head of the lakes in good stead for over a quarter of a century.*

While connection with Duluth had been maintained by the passenger boats of the Canada Steamship Line, originally the Northern Navigation Company, it was the America *which did the local, routine work along the north shore, poking her nose into every little harbor on the coast line and keeping communication between the mainland and Isle Royale uninterrupted. While the* Hamonic *was sailing majestically from point to point, the* America *was serving all the places en route. She was like the local train which unloads its freight at every unimportant siding, past which the stately express train glides as if it never existed.*

The *America* had been launched in 1898 at Wyandotte, Michigan, being worth more than $100,000. Despite the fact that she lay in less that 100 feet of water, she was never salvaged, the recent completion of the north shore highway having made her economic future rather questionable. Indeed, there were dark rumors circulated that the sinking was no accident. However, a lengthy federal investigation exonerated her officers and owners, although First Mate Wick, on his first assignment to the *America* and unfamiliar with the local waters, had chosen a course too close to shore in the moonlit darkness and was censured for careless navigation. After World War II, the hull of the *America* became a mecca for sport divers, and one group unsuccessfully tried to raise her.[34]

The remainder of the season brought little unusual. A stranding in thick weather at Parisienne Island on July 24 brought $30,000 in shipyard charges for the 251-foot,

The swift steamer America *was needed to keep a tight schedule on a regular tri-weekly run from Duluth to the Canadian Lakehead and Isle Royale.* COURTESY OF BLAMEY'S STUDIO, DULUTH.

2,309-ton steel steamer *Kiowa.* A brush collision during poor visibility in Whitefish Bay on August 23 brought a $7,000 repair bill to the 418-foot, 4,471-ton *G.J. Grammer* with little injury to the Canadian steamer *Westmount.*

The America *stranded and sank in relatively shallow water in June 1928, but salvage proved elusive for Captain Cornelius O. Flynn of Duluth.* AUTHOR'S COLLECTION.

The 346-foot, 3,582-ton *John Anderson,* formerly the *Luzon,* banged a pier at Duluth on August 28, an $18,000 item. The little nine-ton motor craft *Alice L.* foundered at Grand Portal in the Pictured Rocks on August 30. The 244-foot steamer *Brockton* needed minor bottom work after October 15 when she struck some obstruction off Devils Island. The 380-foot steel steamer *C.W. Watson* also needed some touching up after hitting high seas on November 6 in the eastern lake. After the regular season ended, the Canadians lost the 27-net-ton tug *Anne Ruth* at Pringle Bay, Edward Island, on December 9, a small loss. Indeed, aside from the loss of two veteran ships, this was a rather tame navigation season.

1929

This was the boom year. Until World War II and the shipping season of 1941, the 92,622,017 tons hauled on Lake Superior in 1929 was the all-time record. The total ships in difficulty increased somewhat over 1928. Actually, several widely spaced storm periods brought the end of one major vessel and rather serious damage to a number of others.

Trouble came early. The 580-foot, 7,518-ton *Thomas Walters* grounded in Superior Harbor on April 25 and needed some shipyard attention to the extent of $7,000. Then a wild mid-May gale over the central lake drew double blood from the Great Lakes Transit Corporation of Buffalo. Caught in the snow-laden tempest were the 381-foot, 4,671-ton *Ralph Budd* and the 350-foot, 4,053-ton *J.E. Gorman.* Under Captain Dugald McLeod of Buffalo, the *Budd* had cleared Duluth late on the night of May 14, heading eastward with a mixed cargo of grain, flour and refrigerated goods said to be worth more than a million dollars. She was overwhelmed by the weather monster off Keweenaw Point and hurled aground near Eagle Harbor about 10:30 p.m., May 15. Her 31-man crew was safely removed by Eagle Harbor Coast Guard, but the ship was badly battered. Canadian salvor Tom Reid eventually took her off. While no loss figure is available, this probably was an insurance item exceeding $500,000, including salvage and rebuilding charges together with cargo lost or damaged. Because she carried tons of butter which floated away from the wreck along with wood shingles, chicken, bran and flour onto the nearby beaches, the *Budd* wreck was known locally, and is still recalled by some along the Keweenaw, as the "butter boat wreck." Needless to say, there were many area sheds sporting new roofs that summer.

The *J.E. Gorman* was en route to Duluth with a cargo of automobiles, suffering her anguish in the very same hours. Though a respectable 1,800-horsepower steamer, she was pummeled so harshly that she lost both wheel and rudder and was driven far south of the vessel lanes to be pitched on the rocks at Rock River east of Marquette. Captain W.B. Holmes and the crew were safe, and the Marquette Coast Guard lifeboat under Captain T.E. Deegan soon arrived. The tug *General* pulled her off four days later, and she was towed to Superior for repairs which ran in excess of $125,000.[35]

Thereafter, sailing was routine for several months. A stranding near Duluth on June 16 saw the 266-foot steamer *Griffin* needing some bottom plates replaced, a $16,000 bill. In the mists of July 5, the 381-foot *Alfred H. Smith* banged the 387-foot *George W. Mead* on the open lake, the *Mead* requiring a $15,000 touch up. A harbor plate-bender on July 13 at Duluth was cause for negligible repairs to the 525-foot *Louis W. Hill* and the 396-foot *W.D. Rees.* The 356-foot steamer *Colonel* whacked bottom near Marquette on July 23, needing minor attention. Fog off the north shore on September 10 caused the 406-foot *Maricopa* to be hung up in shoal water, there to be smacked by her barge. It took $15,000 to make her whole again. A typical equinoctial blow on the eastern lake tossed the 266-foot *Griffin* around rather badly, necessitating more than $14,000 in yard work after this encounter with the seas on September 17.

Then a truly wild westerly gale took over on October 22-23. Outbound from Marquette on October 22 in tow of the 142-foot steel tug *Barrallton* was the 251-foot steel lumber barge *Lake Frugality,* a converted steamer. The towline broke and the *Lake Frugality* was whipped ashore four miles west of Au Sable Point. Her crew reached shore safely. She was salvaged without too great difficulty, though undoubtedly at some cost. Both tug and barge were owned by the Ford Motor Company.[36] The rampaging seas also mauled the 2,000-horsepower, 504-foot *James E. Davidson* on October 22, leaving a $35,000 shipyard journey in prospect, one of the highest recorded for storm damage. The 558-foot Pittsburgher *William E. Corey* took a $3,500 battering on the same day.

The worst sufferer on that fateful day was the Great Lakes Transit Corporation's 324-foot, 3,195-ton *Chicago*. Downbound from Duluth under veteran Captain P.C. Farrell, the *Chicago* was engulfed by blinding snow with 50 mph winds and gigantic waves on October 22. Captain Farrell had intended to put into the Portage Lake Ship Canal, but the raging seas prevented an approach to that pierhead. Then the storm gods took over. Obscured in the whiteout and tossed by combers reportedly 30 feet high, the *Chicago* was given an out-of-control ride of more than 150 miles to the east before being deposited on a reef southwest of Michipicoten Island. With his compass completely awry and visibility zero, Captain Farrell was befuddled. He thought he had struck on Parisienne Island although he was actually aground nearly 100 miles to the northwest. Wisely, the captain held his crew aboard through the night. Finally, when the *Chicago* showed signs of sliding off and listing, Captain Farrell ordered two lifeboats launched and all 32 crew members placed therein. Both successfully negotiated the quarter mile of surf to Michipicoten Island. Figuring that rescue might not be immediate, the captain also ordered bedding and food supplies evacuated from the beleaguered ship. They were prepared for an extended camp-out.

While the *Chicago* had been abandoned in midmorning of October 23, it was not until the following day that a crew member was able to climb a peak and signal to the passing Canadian steamer *Goderich*. The *Goderich* came in for a look, but could not get close enough to effect rescue in the wild water. The Canadian tugs *James Whalen* and *Strathbogie* were towing the salvaged *Ralph Budd* when they put in for shelter at Quebec Harbor, Michipicoten Island. When notified of the *Chicago*'s plight, the *Whalen* and *Strathbogie* also went out for a look, but could not make a rescue in the high seas, either. They did, however, notify the U.S. Coast Guard at Sault Ste. Marie, and the Coast Guard cutters *Seminole* and *119* were dispatched. By October 25, eight of the younger crewmen had hiked 10 miles through the forest to Quebec Harbor where they were taken aboard cutter *119*. Lifeboats from the two cutters then proceeded to maneuver through the shoals and took off the remaining 24 at their camp. All personnel were safe, perhaps not too much the worse for their outdoor experience, but the 28-year-old *Chicago* was reported a total loss of $167,500.

Because of its remoteness, the *Chicago* wreck is not as visited as many other Lake Superior shipwrecks, but provides sport divers a rather spectacular steel-hulled wreck dive in relatively shallow water. The *Chicago* rests hard over on her port side in about 55 feet of water with excellent visibility. One of her boilers has fallen out of the hull and her huge quadruple expansion steam engine is fully exposed. What cargo remains is also spilled out of the wreck including zinc ingots clearly stamped "Anaconda Brass Special," along with fence posts and other package freight. Her large rudder and propeller are intact and still shipped. The bow section has the most severe damage from the elements while her hull is generally intact aft of amidships.

Only a mile away is the wreck of the *Strathmore*, lost November 14, 1906. Her twin, one-cylinder engines with shafts and propellers may be one of the only examples of this propulsion system among located and identified Lake Superior shipwrecks.[37]

The lake struck once more this decade. A slashing two-day blizzard with fierce winds and unusually heavy snow hit the central and eastern lake on November 30, downing wire communications and blocking highways along the Michigan south shore. Trapped in the blasts just east of Keweenaw was the 251-foot, 2,309-ton steamer *Kiowa* under Captain Alex T. Young en route from Duluth to Chicago with a cargo of flax. Her 1,300-horsepower engine was no match for the tempest, and she was driven far south of the vessel lane. Her cargo shifted, and she listed badly. Finally, the driving norther cast her up on the Michigan coast at Twelve Mile Beach, five miles west of the Au Sable Lighthouse in 30 feet of water. Apparently, the *Kiowa*'s plight was not observed by the lighthouse keepers that night or the next morning because of the snow veil, or perhaps downed telephone lines prevented a call to the Coast Guard at Grand Marais. At any rate, when help did not arrive the following morning, Captain Young ordered a ship's lifeboat launched, but this quickly capsized and the captain drowned together with four of his crew. Another crewman seemingly crawled back into the lifeboat, only to die of exposure. During the day, some report did reach the Grand Marais Coast Guard Station, and Captain H.G. Fisher ordered the lifeboat out. Proceeding to the west in late afternoon, the Coast Guardsmen discovered the body of the dead crewman in the *Kiowa* lifeboat and, pushing onward, they sighted the wreck. Meanwhile, the keepers at Au Sable Lighthouse were notified, and when the Coast Guard did not appear by afternoon, the keeper ordered the lighthouse power boat and a hunter's gas boat to take off the *Kiowa* survivors. After the captain's death, First Mate Arthur Kronk had held the remaining 18 men aboard, and these were safely taken ashore to the lighthouse, later to be picked up by the Coast Guard. Two of the crew had to be hospitalized at Munising. While the financial record was not given, the *Kiowa* undoubtedly was a property loss, with cargo, in excess of $200,000.[38]

1 *Duluth News-Tribune,* Aug. 22-24, 26, 1920; Homer Wells, *History of Accidents, Casualties and Wrecks on Lake Superior,* (Duluth, Minn., U.S. Army Corps of Engineers, 1938), p. 66.

2 *Duluth News-Tribune,* Nov. 9, 12, 14-16, 19-20, 1920; Wells, *op. cit.,* p. 67.

3 *Duluth News-Tribune,* Nov. 23, 1920; Wells, *op. cit.,* p. 67.

4 *Duluth News-Tribune,* May 15-16, 18, 21, 24, June 13, 17, 1921; *Marquette Mining Journal,* May 16-17, 1921.

5 Clarence J. Monette, *The Keweenaw Waterway* (Lake Linden, Michigan, by Author, September 15, 1980), p. 59; Dominion of Canada, Department of Transport, *Casualties to Vessels Resulting in Total Loss on the Great Lakes, 1870-1957,* p. 58. The *Arbutus* accident is described in an undated clipping in Corps of Engineers scrapbook, files of St. Louis County Historical Society.

6 *Duluth News-Tribune,* May 1, 1922.

7 *Duluth Herald,* May 18-19, 1922; *Duluth News-Tribune,* May 4, 8, 13, 1922; Skip Gillham, "Yesterday's Fleet: *Renfrew"* in *CSL — The World,* December 1987; Wells, *op. cit.,* p. 68.

8 *Duluth Herald,* Sept. 13, 1922.

9 *Duluth News-Tribune,* Dec. 2, 10, 1922; Wells, *op. cit.,* p. 67A.

10 *Duluth News-Tribune,* Dec. 18-20, 1922.

11 *Duluth News-Tribune,* Oct. 12-13, 1923; Wells, *op. cit.,* p. 70.

12 *Duluth News-Tribune,* Oct. 21-22, 24, 1923; Wells, *op. cit.,* p. 71.

13 *Duluth News-Tribune,* Jan. 15, 1964; *Duluth Evening Herald,* Jan. 7, 1924; LaMonte Florentz, "Nobody Got So Much as a Cold" in *The Nor'Easter,* Vol. 3, No. 5, September-October 1978, pp. 3-6; Wells, *op. cit.,* p. 71.

14 *Duluth News-Tribune,* May 18-20, 28, 1924; Wells, *op. cit.,* p. 72.

15 *Duluth News-Tribune,* May 21-22, 1924; Wells, *op. cit.,* p. 72; Ronald Wrigley, *Shipwrecked: Vessels That Met Tragedy on Northern Lake Superior,* (Cobalt, Ontario, Highway Book Shop, 1985), p. 132.

16 *Duluth News-Tribune,* Nov. 3, 1924; Thom Holden, *Above and Below* (Houghton, Michigan, Isle Royale Natural History Association, 1985), pp. 25-27; Thomas Robert Holden, "Park Interpretation as an Environmental Communication Process with a Sample Interpretive Booklet Text on the Maritime Disaster History of Siskiwit Bay, Isle Royale, Lake Superior," (Madison, Wisconsin, University of Wisconsin, 1974), unpublished master's thesis, pp. 81, 134-138; Larry Murphy and Thom Holden, "Shipwrecks of Isle Royale: The Historical Record" in *Submerged Cultural Resources Study: Isle Royale National Park,* Daniel J. Lenihan, ed., (Santa Fe, New Mexico, Submerged Cultural Resources Unit, National Park Service, 1987), pp. 119-126; Larry Murphy, Daniel Lenihan and C. Patrick Labadie, "Shipwrecks of Isle Royale: The Archeological Record" in Lenihan, ed., *ibid.,* pp. 276-284; Wrigley, *Shipwrecked, op. cit.,* pp. 57-61.

17 *Duluth News-Tribune,* Nov. 1-2, 5-6, 1925; Wells, *op. cit.,* p. 73.

18 *Duluth News-Tribune,* Nov. 7-8, 10, 22, 1925; Wells, *op. cit.,* p. 73.

19 Dominion of Canada, Department of Transport, *op. cit.,* p. 61.

20 *Duluth News-Tribune,* May 17, 1926.

21 *Duluth News-Tribune,* Aug. 30, 1926; *Marquette Mining Journal,* Aug. 30, 1926; Wells, *op. cit.,* p. 74

22 *Duluth News-Tribune,* Nov. 1-3, 1926; Wells, *op. cit.,* p. 74.

23 *Duluth News-Tribune,* Nov. 20, Dec. 1-2, 1926; Wells, *op. cit.,* p. 74.

24 *Duluth News-Tribune,* Nov. 29, 1926; Wells, *op. cit.,* p. 75.

25 Howard Bergh, personal interview at Copper Harbor, Michigan, December 9, 1987, recorded by Thom Holden.

26 *Duluth News-Tribune,* Dec. 3, 5, 1926; Wells, *op. cit.,* p. 75. Mac Frimodig presents a fine description of the *City of Bangor* accident in *Shipwrecks Off Keweenaw,* (Lansing, Michigan, Fort Wilkins Natural History Association and Michigan Department of Natural Resources, 1974), pp. 36-39.

27 *Bayfield County Press,* Nov. 3, 10, 1927; *Duluth Herald,* Oct. 13, 1927; *Duluth News-Tribune,* Oct. 13, Nov. 1, 2, 5, 1927; Dominion of Canada, Department of Transport, *op. cit.,* p. 63; Thom Holden, *Apostle Islands Shipwreck Survey List, 1870-1940,* (Bayfield, Wisconsin, Apostle Islands National Lakeshore, National Park Service, 1985). pp. 74-76; James M. Keller, *The "Unholy" Apostles: Tales of Chequamegon Shipwrecks,* (Bayfield, Wisconsin, Apostle Islands Press, 1985), pp. 125-128.

28 *Duluth News-Tribune* Dec. 10-12, 1927; Wells, *op. cit.,* p. 76; an excellent account of the *Oglebay* stranding is given by Frederick Stonehouse in *Marquette Shipwrecks,* (Marquette, Michigan, Harboridge Press, 1974), pp. 84-87.

29 *Duluth News-Tribune,* Dec. 7-12, 14, 1927; Howard Bergh, *op. cit.; Wells, op. cit.,* p. 76.

30 *Duluth News-Tribune,* Dec. 14-18, 24, 1927, May 27-29, 31, June 4, 1928; *Houghton Daily Mining Gazette,* Aug. 15, 1979; "Lake Fails to Hide Long Lost Wreck" in *Milwaukee Journal,* March 26, 1978; "For and About Divers: Discovery of the *Kamloops"* in *The Nor'Easter,* Vol. 2, No. 5, September-October 1977, p. 5; Blair Charnley, *"Kamloops"* Icy Grave Discovered, But Its Sinking Remains a Mystery" in *Minneapolis Star,* Oct. 13, 1977; Ken Engelbrecht and Thom Holden, "Divers Find Freighter Missing Almost 50 Years" in *Sault Ste. Marie (Michigan) Evening News,* Oct. 17, 1977; Skip Gillham, "Yesterday's Fleet: *Kamloops"* in *CSL — The World,* December 1977; Ken Hafner and Thom Holden, *"Kamloops:* Ghost Wreck of Isle Royale" in *Sport Diver Magazine,* Vol. 2, Fourth Quarter 1978, pp. 112-117; Holden, *Above and Below, op. cit.,* pp. 28-32; Murphy and Holden, *op. cit.,* pp. 187-209; Murphy, Lenihan and Labadie, *op. cit.,* pp. 326-333; Gene Onchulenko, *"Kamloops* Brings Back Memories" in *Thunder Bay Lakehead Living,* Dec. 9, 1987, and "Men Saved from Terrible Fate" in *Thunder Bay Lakehead Living,* Dec. 16, 1987; Katie Schuette, *"Kamloops* Goes Missing No Longer" in *Anchor News,* May-June 1979, p. 41; Ron Vilim, *"Kamloops* (1924-1927): Discovery of a Lake Superior Shipwreck" in Thunder Bay Scuba Club's *Sea Pen,* May 1979; Wrigley, *Shipwrecked, op. cit.,* pp. 63-77.

[31] *Duluth News-Tribune,* Dec. 11, 1927; Dominion of Canada, Department of Transport, *op. cit.,* p. 64.

[32] *Duluth News-Tribune,* Dec. 11-12, 16, 1927; Dominion of Canada, Department of Transport, *op. cit.,* p. 64.

[33] Department of Commerce, Bureau of Navigation, *Merchant Vessels of the United States,* 1929, p. 914.

[34] *Canadian Railway and Shipping World,* March 1902; *Detroit Free Press,* May 22, June 18, 1898; *Duluth News-Tribune,* June 8, 13, 1928, May 24, 1929, May 12, 1966; *Houghton Daily Mining Gazette,* Aug. 23, 1976; *Skilling's Mining Review,* June 16, July 14, 1928; Elmer Engman, "A Shallow Grave for the *America*" in *Nordic Diver,* Vol. 1, No. 2, July-August 1974, pp. 1-5; Holden, *Above and Below, op. cit.,* pp. 49-57; Thom Holden, "Above and Below: Steamer *America*" in *The Nor'Easter,* Vol. 3, No. 3, May-June 1977, pp. 1-4 and Vol. 3, No. 4, July-August 1978, pp. 1-5; Thom Holden, "Steamer *America* Wrecked 50 Years Ago: Still Popular, Above or Below" in Superior *Evening Telegram,* June 8, 1978; Thomas Holden, "The *America*" in James R. Marshall, ed. *Shipwrecks of Lake Superior* (Duluth, Minnesota, Lake Superior Port Cities Inc., 1987), pp. 66-71; James R. Marshall, "Salvage of the *America*" in Marshall, ed. *ibid;* Murphy and Holden, *op. cit.,* pp. 127-152; Murphy, Lenihan and Labadie, *op. ct.,* pp. 285-294; Tom Smrekar, "It's Cold, Eerie Down There at 85 Feet, *America* Awaits Salvaging" in *Duluth News-Tribune,* Oct. 17, 1965; *Wells, op. cit.,* p. 77; Wrigley, *Shipwrecked, op. cit.,* pp. 79-82. The Engman article cited above contained the first good illustrations of how the *America* rests on the bottom and the damage done to the vessel by the elements in the decades after she foundered.

[35] *Duluth News-Tribune,* May 17-20, 22-23, 1929; Howard Bergh, *op. cit.;* Wells, *op. cit.,* p. 79.

[36] *Duluth News-Tribune,* Oct. 22-24, 1929; Wells, *op. cit.,* p. 79.

[37] *Duluth News-Tribune,* Oct. 25-28, 1929; Ryan Leblanc, Schreiber, Ontario, personal interview recorded August 31, 1988, by Thom Holden; Wells, *op. cit.,* p. 80; Wrigley, *Shipwrecked, op. cit.,* pp. 133-134.

[38] *Duluth News-Tribune,* Dec. 2-5, 1929; Wells, *op. cit.,* p. 80. *Duluth Evening Herald,* Dec. 2, 1929; transcription of *Log of Au Sable Lighthouse, Dec. 1, 1929,* in files of Bernard J. Gestel, National Park Service, Grand Marais, Minnesota.

The wrecked George M. Cox *remained on a reef long enough for partial salvage of her contents during summer 1933.* AUTHOR'S COLLECTION.

Chapter 8

The Post Depression Era
1930-1959

The Great Depression, ushered in with the stock market crash of October 1929, brought repercussions to the shipping industry on the lake. Tonnage for the decade of the 1930s, at 535 million tons, was nearly one-third less than that of the previous decade. With the exception of 1937, most shipping seasons were poor and several were catastrophic. For instance, tonnage at Duluth-Superior Harbor for 1930 was 25 percent below the figure for 1929, while the record for 1931 was 40 percent down from that for 1930. Tonnage in 1932 was only one-sixth the 1929 total. It took the events of World War II to rebuild the lake's transportation business.[1]

Fewer than two dozen major vessels, together with a handful of fish tugs and recreational craft, have succumbed to all causes since the close of the 1920s. Only a few large ships have sunk in the last six decades. There were a few close calls with substantial financial losses and at least three instances where damage was sufficient to declare the vessels involved to be constructive total losses, that is, too expensive to repair.

1930

The accident pattern changed drastically. To be sure, a great many ships were laid up, especially the smaller, older, less efficient ones, those which might be more accident prone. Naturally, commands were far fewer. It is possible that with fewer ships sailing and commands harder to achieve and retain, only the more careful, competent navigators received commands. At any rate the number of accidents plummeted; shipwrecks became a rarity.

The onset of the Great Depression resulted in a 21 percent drop in tonnage passing through the Canadian and American Soo Locks to 72.8 million tons. Only a handful of ships were troubled in 1930 and most cases were relatively insignificant plate-bender items. There were exceptions, of course. Cleveland Cliffs' 590-foot, 8,158-ton *Frontenac* and Canada Steamship Lines' canaller *Weyburn* came together in Whitefish Bay with moderate damage to both. Just a few days later on May 2, another Cleveland Cliffs vessel went aground on Parisienne Island. The *Munising*, a 380-foot, 3,838-ton vessel, was later released. The canaller *Yorkton* was reported to have collided with an unidentified vessel, holing herself and settling in relatively shallow water on July 11 just a mile from Whitefish Point, but recovered. Later in the month on July 29, the venerable *Robert L. Fryer*, built in 1888 at West Bay City, was set ablaze at the Canadian Lakehead where she had lain idle and decaying for five years or more after spending the previous decade transferring grain between elevators at Fort William and Port Arthur. Her hulk was towed out to the Welcome Islands and set afire, sinking the vessel in quite a public spectacle. Though not a shipwreck *per se*, her hull is reported to be in the shallows near the island and visible in low water.[2] Early fall saw Midland Steamship Company's 420-foot, 4,872-ton *W.G. Pollock* striking the Duluth Ship Canal on September 24.

1931

Tonnage through the St. Marys Falls Canal dropped again, this time an additional 39 percent to just 44 million tons. Traffic had obviously been reduced by the continued decline in the national economy. The early season passed without notable incident. However, one ship met her end and another had an unusual grounding.

During the early morning hours of October 9, the 201-foot, 804-ton lumber steamer *Charles H. Bradley* of the Blodgett line, Duluth, was nosing her way through the Keweenaw Waterway with the 218-foot wooden barge *Grampian* in tow. To his dismay, Captain August Golomblaky discovered that the light near the entrance to Portage River was out. In the blackness of that October night, he misjudged his distance and grounded. Unable to stop, the *Grampian* crashed into her towing steamer, smashing the *Bradley*'s electrical conduits and the steam pipe to the fire pumps. Within moments, fire broke out in bulkheads near the deck house, probably from a short circuit.

Though not a shipwreck per se, *the 42-year-old* Robert L. Fryer *was intentionally set afire at the Canadian Lakehead in mid-summer 1930, her remains settling to the bottom of Thunder Bay. She had been converted to a floating grain elevator when rebuilt in 1922.* C. PATRICK LABADIE COLLECTION.

The crew fought the blaze for hours with fire extinguishers and buckets, to no avail. The 41-year-old *Bradley*, partially loaded with pulpwood, was a flaming wreck. Yawls from the *Grampian* came alongside and removed the 14-man crew when it became obvious that the *Bradley* was doomed. Captain Fred Sollman and Coast Guardsmen from Portage Station took Captain Golomblaky and several of his crew to Chassell to notify the owners. The *Bradley* was en route to a Georgian Bay lumber port for cargo at the time of the accident. Built in 1890 at West Bay City, she likely was worth $20,000 to her owners at the time of her fiery end. The *Charles H. Bradley*'s remains are reported by sport divers to be about 1,700 feet southwesterly of the outer end of the Lower Entry breakwater and off the mouth of the Sturgeon River in 10 to 20 feet of water.[3]

When the *Charles S. Hebard* passed upbound at the Soo on November 22, coal-laden for Duluth, Captain James Phillips and his crew had no idea they would become involved in an unusual and little reported shipping casualty before making their way downbound. They crossed Lake Superior in about 60 hours, arriving in Duluth early on the 26th. Her coal was unloaded over the next 24 hours or so, and the *Hebard* was off to load grain at the Canadian Lakehead. It was somewhere along the Minnesota north shore on the night of the 27th or 28th that she encountered difficulties.

In darkness and with a compass her wheelsmen knew had been awry for three months, the *Hebard* nearly blundered onto the north shore, possibly near Tofte, about 25 miles south of Grand Marais, Minnesota. Soon after 8 p.m. as Wheelsman A.J. Knuckey was getting into his bunk after coming off watch, the ship struck an object and boldly heeled over, sending him to the deck. It was evidently a glancing blow as the ship continued moving. It was apparently another wheelsman, John Wick, who swung the wheel hard over to starboard, preventing a catastrophe. The *Hebard* had struck not at the bow, but near the stern below the firehold, an indication of just how close the entire ship had been to becoming another major casualty on the north shore. Captain Phillips ordered the vessel to proceed slowly ahead at right angles to the beach and all available steam put on the pumps. As soon as the water was under control, crewmen entered the Number 5 ballast tank to pack the hole with all the dunnage they could, allowing them to continue to Fort William. They assumed that once there, they could make better repairs and return to the dry dock in Superior for permanent repairs.

This was not to be the case. Instead, Captain Phillips ordered the crew kept aboard ship when they tied up at the elevator. No one was to discuss the grounding! Needless to say, there was no report to the home office about the incident. While the *Hebard*'s grain capacity was 350,000 bushels, she took on closer to 300,000 before clearing the Canadian Lakehead. Departure was before midnight on November 30 when insurance rates were due to skyrocket for the remainder of the season.

Proceeding at three-quarter speed, the *Hebard* successfully crossed Lake Superior without encountering any of the usual end-of-season foul weather, passing down at the Soo in the wee morning hours of December 2. As soon as the cargo was discharged in Buffalo, the

After being rammed by her tow barge, Grampian, Charles H. Bradley *caught fire and burned to the waterline in October 1931.* AUTHOR'S COLLECTION.

ship went to Cleveland for dry-docking, and the crew was quickly paid and discharged. Crewmen received no bonus for saving a $2 million ship or successfully transporting grain with its $30,000 freight charge.

It was not until the *Hebard* was settled down on the blocks that the real problem became evident. She had picked up a rock in the brief grounding which punctured the hull and lodged there. No ordinary rock, it was a one-

ton chunk of the Minnesota north shore which had obviously helped keep the ship afloat.

The 504-foot, 6,213-ton *Hebard* was back in service the next season, sailing an additional three decades. She

The 600-foot Frontenac *was typical of the Great Lakes fleet from the turn of the century until World War II when the 620-footers came on line.* COURTESY OF WESLEY R. HARKINS MARINE PHOTOGRAPHY, DULUTH.

was built by the American Shipbuilding Company at Cleveland in 1906 and operated in the Wilson Transit fleet of Cleveland at the time of her uncommon excavation of the Minnesota north shore. Parts of the *Hebard* remain in the Twin Ports today, rescued from shipbreakers. Her pilothouse became a familiar landmark atop a store on Garfield Avenue in Duluth. That business was sold and the pilothouse moved to Barker's Island in Superior where it now serves as the ticket office for the Duluth-Superior Excursion Company. The ship's propeller is displayed in Canal Park in Duluth.[4]

1932

Once more the national economy was reflected in a continued dramatic decline in tonnage passing the Soo. The season was off fully 64 percent to just more than 20 million tons, the lowest ebb of the decade. Again, the early season seemed to pass without a substantial casualty. Then a terrific gale in late November brought a pair of mishaps in the eastern lake, one fatal.

Three fish tugs operating out of Grand Marais, Michigan, the *Lydia, Isabella* and *Josephine Addison,* were caught at the fishing grounds in northeastern Lake Superior by a 60 mph blast on November 25. The *Isabella,* under Captain James McDonald, and the *Addison,* under Captain Palmer Masse, sought shelter behind Michipicoten and Caribou islands. The 47-foot, 26-ton *Lydia,* however, under Captain Louis Larson of Racine, Wisconsin, made a run for the safety of Grand Marais. She apparently struck a sand bar on her approach and was almost instantaneously torn to pieces by the raging waters. Captain Larson and his four crewmen were drowned. Coast Guardsmen found wreckage of the *Lydia,* but no bodies. Very likely this was the worst loss of life in the entire history of the Lake Superior fishing fleet. Built at Menominee, the *Lydia* was 19 years old.[5]

The same storm complex continued and drove the 247-foot, 2,484-ton Canadian steamer *Georgian,* under command of Captain D. Hudson, into the shelter of Grand Island. A sudden squall on November 28, however, grounded her near Trout Point. Salvors, using the wrecker *Maplecourt,* were unable to release her until May 29, 1933, with undisclosed damage.[6]

1933

For the first time in the decade, freight through the Soo rose, nearly doubling that of the previous season to more than 40 million tons. The spring of 1933 saw one of the most bizarre mishaps in the history of the lake. In calm weather and a dense, low-hanging fog early on the evening of May 27, the 259-foot steel passenger steamer *George M. Cox* literally ran herself out of the water on Rock of Ages Reef, Isle Royale. Formerly the Lake Michigan steamer *Puritan* of the Graham and Morton Line, the *Cox* had been purchased by the Isle Royale Transportation Company, reconditioned and renamed for the president of the company. Mr. Cox was on board at the time of the disaster since this was his namesake's maiden cruise after having been renamed and rechristened in Chicago. Under Captain George Johnson of Traverse City, Michigan, she was on Lake Superior en route to Port Arthur to pick up a number of Canadian passengers who were headed to the World's Fair Century of Progress Exposition in Chicago.

Deceived by the fog, First Mate Arthur Kronk and Captain Johnson thought they were two-and-a-half miles west of Rock of Ages Light whose alarm signals they had heard when altering course to the northwest to go around the west end of Isle Royale. Unwittingly, they drove the ship at 17 knots onto this treacherous reef, striking so hard that her engines and boilers were torn loose and a large hole ripped in her hull on the port side. Observers estimated that 110 feet of her keel were out of the water. Immediately, the vessel listed sharply to port and her stern submerged in four minutes. Good discipline prevailed. Quickly, five port-side lifeboats were launched along with the life rafts, and 125 persons abandoned ship without incident, although three crewmen had been injured in the crash, one severely.

Coast Guardsman John F. Soldenski, keeper of Rock of Ages Light, had witnessed the accident from his lofty perch, where he could see the top of the ship's masts protruding above the fog, and raced to the scene in the lighthouse power boat. Keeper Soldenski took the life rafts in tow and herded the lifeboats to the shelter of the lighthouse where the survivors were given temporary refuge. Soldenski then radioed the downbound steamer *Morris S. Tremaine* which hove to off the lighthouse and picked up the worst casualties together with owner George M. Cox and Ship's Nurse Adeline Keeling, rushing them to a Port Arthur hospital. Meanwhile, the ship's SOS had been received by the U.S. Coast Guard cutter *Crawford* at Two Harbors and the Coast Guard stations at Portage Canal and Grand Marais, Minnesota. The cutter and lifeboats from the two stations rushed to the stranding site.

The survivors spent an uncomfortable night scattered up and down the winding stairway inside the lighthouse as Mrs. Soldenski did her best to keep them warm and in coffee. The survivors were taken by the Coast Guard first to Singer's resort on nearby Washington Island and then back to Houghton the next day. No lives were lost, though the newly rebuilt *George M. Cox* was a total loss of more than $200,000, as she proved unrecoverable. Many items were recovered from the *Cox* and transported to Port Arthur where her sister ship, the *Isle Royale,* picked them up in midsummer for transport to the lower lakes. The *Cox* eventually broke in two and slid to the bottom of the lake in from 10 to about 100 feet of water.[7]

Only one other American commercial casualty was recorded in 1933, the 195-ton *Scow No. 8* stranding at Au Sable Point on October 11, a minor financial liability. The Canadians also lost the little 19-ton tug *W.J. Emerson* on October 9 at No. 10 Light near Shaganash Island on the north shore.

1934

Lake Superior freight held its own this season, actually increasing nearly 2 million tons to reach a still dismal 42 million tons. There was just one ship involved in casualty this season, Continental Steamship Company's 580-foot, 8,262-ton *L.M. Bowers* striking an obstruction near the Northern Pacific Railway draw bridge between Duluth and Superior on May 19, causing an estimated $21,000 in vessel damage.

1935

Lake Superior tonnage rose for the third successive season, this time by a moderate 14 percent to more than 48 million tons. During the season, several small gas-driven fishing craft met difficulties along with one ore carrier.

The handsome passenger liner George M. Cox *had been christened in Chicago before proceeding onto Lake Superior where she was lost in 1933.* WISCONSIN MARINE HISTORICAL SOCIETY COLLECTION, MILWAUKEE PUBLIC LIBRARY.

Pittsburgh Steamship's 585-foot, 7,962-ton steamer *William J. Filbert* damaged her rudder stock while maneuvering on the east side of the Duluth, Missabe and Northern ore dock in Duluth on May 23. Shipyard attention

A boiler explosion claimed the Canadian crane steamer Neebing *while towing a barge in September 1937.* LOVELADY PHOTO, GENE ONCHULENKO COLLECTION.

brought the bill to $8,000 for what appeared to be a minor incident.

The 45-foot, 14-ton *Dagmar* ran ashore in fog about one mile east of Chippewa Harbor, Isle Royale, on June 1, slipping off into deep water before her crew could return with help. The *Dagmar* had been built in 1914 at Beaver Bay on the Minnesota north shore. While the approximate location of the *Dagmar* loss is fairly well known, the vessel has never been located. Also, the nine-ton *Eleanora* stranded at Keweenaw Point on August 5. Then, the 11-ton *Avis H.* struck at Whitefish Point on September 23.

1936

Once again tonnage on Lake Superior rose, this time to a healthy 69 million tons, up 44 percent over 1935. The early season was largely uneventful except for the beleaguered *William J. Filbert* becoming ice damaged about 20 miles off shore and north-northwest of Portage Lake Ship Canal. Then a costly fire occurred at Duluth on June 2, when the 186-ton hydraulic dredge *Erie* burned at her dock in West Duluth. Owned by the Duluth-Superior Dredging Company, the *Erie* was undergoing repairs when sparks from an acetylene torch ignited her deck. Despite the efforts of the Duluth Fire Department, the *Erie* became a $200,000 bonfire, burning to the water's edge before settling to the bottom.[8]

T.W. Robinson, a 572-foot, 7,726-ton unit of the Bradley Transportation Company, found herself aground in an unusual location on August 22, the Ontonagon River. She got off virtually unscathed. Not so lucky were the 480-

foot *Crete* of the Interlake Steamship fleet and the 454-foot *Cornell* of the Pittsburgh fleet which came together on September 8, about 40 miles west-northwest of Whitefish Point with undisclosed damage to both. Just a day later on September 9, Interlake's 416-foot *Saturn* and Pittsburgh's 580-foot *Henry H. Rogers* repeated the incident, only about six miles southeast of Whitefish Point, again with undisclosed damage to both vessels.

1937

There was another rise in Lake Superior freight traffic, the sixth season in a row, bringing the season total to a substantial 87 million tons. An unusual disaster on September 24 marred an otherwise pleasant season and ended the days of a lakes veteran. Struggling in heavy seas off Moss Island, Nipigon Straits, with the gravel barge *Coteau* in tow, the 193-foot, 908-ton steel Canadian steamer *Neebing* suddenly burst her boiler, the explosion sinking the vessel almost instantly. Captain A.L. Carney and four of his crew went down with the ship. Nine others narrowly escaped by swimming ashore or clinging to portions of their wrecked vessel. It was largely through the heroic maneuvering of a small rowboat by Captain Emil Konderka of the *Coteau* that the survivors were brought aboard the barge which was picked up some three hours after the tragedy by the tug *Strathmore* under Captain Vince McCabe.

Within a few days, the *Neebing* was relocated by dragging in 108 feet of water about one-third of a mile off the mainland and about one-quarter of a mile from the northern tip of Moss Island near Nipigon Strait. A search for the bodies of five missing crewmen successfully recovered only one, that of Walter Smith. Built by Craig at Toledo in 1892, the *Neebing* had previously been the American steamer *John B. Ketchum 2nd.* She was 45 years old at the time of sinking, being owned by the Sin-Mac Lines. She had been converted into a wrecking and towing steamer by adding a derrick on her deck in 1928. After 1937, she was used primarily for loading and towing gravel barges from Nest Island, Paradise Island and others in that vicinity to Red Rock, Ontario.[9]

1938

The improvement of the previous six seasons crashed in on 1938, cutting tonnage more than in half to barely 40 million tons. Iron ore shipments alone accounted for the decrease with shipment of red ore plummeting from 65 to 20 million tons. Once again, it was a season when the small, gasoline engine-driven craft encountered trouble. The 34-foot, 13-ton *Clarence* burned and exploded at Superior on June 30, after filling her 150-gallon tank. A short in the starting motor was said to have caused the blaze which virtually destroyed the vessel. She had been built in 1930 at Bayfield, Wisconsin, as a fish tug, but converted into a harbor supply vessel or bumboat valued at $3,000. The fire caused an estimated $2,000 damage to the boat and an additional $3,000 damage to the $3,500 worth of supplies on board. Captain A.B. Kaner received some bruises and burns about the head, but survived the ordeal. The nearby tanker *Red Crown* had some exciting moments as the blazing gas tank came back to earth just a short distance away.[10]

The brand new 13-ton *Donna Marie* also was lost, foundering on November 11, 1938, after being struck by the 50-foot tug *Sea Bird*. Visibility was reduced considerably by frost fog as the *Donna Marie* was dead in the water lifting nets about 15 miles northeast of Duluth. The *Sea Bird,* failing to keep a proper watch and running by her compass alone, plowed directly into the helpless fish tug. Two passengers and three crewmen were taken aboard the *Sea Bird* and the tug taken in tow, only to sink about five miles closer to Duluth. Captain Theodore Bodin of Washburn reported his vessel a total loss valued at $2,800 plus $1,200 for three lifts of nets left on the stern deck and an added $30 for his lost fish.[11]

1939

Although tonnage rebounded to 69 million tons with a consequent increase in vessel traffic to more than 40,000 transits at the Soo Locks, there were no casualties of consequence to commercial carriers throughout the season, a remarkable record. Even the smaller craft appear to have had an unblemished season.

1940

The fantastic decade of the 1940s witnessed an increase in vessel troubles. Tonnage soared unbelievably, doubling that of the 1930s, and Lake Superior experienced its first billion-ton decade. Of course, World War II was the big stimulant.

The 1940 season saw ore shipments up more than 40 percent with total tonnage for Lake Superior rising to nearly 90 million tons, the best season in a decade. However, the decade's casualty list began early and harshly with the first sinking coming on the night of April 30 when the 244-foot, 1,870-ton steamer *Arlington* of the Burke Towing and Salvage Company, Midland, Ontario, was downbound with grain from the Canadian Lakehead.

She hit utterly vile weather combining terrific gales, snow and hail. Despite the beating his little ship was taking, Captain Fred Burke persisted in sticking to his direct course to Whitefish Point. About daylight, when the *Arlington* was perhaps 12 miles south of Superior Shoal, it was obvious that the vessel would founder. The lifeboat was launched and the crew placed therein. Then came one of the strangest happenings in the history of Lake Superior. Captain Burke refused to leave his ship, waving goodbye to his departing crew from the pilothouse door. Around 5 a.m., the *Arlington* dove to the bottom of the lake, taking her resolute captain with her.

THE BARNES-DULUTH SHIPBUILDING COMPANY

announces the Launching

on October 2, 1943, 12:45 P. M.

(program to start at 12:15 P. M.)

of the United States Maritime Commission Vessel

S. S. "JAMES MILLER"

Sponsored by

MRS. PAUL NIELSEN

Wife of the General Superintendent

Ship launchings were marked with great community celebration in wartime years. CANAL PARK MARINE MUSEUM COLLECTION.

Fortunately, Captain T.J. Carson of the 386-foot Canadian steamer *Collingwood* had been following the *Arlington,* surmising that she was in difficulties. When the *Arlington* crew abandoned ship, Captain Carson placed his large vessel to the windward and quickly picked up the lifeboat crew. While no value was reported, the 27-year-old *Arlington* and her grain cargo must have represented a loss of more than $150,000. Historians and shipping people are still at a loss to explain Captain Burke's behavior.[12]

While Lake Superior was spared the brunt of that catastrophic blizzard known as the Armistice Day Storm of 1940, a gale on November 5 did draw blood. Fighting the rugged northerly seas west of Grand Marais, Michigan, the 380-foot, 3,942-ton steamer *Sparta* under Captain Chester Danielson was hardly making headway despite her 1,450-horsepower engine. She had almost reached the shelter of Grand Island when she was swept onto a reef at the west end of Mosquito Beach, only a mile or so from the Grand Portal of the Pictured Rocks, about 14 miles east of Munising. The seas subsided enough to permit the launching of a lifeboat, and 16 of the crew rowed to Munising for help. The Coast Guard cutter *Ossippee* and wrecking tug *Favorite* quickly responded, and the remaining crew was saved. Yet, the *Sparta* was well hooked on her sandy perch. She was finally taken off in June 1941 by Merritt, Chapman and Scott of Duluth, although her hull proved so badly shattered that she never sailed again. The *Sparta* was converted to a dry dock by the Roen interests of Sturgeon Bay, Wisconsin. She had previously been the Gilchrist steamer *Frank W. Hart.* Her financial loss must have exceeded $150,000.[13]

but September brought triple grief. The first incident involved the foundering of the only sizable motor vessel to be claimed by Lake Superior. At 8 p.m., September 1, the 250-foot, 1,695-ton crane ship *Steelvendor* of the American Steel and Wire Company, a U.S. Steel subsidiary, departed from Duluth under Captain G.L. Kane with a load of steel billets for Waukegan, Illinois. After a day of decent sailing, she met a veritable tempest just east of Ke-

A violent spring storm in 1940 overcame the Arlington *on the eastern lake.* FRANK E. HAMILTON PHOTO, C. PATRICK LABADIE COLLECTION.

1941

Tonnage again increased on Lake Superior reaching an unprecedented 111 million tons. Iron ore shipments alone were up 26 percent to more than 83 million tons. Despite the increase in tonnage handled, the casualty roster grew at a proverbial snail's pace. Only two casualties were reported, and both occurred on the same date, August 31. Though details are lacking, two fish tugs ran into difficulties east of Munising. The *Miners Castle* was reported to have foundered near the Grand Portal of the Pictured Rocks, while the *Otter* was reported having been beached 20 miles east of Munising in 50 mph winds.[14]

1942

New record cargo was handled by ships transiting Lake Superior, more than 120 million tons, the highest for the entire decade. The early season passed with little difficulty,

weenaw Point, about 18 miles off Manitou Island. Her cargo apparently shifted, and she took on a heavy list. Water pouring into the engine room cut off the engineers from the controls, and for several hours the stricken vessel made big circles in the lake, out of control.

Two ships sighted her and followed her around, the large 586-foot *Charles M. Schwab* and the 587-foot *William G. Clyde.* The *B.F. Affleck, E.N. Saunders Jr., Samuel Mather* and *Joliet* also stood by after receiving the *Steelvendor*'s distress call. After two hours or more, water stopped her engine. The larger carriers then pulled alongside as the *Affleck*'s crew took a position to windward and poured storm oil on the wild sea. In a matter of minutes 24 of 25 men were transferred, 22 to the *Schwab* and two to the *Clyde.* One oiler had been swept overboard and drowned. Moments later, the *Steelvendor* slid beneath the surface, just before daylight on September 3. Built in Kearney, New Jersey, the 19-year-old *Steelvendor* was probably worth more than $150,000.[15]

Less than three weeks later on the night of September 21, a howling equinoctial gale claimed two venerable old timers of the lakes, the 254-foot steel barge *City of*

St. Joseph and the 254-foot iron barge *Transport.* Though now reduced to pulpwood barges, both had colorful histories, the *City of St. Joseph,* built in 1889, having been a Lake Michigan passenger ship under that name and as *City of Chicago* for 45 years, while the 62-year-old *Transport* had been a railroad ferry for the Michigan Central and Wabash Lines for more than 55 years in the Detroit area. On their last trip under tow of the 104-foot tug *John Roen* of Sturgeon Bay, the two barges had loaded 1,400 cords of pulpwood at Grand Marais, Minnesota, consigned to Port Huron, Michigan. An ugly storm arose as they moved across the lake. In the raging waters off Keweenaw Point, the rudder chains of the *City of St. Joseph* let go, and she became uncontrollable. Then her towline broke. Both barges were on their own.

About three miles west of Eagle Harbor, the barge crews lighted distress flares which were spotted in the darkness by the Coast Guard lookout at Eagle Harbor. Captain Ernest Bennett and the Eagle Harbor lifeboat crew responded, soon reaching the wallowing pair. As the *Transport* seemed to be in most danger, taking water rapidly, Captain Bennett determined to take her crew off first. He brought the pitching lifeboat alongside the stricken barge at great risk and one by one, the seven-man barge crew under Captain Ray Williamson jumped to safety in the lifeboat.

Those aboard the *City of St. Joseph* fared far worse. She also was leaking faster than her pumps could handle the water. Suddenly, a rampaging wave stripped off her pilothouse.

Vicious storms struck Lake Superior in September 1942, the unusual crane vessel Steelvendor *being just one of the victims.* CANAL PARK MARINE MUSEUM COLLECTION.

The deck loads of both her barges had gone over the side long before, and the lake was strewn with thousands of pulpwood logs. While a heroic fireman had crawled forward over the *City of St. Joseph*'s wave-washed deck to release her anchors, the anchors dragged. Momentarily, she hit a reef and her waterlogged hulk slid from beneath the feet of the six life-jacketed crewmen. Mrs. McLeod,

wife of the barge captain, drowned amidst the tossing debris, but Captain McLeod, two crewmen and two Coast Guardsmen aboard managed to hang onto pulp logs and scramble to the shore not far away. They then spent a mis-

Local shipyards took great pride in the quality and timeliness of their wartime production. CANAL PARK MARINE MUSEUM COLLECTION.

erable several hours crashing through woods and hiking a shore road in the frigid darkness until they reached the Eagle Harbor Coast Guard station. Four of them were rushed to the Hancock hospital suffering from exposure and shock, but rugged Captain McLeod remained until the next day when a Coast Guard beach patrol recovered the body of his drowned wife.

Meanwhile, Captain Bennett on the lifeboat had a tough decision to make. Seeing the *City of St. Joseph* go down close to shore and being unable to assist her people, he sailed for the open lake. To approach Eagle Harbor in such a gale would have been suicidal. Hence, both Coast Guardsmen and the rescued spent a miserable eight hours being tossed about by the seas until Captain Bennett was able to take the lifeboat into the lee of Keweenaw Point. Finally reaching Bete Grise Bay about 8 a.m., he found the large ore carrier *M.A. Hanna* lying in shelter there, and the rescued were placed aboard the big ship before being transferred to the tug *Roen,* which also managed to reach Bete Grise.

After being abandoned, the disabled *Transport* also was driven onto the reef, only a few hundred feet from where the *City of St. Joseph* sank. She likewise was a total loss, though some of her machinery could be salvaged. Beachcombers did manage to recover hundreds of cords of pulpwood for the war effort. Captain E.L. Taylor of the tug *Roen* reported that the blasts had simply overpowered

The canaller Judge Hart *wrecked in November gales of 1942 and has since proved elusive, although there were many witnesses to the event.* UNIVERSITY OF DETROIT MARINE COLLECTION.

his vessel, and he could do nothing to prevent his tow from striking the reefs. The financial liability was not reported, but was probably in excess of $50,000. All three ships belonged to the Roen Steamship Company of Sturgeon Bay, Wisconsin.[16]

Lake Superior claimed one more vessel before the season was completed. Hugging the Canadian north shore to avoid inclement weather, the 250-foot canaller *Judge Hart* of the Upper Lakes and St. Lawrence Transportation Company struck at Fitzsimmons Rocks, Ashburton Bay. She had completed loading grain in Port Arthur on November 24, but delayed her departure while securing the hatches and then come to anchor behind the Welcome Islands waiting for weather. The wait was long, but not long enough. A dramatic drop in barometric pressure on the 25th and 26th brought high winds, and waves routinely washed her decks.

When he thought he was in the vicinity of Otter Island, Captain Frederick M. Burmeister observed his ship making little headway and decided to run for the shelter of Jackfish Bay. With her anchor windlass iced up, the *Judge Hart* used a hand lead to attempt to feel her way along. Suddenly, she fetched up on a reef. Fearing she had holed herself badly and might settle in deep water, Captain Burmeister had the engine kept ahead to hold her in place. When visibility improved, Captain Burmeister observed three other vessels anchored a few miles to the west, the *James B. Eads* of Norris Steamship Company and two Paterson Steamship vessels, *Lavaldoc* and *Fort Willdoc*. As the captain was unsuccessful in getting a coded signal to the *Eads* using the Morse lamp, it was not until daybreak on the 27th that Captain Stanley Tischart of the *Eads* spotted the treacherous rocks off the *Hart*'s bow.

Some of the *Hart*'s crew were transferred to the *Eads* during the day, carrying with them a message for the vessel's owners. At this time, the message was forwarded to Port Arthur, and the *James Whalen* and a derrick barge set out for the scene. Fearing the worst, Captain Burmeister finally gave the abandon ship order on the 28th. When her unattended engine slowed to a halt, the *Hart* slid back from the rocks and drifted about a mile or more before settling to the bottom about seven-eighths of a mile off Barclay Island and about three miles from Fitzsimmons Rock where she had struck. Captain Tischart commented later that as the *Hart* went to the bottom, all of the hatches blew off sending timber and hatch boards flying into the air. The *Whalen* and her barge arrived shortly after the *Hart* went down. Happily, there had been no loss of life. However, the 19-year-old ship and her 101,500 bushels of wheat must have represented a property loss of more than $150,000.[17]

1943

Tonnage fell off four percent, but held at a remarkable 115 million tons for the season. Casualties began in late spring when blinding fog off Isle Royale on June 1 brought the first of the year. Not far from Passage Island, Canada Steamship Lines' 248-foot, 2,357-ton package freighter *Battleford* collided with and sank the larger 356-foot, 3,813-ton bulk carrier *Prindoc* of Paterson Steamships Ltd. of Fort William. Captain A. Simpell and his 21-man crew were saved. The *Prindoc* was the former American freighter *Gilchrist,* built in 1901 at West Bay City and later named *Lupus.* No damage figures were given, but the *Prindoc* must have been worth $200,000 or more.[18]

That same June fog, moving eastward, brought a near tragedy the following day in lower Whitefish Bay, when Buckeye Steamship Company's 513-foot steamer *Harry W. Hosford* and the 532-foot *W.W. Holloway* of Oglebay Norton Company came together. The *Hosford* was beached at Point Iroquois on June 2, to keep her from sinking. No repair costs were reported, but these must have been sizable. A 60 mph gale on eastern Lake Superior followed the fog, bringing an undisclosed amount of damage to the 580-foot *James A. Farrell* of Pittsburgh Steamship Company and the 432-foot *J.J.H. Brown* of Brown and Company.[19]

The *Robert C. Stanley* suffered substantial damage in early November. The *Stanley* was completing her round trip to Lake Superior, having previously cleared Duluth November 5 with 13,766 tons of ore, when she got caught in a gale and cracked across her deck amidships and down both sides for some 12 to 14 feet. She would open up three or four inches in the sea. Cables were run fore and aft and winched at full power to hold her together, while two other ore carriers escorted her back to the shelter of Whitefish Bay and temporary repairs at the Soo. With temporary patching only, the *Stanley* made two trips up the lake, clearing Two Harbors on November 20 with 13,519 tons and again from Two Harbors on November 30 with 13,684 tons of natural ore. The ship laid up in Toledo on December 8. The following spring after fitout on March 22, 1944, the *Stanley* proceeded to Ecorse, Michigan, for major, permanent repairs. Straps were installed on deck the full length of the ship outboard of the hatch coamings, one on either side, approximately three feet wide and two and a half inches thick, as well as doubling the sheer strake. Similar repair modifications were made to the *Stanley*'s sister vessels.[20]

Three smaller craft were also lost during the 1943 season. The 38-foot, 17-ton *Marymaid* foundered off Munising where she had been built in 1936. The 28-foot, 7-ton *Blanche* burned at Marquette. She had been built in Marquette in 1919. The 27-foot, 9-ton *Mary Ann* was destroyed by fire at Two Harbors on November 12. She had been built in the same Minnesota north shore community in 1939.

A slashing December tempest brought the second major casualty for 1943. Fighting frigid gusts and near zero temperatures, the 321-foot, 2,584-ton steamer *Sarnian* of the Upper Lakes and St. Lawrence Navigation Company stranded at Point Isabelle with a cargo of barley on December 10. Buffeted by sledge-hammer waves, she broke in two. The U.S. Coast Guard cutter *Plaintree* and the Eagle Harbor Coast Guard successfully took off her crew. After an attempt to salvage the cargo, the Upper Lakes Company abandoned her, though salvors pulled her free in 1944 for a trip to an Indiana scrap yard. She had previously been the American freighter *Chili* of the Elphicke fleet, launched in 1895.[21]

1944

Tonnage and traffic held steady this season, up slightly to 117 million tons of cargo crossing Lake Superior. Safety during this troubling war year must have been paramount as no casualties were reported to commercial carriers on the upper lake.

1945

Despite the enormous tonnages being handled by the commercial fleet during the war years, this season totaling 113 million tons, shipping losses were held to a minimum. The lake fishermen were not as fortunate as the large commercial carriers.

On May 22, off the pierhead of Grand Marais, Michigan, the 45-foot fish tug *Eddie S.* capsized and sank in a 50 mph gale. The Coast Guard patrol boat saved one crew member, but Captain James McDonald Sr. and the remaining crew member were lost. Tragedy struck again on July 3, a mile off Michigan's Grand Marais Harbor. A sudden squall surprised Captain Frank Vaudreull and three men aboard the fish tug *Rockaway*. Other boats fishing nearby raced to the safety of Grand Marais, but the *Rockaway* was never seen again. The Coast Guard patrol boat put out immediately and sighted a body in a life jacket, but the body slipped from the life preserver before it could be retrieved. Coast Guardsmen picked up scraps of wreckage which seemed to indicate an explosion. Other fishermen recalled that the *Rockaway* had experienced engine and fuel line trouble only a few days before. At any rate, three more commercial fishermen and a Lansing tourist had succumbed to Lake Superior.[22]

1946

The remarkable safety record of the previous two seasons continued, perhaps aided by a downturn of nearly 20 percent in Lake Superior freight to 91 million tons and subsequently fewer ships crossing the lake. Only two incidents were recorded, both relatively minor. Great Lakes Steamship Company's 504-foot, 6,673-ton *Norway* whacked the Soo Line ore dock in Superior in strong St. Louis River current. A few weeks later, June 26, Bethlehem Steel's 504-foot, 6,287-ton *Cambria* came together with Wilson Transit's 520-foot, 6,294-ton *Edward S. Kendrick*, damaging the latter at the Great Northern ore dock in Superior.

1947

A healthy 31 percent increase in iron ore shipment boosted Lake Superior traffic to 110 million tons. The first casualty of the season occurred on May 29, when a small gasoline-driven craft encountered trouble. The 33-foot, 10-ton *Favorite* was driven aground at Presque Isle in Marquette. The Marquette Coast Guard rushed to the rescue, but their picket boat also was grounded and smashed by the seas. The single occupant of the *Favorite* and the Coast Guard crew were safe, though the Coast Guard cutter *Woodrush* had to be brought down from the Head of the Lakes to release the damaged small craft. The *Favorite* had been built in 1927 at Chassell, Michigan, on the Keweenaw waterway.[23]

A major disaster occurred the following week, one that is still hard to explain. In thick weather early on the morning of June 4, the 525-foot, 7,031-ton steamer *Emperor* of Canada Steamship Lines crashed onto Canoe Rocks Reef off the northeastern tip of Isle Royale. En route from Port Arthur to Ashtabula with iron ore, the 36-year-old

Canada Steamship Lines' Emperor *fell victim to Isle Royale reefs while running in heavy weather without a second mate in June 1947.* AUTHOR'S COLLECTION

vessel struck so hard that she broke in two at Number 4 hatch, sinking so rapidly that she took Captain Eldon Walkinshaw and 11 crew members down with her. Escape for the 21 others was little short of miraculous. Purely by chance, the U.S. Coast Guard cutter *Kimball* was in the area putting out channel markers. Receiving the SOS, the *Kimball* raced around Blake Point to the sinking site in only 25 minutes, picking seven survivors off Canoe Rocks and 14 more from two damaged and sinking lifeboats. Built in 1911 at Collingwood, the *Emperor* was one of the larger bulk carriers in Canada Steamship Lines.

The accident is hard to explain, as her officers knew well the zig-zag course out of Fort William and Port Arthur and around Isle Royale. Yet, she struck with her throttle at three-quarters speed. Someone had missed a turn. The two crewmen who could have given the clearest information on the events leading up to the loss, First Mate James Morey and Wheelsman John Prokup, were among those lost. However, the principal blame was placed by the Court of Investigation on the first mate for failing to keep a proper watch, though the court also noted that the mate had been in charge of the entire loading process while in port when he should have been off duty and that his regular watch was resumed shortly after leaving port. He had simply been overtired and possibly dozed off in the pilothouse when he should have made a course change at Thunder Cape Light which was apparently not made until opposite Trowbridge Island. That one error put the *Emperor* on a collision course with Canoe Rocks reef. A warning light for Canoe Rocks had been established on Blake Point several years after the *Monarch*'s loss in this vicinity and a year before the *Chester A. Congdon* was lost at the western end of this same reef. It failed to alert this crew. While no damage figures were given, the vessel undoubtedly was valued at more than $300,000.[24]

1948

A new peacetime record for tonnage passing through the Soo Locks was set this season at 115 million tons. Nevertheless, nearly a year after the *Emperor*'s loss, an early summer fog on June 23 brought a rash of collisions on western Lake Superior, one of them fatal. At 5 a.m., 135 miles east of Duluth and 30 miles northwest of Portage Lake Ship Canal, the 580-foot, 7,694-ton steel Pittsburgher *J. Pierpont Morgan Jr.* collided nearly bows-on with the 480-foot, 6,030-ton steel *Crete* of the Interlake Steamship Company, managed by Pickands Mather. While the *Crete* was light, the *Morgan Jr.* was loaded with 12,888 tons of iron ore downbound from Duluth Harbor which she cleared on June 22. The bow of the *Crete* crashed through the forward crew quarters of the *Morgan Jr.* killing two men and injuring three others, smashing the whole forward cabin complex. The *Crete*'s bow was pushed back 20 feet. The two ships separated instantly.

Groping around trying to find the *Morgan Jr.* in the fog, the *Crete* came close to being struck a second time by the steamer *Harry L. Findlay*. The *Morgan Jr.* was badly hurt with her forward compartment flooded. However, the collision bulkhead held. The U.S. Coast Guard cutter *Woodrush* raced to the scene. Meanwhile, the *Morgan Jr.* limped into Portage Lake Ship Canal where she was assisted in reaching Houghton by the Corps of Engineers' 85-foot diesel tug *Barlow*. The *Crete* made dry dock in Superior where her lacerated bow was rebuilt. The *Morgan Jr.* had a major reconstruction job. Repairs to the two were estimated to exceed half a million dollars, making this the most costly Lake Superior collision of record where a ship was not sunk. And two men had died. The *Morgan Jr.* returned to active service on September 5, 1948, loading 12,659 tons of ore at Two Harbors.[25]

The same June 23 fog produced a multiple collision to the west of the Apostle Islands when the 560-foot downbound steamer *E.A.S. Clarke* was struck by the 412-foot Canadian steamer *Altadoc* and her 378-foot barge *Kenordoc*. Injuries here were relatively minor, the *Clarke* returning to Superior for repairs, the *Altadoc* and *Kenordoc* proceeding to the Canadian Lakehead.

1949

This season saw a 17 percent decline in tonnage crossing Lake Superior with just 96 million tons passing through the Soo. Only one significant casualty was reported in the year, and that one unusual. A Memorial Day weekend cruise by the Duluth contingent of the U.S. Naval Reserve brought a flurry of excitement when the Naval Reserve Training Ship *PC 782* struck a reef in Siskiwit Bay, Isle Royale, on the night of May 28 and stuck hard.

Weather was calm and pleasant for the 75 persons aboard, including regular Navy advisers, ranking Duluth Naval Reservists, 15 Sea Scouts from Little Falls, Minnesota, and other adult guests, besides the crew. Despite the best efforts of the Coast Guard cutter *Woodrush,* the little vessel clung stubbornly to her perch.

Since weather in the Isle Royale area is subject to dangerous fluctuations at that time of the year, a veritable

1950

The shipping seasons of the early 1950s were good for shippers, with 100-million-ton seasons becoming the norm and for the most part remarkably accident free. More than a billion tons of freight were handled in Lake Superior ports during the decade. The opening season of the decade saw 106 million tons being handled. Only the

Pilothouse awash, the sunken Emperor*'s crew was fortunate that the Coast Guard was near at hand.* THOM HOLDEN COLLECTION.

flotilla of Coast Guard, Corps of Engineers and Navy vessels raced to the spot. Included were the Coast Guard cutter *Mesquite,* augmenting the *Woodrush,* a Corps of Engineers' tug from Marquette, the derrick-barge *Faith* with her 90-ton crane, the Naval Reserve training ship *AMS 51* from Hancock and even the big wrecking tug *Favorite* from the Soo and the Coast Guard icebreaker *Mackinaw* from the lower lakes. Some had not arrived before the cutter *Mesquite* coaxed the *PC 782* off the rocks. Though damaged considerably, the *PC 782* under Commander E.E. Havlik sailed to the dry dock in Superior under her own power with a Coast Guard and Naval Reserve escort.

While the whole experience was a lark for the Sea Scouts and an embarrassingly long weekend for the Naval Reservists, the affair was expensive for the Navy. Repairs to *PC 782* may have exceeded $50,000. The vessel shortly thereafter was withdrawn from Duluth, leaving the Duluth Naval Reserve without a training ship, a situation which still exists.[26]

33-foot, 13-ton diesel-powered fish tug *Vernon* became a casualty, foundering on August 5 when 29 miles northeast of Grand Marais, Michigan. The *Vernon* was owned by Lyle A. McDonald of Grand Marais, having been built in 1932 at Kenosha, Wisconsin.

1951

Tonnage transiting Lake Superior rose a healthy 13 percent to 120 million tons with iron ore accounting for more than 90 million of those tons, second only to the 1942 season, and lakers once again added to the casualty roster. On May 2, Pioneer Steamship's 504-foot, 6,390-ton *A.A. Augustus* struck bottom in the Superior Harbor Basin causing costly damage to her rudder and steering gear. September saw the *B.F. Jones,* a 538-foot unit of Jones & Laughlin Steel, colliding with Great Northern ore dock No. 2 in Superior, causing substantial damage to her shell plating and setting in several structural frames on the 4th. Later in the month on September 19, the 525-foot *Donald B. Gillies* of the Pioneer Steamship fleet virtually repeated the previous incident at Great Northern Dock

The bulk freighter Henry Steinbrenner *shown unloading coal at the Reiss dock in Ashland a decade before her foundering in wild May seas of 1953.* ALLEN BORN PHOTO, AL SMILES COLLECTION.

No. 1 in Superior. Superior was also the scene of the last casualty of the season, occurring on October 23 when the 474-foot, 5,057-ton *Cuyler Adams* of the Globe Steamship Company rammed the north breakwall at the harbor entry, damaging her bow.

1952

More than 23,000 vessels transited the Soo Locks carrying 107 million tons of cargo, a drop of 11 percent, but still a solid season. It was an accident-free season on Lake Superior.

1953

Lake Superior tonnage increased to 128 million tons this season, but two more ships joined the undersea fleet and a third had a mighty close call. Residents of Duluth and Superior were basking in midsummer weather on Saturday, May 9 as the 427-foot steamer *Henry Steinbrenner* was taking on iron ore at the Great Northern Railway docks in Allouez. The thermometer stood at a magnificent 78 degrees F on Saturday, and it was still 65 above at 7 a.m. Sunday, shortly before the *Steinbrenner* sailed. Nevertheless, a cold front was approaching and gale warnings were raised with fresh to strong southerly and southeasterly winds forecast. Still, there was really nothing to suggest to Captain Albert Stiglin of the *Steinbrenner* that the weather was conjuring anything more than

a typically unpleasant May blow, which was not especially dangerous to steel vessels.

Unfortunately, this was an exception. As the *Steinbrenner* steamed her way eastward on Sunday afternoon and evening, a violent thunderstorm complex with winds up to 72 mph struck Duluth at 6:30 p.m. Western Lake Superior was riled by blasts ranging from 38 to 60 mph steadily for the next six hours. Rain fell in torrents. The gales grew worse as the storm moved eastward over the lake. Captain George Fisher of the huge 650-foot ore carrier *Wilfred Sykes* reported waves up to 19 feet. Meanwhile, the temperature was plummeting, Duluth recording a drop of 19 degrees during midday. The next day brought blinding snow.

The 52-year-old *Steinbrenner* was having hard sledding. Only a quarter of the crew was able to get to the galley for the evening meal. While First Mate Andrew Croft had verified the hatch covers secure, they were not tarped down and, under continuous pounding from sky-high waves during the night, began to admit water to the cargo hold. Captain Stiglin maneuvered the vessel as best he could during the hours of darkness, but as daybreak came, he was conscious of the ship's sluggish handling. He could see in the early light that she was riding very low.

The *Steinbrenner* was now approximately 14 to 15 miles south of Isle Royale Light on Menagerie Island midway along Isle Royale's southeasterly shore. Suddenly, a monstrous wave stripped the covers off the three sternmost hatches, and the foundering vessel was taking water over the top. Desperately, Captain Stiglin began to call for help over his radio-telephone, reporting the deteriorating situation. Fortuitously, within hailing distance were several giants of the lakes, the 682-foot *Joseph H. Thompson,* the 650-foot *Wilfred Sykes* and the 580-foot *D.M. Clemson.* In the 70 mph winds, however, they were several hours away. As the would-be rescuers rushed to the *Steinbrenner*'s location, the venomous waves were victorious. Captain Stiglin ordered the ship abandoned at 6:25 a.m., but before this could be accomplished in an orderly manner, the *Steinbrenner* slid to the bottom stern first, her boilers exploding and her pilothouse disintegrating from air pressure. By 6:30 a.m., she was gone.

A life raft and two lifeboats had gotten free. These held only 17 of the 31 aboard. Captain Stiglin and Second Cook Bernard Oberoski were actually sucked down as the vessel sank beneath their feet. Both broke the suction hold and popped to the surface. Captain Stiglin boarded the raft with others, and Oberoski pulled himself into a lifeboat which held only two others.

Then followed four terrible hours in near freezing cold with icy breakers spewing over all. Two men succumbed to exposure aboard the raft and another in a lifeboat. Happily, shortly after 10 a.m., through the spray and snow loomed the hulks of the rescue ships, the *Thompson* picking up the raft containing Captain Stiglin and four men, the *Clemson* bringing aboard seven men from one lifeboat and the *Sykes,* after most difficult maneuvering, retrieving two more from the second lifeboat, together with the body of a sailor who had expired. The *Sykes* actually had to launch a lifeboat of her own to effect the rescue.

Other lake carriers swarmed into the area searching for the 14 missing crewmen, including the *Imperial Leduc, Hochelaga, Pathfinder* and *Ontadoc.* Later in the day, the U.S. Coast Guard lifeboats from Portage Canal, Grand Marais, Minnesota, and Two Harbors combed the waters. Altogether, 10 bodies were recovered, that of Third Mate Arthur J. Morse being found 17 miles southeast of the sinking site four days later by the steamer *Clifford Hood.* Morse had launched a stern lifeboat but had been sucked down by the ship before he could jump. Some crewmen apparently were reticent about getting into the lifeboats, thinking their ship a better gamble in the tumultuous waves. The final tally was 14 rescued and 17 dead. While no property loss was recorded, the old ship must have been worth more than $150,000.[27]

Only six weeks later came another fatal mishap. In dense fog on Thunder Bay, June 21, two Canadian steamers came together, the 444-foot *Burlington* of Canada Steamship Lines ramming and sinking the 416-foot *Scotiadoc* of Paterson Steamship Lines. Luckily, the *Scotiadoc* remained afloat long enough to permit the launching of lifeboats, although Seaman Wallace McDermid of the *Scotiadoc* was drowned as a lifeboat capsized in launching. The other 29 members of the *Scotiadoc* crew were picked up by the *Burlington* and brought to the Canadian Lakehead. Both ships formerly were on the American registry, the *Burlington* having been the *Henry W. Oliver* and *S.H. Robbins,* last of the Wilson Transit Company, and the *Scotiadoc* being the former *Martin Mullen* of the Pioneer Steamship Company. The 49-year-old *Scotiadoc* carried a wheat cargo worth more than $500,000, and the ship herself must have been valued at $175,000 or more.[28]

Lake Superior struggled madly to seize a major carrier once more this season. In the early morning hours of September 12, a tempestuous freak squall struck the 530-foot steamer *Maryland* of the Bethlehem Transportation Company when she was off Grand Island, about 40 miles east of Marquette. For more than five hours, mountainous waves propelled by winds of 55 mph slapped the substantial steamer as she painfully made her way toward Marquette and safety. Then, the menacing combers ripped off two hatch covers, allowing water to pour into the cargo hold. In a risky damage control effort, the crew replaced the hatch covers, but not before several feet of water flooded into the hold. Thereafter, Captain A.P. Goodrow could not hold her on course or avoid the trough.

Knowing the terrain in the vicinity of Marquette, he was aware that a ruinous rocky shore lay northwest of the port, while dangerous rocks also existed from Shot Point to the east. A band of sandy beach stretches between the city and Shot Point. Accordingly, the captain so maneuvered the *Maryland* that if she were to go ashore, she would hit the sand.

That is the way it turned out. Overpowered by the gale, anchors dragging, the *Maryland* hit the sands at 9:50 a.m. about eight miles east of Marquette between Lakewood and Gordon. Alerted by radio, the Marquette Coast

Too few survived the sinking of Henry Steinbrenner *in 1953, despite heroic efforts of several lake vessels which risked peril when they changed course for the wreck scene.* CAPTAIN J.A. ROBINSON COLLECTION.

Guard crew, augmented by 25 Michigan State Policemen and Marquette County Sheriff's deputies, was on hand. Because of the raging seas, the Coast Guardsmen decided to use a breeches buoy in the rescue attempt. Their second shot put a line aboard the *Maryland* and, within several hours, 21 of the crew were brought safely ashore.

Suddenly, an unusually towering comber struck the *Maryland,* lifted her high and broke the life lines. Indeed, the gale was now too strong to permit the Coast Guardsmen to shoot another line. There were still 11 men aboard. But the Marquette Coast Guard commander, Chief Boatswain John Kinnunen, had anticipated just such a situation. Hours before, he had radioed to the Coast Guard base at Traverse City on the east side of Lake Michigan and requested the Coast Guard helicopter. This was airborne, reaching Marquette in good time and standing by when the emergency occurred. The last 11 *Maryland* crewmen were brought ashore by helicopter, apparently the first helicopter rescue in Lake Superior history. The Coast Guard cutter *Woodrush* and icebreaker *Mackinaw* hurried to Marquette, as did the salvage tug *Favorite.* They had the *Maryland* afloat in five days before the lake could break her to pieces. She was towed to Superior for rebuilding, repairs aggregating $250,000. She was then sold and renamed *Henry LaLiberte,* serving in the clinker trade for the Duluth cement industry more than 20 years before being retired in 1973.[29]

En route to the *Maryland* rescue, the Coast Guard icebreaker *Mackinaw* performed another rescue feat. In the same storm which bedeviled the *Maryland,* the 100-foot dredge *Howard M. Jr.* broke away from the tug

The breeches-buoy rescue in September 1953 of the Maryland *crew stranded near Marquette may have been the last use of that lifesaving method on Lake Superior.* AUTHOR'S COLLECTION.

George Purvis of Gore Bay, Ontario. The tug managed to remove six men from the dredge, but nine others remained aboard for the nightmarish ride from just west of Caribou Island to within 12 miles of Au Sable Point, where the *Mackinaw* succeeded in putting a line aboard and towing the dredge to safety. Lake Superior was cheated again. The *Howard M. Jr.* was owned by the McNamara Construction Company of Toronto and was bound for Port Arthur when the troubles occurred.[30]

1954

Following a season of exceptionally good tonnage and a poor safety record was one with a drop of 36 million tons in ore shipments to just 62 million and a season freight total of only 85 million tons. Fewer lakers on the water apparently allowed the season to progress without incident. Casualties involving small craft would predominate for more than 20 years after the flurry of shipwreck action in 1953. On June 8, 1954, the 76-foot, 113-ton steel Canadian tug *Edward C. Whalen* made the final dive a half mile southeast of Corbeil Point. No loss of life was reported.

1955

Iron ore shipments rose to 89 million tons this season bolstering tonnage through the Soo to a respectable 114

million tons. The larger carriers remained without reported incident despite their increased number. However, on May 9, 1955, the diminutive 37-foot, 13-ton *Eileen G.* sank near Tunnel Island. The *Eileen G.* had been built at Owen Sound in 1944 and was owned by J.J. McFadden Lumber Company of Blind River, Ontario.

1956

Despite more than 21,000 vessels transiting Lake Superior carrying 109 million tons of freight, both large and small vessels avoided adding to the lake's casualty roster.

1957

Lake Superior freight shipments remained relatively stable, closing at 111 million tons, and the large vessels for the most part again avoided difficulty. Only one of the smaller vessels was lost. A small Canadian tug, the 47-foot, 13-ton *D & C,* stranded and sank at Grenfell Rock on November 19. She was built in 1950 at Owen Sound and owned by David A. Drever of Collingwood. Earlier in the season, Pittsburgh Steamship's 589-foot, 7,700-ton *Thomas F. Cole* was ice damaged while dockside in Superior on April 22, and in midsummer on July 7 this same vessel collided with the Duluth-Superior Interstate Bridge, damage being minimal.

1958

Lake Superior tonnage fell off by 31 percent this season to 76 million tons, the lowest since 1939. Only 17,000 vessels transited the Soo Locks. Vessels both large and small avoided incident.

1959

A new era was ushered onto Lake Superior and the rest of the Great Lakes as the modern St. Lawrence Seaway came into full deep-draft operation on April 25, 1959. This certainly was not the first time ocean vessels were able to enter the lakes, for they had been doing so for more than a half century, but it marked the beginning of 26-foot drafts and 730-foot vessels throughout the Great Lakes-St. Lawrence Seaway System. Portions of some harbors were still several years from the full 26-foot draft, but the locks and connecting channels were ready for an

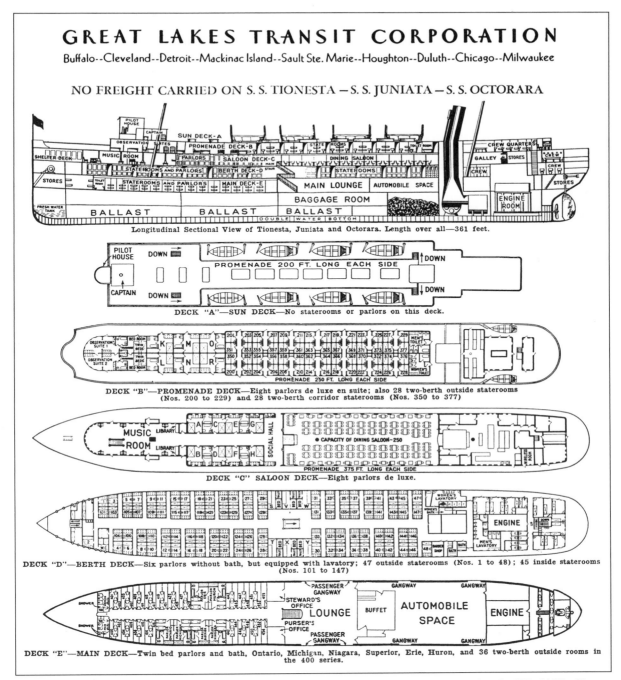

Great Lakes Transit Company's popular sisters called at U.S. Lake Superior ports until the outbreak of World War II.
CANAL PARK MARINE MUSEUM COLLECTION.

expected onslaught of the big ocean-going ships, or "salties." Almost 17 million tons of bulk cargo and nearly 2 million tons of general cargo transited the St. Lawrence Seaway in its first season.[31] More than 19,000 vessels transited the Soo Locks carrying 71 million tons of freight. Some 198 of the salties entered Lake Superior, representing 16 nations on their 350 round trips to American and Canadian Lakehead harbors.

The season was remarkably accident-free, and the salties seemed to adapt well to the ways of fresh-water sailing. Both lakers and salties avoided incident. However, the decade could not close without Lake Superior adding some record of tragedy. Trapped in the west channel of Munising Bay on May 11, 1959, an unnamed 20-foot fishing boat was overwhelmed by a roaring northwest squall, drowning three sports fishermen from Munising.[32]

1 Lake Carriers' Association, *Annual Report* (Cleveland, Ohio, Lake Carriers' Association, 1930-1959).

2 Ronald H. Wrigley, *Northern Superior Shipwrecks,* 198 pp., unpublished manuscript, ca. 1979, pp. 11-12.

3 *Duluth News-Tribune,* Oct. 10, 1931; Frederick Stonehouse, *Keweenaw Shipwrecks,* (Au Train, Michigan, Avery Color Studios, 1988), p. 300.

4 *Duluth News-Tribune,* Nov. 23, 27, 29, Dec. 2-4, 1931; Fred W. Green, *Green's Marine Directory of the Great Lakes* (Cleveland, Fred W. Green, 26th ed., 1934), pp. 113, 154, 200, 391; A.J. "Bud" Knuckey, "Scuttlebutt... The Perils of a Pinched Purse" in *Lake Superior Port Cities* Magazine, Vol. 5, No. 2, Fall 1983, pp. 49-50. Wheelsman John Wick of the *Hebard* is the same John Wick who was first mate on the *America* when she was lost at Isle Royale in June 1928.

5 *Duluth News-Tribune,* Nov. 26-27, 30, 1932; C. Patrick Labadie, *Submerged Cultural Resources Study: Pictured Rocks National Lakeshore,* (Santa Fe, New Mexico, Submerged Cultural Resources Unit, National Park Service, 1989), p. 173.

6 *Duluth News-Tribune,* Nov. 30, 1932. A small portion of the *Josephine Addison*'s hull plus her boiler, one-cylinder steam engine, shaft and propeller were abandoned on the Bayfield waterfront at the former site of the Halvor Reiten boatyard, but were moved in 1989 as a step toward preservation.

7 *Duluth News-Tribune,* May 28-31, June 2, 9, 1933; Thom Holden, "Reef of the Three C's: Part III, Sinking of the *George M. Cox*" in *The Nor'Easter,* Vol. 8, No. 3, May-June 1983, pp. 1-5, 8; Thom Holden, "A Maiden Voyage into History" in *Telescope,* Journal of the Great Lakes Maritime Institute, Detroit, Vol. 23, No. 1, January-February 1984, pp. 3-10; Thom Holden, *Above and Below* (Houghton, Michigan, Isle Royale Natural History Association, 1985), pp. 35, 41-48; Ryan Leblanc, Schreiber, Ontario, personal interview recorded August 31, 1988, by Thom Holden; Larry Murphy and Thom Holden, "Shipwrecks of Isle Royale: The Historical Record" in *Submerged Cultural Resources Study: Isle Royale National Park,* Daniel J. Lenihan, ed., (Santa Fe, New Mexico, Submerged Cultural Resources Unit, National Park Service, 1987), pp. 153-168; Larry Murphy, Daniel Lenihan and C. Patrick Labadie, "Shipwrecks of Isle Royale: The Archeological Record" in Lenihan, ed., *ibid.,* pp. 292-305. One curious element in the *Cox* loss was a note in Canadian records indicating scuttling in Thunder Bay of a boiler believed to have been removed from the ship during commercial salvage.

8 *Duluth News-Tribune,* June 3, 1935.

9 *Duluth News-Tribune,* Sept. 25, 1937; Dominion of Canada, Department of Transport, *Casualties to Vessels Resulting in Total Loss on the Great Lakes, 1870-1957,* p. 70; Ronald Wrigley, *Shipwrecked: Vessels that met tragedy on Northern Lake Superior,* (Cobalt, Ontario, Highway Book Shop, 1985), p. 93-101.

10 *Duluth News-Tribune,* June 2, 1938.

11 Bureau of Navigation, Department of Commerce, *Merchant Vessels of the United States,* 1939, p. 511.

12 *Duluth News-Tribune,* May 3-4, 1940; Dominion of Canada, Department of Transport, *op. cit.,* p. 71. Dwight Boyer presents a fascinating analysis of the *Arlington* affair as "The Enigma of 'Tatey Bug' Burke" in *True Tales of the Great Lakes* (New York, Dodd, Mead, 1971), pp. 1-26.

13 *Duluth News-Tribune,* Nov. 9-10, 1940; Labadie, *op. cit.,* p. 173.

14 Details of the two incidents cited were so sketchy that neither vessel could be positively identified from available records. Labadie, *ibid.*

15 *Duluth News-Tribune,* Sept. 4, 7, 1942; Stonehouse, *op. cit.,* p. 301-302.

16 *Duluth News-Tribune,* Sept. 23, 1942; Stonehouse, *op. cit.,* pp. 303-308.

17 *Duluth News-Tribune,* Dec. 1, 1942; Supervising Examiner of Master and Mates for Inland Waters, Department of Transport, "Preliminary Inquiry — Steamer *Judge Hart* Sinking," December 24, 1942; Captain Frederick M. Burmeister, "Shipping Casualties — Strandings, Wr.1 (g), *Judge Hart*," December 2, 1942; Wrigley, *Northern Superior Shipwrecks, op. cit.,* pp. 103-106.

18 *Duluth News-Tribune,* June 2, 1943; Dominion of Canada, Department of Transport, *op. cit.,* p. 73.

19 *Duluth News-Tribune,* June 3, 1943.

20 *Lake Log Chips,* Dec. 27, 1986; correspondence, Leo Gallagher to Institute for Great Lakes Research, Bowling Green State University, Nov. 21, 1986.

21 *Duluth News-Tribune,* Dec. 13, 1943.

22 *Marquette Mining Journal,* May 23, July 6, 1945; Labadie, *op. cit.,* p. 173.

23 *Duluth News-Tribune,* June 1, 1947.

24 *Duluth News-Tribune,* June 5-6, 1947; Jerry Eliason, "Ships That No Longer Sail" in *Lake Superior Port Cities* Magazine, Vol. 4, No. 4, 1983, pp. 29-34; Holden, *Above and Below, op. cit.,* pp. 20-22; Murphy and Holden, *op. cit.,* pp. 175-186; Murphy, Lenihan and Labadie, *op. cit.,* pp. 312-325; Wrigley, *Northern Superior Shipwrecks, op. cit.,* pp. 107-114.

25 *Duluth News-Tribune,* June 24-26, 1948; *Marquette Mining Journal,* June 24, 1948.

26 *Duluth News-Tribune,* May 29-31, June 1-4, 1949; Sam Rude, personal interview at Duluth, Minnesota, ca. December 1973, conducted by Thom Holden.

27 *Duluth News-Tribune,* May 10-12, 15-17, 19, 1953.

28 *Duluth News-Tribune,* June 22, 1953; Dominion of Canada, Department of Transport, *op. cit.,* p. 77.

29 *Duluth News-Tribune,* Sept. 13, 1953; *Marquette Mining Journal,* Sept. 12, 14-15, 17, 19, 22, 1953.

30 *Duluth News-Tribune,* Sept. 14, 1953.

31 Jacques Lesstrang, "The Thirtieth Season: A Retrospective" in *Seaway Review,* Vol. 17, No. 2, Summer 1988, pp. 37-47; "St. Lawrence Seaway: Chronology of Significant Events" in *Seaway Review, op. cit.,* pp. 53-66; "The Seaway at Twenty: An Anniversary Overview" in *Seaway Review,* Vol. 8, No. 4, Summer 1979, pp. 17-27.

32 Records of the Canadian tug losses are reported in Dominion of Canada, Department of Transport, *op. cit.,* pp. 78-80; the Munising accident was covered in *Munising News,* May 13, 1959.

The Italian Fucinitore *typifies salties entering the Great Lakes trade in the first two decades of the new Seaway.* HARBOR REFLECTIONS PHOTO BY TIM SLATTERY, DULUTH.

Chapter 9

The Lakes-Seaway System Emerges
1960-1975

The decade of the 1960s fully opened the Great Lakes-St. Lawrence Seaway system which allowed vessels from around the world to trade alongside familiar U.S. and Canadian lakers coming into the heartland of the continent from virtually all corners of the world. Lake Superior traffic for the decade reached 911,448,603 tons while the novel Seaway traffic for the same period reached 331,305,970 tons.[1]

The pattern of minor incidents continued throughout the 1960s and into the 1970s.

1960

Tonnage was up at the Soo in 1960 to more than 91 million tons, showing a substantial 29 percent increase on the dismal 1959 season which had been the lowest on record since 1939. Seaway traffic held rather steady at 18.4 million tons, a slight decrease from 1959. Ice posed some problems on Lake Superior, particularly in April between the 13th and 17th, for the most part delaying rather than

207

damaging vessels. However, many difficulties for the large commercial vessels occurred in Whitefish Bay or in the Upper St. Marys River above the Soo Locks where early and late season ice compounded problems in these heavily used shipping areas.

The John O. McKellar *was one of two ships which experienced cracked plates as she worked in the Lake Superior storm of December 9, 1960, the other being the* Starbelle. CANAL PARK MARINE MUSEUM COLLECTION.

The casualty season opened on the Canadian shore with Mohawk Navigation's 542-foot *Captain C.D. Secord* having to return to port on April 12, after finding a cracked hull plate up forward when off Hare Island. The damage was probably caused by ice, either on her journey up the lake or immediately after having cleared Port Arthur. She was in no danger of sinking and damage was minimal. Shipyard workers had to have some cargo removed so the *Secord* could be ballasted down aft to bring the damaged area above the waterline for repair and reinforcing.

On April 18, the 603-foot, 9,057-ton *Robert C. Stanley* of U.S. Steel's Pittsburgh Steamship Company ripped her bottom at Vidal Shoal, but limped into the Soo for inspection and temporary repairs. Later in the season on September 17, fleetmate *Richard V. Lindabury* also grounded on Vidal Shoal, although the extent of damage was unreported. On October 30, Pickands Mather's 690-foot, 14,114-ton *John Sherwin,* with 21,500 tons of ore aboard, snagged rocks and sank in the St. Marys River eight miles above the Soo. The next day, October 31, the 585-foot, 9,115-ton *Tom M. Girdler* hit some obstruction near the west approach to the locks, going aground. Salvors got them off, though the *Sherwin* could have been a moderately expensive operation.

The Liberian saltie *National Hope* had a brush collision on October 20 with the Duluth-Superior Interstate Bridge, neither suffering extensively. A rousing gale on December 9 caused some anxiety as two Canadian ships, the *Starbelle* and *John O. McKellar,* reported they had suffered cracking due to stress of weather. The 110-foot Coast Guard cutter *Naugatuck* went into the eastern lake

to escort the *Starbelle* to safety. The 47-year-old 250-foot, 2,274-ton *Starbelle* was owned by K.A. Powell (Canada) Ltd. of Winnipeg. Scott Misener Steamships' 660-foot, 13,884-ton *McKellar* apparently continued on her own.[2]

1961

Reported casualties dropped this season, one far exceeding the financial damage with its intriguing week-long chain of rescue events. Roles were reversed this season between Lake Superior tonnage and that of the Seaway, with the latter up a whopping 15 percent to more than 21 million tons while traffic through the Soo canals dropped off 12 percent to little more than 81 million tons.

Problems continued to occur in the eastern lake above the Soo. One of the costliest mishaps involved the five-year-old 461-foot, 8,671-ton British saltie *Crystal Jewel* which raked a reef at Gros Cap, putting a 300-foot slash in her hull on May 6. Her captain first beached her to keep from foundering; then U.S. Coast Guard cutters brought powerful pumps to keep her afloat until she reached the Soo. Repairs must have been expensive. Another saltie, the Greek ship *Anvarkikos,* grounded on Pancake Shoal November 26, needing the services of salvors.

The Isle Royale passenger ferry *Voyageur* settled at dockside on May 26 at Grand Portage near the Canadian border, but the wooden vessel was quickly retrieved with minimal damage. The *Joseph H. Thompson* struck an obstruction in Superior Harbor on September 14 with damage estimated to be in excess of $27,000 to the 696-foot,

The Captain C.D. Secord *wallowed helplessly as several vessels worked to get her in tow during an early December 1961 storm off Isle Royale.* COURTESY OF WESLEY R. HARKINS MARINE PHOTOGRAPHY, DULUTH.

12,217-ton bulk freighter which had been converted from a C-4 saltie named *Marine Robin* in 1952.[3] Reiss Steamship's 430-foot, 4,510-ton *Otto M. Reiss,* formerly the *James S. Dunham* built in 1906, hit some submerged object and suffered minor hull damage at Ashland in October. The 18-year-old 7,139-ton British saltie *Oak Hill* found what was becoming a favorite haunt for foreign vessels, the Duluth-Superior Interstate Bridge, on November 22, fortunately with minimal damage.

The season closed dramatically with several lake carriers and the U.S. Coast Guard working together to rescue a dead ship adrift with 28 crewmen aboard wallowing in high wind and sea off Rock of Ages Light. While upbound in the St. Marys River on December 2, the 542-foot, 6,943-ton Canadian bulk freighter *Captain C.D. Secord* experienced problems resulting in propeller and machinery damage. Captain Basil Jarvis contacted *Sir Thomas Shaughnessy,* a fleetmate in the Mohawk Navigation Company Ltd. which was also upbound light for the Canadian Lakehead, to see if she could tow the *Secord* up the lake. Meanwhile, the *Secord* had come to anchor in the river. The *Shaughnessy* put a line out to the *Secord* on the afternoon of the 2nd, towing her up through the canal and onto Lake Superior.

Both the *Shaughnessy* and *Secord* masters had previous experience with consorts, so towing was nothing new. However, the 1,200-horsepower *Shaughnessy* had slow going up the lake on December 3rd and into the 4th with weather conditions deteriorating. A storm out of the northwest finally caught the two vessels, putting a strain on the tow line until it finally parted in 40 mph winds and 15-foot seas when the two were about 10 miles southeasterly of Rock of Ages off the southwest end of Isle Royale and about 58 miles east of Grand Marais, Minnesota.

The call for assistance was picked up at the U.S. Coast Guard's North Superior station in Grand Marais and relayed to Lieutenant Commander C. Gil Porter of Duluth, captain of the *Woodrush.* Captain Porter's crew of 42 had just returned from a logistics run and had been given shore passes but an hour before. However, within two hours, the crew was reassembled and the 180-foot *Woodrush* was under way. A memorable, storm-tossed journey of 165 miles was ahead of the crew before they caught up with the *Secord,* drifting at about three mph toward the Keweenaw Peninsula, fortunately with nothing but open water in her path.

Meanwhile, another running mate of the *Secord,* the *Golden Hind,* had completed loading in Port Arthur and set out for the scene. *Golden Hind* reached her stricken sister in the early morning hours of the 5th, positioning herself to windward along with the *Shaughnessy* to take the worst of the seas even though they, too, were taking quite a beating. The *Woodrush* arrived about two hours after the *Golden Hind* and succeeded in getting a line onto the *Secord.* They set course for Duluth. Even though the wind had dropped to 25 mph, the seas had only dropped to 10 feet. Captain Porter elected to change course for the Keweenaw and run downwind for the shelter of Bete Grise rather than running in the trough fully 150 miles to her home base.

The Coast Guard cutter *Woodrush* was successful in getting her charge into the sheltered waters behind Keweenaw Point. There, another *Secord* fleetmate, the 451-foot *Mohawk Deer,* arrived to take up the tow to the Ca-

The Golden Hind *was one of several vessels which assisted in rescuing* Captain C.D. Secord *in December 1961 storm.* BARRY ANDERSEN PHOTO, E.B. GILLHAM COLLECTION.

nadian Lakehead where the *Secord* could be repaired. However, weather continued to rile the lake with 30 mph winds and heavy snow until they were finally able to set out on December 8 with the *Woodrush* as escort. They arrived safely after crossing 120 miles of open lake without further incident. Port Arthur shipyard workers found extensive damage to the *Secord*'s machinery, delaying her reentering service until June 1962.[4]

1962

Lake Superior tonnage fell only one percent from the previous season, but reached the lowest for the entire decade at 80.3 million tons while tonnage handled on the St. Lawrence Seaway improved nine percent to 23.2 million tons. There was an American passenger vessel, one government vessel and a Norwegian saltie among reported casualties involving mostly a host of the usual dock strikings at Duluth, Superior and Two Harbors.

While working the Duluth-Superior Harbor on April 28, the 180-foot, 1,200-horsepower U.S. Coast Guard cutter *Woodrush* found herself aground, though released undamaged. Later in the summer on July 31, the 290-foot, 2,662-ton passenger vessel *South American* suffered propeller damage en route on the open lake from the Twin Ports to Munising, Michigan. The incident added some excitement for her myriad passengers who had expected a memorable cruise on the Chicago, Duluth & Georgian

Bay Transit liner, but more for the scenery, accommodations and relaxation. The *Otto M. Reiss* grounded in Ashland Harbor on September 3 with damage estimated at $87,000.[5] An apparent brush collision in Duluth Harbor

The Otto. M. Reiss *saw better July sailing than that in 1965 when she first brushed the Interstate Bridge in Duluth-Superior and a few weeks later grounded lightly in Ashland.* HAROLD ANDRESEN PHOTO, CANAL PARK MARINE MUSEUM COLLECTION.

between the 56-year-old 4,510-ton *Otto M. Reiss* and the two-year-old 7,050-ton Norwegian saltie *Carina* on November 8 persisted in highlighting the presence of foreign vessels whose numbers continued to increase as the St. Lawrence Seaway aspired to reach its potential.

One sad incident in 1962 served as a reminder of the often devastating catastrophies involving small craft. A young Negaunee, Michigan, mining engineer took his three sons, ages six to 10, for a late afternoon cruise east of Marquette on July 13. A rugged squall swept in. Seemingly, the father had not informed the Marquette Coast Guard of his trip. Consequently, no search was launched when he failed to return at nightfall until relatives reported the boat missing. Searchers discovered the little craft capsized off the mouth of Chocolay River, four miles east of Marquette, with the boys dead in their life jackets and the father missing and presumed drowned. A number of other recreational boaters have come to grief over the years at various points around the lake.[6]

1963

This was a season in which Lake Superior regained some of the tonnage it had lost over the previous two seasons, improving seven percent to 86 million tons while the Seaway also showed considerable improvement, increasing 21 percent to a new record high of 23.2 million tons.

Two bridges crossing the Duluth-Superior Harbor were smacked, however lightly, during the season. The 586-foot, 7,940-ton Pittsburgher *Richard V. Lindabury* was first on May 5 when her rudder stock failed, sending her aground while also colliding with the old Northern Pacific Railroad swing bridge. Toward the end of the season on November 16, fleetmate *William P. Palmer* struck the Interstate Bridge lightly, the 580-foot, 7,602-ton vessel suffering little apparent damage. An unusual collision in the Duluth Harbor on May 18 saw the seven-year-old 6,156-ton Greek *Maria K.* strike a suction dredging pipeline, disrupting work for only a short while and causing no apparent damage to the saltie.

1964

Drift ice in the Upper St. Marys River and Whitefish Bay posed some problems during the early season from April 1-17, but tonnage improved again to 94 million tons, an increase of 10 percent. Traffic through the Seaway set another record, the fourth in a row, at 35.6 million tons, an increase of 27 percent from 1963.

The Northern Pacific Railroad Bridge across the St. Louis River in the Duluth-Superior Harbor was struck twice during the 1964 season. The William P. Palmer *was first with a light May 1 brush.* CANAL PARK MARINE MUSEUM COLLECTION.

The only casualty of some consequence befell the Bradley Transportation fleet's *Calcite II,* the former *William G. Clyde* built in 1929, which sustained bottom damage when she stranded hard in the upper St. Marys River above the locks on August 28, requiring salvage assistance for the 587-foot, 8,243-ton self-unloader. Damage was undisclosed, but she was dry-docked in Superior at Fraser Shipyards. Earlier in the season on May 1, the Pittsburgher *William P. Palmer* had a minor collision with the Northern Pacific Railroad Bridge in Duluth-Superior Harbor. A similar event on November 18 involved the 504-foot, 6,423-ton *William H. Donner*. Cleveland-Cliffs' 716-foot, 13,122-ton *Walter A. Sterling* was reported aground in Whitefish Bay off Point Iroquois on May 8. Her 580-foot, 7,918-ton fleetmate *Pontiac* struck a breakwall at Marquette on July 31. A gentle collision between the Greek *Constantia* and the 586-foot, 7,694-ton *J.P. Morgan Jr.* was of little consequence in Duluth Harbor on November 3. The 30-foot cruiser *Markay* also was reported as having foundered in a storm five miles east of Whitefish Point on September 26.

1965

Lake Superior tonnage was virtually unchanged this season from last, although an improvement of one percent boosted it to 95.3 million tons. Another record, the fifth in a row, was set on the Seaway with a 10 percent increase to 39.3 million tons.

Spring saw the 28-foot fish tug *Wigeon* suffering weather damage while sheltering in Grand Traverse Bay on the east side of the Keweenaw Peninsula.[7] Cleveland Tankers' 52-year-old 349-foot tanker *Rocket* grounded lightly in Superior on April 30. Columbia's *Reserve* struck a pier at Sault Ste. Marie, Michigan, on May 18 with damage estimated at $46,000.[8] U.S. Steel's *Peter A.B. Widener* nearly repeated her adventures of November 1926 when the steering gear failed on the 585-foot, 7,670-ton bulk freighter off Rock of Ages Light near Isle Royale on September 15, making for another miraculous bit of seamanship. The 25-year-old 4,934-ton British saltie *Glaisdale* reported a minor grounding in Duluth on October 3. Ashland Harbor had been the scene of several minor groundings with Reiss Steamship's 580-foot, 8,220-ton *Raymond H. Reiss* grounded and released on May 1, Columbia Transportation's 533-foot, 6,551-ton *J. Clare Miller* similarly involved on June 14 and another Reiss boat, the 430-foot, 4,510-ton *Otto M. Reiss,* likewise on July 27. Less than three weeks earlier, July 8, the *Otto M. Reiss* had brushed the Duluth-Superior Interstate Bridge. The season closed with the U.S. Coast Guard cutter *Woodrush* reporting damage from a grounding at an undisclosed location on Lake Superior, December 4.

1966

This was a season for Lake Superior traffic to shine with the highest tonnage for the decade and the highest since

1957 at 103.6 million tons. This was accompanied by another record year on the Seaway with 44.6 million tons transiting its myriad locks.

The season started early when National Steel's 710-foot, 12,626-ton bulk freighter *Paul H. Carnahan* struck a dock in Superior on April 26 with damage estimated at $42,800. She was previously the *Honey Hill,* a coastwise tanker, rebuilt just five years before.[9]

An old stamp sand reclaiming dredge settled to the bottom of Torch Lake in 1968 where it remains. WILDERNESS PORT SHIPWRECKS PHOTO BY THOM HOLDEN, CANAL PARK MARINE MUSEUM COLLECTION.

After a substantial period of calm in reported casualties, excitement filled the radio air waves on September 15 as Bethlehem Steel's 603-foot, 9,057-ton steamer *Lehigh* reported a boiler explosion 10 miles south of Caribou Island with a man badly injured and all power lost. Wilson Marine Transit's 585-foot steamer *Tom M. Girdler* stood by as the 110-foot U.S. Coast Guard cutter *Naugatuck* raced toward the scene and a Coast Guard amphibious plane landed and picked up the injured seaman. Her crew repaired a portion of the damage, and the *Lehigh* limped to the Soo.

The rest of the season was much like those in the first half of this decade with myriad dock strikings and minor groundings. Kinsman Marine Transit's 480-foot, 6,053-ton *Peavey Pioneer,* the former *Stephen M. Clement,* was aground twice in Ashland Harbor, first on April 20 and then again on May 31. She was apparently little damaged in either incident. Reiss Steamship's 601-foot, 10,849-ton *William A. Reiss* hit a submerged object at Taconite Harbor on April 30 and just a week later was damaged by a fire at Superior. The May 6 blaze resulted in damages of $50,937.[10] Great Lakes Towing's 81-foot, 1,200-horsepower tug *Texas* also struck some submerged object off Two Harbors on September 20. The Duluth Ship Canal was smitten twice during 1966, U.S. Steel's 24-year-old 622-foot, 10,294-ton *Benjamin F. Fairless* hitting the north pier on July 6 and the 23-year-old 511-foot, 8,602-ton Liberian *Delos Glory* striking the south pier on September 23. The season was drawing to a close on December 6 when the *Reiss Brothers* was weather damaged on the open lake to the tune of $50,000.[11]

1967

Tonnage fell off on both the Seaway and lakes this season. Seaway traffic was down one percent to 39.9 million tons while that through the locks at the Soo fell 13 percent to 90.4 million tons.

The Tom M. Girdler *stood by the stricken* Lehigh *off Caribou Island after a devastating boiler explosion.* CANAL PARK MARINE MUSEUM COLLECTION.

Despite fewer ships hauling less cargo, the Canadians had a scare on June 6 when Hall Corporation's new 712-foot, 17,819-ton carrier *Frankcliffe Hall,* laden with 900,000 bushels of wheat, grounded in heavy fog two miles off Thunder Cape. Salvors released her after five days, but then she had to be unloaded before repairs could be made. All of this amounted to a costly salvage endeavor. Early fall saw the Apostle Islands Cruise Service's 61-foot passenger ferry *Chippewa,* the former *Mary Margaret,* reporting a light grounding off Bayfield. Later in the fall, Wilson Marine Transit's 580-foot, 8,047-ton *A.T. Lawson,* the former *B.W. Druckenmiller,* suffered undisclosed weather damage fighting the big lake on November 27.

1968

There was a leveling off of Lake Superior tonnage this season at 89.3 million tons, just one percent below 1967. Meanwhile, Seaway tonnage improved nine percent to 43.5 million tons, though still shy of the record 44 million tons set in 1966.

Two ore carriers sustained similar injuries at north shore ports in blustery weather on April 20, Interlake

Steamship Company's 615-foot *Harry Coulby* smashing her bow against the dock at Taconite Harbor, while to the southwest at Silver Bay, Oglebay Norton Company's 706-foot *Middletown* did the same. Both had to go to Superior for fixing. Only days earlier on April 16, Cleveland Cliffs' 601-foot, 8,653-ton *William G. Mather* reported having grounded at Marquette. Duluth-Superior's Interstate Bridge received another dusting on June 7, this time by U.S. Steel's 587-foot, 7,918-ton *Horace Johnson.* Late in the fall, too, Quincy Mining Company's dredge *No. 2,* used to reclaim stamp sand from earlier copper mining operations for additional processing, settled to the bottom near shore adjacent to Hubbell, Michigan, in Torch Lake on the Keweenaw Waterway, where it remains abandoned.[12]

1969

There was an improvement of 10 percent in Lake Superior tonnage to 98.5 million tons. Among 1969's pace-setting carriers was Columbia Transportation's 11-year-old *Edmund Fitzgerald,* once the largest carrier on the lakes, which this season carried a Soo Locks record tonnage for all cargoes of 30,690 short tons. Seaway traffic could not keep pace and fell off 14 percent to 37.2 million tons. Casualty reports held steady with one, a career-ending grounding. The decade closed with a long-awaited change at the Soo. Finally dedicated on June 26, 1969, was the new Poe Lock. It was designed to handle leviathans of the lakes which had not yet arrived, vessels 1,000 feet long and 105 feet wide with carrying capacities of 60,000 to 70,000 tons.

Reiss Steamships' 504-foot, 6,432-ton *John P. Reiss* reported grounding in the channels at Ashland on July 7, releasing herself undamaged. The Interstate Bridge in Duluth-Superior was once again struck, this time by Kinsman Marine's 556-foot, 6,584-ton *R.E. Webster* on October 14. Silver Bay and Taconite Harbor each reported incidents in October, Bethlehem's 683-foot *Johnstown* striking the Reserve Mining Company dock at Silver Bay on October 17, and the next day her 580-foot fleetmate *Bethlehem* striking the Erie Mining Company dock at Taconite Harbor, both incidents being relatively minor.

The season's finale eventually resulted in the rescue of the last survivor of Alexander McDougall's famous fleet of unique whalebacks, the *Meteor,* formerly the whaleback ore carrier *Frank Rockefeller* built at Superior in 1896. Under command of Captain Michael Pavokovich, the 366-foot, 3,383-ton *Meteor,* having been converted to a tanker for Cleveland Tankers, ran aground on Gull Island Shoal off Marquette on November 21. Damage was significant. At the same time the U.S. Coast Guard lost enthusiasm for allowing single-bottomed tankers on the lakes with their potential for environmental damage. The

Meteor was pulled off and retired. She was acquired by the city of Superior and towed back to her home port on September 11, 1972, where she was put in dry dock at Fraser Shipyards prior to being permanently docked on Barker's Island in 1973 as a museum vessel, the last surviving whaleback. Like the museum vessels *William A. Irvin* in Duluth and the *Valley Camp* at the Soo, the whaleback *Meteor* is open for public tours in season.[13]

On January 13, well before the season opened, U.S. Steel's 604-foot, 8,758-ton *Sewell Avery* settled to the bottom in Duluth Harbor, flooding her lower machinery spaces. Damage was minimal, but the cleanup process was messy at best. Ice-damaged vessels were common in the early season; Republic Steel's 525-foot, 7,031-ton *Silver Bay* was damaged while being escorted by the U.S. Coast Guard cutter *Mackinaw* through windrowed ice in

Alexander McDougall's old whaleback, Meteor, *ended her career when she grounded hard near Marquette in November 1969, the death blow for a single-bottom tanker.* Harold Andresen collection, Canal Park Marine Museum.

1970

Like the 1960s, the early 1970s saw each season accumulate its share of collisions, groundings and dock strikings, all of comparatively little consequence, while carrying immense tonnages. Nearly 600 million tons of cargo were carried on Lake Superior from 1970 through 1975 while vessels using the Seaway in the early years of its second decade would carry almost 280 million tons. Whole new classes of lake carriers came into being with the launching of Bethlehem Steel's "thousand-footer," the 989-foot, 32,930-ton *Stewart J. Cort,* and U.S. Steel's smaller, but still massive, 833-foot, 22,041-ton *Roger Blough.*

Vessels transiting Lake Superior this season carried the highest tonnage since 1966, up three percent from 1969 to 101.4 million tons. Lake and ocean vessels using the St. Lawrence Seaway carried 25 percent more than in the previous season and set a new record of 46.4 million tons. Casualty numbers doubled to eight.

Whitefish Bay. Even the 290-foot, 10,000-horsepower "Mighty Mac" received some damage from ice. The *John Sherwin* of Pickands Mather's Interlake fleet also reported ice damage on Lake Superior on or about April 11, as did her 664-foot fleetmate *Charles M. Schwab* on April 14. Reiss Steamship's 588-foot, 8,195-ton *George D. Goble,* formerly the *Reiss Brothers,* also reported a modest grounding near Ashland Harbor on April 24. A minor collision was reported between Kinsman's 591-foot *Kinsman Independent* and U.S. Steel's 585-foot *William J. Filbert* in Superior on July 18, and Red Arrow Steamship's 420-foot *Joe S. Morrow* reported grounding in Superior on October 9.

1971

Lake Superior freight traffic slipped by eight percent through the season to 92.9 million tons while traffic

Launched in the early 1970s was the unique Roger Blough, *a massive ore carrier stretching to 858 feet.* Canal Park Marine Museum collection.

through the Seaway resulted in another record high of 48 million tons. Early season ice both on eastern Lake Superior and in the harbors caused vessel problems, particularly in April and through the first week of May.

Pickands Mather's 670-foot *Herbert C. Jackson* sustained propeller damage in ice on April 22 while transiting Whitefish Bay. On the same day in Superior Harbor, U.S. Steel's 580-foot, 7,602-ton *William P. Palmer* and Hanna Mining Company's 595-foot, 8,318-ton *Matthew Andrews* came together. Two days later on April 24, Pickands Mather's 683-foot *Elton Hoyt 2nd* sustained propeller damage in Whitefish Bay ice.

Hall Corporation's 712-foot, 17,917-ton *Lawrencecliffe Hall* grazed the Duluth-Superior Interstate Bridge on May 2, a persistent trouble spot and bottleneck in the harbor. Just upstream, the Wisconsin draw of the Northern Pacific Railroad bridge was struck on October 27 by the 531-foot, 6,945-ton *Harry L. Allen*. Over in the eastern lake, the Upper St. Marys River continued to be a trouble spot. On July 2, the brand new 645-foot, 17,510-ton Greek saltie *Maritsa P. Lemos* slashed her bottom in a grounding and had to be pumped out before entering the Soo Locks.

Harbor entries with two Liberian vessels taking honors. The eight-year-old 583-foot, 13,516-ton saltie *Ionian Mariner* struck the Superior Entry south pier while a nearly identical eight-year-old 583-foot, 13,203-ton saltie

The colossal Stewart J. Cort *became the first of 13 1,000-footers to roam the lakes by the end of the 1980s. With traditional fore 'n aft cabins, she entered service in 1972 for Bethlehem Steel.* CANAL PARK MARINE MUSEUM COLLECTION.

1972

For the third season in a row, St. Lawrence Seaway freight set a record high at 48.6 million tons. Lake Superior freight also rose by six percent to 98.1 million tons. While seasonal fluctuations continued, it appeared shippers were on a roll. Two new giants, leviathans of the lakes, entered active service. The "thousand-footer" *Stewart J. Cort,* 1,000 feet in overall length and 105 feet in beam, a member of Bethlehem Steel's Great Lakes fleet, first passed through the new Poe Lock upbound on May 3. Scarcely six weeks later on June 17, U.S. Steel's *Roger Blough,* 858 feet in overall length and also 105 feet in beam, first tasted Lake Superior waters. While most of the giants to follow were near look-alikes, these first two were unique and carried on the tradition of the old style lakers having pilothouses forward and cabins aft. They had carrying capacities unlike anything which had previously floated on the lakes, the *Cort* able to carry 58,000 tons per trip while the *Blough* transported 44,500 tons. Another new era had opened.

U.S. Steel's 580-foot *William A. McGonagle* was the chief victim of ice on the eastern lake in the spring, suffering damage both in the St. Marys River and on Lake Superior between April 20 and 25. About the same time, April 25, Wilson Marine's 604-foot, 8,758-ton *Thomas Wilson* and U.S. Steel's 580-foot, 7,969-ton *August Ziesing* came together in the waters off Two Harbors.

June saw the first double hit for the Duluth-Superior

Saturn struck the Duluth Ship Canal pier. While both canal piers had been struck many times before, this is the first instance where both were struck on the same date. Fortunately, damage was minimal all around.

Western Lake Superior was the scene of frantic searching in gale and snow on November 2 as Wilson's 525-foot grain-laden barge *A.E. Nettleton,* a converted steamer, broke her tow line from the powerful 120-foot, 2,000-horsepower tug *Olive L. Moore* of Escanaba Towing Company and began drifting toward the dreaded reefs off the northwestern shore of Keweenaw Point. Concern was felt for the five crewmen aboard, since an aerial observation indicated the barge had begun to list due to her cargo shifting. Moderation of the gale, however, permitted a U.S. Coast Guard helicopter to transfer three men from the barge to the tug where they assisted in rerigging the towline which was then passed to the barge; the tow resumed to the Keweenaw Waterway where the grain cargo was trimmed. The *Moore* and *Nettleton* were undamaged and eventually able to continue their eastbound voyage.

The Boutin tug *Nor'easter* became ice cut on December 11 while attempting to maneuver between floes off Bayfield and Madeline Island, successfully reaching the Bayfield dock before settling to the bottom. The 29-foot, 10-ton fish tug which had been built in nearby La Pointe in 1948 was raised successfully, but subsequently abandoned.

Ice also captured the 103-foot *Outer Island* on December 16. Returning in the late season from work on the lower lakes, the *Outer Island* found herself in the midst of a substantial storm and horrendous ice conditions west of the Keweenaw en route to her home port of Bayfield. Ice not only built up on her open deck and all the equipment there including a crane, truck, snowmobiles and

Lake Superior wind and massive ice floes nearly swallowed the Outer Island *in December 1972.* Courtesy of Wesley R. Harkins Marine Photography, Duluth.

other construction gear, but also surrounded her. She became entrapped in a giant ice floe, turned completely around and pushed closer and closer to the shore until fetching up a mile or two east of Silver City, Michigan, just to the west of Ontonagon. It was a harrowing experience for Captain Richard Erickson, son of the owner, and his crew of three. Yet luck was with them.

They had been driven ashore on one of the few stretches of beach where the highway comes close to the lake. When Erickson, Elvis Moe, James Boutin and Wilmer Compton made their way over mountainous ice, they found themselves being greeted by a passing highway patrolman. The *Woodrush* came out from Duluth to try to assist, but found the offshore waters too shallow, and was forced to watch instead of participate.

As the damage to the *Outer Island* was assessed in the following days, it appeared she could become a total loss, possibly broken in two. But owner Captain Ed Erickson was not about to give up on his strange little craft. Over the next few weeks, much of her deck load was removed along with tons of ice. Though badly listed with part of her engine room flooded, he succeeded in getting the starboard engine running. He worked the vessel free and made the safety of the Ontonagon Harbor where she spent the winter. The former LCT (Landing Craft Tank), built for the government in 1942, had survived to work another decade and move in places where most vessels cannot go.

1973

Not to be outdone by the previous substantial season, Soo Locks tonnage climbed 14 percent to an unbelievable

111.7 million tons while Seaway freight rose seven percent for another record high of 52.8 million tons. As the new *Cort* and *Blough* neared the end of their second seasons, a new face joined the leviathans, that of a unique tug-barge combination "thousand-footer" capable of carrying 57,500 tons, the *Presque Isle.* The vessel consists of a 141-foot, 14,840-horsepower tug built in New Orleans and nestled into a notched, 974-foot, 22,621-ton barge built in Erie, Pennsylvania. Litton Great Lakes Corporation's *Presque Isle* made but one late season voyage to Lake Superior, being upbound on December 18 and down on the 23rd. A smaller, equally unique vessel jumped into the Great Lakes scene earlier in the season as Pringle Transit's self-unloader *William R. Roesch* was christened in Lorain, Ohio, on June 22. The *Roesch,* 630 feet in overall length, became the first of the distinctive new "River Class" ships. Her "P-Ring-Gull" stack insignia remains the most imaginative and attractive on the lakes.

The casualty season started early in 1973 with the 103-foot *Sandcraft,* another former LCT built for the government in 1942, settling dockside at Chassell, Michigan, on the Portage Lake Ship Canal as ice melted on March 26. On June 1, Upper Lakes Shipping's 712-foot, 17,646-ton grain carrier *Quebecois* came together lightly with the 602-foot, 15,028-ton Liberian saltie *Marathonian* at Duluth's Cargill Elevator "D."

The Northern Pacific railroad bridge in Duluth-Superior Harbor was struck by the Harry L. Allen *in October 1971, but survived to continue as the harbor's main bottleneck for shipping.* Bruce Everett photo, Canal Park Marine Museum.

In July a tug turned pleasure boat ran into a number of problems during the first two days of the month at Cornucopia Harbor, Wisconsin. The *Sherman VI* ran aground there on the first of the month and the following day was involved in a collision with two unnamed Minnesota-registered motorboats. Later in the summer, Inland Steel's 661-foot *Wilfred Sykes* reported having grounded at Thunder Bay on August 5.

Off Mosquito Bay in the Upper St. Marys River on September 28, Kinsman's 62-year-old 580-foot, 7,763-ton grain carrier *Frank R. Denton* sideswiped the seven-year-old 681-foot, 19,644-ton Belgian motor vessel *Federal Schelde,* both sustaining some injury as they groped through heavy fog.

Twin Ports bridges were the scene of two accidents, U.S. Steel's 622-foot *Leon Fraser* bumping the Wisconsin section of the Burlington Northern Railway bridge on September 15 and Kinsman's 554-foot *Peter Robertson* striking the old Arrowhead Bridge.

1974

As substantial as the 1973 season had been, it seems that there was little way to avoid a downturn. Soo Locks traffic was off eight percent from 1973 but remained at a respectable high of 102 million tons, while Seaway traffic fell dramatically to 40 million tons, a plunge of 23 percent. Reported casualties declined.

The Lake Superior casualty season opened with the troublesome tug *Sherman VI* settling to the bottom at her dock in Duluth on April 19. She was later pumped out, refloated and moved to Fraser Shipyards. There the 67-foot, 59-ton tug remained idle for some time before her 450-horsepower diesel engine was removed and sold and her pilothouse cut away to become an addition to a summer cottage in northern Wisconsin. Her remains were finally pulled out and cut up when changes in the shipyard's land use called for filling in the old slip where she had been abandoned.

Twin Ports railway bridges again got in the way of ship traffic, Kinsman Marine Transit's 532-foot *Paul L Tietjen* striking the Grassy Point Bridge on May 14 and her 556-foot fleetmate *George M. Steinbrenner* striking the Wisconsin side on June 12. Two minor saltie groundings in Duluth-Superior Harbor also marred the summer season. The year-old 510-foot, 12,982-ton British saltie *Surenes* grounded on July 2 and two-year-old 591-foot, 16,018-ton Danish saltie *Torm Kristina* reported grounding on September 30.

On October 30, Scott Misener Steamships' 660-foot, 13,884-ton grain carrier *John O. McKellar* stranded in the Mosquito Bay area of the Upper St. Marys River and had to be lightered before she could be taken off for repairs to her bottom.

1975

Tonnage improvements were in store on the Seaway in 1975 with a rise of nine percent above the previous sea-

son's slump to 43.5 million tons. Lake Superior freight, however, fell off 11 percent to 91.5 million tons.

There were certainly minor emergencies, some involving ice in the Upper St. Marys River and lower Whitefish

The Belgian Federal Schelde *survived a minor collision in the Upper St. Marys River in September 1973 to complete her journey to the Twin Ports.* HAROLD ANDRESEN PHOTO, CANAL PARK MARINE MUSEUM COLLECTION.

Bay, plus occasional simple groundings, dockside founderings and light collisions throughout the 1960s and early 1970s, but Lake Superior had failed to claim a major commercial ship for 22 years. Things changed by the end of navigation in 1975, with a dramatic, still not fully explained foundering of a major bulk carrier of the American fleet.

Columbia Transportation's 603-foot *Ashland* grounded at Silver Bay on May 21 while her 604-foot fleetmate *J. Burton Ayers* reported a similar incident at Ashland on June 28. The 13-year-old 559-foot, 12,757-ton Norwegian *Aniara* bumped into the aging Arrowhead Bridge on the Upper St. Louis River.

A destructive boat shed fire at Port Wing, Wisconsin, on July 9 destroyed the 42-foot diesel-powered fishing boat *Roamer* and the 36-foot troller *Tailwinds,* together with a quantity of fishing equipment. Loss estimates exceeded $200,000, high for fishing boats. The *Vera Jane* also foundered near Pilot Harbor on September 2. She may have been recovered.[14]

A sinister reminder that Lake Superior could still be the Grim Reaper came on the evening of November 10. The 729-foot *Edmund Fitzgerald,* flagship of the Columbia Transportation fleet, Oglebay Norton Company, mysteriously plunged to the bottom in the midst of an intense storm hovering over the eastern lake. Lost with the *Fitzgerald* were Captain Ernest M. McSorley of Toledo and his 28-man crew. The financial loss was the greatest in history of Great Lakes sailing, the ship being worth $8 million when new in 1958 and replacement costs at the time of loss running more than three times that figure. A taconite cargo of 26,116 tons was lost with her.[15]

The sinking of the "Big *Fitz*," as sailors termed her, is perhaps one of the strangest shipwreck incidents in all of Lake Superior's history. She cleared the Superior Entry after loading at the Burlington Northern ore dock on Allouez Bay in Superior on November 9, at 2:15 p.m. in calm weather.[16]

The troublesome tug turned pleasure craft Sherman VI *went to the bottom in a Duluth Harbor slip in the spring of 1974, ending her distress.* CANAL PARK MARINE MUSEUM COLLECTION.

Loaded at the Two Harbors ore dock and departing about the same time was U.S. Steel's newly lengthened 767-foot *Arthur M. Anderson.* The late Indian summer weather of the day seemed just too nice for November on western Lake Superior. The weather forecast called for small craft warnings and a storm to pass over the eastern lake, but nothing extraordinary for November sailing. However, hours after the *Anderson* and *Fitzgerald* sailed, the Weather Bureau upgraded the forecast, posting gale warnings.[17]

The storm hit the western lake about 7 p.m. on the 9th and blew for a number of hours out of the northeast, though it was not particularly severe, leaving an inch or so of snow on shore after gusty winds subsided. The *Anderson* and *Fitzgerald* were beset by the blasts when about 20 miles south of Isle Royale and well north of Keweenaw Point. Captain McSorley reported at 1 a.m., November 10 that his ship was meeting winds of 52 knots on a bearing of 30 degrees true with 10-foot waves. Still, she appeared to be riding the weather well. The *Fitzgerald* radioed again six hours later when 45 miles north of Copper Harbor that the wind had dropped to 35 knots with continuing 10-foot waves. Presumably the worst was past, although in fact they were simply approaching the calmer eye of the storm.

Nevertheless, this particular weather mass adopted a strange deviation. National Weather Service forecasters originally had expected the storm to pass northeasterly over Marquette at about 7 a.m., November 10 and then move rapidly across the lake and off into Ontario. Instead, the weather system slowed markedly, hovering over the eastern lake and intensifying as the day progressed. Gale warnings were upgraded to storm warnings at 2 a.m. on the 10th. Hurricane-like winds developed, the gusts being officially clocked in the Soo at 71 mph at 7:41 p.m. Unofficial reports declared gusts reached 80 and 90 miles per hour out on the lake. Lake captains estimated the waves at 25 to 30 feet high. Captain Jesse B. "Bernie" Cooper's log on the *Arthur M. Anderson* shows that at 1:50 p.m., when just north of Michipicoten Island, winds were northwest by west at five knots. About an hour later, at 2:45 p.m., the log shows that they were west of Michipicoten with northwest winds at 42 knots. Another weather entry was logged at 3:20 p.m. when the *Anderson* was just south of Michipicoten Island and approaching Caribou Island showing that the wind was northwest at 43 knots. Another weather entry at 4:52 p.m., when the *Anderson* was northeast of Caribou Island, having passed several miles to the north of it, notes winds continued out of the northwest, but had increased to 52 knots.[18]

In later testimony, Captain Cooper noted considerable change in wave conditions as his vessel cleared Caribou Island and wind gusts increased to 70 to 75 knots. He stated that when 10 or 12 miles north of Caribou Island, seas were 12 to 18 feet and that the seas increased to 18 to 25 feet as they progressed south of the island. Wind and sea conditions had indeed deteriorated as the two vessels rounded Caribou Island, moving into the backside of the intense low pressure area which formed the eye of the storm.[19]

The *Fitzgerald* was the first of a line of large carriers to negotiate the worst of the storm area, being followed by the 767-foot *Arthur M. Anderson,* with the 858-foot *Roger Blough,* the 650-foot *Wilfred Sykes* and the 488-foot Canadian *Fort William* also out on the lake. The 730-foot *Simcoe* had been about 15 miles southwest of the *Anderson* in the early afternoon, and the 642-foot *Ernest R. Breech* was downbound about three hours ahead of the *Anderson* and *Fitzgerald.* The 767-foot *Philip R. Clarke* also had passed through the area several hours earlier and was eventually the last vessel allowed down through the Soo Locks before the Corps of Engineers closed them due to the intensity of the storm there.[20]

Closest to the *Fitzgerald,* though, was the *Anderson,* trailing at a 10- to 15-mile interval. In an effort to avoid the worst seas, the ships were sailing well north of the customary vessel lane as is common practice either in or in anticipation of foul weather, passing south of Isle Royale and then to the north and east of Caribou Island, passing between Michipicoten and Caribou islands.

About 3:30 p.m. on the 10th, Captain McSorley radioed to the *Anderson* that the *Fitzgerald* had lost two vent covers and some railings to the giant waves and that she was taking water and developing a list (leaning over to one side). It should be noted that this was several hours after passing anywhere near the Superior Shoal area in the northern part of the lake where there is some speculation that the *Fitzgerald* may have grounded.[21] It should be further noted that the *Fitzgerald*'s pumping equipment consisted of four 7,000 gallon-per-minute main pumps and two 2,000 gallon-per-minute auxiliary pumps, or 32,000 gallons-per-minute total pumping capacity. Still, this was insufficient to eliminate or even reduce the list as reported by Captain McSorley.

Twenty minutes later at about 3:50 p.m., Captain McSorley called the *Anderson* again, reporting that his radar was not working, although he had two sets aboard. He requested that the *Anderson* shadow the *Fitzgerald* down the lake, that is, keep them in sight, and indicated that he would check his ship down so the *Anderson* could close the gap between them. This was within minutes of passing the Six Fathom Shoal area north of Caribou Island. Captain Cooper agreed to keep an eye on the *Fitzgerald* and gave McSorley fixes on his position, that is, his loca-

tions, although not requested to provide courses to steer. Captain McSorley was still navigating his own vessel. The afternoon went by with the winds out of the northwest and the seas getting rougher.

Periodically, the *Anderson* radioed navigational position information to the *Fitzgerald*. To those in the wheelhouse of the *Anderson*, it appeared that they were gaining on the *Fitzgerald* as was the plan, although under ordinary circumstances a vessel would not check down in a following sea. The ships closed to approximately 10 miles apart.

After 4 p.m. and between radio conversations with the *Anderson*, Captain McSorley had raised the U.S. Coast Guard station at Grand Marais, Michigan, and then hailed any ships in the vicinity of Whitefish Point, inquiring if the Whitefish Point light or radio beacon were operational. Actually, due to electrical trouble with the land lines, the automated light and beacon were on and off intermittently. The pilot of the upbound Swedish saltie *Avafors*, Captain Cedric Woodard of Duluth, a retired lakes captain, answered the call when his ship was off Whitefish Point. Captain Woodard reported that both the light and the radio direction beacon were out at that moment.

An hour or more later, Woodard called the *Fitzgerald*

DULUTH HERALD

Vol. 91 — No. 169   TUESDAY, NOVEMBER 11, 1975   Price 15 cents

Laker sinks; 29 lost

The U.S. Coast Guard today reported the Edmund Fitzgerald, a Great Lakes bulk carrier, has sunk after disappearing from radar about 7:10 p.m. Monday with 29 persons aboard. (Related stories on Pages 2 and 9.)

"It has sunk. The ship disappeared off the radar scopes in the area, and we've searched 18 hours for the vessel. We classify it as sunk," said a spokesman at Coast Guard headquarters in Washington.

The Coast Guard determined that the vessel sunk after making positive identification of a life raft from serial numbers found on it.

No presumption of the crew's fate had been made as of noon, CST, said Chief Jere Bennett, officer of the day at U.S. Coast Guard Operations Center in Sault Ste. Marie, Mich.

The last known location of the Fitzgerald was 14 miles northwest of Copper Mine Point, Ont., about 65 miles from the Soo.

Bennett said debris from the ship washed up this morning on Pancake Point, Ont. He said the Ontario Provincial Police were searching the beaches in the area for more traces of the vessel.

Bennett said it was not known whether the crew was unable to dispatch the life boats or whether the high seas overturned them.

On the scene at noon today were several Coast Guard aircraft, two Coast Guard cutters, a 40-foot utility boat and several civilian freighters.

The sea was captain's life

TOLEDO, Ohio (AP) — E. R. McSorley, captain of the sunken ore carrier Edmund Fitzgerald, first experienced a sailor's life 44 years ago.

"The sea was his life," his stepdaugh-

Still, several helicopters, several fixed-wing aircraft and at least two other Great Lakes vessels were criss-crossing the eastern tip of Lake Superior today, looking for the vessel or survivors.

A spokesman said so far no bodies or survivors had been found.

The water temperature was 51 degrees Monday night when the vessel disappeared from the radar screem of the U.S. Steel laker Arthur M. Anderson, which was about five miles away. The air temperature was in the 38 to 40-degree range.

Contact with the Fitzgerald was lost in 70-plus mile-an-hour winds and following seas as high as 25 feet.

The ship radioed it was taking on some water and its vent covers had blown off, but said it was in no immediate danger.

An oil slick, two lifeboats, a life raft, part of a broken life ring-buoy, as well as other debris and boat planking were found today by searchers, the Coast Guard reported.

But, said a spokesman, "We haven't found a bow section, or any part of the vessel, itself."

A shoreline search in the area the Fitzgerald was last sighted—near Copper Mine Point on the Canadian shore, about 65 miles from Sault Ste. Marie, Mich.—was being conducted today for survivors.

A spokesman for Oglebay Norton Co.,

See **BULK**, Page 2

Lake holds secret

By JACK TYLLIA
Of the Herald Staff

It may never be known what happened Monday to the laker Edmund Fitzgerald.

The 729-foot Great Lakes bulk carrier presumably went to the bottom of Lake Superior about 7:10 p.m. after reporting taking on some water. At that time, the vessel reported her pumps were taking

This is a file photo of Great Lakes freighter Edmund Fitzgerald which disappeared Monday night.

The "Toledo Express" was what her crewmen sometimes called the Edmund Fitzgerald *because of her routine Silver Bay-Toledo voyages.* OGLEBAY NORTON COMPANY PHOTO, CANAL PARK MARINE MUSEUM COLLECTION.

to say the light had come on again, but not the directional beacon. In replying, Captain McSorley commented, "We're in a big sea. I've never seen anything like it in my life." He had sailed 44 years. Woodard, who had talked with the *Fitzgerald*'s captain many times by radio, thought that McSorley's voice sounded worried, although there was no indication that anything was seriously awry. This conversation was probably between 5:30 and 6:00 p.m. Apparently it was Captain McSorley's last detailed communication with the outside world, though there would be one more short response.

The temperature was above freezing, but heavy snow squalls at times cut off visibility. About 7:10 p.m., with the *Fitzgerald* still prominent on the *Anderson*'s radar screen, First Mate Morgan Clark of the *Anderson* radioed the *Fitzgerald*, notifying her of an upbound ship ahead and inquiring how the *Fitzgerald* was doing. Captain McSorley's calm voice replied, "We're holding our own." This may have been the last word from the *Fitzgerald*. Then a heavy snow squall cut visibility with the naked eye and blotted out the *Fitzgerald*'s image on the radar screen.

Not long after 7:15 p.m., just a few minutes after the last brief radio conversation with the *Fitzgerald*, the heavy snow squall cleared and the *Anderson*'s radar image once again sharpened. The officers of the *Anderson* were aghast. The *Fitzgerald*'s image had disappeared. Although other more distant upbound ships could be plotted, the *Fitzgerald*'s shadow did not appear on the radar screen. There were no distant lights of the *Fitzgerald*. There was no reply to the *Anderson*'s radio hail. In less than 10 minutes after the last contact with the *Anderson*, the *Fitzgerald* had simply disappeared.

Captain Cooper radioed other ships in the area at 7:25 p.m. inquiring if they could see the *Fitzgerald*. All replies were negative. Inquiries to vessels in shelter at Whitefish Bay likewise brought negative replies. The *Fitzgerald* had not reached shelter. Finally, at 8:25 p.m. Captain Cooper managed to contact U.S. Coast Guard headquarters at the Soo, reporting his fears that the *Fitzgerald* had gone down. The Coast Guard then began repeated attempts to reach the *Fitzgerald* by radio, to no avail. The Coast Guard listed the *Fitzgerald* as missing at 9:25 p.m., November 10, 1975.

Thereupon, the Coast Guard commander at Sault Ste. Marie requested all ships in the area of Whitefish Point to comb the vicinity of the presumed sinking for survivors or signs of wreckage. The upbound salties, *Nanfri, Benfri* and *Avafors* already had passed through that sector of the lake without sighting anything. The downbound vessels following the *Fitzgerald*, namely the *Anderson, Blough* and *Wilfred Sykes*, spent hours searching the storm-tossed lake. True to lakes tradition, Captain Donald E. Erickson brought the *William Clay Ford* out from the shelter of Whitefish Bay at considerable risk to

join in the search. The Canadian *Hilda Marjanne* also weighed anchor from her position near the *Ford*, but had to turn back due to the pounding she was receiving. Several other vessels actively participated in subsequent

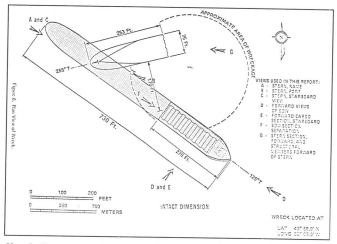

Sketch illustrates orientation of the Fitzgerald's *remains.* NATIONAL TRANSPORTATION SAFETY BOARD.

search efforts including the *Armco* and *William R. Roesch* and Canadians *Murray Bay* and *Frontenac* along with Ferroclad Fisheries' 64-foot steel fish tug *James D.*[22]

It is one thing to come out of shelter, but another to nearly reach shelter and turn back out knowing full well that another turn had to be made out on the lake in order to get back to sheltered waters. To the immense credit of Captain Bernie Cooper and the entire crew of the *Arthur M. Anderson*, they turned back onto the lake after searching all the way to Whitefish Bay. Despite the intense effort and incredible seamanship of those commanding the vessels struggling to find their stricken sister, no survivors were found.

U.S. and Canadian Coast Guard planes and helicopters joined the search, sweeping over the eastern lake within a few hours. The only available Coast Guard cutter was the 180-foot *Woodrush* at Duluth which was ordered to the scene at full speed, though in the gale and high seas she would be 24 hours in reaching the scene.[23] Meanwhile, the Ontario Provincial Police established and maintained a beach patrol all along the eastern shore of the lake. Still no survivors, but enough flotsam was eventually recovered along the Canadian shore and by search vessels to fill a three-ton truck, including both life boats, both fully inflated life rafts and dozens of life jackets and life rings — all unused. Planes patrolled in vain for three days.

On the fourth day, an anti-submarine patrol plane detailed to the search by the U.S. Navy located an object on the lake bottom in 530 feet of water about 17 miles north-northwest of Whitefish Point, roughly 1.8 miles from where the *Anderson* had last reported the *Fitzgerald*.[24]

Subsequent examination by sidescan sonar aboard the cutter *Woodrush* clearly identified a broken hulk on the bottom. The sonar unit was provided by the Coast Guard's own Research and Development Center at Groton, Connecticut, and operated by a three-man team of experts which accompanied it to the Soo. Potentially violent weather in November precluded additional on-scene investigation in 1975, but the wreck had been located at 46 degrees, 59.9 minutes north latitude, and 85 degrees, 06.6 minutes west longitude, just into Canadian waters west of Coppermine Point, Ontario, and north of Whitefish Point, Michigan.[25]

Arthur M. Anderson, *shown here on her maiden voyage in 1952, was lengthened 120 feet over the winter prior to her fateful journey with the* Edmund Fitzgerald *across Lake Superior.* USS GREAT LAKES FLEET PHOTO, CANAL PARK MARINE MUSEUM COLLECTION.

The following May, however, the *Woodrush* returned with a CURV-III (Cable-controlled Underwater Research Vehicle) and minutely examined the underwater object with logistics support provided by the Coast Guard's *Point Steel* (WPB 82359).[26] It was the *Fitzgerald,* all right, broken in two major sections and several associated parts. The stern section was upside-down, though adjacent to the rest. The entire identified wreckage field was in a circle the diameter of which is less than the *Fitzgerald*'s length. As had been expected from the beginning, the vessel was well beyond normal commercial salvage.[27]

The CURV-III logged a dozen dives in 500 feet of water with more than 56 hours of bottom time, making 43,000 feet of videotape recording of the wreckage plus 895 still color photographs. The underwater examination was termed successful in documenting the wreck's condition even though somewhat hampered by mud. It was impossible to study the lower hull since the wreckage lay in 27 feet of silt. It was concluded by the observers on site that "there was more damage than expected." However, the cause of the sinking remained nearly as large a mystery as ever.

A formal U.S. Coast Guard inquiry into the loss of the *Edmund Fitzgerald* was convened almost immediately after the casualty. But, also from the beginning, there were parties, particularly representing the various labor organizations and some of the families, who believed the Coast Guard findings could be tainted since there were serious questions of their own preparedness as well as licensing and rules changes, among other matters. Seafarers International Union, Marine Engineers Beneficial Association and United Steelworkers of America all called for the National Transportation Safety Board to begin a parallel, impartial inquiry.[28]

Vocal Detroit attorney Victor G. Hanson, representing two of the families, also called for independent investigation. Hanson stated:

We question whether the [Coast Guard] *panel can sit impartially in judgment when there may be careless conduct on the part of the Coast Guard.*

Should they judge themselves on the competency of the rescue attempt, if safety equipment in the [sunken] *ship was adequate, or if the ship should have been even sailing in such rough weather?*

They may be passing judgment on their own actions and negligence in similar [Great Lakes] *tragedies in the past.*

By licensing the master [ship captain], *the Coast Guard can regulate under what conditions a ship can sail.*[29]

A Coast Guard spokesman countered part of Hanson's statement saying that his agency could only warn about rough sailing conditions and that each captain determined his own actions.

Melvin H. Pelfrey, a vice president for Marine Engineers Beneficial Association, District No. 2, and Stephen F. Nowalski, sub-district director for United Steelworkers, charged that "seamen die more often than not because of quirks of nature or risks taken by others whom they are duty-bound to follow." Continuing in a prepared statement, Pelfrey and Nowalski said, "All ships are dangerous, yet there are ways to make them less dangerous. All gales and storms at sea can produce destruction. Yet there are ways to minimize their destructive capabilities. Ships will go down at sea, but there are ways to ensure that lives are saved even if the ship is not."[30]

In a separate statement, Pelfrey said he expected delays in the Coast Guard investigation and that nothing would be done to improve the structural integrity of Great Lakes vessels, particularly installation of watertight bulkheads between cargo holds. His organization took essentially the same position following the 1958 sinking of the *Carl D. Bradley* in heavy weather with structural failure of the hull on Lake Michigan and the 1966 sinking of the *Daniel J. Morrell* on Lake Huron, also with structural failure of the hull.[31]

As might have been expected, the Lake Carriers' Association, consisting primarily of vessel owners, was against the costly retrofit procedure of "subdividing" vessels with watertight bulkheads in the hold, claiming it was unnecessary, particularly citing the demonstrated safety record for vessels similar to the *Fitzgerald*.[32]

However, *Seaway Review* columnist and professor of Naval Architecture Harry Benford posed an intriguing scenario a few years after the *Fitzgerald* loss.[33] Benford suggested that marine underwriters and the level of premiums they imposed for certain vessel conditions and configurations could bring about substantial change in the industry even without government regulation. Quoting J.M. Murray, Benford's column said:

> *It would be an insult to the science of the present day to assert that shipbuilders cannot build vessels capable of coping with the worst weather they are ever likely to encounter. But such vessels require good workmanship, good materials, good stowing and good management, to say nothing of good design — in fact, to be thoroughly seaworthy — while competition encourages slovenly work, cheap materials, rapid and deep loading, undermanning and a form that will earn the greatest amount of freight upon the smallest expenditure of capital.*
>
> *These latter qualifications are not all conducive to seaworthiness; but if the underwriters would only combine to insist upon the seaworthiness of the vessels they underwrite, I feel confident the naval architects would not be behindhand in producing the article that is required.*[34]

What makes this scenario so ironically intriguing is that J.M. Murray's original statement was made well over a century before the *Fitzgerald* casualty occurred.

Prior to formal release of findings by the Coast Guard Board of Inquiry appointed to review the *Fitzgerald* disaster, only piecemeal information on the underwater examination was released. Coast Guard officers confirmed the fact that the cutter *Woodrush,* using the CURV-III vehicle, had made 19 hours of television tapes of the *Fitzgerald*'s broken hull. Also, although silt was a complicating factor in some cases, much of the underwater photography was clear. A battery of marine experts studied the pictorial evidence and weighed hundreds of pages of testimony for more than a year, compiling a detailed report for the Board of Inquiry which, in turn, passed its findings to the National Transportation Safety Board appointed to independently review the casualty. The Coast Guard blamed sinking in large part on "ineffective hatch closures" which permitted water into the cargo hold. They further determined that there was no evidence of misconduct or negligence on the part of any licensed personnel and, further, that no government agency contributed to the sinking.[35]

The U.S. Coast Guard finally presented its formal casualty report in July 1977. The Coast Guard deduced that the *Fitzgerald* foundered suddenly due to loss of buoyancy possibly caused by water penetrating into the cargo

hold through improperly sealed hatches. The ship had "dunked," that is, nosed, into a giant wave and, without adequate reserve buoyancy, continued to the bottom, striking so hard that she shattered amidships and her stern

The William Clay Ford *emerged from the sheltered safety of Whitefish Bay to search for survivors of the* Edmund Fitzgerald *at risk to herself and crew.* TERRY SECHEN PHOTO, CANAL PARK MARINE MUSEUM COLLECTION.

wrenched off. The foundering had been almost instantaneous, and the crew had no chance to escape. The report went on to recommend a series of operational limitations on lake carriers in rough weather and numerous other recommendations to increase safety for vessels and crewmen. Notable among its recommendations was the rescinding of the reduction in minimum freeboard brought about by load line regulation changes in 1969, 1971 and 1973, all of which had permitted the *Fitzgerald* to load deeper than her original design and original certificate had allowed. Other recommendations dealt with the need to develop loading manuals to reduce hull stress during the loading process, cooperation among vessel owners and operators and the unions and training schools for more and better training of all personnel to deal with emergency situations and in the use of all available lifesaving equipment. A recommendation was also included for the requirement of survival or all-weather exposure suits which were commercially available at the time of the *Fitzgerald*'s loss, but not required and thus not provided on this particular vessel, although other similar vessels in other Great Lakes fleets did have them on board at the time. The Coast Guard also proposed enclosed lifeboats. The *George A. Stinson,* built in 1978 for the National Steel Corporation fleet, was the first vessel built on the lakes to be originally equipped with an enclosed lifeboat. It appears that only three other American lake carriers had them by the end of the 1980s.[36]

The recommendations set forth in the Coast Guard's final report echoed many of the recommendations made more than a year earlier by union representatives. In April

1976, Melvin H. Pelfrey of the Marine Engineers Beneficial Association had recommended the following:

1) requirement for watertight bulkheads between cargo holds;
2) Coast Guard require all vessels to be equipped with the Brucker-type capsule lifeboat instead of the open lifeboat;
3) cold-resistant, self-inflating life rafts should be installed on all vessels which do not have them;
4) survival suits and life jackets of a practical type should be issued to all personnel on Great Lakes ships;
5) Coast Guard should seriously reexamine its load line limits for all Great Lakes vessels;
6) stress and "King" gauges should be installed on vessels which do not already have them;
7) Great Lakes shipping operations should be restricted during November;
8) a large-craft weather warning advisory system should be put into effect on the lakes;
9) every possible effort should be made to minimize icing on topside navigational, safety and rescue gear aboard ship;
10) comprehensive measures should be implemented to reduce hazards at loading and unloading docks and, finally;
11) officers and unlicensed shipboard personnel should receive comprehensive training in "abandon ship" procedures and survival techniques.[37]

The upbound saltie Benfri *searched for the stricken* Edmund Fitzgerald *along with two other salties, the* Nanfri *and* Avafors. H.G. WEIS PHOTO COURTESY SHIP VIEW PHOTO, DULUTH.

The U.S. Coast Guard document provoked a storm of disagreement from the Lake Carriers' Association. Vice Admiral Paul E. Trimble, USCG (Ret.), president of the association, issued an 18-page rebuttal to the Coast Guard's final report. The Lake Carriers agreed with the concept of a sudden foundering, but denied emphatically that hatch cover leakage could have sunk a ship of this size, especially in view of the remarkable safety record for vessels using that particular design. Rather, they were convinced that shoaling in the area of Six Fathom Shoal northwest of Caribou Island was a more probable cause

of sinking, particularly after a Canadian hydrographic survey in 1976 had disclosed a hitherto unknown shoal running a mile farther east of Six Fathom Shoal than was shown on Canadian charts.[38] The *Fitzgerald* had sailed through that very area, according to the observations of the *Anderson*'s officers who were closest to the scene. With no Whitefish Point Light or radio direction beacon to guide them, the *Fitzgerald* may have unknowingly raked a reef in rounding Caribou Island. Oddly enough, this same explanation had been offered by other high ranking retired Coast Guard officers more than six months before the U.S. Coast Guard report was issued.[39]

Following release of the formal Coast Guard report, the National Transportation Safety Board came more fully into play, particularly after reviewing the Coast Guard's largely inconclusive findings. However, after nearly a year of additional study, the National Transportation Safety Board report included many similar findings and recommendations, but, more importantly, added some insights not previously alluded to. The Safety Board concluded, as did the Coast Guard, that the *Fitzgerald* sank because of massive flooding of the cargo hold, but not due to ineffective hatch closure and topside leakage. Rather, they concluded that the flooding was due to the collapse of one or more hatch covers under the weight of giant boarding seas. The hatch covers had been designed to withstand a four-foot static head of water, not pounding seas several times that depth. Water, too, especially toward the end, may have been piling up on deck behind the forward cabins resulting in failure of one or more hatch covers. The Number 1 hatch cover stands upright inside the cargo hold, an unlikely position if it had been "blown off" by air pressure in the sudden sinking. National Transportation Safety Board member Philip A. Hogue, in a dissenting opinion included in the final report, was also firmly convinced that the vessel suffered from significantly reduced freeboard which could only have come from exterior damage to the shell plating and cargo bottom through shoaling, probably near Caribou Island where the vessel passed less than four hours prior to loss. This damage must have been significant and possibly progressively worsening in that the ship's pumps were incapable of eliminating the water fast enough to overcome the list reported by Captain McSorley. Hogue concluded that towering seas regularly boarded the slowly sinking vessel until one or more hatch covers collapsed, allowing literally tons of water to flood into the cargo hold. The ship quickly became very heavy at the bow and lacked sufficient reserve buoyancy to remain afloat.[40]

The *Edmund Fitzgerald* was built in 1958 at River Rouge, Michigan, by Great Lakes Engineering Works as the largest vessel ever built on the lakes. She was a straight decker, or conventional bulk cargo carrier, with cabins fore and aft. Her 7,500-horsepower steam turbine engine was originally coal-fired, but later converted to oil. She

Ocean vessels from many nations poured into the lakes in the first years of the Seaway era. CANAL PARK MARINE MUSEUM COLLECTION.

was 729 feet in overall length with a breadth of 75 feet and depth of 39 feet. She had three cargo compartments in her hold, divided by screen or non-watertight bulkheads. Twelve hatch openings 48 feet by 11 feet were fitted on deck with 24-inch high hatch coamings. The hatch covers were fabricated of 5/16-inch steel and weighed seven tons each, requiring the use of a mobile hatch crane or "iron deck hand" to remove and replace them. Each hatch cover was secured to the coaming with 68 manually closed Kestner clamps spaced on two-foot centers, an industry standard. Ballast pumping was accomplished with four main pumps and two auxiliary pumps. Navigational and communication equipment included the usual radios for voice communication, a radio direction finder and two radar units. Lifesaving equipment included two 50-person open lifeboats located aft on either side, two 25-person, self-inflating life rafts, one forward and the other aft, as well as numerous life rings and life jackets. She met all U.S. Coast Guard standards in every respect.

The *Fitzgerald*'s crew was headed by Captain McSorley, a veteran of 44 years on the lakes, 38 of those years as captain. Although known as a "weather captain" more than willing to be out when others were in, there is little doubt of his skills as a vessel master. First Mate John H. McCarthy was likewise a licensed master for 34 years. Each also held an unlimited tonnage pilot's license for all Great Lakes. Second Mate James A. Pratt and Third Mate Michael E. Armagost also held pilot's licenses. Chief Engineer George J. Holl and his four assistants were experienced officers. Twenty of the crew were unlicensed personnel, including Deck Cadet David E. Weiss, 22 years old, in training to become an officer.[41]

While operated in the Columbia Transportation Division of Oglebay Norton Company, the *Fitzgerald* was actually owned by the Northwestern Mutual Life Insurance Company of Milwaukee, an early and strong investor in the Minnesota taconite industry, whose chief executive officer was the vessel's namesake. Mr. Edmund Fitzgerald passed away in Milwaukee in 1985. The vessel was under 25-year charter to Oglebay Norton at the time of her loss.

Despite formal investigations by the U.S. Coast Guard, the National Transportation Safety Board, the U.S. Navy Supervisor of Salvage, the Naval Undersea Center and Seaward Inc., an engineering consultant firm, there remains no certainty as to exactly what sank this fine ship with the loss of her 29-man crew. Opinions and theories about the sinking and contributing factors continue to come to the fore.

One of the theories involves the concept of the "Three Sisters." This phenomenon, perhaps peculiar to Lake Superior, suggests that in particularly severe storms, primarily on the eastern lake, extraordinarily large, rogue waves develop, running generally in a series of three. Primary proponent of this theory as a contributing factor

in the *Fitzgerald* loss is Lyle A. McDonald, a commercial fisherman of Laurium, Michigan. In testimony before the House Subcommittee on Coast Guard and Navigation, McDonald stated: "I respectfully submit that the *Fitzgerald* did sink to the bottom of Lake Superior as the result of her having been caught precisely by the Three Sisters, or three big waves. The *Fitzgerald* submarined!" He added, "I am amazed that the phenomenon of the Three Sisters is not more widely known. Most certainly the older sailors are fully cognizant of the fact that the Three Sisters are a reality on Lake Superior."

McDonald explained that at irregular intervals during a storm, three waves will occur, possibly one-third larger than the average seas of the moment. The first of these waves will hit the deck, and before the backwash can clear, a second wave hits. The two accumulated backwashes are then hit by the third incoming wave. The deck was suddenly so overloaded with an estimated 5,000 tons of water added to the *Fitzgerald*'s 26,000-ton load for fully 20 seconds that it caused her bow to drop as much as 15 degrees below horizontal, allowing inertia to prevail and causing her to submarine or dive directly to the bottom. McDonald noted, "The Three Sisters swept up the full length of her decks and piled up against the after side of the pilot house. These seas were traveling twice as fast as the ship, and this permitted a tremendous weight to remain on the forward section."[42]

It may be observed that McDonald's theory of the Three Sisters is not inconsistent with the dissenting opinion of Philip Hogue in the National Transportation Safety Board report[43] or with the observations of Captain Cooper[44] or with the direct experience of some small craft sailors.[45]

Captain Cooper, who comes closest to being an eyewitness to the event, is convinced that the *Fitzgerald* received a mortal wound at about 3:30 p.m. on the 10th, the approximate time the vessel was passing to the north of Caribou Island. He said, ". . .at that time, she either grounded upon a shoal, an unknown shoal up there, or had a stress crack in the hull, because the water poured into her faster than the pumps could take it out." As his vessel, *Arthur M. Anderson,* passed through the same area, although somewhat north of the *Fitzgerald*'s track, he observed winds blowing at 69 mph, but gusting to more than 100 mph, and waves generally running 16 to 26 feet. Waves were routinely boarding the *Anderson* with as much as 12 feet of "green" water on deck. Then the *Anderson* was "hit by two 30- to 35-foot seas about 6:30 p.m., one burying the after cabins and damaging a lifeboat by pushing it right down onto the saddle. The second wave of this size, perhaps 35 feet, came over the bridge deck." He noted that the "second wave put green water on our bridge deck" which was about 35 feet above the waterline. Captain Cooper observed that if these two waves, and possibly a third, continued in the direction and speed with which they struck his vessel, they would have struck the *Fitzgerald* at about the time she was lost, perhaps inflicting the final fatal blow for the *Fitzgerald* and her crew.[46]

This identified pair of the devastating rogue triplets certainly would have compounded problems already complicated somewhat by the *Fitzgerald's* known list and her having slowed down in a following sea, which allows water to stay on deck for a longer period of time, substantially increasing the draft and dynamic stresses on the hull.

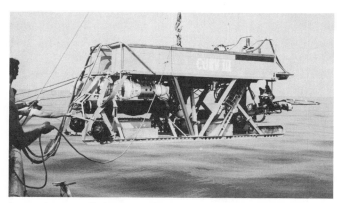

Remotely controlled submersible CURV-III examined the Edmund Fitzgerald *wreckage with the U.S. Coast Guard cutter* Woodrush *serving as mother ship in spring 1976. A high tech mini-rover, considerably smaller and more advanced than her predecessors, would examine this wreck again in 1989, perhaps shedding new light on sinking.* U.S. NAVY PHOTO, CANAL PARK MARINE MUSEUM COLLECTION.

Questions have also been raised about the structural integrity of the *Fitzgerald,* not only in this particular storm and what may have occurred to her then, but from observations made in the last few years she sailed. Note that Captain Cooper stated that the *Fitzgerald* may have "had a stress crack in the hull, because the water poured into her faster than the pumps could take it out." Stress cracks, while not common, are not unheard of on Great Lakes vessels. For instance the *Silver Isle* experienced this phenomenon on Lake Superior in the spring of 1984 and the *Starbelle* and *John O. McKellar* in 1975. The *Robert C. Stanley* also experienced dramatic stress cracking in the fall of 1943.[47] Weather was a major contributing factor in each of these instances, but materials used and design factors were also part of the problem. Fortunately, these four vessels survived their ordeals to be repaired, reinforced and to reenter service.

Added to this suspicion of a stress fracture are observations related by two of the *Fitzgerald's* former crewmen. Former *Fitzgerald* Second Mate Richard Orgel described a phenomenon peculiar to the ship which was termed "the wiggling thing" by Captain McSorley.

Mate Orgel, in testifying before the Marine Board of Inquiry, recalled a storm in November 1973 when the *Fitz-gerald* was upbound light out of Whitefish Bay and the ship was "bending, whipping, and twisting." In further describing the wiggling thing, Orgel said that the ship had a tendency to bend and spring during storms "like a diving board after somebody has jumped off."

In that particular November storm, he said that "by looking aft there was quite a bit of action there. She bends and springs considerably." He commented further that the movement seemed a little excessive to him, considering they were running in only 10-foot seas.

Orgel testified that when Captain McSorley left the bridge in that particular storm, the mate was ordered to alert the captain if it started. McSorley said, "If she starts to do the wiggling thing, let me know. This thing scares me sometimes." The wiggling thing did occur, and Orgel was later instructed by McSorley to change course and slow down.[48]

Another former crew member, who had gotten off the *Fitzgerald* early in the fall of 1975, also described the wiggling thing as well as other observations on the structural integrity of the *Fitzgerald.*

Former Chief Steward George H. (Red) Burgner sailed for Oglebay Norton since 1942 except for a hitch in the Army. He became steward on the *Fitzgerald* in 1966 and remained in that position until he got off in the late summer of 1975, although he did not retire from the company until 1976.

Of particular interest in Steward Burgner's career was not so much his nearly 10 seasons of sailing aboard the *Fitzgerald* and twice that many years on other Columbia vessels, but that he was also winter shipkeeper aboard the *Fitzgerald* from 1966 through fitout in 1973. During all those winters, the ship laid up at the shipyard in Superior, Wisconsin, Burgner's home town.[49]

Burgner surprisingly was not called as a witness in either the Coast Guard or National Transportation Safety Board investigations. He was asked later by attorneys for one of the families to provide a formal deposition. Burgner noted in his statement that the *Fitzgerald* was known among the crew as the "Toledo Express" because of its usual run between the loading port of Silver Bay, Minnesota, and the unloading port of Toledo, Ohio. In describing the loading routine, Burgner noted that he was unaware of any printed loading manual that could be followed by the mate in the loading procedure. Instead, he said the mates frequently asked him or the steward staff to save the cardboard stiffeners that came in their shirts when they were returned from the laundry. The mates routinely kept track of the loading procedure on these white cardboard discards.[50]

When asked if, under Captain McSorley's command, the ship had ever sailed without its hatch covers fully clamped down, Burgner said "yes" and that this occurred even in foul weather, particularly on weekend departures or any time it required overtime to get all of the 68 clamps per hatch cover locked in place. It was common that only a dozen clamps would be set on each cover, that is, two at each corner and two on each of the long sides. It might be a day or more before all the clamps were eventually set, weather permitting. Taconite pellets strewn on deck in the loading process would not even be hosed off if it required overtime. The crew would use the inboard tunnels to get fore and aft rather than risk the danger of slipping on the deck.[51]

Captain McSorley was described as a good navigator, knowledgeable of Lake Superior and the Great Lakes as was First Mate McCarthy. However, Burgner went on to say that Captain McSorley "beat hell" out of the *Fitzgerald* and "very seldom ever hauled up for weather."[52]

In describing the condition of the *Edmund Fitzgerald* and repairs done to the ship while he was aboard either in his capacity as steward or as winter shipkeeper, Burgner noted that there was a definite difference between routine shipboard maintenance done during the seasons he sailed the *Fitzgerald* under Captain Pulcer, her previous master, and that done under Captain McSorley. Captain Pulcer's attitude was simply that if it needed to be done, it was done. Pulcer kept after the mates and men until the work was completed.[53] However, Captain McSorley did not keep up on the routine maintenance. He did not seem to have an interest in keeping the vessel up and, thus, neither did the crew. He knew what needed to be done, but seemingly could not confront the mates about the work not getting done. Morale was low among the crew.[54]

A potential structural problem with the *Fitzgerald* is a possible contributing factor in the vessel's loss, according to Burgner. Welds along the keel and sister keelsons were only tack welded or strip welded rather than running a continuous weld bead between the keel and the inside of the shell plating. Burgner personally observed many of these welds which were broken. He refers to this problem as the *Fitzgerald* having a "loose keel."[55] While shipkeeper in 1972-73 and during a Coast Guard and American Bureau of Shipping inspection while the *Fitzgerald* was in dry dock, they did make some repairs to the keel. He observed the problem along with a representative of the shipyard.

"When they opened up the holes in the cargo hold and went down there," he said, and a shipyard foreman "showed me — shoved the crowbar right under it [the keel], and what he pushed out of there was welding rods and everything else [from] when the ship was built." He added, "And if that's loose, the outer shell, the keel would be steady, but the outer hull, it would crack some of the frames and that in the bottom down there. The hull could move."[56] Some of the broken welds were repaired using small plates and bar stock to make up the gap between the keel and shell plating, at least for two sections of the ship's bottom, but not all the work was completed that season. The ship was apparently certified as seaworthy

on the condition that the remaining repairs would be completed the following winter.[57]

American Society for Testing Metals President August G. Hebel Jr. stated that welds on the *Fitzgerald* were cracked and that photos of the vessel show cracked welds were never repaired, but rather riveted plates were used to "patch up" the faulty welds. He noted that most weld failures are due to improper stress relief, particularly in large weldments. He further stated, "The hull was just being held together with patching plates."[58]

It should be noted that these observations regarding the integrity of the keel were made during a time when the *Fitzgerald*'s load line was being increased for the second and third time by the Coast Guard, thus reducing freeboard and the amount of critical reserve buoyancy. The *Fitzgerald* was said to be a good riding ship until the Coast Guard began allowing increased load lines. Afterward, the vessel was more sluggish, slower to respond or recover, particularly in heavy weather. Even Captain McSorley did not like the action of the ship, the "wiggling thing" that scared him. The bow hooked to one side or the other in heavy seas and would not return in the few seconds it normally took a ship to recover.[59] "But the *Fitzgerald,* it seemed like the bow would just never get back there again and another one [wave] would hit it; she'd go back over again . . . She had an awful lot of movement to her or action to her," Burgner said.[60] The *Fitzgerald* "groaned" as well, more than most ships, he said, like "she was hurting herself, you know, in rough seas." It was a groaning not really heard on other ships.[61]

At any rate, ruptured shell plating, perhaps damage to the weather or spar deck or failure of some internal structural elements may have admitted water into the tunnels running the full length of the hold on both sides between the main and spar decks or to the hold itself or into the bottom tanks, adding to the *Fitzgerald*'s list, its slowing speed, its deeper draft and its diminishing freeboard just prior to her foundering.

Out of the *Edmund Fitzgerald* tragedy have emerged a number of items designed to increase safety for Great Lakes seamen. Heightened awareness of the continuing possibility of such a disaster recurring has also brought increased caution. Improvements since this loss include:
1) final U.S. Coast Guard approval of and requirement for survival or exposure suits to be carried aboard ship for all personnel and sufficient extras so that there is one in each man's quarters as well as in his customary work station;
2) the requirement for strobe lights to be attached to life jackets and survival suits to improve visibility in darkness;
3) completion of the installation of the extremely accurate LORAN-C (Long Range Aid to Navigation) positioning system to cover the Great Lakes;
4) requirement that all Great Lakes vessels carry Emergen-

cy Position Indicating Radio Beacons (EPIRB) so that a sinking site can be quickly and accurately determined using satellite-relayed data.

Also, National Oceanic and Atmospheric Administration charts of Lake Superior and particularly the area surrounding Caribou Island have been improved to reflect greater detail of the shoals found in that area, especially to the north and northwest. Further, NOAA's National Weather Service revised its method of estimating wave heights in foul weather to better reflect true heights. This tragedy also provided impetus for the long overdue improvement in the U.S. Coast Guard's multipurpose vessels available for search and rescue work in virtually any sea condition, particularly replacement of the aging 110-footers such as the *Naugatuck* with the new 140-foot Bay-

class vessels like the *Katmai Bay,* now stationed at Sault Ste. Marie, Michigan.[62]

Seldom, if ever, has a Lake Superior shipwreck attracted such widespread and seemingly unending public attention and speculation as to its cause. The *Fitzgerald* incident may remain one of the all-time mysteries of Lake Superior with interest in this casualty remaining high for decades to come. Despite the interest in and uncertainties surrounding the loss of the *Edmund Fitzgerald,* this was not to be the last ship to end her career on Lake Superior, nor would her sailors be the last lost in what is overwhelmingly a safety conscious industry. Media coverage of the occasional, rare casualty can be misleading. More typical routine voyages, year in and year out, attract little attention.[63]

Foreign-flagged visitors vary from turn-of-the-century relics to modern carriers like the Norwegian Sistina. CANAL PARK MARINE MUSEUM COLLECTION.

[1] Many of the minor mishaps are listed in various Great Lakes newsletters. Most of these and information from U.S. and Canadian government sources as well as first-hand observations have been compiled into a briefly annotated "Running Chronology of Lake Superior Marine Casualties." Among the many Great Lakes journals and newsletters carrying casualty information are *Telescope,* journal of the Great Lakes Maritime Institute at Dossin Great Lakes Museum in Detroit, *Lake Log Chips,* prepared by the Institute for Great Lakes Research, Bowling Green State University, at their research facility near Toledo through 1988; *Inland Seas,* Journal of the Great Lakes Historical Society of Vermilion and Cleveland, Ohio; *Marine Historian,* newsletter of the Marine Historical Society of Detroit; *Soundings,* newsletter of the Wisconsin Marine Historical Society at the Milwaukee Public Library, *Scanner,* Journal of the Toronto Marine Historical Society; *Lake Superior Newsletter,* a special interest publication of *Lake Superior Magazine* in Duluth; and *The Nor'Easter,* journal of the Lake Superior Marine Museum Association of Duluth. The latter two are the only two of these periodicals specifically concentrating on Lake Superior events.

[2] Lake Carriers' Association, *Annual Report,* (Cleveland, Ohio, Lake Carriers' Association, 1959-1975); Thom Holden, "Running Chronology of Lake Superior Marine Casualties," unpublished manuscript, 1973, revised 1988; Jacques Lesstrang, "The Thirtieth Season: A Retrospective" in *Seaway Review,* Vol. 17, No. 2, Summer 1988, pp. 37-47.

[3] Great Lakes Protective Association, *Annual Report* (Cleveland, Ohio, Great Lakes Protective Association, 1961), p. 13.

[4] *Duluth News-Tribune,* Dec. 5-8, 12, 1961; John Bascom, "The Ship with the Golden Rivets — Ship of the Month No. 38" in *The Scanner,* Vol. 6, No. 6, March 1974; James Kidd, "More About the Ship with the Golden Rivets" in *The Scanner,* Vol. 6, No. 7, April 1974, p. 7. An excellent account of the *Secord* incident is presented by retired vessel agent Richard D. Bibby as "*Secord*'s Last Trip of the 1961 Season" in *The Nor'Easter,* Vol. 7, No. 2, March-April 1982, pp. 1-3.

[5] Great Lakes Protective Association, *op. cit.,* 1962, p. 13.

[6] *Duluth News-Tribune,* July 15, 1962.

[7] The *Wigeon* was a 28-foot steel fish tug built at Traverse Bay, Michigan, in 1939 and owned by Waino Asonmaa of Sault Ste. Marie, Michigan.

[8] Great Lakes Protective Association, *op. cit.,* 1965, p. 13.

[9] Great Lakes Protective Association, *op.cit.,* 1966, p. 13.

[10] *ibid.*

[11] *ibid.*

[12] Frederick Stonehouse, *Keweenaw Shipwrecks,* (Au Train, Michigan, Avery Color Studios, 1988), p. 311. It is not clear if this is the same dredge which settled in Torch Lake on Jan. 15, 1956.

[13] Ryck Lydecker, *Pigboat: The Story of The Whalebacks* (Duluth, Minnesota, Sweetwater Press, 1973), pp. 27-33.

[14] *Duluth News-Tribune,* July 10, 1975. Positive identification of the *Vera Jane* has not been made, as a vessel of this name does not appear in contemporary U.S. or Canadian registries, although a 23-year-old 38-foot steel fish tug owned by John Prouix of Killarney, Ontario, named *Verna Jane* does appear in the 1975 *Canadian List of Shipping.* The latter vessel was still listed in the 1980 edition.

[15] The *Edmund Fitzgerald* loss was given exhaustive newspaper coverage. See *Duluth News-Tribune,* Nov. 11-13, 15-17, 19-21, 24-25, 27-28, Dec. 10-11, 1975; Feb. 7, May 12, 20-23, 26, 31, June 12, 1976; *Duluth Herald,* Nov. 11-13, 17-18, 20-21, 24-25, Dec. 11-12, 1975, May 11, 1976; *Cleveland Plain Dealer,* Nov. 11, 17, 19, 22-23, 25-27, Dec. 11-13, 1975; *Minneapolis Tribune* Dec. 14, 1975; *Superior Evening Telegram,* Nov. 14, 1975. Also, on or about the casualty anniversary over the next decade and more in many Great Lakes port city newspapers.

[16] All times relating to the *Fitzgerald* casualty are Eastern Standard Time.

[17] National Transportation Safety Board, Bureau of Accident Investigation, *Marine Accident Report: SS* Edmund Fitzgerald *Sinking in Lake Superior, November 10, 1975* (Washington, D.C., May 4, 1978), Report Number: NTSB-MAR-78-3, pp. 11-12; U.S. Coast Guard, Department of Transportation, *Marine Casualty Report: SS* Edmund Fitzgerald; *Sinking in Lake Superior on 10 November 1975 with Loss of Life: Marine Board of Investigation Report and Commandant's Action* (Washington, D.C., July 26, 1977), Report Number: USCG 16732/64216, pp. 18-21.

[18] National Transportation Safety Board, *op.cit.,* p. 12.

[19] *ibid.*

[20] *Evening News,* Sault Ste. Marie, Mich., Nov. 11, 1975; radio broadcast interview on Nov. 10, 1988, from Duluth with Chief Engineer Clem Lesota, formerly on the *Philip R. Clarke.*

[21] *Evening News,* Sault Ste. Marie, Mich., Nov. 10, 1982.

[22] *Duluth News-Tribune,* Nov. 13, 1975; U.S. Coast Guard, *Marine Casualty Report, op. cit.,* pp. 334-38. Captain Erickson knew his vessel extremely well, having come aboard as second mate in 1953 when she went into service, becoming her master in 1964.

[23] U.S. Coast Guard, *Marine Casualty Report, op. cit.,* pp. 34-39. Another account of the U.S. Coast Guard's preparedness at the time of the *Fitzgerald* casualty appears as "An Epilog: A Conspiracy of Ineptitude" in Frederick Stonehouse's *The Wreck of the* Edmund Fitzgerald (Au Train, Michigan, Avery Color Studios, 1982, third edition), pp. 97-120.

[24] Richard L. Pomeroy, "Plane Reports Possible *Fitz* Site" in *Duluth News-Tribune,* Nov. 14, 1975.

[25] *Minneapolis Tribune,* Dec. 14, 1975.

[26] Seaward Inc., *Observations made of the wreck of the S/S* Edmund Fitzgerald *in Lake Superior, Michigan, 19-28 May 1976, prepared under U.S. Navy Supervisor of Salvage Contract N0024-76-A-2015* (Falls Church, Virginia, July 1976), pp. 1-15; U.S. Coast Guard, Dept. of Transportation, "Summary of Results of Survey of Wreckage of *Edmund Fitzgerald,*" eight-page mimeo; U.S. Coast Guard, Dept. of Transportation, "Proceedings of the Marine Safety Council," Vol. 33, No. 7, July 1976, unpaged clipping.

[27] Charles W. Theisen, "*Fitzgerald*'s Salvage Called Hopeless Task" in *Detroit News,* Nov. 12, 1975.

28 James L. Kerwin, "Coast Guard Remiss: Possible Laxity Cited in Sinking" in *Detroit News,* Nov. 14, 1975; Superior *Evening Telegram,* Nov. 19, 1975; Melvin H. Pelfrey, "*Fitz* Inquiry Stalls, Photos Reveal Nothing" in *American Maritime Officer,* November 1976, p. 8.

29 Kerwin, "Coast Guard Remiss," *op. cit.*

30 Superior *Evening Telegram,* Nov. 19, 1975.

31 Melvin H. Pelfrey, "*Fitz* Inquiry Stalls," *op. cit.*

32 "Subdividing an Ore Boat Will Not Make it Safer" in *Seaway Review,* Winter 1981, pp. 33, 35, 37.

33 Harry Benford, "Random thoughts on the safety of ships" in *Seaway Review,* Vol. 8, No. 4, Summer 1979, pp. 61-63.

34 J.M. Murray, "A Hundred Years of Lloyd's Register Ship Rules" in *Transactions, Royal Institution of Naval Architects,* Vol. 97, 1955, in Benford, *ibid.*

35 *Duluth Herald,* July 15, Dec. 28, 1976; *Duluth News-Tribune,* July 16-17, Dec. 29, 1976; *Evening News,* Sault Ste. Marie, Mich., Aug. 2, 1977.

36 U.S. Coast Guard, *Marine Casualty Report, op. cit.,* pp. ii-ix.

37 Melvin H. Pelfrey, "District 2's Proposals on Great Lakes Safety" in *American Maritime Officer,* April 1976, pp. 8, 10.

38 National Transportation Safety Board, *op. cit.,* pp. 21-22; Marlin Bree, *In the Teeth of the Northeaster: A Solo Voyage on Lake Superior* (New York, Clarkson N. Potter, 1988), pp. 123-129.

39 "The *Fitzgerald* Sinking: Two Views" in *Seaway Review,* Vol. 7, No. 1, Autumn 1977, pp. 21-24; "Lake Carriers Dispute U.S. Coast Guard Panel's Findings, Assert *Edmund Fitzgerald* Struck Caribou Island Shoal" in *American Maritime Officer,* October 1977, p. 8; "LCA's President Rebuts Coast Guard's *Fitzgerald* Findings" in Lake Carriers' Association *The Bulletin,* September-October-November 1977, Vol. 66, No. 3, pp. 2, 5-7, 13-18; Richard L. Pomeroy, "Lake Carriers Reject *Fitz* Theory" in *Duluth Herald,* Sept. 29, 1977, and also appearing in *Duluth News-Tribune,* Sept 29, 1977; Paul E. Trimble, Vice Admiral USCG (Ret.), President, Lake Carriers' Association, correspondence to Mr. Webster B. Todd Jr., Chairman, National Transportation Safety Board, dated September 16, 1977, 18 pp., as amended; "What Happened to the S.S. *Edmund Fitzgerald?*" in *Interlake Log,* Winter 1977, pp. 6-7.

40 *National Transportation Safety Board, op. cit.,* pp. 44-48; Dr. Julius F. Wolff Jr., "Transportation Safety Board Reports on *Edmund Fitzgerald* Disaster" in *The Nor'Easter,* Vol. 5, No. 1, January-February 1980, pp. 1-4, 8; Dr. Julius F. Wolff Jr., "The *Fitzgerald* Board Report" in James R. Marshall, ed., *Shipwrecks of Lake Superior* (Duluth, Minnesota, Lake Superior Port Cities Inc., 1987), pp. 62-65.

41 Playwright Steven Dietz wrote in his moving play "Ten November," "I do not know them as individuals. I have read the books and heard the song and seen the list of names. But the names do not make the faces appear. They remain a group. Working men made fallible by fate." In the spirit of remembrance in which those words were penned, the crew of the *Edmund Fitzgerald*:
Third Mate Michael E. Armagost, 37, Iron River, Wisconsin;
Porter Frederick J. Beetcher, 56, Superior, Wisconsin;
Oiler Thomas Bentsen, 23, St. Joseph, Michigan;

First Assistant Engineer Edward F. Bindon, 47, Fairport Harbor, Ohio;
AB Maintenance Man Thomas D. Borgeson, 41, Duluth, Minnesota;
Third Assistant Engineer Oliver J. Champeau, 41, Milwaukee, Wisconsin;
Porter Nolan F. Church, 55, Silver Bay, Minnesota;
Watchman Ransom E. Cundy, 53, Superior, Wisconsin;
Second Assistant Engineer Thomas E. Edwards, 50, Oregon, Ohio;
Second Assistant Engineer Russell G. Haskell, 40, Millbury, Ohio;
Chief Engineer George J. Holl, 60, Berea, Ohio, and Cabot, Pennsylvania;
Deckhand Bruce L. Hudson, 22, Olmsted, Ohio;
Second Cook Allen G. Kalmon, 43, Washburn, Wisconsin;
Wiper Gordon F. MacLellan, 30, Clearwater, Florida;
Special Maintenance Man Joseph W. Mazes, 59, Ashland, Wisconsin;
First Mate John H. McCarthy, 62, Bay Village, Ohio;
Captain Ernest M. McSorley, master, 63, Toledo, Ohio;
Wheelsman Eugene W. O'Brien, 50, St. Paul, Minnesota, and Toledo, Ohio;
Watchman Karl A. Peckol, 55, Ashtabula, Ohio;
Wheelsman John J. Poviach, 59, Bradenton, Florida;
Second Mate James A. Pratt, 44, Lakewood, Ohio;
Steward Robert C. Rafferty, 62, Toledo, Ohio;
Deckhand Paul M. Riipa, 22, Ashtabula, Ohio;
Wheelsman John D. Simmons, 60, Ashland, Wisconsin;
Watchman William J. Spengler, 59, Toledo, Ohio;
Deckhand Mark A. Thomas, 21, Richmond Heights, Ohio;
Oiler Ralph G. Walton, 58, Fremont, Ohio;
Deck Cadet David E. Weiss, 22, Agoura, California;
Oiler Blaine H. Wilhelm, 52, Moquah, Wisconsin.
Duluth News-Tribune, Nov. 13, 1975; U.S. Coast Guard, *Marine Casualty Report, op. cit.,* pp. 13-17; Steven Dietz, "Ten November" (Minneapolis, 1987), 84 pp. manuscript, p. 6.

42 *Duluth News-Tribune,* Sept. 24, 1978; unidentified clipping in the files of the Corps of Engineers' Canal Park Visitor Center and Marine Museum in Duluth, dated, Sept. 22, 1978, possibly from Houghton *Daily Mining Gazette.*

43 *National Transportation Safety Board, op. cit.,* pp. 44-48.

44 Jesse B. "Bernie" Cooper, "Sinking of the SS *Edmund Fitzgerald,*" transcript of speech delivered to the Wisconsin Marine Historical Society in Milwaukee, Wisconsin, on November 7, 1985, 13 pages, copy in the files of the Corps of Engineers' Canal Park Visitor Center and Marine Museum in Duluth; Captain Jesse B. Cooper, "SS *Arthur M. Anderson:* November 10, 1975" in Marshall, ed., *Shipwrecks of Lake Superior, op. cit.,* pp. 60-61.

45 James R. Marshall, radio interviews from Duluth on Nov. 10, 1985, and Nov. 10, 1988.

46 Cooper, "Sinking of the SS *Edmund Fitzgerald,*" *op. cit.*; Cooper, "SS *Arthur M. Anderson:* November 10, 1975," *op. cit.*

47 The *Silver Isle*'s incident is little reported other than that it occurred on May 1, 1984, and that repairs were completed in early May. The *Starbelle* and *McKellar* incidents are previously noted. However, there is better documentation on the incident involving the *Robert C. Stanley.* See Leo Gallagher, wheelsman, correspondence of November 21, 1986, to *Lake Log Chips,* Institute for Great Lakes Research collection, Bowling Green State University, and *Lake Log Chips,* Dec. 27, 1986, p. 2. An incident similar to the *Stanley*'s also occurred on the *George A. Sloan* in July 1943, although while on Lake Huron. See W.R. Oehlen-

schlager, second engineer, correspondence of Dec. 27, 1986, to *Lake Log Chips,* Institute for Great Lakes Research collection, Bowling Green State University, and *Lake Log Chips,* Mar. 7, 1987, p. 5.

[48] Houghton *Daily Mining Gazette,* Dec. 1, 1975; unidentified clipping dated December 11, 1975, in files of the Corps of Engineers' Canal Park Visitor Center and Marine Museum in Duluth.

[49] George H. Burgner, "Transcript of Discovery Deposition, U.S. District Court, Northern District of Ohio, Eastern Division, December 13, 1977," given at Minneapolis, Minn., 99 pp. typewritten manuscript, pp. 2-11.

[50] Burgner, *ibid,* pp. 20-23.

[51] Burgner, *ibid,* pp. 23-26, 56-57.

[52] Burgner, *ibid,* p. 27.

[53] Burgner, *ibid,* pp. 26, 28.

[54] Burgner, *ibid,* p. 26, 29.

[55] Burgner, *ibid,* p. 31.

[56] Burgner, *ibid,* pp. 31-34, 39-40, 44-45.

[57] Burgner, *ibid,* pp. 37-42, 47.

[58] "Faulty Welds Blamed for *Fitzgerald* Wreck" in *American Maritime Officer,* November 1976.

[59] Burgner, *op. cit.,* pp. 49-55; Houghton *Daily Mining Gazette,* Dec. 1, 1975; unidentified clipping dated Dec. 11, 1975, in files of the Corps of Engineers' Canal Park Visitor Center and Marine Museum in Duluth.

[60] Burgner, *op. cit.,* p. 53.

[61] Burgner, *ibid,* p. 55.

[62] James R. Marshall, "The *Edmund Fitzgerald* Tragedy" in Marshall, ed., *op. cit.,* pp. 64-65

[63] The *Fitzgerald* discussion has produced some valuable lakes literature. A very interesting exploration is presented by Frederick Stonehouse in *The Wreck of the* Edmund Fitzgerald, previously noted. For the technical scholar, Robert E. Lee, editor of *Telescope,* has published Edmund Fitzgerald, *1957-1975* (Detroit, Great Lakes Maritime Institute, 1977, 59 pp.). A more popularized account is found in William Ratigan's *Great Lakes Shipwrecks and Survivals,* (Grand Rapids, Michigan, Wm. B. Eerdmans Publishing Company, 1978, *Edmund Fitzgerald* edition, 384 pp.).

A wild November 1985 storm was too much for the anchored Liberian Socrates. *Dredging and seven tugs were needed to free her.* DULUTH NEWS TRIBUNE PHOTO, CANAL PARK MARINE MUSEUM COLLECTION.

Chapter 10

The Legacy Continues
1976-1989

In the 15 years since the tragic loss of the *Edmund Fitzgerald* with all hands in November 1975, truly catastrophic shipwrecks have numbered only a handful on Lake Superior. Still, there have been a number of significant casualties along with numerous lesser events. There were times when media coverage of an event would overplay the actual significance of a particular casualty and numerous times when lesser casualties were completely overlooked.

Improved reporting of casualties coupled with increased access to available records made the overall casualty roster appear longer than one would have expected

with the continual move to newer, better designed and better built vessels with more fully trained crews and dramatic moves forward in lifesaving, communication and navigation equipment as well as weather prediction.

Dollar figures for casualties are not as readily available in this time period as they were in the early years, so this criterion for inclusion or exclusion has been eliminated. Today, a typical "fender bender" runs into the tens of thousands of dollars with light groundings often exceeding a quarter of a million dollars in repairs.

Length overall will be used to describe vessels hereafter unless otherwise specifically stated.[1]

1976

Freight tonnage through the Soo Locks held nearly steady at 90.9 million tons, a decline of only one percent. Traffic through the Seaway, however, improved 13 percent to 49.3 million tons. Shipbuilding activity increased on both sides of the blue water boundary, more so on the U.S. side with more vessels delivered or under construction than there had been since the early 1950s.

There were 19 vessels involved in casualties throughout the season including one Panamanian, one Greek and three Liberian salties.[2]

Leaky rivets kept the Chicago Tribune *in Thunder Bay on May 18, 1976.* GENE ONCHULENKO PHOTO, CANAL PARK MARINE MUSEUM COLLECTION.

The Coast Guard's big icebreaker *Mackinaw* was involved in the first reported casualty of the season on March 21, when she and the 767-foot *Philip R. Clarke* sideswiped while working in heavy ice at Whitefish Bay. The *Clarke* received several creased plates and the *Mackinaw* had minimal damage which was repaired at the Soo. The *Clarke* was reported as being unable to stop when the *Mackinaw* was slowed by windrowed ice.

Cleveland-Cliffs' 600-foot *Pontiac* encountered difficulties on April 23 while downbound from Two Harbors to Cleveland with taconite. A cracked bottom plate on her starboard side was discovered which allowed water to enter the hull in ballast tank No. 5 at the rate of one foot per hour, despite pumps. The *Pontiac* was escorted into Duluth-Superior Harbor on the 24th by the Coast Guard cutter *Woodrush*.

The 319-foot *Chicago Tribune* was found to be taking water while loading at Canada Malt Elevator in Thunder Bay Harbour on May 18. Her leaky rivets were repaired, and she cleared the following day. The 600-foot *Eugene W. Pargny* reported striking a submerged obstruction in Duluth Harbor on the same day. The Liberian saltie *Ham-burger Senator* struck the Great Lakes Storage & Contracting dock in Superior on June 7.

After loading 22,900 tons of pellets at the Missabe Ore Dock, the 698-foot *Sparrows Point* grounded in Duluth Harbor on September 1 twisting her rudder. She had to unload before repairs in dry dock. A few days later on September 7 at nearby Hallett Dock No. 5, the 611-foot *Ralph H. Watson* struck the dock corner while making her approach, damaging her port bow.

Damage was relatively light on October 14 when 663-foot *Gordon C. Leitch* collided with the 730-foot *Rimouski* near Manitoba Pool No. 1 and McCabe grain elevators in Thunder Bay. The *Leitch*'s bow came in contact with the *Rimouski*'s stern in strong, gusty wind.

The Greek saltie *Aegis Destiny* struck the inner end of the north pier of the Duluth Ship Canal on her departure November 3, though neither sustained serious damage. Liberian saltie *Ocean Sovereign* had difficulties when downbound at the Soo Locks on November 13. She sheared off the southwest pier in current and became wedged across the entry to the MacArthur and Poe locks with her bow across the end of the west center pier and her stern wedged against the southwest pier. Tugs were able to free her, although traffic was blocked for several hours.[3] On the same day in the nearby upper portion of the St. Marys River, the 620-foot *Sewell Avery* and self-unloader *Hochelaga* collided near Big Point buoy. The *Hochelaga* got the worst of it, though not badly damaged. November closed with Columbia's *Ashland* striking the dock on the 30th at Taconite Harbor after loading. She proceeded to Duluth for shipyard attention to her damaged bow.

The Sewell Avery, *being assisted by* Edna G. *at Two Harbors.* ZWEIFEL-ROLEFF STUDIO PHOTO, CANAL PARK MARINE MUSEUM COLLECTION.

The tug *Robert John* got the worst of a minor collision with the Panamanian saltie *Adriatik* in Thunder Bay Harbour just off the breakwater. The saltie was reported as having suffered a cracked plate in the December 2 incident.

Thunder Bay was the scene of another incident as the season was drawing to a close. The Liberian *Unimar* was apparently loaded right into the bottom at Saskatchewan Pool 7B elevator on December 7. The following day she was reported aground off the Keefer Terminal, requiring three tugs and some lightering before being refloated. The beleaguered *Unimar* finally left the harbor on December 11, but was reported aground in the St. Marys River on the 13th, requiring nearly a day to get off.

The outbound 730-foot *Canadian Hunter* went aground in the Duluth-Superior Harbor on December 14, requiring the Coast Guard cutter *Woodrush* and Great Lakes Towing Company tugs to free her some two and a half hours later.

1977

The St. Lawrence Seaway again posted an increase in freight traffic, up 16 percent, to a new record high for the decade and for all time at 57.4 million tons. Meanwhile, traffic crossing Lake Superior fell again, this time by a more significant 14 percent to 78.1 million tons.

Five new lakes vessels were added to the registry, two American and three Canadian. There were four salties among the 18 casualties reported for this season with one each from Great Britain, Germany, Finland and Yugoslavia.[4]

U.S. Steel's *Benjamin F. Fairless* topped the early season near misses when she was trapped in ice for some 16 hours off Devils Island on January 10. The Canadian Coast Guard cutter *Alexander Henry* was able to release her.

The rest of the early season seems to have gone by relatively unimpaired, although the *John G. Munson* reported moderate hull damage while transiting Lake Superior and Lake Michigan in ice during early April, and *Canadian Leader* was grounded off Thunder Bay's Searle Elevator on April 21. The veteran landing craft *Outer Island* suffered an explosion and some fire damage at Bayfield on April 29.

May saw a pair of small dockside incidents with the little 382-foot *Black River* hitting a dock crane in the Duluth-Superior Harbor on May 13 and the British saltie *Anchises* striking an elevator dock in Thunder Bay while coming alongside.

Thunder Bay was the scene of a grounding on June 3 when the 730-foot *Senneville* came to rest amidships on a rock off the Saskatchewan Pool 4 elevator. She was able to release herself the next day after lightering a substantial portion of her grain cargo. She sustained some hull damage, including a cracked bottom plate. Water levels were the lowest they had been in a decade. Upper Lakes' *Canadian Leader* reported striking the Pool No. 4 dock on June 21.

Two Canadian tugs boosted the casualty roster in July with the *W.J. Ivan Purvis* grounding at Bateau Rock on July 16 and *Annis Lee* grounding in Nipigon Strait on July 18. That same day, the *Copper Queen* grounded at

The Benjamin F. Fairless *became trapped in ice off Devils Island in January 1977.* H.G. WEIS PHOTO COURTESY OF SHIP VIEW PHOTO, DULUTH.

Copper Harbor. Low water was undoubtedly a factor in each incident.

A more significant event occurred on July 18. This one involved Paterson's *Quedoc* when she banged the dock at Saskatchewan Pool No. 6 elevator in Thunder Bay, sustaining a 10-inch crack near her port bow. Strong, gusty winds apparently caught her before she was able to reverse her engines.

A pair of dockside incidents, one each at the Canadian and American lakeheads, rounded out the summer season. The *Elmglen* struck a dock and was damaged slightly on August 15 in Thunder Bay, while Ford Motor Company's *John Dykstra* struck the ore dock in Superior on August 22.

Only one incident occurred in the early fall, as former fish tug *Neptune* foundered at dockside in Superior. Although the wooden vessel was raised, she was dismantled during the decade following the casualty.

Two salties came together in the anchorage at Thunder Bay on November 10. The German-flagged *Normania* collided with the Yugoslavian *Trinaesti Juli* while both were anchored. It appeared that neither sustained any significant damage. Another saltie, the Finnish-flagged *Kelo*, reportedly hit the MacArthur Lock at the Soo on November 30, with but slight injury, closing out the season.

1978

There was tremendous turnaround in Lake Superior freight passing through the Soo Locks with a dramatic increase to 106.7 million tons, up 37 percent over the previous season. Seaway traffic remained almost unchanged at 56.9 million tons, a decline from the 1977 all-time record of only one percent. This was a historic year in which a 365-day shipping season was achieved on Lake Superior. The season opened April 1, 1977, and closed on March 31, 1978.

In January 1978, an inferno at Capitol Elevator No. 4 in Duluth collapsed onto the Harry L. Allen, *finishing her nearly 70-year career.* MARY T. GEORGE PHOTO, CANAL PARK MARINE MUSEUM COLLECTION.

The 1,000-footer *Belle River* set a new tonnage record for Lake Superior when she locked down on September 22 with 68,553 net tons of coal from Superior's Midwest Energy Terminal, a cargo four or five times that carried by her turn-of-the-century predecessors. The new *Lewis Wilson Foy* upped the upper lakes ore record to 67,415 tons. The season saw 26 vessels involved in casualty, 10 of them salties.[5]

The casualty roster began to build earlier. Hanna's *Leon Falk Jr.* damaged her propeller while working in ice at Superior's Burlington Northern ore docks on January 4. She had to off-load 2,000 tons of taconite in Duluth before receiving temporary repairs.

Only five days later on January 9, Interlake Steamship's 1,000-foot *Mesabi Miner* touched bottom at Taconite Harbor when she was apparently overloaded at the Erie Mining dock there. Part of her cargo was unloaded before inspection revealed little or no actual damage.

The first two January incidents were little in comparison to a spectacular blaze on Duluth's waterfront on

January 21. A grain elevator fire which began in Capitol Elevator No. 4 engulfed the entire structure in the late afternoon and early evening. As the elevator weakened, the head house toppled onto the deck of the 545-foot *Harry L. Allen* which had been berthed at the adjacent dock for the winter. On a bitterly cold evening, cold water pumped onto the cherry-red deck and side of the *Allen* by local fire fighters cracked and warped her steel plating. Flames also spread into her pilothouse and were extinguished only after extensive damage.

When the smoke cleared and the extent of damage was determined, *Harry L. Allen* was declared a constructive total loss. By season's end the ship had been moved to the nearby Hyman Michaels scrap yard where she was dismantled. On April 15, 1981, more than three years after the incident, International Multifoods Corp., owner and operator of the elevator, was found negligent and thus responsible for the fire. The damage assessment was estimated at $635,000. This sum included $449,550.66 in actual damage plus interest at 12.5 percent.[6]

More typical casualties began to appear in April with ice damage sustained by the *Philip R. Clarke* on April 3, *Middletown* on April 9 and *Benjamin F. Fairless* on April 14, all while transiting Lake Superior. The Greek saltie *Archangelos* suffered a minor grounding on April 22 in the Duluth Harbor.

The month closed with a grounding on the Kaministiquia River in Thunder Bay near the Great Lakes Paper Company dock. On April 29-30 the *E.B. Barber* grounded while carrying 10,587 tons of limestone through the harbor. Tugs were able to free her eight hours after the incident.

A collision occurred in Thunder Bay on May 24. Carryore's *Carol Lake* collided with the British saltie *Upwey Grange* which was docked. Presumably neither vessel sustained significant damage. On the same day in the same harbor, the Finnish saltie *Karl* struck the Searle elevator dock while making her berth there, sustaining stem damage.

On May 28-29, Interlake's *Herbert C. Jackson* grounded while backing away from the dock at Taconite Harbor, badly damaging her rudder. Fleetmate *Charles M. Beeghly* towed her disabled sister into the Duluth-Superior Harbor on May 30 for permanent repairs.

The Greek-flagged *Velos* hit the Blatnik Interstate Bridge in Duluth-Superior Harbor on June 2, causing slight damage. This was the same location where the Liberian saltie *Scan Fugi* hit on May 26. In neither case was damage significant. Another saltie, Panamanian-registered *Alexandra,* grounded in the Upper St. Marys River on June 26, being freed with the help of the tug *Ste. Marie I.*

July saw two incidents also involving salties. The Greek *Aegis Kudu* struck a dock in Thunder Bay on July 17 causing damage to her shell plating. Then on July 28 the Danish *Arctic Skou* grounded in Duluth-Superior Harbor.

Misener Steamship's *George M. Carl* hit either the dock or the bottom near Saskatchewan Pool No. 8 in Thunder Bay on August 1, damaging her rudder and steering gear. Just a week later on August 8, the 730-foot *Maplecliffe*

The Charles M. Beeghly *holed herself in the Duluth Ship Canal, but made it back into the harbor.* THOM HOLDEN PHOTO, CANAL PARK MARINE MUSEUM COLLECTION.

Hall collided with the tug *George N. Carleton* and was holed in Thunder Bay, again off Pool No. 8.

The *Outer Island* was again fire damaged, this time on September 18 near Red Cliff Bay outside Bayfield. The starboard bow of Upper Lakes' *Canadian Prospector* was damaged when she hit a dock in Thunder Bay on September 21. The *Algobay* grounded on Vidal Shoals in the Upper St. Marys on October 31 due to failure of her main engine. No report on the extent of hull damage, if any.

November casualties were concentrated in the last few days of the month. On November 24 Bethlehem's *Arthur B. Homer* struck the Burlington Northern ore dock in Superior. Then on November 30, the Greek *Rosario* and British *Welsh Voyager* experienced a slight collision in Duluth Harbor.

Fire broke out in the after end of the 663-foot *Stadacona* on December 2, gutting the galley and some of her accommodations. The ship was off the Keweenaw Peninsula at the time. A cook and a porter, two crewmen who led fire fighting efforts, were both airlifted to a hospital in Hancock suffering from smoke inhalation. Meanwhile, *Stadacona* proceeded to Thunder Bay for repairs to her self-unloading machinery, her side and quarters.

Fire again came into play just a few days later when Interlake's 647-foot *J.L. Mauthe* returned to Duluth Harbor. She was about 30 miles out on December 6 when a crewman discovered a hot bulkhead separating the forward end from the cargo hold. After inspection, it was determined that an overheated bow thruster exhaust pipe had caused some of her cargo to begin smoldering.

The *McKee Sons* was reported aground and later released in Thunder Bay on December 11. December 13 found U.S. Steel's *Eugene W. Pargny* colliding with Hallett Dock No. 5 in Duluth. Just two days before she was aground in the St. Marys River, perhaps causing some of the mechanical problems which prevented her from reversing her engines in the docking maneuver. Damage from the dock striking was superficial.

The 806-foot *Charles M. Beeghly* collided with the north pier of the Duluth Ship Canal while outbound with taconite on December 22, careening off the north wall into the south pier. She was holed below the waterline in the forward ballast tanks. Captain Richard Gowan was able to reverse her course, back into the harbor and turn before settling to the bottom in 32 feet of water. The next day the Coast Guard cutter *Mesquite* put air compressors aboard the sunken vessel which was nearly awash at the weather deck and, with the assistance of two tugs, refloated the *Beeghly*. She needed dry-docking to complete repairs, but had to wait until the following spring.

1979

Both Seaway and Lake Superior freight tonnages remained comparatively stable for the season with tonnage at the Soo Locks up two percent to 108.8 million tons while Seaway tonnage was off but three percent to 55.2 million tons.

The steam tug Edna G. *suffered multiple wounds due to January and February 1979 ice.* THOM HOLDEN PHOTO, CANAL PARK MARINE MUSEUM COLLECTION.

Three U.S. and three Dominion vessels joined lakes' fleets this season. The new 1,000-footer *Indiana Harbor* set a record high for the Great Lakes when she passed down at the Soo on September 14 with 70,171 tons of taconite.

Over the course of the season, the first visible signs of improvement in Coast Guard search and rescue craft since the sinking of the *Edmund Fitzgerald* also entered service. The new vessels are capable of operating in ice and

The broad-beamed Roger Blough *broke heavy ice in March 1979.* TERRY SECHEN PHOTO, CANAL PARK MARINE MUSEUM COLLECTION.

moderately heavy weather on all of the Great Lakes. The Coast Guard cutter *Katmai Bay,* first of the new 140-foot Bay Class ice-breaking tugs, was stationed at Sault Ste. Marie, a replacement for older 110-footers such as the *Naugatuck.*

The season was marred significantly by a midseason fire aboard *Cartiercliffe Hall* with loss of life and significant damage to the vessel and, toward the end of the season, with the grounding and ultimate retirement of Cleveland-Cliffs' *Frontenac.* In all there were 37 vessels involved in casualties this season. Salties were involved in fewer incidents than were expected.[7]

Venerable steam tug *Edna G.* was called out from Two Harbors on January 2 to assist the 730-foot *Paul H. Carnahan* through six inches of solid ice in getting to the Reserve Mining dock at Silver Bay. The *Edna G.* lost one of her propeller blades during the assist. The tug *Western Engineer* became the second member on the early season casualty register when she was damaged in an explosion while getting winter work at the Western Engineering dock in Thunder Bay on January 12. A crew was preparing to lift her out of the water for hull inspection when the incident occurred. U.S. Steel's *A.H. Ferbert,* part of the extended navigation winter fleet, sustained some damage to her steering gear in ice at Two Harbors on January 18.

The 767-foot *Philip R. Clarke* suffered steering gear damage while transiting Lake Superior on February 19. Winter ice on Lake Superior was also unkind to the brand new addition to U.S. Steel's Great Lakes Fleet, the *Edwin H. Gott,* after she was upbound light at the Soo for the first time. Battling ice all the way in accompaniment with the *Philip R. Clarke, John G. Munson, Cason J. Calla-*

way and *Mackinaw,* the *Gott* arrived in Two Harbors on February 21. The *Callaway* suffered ice damage the day before. The already limping steam tug *Edna G.* was called out to break ice off Two Harbors, losing another propeller blade on February 23. Even the *Mackinaw* suffered damage to her port propeller shaft, necessitating shipyard repairs. During her upbound journey through blue ice 12 to 16 inches thick, the *Gott* sustained damage to her side tanks, possibly from improper ballasting, and was taking water as well as having lost one of her twin rudders somewhere out on the lake. Some or all of her hull damage may have begun in St. Marys River ice. It was a costly journey for the U.S. Steel fleet, and the *Gott* had yet to take on her first paying cargo. The *Edwin H. Gott* finally cleared Two Harbors with her first cargo on April 21 after two months dockside undergoing repairs and rudder replacement.

Ice continued to plague the U.S. Steel fleet as the 858-foot *Roger Blough* and 767-foot *Cason J. Callaway* came together on March 20 while operating in convoy across Lake Superior. The *Scott Misener* joined the ranks of ice-damaged vessels on April 9 when she bent the blades of her propeller working in the ice of Whitefish Bay. The *Arthur M. Anderson* also received ice damage on April 12 when transiting the lake.

While it appeared that the melting ice of spring would bring good news to lake shippers, Kinsman's 603-foot *Alastair Guthrie* foundered dockside at International Multifoods Capitol Elevator slip in Duluth, settling to the bottom. Nearly 15 feet of water entered the engine room through a broken intake valve, causing her to settle at the stern, damaging her electrical and boiler equipment.

Salties returned to the casualty list on April 23 when the Greek *Kapodistrias* came together in a minor collision with the little refueling tanker *Reiss Marine* in the Duluth Harbor. Neither sustained damage.

Ice problems continued into May, particularly plaguing the 620-foot *Ashland* on May 9 when she was loaded and outbound through the Duluth Ship Canal. Ice, wind and current combined to drive her into the north wall of the Canal. She dropped her anchor to lessen the impact, but drifted over the flukes, ripping a hole in her port-side bottom up forward. Still, she was able to proceed out into the lake, turn and make a normal inbound approach to the Canal where she was assisted by tugs to the Duluth Port Terminal for inspection.

Perhaps a prelude to an event only a week away, Cleveland Cliffs' *Champlain* suffered a fire in her galley while crossing Lake Superior late in May. There were no major injuries.

Fire is clearly the nemesis of any sailor, fresh or salt water. In the early morning light of June 5 the forward crew of U.S. Steel's *Thomas W. Lamont* spotted thick black smoke billowing up from the lake in the downbound vessel lane north of Copper Harbor. It proved to be Hall Corporation's 730-foot *Cartiercliffe Hall.* Fire had broken out in the crew quarters and spread rapidly throughout the accommodations. Six sailors died in the conflagration. A seventh died later of burns suffered in the ordeal. Several others of the 19 survivors were badly burned, including Captain Raymond Boudreault. The *Thomas W. Lamont* and *Louis R. Desmarais* both took survivors aboard. Captain John Ala's Coast Guard Auxiliary boat *Rebecca* out of Copper Harbor brought sur-

Columbia's *Wolverine* grounded on the muddy bottom of the channel leading into Ashland on June 21. She was able to work herself free undamaged.

The Algerian saltie *Biban* suffered a pair of incidents on her visit to the upper lake. She had mechanical problems while upbound and then on July 7 had a minor fire in the cargo hold. After more than a week of attempts to complete repairs, the *Biban* was towed from Duluth's

Still smoldering, the Cartiercliffe Hall *is assisted into Thunder Bay.* GENE ONCHULENKO PHOTO, CANAL PARK MARINE MUSEUM COLLECTION.

vivors into that tiny port which had many times before welcomed and cared for shipwrecked sailors.

Meanwhile, the still smoldering vessel was towed into Thunder Bay Harbour where fire fighters quenched the blaze. Shipyard workers in Thunder Bay cut away the entire accommodations section. The hulk was towed down the lakes for rebuilding at Collingwood. Captain Raymond Boudreault returned to command the rebuilt *Cartiercliffe Hall* in 1980.

Both United States and Canadian Coast Guards and the National Transportation Safety Board conducted formal investigations into the casualty. They concluded that there were apparent laxities in both vessel inspection and training of crew. Canadian Coast Guards placed blame on the owners, captain and officers of the vessel.[8]

Later on in the month, two Liberian vessels rubbed against one another in the Duluth-Superior Harbor. Participants in the minor collision on June 20 were the *Grand Justice* and *Righteous.* Apparently, neither was damaged.

port terminal to Montreal where her cargo was off-loaded and permanent repairs undertaken.

On July 17 the 730-foot *Canadian Hunter* damaged her shell plating when she hit the Richardson elevator dock in Thunder Bay. On the same day the 730-foot *Ottercliffe Hall* suffered a shipboard fire while under way on the open lake, but it was quickly contained and damage minimized. On July 27, three vessels were involved in incidents. At Thunder Bay, *L.E. Block* collided with tug *George N. Carleton,* neither apparently suffering more than minor damage, and *Paul H. Carnahan* found herself briefly grounded in Duluth Harbor.

Winds of 80 mph in the Twin Ports were major contributing factors in three incidents at the end of August. The 30-foot *Tarantau* struck the ore dock in Superior on August 30. The following day Yugoslavian saltie *Krpan* was blown from the Duluth Harbor anchorage into the shallows off the Lakehead Boat Basin. Meanwhile, the Finnish saltie *Puhos* parted her mooring cables at the Duluth port terminal and began drifting across the bay. She was able to set an anchor before being driven ashore. Apparently no damage was reported to either saltie. On September 2 the *Champlain* and *Reserve* were involved in

The Frontenac *ended her days in the Fraser shipyard following a November 1979 grounding.* AL SWEIGERT PHOTO, CANAL PARK MARINE MUSEUM COLLECTION.

a light collision at Silver Bay with wind continuing to be a factor. The month closed with the 618-foot *Joseph H. Frantz* grounding and releasing herself at Ashland on September 28 and then suffering topside damage in Duluth on the 30th when a hatch coaming was damaged by a loading chute at the Missabe ore docks.

A season already marred by tragedy seemed destined to close in similar fashion. The *Tadoussac* struck a dock on November 22 at Duluth in heavy wind and sea conditions, although damage was modest for the 730-footer. Columbia's *Middletown* repeated that type of incident at the ore docks in Duluth on November 29.

The month's primary casualty occurred on November 22. The bulk freighter *Frontenac* was upbound for the Reserve Mining Company dock at Silver Bay. The trip went well until the *Frontenac* arrived off Silver Bay that night.

Captain Clyde Trueax, a sailing veteran of more than three decades, assessed the weather situation. He radioed the Reserve dock and the skipper of the *Armco* which had entered the harbor about an hour and a half earlier. Their observations were similar to what had been forecast. There was a 25 to 30 mph northeast wind with 6- to 12-foot seas and occasional light snow. Generally, though, visibility was good. Captain Trueax relieved Third Mate Peter Zeiher, leaving only himself and Wheelsman William Pollard, a five-year veteran, in the pilothouse.

The *Armco* had reported heavy rolling on her direct approach into the harbor. Captain Trueax determined that

the course which would give the *Frontenac* the least roll time would be to pass Silver Bay from the northeast and come about on a hard right wheel when about three miles beyond the entry and about three miles off shore. The turn was completed without encountering anything unexpected.

The *Frontenac* was then on a roughly reciprocal northeast course heading back toward the entry to Silver Bay. As the *Frontenac* came closer to Silver Bay, Captain Trueax still had not made a final decision as to whether or not he was definitely taking the *Frontenac* in. He was about six or seven minutes from having to make the decision when a sudden snow squall, perhaps with a slight increase in wind velocity, engulfed the *Frontenac*. Visibility was instantly reduced to only a few hundred feet and the radar was useless. Third Mate Peter Zeiher along with First Mate Edward Gaynor and Watchman Donald Walker were then on the bow maintaining a lookout as well as readying the anchor. They caught a faint glimpse of Pellet Island just before the whiteout. They could still see a flashing green light on the entry buoy ahead. Captain Trueax could see that light as well. A second light, which was much needed at this time, was the Pellet Island light, a privately maintained aid to navigation. As fate would have it, that light was burned out.

Five minutes after the squall hit, so did the *Frontenac*. She ran aground at 9:40 p.m. on a reef extending outward from Pellet Island, striking on the port side just aft of amidships. Working the engine and bow thruster proved fruitless and may have caused even more damage to the ship's bottom.

The wind started to swing the *Frontenac*'s bow more toward shore, and she began to roll. The damage spread. Water was coming into the No. 3 hold. Over the course of the next three hours, wind and waves wreaked havoc with the *Frontenac*, constantly uplifting and pounding her over the reef. Her water bottom was thoroughly gutted. The No. 3 hold was full of water and leaking into No. 4.

By 7:45 in the morning the Coast Guard cutter *Mesquite* arrived from Duluth and was alongside. Pumps were put aboard the *Frontenac*. Cracks began appearing on the deck. There were also two severe buckles amidships, one on either side.

About 23 hours after the initial impact, the fuel lighter *Reiss Marine* of Duluth came alongside and began pumping off the main supply of Bunker C fuel. When about two-thirds of the fuel was off, the *Frontenac* began to work free. Fuel lightering was completed by midnight, and the *Frontenac* moved to the nearby Reserve dock, with the *Mesquite*'s line on her stern.

Fraser Shipyards crews went aboard and welded reinforcing plates onto the hull and deck. Repairs continued over the course of the next few days.

Coast Guard officials determined that the *Frontenac* could proceed to Duluth under her own power. Early on the morning of the 28th, the *Frontenac* left Silver Bay Harbor with her escorts, fleetmate *Pontiac* and tug *Peninsula* out of Thunder Bay bound for Duluth.

Dry-docking showed damage considerably more extensive than the Coast Guard had been led to believe. Primary damage extended from beneath hatch No. 7 through No. 18, with the worst of it amidships. She was buckled inward on one side and outward on the other and her hull was twisted and bent like a milk carton. Her back was broken and the keel shoved upward some four feet, which made it difficult to get her on the blocks at the shipyard.

A hearing against Captain Trueax's license was held in January at Cleveland during which he was found negligent and the license put on probation.

While in dry dock, Fraser Shipyards' crews cut away some of the torn bottom plating and covered almost the entire bottom of the *Frontenac* with 5/16-inch steel plating. The *Frontenac* was floated out on December 13. She was towed to a nearby berth in Superior where she was nosed into the muddy bottom for the winter. Although her temporary bottom plating seemed to hold well, the *Frontenac* took on a noticeable port list over the next 10 days.

The *Frontenac* had been built in 1923 by Great Lakes Engineering Works at River Rouge, Michigan. The vessel was scrapped in Superior during 1985. Her pilothouse was moved to Two Harbors in 1987 where it now overlooks the lake behind the lighthouse.[9]

The *Ashland* was in trouble again near the close of the 1979 season. On December 10, when about 11 miles off Manitou Island in heavy weather, she apparently stalled her engines due to an electrical failure. True to lakes tradition, her distress call was answered by the *Lewis Wilson Foy*, *Edwin H. Gott* and *Willis B. Boyer* while the Coast Guard cutter *Mesquite* made her way halfway across the lake from Duluth. The next day, the tug *Peninsula* had the *Ashland* in tow to Thunder Bay with partial power restored. They arrived on the 12th, and the *Ashland* was repaired overnight, clearing the next day for Ashtabula.

1980

The decade of the 1980s opened with less than spectacular cargo statistics. A slump in ore demand was reflected in Lake Superior freight traffic falling off 12 percent to a still healthy 96.2 million tons, while Seaway tonnages fell off similarly by 11 percent to 49.4 million tons.

Fortunately, there were fewer recorded casualties on Lake Superior and none as devastatingly destructive of life and property as those of the previous year.[10]

A small fire burned aboard the 620-foot Interlake steamer *Samuel Mather* while she was undergoing repairs at General Mills A Elevator in Duluth on March 3. Actual vessel damage was minimal and confined to a small area.

A number of casualties occurred during April, but none as sensational as that involving Columbia's 690-foot *Courtney Burton* on April 8. For several days, easterly winds drove brash ice into the western lake, packing it in with

The *Ashland ventured out the Duluth Ship Canal, only to return with bottom damage.* C. Patrick Labadie photo, Canal Park Marine Museum collection.

tremendous force. The *Courtney Burton* attempted to negotiate the Duluth Ship Canal in midafternoon, although it was packed with ice. Her bow sliced through the ice handily until she was about midlength into the piers. At that point she abruptly stopped. Great Lakes Towing's tugs *Vermont* and *Rhode Island* were pressed into service. They, too, were mired down only halfway out of the canal, unable to reach the *Burton*. Captain Sam Ring started slowly backing the *Burton* out of the canal. Continued wind and wave action began to work the stern toward the north.

As the *Burton* continued to extricate herself from the canal, her stern swung further and further to the north. She was completely crosswise to the canal when she finally emerged, rolling heavily at roughly 30 degrees.

With each roll the ship was being driven closer and closer to the pierhead. She came within about 150 yards of disaster before gaining headway. She progressed slowly and worked her way back out toward the open lake. The *Burton* came to anchor safely about a mile and a half off shore.[11]

The same storm that worked on *Courtney Burton* off Duluth caught Canada Steamship Lines' 461-foot package freighter *Fort York* in Thunder Bay Harbour where wind slammed her bow against the dock while berthing. Her stem was damaged, and she was holed above the waterline in the presumed safety of the harbor on April 8.

Ice conditions were responsible for at least four more incidents in mid-April. The *Meldrum Bay* suffered ice damage to her rudder as she maneuvered just outside Thunder Bay Harbour on April 11. The *Algolake* was damaged in ice just off the Welcome Islands, holing herself in the port side fore peak on April 12. The same

Spring was in the air, but ice in the water as the Courtney Burton *was stopped cold at the Duluth Ship Canal.* JOHN T. SAUNDERS COLLECTION, CANAL PARK MARINE MUSEUM.

day, the 319-foot *Chicago Tribune* received ice damage to her bow while outbound from Thunder Bay. Ice in the harbor continued to be a problem at Thunder Bay. On April 16 the 717-foot *Seaway Queen* hit bottom and rubbed her starboard side along the edge of the dredged channel at the harbor entrance trying to maneuver in heavy ice. The *Arthur B. Homer* grounded and damaged her bow early on April 23 when her bow thruster failed while maneuvering through brash ice into Taconite Harbor, also slicing open one ballast tank. The 826-footer required a trip to dry dock in Superior for permanent repairs. The month closed with the 730-foot *Louis R. Desmarais* striking the Algoma Steel dock above the Soo on April 26. Damage, if any, was not disclosed.

The outbound *Lake Winnipeg* collided with the inner end of the north pier at Duluth Ship Canal on May 23, damaging both herself and the concrete pier. The 730-footer had her stem driven back nearly a foot, though well above the waterline, while her steering pole skewered a lamp post atop the pier. She was carrying about 23,000 metric tons of wheat to Baie Comeau at the time of the episode.

June and July passed without report of casualty. Then on August 26 the Ford fleet's 642-foot *Ernest R. Breech* struck the Burlington Northern ore dock in Superior. The Greek saltie *Common Venture* found herself aground in Duluth on September 22, but was quickly released. The following day at about 1:30 a.m., the Canadian tug *Tusker* had U.S. Steel's retired *D.G. Kerr* in tow from Duluth toward overseas shipbreakers when she lost control and the *Kerr* slammed hard into the Duluth Ship Canal within 75 feet of the spot struck by *Lake Winnipeg*. The *Kerr* was

loaded with about 5,000 tons of scrap iron. Army Corps of Engineers officials reported in October that it would cost about $200,000 to repair the Duluth Ship Canal as a result of the collisions by *Lake Winnipeg* and *D.G. Kerr*. Apparently reluctant to leave the lakes, the *D.G. Kerr* foundered in heavy weather on December 12 in the Atlantic.

On September 25, the big tug *Ohio* had U.S. Steel's *Irvin L. Clymer* in tow up the lake to the shipyard where she was to be refurbished. They encountered horrendous weather east of the Keweenaw and started to put in there for shelter. It was all the tug crew could do to get the 552-foot self-unloader safely sheltered. They were successful in settling the *Clymer* down and eventually getting her to the shipyard at Superior.

The 42-foot American gill net fish tug *Sallie* was reported stranded in Whitefish Bay on October 8. She presumably was freed, although her disposition was not disclosed. *Tadoussac* slammed into a dock in Thunder Bay on October 27, cracking some of her shell plating. Then, on November 3, Shell Canadian Tankers' 399-foot *Lakeshell* struck a dock and grounded in Marathon Harbour, but was able to free herself without substantial damage.

1981

Freight tonnages held steady on Lake Superior this season with 96.2 million tons passing through the Soo Locks while Seaway tonnages showed a modest increase of two percent to 50.5 million tons.

Carryore's *Lake Wabush* set three records this season for Seaway ore cargo at 30,831 tons, wheat at 1,024,482 bushels and corn at 1,099,000 bushels. The number of reported casualties remained stable, increasing by just four to 19 with just a couple out of the ordinary. Again, only one saltie was involved in a casualty.[12]

A tug joined the pre-season casualty roster when she foundered at dockside in Duluth. The *Erich R. Luedtke* went to the harbor bottom on March 17, but was recovered handily. The *Cason J. Callaway* was damaged slightly by a loading chute at the ore dock in Duluth on April 8.

It was left to the 716-foot *Cliffs Victory* to provide the season's first near brush with catastrophe. While ore laden and outbound from Duluth on May 13, she was extremely slow in responding to her helm and went aground inside Minnesota Point. Two tugs were able to release her unscathed without lightering.

The *Irvin L. Clymer* was resurrected from nearly eight years of retirement through extensive shipyard renovation in Superior. She left the yard on May 15 and the following day completed loading 11,154 tons of taconite at the Missabe ore docks in Duluth. She began taking water unexpectedly in her ballast tanks several hours out while bucking 35 mph winds and 10-foot seas. She came about and returned to Duluth where it was found a single leaky rivet had caused the problem. She was quickly repaired.

The same day the *Clymer* left, winds caused the 730-foot *Leon Falk Jr.* to strike the ore docks in Superior. Damage was light. Three days later on May 19, U.S. Steel's 620-foot *Robert C. Stanley* lost her propeller just off the Missabe ore docks in Duluth while making the dock. She had to be towed to Fraser Shipyards for dry-docking and evaluation of the damage.

The Cason J. Callaway *rescued the* Eugene P. Thomas, *powerless off the south shore.* HARBOR REFLECTIONS PHOTO BY TIM SLATTERY, DULUTH.

Canada Steamship's *Nipigon Bay* grounded and holed herself while shifting in Slip No. 2 in Thunder Bay on June 15. The *Senneville* added her name to the Canadian casualty list when the 730-footer struck bottom and damaged her hull while backing out of Saskatchewan Pool 4 on June 19. The *Arthur M. Anderson* bumped the ore dock in Duluth on June 23 with negligible damage. The same day, *Samuel Mather* suffered an explosion in the crankcase of her main engine while sailing on the open lake. No specific damage report was disclosed.

Another main engine failure, this one aboard U.S. Steel's *Eugene P. Thomas* on July 23, sidelined her. She was picked up by fleetmate *Cason J. Callaway* off Bark Point on the south shore and brought alongside for tow to Duluth. The *Quetico* apparently backed over the turning buoy in her attempt to get into the Duluth Harbor on July 29, fouling the chain in her rudder and propeller.

The brand new steel-hulled 74-foot (registered), 141-ton Canadian fish tug *Last Time* was reported aground and damaged in the Slate Islands on August 8, although subsequently repaired and put back in service. Later in the month on August 24, Columbia Transportation's 767-foot

Reserve was reported as having hit the Duluth ore docks.

Thunder Bay harbor tug *Robert John* received some damage on September 1 when she grounded in the Kaministiquia River while towing saltie *Hercegovina* in strong wind. Bethlehem's 1,000-foot *Lewis Wilson Foy* and Algoma Central Railway's 574-foot *E.B. Barber* tried to be in the same spot at the same time just above the Soo Locks on September 15. The *Foy* was about to enter the Poe Lock as the *Barber* was leaving the MacArthur Lock when they collided. The smaller *Barber* was undamaged while the larger *Foy* was holed in three places above the waterline.

The Greek-flagged *Rea* slammed into the approach pier for the Poe Lock on September 25, denting herself badly, but avoiding any breech of her hull. A 31-foot cruiser known as *Dad's Pad* was reported missing from the marina at Knife River on September 29 only to be found in a sinking condition off shore, probably the work of vandals.

The fall closed rather quietly with the 640-foot *Meldrum Bay* slamming into the McCabe Elevator dock at Thunder Bay on October 16, damaging her hull. Two days later the Canadian *Frontenac* ran over the shoals off Point Iroquois in the Upper St. Marys River, ruffling her bottom. The saltie *Angeatlantic* closed the season's roster by running over a buoy in the Duluth Harbor on December 1.

1982

Lake Superior freight shipments fell dramatically from the previous season to 66.4 million tons, just 69 percent of that in 1981. Seaway traffic was also off, but only 15 percent to 42.8 million tons. There was less traffic on the lake, but an increase in the number of reported casualties.[13]

Heavy ice got the best of Coast Guard cutter *Sundew* on March 24 as she was attempting to break through ice at Portage Entry to pick up personnel to service area lighthouses. She was forced to return to Duluth to make engine repairs. An unusual event involving an uncommon vessel opened the season's toll of casualties for commercial vessels. Upper Peninsula Shipbuilding Company's (UPSCO) floating dry dock *FDD1* broke away from her moorings at the company's dock in Ontonagon in high winds and was blown up the Ontonagon River a couple hundred yards until it crashed into the highway bridge upstream where it stopped. An UPSCO bulldozer was pressed into service as rescue vehicle and the wayward dry dock returned to her berth within a few hours without apparent damage to dry dock or bridge.

Ice caused a reported 18-foot gash in the 730-foot *Tadoussac* while she was downbound from Superior to the Canadian Soo on April 14-15, although it was not discovered until the 16th when she was upbound for Thunder Bay. She was repaired at the Thunder Bay shipyard.

Drifting ice continued to be a problem, this time damaging the rudder and propeller of the Canadian fish tug *Manville L.* about three and a half miles south-southwest of Pancake Point on the far eastern end of the lake on April 19. She was taken in tow by another fish tug, the *Pride,* and returned to the Soo. The Panamanian saltie *Adriatik* experienced propeller damage in ice while upbound for Duluth on April 21-22. She made repairs and cleared on the 28th. The Greek saltie *Violetta* was damaged in ice while shifting several times to different loading berths in Thunder Bay between April 23 and 27. Thunder Bay was also the scene of a grounding on April 29 when the 730-foot *Lake Manitoba* was damaged in excess of $155,000.[14]

Ice continued to be a problem into early May. The 34-foot Canadian fish tug *Gerry S.* struck submerged ice off Otterhead on May 5, causing damage to her bottom and running gear. The 730-foot *Canadian Prospector* touched bottom and holed herself on May 21 while backing away from Saskatchewan Pool No. 15 elevator in Thunder Bay. Thunder Bay was again the scene of a June 9 incident in which the Greek saltie *Captain Panapagos DP* struck the dock at Pool No. 15 elevator. She dented her hull while backing away, but apparently was not holed. Derrick barge *Adelle* was reported as having grounded on St. Louis Bay in Duluth Harbor on June 24, but came away unscathed.

Bethlehem's 1,000-foot *Lewis Wilson Foy* damaged her bottom and steering gear when she collided with the breakwall at Taconite Harbor on July 5. She proceeded to Duluth where divers found an 8 x 10-foot area of her bottom set up six to 12 inches along with a series of small cracks.

Dense fog resulted in the grounding of the passenger vessel *Isle Royale Queen II* which was negotiating the Smithwick Channel at Isle Royale on August 15. All passengers were taken off by the National Park Concessions' vessel *Sandy* while the 65-foot *Queen* was pulled free by National Park Service vessels. Some minor dents and scrapes were the net result of damage. Another grounding in Thunder Bay closed the month. Upper Lakes' 730-foot *Quebecois* was driven out of the channel on the Mission River by wind and current on August 26.

Kinsman's *Merle M. McCurdy* smacked a dolphin protecting the Blatnik Interstate Bridge in Duluth-Superior Harbor on September 14, although both apparently were undamaged. The 47-foot Canadian fish tug *Dorothy May* experienced an explosion and fire in her engine compartment when the governor failed off Michipicoten Harbour on October 13. The Panamanian saltie *Lugano* experienced some heavy weather while transiting Lake Superior on November 16, resulting in cracks appearing in her main deck. The *Adventure IV* was reported aground on November 20 at Goulais Bay on the far eastern Canadian shoreline. Ford's 642-foot *Ernest R. Breech* reported a light grounding while making the entry to the Keweenaw

Waterway on December 10. Ice may have been a problem there as it was in Thunder Bay on December 12 when the 729-foot *Canadian Navigator* stove in her bow a modest four inches while working her way into an elevator slip.

1983

Lake Superior traffic made a partial recovery from the previous season, posting an 18 percent gain to 78.6 million tons while Seaway tonnage made a moderate gain of five percent to 45.1 tons. *Columbia Star* carried the largest cargo of taconite through the Soo Locks of any vessel so far with 70,524 tons in a single voyage. The top Seaway ore load was up again to 31,250 and again delivered by the *Lake Wabush.* The *Belle River* boosted the coal record to 69,054 tons with a cargo from Superior's Midwest Energy Terminal. A remarkable number of incidents were

The George N. Carleton *was one of six tugs needed to free* Willowglen *at Thunder Bay in early June 1983.* THOM HOLDEN PHOTO, CANAL PARK MARINE MUSEUM COLLECTION.

recorded for Thunder Bay compared to any other area on the lake this season, yet overall casualties declined.[15]

Cleveland Cliffs' 767-foot self-unloader *Edward B. Greene* became the season's first casualty with extensive machinery damage while transiting Lake Superior on April 7. Repairs approached a quarter of a million dollars.[16] Ice caused the 730-foot *Algowood* to run out of the channel and go aground on the Mission River in Thunder Bay on April 13. Over on the south shore, the *Agawa Canyon* slammed into the Lake Superior & Ishpeming ore dock at Marquette in strong winds on April 18, causing some damage to her forward end and the dock. There were only a couple of incidents in May with the 730-foot *Canadian Pioneer's* bow thruster sucking in a buoy near the Searles slip in Thunder Bay on the 8th and the 730-foot *Algocen* striking the Manitoba Pool No. 3 elevator dock there in wind and current on the 13th.

The 620-foot *Willowglen* ran solidly aground on June 2

The Canadian Silver Isle *experienced hull failure due to the stress of weather in May 1984.* HAROLD ANDRESEN PHOTO, CANAL PARK MARINE MUSEUM COLLECTION.

about 1,000 to 1,500 feet off Saskatchewan Wheat Pool 6 elevator in Thunder Bay. Six tugs were called in to assist her off, including the *Robert John, George N. Carleton, Thunder Cape, Donald Mac, Peninsula* and *Rosalee D.* They were successful in releasing her on the 3rd with only minor damage. Meanwhile, fleetmate *Birchglen* was called in to assist, but she too ran aground while backing away from Saskatchewan Pool No. 7A elevator on the 3rd. The *Birchglen* was readily released. The Canadian Pacific Railway's jackknife bridge over the Kaministiquia River in Thunder Bay was struck a glancing blow by the Greek saltie *Anangel Might* on June 24. She damaged her starboard bridge wing in the process. Minor casualties continued in Thunder Bay with the 730-foot *Algobay* pushing in some shell plating on June 28 when she struck the dock at Pool No. 4.

The summer of Thunder Bay occurrences continued with the 680-foot *Beechglen* striking the ore dock on August 8. This activity continued into the fall with the 730-foot *Algolake* ramming a dolphin and holing herself near Coal Terminal No. 2 in Thunder Bay on October 12. Six days later she damaged her Kort nozzle when coupling bolts on her propeller failed while she was downbound on Lake Superior.

The downbound Greek saltie *Anangel Spirit* glanced off a pier and collided with the 1,000-foot *Indiana Harbor* at the Soo on November 27 just as the *Indiana Harbor* was emerging from the Poe Lock. The *Indiana Harbor* received an eight-foot gash in her hull above the waterline

while the much smaller saltie suffered only an eight-foot-long dent.

Great Lakes Towing's tug *Vermont* lost a stern tube seal late on December 16 as she was breaking ice at the Globe Elevator slip in Superior. The *Vermont* was nosed hard into the muddy bank to keep her from sinking in deeper water. She was tugged over to her normal berth the following day. The *Algolake* concluded the casualty season on December 28 with damage to her controllable pitch propeller when off the Thunder Bay Terminals coal dock while working in ice.

1984

Both Lake Superior and St. Lawrence Seaway tonnages posted five percent increases over the 1983 season. Freight through the locks at the Soo stood at 82.3 million tons while that on the St. Lawrence was 47.5 million tons.

Casualties for the season fell again despite increased tonnages. There were eight lakers and four salties involved in incidents this season.[17]

The steel-hulled 48-foot fish tug *Energy* out of Bayfield was first into the news of casualties on Lake Superior, although, in the end, her damage was minuscule. March 1 found the *Energy* stranded in ice immediately adjacent to Devils Island in the Apostles archipelago. She had been caught there in ice flows and was pushed completely out of the water, tipping somewhat on her starboard side. No one aboard was in any great danger since the vessel's hull had not been penetrated. The Coast Guard cutter *Sundew* responded and cautiously worked the ice around the tug, freeing her on the third attempt.[18]

As the regular season got under way the saltie *Federal Maas* and the 644-foot *Benson Ford* both found a shoal developing in the East Gate Basin of Duluth-Superior Harbor on April 15. Neither sustained noteworthy damage.

Interlake's *Charles M. Beeghly*, under command of Captain Richard W. Gowan, moved to the Burlington Northern ore docks on April 25 to begin loading. As she began backing away on April 27 her stern was caught in strong, confused currents and swung into the inner end of the northwest pier at about 8:20 a.m. Her stern was holed above the waterline and the stern anchor dropped away as she contacted the pier. Her bow swung around so that it nearly came in contact with the southeast pier, being held off only by the stabilizing rubble mound of rock below the water. After working more than five hours in the extremely strong current, tugs were able to release the *Beeghly* and move her to the Duluth Port Terminal for inspection. Captain Gowan was cleared by the Coast Guard of any misconduct in the incident, but damage was estimated at $50,000 to his ship and an additional $25,000 to the piers.

Heavy weather caught the 730-foot *Silver Isle* transiting the lake upbound light on May 1. Her main deck fractured as she worked in the seas west of Caribou Island. Quick work by her crew and careful navigation allowed her to safely gain refuge in Thunder Bay where she entered the shipyard. She was loaded and downbound 15 days later.

case explosion which badly injured Chief Engineer William King. The vessel made the dock safely, but was later moved to the port terminal in Duluth for inspection and repairs.

The Burlington Northern "S" elevator in Superior was

The record-breaking Belle River *was but one of four vessels hung up on shoals in Duluth Harbor April 1985.* HARBOR REFLECTIONS PHOTO BY TIM SLATTERY, DULUTH.

The French saltie *Philippe L.D.* was being towed into the Burlington Northern "S" elevator in Superior on July 11 when something went awry and she collided with the Superior Midwest Energy Terminal coal dock. The saltie received a gash across her stem and several bent frames, fortunately all above the waterline. Two days later, she entered the shipyard for repairs. At Thunder Bay on July 25, the 349-foot *Eva Desgagnes* suffered an engine room fire when her generator overheated and shorted out. The Greek saltie *Kasos* was reported aground on July 27 at Vidal Shoal, but was able to release herself apparently undamaged. *Eva Desgagnes* continued to have a hard time of it. She slammed the dock at Algoma's steel plant at the Canadian Soo, badly denting her hull on September 6.

As the 730-foot *Steelcliffe Hall* was maneuvering into the Cargill Elevator B-1 dock in Duluth on October 2, her engine room was wracked by a scavenger fire and crank-

again the scene of a dock encounter as the Yugoslavian saltie *Danilovgrad* was making the dock under tow on December 3, the last reported casualty of the season.

1985

Lake Superior's waterborne commerce fell off a full 10 percent this season to 74.1 million tons while Seaway traffic declined even more sharply to 37.3 million tons, a drop of 21 percent. Despite the season totals, there were new tonnage records set for taconite pellets with the *Columbia Star* carrying 71,891 tons and the *Belle River* establishing a new coal record with a cargo of 70,522 tons. The wheat carrying record also jumped to 1,058,867 bushels carried by the *Paterson,* bettering the 1983 record by 11,000 bushels.

The season saw the usual casualty types, but ended dramatically with a Liberian saltie involved in what turned out to be a unique incident even though it appeared to have all the trappings of groundings more common decades ago.[19]

A pre-season casualty occurred aboard the long-retired 601-foot *William B. Schiller* as she was being scrapped in Duluth. A cutting torch started a small fire which was quickly contained and extinguished on January 11. Things were quiet until spring ice damaged the forepeak of Algoma's 730-foot *John B. Aird* on April 1 while maneuvering through Whitefish Bay. The *Philip R. Clarke* damaged her rudder and steering gear while backing away from the Two Harbors ore docks on April 3.

The *Indiana Harbor* was aground for three or four hours while attempting to clear Duluth Harbor on April 14. She apparently swung too far north of the channel just inside the Aerial Bridge and found a shoal. The same shoal spot was discovered on April 18 by Panamanian saltie *Blue Pine*. Three days later, *William J. DeLancey* grounded briefly on the same shoal. The very next day, April 22, the 1,000-foot *Belle River* hung up on the shoal, the fourth such incident in eight days. U.S. Army Corps of Engineer's derrick barge *Coleman* began removing the shoal that day. An estimated 10,000 or more cubic yards of sediment had built up in the area.

The Coast Guard cutter *Sundew* became totally disabled on May 2 when her second main engine failed while working off Munising. The 663-foot *Stadacona* was reported to have grounded near the Algoma Steel dock above the Canadian Soo on May 18 when her main engine also failed.

June and July casualties highlighted a single vessel, the *Arctic*. This unique Canadian ice-breaking bulk carrier was briefly driven aground in high wind while shifting berths at Thunder Bay on June 2. On July 20 she was the victim of a collision with the 730-foot *Manitoulin* while she was berthed in Thunder Bay. Both vessels received only minor scratches. The American cabin cruiser *Gemini III* caught fire earlier in the month. All seven persons aboard were taken off the 38-foot vessel before she foundered in about 90 feet of water off the Superior Entry on July 7.

The *St. Clair* narrowly missed striking the Duluth Ship Canal piers on September 2 when a loose wire shut down her main engine just as she was about to pass beneath the Aerial Bridge. Captain Pete Gronwall dropped both anchors and held the 770-foot ship in position with her thrusters despite 45 mph winds. Wind forced the ship backward under the bridge and into the harbor again during which she scraped stone at the base of the piers. This caused a 35-foot long dent in her hull at the turn of the bilge. Tugs nursed her into the Port Terminal for repairs. Damage was estimated at more than $50,000 in the incident.[20]

The Liberian saltie *Federal Rhine* grazed the *Belle River* on September 26 at the St. Lawrence Cement dock in Duluth. *Belle River*'s forward port-side hull was somewhat dented.

Local weather forecasts predicted stormy conditions on the western lake for the night of November 18. There were obvious indications of the impending weather throughout the day. Captain Ioannis Kukanaris of the Liberian saltie *Socrates* had ordered Chief Engineer Peter Velissaratos to have the engines available on 30 minutes notice. Winds increased dramatically between 7 and 8 p.m. to more than 50 mph with 10-foot seas. During this time, the *Socrates* began to drag her anchor and slowly drifted from the spot where she had been for the previous couple of days toward the beach along Minnesota Point a mile away. When it became clear that the vessel was drifting, the captain ordered up the engines and lifted anchor. But, before *Socrates* gained any forward momentum, wind swung her bow around 120 degrees. Just minutes later, she was hard aground about 150 yards off the beach. In an attempt to keep off the beach, the bow anchors were dropped again, but the forepeak drifted over one of them, causing a hole in her bulbous bow. Waves crashed over the vessel as she came to rest. She had a noticeable list and was aground over much of her midships bottom.

The Coast Guard was quickly on the scene preparing to evacuate the crew if necessary. Lines were put aboard from shore so that a breeches buoy could be used if necessary. Spotlights were set up on shore. Her crew was removed by the Coast Guard the following day after tugs were unsuccessful in budging her.

Salvage plans were worked out and the engine crew put back aboard to determine if the ship's main engines could be started. Their intake cooling valves had been jammed with sand. On November 22 the salvors enlisted all of the port's seven available tugs including the *Sioux, Dakota, New Jersey, Rhode Island, Illinois, Louisiana* and *Arkansas* in a combined effort to free the vessel. The tugs tried relentlessly to free the vessel. They were successful in turning her bow back out toward Lake Superior.

After nearly 24 hours of continuous dredging around the ship, *Socrates* was freed on November 24. Repairs consisted of patching small holes in her bulbous bow.

The Coast Guard had succeeded in its three main objectives of saving the crew, saving the ship and preventing any pollution. The Coast Guard cutter *Sundew,* Group Duluth, Station Duluth and Marine Safety Office-Duluth were each recipients of commendations for their assistance to the *Socrates* and her crew.

Several days later, *Socrates* was loaded and bid farewell to the Twin Ports. Representatives of the Durocher Dock & Dredge, the salvage company, said of the release efforts, "The dredging helped, the tugs helped, the anchors helped, the ship's main engine helped. It was a matter of using every trick in the book." They estimated salvage at nearly a half million dollars including lost time for the ship and crew.[21]

Only two minor casualties were reported at the end of

the season. *Canadoc* hit a dock while berthing in Richardson Harbour on November 22, and the *John G. Munson* was aground a couple of hours while negotiating the channels of Chequamegon Bay in darkness en route to Ashland with 18,516 tons of coal.

1986

Lake Superior freight through the Soo Locks fell off six percent to 69.6 million tons, while freight through the St. Lawrence remained virtually unchanged from the 1985 slump at 37.5 million tons, an improvement of one percent. Several new record cargoes were delivered during the season. There were 22 casualties throughout the season with none involving ocean vessels.[22]

June and July 1985 were hard on the unusual ice-breaking bulk freighter Arctic. THOM HOLDEN PHOTO, CANAL PARK MARINE MUSEUM COLLECTION.

The excursion boat *Sieur Du Lhut*, foundered dockside on April 9 in Duluth. She was the apparent victim of frozen piping following a hasty lay-up the previous fall. A crane lifted *Sieur Du Lhut* from the harbor bottom two days later.[23] The long-idle *Telson Queen* fell victim to a similar incident. The *Queen* foundered dockside in Superior on April 13 opposite the Harvest States Cooperatives grain elevator. B & B Contracting of Duluth finally salvaged the vessel more than two months after the event.

The *Indiana Harbor* had a tough time getting back in harness this spring after having gone to the wall at Ashland on May 29, 1985. As she began to back away from the old ore dock on May 8, she was blown against the dock and knocked down about 30 feet of her railing on the port bow and raked two old loading chutes, too. Two hours later, she extricated herself and began her journey through picturesque Chequamegon Bay.

On June 20 as the *Wolverine* was maneuvering near the ore dock in Marquette, she backed out of the channel and damaged her rudder and shoe. The tug *Chippewa* came up from the Soo to tow the 630-foot vessel into Duluth-Superior Harbor three days later for shipyard repairs. Vessel damage was well in excess of $200,000.[24]

Westerly winds up to 86 mph hit the Twin Ports early in the evening of June 21 causing power outages and much damage throughout the area. Harvest States Cooperatives elevator in Superior had a conveyor system virtually disintegrate into a pile of rubble right next to a saltie which managed to avoid any damage. The Coast Guard was kept busy with small craft problems throughout the harbor. Retired ore carrier *Joshua A. Hatfield,* moored at Azcon/Hyman Michaels scrap yard in Duluth, was blown across the bay and grounded in the shallows off Park Point. Meanwhile, Interlake's idle *Harry Coulby* and *John Sherwin* parted lines and dragged across their slip in Superior. The also idle *A.H. Ferbert, Irving S. Olds* and *Enders M. Voorhees* broke loose from their moorings at Hallett Dock No. 5 in West Duluth. The trio raked the ore chutes on the east side of the Missabe Ore Dock No. 5 and blew across the bay where they grounded in Superior, still tethered together. Tugs rescued the runaways. North American Towing's (Noramtow) tugs found the *Hatfield* too hard aground for quick recovery, some 400 feet of her keel resting comfortably in the sand. On July 11, strong easterly winds began pushing water into the bay, making it possible for tugs to finally recover the *Hatfield* and return her to the scrap yard.[25]

There was little excitement during the next month although the 730-foot *Algowest* smacked a buoy during a heavy rain squall in Thunder Bay on July 13 just off Pool No. 6 elevator. Later in the month, the *Vista Queen* collided with the Aerial Lift Bridge on August 17, raking her after cabin sun roof. The bridge was undamaged. Wind and current played a part in the casualty. The *Vista Queen* was back in service within two days after some prompt shipyard attention and fresh paint.

The 37-foot Canadian tug *Radville*'s engine seized in Thunder Bay Harbour near the breakwall on September 17 and she drifted aground. At the American lakehead the 610-foot museum vessel *William A. Irvin* parted her steel mooring cables on September 26 and dragged an anchor in 55 mph winds while moored on the bay front. She was moved into a permanent berth in the Lake Avenue slip in mid-October.

Much as the *Joshua A. Hatfield* had done in June, *B.F. Affleck* broke loose on October 31 from the Azcon/Hyman Michaels scrap dock in Duluth and blew across the bay, grounding near the Coast Guard station on Minnesota Point, just 30 feet astern of Coast Guard cutter *Sundew*. This time, though, tugs had the wayward 604-foot vessel back at her berth within five hours, but 10 days later, she was back in the news.[26]

The tug *Thunder Cape* had the *Affleck* outbound in the Duluth Ship Canal assisted by tug *Arkansas* on November 6 bound for Port Colborne. The duo encountered heavy weather off the Keweenaw Peninsula on Novem-

Tugs retrieved the Enders M. Voorhees, Irving S. Olds *and* A.H. Ferbert *from across the bay in June 1986*. WILDERNESS PORT SHIPWRECKS PHOTO BY THOM HOLDEN.

ber 8, and *Thunder Cape* began losing power. The Coast Guard was called out from Portage Station in Hancock and took the crew off the *Affleck* which appeared to be in danger of capsizing and foundering. Then they stood by the tug until the tanker *Eastern Shell* took her in tow. Purvis Marine's tug *Avenger IV* came up from the Soo to search for the drifting *Affleck* and take her in tow to the Soo. Once under tow again, the new duo was escorted down the lake by the *Mackinaw,* which had been in the area on a training mission.[27]

A fire in the electrical system of the freighter *Maplecliffe Hall* was contained and damage limited in Thunder Bay on November 11. The giant *William J. DeLancey* reported a modest grounding on St. Louis Bay in Duluth-Superior Harbor on November 16. A.B. McLean's tug *Wilfred M. Cohen* broke down on November 30 on the western lake while towing a barge. *Avenger IV* came out of the Soo along with the tug *Miseford,* to assist. *Avenger IV* put a line on the barge while the *Miseford* took the disabled *Cohen* in tow back to the Soo.

1987

There was a dramatic upswing in Lake Superior tonnage this season. Freight through the Soo Locks increased 23 percent to 85.7 million tons. Seaway tonnage was up, but not as dramatically, with a six percent gain to 39.9 million tons. Despite the increased tonnage, there were fewer accidents reported than in any season from 1976 through 1989.[28]

As the *Algocen* was getting to United Grain Growers M elevator in Thunder Bay on March 30, she slammed into the dock, ice jamming her bow thruster. She fractured her stem bar and holed herself in the bow above the waterline. The dock also received some minor damage. Repairs were made within five days.

Parrish & Heimbecker's handsome *Willowglen* got caught in tricky current and strong northwesterly winds at the Soo which caused her to sheer into the pier separating the MacArthur and Poe locks on April 27. The pier came out of it unblemished, but the *Willowglen* had a 12- to 15-foot gash in her port bow and was taking water, although in controllable quantity. She made temporary repairs at the Soo's Carbide Dock and was under way toward Port Colborne with her grain cargo the next day.

The 826-foot *William Clay Ford* had some difficulty making the Missabe ore dock in Duluth on May 18 in 40- to 45-knot winds. She dropped her anchor to assist in making the dock approach and lost it along with some 360 feet of chain. The following day two crewmen were injured at Duluth while fitting out USS Great Lakes Fleet's *Edgar B. Speer* when an air compressor pipe exploded in the engine room.

The Altadoc *pilothouse stood for many years in Copper Harbor until it burned on April 22, 1987*. THOM HOLDEN PHOTO, CANAL PARK MARINE MUSEUM COLLECTION.

On July 20, 767-foot *Reserve* and 730-foot *Canadian Enterprise* collided near the western approach to the Soo locks. Neither vessel was damaged in the brush collision.

Selvick Marine Towing's 118-foot tug *John M. Selvick* was reported broken down with engine problems just west of the Soo on August 14 while towing two stone-laden barges to the Keweenaw Waterway. The tug *Chippewa* took over the tow as the *Selvick* limped into the Soo.

On September 27 the 40-foot American cruiser *Sassy Suzy* began taking water when about two and a half miles off Port Wing. Two other local craft had the two occupants aboard and the *Julie Ann,* a 58-foot vessel, then towed the vessel to within 20 feet of the dock, where it was later recovered.

American Steamship's 680-foot *Charles E. Wilson* went aground in Ontonagon on October 8. Fleetmate *St. Clair* was diverted to help get her off undamaged. Later in the month, the dredge *Argessy* was working at the site of a new materials handling dock above the Canadian Soo when fire broke out on October 20. It took five local fire trucks to put out the blaze which did serious damage to the engine room. The next day in Duluth Harbor, the Polish saltie *Ziemia Gniieznienska* was apparently loaded into the bottom at a Duluth grain elevator. Tugs *Arkansas* and *Rhode Island* pulled her free, undamaged. She completed loading and cleared the next day to conclude a season of light casualties.

1988

Soo Locks tonnage showed a six percent increase over 1987, but also included 1.5 million tons of cargo carried in January 1989. The end of season total reached 90.6 million tons. Seaway tonnage showed a modest one percent gain to 40.5 million tons. Lake Superior casualties increased to 16, involving three salties.[29]

The *Richilieu* opened the season's manifest of mishaps by striking a submerged obstruction in the channel off Saskatchewan Pool 6 elevator at Thunder Bay on the evening of April 7. The 730-footer was fully loaded when she struck on her forward port side. Temporary repairs were made, and she was under way again within two days. Canada Steamship Lines' 730-foot *Winnipeg* grounded in Thunder Bay on the night of April 10 with some damage to her hull, although she was able to free herself. Low water levels were a contributing factor in the incident. Discovered later were two large rocks located in the Grand Trunk Mission turning basin. The 767-foot *Philip R. Clarke* struck and toppled a dolphin designed to protect the Major Richard I. Bong Memorial Bridge in darkness on May 7. There was no damage to the *Clarke*'s starboard bow. She apparently had touched bottom and sheered into the dolphin before being able to come to a stop. Another grounding was reported in mid-May at Thunder Bay involving the 730-foot *Algosound*. She received propeller damage but was able to go to Sarnia for repairs. June slipped by without a reported grounding at the Canadian Lakehead, but *Manitoulin* did foul a cable in her wheel at the Algoma Steel dock at the Soo. Divers

removed it without any damage.

American Steamship's 680-foot *Roger M. Kyes* experienced some difficulty getting through the channel into Ashland Harbor on August 16. She was carrying 17,600 tons of stone at the time. Docking took more than four hours as she kept working herself off the bottom. The following day, August 17, outbound Yugoslavian saltie *Bijelo Polje* got caught in gusty wind and current near Duluth's Aerial Lift Bridge soon after tugs let go their lines. Her bulbous bow swung quickly to port and she rammed the newly remodeled Duluth Ship Canal piers, despite dropping both bow anchors in an attempt to avert the collision. The saltie was undamaged, but there was substantial damage to the pier. Later in the month, a Thunder Bay shipyard worker's welding torch ignited hydraulic fluid on the 730-foot *Canadian Transport,* but the August 23 fire was quickly contained.

The Yugoslavian Bijelo Polje *struck the Duluth Ship Canal pier while outbound in August 1988.* THOM HOLDEN PHOTO, CANAL PARK MARINE MUSEUM COLLECTION.

The following month the 55-foot Canadian tug *Annis Lee* got caught on September 12 in eight-foot seas, the result of an unexpected storm over northern Lake Superior. The *Annis Lee* was towing two 60-foot diameter oil storage tanks from Thunder Bay down the lake at the time. One broke free, and Captain Fred Broennle ordered the other tank cut loose while the tug ran for shelter behind Moss Island with her four crewmen. The two storage tanks were spotted by helicopter the next day aground off Longcroft Island. The *Annis Lee* corralled them and towed them into Rossport for damage survey and repairs. The *Annis Lee* successfully locked down at the Soo with one of the tanks on October 6 while the other tank was still being repaired.

Current was said to have been a contributing factor when another saltie, the Cypriot-flagged *Maria Angelicoussi*, grazed the Duluth Ship Canal while outbound on October 5. She was little damaged, but some additional damage was done to the pier in almost the same location where *Bijelo Polje* collided with it about six weeks earlier.

Interlake's 1,000-foot *Mesabi Miner* grounded while entering Taconite Harbor on November 19. She put a substantial gash in her bottom. The Coast Guard would not let her load, but she proceeded under her own power to Sturgeon Bay for repairs.

A partially lowered cable boom at the Soo Locks snagged the bridge wing of the 1,000-foot *Columbia Star* on December 18, causing some damage. A Christmas Eve encounter with the Two Harbors ore dock left the *James R. Barker* with a six-foot long, crescent-shaped crack in her bow just forward of the starboard anchor pocket. Strong easterly winds and no stern thruster were contributing factors. The 1,000-foot *Barker* went to the wall at Duluth a trip earlier than planned. Repairs were made over the winter.

1989

The Soo Locks, which had only closed on January 15, were reopened on March 15. The Lake Carriers' Associa-

The foundering of two tugs remained unexplained even after the Louisiana *reached the surface in a Duluth Harbor slip.* WILDERNESS PORT SHIPWRECKS PHOTO BY THOM HOLDEN, CANAL PARK MARINE MUSEUM COLLECTION.

tion reported in March that 63 of their 69 member vessels were to see action this season and possibly two others later in the year. However, the Canadian grain trade had fallen off dramatically the previous year and worse was

expected this year. Thunder Bay grain shipments dropped to a 20-year low, off nearly 4 million metric tons from a modest 1988 season which saw shipment of 10.8 million metric tons pass through the port. Vessel traffic alone was off some 17 percent.[30]

Season tonnages for both the Seaway and the Soo Locks tumbled primarily due to the dramatic fall-off of grain shipments from the Canadian Lakehead. Tonnages through the Soo Locks also declined due to early closing, knocking two and a half weeks off the expected season. The Soo Locks closed with nearly 85 million tons, a decline of six percent from the 90.6 million tons carried last season.[31]

Because of ice, the Coast Guard's 140-footers *Bristol Bay, Biscayne Bay* and *Neah Bay* were sidelined with damage ranging from broken welds to damaged engines during March. Columbia's *Middletown* was stuck in ice off the Duluth entry as late at April 4, requiring the cutter *Sundew* to break her free.

In darkness and ice on April 5, the *Canadian Leader* crashed into the Peavey Connors Point Elevator dock in Superior, holing her starboard bow just above the waterline. The 767-foot *Reserve* put in at the Duluth Port Terminal on April 5 with apparent propeller problems, but was able to clear the next day. The Polish saltie *Ziemia Krakowska* suffered main engine problems on April 7 and sheltered behind Keweenaw Point for nearly two days before getting under way again for Duluth.

Shortly after 8 a.m. on March 27, Great Lakes Towing's tugs *Arkansas* and *Louisiana* settled to the bottom at their berths in the 7th Avenue Slip in Duluth. A Coast Guardsman attempting to start pumps aboard one of the tugs was nearly trapped inside.

A salvage contract had been awarded but no activity beyond oil spill cleanup and containment was visible until April 8 when divers examined the vessels. Using a barge on one side and piling driven between the tugs, hydraulic jacks were used to raise the tugs in slings. The lifting rig was tested on April 13 with the real lift set for the following day. Tug *Arkansas* reached the surface at midday on April 15. She floated freely, apparently undamaged.

The salvage rig was moved over the *Louisiana* on April 17; it was successfully raised two days later. The Coast Guard again found no probable cause for the sinking; it remains a mystery. The two tugs were prepared for towing to the Company's shipyard in Cleveland. The *Ohio* arrived on May 8 and cleared the same day with the infamous *Arkansas* and *Louisiana* in tow.[32]

Once the spring troubles were over, the season went relatively safely, albeit, with somewhat fewer vessels operating than in past seasons. On May 2 the Coast Guard successfully rescued the crew of the disabled fish tug *North Star* operating out of Black River Harbor on the south shore. Severe winds engulfed the Duluth-Superior area on May 24 and 25 with the *Lewis Wilson Foy* reporting 74 mph winds just off the Duluth Ship Canal on the 24th. The next day the Canadian *Silver Isle* was blown virtually aground off the Lakehead Boat Basin in Duluth as she backed out of an elevator and prepared to leave the harbor. After recovering, she went out the Superior Entry.

Wind was again the culprit on June 13 as the *Black Bay* got caught in gusts on her approach to the Burlington Northern Ore Dock in Superior. Although assisted by tugs, she got away from them and her port bow snagged shuttle *No. 27,* putting it out of commission as well as causing some relatively cosmetic damage to the vessel.

On July 29, American Steamship's *Belle River* hooked a buoy in her rudder on arrival in early morning darkness. Needless to say, the buoy got the worst of it.

Generally, there were no casualties of real consequence over the summer until an unusual combination of foul weather saw a dredge under tow founder. Tug *William J. Dugan,* a veteran of the Revenue Cutter Service dating back to 1894 when she was launched as the *Tioga,* passed up at the Soo Locks en route to Duluth on August 28 with the old Dunbar & Sullivan dredge *Niagara* in tow. During the night, seas began running eight to 12 feet with 30 to 40 knot winds. The 135-foot, 827-gross-ton *Niagara,* built in 1913 in Manitowoc, Wisconsin, began taking some water that night, August 29. When daylight came, the old dredge was taking water fast, although the weather had subsided to four- to eight-foot seas and 20 to 25 knot winds.

As the tug crew assessed the situation it appeared that the *Niagara* was in imminent danger of foundering and dragging the *Dugan* down with her. The towline was cut. The *Niagara* settled to the bottom soon afterward roughly 13 nautical miles due north of Grand Island Light in nearly a hundred fathoms of water.

The *Windoc,* the former *Rhine Ore,* was aground in Thunder Bay Harbor on September 11 near the harbor's main entrance. Tug *W.J. Ivan Purvis* assisted her off relatively undamaged within a few hours. Just two days later on September 13, *Richilieu* experienced an engine failure as she was leaving United Grain Growers Elevator A and the *Purvis* again came to the rescue, tugging her to the Keefer Terminal for repairs.

The early fall went by with few casualties, but a cold, stormy November slowed ships on the upper and lower lakes, at times finding several remaining in port or seeking shelter. Then followed a bitter cold, equally stormy December and a casualty unique in the history of Lake Superior.

Normally stationed at Duluth, the Coast Guard cutter *Sundew* was in the shipyard at Sturgeon Bay, Wisconsin, when many of the buoys had to be pulled from Lake Superior late in the season. In the *Sundew*'s stead was her 180-foot sister vessel, *Mesquite,* home-based at Charlevoix, Michigan.

On December 4, the *Mesquite* and her crew had successfully hoisted a weather buoy about 1 a.m. and then proceeded to another buoy which marked a three-foot shoal off the tip of Keweenaw Point. The conditions were not ideal. It was dark with three- to six-foot seas and 15 to 25 mph winds. Buoys are not normally worked at

Shipyard crew works to repair the Canadian Leader*'s starboard bow.* WILDERNESS PORT SHIPWRECKS PHOTO BY THOM HOLDEN, CANAL PARK MARINE MUSEUM COLLECTION.

night, but in this case the crew was working against declining weather and with the knowledge that much of their own work was waiting for them when they returned to Lake Michigan.

About 2 a.m. on December 4, the buoy was wrestled aboard and work began to secure it. Floodlights illuminated the buoy deck as if it were midday. Over the course of the next 30 minutes, the *Mesquite* and her crew crept onto the roster of Lake Superior shipwrecks.

It appears a series of small navigational errors were made by several persons sometime between when the preliminary work of securing the buoy was completed and when the *Mesquite* got under way. At the time of the accident, *Mesquite* captain LCDR John Richard Lynch had retired to the mess hall leaving Ensign Susan Subocz in command of the vessel. He had stood by coaching Ensign

Subocz on the buoy approach and then told her to back the vessel off about 1,000 yards. She began backing at about three knots with Captain Lynch standing by her. When he thought they had backed off enough, the captain then said good night to the wheelhouse crew and proceeded to the mess deck en route to his quarters.

Lynch said, "There was a loud noise and you could feel the impact. I knew what had happened." The *Mesquite*

back five or 10 miles at full speed to reach the scene. Captain S.V. Pohonerkar, himself just 33 years old and in command of his own ship only three months, circled with the *Desai* to take the crew aboard, each time picking up about 15 crewmen.

The *Mangal Desai* brought the survivors safely into Duluth early the following morning. In addition to 47 crew members normally assigned to the *Mesquite,* there

The U.S. Coast Guard cutter Mesquite *grounded off Michigan's Keweenaw Point while retrieving buoys on December 4, 1989. She was declared a constructive total loss.* PA1 FRANK JENNINGS, U.S. COAST GUARD, *LAKE SUPERIOR MAGAZINE* COLLECTION.

seems to have drifted in the current or was set over by the weather, a factor which was not fully accounted for when the vessel got under way. The captain said later that he had failed to get a fix on the vessel's position during and after lifting the buoy. The Gull Rock Light just off Manitou Island was not lighted, making a visual fix difficult.

A damage survey found three compartments flooded or flooding, including the engine and motor rooms, the refrigerator units and dry storage area. The crew worked more than three hours to save their ship, but were finally ordered to abandon her at 6:17 a.m. when Captain Lynch determined it was too dangerous to remain aboard. The crew of 53 went over the side in survival suits into three inflatable life rafts along with their motor surfboat.

The upbound Indian vessel *Mangal Desai* answered the *Mesquite*'s distress call, coming about and running

were three crewmen from the *Sundew* to provide local knowledge in tending the buoys, two civilians and one person attached to NOAA. There were three injured crewmen who were airlifted from the deck of the *Desai* to the hospital in Hancock, Michigan, though the injuries were not reported as severe. Captain Lynch and two other officers also went to Hancock to assist in salvage plans. In addition to two HH-3F helicopters out of Traverse City which transported the injured crewmen and the other officers, the 140-foot cutters *Katmai Bay* and *Mobile Bay* proceeded to the scene as did the *Mesquite*'s 180-foot sister, *Acacia*. The Canadian cutter *Samuel Risley* also proceeded to the wreck site.

Initial evaluation of the *Mesquite*'s condition indicated salvage as a possibility, but a devastating series of storms ravaged the vessel. Removing the estimated 19,000 gallons of fuel remaining aboard was constantly hampered, sending Purvis Marine's large tug *Anglian Lady* from Sault Ste. Marie, Ontario, to shelter in Lac La Belle Harbor along with the National Park Service's tug *Joe Colombe* and barge *Beaver,* leaving only *Acacia* on scene. It was not until December 12 that the Atlantic Strike Force, working with the *Anglian Lady* and a Corps of Engineers fuel barge, was able to remove the *Mesquite*'s fuel.

Several days of seas from 10 to 18 feet and winds of up to 50 mph racked the ice-covered *Mesquite* as she lay helpless. Her mast was toppled, her rudder ripped from the stern. Her center fuel tank was holed, although the port and starboard ones remained intact. Her bottom was further shattered. Frames and shell plating were dislodged and lay on the bottom. Portions of the deck and bulkheads buckled. With every day that passed the *Mesquite* was literally pounding herself to pieces, grinding away the sandstone on which she rested with every wave that struck her. As she rolled and pitched, the water surrounding her was filled with reddish brown sandstone silt; the life blood of a fine ship, pride of her crew, was being sucked from within her. An ice shroud gave her a spectral appearance.

The *Mesquite* was decommissioned on January 31, 1990, an administrative necessity so that her crew could be reassigned. Admiral Paul Yost, Commandant of the Coast Guard, said that the *Mesquite* was "written off as far as to refloating, re-doing and re-using the ship at this point. We will look at the ship again in the spring to see what salvage efforts can be made."

In April 1990, the Coast Guard announced it would move the *Mesquite* off the ledge it was resting on and sink it in about 100 feet of water, contributing the wreck to a yet-to-be-designated underwater preserve off Keweenaw Point.

Never before in the history of Lake Superior shipwrecks had the U.S. Coast Guard or its predecessor agencies lost a major vessel. Only once before in the history of the Great Lakes had a similar U.S. vessel been decommissioned because of a casualty. That was the *Lightship No. 82,* stationed at Waverly Shoal, a November 10, 1913, storm casualty on Lake Erie about 13 miles southwest of Buffalo. There had been previous accidents dating back to the U.S. Lighthouse Board's *Lamplighter,* which stranded at Isle Royale and later at Whitefish Point in 1857, but not a loss such as this. The Canadian Lighthouse Service lost their tender *Lambton* on the eastern shore of the lake in the spring of 1922.[33]

Epilogue

These are the important shipping accidents of Lake Superior, or an overwhelming majority of them anyway. Thus far, one can document approximately 350 total vessel losses on Lake Superior. With the inexactitude of records, however, particularly prior to 1890, some could have been missed. Casualty occurrences are also unequally reported around the lake, particularly on the far eastern shore. There are also time periods in which it appears there was less than adequate reporting, particularly in the 1930s through 1950s. Then too, there is always the question of what unregistered vessels were destroyed, especially those in the rum-running trade during the American Prohibition. Rumors still float around.

Human casualties from Lake Superior shipwrecks exceed 1,000, with more dozens lost in shipboard accidents which this study did not attempt to record. Mariners have paid a substantial price in attempting to master the big lake.

Still, our sailing people have succeeded. They have made the forest and agricultural products and minerals of upper Middle America and western Canada available to the economies of both nations, and now to the nations of the world. Also, prior to the development of the railroads, highways and air traffic, they made possible the flowering of civilization in the Lake Superior basin and in the country to the west. Millions of Americans and Canadians, both past and present, owe a tremendous debt of gratitude to the maritime people who traversed Lake Superior.

As the research and writing of this book were in the final stages came grim reminders of the importance of adding special thanks to all the sport divers who, often at great risk, locate, explore, photograph and share their intimate experiences with the shipwrecks of Lake Superior.[34]

1   Many of the minor mishaps noted in this chapter are reported in the various Great Lakes newsletters and journals listed below. Most of these notations along with information from United States and Canadian government sources in addition to the contributing editor's first-hand observations have been compiled into a briefly annotated "Running Chronology of Lake Superior Marine Casualties" which became the primary reference source in preparing this chapter. Both the regular "Observations" column in *The Nor'Easter,* prepared by the author over much of the past decade with the assistance of numerous contributors, and *Lake Log Chips* are so chronological in their reporting, thus readily accessed by casualty date, and so frequently used herein, that specific citations to both have been limited to their feature articles. Extensive, but brief, manuscript casualty notes from both the United States and Canadian Coast Guards were also extensively used and not specifically cited below since they, too, were assimilated into the "Running Chronology."

2   Lake Carriers' Association, *Annual Report, 1976* (Cleveland, Ohio, Lake Carriers' Association), pp. 24-27; John O. Greenwood and Michael J. Dills, *Greenwood's and Dills' Lake Boats '76* (Cleveland, Ohio, Freshwater Press, 1976); Thom Holden, "Running Chronology of Lake Superior Marine Casualties," unpublished manuscript, 1989.

3   Lake Carriers' Association, *op. cit., 1976,* p. 67.

4   Lake Carriers' Association, *op. cit., 1977,* pp. 22-23, 61; John O. Greenwood and Michael J. Dills, *Greenwood's and Dills' Lake Boats '77* (Cleveland, Ohio, Freshwater Press, 1977); Holden, "Running Chronology," *op. cit.*

5   Lake Carriers' Association, *op. cit., 1978,* pp. 23-25, 66-67; John O. Greenwood and Michael J. Dills, *Greenwood's and Dills' Lake Boats '78* (Cleveland, Ohio, Freshwater Press, 1978); Holden, "Running Chronology," *op. cit.*

6   Arvid Morken, "Harry L. Allen — A Soliloquy" in *Nor'Easter,* Vol. 3, No. 1, January-February 1978, pp. 1-3, 5; Charles Bernen, "It Started Quickly, Ended Slow" in *Duluth News-Tribune,* Jan. 22, 1978; Richard L. Pomeroy, "Fire Consumes City Grain Elevator" in *Duluth News-Tribune,* Jan. 22, 1978; *Duluth News-Tribune,* Jan. 23, April 2, 1978.

7   Lake Carriers' Association, *op. cit., 1979,* pp. 20-23, 58-59, 83-84; John O. Greenwood and Michael J. Dills, *Greenwood's and Dills' Lake Boats '79* (Cleveland, Ohio, Freshwater Press, 1979); Holden, "Running Chronology," *op. cit.*

8   "Transcript of Proceeding: Formal Coast Guard Casualty investigation into Circumstances Involving the Fire on Boat Motor Vessel *Cartiercliffe Hall* 10 Miles North of Copper Harbor, Michigan, on June 5, 1979," five-volume, 579-page manuscript, copy in U.S. Army Corps of Engineers' Canal Park Visitor Center ship history files; K.C. Mackay, *et al.,* Transport Canada, "*Cartiercliffe Hall:* Report of Formal Investigation (No. 105)," dated June 5, 1980, 53 pp.; Thom Holden, "Last of the 1980-81 Season" in *Nor'Easter,* Vol. 6, No. 4, July-August 1981, pp. 1-3, 6; U.S. Coast Guard, "Casualty Investigation Report, *Cartiercliffe Hall,*" 14-page manuscript dated October 11, 1979, copy in U.S. Army Corps of Engineers' Canal Park Visitor Center ship history files; *American Maritime Officer,* January, June 1980; *Thunder Bay Chronicle-Journal,* Aug. 28, Dec. 8, 15, 1979, Jan. 5, 1981; Doug Smith, "Fire Caught Ship Unaware, Sailors Claim" in *Duluth News-Tribune,* June 10, 1979; Doug Smith, "$37.5 Million Suit Filed in Ship Fire" in *Duluth News-Tribune,* Dec. 8, 1979;

Captain H.F. Norton Jr., "Fire at Sea — A Casualty Visited" in *Proceedings of the Marine Safety Council,* U.S. Coast Guard, U.S. Dept. of Transportation, CG-129, Vol. 38, No. 3, May 1981, pp. 60-63; Houghton *Daily Mining Gazette,* Oct. 26, Dec. 8, 1979; Mar. 28, 1981.

9   National Transportation Safety Board, Marine Accident Report, *Grounding of the SS* Frontenac *in Lake Superior, Silver Bay, Minnesota, November 22, 1979,* NTSB-MAR-80-13, 30 pages; Georgia Swing, "Safely in Port, *Frontenac* Awaits Verdict on its Fate" in *Duluth News-Tribune,* Nov. 29, 1979; Georgia Swing, "Lack of Light May Have Imperiled Ship" in *Duluth News-Tribune,* Nov. 30, 1979; Georgia Swing, "*Frontenac* Piled Nearly Blind Onto Rocky Shoal" in *Duluth News-Tribune,* Dec. 1, 1979; Georgia Swing, "Wounded *Frontenac* Awaits Its Final Call" in *Duluth News-Tribune,* Dec. 2, 1979; Mike Payton, "*Frontenac* Won't Be Repaired, But Some Salvage Planned" in Superior *Evening Telegram,* Nov. 30, 1979; Thom Holden, "A Thanksgiving to Remember," *The Nor'Easter,* Vol. 4, No. 6, November-December 1979, pp. 1-4; Thom Holden, "Wreck of the *Frontenac:* A Thanksgiving Remembered" in Superior *Evening Telegram,* Nov. 25, 1982; Thom Holden, "The Fate of the *Frontenac*" in *Minnesota's World Port,* Vol. 5, No. 1, Spring 1980, pp. 6-8; Houghton *Daily Mining Gazette,* Nov. 30, Dec. 1, 1979; Jan. 7, 1981; Sault Ste. Marie *Evening News,* Nov. 26, 30, 1979; *Duluth Evening Herald,* Jan. 7, 1980; *Duluth News-Tribune,* Oct. 5, 1985.

10 Lake Carriers' Association, *op. cit., 1980,* pp. 24, 60; John O. Greenwood and Michael J. Dills, *Greenwood's and Dills' Lake Boats '80* (Cleveland, Ohio, Freshwater Press, 1980); Holden, "Running Chronology," *op. cit.*

11 U.S. Coast Guard "Casualty Investigation Report, *Courtney Burton,* April 11, 1980," two-page manuscript; "Some Days Nothin' Goes Right . . ." in *Minnesota's World Port,* Fall 1980, p. 18; *American Maritime Officer,* May 1980; Wayne Nelson, "An Anxious Hour for Ship Caught by Ice and Wind" in *Duluth News-Tribune,* April 9, 1980.

12 Lake Carriers' Association, *op. cit., 1981,* pp. 15-16, 48-49; John O. Greenwood and Michael J. Dills, *Greenwood's and Dills' Lake Boats '81* (Cleveland, Ohio, Freshwater Press, 1981); Holden, "Running Chronology," *op. cit.*

13 Lake Carriers' Association, *op. cit., 1982,* pp. 10, 34; John O. Greenwood and Michael J. Dills, *Greenwood's and Dills' Lake Boats '82* (Cleveland, Ohio, Freshwater Press, 1982); Holden, "Running Chronology," *op. cit.*

14 Great Lakes Protective Association, *Annual Report, 1982* (Cleveland, Ohio, Great Lakes Protective Association), p. 9.

15 Lake Carriers' Association, *op. cit., 1983,* pp. 33, 51; John O. Greenwood and Michael J. Dills, *Greenwood's and Dills' Lake Boats '83* (Cleveland, Ohio, Freshwater Press, 1983); Holden, "Running Chronology," *op. cit.*

16 Great Lakes Protective Association, *op. cit., 1983,* p. 9.

17 Lake Carriers' Association, *op. cit., 1984,* pp. 39, 66; John O. Greenwood and Michael J. Dills, *Greenwood's and Dills' Lake Boats '84* (Cleveland, Ohio, Freshwater Press, 1984); Holden, "Running Chronology," *op. cit.*

18 Robert Grunst, "A Fish Tug Named *Energy*" in *Inland Seas,* Vol. 41, No. 2, Summer 1985, pp. 82-85; Patricia Neubauer, "Fishing Boat Stranded on Lake Ice Floe" in *Duluth News-Tribune,* Mar. 3, 1984; Patricia Neubauer, "Icy Ordeal Over for Bayfield Fishermen" in *Duluth*

News-Tribune, Mar. 6, 1984; *Duluth News-Tribune,* Mar. 5, 1984.

[19] Lake Carriers' Association, *op. cit., 1985,* pp. 43, 70; John O. Greenwood and Michael J. Dills, *Greenwood's and Dills' Lake Boats '85* (Cleveland, Ohio, Freshwater Press, 1985); Holden, "Running Chronology," *op. cit.*

[20] Great Lakes Protective Association, *op. cit., 1985,* p. 9.

[21] U.S. Coast Guard "Casualty Report on *Socrates* Grounding, Jan. 13, 1986," six-page manuscript; U.S. Coast Guard, Marine Safety Office-Duluth, "Chronology of M/V *Socrates,* Nov. 18 through Nov. 24, 1985," 12-page manuscript; Al Miller, "Tugs Fail to Budge Grounded Ship" in Duluth *News-Tribune & Herald,* Nov. 20, 1985; Al Miller, "Ship's Crew Evacuated" in Duluth *News-Tribune & Herald,* Nov. 20, 1985; Al Miller, "Tugboat Fleet to Attempt Freighter Rescue" in *St. Paul Pioneer Press Dispatch,* Nov. 21, 1985; Al Miller, "Tugs Loosen Shore's Grip on Ship" in Duluth *News-Tribune & Herald,* Nov. 23, 1985; Al Miller, "Salvor Says It Took Every Trick to Free *Socrates*" in Duluth *News-Tribune & Herald,* Nov. 27, 1985; Bob Ashenmacher, "Grounding Launched Big Beach Party" in Duluth *News-Tribune & Herald,* Nov. 20, 1985; Dick Pomeroy, "*Socrates*' Skipper Failed to Take Early, Positive Action" in Superior *Evening Telegram,* Jan. 17, 1986; Susan Stanich, "Wind, Waves Push Ship Aground" in Duluth *News-Tribune & Herald,* Nov. 19, 1985; Tom Dennis, "Tugs Free Freighter from Sand" in Duluth *News-Tribune & Herald,* Nov. 25, 1985; *St. Paul Pioneer Press Dispatch,* Nov. 26, 1985; Henry Boyd Hall, "Plans to Free *Socrates* Swamp Coast Guards" in *St. Paul Pioneer Press Dispatch,* Nov. 24, 1985; Henry Boyd Hall, "Six Tugboats Free Freighter" in *St. Paul Pioneer Press Dispatch,* Nov. 25, 1985; Joe Soucheray, "Suddenly, A Ship Was in Their Yard" in *St. Paul Pioneer Press Dispatch,* Nov. 22, 1985; Pat Prince, "Power is Restored to Grounded Ship as Storm Moves In" in *Minneapolis Star Tribune,* Nov. 22, 1985; Carol Byrne, "Ship's Plight Becomes Tourist Bonanza for Duluth" in *Minneapolis Star Tribune,* Nov. 22, 1985.

[22] Lake Carriers' Association, *op. cit., 1986,* pp. 55, 91; John O. Greenwood and Michael J. Dills, *Greenwood's and Dills' Lake Boats '86* (Cleveland, Ohio, Freshwater Press, 1986); Holden, "Running Chronology," *op. cit.*

[23] *Duluth News-Tribune,* Apr. 10, 1986.

[24] Great Lakes Protective Association, *op. cit., 1986,* p. 9.

[25] *Duluth News-Tribune,* June 25, July 12, 1986.

[26] Dick Pomeroy, "Laker Adrift Vexes Port Safety Officer" in Superior *Evening Telegram,* Oct. 31, 1986; Al Miller, "Freighter Drifts Across Bay After Strong Winds Set It Free" in Duluth *News-Tribune & Herald,* Nov. 1, 1986.

[27] PA3 Mike Milliken (USCG), "A Daring Rescue" in *USCG Shipmates,* Vol. 9, No. 3, January 1987, pp. 2-3; Mike Hughlett, "Drifting Tug, Ship Taken Under Tow" in Duluth *News-Tribune & Herald,* Nov. 10, 1986; *Thunder Bay News Chronicle,* Nov. 10, 11, 1986; Sault Ste. Marie *Evening News,* Nov. 10, 28, 1986; Houghton *Daily Mining Gazette,* Nov. 10, 1986; Superior *Evening Telegram,* Nov. 10, 1986.

[28] Lake Carriers' Association, *op. cit., 1987,* p. 79; John O. Greenwood and Michael J. Dills, *Greenwood's and Dills' Lake Boats '87* (Cleveland, Ohio, Freshwater Press, 1987); Holden, "Running Chronology," *op. cit.*

[29] Lake Carriers' Association, *op. cit., 1988,* p. 86; John O. Greenwood and Michael J. Dills, *Greenwood's and Dills' Lake Boats '88* (Cleveland, Ohio, Freshwater Press, 1988); Holden, "Running Chronology," *op. cit.;* "The System Soars" in *Seaway Review,* Vol. 17, No. 4, Winter 1989, pp. 5-8, 11-12; "The Seaway at Twenty: An Anniversary Overview" in *Seaway Review,* Vol. 8, No. 4, Summer 1979, pp. 17-27; "St. Lawrence Seaway: Chronology of Significant Events" in *Seaway Review,* Vol. 17, No. 2, Summer 1988, pp. 53-66; Holden, "Running Chronology," *op. cit.*

[30] Sault St. Marie *Evening News,* Dec. 22, 26, 1989; Superior *Evening Telegram; Duluth News-Tribune,* Dec. 14, 29, 1989.

[31] *Duluth News-Tribune,* Jan. 3, 1990.

[32] U.S. Coast Guard, "Pollution Reports 27 March 1989 — 21 April 1989, Regarding Tugs *Arkansas* and *Louisiana* Sunk at Duluth, Minnesota," 16-page unpublished manuscript; John O. Greenwood and Michael J. Dills, *Greenwood's and Dills' Lake Boats '89* (Cleveland, Ohio, Freshwater Press, 1989); Holden, "Running Chronology," *op. cit.; Duluth News-Tribune,* April 2, 16, 1989; Superior *Evening Telegram,* April 11, 1989; Mike Hughlett, "Sunken Tugs Prove Tough to Salvage" in *Duluth News-Tribune,* April 11, 1989; Mike Hughlett, "Tugs Yield No Clues About Sinking" in *Duluth News-Tribune,* April 19, 1989; Don Jacobson, "Raised Tug Yields No Clues to Mysterious Sinking" in *Duluth News-Tribune,* April 16, 1989;

[33] *Duluth News-Tribune,* Dec. 5, 7, 15-16, 20, 22, 1989, Jan. 6, 11, 1990; Houghton *Daily Mining Gazette,* Dec. 4-5, 15, 21-22, 30, 1989, Jan. 5, 1990; Sault Ste. Marie *Evening News,* Dec. 6, 8, 11, 22, 1989; Superior *Evening Telegram,* Dec. 4-7, 12, 14-15, 21, 1989; U.S. Coast Guard, "Local Notice to Mariners, LNM 41/89," Dec. 15, 1989; U.S. Coast Guard, "Local Notice to Mariners, LNM 42/89," Dec. 22, 1989; Lisa Babcock, "*Mesquite* Crew Abandons Ship" in *Petoskey News-Review,* Dec. 4, 1989; Lisa Babcock, "*Mesquite* Fuel Oil Leaking Into Lake Superior" in *Petoskey News-Review,* Dec. 5, 1989; Lisa Babcock, "*Mesquite* Study, Salvage Continue" in *Petoskey News-Review,* Dec. 6, 1989; Lisa Babcock, "*Mesquite* Salvage Continues; Crew Home" in *Petoskey News-Review,* Dec. 7, 1989; Lisa Babcock, "*Mesquite* Crew Working Out of Temporary Offices" in *Petoskey News-Review,* Dec. 8, 1989; Lisa Babcock, "*Mesquite* Salvage Delayed 'til Spring?" in *Petoskey News-Review,* Dec. 11, 1989; Lisa Babcock, "Salvage of *Mesquite* Appears Unlikely" in *Petoskey News-Review,* Dec. 12, 1989; Lisa Babcock, "Indian Skipper Glad to Help But Doesn't Want Repeat" in *Petoskey News-Review,* Dec. 12, 1989; Lisa Babcock, "*Mesquite* Salvage Delayed 'til Spring" in *Petoskey News-Review,* Dec. 13, 1989; Lisa Babcock, "*Mesquite* Crew Keys on Inquiries as Salvage Stops" in *Petoskey News-Review,* Dec. 15, 1989; Lisa Babcock, "Currents May Have Caused Ship Grounding" in *Petoskey News-Review,* Dec. 18, 1989; Lisa Babcock, "*Mesquite* Commander Testifies at Hearing" in *Petoskey News-Review,* Dec. 20, 1989; Lisa Babcock, "Charlevoix Laments Ship Loss" in *Petoskey News-Review,* Dec. 21, 1989; Lisa Babcock, "*Mesquite* Crewmen Leaving" in *Petoskey News-Review,* Dec. 27, 1989; John Flesher, "Coast Guard Panel Eyes Fleet Update" in Superior *Evening Telegram,* Dec. 8, 1989; Paul Furiga, "Subcommittee to Probe Grounding of *Mesquite*" in Houghton *Daily Mining Gazette,* Dec. 9, 1989; Paul Furiga, "*Acacia* to Replace *Mesquite*" in Houghton *Daily Mining Gazette,* Jan. 10, 1990; Don Jacobson, "Coast Guard Praises 'Superb Seamanship' of *Mesquite* Rescuer" in *Duluth News-Tribune,* Dec. 8, 1989; Don Jacobson, "Weather Halts Oil Retrieval" in *Duluth News-Tribune,* Dec. 9, 1989; Don Jacobson, "Strikers Rush to Ship's Aid" in

Duluth News-Tribune, Dec. 9, 1989; Roger Komula, "Coast Guard Cutter Leaking Fuel Oil" in Houghton *Daily Mining Gazette,* Dec. 5, 1989; Roger Komula, "Weather, Fuel Shortage Hamper Salvage" in Houghton *Daily Mining Gazette,* Dec. 6, 1989; Roger Komula, "Damage Report on Grounded Cutter Due Friday" in Houghton *Daily Mining Gazette,* Dec. 7, 1989; Roger Komula, "Cutter in Race With Winter" in Houghton *Daily Mining Gazette,* Dec. 8, 1989; Roger Komula, "Salvage Efforts Continue" in Houghton *Daily Mining Gazette,* Dec. 9, 1989; Roger Komula, "Weather Takes Toll on Grounded Cutter" in Houghton *Daily Mining Gazette,* Dec. 11, 1989; Roger Komula, "Coast Guard Leaves Cutter" in Houghton *Daily Mining Gazette,* Dec. 13, 1989; Roger Komula, "*Mesquite* Eyed for Preserve" in Houghton *Daily Mining Gazette,* Dec. 14, 1989; Roger Losey, "The Coast Guard Cutter *Mackinaw*" in *The Nor'Easter,* Vol. 7, No. 6, November-December 1982, pp. 1-5; Roger Losey, "Ice and the 140s — The Story of the 'Bay Class'" in *The Nor'Easter,* Vol. 8, No. 6, November-December 1983, pp. 1-5; Roger Losey, "Pride of the Coast Guard — The 180s from Duluth" in *The Nor'Easter,* Vol. 10, No. 4, July-August 1985, pp. 1-5; Patrick Murphy, "The Loss of *Lightship No. 82*" in *Shipmates,* January-February 1975, pp. 2-7; Wayne Nelson, "Storm Damages Coast Guard Cutter: Crews Pump Fuel from the *Mesquite*" in *Duluth News-Tribune,* Dec. 12, 1989; Katy Read, "Sailors Savor Safety Ashore" in *Duluth News-Tribune, Dec. 6, 1989; Jack* Storey, "*Mesquite* Grounded Off Keweenaw," Sault Ste. Marie *Evening News,* Dec. 4, 1989; Jack Storey, "Law of the Sea is Still a Binding Code" in Sault Ste. Marie *Evening News,* Dec. 24, 1989; Jackie Tomchak, "*Mesquite* Oil Leak Toll Unknown" in Houghton *Daily Mining Gazette,* Dec. 8, 1989.

[34] Doug Ferguson, "Toronto Diver Exploring Sunken Luxury Yacht *Gunilda* Presumed Drowned Near Rossport" in *Thunder Bay Chronicle-Journal,* Aug. 14, 1989; James R. Marshall, "Danger at 140 Feet: Jerry Eliason Survives Free Ascent" in *Lake Superior Newsletter,* Fall 1989, pp. 1-3.

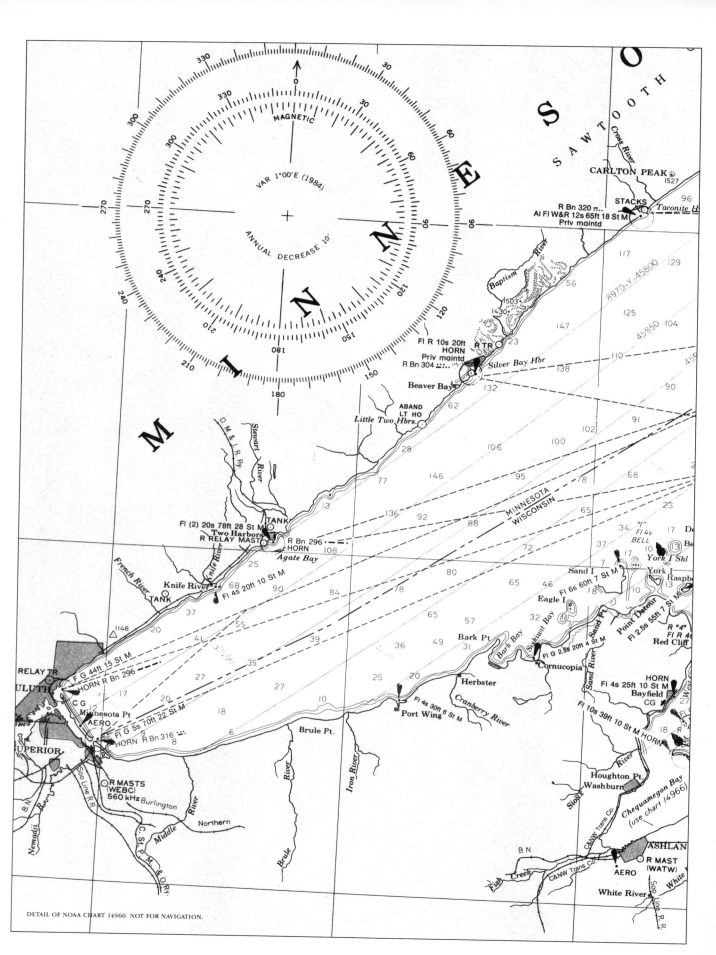

VAR 1°00'E (1984)

ANNUAL DECREASE 10'

MAGNETIC

MINNESOTA

SAWTOOTH

Cross River

CARLTON PEAK ☼
1527

R Bn 320 ⁻·⁻ STACKS
Al Fl W&R 12s 65ft 18 St M   Taconite H
Priv maintd   96

117

8970-Y-45800   129

Baptism River   56
1503   125
1430   147
45550   104

Fl R 10s 20ft   R TR   23
HORN
Priv maintd   110
R Bn 304 ⁻··⁻   Silver Bay Hbr   138
                                      459
Beaver Bay   132   90

ABAND
LT HO   62
Little Two Hbrs.   91

Stewart River   102
D. M. & I. R. Ry.   28   106   100

77   95   78   68

13   146   92   88   65   23

Fl (2) 20s 78ft 28 St M   TANK   34 "I"   17   De
Two Harbors   R Bn 296 ⁻ ⁻   36   Fl 4s   17
R RELAY MAST   72   37   BELL   Be
HORN   108   York I Shl
Agate Bay   80   Sand I 7 St M   10
25   7   17   York I
French River   46   Fl 6s 60ft 7 St M   Raspb
Knife River   68 20ft 10 St M   18   10
TANK   Fl 4s 20ft 10 St M   90   Eagle I   Point Detour
37   84   65   57   32 Siskiwit Bay   Fl 2.5s 55ft 7 St M
Knife River   55   36   49   Bark Pt   Bark Bay   R "4"
1148 △   41   39   31   Sioux River   Fl R 4
RELAY TR   35   27   Sand River   Red Cliff
F G 44ft 15 St M   27   25   20   Cornucopia
DULUTH   HORN R Bn 296   17   Fl G 2.5s 20ft 4 St M
C G   12   20   27   Herbster   HORN
Minnesota Pt   18   10   Fl 4s 25ft 10 St M
AERO   6   Bayfield
F G 5s 70ft 22 St M   Cranberry River   CG
HORN R Bn 316 ⁻··⁻   8   Fl 4s 30ft 6 St M   Fl 10s 39ft 10 St M HORN
SUPERIOR   Brule Pt.   Port Wing   18

Houghton Pt.
Washburn
R MASTS   Iron River   Chequamegon Bay
(WEBC)   Sioux River   (use chart 14966)
560 kHz   Burlington
B.N.   C&NW Trans Co.   ASHLAN
Nemadji   Middle River   Northern   R MAST
C. St. P. M. & O. Ry.   Brule   B.N.   C&NW Trans Co.   (WATW)
AERO
Fish Creek   White River   White
Soo Line R.R.

DETAIL OF NOAA CHART 14960. NOT FOR NAVIGATION.

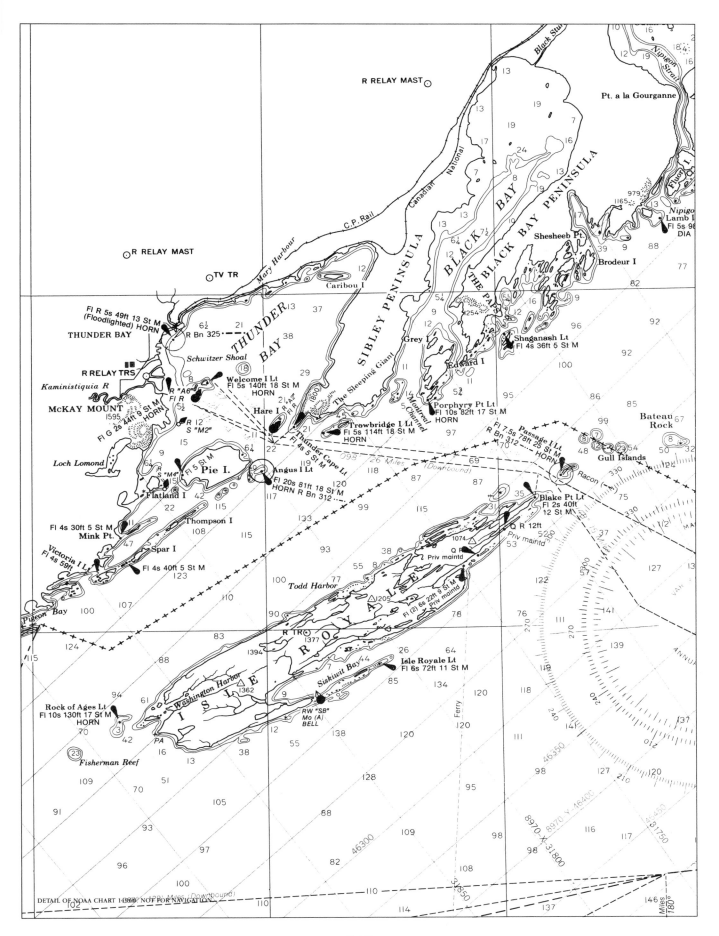

R RELAY MAST

Pt. a la Gourganne

Nipigo
Strait

Black Stur

Canadian National

C.P. Rail

Mary Harbour

R RELAY MAST

TV TR

Caribou I

SIBLEY PENINSULA

BLACK BAY

BLACK BAY PENINSULA

THE PASS

Shesheeb Pt.

Brodeur I

Nipigo
Lamb I
Fl 5s 98
DIA

Fl R 5s 49ft 13 St M
(Floodlighted) HORN

THUNDER BAY

R Bn 325

Schwitzer Shoal

THUNDER BAY

Grey I

Shaganash Lt
Fl 4s 36ft 5 St M

R RELAY TRS

Kaministiquia R

McKAY MOUNT

Fl G 2s 44ft 9 St M
HORN

R "A6"
Fl R

Welcome I Lt
Fl 5s 140ft 18 St M
HORN

The Sleeping Giant

Edward I

Montreal
Channel

Porphyry Pt Lt
Fl 10s 82ft 17 St M
HORN

Bateau
Rock

Hare I

R "A2"
Fl R

R 12
S "M2"

Trowbridge I Lt
Fl 5s 114ft 18 St M
HORN

Passage I Lt
Fl 7.5s 78ft 25 St M
R Bn 312 HORN

Gull Islands

Loch Lomond

R
S "M4"

Fl 5 St M

Pie I.

Angus I Lt
Fl 20s 81ft 18 St M
HORN R Bn 312

Thunder Cape Lt
Fl 5s 5 St M

093° 26 Miles (Downbound)

Racon

Blake Pt Lt
Fl 2s 40ft
12 St M

Flatland I

Thompson I

Q R 12ft
Priv maintd

Priv maintd

Fl 4s 30ft 5 St M
Mink Pt.

Spar I

Fl 4s 40ft 5 St M

ROYALE

Q R
Priv maintd

Fl (2) 6s 22ft 9 St M
Priv maintd

Victoria I L
Fl 4s 59ft

Todd Harbor

R TR

Pigeon Bay

ISLE

Washington Harbor

Siskiwit Bay

Isle Royale Lt
Fl 6s 72ft 11 St M

Rock of Ages Lt
Fl 10s 130ft 17 St M
HORN

Ferry

RW "SB"
Mo (A)
BELL

Fisherman Reef

46350
8970-X-31800
8970-Y-46400

46300

32850

DETAIL OF NOAA CHART 14900 NOT FOR NAVIGATION

093° 26 Miles (Downbound)

180°
Miles

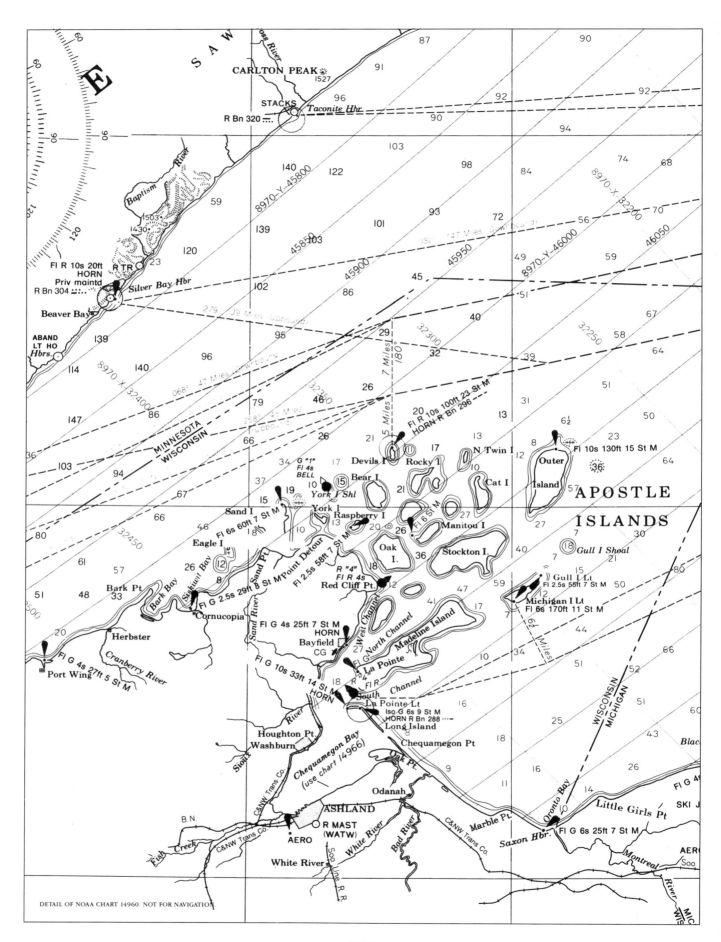

260

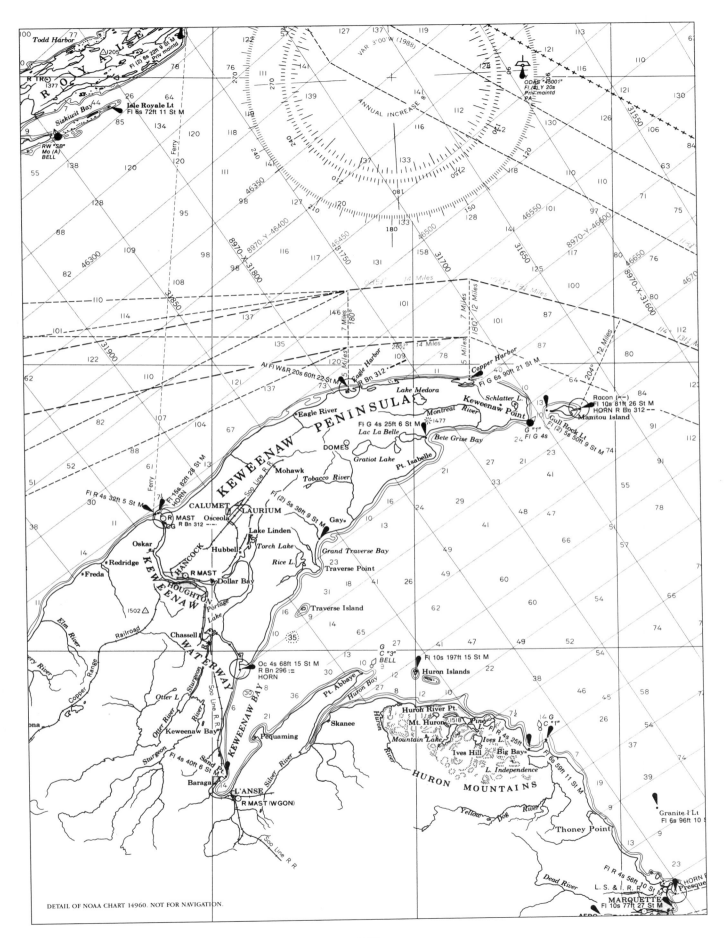

DETAIL OF NOAA CHART 14960. NOT FOR NAVIGATION.

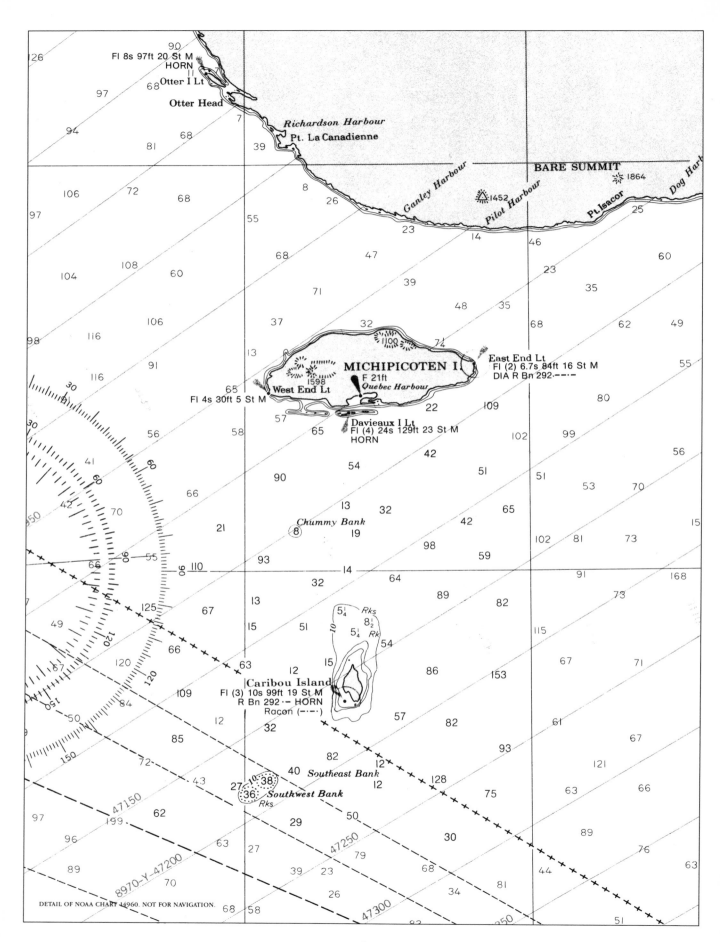

Fl 8s 97ft 20 St M
HORN
Otter I Lt

Otter Head

90
26
97
68
7
94
81
68
39

Richardson Harbour
Pt. La Canadienne

Ganley Harbour
BARE SUMMIT
△ 1452 *Pilot Harbour*
✴ 1864
Pt. Isacor
Dog Harb

106   72   68
97   55
8   26   23   14   46   25   60
68   47
71   39   23   35
104   108   60
48   35
98   116   37   32   1100   74   68   62   49
13   1598   East End Lt
91   106   West End Lt   Fl (2) 6.7s 84ft 16 St M
MICHIPICOTEN I.   DIA R Bn 292·-·-
F 21ft
65   *Quebec Harbour*
Fl 4s 30ft 5 St M   57   22   109   80   55
30   58   Davieaux I Lt   65
30   Fl (4) 24s 129ft 23 St M   42   102   99   56
41   66   HORN
60   90   54   51   51   53   70
70   13   32   65   15
55   21   *Chummy Bank*   42   102   81   73
⑧   19   98   59
110   93   14   64   91   168
125   32   89   82   73
67   13   5¼   *Rks*   67   71
49   15   8½   54   153
120   63   51   5¼   *Rk*   86
66   12   15   57   67
120   109   **Caribou Island**   82   61   67
84   Fl (3) 10s 99ft 19 St M   93   121
50   12   R Bn 292·- HORN   82   75   63   66
85   Racon (-·-·)   32   12   128
72   40   *Southeast Bank*   12   75
43   10   ③⑧   29   50   30   89   76
36   *Southwest Bank*   79   68   44   63
62   *Rks*   39   23   81
97   27   26   34   51
96   63
89   70   68   58

DETAIL OF NOAA CHART 14960. NOT FOR NAVIGATION.

8970-Y-47200   47150   47250   47300   350

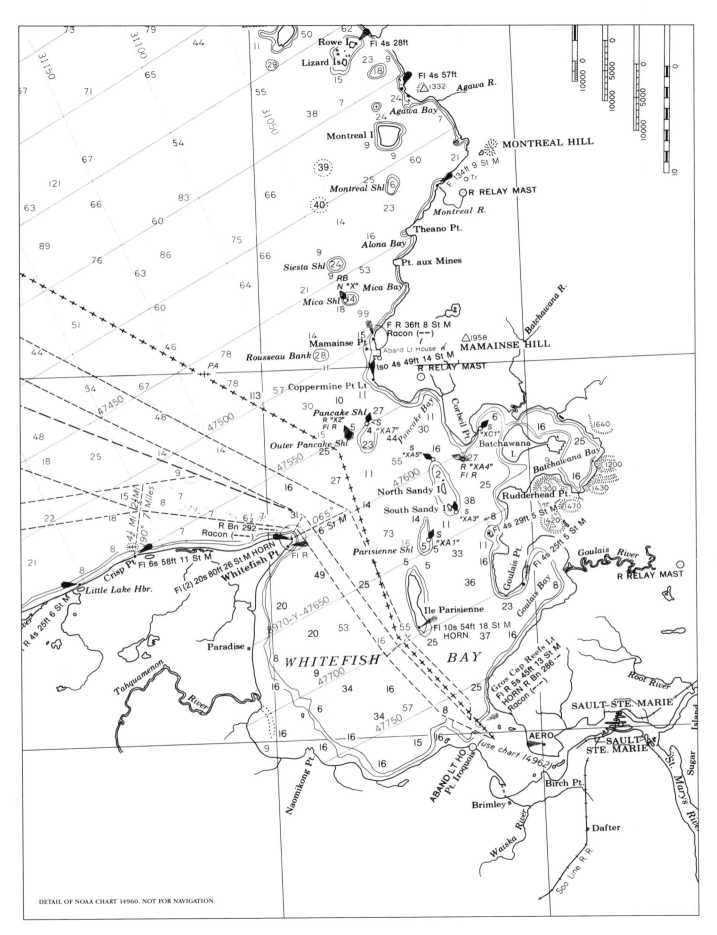

DETAIL OF NOAA CHART 14960. NOT FOR NAVIGATION.

Glossary

ACCOMMODATIONS — Berths, cabins or quarters aboard ship.

ARCH — Large, curved truss used to strengthen wooden HULL.

AUXILIARIES — Secondary machinery such as pumps, condensers, dynamos.

BALLAST — Bulk material carried for weight to stabilize ships, usually water.

BARK (BARQUE) — Sailing ship with three masts, two of which are square-rigged. On the Great Lakes the term is applied to BARKANTINES.

BARKANTINE — Sailing ship with three masts, the FOREmost of which is square-rigged. On the Great Lakes usually called BARKS.

BAROMETER — Instrument for measuring atmospheric pressure.

BILGE — In general, the bottom of a ship. Specifically, the "corner" where the bottom meets the side.

BITTS (Mooring) — Posts on ship's deck for tying up mooring or towing lines.

BLOOM — Thick mass of iron ready for working into bars, sheets or beams.

BOILER — Steam generator. Large iron drum to create steam to drive machinery.

BOOM — Horizontal SPAR used at foot of sail or for a derrick. Also, string of logs fastened end-to-end for enclosure of a log RAFT.

BOW — Front of a ship.

BOWSPRIT — SPAR overhanging a ship's BOW to carry headsails (JIBS).

BOW THRUSTER — Small PROPELLER fixed sideways in ship's BOW to assist with maneuvering.

BREECHES-BUOY — A lifesaving device using a harness suspended from overhead lines to lift survivors from shipwrecks. The lines are fired out to the wreck with a LYLE GUN.

BROACH — To lose control of a vessel by being turned broadside to the waves, also called "falling into the TROUGH" of the seas.

BULBOUS BOW — Ship's BOW which forms a bulb-shape below the waterline, designed to minimize DRAG caused by large bow-wave at high speed. Used only in vessels built for more than 20 miles per hour speed.

BULK FREIGHTER — 200- to 1,000-foot ship designed to carry loose cargo such as coal, ore, limestone or grain, which is simply dumped into HOLDS.

BULWARKS — Solid rail around the DECKS of a ship. Protective extension of ship's side which runs from deck to rail.

BULKHEAD — Wall or partition between portions of ship's HULL.

BUNKER — Space for storage of fuel, such as coal or oil.

CANALLER — A ship designed to pass through the locks of the St. Lawrence River canals. From 1845 to 1884 measuring 145 x 26 feet; from 1884 to 1958 measuring 254 x 45 feet; and since 1958 measuring 730 x 75 feet.

CAPSIZE — To roll onto one side or to turn over.

CAPSTAN — A type of WINCH stood vertically. Deck device used to haul on heavy lines for mooring, towing or handling sails, using several deck hands with long wooden bars.

CHAINS — Anchor chains, or steering chains. Used to connect steering wheel with rudder.

CENTERBOARD — Large board suspended vertically through a well in a ship's bottom, used to stabilize the vessel and to prevent drifting sideways, especially while under sail.

CHUTE — Loading spout at ore docks.

COAMING — Raised edge around a HATCH or deck opening, meant to keep out water.

COMBER — A wave with a crest or foam on top.

COMPANIONWAY — Deck opening for a stair or ladder.

COMPOSITE — Method of constructing ship's HULLS, using metal FRAMES and wooden planking.

CONSORT — A towbarge.

CONSTRUCTIVE TOTAL LOSS — Vessel damaged so badly that repair is not economically worthwhile. Damage exceeds value of the ship.

COSTON GUN — Flare gun, used to fire distress signals.

CRAB — To jamb or snag an oar while rowing a boat. Failing to clear the water with an oar during the backstroke.

DAVIT — Small fixed derrick used to raise and swing out lifeboats.

DECKS:

BOAT — Deck where lifeboats are carried, usually upper deck. Often a short one.

HURRICANE — Highest deck. Can be same as weather or boat deck.

MAIN — Lowest full-length deck in a ship's HULL.

SPAR — In BULK FREIGHTERS, the upper full-length deck. Where HATCHES are located.

WEATHER — Highest decks, those exposed to weather.

DERELICT — A ship which has been abandoned. Out of control.

DOLPHIN — Large pedestal which forms the foundation for a bridge or dock structure. A fixed structure for mooring ships.

DONKEY BOILER — Auxiliary BOILER to furnish steam for WINDLASS and/or deck equipment.

DRAG — To move downwind when anchors fail to hold. To drag ashore.

ELEVATOR — Building designed for sorting, storage, weighing and loading of grain products.

EQUINOX, EQUINOCTIAL — Time of the year when the sun crosses the equator, marking transition of seasons: vernal equinox about March 12, autumnal equinox about September 22. A time for unusual storms.

FLOOD — To fill with water.

FLOTSAM — Floating debris.

FORE-AND-AFT — Running in a front-to-back direction, BOW-to-STERN. Schooner-rigged as opposed to square-rigged sailing vessel.

FORECASTLE — Raised portion of a ship's BOW, used for WINDLASS and anchor stowage in modern vessels, largely for crew quarters in nineteenth-century craft.

FOREPEAK — Watertight compartment at BOW of a ship. Furthest forward portion of HULL.

FORE... — Foremost, furthest forward, as in ...MAST, SAIL, etc.

FOUNDER — To fill and sink. To SWAMP.

FRAMES — The ribs or transverse members which make up the backbone structure of a ship.

FREEBOARD — Height of a ship's HULL above surface of the water, usually measured amidships.

GAFF — Horizontal SPAR standing out from a mast and used to suspend top of a FORE-AND-AFT sail.

GANGWAY — Opening in the side of a ship's HULL for loading passengers and/or PACKAGE FREIGHT.

GROSS (TONS) — Measurement of ship's entire capacity in REGISTER TONS, where one ton equals 100 cubic feet of space. Register tons are not a measure of weight.

GROUNDING — Running aground. Striking or rubbing bottom.

GYROCOMPASS — Electronic compass. A modern form of compass which is unaffected by magnetic deviation or variation, and therefore is more reliable than old style magnetic compasses.

HATCH — Deck opening, usually for loading cargo.

HAWSEPIPE — Tube for anchor CHAINS, passing from outside of HULL to FORECASTLE deck, where anchor-WINDLASS (hoist) is located.

264

GLOSSARY

HAWSER — Anchor line or towing line. Heavy rope, cable or chain.

HOLD — Portion of ship's HULL used for carrying and stowing cargo.

HOOKER — STEAMBARGE. Small wooden ship used for carrying lumber. Single-decked steamer of 130 to 200 feet with raised poop deck.

HULL — Main structure of a ship. "Body" of the vessel where machinery and cargo are placed.

JETTISON — To throw overboard.

JIB — Headsail. Small triangular sail carried forward of ship's FOREmast.

JIBBOOM — Light SPAR which projects out over a sailing ship's BOW to carry the headsails (JIBS), fixed on the end of the heavier BOWSPRIT. FOREmost feature of a sailing vessel.

KEDGE — A light anchor.

KEEL — The backbone of a ship. A girder which runs down the centerline in a ship's bottom, from STEM to STERN.

KEELSON — Inner portion of a ship's KEEL.

LIGHTER — A small salvage vessel used to remove cargo from ship in distress. To remove cargo.

LORAN — "LOng RAnge Navigation;" an electronic positioning system for ships and aircraft, which provides accurate locational data.

LYLE GUN — Small canon used to shoot a projectile with a light line to vessels in distress.

MACKINAW BOAT — Class of small working boats used for commercial fishing and coastal freighting trades. Two-masted "cat-ketch" sailing vessel, from 24 to about 40 feet long.

MASTER — Captain.

MATE — Assistant to Captain.

MIZZEN — Third mast in a three-masted sailing craft.

MONTREAL CANOE — 36-foot canoe used for freighting over open water, principally in the fur trade.

NET (TONS) — Measurement of ship's earning capacity in REGISTER TONS, where one ton equals 100 cubic feet of space. NET tonnage includes cargo HOLDS only, and not machinery, crew or fuel spaces. Register tons are not a measure of weight, but of space. Also see GROSS TONS.

PACKET — Small passenger and cargo steamer which ran on local routes on a regular, repetitive basis.

PACKAGE FREIGHT — Cargo that is packaged in barrels, boxes or bags. Also called "General Cargo."

PAINTER — Very light rope.

PICKET BOAT — Class of small, gasoline-powered patrol vessels measuring about 40 feet in length.

PIG IRON — Small cylinder of iron cast at a smelter, usually about 10 pounds.

PLIMSOLL MARK — Symbol marked on the side of a merchant ship to specify maximum depth to which the vessel can be safely loaded.

PORT — Left side when facing ship's BOW.

PROPELLER — Screw used to drive a ship through the water. Type of ship driven by a screw, usually a "passenger and freight propeller."

PURSER — Ship's officer responsible for passenger tickets and ship's books.

RADAR — Electronic device using transmitted and reflected radio waves to locate objects such as ships, obstructions or shoreline features for navigation.

RAFTING — Towing logs in a raft, large numbers of which are enclosed in a BOOM and floated long distances to lumber mills. Common between 1870 and 1930.

REEF — Shallow area with rocky bottom.

RIGGING — Wire or hemp rope used to support masts or to operate sails. Also stays for smokestack, etc.

R.O.V. — Remote Operated Video. Small submersible vehicle with video equipment, used to explore and document underwater features.

RUDDER SHOE — Support for ship's rudder. Short stout extension of ship's KEEL at the STERN.

SCHOONER — Sailing craft with two or more masts, rigged with FORE-AND-AFT sails, 60 to 200 feet long.

SCOW — Square-built vessel with flat sides, usually a flat bottom.

SCUBA — Self Contained Underwater Breathing Apparatus.

SCUTTLE — To sink a ship, usually by opening the sea cock, a water intake valve in the engine room.

SHELL-PLATING — Steel plates which form the skin or "shell" of a vessel's HULL.

SHOAL — Shallow, sandy or muddy spot in a body of water.

SKIFF — Rowboat.

SLOOP — Sailing craft with one mast, ordinarily no more than 40 feet in length.

SONAR — Echo-sounder. Device which uses transmitted sound waves to locate objects in water or to measure depth to bottom.

SOUNDINGS — Depth measurements.

SPAR — A pole or mast used to support or spread sails or to carry lights or flags.

STARBOARD — Right side of a vessel when facing forward.

STEAMBARGE — A small wooden ship used for carrying lumber products. Also see HOOKER.

STEM — FOREmost portion of the BOW of a ship. The vertical member to which side plates are fastened at the bow.

STERN — After (rear) end of a ship.

STORM OIL — Light oil dribbled onto stormy water to calm its surface. The oil spreads quickly downwind and flattens out the breakers.

STEWARD — Officer in charge of passengers' meals and ACCOMMODATIONS.

STRAND — To run ashore or aground. To become stuck on an obstruction or a beach.

SUPERSTRUCTURE — Cabins or "upper works" of a vessel. That part which projects above the HULL.

SURFBOAT — Small rescue craft meant to be launched from a beach, carried on a beach-cart or trailer, usually horse-drawn. Powered by oars or small gasoline engine.

SWAMP — To fill with water to the point of sinking. Similar to WATERLOGGING.

TACONITE — Low-grade iron ore containing hematite or magnetite. Shipped in pellets after concentrating and processing near the mines.

TONS:
DISPLACEMENT — Actual weight of a ship where one ton equals 2,000 pounds.

DEADWEIGHT — Weight of cargo.

REGISTER — One ton equals 100 cubic feet of space (not weight).

GROSS — Entire capacity of ship.

NET — Capacity of ship's earning spaces.

TOPMAST — Upper portion of a two-piece mast.

TOW — A CONSORT or barge towed behind a steam vessel. Act of towing or pulling a second vessel.

TROUGH — The low point between two waves. Being "caught in the trough" means to become helplessly out of control by swinging crosswise to the waves.

VENT — A pipe used to ventilate HOLDS or BALLAST tanks, usually projecting just above deck level.

WATERLOG — To fill with water. Similar to SWAMPING.

WHALEBACK — Unusual ship design with steel HULLS and rounded DECKS introduced by Captain Alexander McDougall of Duluth in 1888. McDougall's American Steel Barge Company built whaleback barges and steamers between 1888 and 1896. Several were also built on the East Coast.

WINCH — Mechanical device used to haul on lines for mooring, towing or for handling sails or cargoes. May be steam or electrically powered.

WINDLASS — Mechanical device used to haul on anchor CHAINS, located at BOW of ship and operated by hand or by steam or electrical power.

YAWL — Small SKIFF or lifeboat. In modern parlance a two-masted sailing craft with a short MIZZEN-mast astern of the rudder post.

Index to Vessel Names

Page listings refer to an illustration, picture or to first mention of a vessel for any specific incident. Vessels are listed alphabetically by given or last name. Some vessels may have more than one listing due to lack of detail available for a specific incident. For instance, *M.D. Carrington* is listed under "C" as *Carrington, M.D.*, but may also be listed simply as *Carrington* if that were the only information available. Some vessels have more than one listing due to name structure. The *Lady Elgin* is listed under both "L" and "E."

Bibliography

Books and Pamphlets

Barcus, Frank. *Fresh Water Fury*. Detroit. Wayne State University Press. 1960. 166 pp.

Bigsby, Dr. John J. *The Shoe and Canoe, II*. London.Chapman & Hall. 1850. p. 234.

Bowen, Dana Thomas. *Lore of the Lakes*. Daytona Beach, Florida. Dana T. Bowen. 1940. 314 pp.

Bowen, Dana Thomas. *Memories of the Lakes*. Daytona Beach, Florida. Dana T. Bowen. 1946. 292 pp.

Bowen, Dana Thomas. *Shipwrecks of the Lakes*. Daytona Beach, Florida. Dana T. Bowen. 1952. 368 pp.

Boyer, Dwight. *Ghost Ships of the Great Lakes*. New York. Dodd, Mead Co. 1968. 294 pp.

Boyer, Dwight. *Great Stories of the Great Lakes*. New York. Dodd, Mead Co. 1966. 242 pp.

Boyer, Dwight. *True Tales of the Great Lakes*. New York. Dodd, Mead Co. 1971. 340 pp.

Bree, Marlin. *In the Teeth of the Northeaster: A Solo Voyage on Lake Superior* New York. Clarkson N. Potter. 1988.

Bryce, George. *The Remarkable History of Hudson's Bay Company*. New York. Burt Franklin. 1904 (1968 reprint).

Burnham, Guy M. *The Lake Superior Country in History and in Story*. Ann Arbor, Mich. Brower Books. 1975. 464 pp.

Campbell, Marjorie W. *McGillivray Lord of the Northwest*. Toronto. Irwin & Co. 1962. p. 244.

Carter, James L. *Voyageurs Harbor; Grand Marais*. Grand Marais, Mich. Pilot Press. 1967. 66 pp.

Castle, Beatrice Hanscom. (James L. Carter, ed.). *The Grand Island Story*. Marquette, Mich. John M. Longyear Research Library. 1974. 110 pp.

Cooley, Jerome E. *Recollections of Early Days in Duluth*. Duluth. Jerome E. Cooley. 1925. 99 pp.

Coues, Elliott. *Manuscript Journal of Alexander Henry and David Thompson, 1799-1814*. New York. Francis P. Harper. 1897.

Curwood, James Oliver. *The Great Lakes*. 1909 (1967 reprint). Detroit. Archives of James Pergliese. 227 pp.

Davidson, Gordon C. *The Northwest Company*. New York. Russell and Russell. 1918 (reissued 1967).

Delafield, Major Joseph. *The Unfortified Boundary*, edited by Robert McElroy and Thomas Riggs. New York, privately published, 1943. Book 10 and Book 11.

Disturnell, John. *Sailing on the Great Lakes and Rivers of America*. Philadelphia. 1874. 280 pp.

Doner, Mary Frances. *The Salvager*. Minneapolis. Ross and Haines Inc. 1955. 312 pp.

Engman, Elmer. *In the Belly of the Whale*. Duluth, Minn. Innerspace. 1976. 48 pp.

Engman, Elmer. *Shipwreck Guide to the Western Half of Lake Superior*. Duluth, Minn. Innerspace. 1976. 48 pp.

Frimodig, Mac (D.M.). *Shipwrecks Off Keweenaw*. Lansing, Mich. Fort Wilkins Natural History Association and Michigan Department of Natural Resources. 1974. 48 pp.

Harmon, Daniel W. *A Journal of Voyages and Travels in the Interior of North America*. New York. Allerton Book Co. 1905.

Hatcher, Harlan. *The Great Lakes*. New York. Oxford University Press. 1944. 384 pp.

Havighurst, Walter. *The Great Lakes Reader*. New York. Macmillan Co. 1966. 421 pp.

Holden, Thom. *Above and Below*. Houghton, Mich. Isle Royale Natural History Association. 1985. 66 pp.

Jamison, James K. *By Cross and Anchor*. Paterson, N.J. St. Anthony Guild Press. 1946. 225 pp.

Keller, James M. *The "Unholy" Apostles: Tales of Chequamegon Shipwrecks*. Bayfield, Wis., Apostle Islands Press. 1984.

Lee, Robert E. *Edmund Fitzgerald, 1957-1975*. Detroit, Great Lakes Maritime Institute. 1977. 59 pp.

Longstreth, T. Morris. *The Lake Superior Country*. New York. The Century Company. 1924. 360 pp.

Lydecker, Ryck. *Pigboat: The Story of The Whalebacks*. Duluth, Minn. Sweetwater Press. 1973.

Lytle, William M. and Forrest R. Holdcamper, *Merchant Steam Vessels of the United States, 1790-1868*, C. Bradford Mitchel, ed. Staten Island, N.Y. The Steamship Historical Society of America. 1975.

MacKenzie, Alexander. *Voyages from Montreal on River St. Laurence Through the Continent of North America, 1789 and 1793*. London. T. Codell Jr. and W. Davis, et al. 1801.

Mansfield, John B., ed. *History of the Great Lakes*. Chicago. J.H. Beers & Co. 1899. 2 vols.

Marshall, James R., ed. *Shipwrecks of Lake Superior* Duluth, Minn. Lake Superior Port Cities Inc. 1987.

Marshall, Rose Mary, ed. *Great Lakes Ship Wrecks* (selections from *Great Lakes Gazette*). Grand Marais, Mich. The Voyager Press. 1977. 52 pp.

Mills, James C. *Our Inland Seas*. Chicago. A.C. McClurg Co. 1910. 380 pp.

Mills, John M. *Canadian Coastal and Inland Steam Vessels, 1809-1930*. Providence, Rhode Island. The Steamship Historical Society of America. 1979.

Monette, Clarence J. *The Keweenaw Waterway*. Lake Linden, Mich. 1980.

Nute, Grace Lee. *Lake Superior*. Indianapolis. Bobbs-Merrill Co. 1944. 376 pp.

Parsons, Earl. *Stories of the Great Lakes*. Canton, O. Rob-Roy Graphic Arts. 1963. 128 pp.

Ratigan, William. *Great Lakes Shipwrecks and Survivals*. Grand Rapids, Mich. Wm. B. Eerdmans Publishing Co. 1960, 1978, *Edmund Fitzgerald* edition. 384 pp.

Ross, Hamilton Nelson. *La Pointe*. St. Paul. North Central Publishing Co. 1960. 200 pp.

Scott, William E. *The Wreck of the Lafayette*. Two Harbors, Minn. Scott-Mitchell Publishing Co. 1959. 43 pp.

Stonehouse, Frederick. *Marquette Shipwrecks*. Marquette Mich. Harboridge Press. 1974. 98 pp.

Stonehouse, Frederick. *Keweenaw Shipwrecks*. Au Train, Mich. Avery Color Studios. 1988.

Stonehouse, Frederick. *Munising Shipwrecks*. Au Train, Mich. Avery Color Studios. 1983.

Stonehouse, Frederick. *Went Missing*. Au Train, Mich. Avery Color Studios. 1984.

Stonehouse, Frederick. *The Wreck of the* Edmund Fitzgerald. Au Train, Mich. Avery Color Studios. 1982, third edition.

Wolff, Jr., Julius F. *Lake Superior Shipwrecks of the 1890s*. Duluth. Pamphlet No. 6, Social Science Research Fund, University of Minnesota, Duluth. 1961. 23 pp.

Wrigley, Ronald. *Shipwrecked: Vessels that met tragedy on Northern Lake Superior*. Cobalt, Ontario. Highway Book Shop. 1985.

BIBLIOGRAPHY

Periodicals

Anon. "*Indiana,*" American Bureau of Shipping, *Surveyor,* Vol. 14, No. 3, August 1980, p. 20.

Anon. "Diary of Nicholas Garry," *Proceedings of the Royal Society of Canada, Second Series.* Ottawa. James Hope & Son. 1900. pp. 78, 113.

Anon. "Narrative of Jean Baptiste Perrault" in John S. Fox, ed. *Michigan Pioneer and Historical Collections,* Vol. 37, p. 615, 1909-1910.

Anon. "St. Lawrence Seaway: Chronology of Significant Events" in *Seaway Review,* Vol. 17, No. 2, Summer 1988, pp. 53-66.

Anon. "The Seaway at Twenty: An Anniversary Overview" in *Seaway Review,* Vol. 8, No. 4, Summer 1979, pp. 17-27.

Anon. "The System Soars" in *Seaway Review,* Vol. 17, No. 4, Winter 1989, pp 5-8, 11, 12.

Anon. "*Onoko* Mystery" in Lake Carriers' Association *Bulletin,* November 1958, pp. 5-8.

Anon. "$3,500,000 in Lake Superior: Finder's Keepers," *Argosy,* December 1971, pp. 36-38.

Anon. "*Pretoria*'s Bell Found," *Inland Seas,* Vol. 4, No. 3, p. 207, Fall 1948.

Anon. "Captain William Blattner of Vermilion, Ohio, A Steamboat Man of Nerve," *Marine Review,* Sept. 23, 1897-reprinted in *Inland Seas,* Vol. 13, No. 4, p. 315, Winter 1957.

Anon. "Captain William Blattner of Vermilion, Ohio, A Steamboat Man of Nerve," *Marine Review,* Sept. 23, 1897, reprinted in *Inland Seas,* Vol. 13, No. 4, p. 315, Winter 1957.

Anon. "Faulty Welds Blamed for *Fitzgerald* Wreck," *American Maritime Officer,* Nov. 1976.

Anon. "For and About Divers: Discovery of the *Kamloops,*" *The Nor'Easter,* Vol. 2, No. 5, Sept.-Oct. 1977, p. 5.

Anon. "Lake Carriers Dispute U.S. Coast Guard Panel's Findings, Assert *Edmund Fitzgerald* Struck Caribou Island Shoal," *American Maritime Officer,* Oct. 1977, p. 8.

Anon. "Lake Fails to Hide Long Lost Wreck," *Milwaukee Journal,* Mar. 26, 1978.

Anon. "LCA's President Rebuts Coast Guard's *Fitzgerald* Findings," Lake Carriers' Association *The Bulletin,* Sept.-Oct.-Nov. 1977, Vol. 66, No. 3, pp. 2, 5-7, 13-18.

Anon. "Narrative of Jean Baptiste Perrault," *Michigan Pioneer and Historical Collections,* Vol. 37, 1909-1910, p. 615.

Anon. "Old Wreck of Steamer *Winnipeg,*" *Inland Seas,* Vol. 26, No. 3, p. 232, Fall 1970.

Anon. "*Pretoria*'s Bell Found," *Inland Seas,* Vol. 4, No. 3, p. 207; Fall 1948.

Anon. "Soo Park's Propeller Recalls Story of Steamer *Independence,*" Lake Carriers' Association, *The Bulletin,* July 1953, pp. 17-19.

Anon. "St. Lawrence Seaway: Chronology of Significant Events," *Seaway Review,* Vol. 17, No. 2, Summer 1988, pp. 53-66.

Anon. "Statement of Commerce Through the St. Mary's Falls Canal For Each Calendar Year Since 1870," *Blue Book of American Shipping* (Cleveland, Marine Review Publishing Co., 1901), p. 266.

Anon. "Subdividing an Ore Boat Will Not Make it Safer," *Seaway Review,* Winter 1981, pp. 33, 35, 37.

Anon. "Sworn Statement of H.W. Stewart," *Marine Review,* Vol. 6, No. 11, Sept. 15, 1892, p. 7.

Anon. "The *Fitzgerald* Sinking: Two Views," *Seaway Review,* Vol. 7, No. 1, Autumn 1977, pp. 21-24.

Anon. "The Seaway at Twenty: An Anniversary Overview," *Seaway Review,* Vol. 8, No. 4, Summer 1979, pp. 17-27.

Anon. "Three Strikes on the *Mohawk Deer,*" *Scanner: Journal of the Toronto Marine Historical Society,* Vol. 3, No. 2, Nov. 1970, pp. 5-7.

Anon. "What Happened to the S.S. *Edmund Fitzgerald?,*" *Interlake Log,* Winter 1977, pp. 6-7.

Anon. "Wreck of the *Monticello,*" *Inland Seas,* Vol. 24, No. 1, Spring 1968, p. 34.

Anon. "Some Days Nothin' Goes Right. . .," *Minnesota's World Port,* Fall 1980, p. 18.

Ashenmacher, Bob. "Grounding Launched Big Beach Party," Duluth *News-Tribune & Herald,* Nov. 20, 1985.

Babcock, Lisa. "*Mesquite* Crew Abandons Ship," *Petoskey News-Review,* Dec. 4, 1989.

Babcock, Lisa. "*Mesquite* Fuel Oil Leaking Into Lake Superior," *Petoskey News-Review,* Dec. 5, 1989.

Babcock, Lisa. "*Mesquite* Study, Salvage Continue," *Petoskey News-Review,* Dec. 6, 1989.

Babcock, Lisa. "*Mesquite* Salvage Continues; Crew Home," *Petoskey News-Review,* Dec. 7, 1989,

Babcock, Lisa. "*Mesquite* Crew Working Out of Temporary Offices," *Petoskey News-Review,* Dec. 8, 1989.

Babcock, Lisa. "*Mesquite* Salvage Delayed 'til Spring?" *Petoskey News-Review,* Dec. 11, 1989.

Babcock, Lisa. "Salvage of *Mesquite* Appears Unlikely," *Petoskey News-Review,* Dec. 12, 1989.

Babcock, Lisa. "Indian Skipper Glad to Help But Doesn't Want Repeat," *Petoskey News-Review,* Dec. 12, 1989.

Babcock, Lisa. "*Mesquite* Salvage Delayed 'til Spring," *Petoskey News-Review,* Dec. 13, 1989.

Babcock, Lisa. "*Mesquite* Crew Keys on Inquiries as Salvage Stops," *Petoskey News-Review,* Dec. 15, 1989.

Babcock, Lisa. "Currents May Have Caused Ship Grounding," *Petoskey News-Review,* Dec. 18, 1989.

Babcock, Lisa. "*Mesquite* Commander Testifies at Hearing," *Petoskey News-Review,* Dec. 20, 1989.

Babcock, Lisa. "Charlevoix Laments Ship Loss," *Petoskey News-Review,* Dec. 21, 1989.

Babcock, Lisa. "*Mesquite* Crewmen Leaving," *Petoskey News-Review,* Dec. 27, 1989.

Bancroft, William L. "Memoirs of Captain Samuel Ward," *Michigan Pioneer and Historical Collections,* Vol. 21, 1892, pp. 336-367.

Bascom, John. "The Ship with the Golden Rivets — Ship of the Month No. 38," *The Scanner,* Vol. 6 No. 6, Mar. 1974.

Benford, Harry. "Random Thoughts on the Safety of Ships," *Seaway Review,* Vol. 8, No. 4, Summer 1979, pp. 61-63.

Bernen, Charles. "It Started Quickly, Ended Slow," *Duluth News-Tribune,* Jan. 22, 1978.

Bibb, A.B. "The Life-Saving Service on the Great Lakes," *Frank Leslie's Popular Monthly,* XIII: 4, pp. 386-398, Apr. 1882.

Bibby, Richard D. "*Secord*'s Last Trip of the 1961 Season," *The Nor'Easter,* Vol. 7, No. 2, Mar.-Apr. 1982, pp. 1-3.

Bigsby, Dr. John J. *The Shoe and Canoe, II.* London. Chapman & Hall. 1850.

Brotherton, R.A. "The Wreck of the *Kershaw, Moonlight,* and *Kent,*" *Inland Seas,* Vol. 4, No. 2, pp. 124-126, Summer 1948.

Brown, Edwin T. "Shipwrecked Crew Saved by a Bathtub," *Inland Seas,* Vol. 4, No. 1, Spring 1948, pp. 65-66.

Brown, W. Russell. "Ships at Port Arthur and Fort William," *Inland Seas,* Vol. 1, No. 4, Oct. 1945, pp. 45-51.

Byrne, Carol. "Ship's Plight Becomes Tourist Bonanza for Duluth," *Minneapolis Star Tribune,* Nov. 22, 1985.

Carter, James L. "Au Sable Light, Sentinel of the 'Great Sands,'" *Inland Seas,* Vol. 33, No. 2, Summer 1977, pp. 96-105.

Carus, Captain Edward. "100 Years of Disasters on the Great Lakes," *Manitowoc Herald-News,* Nov. 19, 1931.

Charnley, Blair. "*Kamloops'* Icy Grave Discovered, But Its Sinking Remains a Mystery," *Minneapolis Star,* Oct. 13, 1977.

Cooper, Captain Jesse B. "SS *Arthur M. Anderson:* November 10, 1975" in James R. Marshall, ed., *Shipwrecks of Lake Superior* (Duluth, Minnesota, Lake Superior Port Cities Inc., 1987), pp. 60-61.

Cooper, Jesse B. "Bernie." "Sinking of the SS *Edmund Fitzgerald,*" transcript of speech delivered to the Wisconsin Marine Historical Society in Milwaukee, Wisconsin, on Nov. 7, 1985, 13 pp. Copy in the files of U.S. Army Corps of Engineers' Canal Park Visitor Center and Marine Museum ship history files, Duluth.

Dennis, Tom. "Tugs Free Freighter from Sand," Duluth *News-Tribune & Herald,* Nov. 25, 1985.

Dowling, Rev. Edward J. "The Tin Stackers," *Inland Seas,* Vol. 9, No. 2, Summer 1953, pp. 79-85.

Dunathan, Clint. "Coast Guard Service in the Twenties," *Inland Seas,* Vol. 28, No. 2, Summer 1972, pp. 96-101.

Dutton, Fred W. "The *William C. Moreland,* Part I," *Inland Seas,* Vol. 5, No. 1, Spring 1949, pp. 12-17; Part II, Vol. 5, No. 2, Summer 1949, pp. 76-82.

Eliason, Jerry. "Ships That No Longer Sail," *Lake Superior Port Cities* Magazine, Vol. 4, No. 4, 1983, pp. 29-34.

Engelbrecht, Ken and Thom Holden. "Divers Find Freighter Missing Almost 50 Years," Sault Ste. Marie *Evening News,* Oct. 17, 1977.

Engman, Elmer. "A Shallow Grave for the *America,*" *Nordic Diver,* Vol. 1, No. 2, Jul.-Aug. 1974, pp. 1-5.

Ferguson, Doug. "Toronto Diver Exploring Sunken Luxury Yacht *Gunilda* Presumed Drowned Near Rossport," *Thunder Bay Chronicle-Journal,* Aug. 14, 1989.

Fleming, Roy F. "Propeller *Independence* Wrecked on Lake Superior," *Inland Seas,* Vol. 14, No. 2, Summer 1960, pp. 131-135.

Flesher, John. "Coast Guard Panel Eyes Fleet Update," Superior *Evening Telegram,* Dec. 8, 1989.

Florentz, LaMonte. "Nobody Got So Much as a Cold" in *The Nor'Easter,* Vol. 3, No. 5, Sept.-Oct. 1978, pp. 3-6.

Furiga, Paul. "Subcommittee to Probe Grounding of *Mesquite,*" Houghton *Daily Mining Gazette,* Dec. 9, 1989.

Furiga, Paul. "*Acacia* to Replace *Mesquite,*" Houghton *Daily Mining Gazette,* Jan. 10, 1990.

Gerred, Janice H. "Wreck of the *Chauncy Hurlbut* Recalled," *Inland Seas,* Vol. 33, No. 4, Winter 1977, p. 333.

Gerred, Janice H. "Vermilion: A Lake Superior Ghost Town," *Inland Seas* Vol. 30, No. 1, Spring 1974, pp. 48-49.

Gerred, Janice H., "Wreck of the *Alex Nimick,*" *Inland Seas,* Vol. 31, No. 2, Summer 1975, pp. 139-140.

Gillham, Skip. "Yesterday's Fleet: *Kamloops,*" *CSL — The World,* Dec. 1977.

Gillham, Skip. "Yesterday's Fleet: *Renfrew,*" *CSL — The World,* Dec. 1987.

Grunst, Robert. "A Fish Tug Named *Energy,*" *Inland Seas,* Vol. 41, No. 2, Summer 1985, pp. 82-85.

Hafner, Ken, and Thom Holden. "*Kamloops:* Ghost Wreck of Isle Royale," *Sport Diver Magazine,* Vol. 2, Fourth Quarter 1978, pp. 112-117.

Hall, Henry Boyd. "Plans to Free *Socrates* Swamp Coast Guard," *St. Paul Pioneer Press Dispatch,* Nov. 24, 1985.

Hall, Henry Boyd. "Six Tugboats Free Freighter," *St. Paul Pioneer Press Dispatch,* Nov. 25, 1985.

Holden, Thom. "A Thanksgiving to Remember," *The Nor'Easter,* Vol. 4, No. 6, Nov.-Dec. 1979, pp. 1-4.

Holden, Thom. "Last of the 1980-81 Season," *The Nor'Easter,* Vol. 6, No. 4, Jul.-Aug. 1981, pp. 1-3, 6.

Holden, Thom. "The Fate of the *Frontenac,*" *Minnesota's World Port,* Vol. 5, No. 1, Spring 1980, pp. 6-8.

Holden, Thom. "Wreck of the *Frontenac:* A Thanksgiving Remembered," Superior *Evening Telegram,* Nov. 25, 1982.

Holden, Thom. "A Maiden Voyage into History," *Telescope,* Journal of the Great Lakes Maritime Institute, Detroit, Vol. 23, No. 1, Jan.-Feb. 1984, pp. 3-10.

Holden, Thom. "Above and Below: Steamer *America,*" *The Nor'Easter,* Vol. 3, No. 3, May-Jun. 1977, pp. 1-4 and Vol. 3, No. 4, Jul.-Aug. 1978, pp. 1-5.

Holden, Thom. "Fall of 1840, the *Siskawit* Stranding," *Nordic Diver,* Superior, Wisc., Jul.-Aug. 1974, pp. 8-9.

Holden, Thom. "Home for Christmas: *Dunelm* Stranding," *Nordic Diver,* Vol. 1, No. 4, Winter 1975, pp. 3, 6-7.

Holden, Thom. "One Cylinder Steam Engine Target of Recovery Teams," Superior *Evening Telegram,* Aug. 7, 1979.

Holden, Thom. "Reef of the Three C's: Part I, Wreck of the *Cumberland,*" *The Nor'Easter,* Vol. 2, No. 4, Jul.-Aug. 1977, pp. 1, 4-6.

Holden, Thom. "Reef of the Three C's: Part II, Wreck of the *Henry Chisholm,*" *The Nor'Easter,* Vol. 3, No. 2, Mar.-Apr. 1978, pp. 1-3, 5.

Holden, Thom. "Reef of the Three C's: Part III, Sinking of the *George M. Cox,*" *The Nor'Easter* , Vol. 8, No. 3, May-Jun. 1983, pp. 1-5, 8.

Holden, Thom. "Wilderness Port Wreck of the *Glenlyon,*" *Soundings,* Vol. 15, No. 1, pp. 1-4, 1974.

Holden, Thom. "Steamer *America* Wrecked 50 Years Ago: Still Popular, Above or Below," Superior *Evening Telegram,* Jun. 8, 1978.

Holden, Thomas. "The *America*" in James R. Marshall, ed. *Shipwrecks of Lake Superior.* Duluth, Minn. Lake Superior Port Cities Inc. 1987. pp. 66-71.

Hopkins, Loren. "The Wreck of the *Monticello,*" *Inland Seas,* Vol. 24, No. 1, Spring 1968, pp. 34-40, 49.

Hrthe, Walter M. "Shipbuilding on Little Sturgeon Bay, 1866 to 1874," *Inland Seas,* Vol. 32, No. 4, pp. 270-280, Winter 1976.

Hughlett, Mike. "Drifting Tug, Ship Taken Under Tow," Duluth *News-Tribune & Herald,* Nov. 10, 1986.

Hughlett, Mike. "Sunken Tugs Prove Tough to Salvage," *Duluth News-Tribune,* April 11, 1989.

Hughlett, Mike. "Tugs Yield No Clues About Sinking," *Duluth News-Tribune,* April 19, 1989.

Jacobson, Don. "Raised Tug Yields No Clues to Mysterious Sinking," *Duluth News-Tribune,* April 16, 1989.

Jacobson, Don. "Coast Guard Praises 'Superb Seamanship' of *Mesquite* Rescuer," *Duluth News-Tribune,* Dec. 8, 1989.

Jacobson, Don. "Weather Halts Oil Retrieval," *Duluth News-Tribune,* Dec. 9, 1989.

Jacobson, Don. "Strikers Rush to Ship's Aid," *Duluth News-Tribune,* Dec. 9, 1989.

Jennison, E.N. "Reminiscences of the Keweenaw Waterway," *Inland Seas,* Vol. 9, No. 2, Summer 1953, p. 144.

Kerwin, James L. "Coast Guard Remiss: Possible Laxity Cited in Sinking," *Detroit News,* Nov. 14, 1975.

Kidd, James. "More About the Ship with the Golden Rivets," *The Scanner,* Vol. 6, No. 7, Apr. 1974, p. 7.

Knuckey, A.J. "Bud." "Scuttlebutt. . .The Perils of a Pinched Purse," *Lake Superior Port Cities Magazine,* Vol. 5, No. 2, Fall 1983, pp. 49-50.

Komula, Roger. "Coast Guard Cutter Leaking Fuel Oil," Houghton *Daily Mining Gazette,* Dec. 5, 1989.

Komula, Roger. "Weather, Fuel Shortage Hamper Salvage," Houghton *Daily Mining Gazette,* Dec. 6, 1989.

Komula, Roger. "Damage Report on Grounded Cutter Due Friday," Houghton *Daily Mining Gazette,* Dec. 7, 1989.

Komula, Roger. "Cutter in Race With Winter," Houghton *Daily Mining Gazette,* Dec. 8, 1989.

Komula, Roger. "Salvage Efforts Continue," Houghton *Daily Mining Gazette,* Dec. 9, 1989.

Komula, Roger. "Weather Takes Toll on Grounded Cutter," Houghton *Daily Mining Gazette,* Dec. 11, 1989.

Komula, Roger. "Coast Guard Leaves Cutter," Houghton *Daily Mining Gazette,* Dec. 13, 1989.

Komula, Roger. "*Mesquite* Eyed for Preserve," Houghton *Daily Mining Gazette,* Dec. 14, 1989.

Landon, Fred. "Loss of the *Western Reserve,*" *Inland Seas,* Vol. 20, No. 4, Winter 1964, pp. 323-326.

Landon, Fred. "Shipwreck on Isle Royale," *Inland Seas,* Vol. 16, No. 1, Spring 1960, pp. 60-62.

Landon, Fred. "Sixty Years of the CPR Great Lakes Fleet," *Inland Seas,* Vol. 1, No. 1, Jan. 1945, pp. 3-7.

Landon, Fred. "Loss of the *Bannockburn,*" *Inland Seas,* Vol. 13, No. 4, Winter 1957, pp. 303-305.

Law, W.H., "Captain Wright's Story of the *Lafayette,*" *Inland Seas,* Vol. 13, No. 1, Spring 1957, p. 67.

Lesstrang, Jacques. "St. Lawrence Seaway: Chronology of Significant Events," *Seaway Review,* Vol. 17, No. 2, Summer 1988, pp. 53-66.

Lesstrang, Jacques. "The Seaway at Twenty: An Anniversary Overview," *Seaway Review,* Vol. 8, No. 4, Summer 1979, pp. 17-27.

Lesstrang, Jacques. "The Thirtieth Season: A Retrospective," *Seaway Review,* Vol. 17, No. 2, Summer 1988, pp. 37-47.

Lonsdale, Captain Adrian L. "Rescue in '86," *Inland Seas,* Vol. 30, No. 1, Spring 1974, pp. 29-34.

Losey, Roger. "The Coast Guard Cutter *Mackinaw*" in *The Nor'Easter,* Vol. 7, No. 6, November-December 1982, pp. 1-5.

Losey, Roger. "Ice an the 140s — The Story of the 'Bay Class,'" *The Nor'Easter,* Vol. 8, No. 6, November-December 1983, pp. 1-5.

Losey, Roger. "Pride of the Coast Guard — The 180s from Duluth," *The Nor'Easter,* Vol. 10, No. 4, July-August 1985, pp. 1-5.

Marshall, James R. "Danger at 140 Feet: Jerry Eliason Survives Free Ascent," *Lake Superior Newsletter,* Fall 1989, pp. 1-3.

Marshall, James R., ed. "The Hunt for the *Benjamin Noble,*" *Lake Superior Newsletter,* Vol. 1, No. 1, Fall 1987, pp. 1-3.

Marshall, James R. "Jerry Eliason finds the *Onoko* — in 207 feet of Water," *Lake Superior Newsletter,* No. 4, Summer 1988, pp. 1-3, 8.

Marshall, James R. "Salvage of the *America*" in James R. Marshall, ed., *Shipwrecks of Lake Superior.* Duluth, Minn. Lake Superior Port Cities Inc. 1987.

Marshall, James R. "Ships That No Longer Sail" in James R. Marshall, ed., *Shipwrecks of Lake Superior.* Duluth, Minn. Lake Superior Port Cities Inc. 1987.

Marshall, James R. "The *Edmund Fitzgerald* Tragedy," in James R. Marshall, ed., *Shipwrecks of Lake Superior.* Duluth, Minn. Lake Superior Port Cities Inc. 1987. pp. 49-59.

Marshall, James R. "The Deep Dive" in James R. Marshall, ed., *Shipwrecks of Lake Superior.* Duluth, Minn. Lake Superior Port Cities Inc. 1987. pp. 24-29.

Marvill, Lewis. "First Trip by Steam to Lake Superior," *Michigan Pioneer and Historical Collections,* Vol. 4, 1881, pp. 67-69.

Mason, George C. "A List of Hulls Built by F.W. Wheeler & Co., Bay City, Michigan," *Inland Seas,* Vol. 1, No. 4, 1945, p. 54.

Miller, Al. "Freighter Drifts Across Bay After Strong Winds Set It Free," Duluth *News-Tribune & Herald,* Nov. 1, 1986.

Miller, Al. "Salvor Says It Took Every Trick to Free *Socrates,*" Duluth *News-Tribune & Herald,* Nov. 27, 1985.

Miller, Al. "Ship's Crew Evacuated," Duluth *News-Tribune & Herald,* Nov. 20, 1985.

Miller, Al. "Tugboat Fleet to Attempt Freighter Rescue," *St. Paul Pioneer Press Dispatch,* Nov. 21, 1985.

Miller, Al. "Tugs Fail to Budge Grounded Ship," Duluth *News-Tribune & Herald,* Nov. 20, 1985.

Miller, Al. "Tugs Loosen Shore's Grip on Ship," Duluth *News-Tribune & Herald,* Nov. 23, 1985.

Miller, Alan W. "*Winslow:* Gone, But Not Forgotten," *The Nor'Easter,* Vol. 13, No. 1, January-February 1988, pp. 1-4.

Milliken (USCG), PA3 Mike. "A Daring Rescue," *USCG Shipmates,* Vol. 9, No. 3, January 1987, pp. 2-3.

Morken, Arvid. "*Harry L. Allen* — A Soliloquy," *Nor'Easter,* Vol. 3. No. 1, January-February 1978, pp. 1-3, 5.

Murphy, Larry, and Thom Holden. "Shipwrecks of Isle Royale: The Historical Record" in *Submerged Cultural Resources Study: Isle Royale National Park,* Daniel J. Lenihan, ed. Santa Fe, New Mexico. Submerged Cultural Resources Unit, National Park Service. 1987.

Murphy, Larry, Daniel Lenihan, and C. Patrick Labadie. "Shipwrecks of Isle Royale: The Archeological Record" in *Submerged Cultural Resources Study: Isle Royale National Park,* Daniel J. Lenihan, ed. Santa Fe, New Mexico. Submerged Cultural Resources Unit, National Park Service. 1987.

Murphy, Patrick. "The Loss of *Lightship No. 82,*" *Shipmates,* January-February 1975, pp. 2-7.

Murray, J.M. "A Hundred Years of Lloyd's Register Ship Rules," *Transactions Royal Institution of Naval Architects,* Vol. 97, 1955, in Harry Benford, "Random Thoughts on the Safety of Ships," *Seaway Review,* Vol. 8, No. 4, Summer 1979, pp. 61-63.

Nelson, Wayne. "An Anxious Hour for Ship Caught by Ice and Wind," *Duluth News-Tribune,* Apr. 9, 1980.

Nelson, Wayne. "Storm Damages Coast Guard Cutter: Crews Pump Fuel from the *Mesquite,*" *Duluth News-Tribune,* Dec. 12, 1989.

Neubauer, Patricia. "Fishing Boat Stranded on Lake Ice Floe," *Duluth News-Tribune,* Mar. 3, 1984.

Neubauer, Patricia. "Icy Ordeal Over for Bayfield Fishermen," *Duluth News-Tribune,* Mar. 6, 1984.

Norton, Jr., Captain H.F. "Fire at Sea — A Casualty Visited," *Proceedings of the Marine Safety Council,* U.S. Coast Guard, U.S. Dept. of Transportation, CG-129, Vol. 38, No. 3, May 1981, pp. 60-63.

Onchulenko, Gene. "*Kamloops* Brings Back Memories," *Thunder Bay Lakehead Living,* Dec. 9, 1987.

Onchulenko, Gene. "Men Saved from Terrible Fate," *Thunder Bay Lakehead Living,* Dec. 16, 1987.

Parker, John G. "Autobiography of Captain John G. Parker," *Michigan Pioneer and Historical Collections.* Vol. 30, pp. 582-585, 1905.

Payton, Mike. "*Frontenac* Won't Be Repaired, But Some Salvage Planned," Superior *Evening Telegram,* Nov. 30, 1979.

Pelfrey, Melvin H. "District 2's Proposals on Great Lakes Safety," *American Maritime Officer,* Apr. 1976, pp. 8, 10.

Pelfrey, Melvin H. "*Fitz* Inquiry Stalls, Photos Reveal Nothing," *American Maritime Officer,* Nov. 1976, p. 8.

Pomeroy, Dick. "*Socrates'* Skipper Failed to Take Early, Positive Action," Superior *Evening Telegram,* Jan. 17, 1986.

Pomeroy, Dick. "Laker Adrift Vexes Port Safety Officer," Superior *Evening Telegram,* Oct. 31, 1986.

Pomeroy, Richard L. "Fire Consumes City Grain Elevator," *Duluth News-Tribune,* Jan. 22, 1978.

Pomeroy, Richard L. "Lake Carriers Reject *Fitz* Theory," *Duluth Herald,* Sept. 29, 1977.

Pomeroy, Richard L. "Plane Reports Possible *Fitz* Site," *Duluth News-Tribune,* Nov. 14, 1975.

Prince, Pat. "Power is Restored to grounded Ship as Storm Moves In," Minneapolis *Star Tribune*, Nov. 22, 1985.

Rankin, Sr., Ernest H. "Captain Cleary, Lifesaver-Showman," *Inland Seas*, Vol. 33, No. 1, Spring 1977, pp. 4-11; Vol. 33, No. 2, Summer 1977, pp. 128-130, 139-141.

Rankin, Sr., Ernest H. "The Wreck of the *Independence*," *Inland Seas*, Vol. 22, No. 1, Spring 1966, pp. 35-40.

Read, Katy. "Sailors Savor Safety Ashore," *Duluth News-Tribune*, Dec. 6, 1989.

Remick, Teddy. "Loss of the *Cyprus* and Her Captain," *Inland Seas*, Vol. 21, No. 2, Summer 1965, pp. 126-128.

Ripley, James M. "Whitefish Point Light," *Inland Seas*, Vol. 24, No. 4, Winter 1968, pp. 279-284.

Russell, Ann Z. and Yvonne Nissen, "The Elusive Algoma Bow," *Lake Superior Port Cities Magazine*, Vol. 8, No. 1, Winter 1985-86, pp. 10-15.

Sandvik, Glenn. "A Brief History of the Split Rock Lighthouse," *Inland Seas*, Vol. 28, No. 3, Fall 1972, pp. 206-208, 217-222.

Schuette, Katie. "*Kamloops* Goes Missing No Longer," *Anchor News*, May-Jun. 1979, p. 41.

Smith, Doug. "$37.5 Million Suit Filed in Ship Fire," *Duluth News-Tribune*, Dec. 8, 1979.

Smith, Doug. "Fire Caught Ship Unaware, Sailors Claim," *Duluth News-Tribune*, Jun. 10, 1979.

Smrekar, Tom. "It's Cold, Eerie Down There at 85 Feet, *America* Awaits Salvaging," *Duluth News-Tribune*, Oct. 17, 1965.

Soucheray, Joe. "Suddenly, A Ship Was in Their Yard," *St. Paul Pioneer Press Dispatch*, Nov. 22, 1985.

Stanich, Susan. "Wind, Waves Push Ship Aground," Duluth *News-Tribune & Herald*, Nov. 19, 1985.

Storey, Jack. "*Mesquite* Grounded Off Keweenaw," Sault Ste. Marie *Evening News*, Dec. 4, 1989.

Storey, Jack. "Law of the Sea is Still a Binding Code," Sault Ste. Marie *Evening News*, Dec. 24, 1989.

Swing, Georgia. "*Frontenac* Piled Nearly Blind Onto Rocky Shoal," *Duluth News-Tribune*, Dec. 1, 1979.

Swing, Georgia. "Lack of Light May Have Imperiled Ship," *Duluth News-Tribune*, Nov. 30, 1979.

Swing, Georgia. "Safely in Port, *Frontenac* Awaits Verdict on its Fate," *Duluth News-Tribune*, Nov. 29, 1979.

Swing, Georgia. "Wounded *Frontenac* Awaits Its Final Call," *Duluth News-Tribune*, Dec. 2, 1979.

Ten Broek, Rev. J.A. "Old Keweenaw," *Michigan Pioneer and Historical Collections*, Vol. 30, 1905, pp. 139-149.

Thayer, George W. "From Vermont to Lake Superior," *Michigan Pioneer and Historical Collections*, Vol. 30, 1905, p. 564.

Theisen, Charles W. "*Fitzgerald*'s Salvage Called Hopeless Task," *Detroit News*, Nov. 12, 1975.

Thom, Robert W. "The Sinking of the *Ottawa*," *Inland Seas*, Vol. 9, No. 4, Winter 1953, pp. 296-297.

Timmer, Amy. "The Search for the *Onoko*," *Lake Superior Newsletter*, No. 3, Spring 1988, pp. 3-4.

Tomchak, Jackie. "*Mesquite* Oil Leak Toll Unknown," Houghton *Daily Mining Gazette*, Dec. 8, 1989.

Vilim, Ron. "*Kamloops* (1924-1927): Discovery of a Lake Superior Shipwreck" in Thunder Bay Scuba Club's *Sea Pen*, May 1979.

White, Lt. Richard D., and Truman Stobridge. "Nineteenth Century Lighthouse Tenders on the Great Lakes," *Inland Seas*, Vol. 31, No. 2, Summer 1975, pp. 87-96.

Williams, Ralph D. "Commerce of the Great Lakes" in Charles Moore, ed., *Saint Mary's Falls Canal Semicentennial 1905*. Detroit. Semicentennial Commission, 1907, p. 193.

Williams, W.R. "Colonel McKnight's Lake Superior Line," *Inland Seas*, Vol. 16, No. 2, Summer 1960, pp. 138-144.

Williams, W.R. "Shipwrecks at Isle Royale," *Inland Seas*, Vol. 12, No. 4, Winter 1956, p. 254.

Williams, W.R. "The *Leafield* Was Unlucky," *Inland Seas*, Vol. 3, No. 3, Fall 1948, pp. 143-144.

Wolff, Jr., Julius F. "1905-Lake Superior At Its Worst," *Inland Seas*, Vol. 18, No. 3, Fall 1962, pp. 190-198; Vol. 18, No. 4, Winter 1962, pp. 267-272.

Wolff, Jr., Julius F. "A Coastal Packet on Lake Superior," *Inland Seas*, Vol. 22, No. 3, Fall 1966, pp. 183-184.

Wolff, Jr., Julius F. "A Lake Superior Lifesaver Reminisces," *Inland Seas*, Vol. 24, No. 2, Summer 1968, pp. 108-117.

Wolff, Jr., Julius F. "Before the Days of Radar: The Ship Collisions on Lake Superior," *Inland Seas*, Vol. 25, No. 2, Summer 1969, pp. 137-149.

Wolff, Jr., Julius F. "Canadian Shipwrecks of Lake Superior," *Inland Seas*, Vol. 34, No. 1, Spring 1978, pp. 34-42; Vol. 34, No. 2, Summer 1978, pp. 113-120; Vol. 34, No. 3, Fall 1978, pp. 200-206; Vol. 34, No. 4, Winter 1978, pp. 275-283.

Wolff, Jr., Julius F. "Collision Off the Pierhead," *Inland Seas*, Vol. 20, No. 1, Spring 1964, pp. 15-20.

Wolff, Jr., Julius F. "Danger Rides the Waves," *Duluthian*, Vol. 3, No. 6, November-December 1967, pp. 6-9; Vol. 4, No. 1, January-February 1968, pp. 14-17.

Wolff, Jr., Julius F. "Grim November," in Walter Havighurst, *Great Lakes Reader*, New Yor. Macmillion Co. 1966. pp. 315-320.

Wolff, Jr., Julius F. "In Retrospect," *Inland Seas*, Vol. 32, No. 2, Summer 1976, pp. 122-124.

Wolff, Jr., Julius F. "Lake Superior Shipwrecks, 1900-1909," *Inland Seas*, Vol. 27, No. 1, Spring 1971, pp. 28-38; Vol. 27, No. 2, Summer 1971, pp. 113-118, 127-130; Vol. 27, No. 3, Fall 1971, pp. 174-187; Vol. 27, No. 4, Winter 1971, pp. 297-306; Vol. 28, No. 1, Spring 1972, pp. 51-63.

Wolff, Jr., Julius F. "Mayday on Lake Superior," *Minnesota Volunteer*, Minnesota Department of Natural Resources, Vol. 41, No. 239, July-August 1978, pp. 44-49.

Wolff, Jr., Julius F. "One Hundred Years of Rescues: The Coast Guard on Lake Superior," *Inland Seas*, Vol. 31, No. 4, Winter 1975, pp. 225-265; Vol. 32, No. 1, Spring 1976, pp. 32-40, 49-51.

Wolff, Jr., Julius F. "Shipwreck County Revisited," *Inland Seas*, Vol. 23, No. 2, Summer 1967, pp. 104, 113.

Wolff, Jr., Julius F. "Shipwrecks on the North Shore of Lake Superior," *Telescope*, Vol. 5, No. 5, May 1956, pp. 3-7; Vol. 5, No. 6, June 1956, pp. 3-12.

Wolff, Jr., Julius F. "Skin Diving and Historical Research," *Minnesota History*, Vol. 35, No. 6, June 1957, pp. 278-281.

Wolff, Jr., Julius F. "Some Noted Shipwrecks on Lake Superior," *Telescope*, Vol. 19, No. 2, March-April 1970, pp. 35-44.

Wolff, Jr., Julius F. "Some Noted Shipwrecks on the Michigan Coast of Lake Superior," *Inland Seas*, Vol. 16, No. 3, Fall 1960, pp. 172-179.

Wolff, Jr., Julius F. "Some Shipwrecks on the Pioneer North Shore of Lake Superior," *Inland Seas*, Vol. 17, No. 2, Summer 1961, pp. 114-122.

Wolff, Jr., Julius F. "The *Fitzgerald* Board Report" in James R. Marshall, ed., *Shipwrecks of Lake Superior*, Duluth, Minn., Lake Superior Port Cities Inc., 1987, pp. 62-65.

Wolff, Jr., Julius F. "Stranding of the Steamer *Frontenac*," *Inland Seas*, Vol. 36, No. 1, Spring 1980, pp. 29-30.

Wolff, Jr., Julius F. "The *George T. Hope*," *Inland Seas*, Vol. 22, No. 2, Summer 1966, pp. 144-145.

Wolff, Jr., Julius F. "The Coast Guard Comes to Lake Superior, 1874-1875," *Inland Seas*, Vol. 21, No. 1, Spring 1965, pp. 14-21.

Wolff, Jr., Julius F. "The *Cartiercliffe* Fire," *Inland Seas*, Vol. 35, No. 3, Fall 1979, pp. 196-200.

Wolff, Jr., Julius F. "The Ships and Duluth," in *Duluth-Sketches of the Past*. Duluth. American Revolution Bicentennial Commission. 1976. pp. 142-163.

Wolff, Jr., Julius F. "The Shipwrecks of Lake Superior, 1822-1889, *Telescope*, Vol. 9, No. 9, September 1960, pp. 155-164; Vol. 9, No. 10, October 1960, pp. 178-181; Vol. 9, No. 11, November 1960, pp. 199-203.

Wolff, Jr., Julius F. "The Thresher Lifering," *Inland Seas*, Vol. 28, No. 4, Winter 1972, pp. 317-319.

Wolff, Jr., Julius F. "They Sailed Away on Lake Superior," *Inland Seas*, Vol. 29, No. 4, Winter 1973, pp. 262-274, 283-285.

Wolff, Jr., Julius F. "Transportation Safety Board Reports on *Edmund Fitzgerald* Disaster," *The Nor'Easter*, Vol. 5, No. 1, Jan.-Feb. 1980, pp. 1-4, 8.

Wright, Richard J. "A History of Shipbuilding in Cleveland," *Inland Seas*, Vol. 13, No. 1, Spring 1957, pp. 29-37.

Wright, Steven J. "The Forgotten November Storm," *The Nor'easter*, Vol. 12, No. 5, September-October 1987, pp. 1-3.

Zehnder, Chuck. "$3,500,000 in Lake Superior; Finders Keepers," *Argosy*, pp. 36-38, December 1971.

Zehnder, Chuck. "Lake Superior's Richest Wreck," *Treasure World*, February-March 1972, pp. 23-25.

Manuscripts, Letters, Diaries

Anon. Log of Au Sable Lighthouse Keepers. In files of Bernard J. Gestel, National Park Service, Grand Marais, Minnesota.

Anon. "Diary of Nicholas Garry" in *Proceedings of the Royal Society of Canada*, Second Series. Ottawa. James Hope & Son. 1900, pp. 78, 113.

Bardon, John A. "Early Pioneering Along the North Shore." Unpublished manuscript in files of St. Louis County Historical Society, Duluth.

Bardon, John A. "Wreck of the Propeller *Sunbeam*." Unpublished manuscript in files of St. Louis County Historical Society, Duluth. Recollections of survivor John Fregeau.

Belle River Ship's Log, March 18-26, 1989.

Bergh, Howard, personal interview at Copper Harbor, Michigan, Dec. 9, 1987, recorded by Thom Holden.

Burgner, George H. "Transcript of Discovery Deposition, U.S. District Court, Northern District of Ohio, Eastern Division, December 13, 1977," given at Minneapolis, Minnesota, 99 pp. typewritten manuscript.

Burmeister, Capt. Frederick M. "Shipping Casualties — Strandings, Wr.1 (g), *Judge Hart*, December 2, 1942;"

Dietz, Steven. "Ten November." Minneapolis. 1987, 84 pp. manuscript.

Eliason, Jerry. Personal interview recorded on Sept. 6, 1988, by Thom Holden.

Gallagher, Leo. Correspondence of Nov. 21, 1986, to *Lake Log Chips*, Institute for Great Lakes Research collection, Bowling Green State University, and *Lake Log Chips*, Dec. 27, 1986, p. 2.

Goldish, Harry. Personal interviews by Thom Holden in Duluth on Mar. 6, 15, 1984.

Hastings, First Mate Joseph Buckley. Letter to Miss McKenzie, sister of Alex McKenzie, Purser, Nov. 18, 1885.

Holden, Thom. "Running Chronology of Lake Superior Marine Casualties," unpublished manuscript, 1973, revised 1989.

Holden, Thom. *Apostle Islands Shipwreck Survey List, 1870-1940*. Bayfield, Wisconsin. Apostle Islands National Lakeshore, National Park Service. 1985.

Holden, Thom. *Summary List of Shipwrecks and Marine Casualties on Lake Superior Resulting from the Storm of November 27-29, 1905*, unpublished manuscript, ca. 1980, 3 pp.

Holden, Thom. Transcript of exhibit labels on the *Indiana* machinery displayed in Smithsonian Institution, Dec. 1982.

Holden, Thomas Robert. *Park Interpretation as an Environmental Communication Process with a Sample Interpretive Booklet Text on the Maritime Disaster History of Siskiwit Bay, Isle Royale, Lake Superior*, 195 pp., unpublished master's thesis, University of Wisconsin, Madison, 1974.

Hulse, Charles Allen. *A Spatial Analysis of Lake Superior Shipwrecks: A Study in the Formative Process of the Archaeological Record*, 255 pp., unpublished doctoral dissertation, Michigan State University, East Lansing, 1981.

Keast, John E., "Early Navigation on Lake Superior." Unpublished manuscript in files of Marquette County Historical Society, Marquette, Mich., Oct. 20, 1942.

Lake Carriers Association, "Coast Guard Investigation Report Dated July 26, 1977, on *Fitzgerald* Sinking." 18 pp. (typewritten).

Leblanc, Ryan. Schreiber, Ontario, personal interview recorded Aug. 31, 1988, by Thom Holden.

Lasota, Chief Engineer Clem. Radio broadcast interview on WEBC from Duluth on Nov. 10, 1988.

Marshall, James R. Radio interview broadcast on WEBC from Duluth on Nov. 10, 1985.

Marshall, James R. Radio interview broadcast on WEBC from Duluth on Nov. 10, 1988.

Middleton, Edward N. Collection notes housed in U.S. Army Corps of Engineers' Canal Park Visitor Center, Duluth, Minn.

Moore, John. *Marine Protest, Dominion of Canada, Province of Ontario, District of Thunder Bay, John Malcolm Munro, Notary Public, by John S. Moore, Master*, Nov. 9, 1885.

Oehlenschlager, W.R. Correspondence of Dec. 27, 1986, to *Lake Log Chips*, Institute for Great Lakes Research collection, Bowling Green State University, and *Lake Log Chips*, Mar. 7, 1987, p. 5.

Rude, Sam. Personal interview at Duluth, Minnesota, ca. Dec. 1973, conducted by Thom Holden.

Shields, C.M. "An Account by My Father of Shipwreck," a copy of which is on file in the Peter White Public Library, Marquette, Michigan.

Smith, Judge W.E. Extracts of newspaper clippings, collection, Nov. 1885, in files of D.M. Frimodig, Marquette County Historical Society.

Stoddard, Captain Benjamin C. Letter to Ramsay Crooks, President of American Fur Company, Sept. 27, 1844. Photocopy from Papers of American Fur Company, in files of David A. LaPointe, Park Manager, Fort Wilkins State Park, Copper Harbor, Mich.

Trimble, Vice Admiral USCG (Ret.) Paul E., President, Lake Carriers' Association, correspondence to Mr. Webster B. Todd, Jr., Chairman, National Transportation Safety Board, dated Sept. 16, 1977, 18 pp., as amended.

U.S. Army Corps of Engineers' Canal Park Visitor Center and Marine Museum ship history fies in Duluth, Minnesota.

U.S. Army Corps of Engineers' scrapbook, files of St. Louis County Historical Society.

Wieland, Otto E. "The *Stranger*." Unpublished manuscript in files of St. Louis County Historical Society, Duluth.

Wisconsin Marine Historical Society, Herman G. Runge Collection vessel history files, Milwaukee Public Library.

Wrigley, Ronald H. *Northern Superior Shipwrecks*, 198 pp., unpublished manuscript, ca. 1979.

Government Documents and Reports

Carrell, Toni. *Shipwrecks of Isle Royale National Park: Thematic Group Nomination to the National Register of Historic Places*, (Santa Fe, New Mexico, Submerged Cultural Resources Unit, National Park Service, 1983, 172 page typewritten manuscript).

Carrell, Toni. *Submerged Cultural Resources Site Report:* Noquebay (Santa Fe, New Mexico, National Park Service, 1985).

Dominion of Canada, Department of Marine and Fisheries. *List of Shipping, 1913,* p. 305, as *Sessional Paper 21-b,* (Ottawa, 1914).

Dominion of Canada, Department of Marine and Fisheries. *Report of the Wreck Commissioner: Inland Waters Wrecks,* p. 207, as *Sessional Paper 21* (Ottawa, 1914).

Dominion of Canada, Department of Transport. *Casualties to Vessels Resulting in Total Loss on the Great Lakes, 1870-1957.*

Dominion of Canada, Department of Transport. *Marine Protest, Province of Ontario, District of Thunder Bay, John Malcolm Munro, Notary Public, by John S. Moore, Master, November 9, 1885.* In files of D.M. Frimodig, Marquette, Mich.

Dominion of Canada, Department of Transport. Supervising Examiner of Master and Mates for Inland Waters, "Preliminary Inquiry — Steamer *Judge Hart* Sinking," Dec. 24, 1942.

Labadie, C. Patrick. *Submerged Cultural Resources Study: Pictured Rocks National Lakeshore.* Santa Fe, New Mexico, Submerged Cultural Resources Unit, National Park Service. 1989. 232 pp.

Lenihan, Daniel J., ed. *Submerged Cultural Resources Study: Isle Royale National Park,* Daniel J. Lenihan, ed., (Santa Fe, New Mexico, Submerged Cultural Resources Unit, National Park Service, 1987). 570 pp.

Lidfors, Kate, Thom Holden, Ellen Maurer, *et. al., Report of a Two-Day Underwater Survey of Selected Historical Sites at Apostle Islands National Lakeshore with Considerations for Future Research,* (Bayfield, Wisconsin, National Park Service, Apostle Islands National Lakeshore, 1982), unpublished manuscript.

Mackay, K.C., *et. al.,* Transport Canada, "*Cartiercliffe Hall:* Report of Formal Investigation (No. 105)," dated June 5, 1980, 53 pp.

Maurer, Ellen. "Rough sketch of an unidentified wooden vessel, possibly a barge, examined on August 17, 1982" in Kate Lidfors, Thom Holden, Ellen Maurer, *et. al., Report of a Two-Day Underwater Survey of Selected Historical Sites at Apostle Islands National Lakeshore with Considerations for Future Research,* (Bayfield, Wisconsin, National Park Service, Apostle Islands National Lakeshore, 1982).

National Transportation Safety Board, Marine Accident Report, *Grounding of the SS* Frontenac *in Lake Superior, Silver Bay, Minnesota, November 22, 1979,* NTSB-MAR-80-13, 30 pp.

National Archives, Microcopy T-729, *Marine Casualties on the Great Lakes, 1863-1873* (Record Group 26, Records of the U.S. Coast Guard). Pages unnumbered.

National Transportation Safety Board, Bureau of Accident Investigation, *Marine Accident Report: SS* Edmund Fitzgerald *Sinking in Lake Superior, November 10, 1975* (Washington, D.C., May 4, 1978), Report Number: NTSB-MAR-78-3.

Seaward Inc., *Observations made of the wreck of the S/S* Edmund Fitzgerald *in Lake Superior, Michigan, 19-28 May 1976, prepared under U.S. Navy Supervisor of Salvage Contract N0024-76-A-2015* (Falls Church, Virginia, July 1976).

Senate Executive Document No. 21, 42nd Congress, 3rd Session, "Government Works in Harbor of Du Luth," pp. 1-6.

United States Army Corps of Engineers, *Chief of Engineers, Annual Report.* Annual, 1870-date.

United States Army Corps of Engineers, U.S. Lake Survey, *Great Lakes Pilot.* (annual)

United States Army Corps of Engineers, Col. A. Riano, *Statistical Report of Lake Commerce Passing Through Canals at Sault Ste. Marie, Michigan and Ontario, During Season of 1946.*

United States Army Corps of Engineers, *Waterborne Commerce of the United States.* (Part III, Waterways and Harbors, Great Lakes) annual.

United States Coast Guard. "Casualty Investigation Report, *Cartiercliffe Hall*," 14-page manuscript dated Oct. 11, 1979, copy in U.S. Army Corps of Engineers' Canal Park Visitor Center ship history files.

United States Coast Guard. "Casualty Investigation Report, *Courtney Burton,* Apr. 11, 1980," 2 pp.

United States Coast Guard. "Casualty Investigation Report, *Socrates,* Jan. 13, 1986, 6 pp.

United States Coast Guard. "Chronology of M/V *Socrates,* Nov. 18 thru Nov. 24, 1985," 12 pp.

United States Coast Guard, "Local Notice to Mariners, LNM 41/89," Dec. 15, 1989.

United States Coast Guard, "Local Notice to Mariners, LNM 42/89," Dec. 22, 1989.

United States Coast Guard. *Marine Casualty Report: SS* Edmund Fitzgerald; *Sinking in Lake Superior on 10 November 1975 with Loss of Life: Marine Board of Investigation Report and Commandant's Action* (Washington, D.C., July 26, 1977), Report Number: USCG 167364216.

United States Coast Guard, "Pollution Reports 27 March 1989 — 21 April 1989, Regarding Tugs *Arkansas* and *Louisiana* Sunk at Duluth, Minnesota," 16-page unpublished manuscript.

United States Coast Guard. "Transcript of Proceeding: Formal Coast Guard Casualty investigation into Circumstances Involving the Fire on Boat Motor Vessel *Cartiercliffe Hall* 10 Miles North of Copper Harbor, Michigan, on June 5, 1979," 5 volumes, 579-page manuscript, copy in files of U.S. Army Corps of Engineers' Canal Park Visitor Center ship history files.

United States Coast Guard. "Summary of Results of Survey of Wreckage of *Edmund Fitzgerald*," 8-page mimeo.

United States Coast Guard. "Proceedings of the Marine Safety Council," Vol. 33, No. 7, Jul. 1976, unpaged clipping in files of U.S. Army Corps of engineers, Duluth, Minn.

United States Coast Guard. *Annual Reports, U.S. Coast Guard.* Annual, 1916-date.

United States Department of Agriculture, Weather Bureau; *Wreck Chart of the Great Lakes, 1886-1891.*

United States Departments of Commerce and Treasury, *Merchant Vessels of the United States,* 1884-1981.

United States Life-Saving Service. *Annual Reports, U.S. Life-Saving Service.* Annual, 1876-1915.

Wells, Homer. "History of Accidents, Casualties, and Wrecks on Lake Superior" (Duluth, Minnesota, Corps of Engineers, U.S. Army, 1938), 90 pp. unpublished typewritten manuscript.

Private Guides and Directories
Blue Book of American Shipping Cleveland, Marine Review Publishing Co. 1901.

Great Lakes Redbook. Annual, 1920-date.

Interlake Log, Interlake Steamship Company, Cleveland, Ohio.

Beeson, Harvey C., *Inland Marine Directory,* 1887-1915.

Great Lakes Protective Association, *Annual Report Cleveland, Ohio.* Various issues, 1937-date.

Green, Fred W. *Green's Marine Directory of the Great Lakes.* Cleveland, Ohio. Annual 1908-1954.

Greenwood, John O., *Greenwood's Guide to Great Lakes Shipping.* Cleveland, Ohio, Freshwater Press, annual, 1960-1989.

Greenwood, John O. and Michael J. Dills, *Greenwood's and Dills' Lake Boats.* Cleveland, Ohio, Freshwater Press, annual 1976-1989.

BIBLIOGRAPHY

International Shipmasters Associaton, *Directory.* Annual, 1906-1963.

Lake Carriers' Association, *Annual Report,* (Cleveland, Ohio, Lake Carriers' Association. Annual, 1917-date.

Lake Carriers' Association *The Bulletin.* Scattered editions, 1959-1985.

Serials

American Maritime Officer.

Ashland Daily News.

Ashland *Press.*

Ashland Weekly News.

Ashland Weekly Press.

Bayfield County Press.

Buffalo Morning Express.

Canadian Railway and Shipping World.

Chicago Democratic Press.

Chicago Tribune.

Cleveland Evening Herald.

Cleveland Herald.

Cleveland *Plain Dealer.*

CSL - The World.

Detroit Daily Free Press.

Detroit Free Press.

Duluth Daily Commonwealth.

Duluth Daily News.

Duluth Daily Tribune.

Duluth Evening Herald.

Duluth Herald.

Duluth Minnesotian-Herald.

Duluth Minnesotian.

Duluth News-Tribune.

Duluth *News-Tribune & Herald.*

Duluth Weekly Herald.

Duluth Weekly Minnesotian.

Duluth Weekly News-Tribune.

Duluth Weekly Tribune.

Escanaba *Daily Press.*

Grand Marais (Michigan) *Herald.*

Houghton *Daily Mining Gazette.*

Houghton Evening Copper Journal.

Houghton Evening Journal.

Houghton Gazette, 1876-1877.

Houghton Mining Gazette.

Inland Seas, journal of the Great Lakes Historical Society of Vermillion and Cleveland, Ohio. Quarterly, 1946-date.

L'Anse Sentinel.

Lake Log Chips, prepared by the Institute for Great Lakes Studies, Bowling Green State University through 1988 and afterward by Harbor House Publishers of Boyne City, Michigan.

Lake Superior Journal.

Lake Superior Magazine.

Lake Superior Miner.

Lake Superior Mining Journal.

Lake Superior News and Journal.

Lake Superior News.

Lake Superior Newsletter, a special interest publication of *Lake Superior Magazine,* Duluth, Minnesota.

Lake Superior Port Cities Magazine.

Lake Superior Review & Weekly Tribune (Duluth).

Manitowoc Herald.

Marine Historian, newsletter of the Detroit Marine Historical Society.

Marine Review.

Marquette *Mining Journal.*

Marquette Weekly Plain Dealer.

Minneapolis *Star Tribune.*

Minneapolis Tribune.

Munising *News.*

New York Daily Times.

Ontonogan *Herald.*

Penetang (Ontario) *Herald.*

Petoskey News-Review

Pontiac Oakland Press.

Port Arthur Daily News.

Portage Lake Mining Gazette.

Sault Ste. Marie *Evening News.*

Skillings' Mining Review.

Soundings, newsletter of the Wisconsin Marine Historical Society at the Milwaukee Public Library.

St. Paul Pioneer Press Dispatch.

Superior Chronicle.

Superior Daily Call.

Superior *Evening Telegram.*

Superior Gazette.

Superior Times.

Telescope, journal of the Great Lakes Maritime Institute at Dossin Great Lakes Museum in Detroit.

The Nor'Easter, journal of the Lake Superior Marine Museum Association of Duluth. Bimonthly, 1976-date.

The Scanner, journal of the Toronto Marine Historical Society.

Thunder Bay *Chronical-Journal.*

Thunder Bay News Chronicle.

Toronto Globe.

Two Harbors Chronicle.

Washburn Bee.

About the Author

Dr. Julius F. Wolff Jr. has spent most of his life in the Lake Superior country. Born at Duluth, Minnesota, in 1918, he attended parochial and public school in that city, was graduated from the University of Notre Dame in 1940 and completed his doctorate at the University of Minnesota in 1949. He served four years with the U.S. Army during World War II and continued his military service in the U.S. Army Reserve, retiring as a colonel in 1975. He has been a member of the Political Science faculty at the University of Minnesota, Duluth, since 1949, presently holding the rank of professor emeritus.

His interest in the ships of Lake Superior was almost hereditary. His maternal ancestors had come to western Lake Superior by ship in 1866. His mother had worked in the Marquette vessel office of the James Pickands Company, predecessor of the renowned ship managers, Pickands-Mather and Company. Dr. Wolff heard stories from his mother about the famous lake captains of the early 20th century and the unfortunate tragedies which beset some of the iron ore ships. His father was a mining engineer for the Oliver Iron Mining Company, which supplied the ships of the Pittsburgh Steamship Company with iron ore for lower lakes steel plants. Growing up in East End Duluth, Dr. Wolff lived a stone's throw from the rocky outcrops beneath which passed every ship entering and leaving the port of Duluth. He spent hours watching the lakes freighters, wondering what happened to them as they passed to the east. He carefully studied every shipwreck story appearing in Duluth newspapers.

Yet, his 30-year study for the University of Minnesota, Duluth, began quite accidentally. While a college student, he had become interested in the wildlife conservation movement, serving as a deputy conservation officer in Indiana and Minnesota for several years. In Minnesota this work made him very familiar with the north shore of Lake Superior. Also, because of his doctoral research on the Minnesota Department of Natural Resources, he was assigned to teach the Government and Conservation course, conducting numerous field trips in northeastern Minnesota. When the Department of History at the University of Minnesota, Duluth, needed a faculty member to lecture on shipping problems along the wild and forested north shore, Dr. Wolff was asked to handle the assignment. Soon afterward, the Graduate School of the University, discovering that ship accidents on Lake Superior had never been explored by Minnesota faculty, designated him to conduct research on a part-time basis. Dr. Wolff has discovered more than 350 vessels lost on Lake Superior. He has investigated many hundreds of shipping accidents on all coasts.

As a volunteer Boy Scout leader in the 1950s and 1960s, Dr. Wolff recruited a number of young men for Lake Superior shipwreck hunts. For 40 years he has guided canoe parties of young people in the Minnesota-Ontario boundary wilderness. But those high school students who wished to participate in canoe expeditions would first spend some days beachcombing eastern Lake Superior, from the Keweenaw to Marquette and east to Sault Ste. Marie. In recent years, some have made treks along the Canadian east and north coasts of the lake as well. These beach explorations have produced numerous artifacts which have reinforced the academic study of shipwrecks.

Dr. Wolff has described his research discoveries in *Telescope, Inland Seas* and *The Nor'Easter.* He is now Senior Editor of *Inland Seas.* He has written extensively for Minnesota publications, newspapers and magazines, including the *Volunteer* and *Minnesota History.* He has appeared on the lecture circuit for the University of Minnesota, Duluth, and has presented programs on radio and television, including documentations for the national American and Canadian networks when major ship tragedies have occurred on Lake Superior.

Dr. Wolff has been a member of the Great Lakes Historical Society, the Great Lakes Maritime Institute, the Minnesota State Historical Society, the St. Louis County (Minnesota) Historical Society, the Marquette County (Michigan) Historical Society and the Lake Superior Marine Museum Association affiliated with the Corps of Engineers' Canal Park Marine Museum. He remains a member of the American Forestry Association and the Minnesota State Forestry Association. He has served on the Minnesota Land Exchange Review Board and the Superior National Forest Advisory Commission.

This book is the result of 30 years of persistent research covering Great Lakes area newspaper files of the last 140 years, available historical documents from libraries and archives, innumerable interviews with Great Lakes maritime people, continuous contact with hard hat and scuba divers and U.S. Coast Guard personnel and personal examination of the isolated stretches of Lake Superior littoral where accidents have occurred over the years.

About the Contributing Editor

Thomas R. (Thom) Holden was born at Delavan, Wisconsin, in 1946. He attended the public schools and graduated with honors in 1965 going on to the University of Wisconsin, Madison, where he majored in Mechanical Engineering and earned his graduate degrees in Recreation Resources Management and Environmental Communications. He lives in Superior, Wisconsin, with his wife, Cindi, and daughter, Rachael.

Thom has worked at the Corps of Engineers' Canal Park Marine Museum for more than a decade, previously having worked for the National Audubon Society in Greenwich, Connecticut, Isle Royale National Park and Michigan Department of Natural Resources. His interest in maritime history grew out of a passion for Isle Royale which evolved into research on local shipwrecks more than two decade ago and now includes research on nearly 4,000 Lake Superior shipwrecks and marine casualties. In his 1974 graduate thesis he acknowledged, "My brightest research hours were spent elbow to elbow with Dr. Julius F.

Wolff Jr., each of us reviewing page after page of newsscript on microfilm searching out period accounts of Lake Superior's marine casualties." Thom is author of *Above and Below: A History of Lighthouses and Shipwrecks of Isle Royale,* prepared especially for the Isle Royale Natural History Association, Houghton, Michigan; a contributor to James R. Marshall's *Shipwrecks of Lake Superior* and to the National Park Service's definitive historical and archaeological report on Isle Royale shipwrecks and author of numerous articles for various Great Lakes historical journals and local and regional newspapers and magazines. He has been interviewed for commentary on shipping events by local and regional radio and television stations, has spoken before numerous groups on the history of Lake Superior shipwrecks and serves as guest editor for *The Nor'Easter,* for which he also prepares the continuing maritime "Observations" column. He also prepared the initial historical survey of marine casualties in the vicinity of the Apostle Islands for the National Park Service and participated in archaeological studies there.

Thom continues to do volunteer work on the history of shipping and marine casualties for Isle Royale National Park, Apostle Islands National Lakeshore, Ontario Ministry of History and Culture and numerous sport divers. He enjoys camping, historical and archaeological research, and does both still and video photographic documentation of the Twin Ports maritime scene in addition to writing and editing.